ISSN 0885-6842

something ABOUT THE AUTHOR

AUTOBIOGRAPHY SERIES

ADELE SARKISSIAN
EDITOR

VOLUME **2**

GALE RESEARCH COMPANY • BOOK TOWER • DETROIT, MICHIGAN 48226

EDITORIAL STAFF

Adele Sarkissian, *Editor*
Christopher J. Momenee, Mark Zadrozny, and Donald E. Zurack, *Assistant Editors*
Marilyn O'Connell, *Research Coordinator*

Mary Beth Trimper, *External Production Supervisor*
Art Chartow, *Art Director*
Vivian Tannenbaum, *Layout Artist*
Darlene Maxey, *External Production Assistant*

Laura Bryant, *Internal Production Supervisor*
Louise Gagné, *Internal Production Associate*
Sandy Rock, *Internal Senior Production Assistant*

Alan Dyer, *Indexer*
Donald G. Dillaman, *Index Program Designer*

Frederick G. Ruffner, Jr., *Publisher*
Dedria Bryfonski, *Editorial Director*
Christine Nasso, *Director, Literature Division*
Adele Sarkissian, *Senior Editor, Autobiography Series*

Copyright © 1986 by Gale Research Company

ISBN 0-8103-4451-3
ISSN 0885-6842

Printed in the United States.

Contents

Preface

Each volume in the *Something about the Author Autobiography Series (SAAS)* presents an original collection of autobiographical essays written especially for the series by prominent authors and illustrators of books for children and young adults. This series takes its place beside other distinguished reference works on young people's literature published by the Gale Research Company: *Children's Literature Review, Children's Book Review Index, Children's Literature Awards and Winners,* the biographical indexes *Children's Authors and Illustrators* and *Writers for Young Adults,* and particularly the highly acclaimed bio-bibliographical series *Something about the Author (SATA),* to which this *Autobiography Series* is a companion.

You may already be familiar with *SATA,* which has long been recognized as the only comprehensive ongoing reference series that deals with the lives and works of the people who create books for young readers. To complement *SATA*'s wide range of detailed information, *SAAS* presents a "close up" view of some of these fascinating people. In *SAAS* authors and illustrators are invited to write about themselves, especially for you, in the form of an extended essay. This is a new and exciting opportunity—for you, for the author, and for the publisher. A reference work that collects autobiographies of this kind has never existed before, and Gale is pleased to fill this information gap with the *SATA Autobiography Series.*

Purpose

This series is designed to be a place where young readers, as well as adults interested in young people's literature, can meet "in person" the men and women who create the books that children and young adults are reading today. Here you can learn about the people and events that influenced these writers' early lives, how they began their careers, what problems they faced in becoming established in their professions, what prompted them to write or illustrate particular books, what they now find most challenging or rewarding in their lives, and what advice they may have for young people interested in following in their footsteps, among many other subjects. In *SAAS* writers can talk directly to you on their own terms. They are free to choose what they will say to you, and the way they will say it. As a result, each essay highlights the individuality of its writer—that special quality that sets one creative person apart from another.

In *SAAS* young readers, adult students of children's literature, teachers, librarians, and parents can learn more about familiar authors and illustrators and make the first acquaintance of many others. Authors who may never write a full-length autobiography have the opportunity in *SAAS* to let their readers know how they see themselves and their work. Even writers who have already published full-length life stories have the opportunity in *SAAS* to bring their readers "up to date," or perhaps to take a different approach in the essay format. At the very least, these essays can help to satisfy every reader's natural curiosity about the "real" person behind the name on the book jacket. Each of these essays offers a distinctive view of the person who wrote it; taken together, the essays in this series offer a new window on young people's literature.

Even though the *SATA Autobiography Series* is still in its youth, we can look forward to what it will accomplish. The series expects to fill a significant information gap—the primary reason behind every reference book. But we expect *SAAS* to do even more: the original essays in these volumes will make *SAAS* a varied and rewarding anthology of contemporary writing for young people.

Scope

Like its parent series, *Something about the Author,* the *SATA Autobiography Series* aims to include writers and artists who produce all the types of books that young people read today. *SAAS* sets out to meet the needs and interests of a broad range of readers from upper elementary school through junior high school and high school. Each volume in the series provides about twenty essays by current writers whose work has special appeal for young readers. We consider it an extraordinary accomplishment that twenty busy writers and artists are able to interrupt their writing, teaching, speaking, traveling, and other schedules to come together in print by a given deadline for any one volume. So it is not always possible to represent every area of young people's literature equally and uniformly in each volume of *SAAS*. Most of the twenty-one writers in Volume 2, for example, specialize in fiction for children and young adults, with the prominent exception of two writers who specialize in nonfiction. However, these categories do not begin to suggest the variety and vitality of their work. Many of the contributors to this volume have also written fiction and nonfiction for adults as well as work for movies, television, radio, newspapers, and journals.

Format

Writers who contribute to *SAAS* are invited to write a "mini-autobiography" of approximately 10,000 words. We deliberately set no pattern for authors to follow in writing their essays, and we do not limit the essays to particular topics. This leaves the way open for the essayists to speak to you in the manner that is most natural and comfortable for each of them. Writers for *SAAS* are also asked to supply a selection of personal photographs, showing themselves at various ages, as well as important people and special moments in their lives. Our contributors have responded graciously and generously, sharing with us some of their most treasured mementoes, as you will see in this volume. This enticing combination of text and photographs makes *SAAS* the kind of reference book that even browsers will find irresistible.

A bibliography appears at the end of each essay, listing the writer's book-length works in chronological order of publication. Each entry in the bibliography includes the publication information for the book's first printing in the United States and Great Britain. Generally, the bibliography does not include later reprintings, new editions, or foreign translations. Also omitted from this bibliography are articles, reviews, and other contributions to magazines and journals. The bibliographies in this volume were compiled by members of the *SAAS* editorial staff from their research and the lists of writings that were provided by many of the authors. Each of the bibliographies was submitted to the author for review.

Each volume of *SAAS* includes a cumulative index that lists all the essayists in the series as well as the subjects mentioned in the essays: personal names, titles of works, geographical names, etc. The index format is designed to make these cumulating references as helpful and easy to use as possible. For every reference that appears *in more than one essay,* the name of the essayist is given before the volume and page number(s). For example, Franklin Delano Roosevelt is mentioned by several essayists in the series. The entry in the index allows you to identify the essay writers by name:

Roosevelt, Franklin Delano
Meltzer **1:** 210, 211
Peck **2:** 179
Sachs **2:** 198

For references that appear *in only one essay,* the volume and page number(s) are given but the name of the essayist is omitted. For example:

Looking Ahead

While each essay in *SAAS* has its own special character and its individual point of view, these life stories take on a new importance when we see them grouped here in one volume. Together they tell us even more than they tell us as separate essays. Common experiences and common themes echo throughout these autobiographies and illuminate our understanding of these writers and their works.

Many of the authors in this volume, for example, tell us something about *how* they create their books. Henry Gregor Felsen describes his unique approach: "The very first character I create is the boy or girl I think would be interested in the story, and I write it for him—or her." P.L. Travers, on the other hand, thinks of her writing a kind of "listening." "You just set yourself to listen for what, with luck, may be told you. Well, luck brought me Mary Poppins. . . ."

For Sonia Levitin, the writing process starts when she forces herself every morning "to go down to my study and *sit there* for five to seven hours, and struggle to fill those pages with something that might be worth saving." Sometimes the struggle fails, but when it succeeds, there are "magic moments when the muse sits on [my] shoulder, whispering encouragement, and all [my] risks pay off. . . .The characters live with me then. The images and people that I created seem like another reality coexisting with my own daily life in a very real way. 'They' are only waiting for me to get back to my typewriter, to share their lives, to give them flesh and a purpose."

Other writers, like Scott Corbett, begin the process very differently. Corbett is one writer who doesn't sit at his typewriter every day. Instead, he tells us, "I spend almost as much time thinking out a story as I do writing it. During that period I seldom make notes. . . .Eventually I write most of a book in my head before I set it down on paper." But getting the ideas is the hard part, Corbett admits. "Thinking back to my own boyhood, thinking what it was like to be a boy, has gotten me started on more than one story."

In John Rowe Townsend's estimation, each of his books is a unique writing experience, but "there are stages to be gone through every time. There's the initial fascination with an idea, ... the first fine careless rapture of writing. Then come the problems: the tendency of every narrative to go its own way and of every character to do what he or she is not supposed to do. . . . There's a period of sheer, dogged slog, when only willpower keeps me going. Then, with luck, comes the recovery—the realization that it can be made to work out after all, the returning enthusiasm, the completion of the first rough draft. . . .For me, completing the final revision is like coming into port at the end of a long voyage."

As a final example, there is Julia Cunningham's reenactment of a skirmish that she witnesses each time she begins writing a book—a war between the "demons" (self-doubt, fear of failure) and the "angels" (self-trust, confidence). "Call them what you will, the demons and the angels are always present, the struggle ongoing. But as long as the pages fill, as the writer writes, the angels are winning."

These are only hints of what you will find in the essays ahead. We invite you to treat yourself to an exceptional reading experience. Turn the page and see what these writers have to say just to you.

Acknowledgments

We wish to acknowledge our special gratitude to each of the authors in this volume. They all have been most kind and cooperative in contributing not only their talents but their enthusiasm and encouragement to this project.

Authors Forthcoming in *SAAS*

Michael Bond (children's book and short story writer, dramatist, and essayist)—Paddington Bear, an acknowledged part of childhood folklore, is Bond's most popular character. Combining "bearishness and boyishness," Bond has created nearly forty books, while Paddington's antics have been made into more than fifty films. Bond's successes include *Paddington Abroad* and *Paddington Takes to the Air.*

Frank Bonham (novelist, short story and nonfiction writer, and screenwriter)—In books like *Durango Street* and *Mystery of the Fat Cat,* Bonham exemplifies his concern for minority youths and the difficulties they face. His cultural mix of characters speaks directly to less fortunate teenagers in books like *Hey, Big Spender.*

Tomie de Paola (picture book writer and illustrator, and novelist)—Recognized as one of the most prolific and popular creators of children's books, de Paola illustrates his works so that children can "read the pictures." Subtle meanings and messages, conveyed by his precise and deliberate use of color, have helped create his award-winning *Strega Nona* and *The Clown of God.*

Lee Kingman (young adult and children's novelist, picture book creator, playwright, and editor)—Kingman has been praised for the accurate portrayal of her characters. Her careful representation of young adults and their parents is seen in books like *The Secret Journey of the Silver Reindeer* and *The Year of the Raccoon.*

Karla Kuskin (children's book writer and illustrator)—Her stories, such as *Roar and More* and *Near the Window Tree,* are written for children who "think complicated thoughts and suffer and laugh." Using techniques like typographical representations of animal sounds, Kuskin aims to elicit the child's participation in her books.

Lois Lowry (young adult novelist and photographer)—Best known for her novel, *A Summer to Die,* Lowry writes fiction that explores topical themes such as an adopted child's quest to find her real mother or a young girl's struggle to cope with her sister's death. Through her work, Lowry attempts to "help adolescents answer their own questions about life, identity, and human relationships."

Sharon Bell Mathis (young adult and children's author)—With critically acclaimed books such as *Teacup Full of Roses* and *The Hundred Penny Box,* Mathis leads the latest trend in children's literature which advocates the realistic portrayal of people and events. Addressing subjects that include drug addiction, senility, and death, Mathis writes "to salute the strength in Black children" and offers—in words and symbols—tales "to grow on."

John Neufeld (novelist, scriptwriter, playwright)—In novels like *Edgar Allan, Touching,* and *Lisa, Bright and Dark,* Neufeld vividly depicts young adults confronting contemporary social problems—mental illness, accepting minorities and the handicapped—as well as the ineffectuality of adults in dealing with those problems.

Jill Paton Walsh (young adult and children's novelist)—An English author who offers a wide range of settings for her novels, from prehistoric times (*Toolmaker*) to the contemporary (*Fireweed*). Idealistic as well as realistic, her coming-of-age stories appeal to young adults who respond to her well-defined characters and her ability to weave the powerful forces of young love with dramatic moments in history.

Joan Phipson (children's novelist)—Books like *Good Luck to the Rider, The Way Home,* and *The Family Conspiracy* have brought honors to Phipson from beyond the shores of her native Australia. Vast landscapes and highly developed characters in her novels have encouraged many young readers to "walkabout" with her.

Ian Serraillier (children's writer and poet)—Praised by critics as one of the finest poets writing for young people today, Serraillier has introduced his readers to such timeless tales as *Beowulf the Warrior* and *The Challenge of the Green Knight,* among his many imaginative retellings of myths and legends.

Ivan Southall (writer of fiction and nonfiction for children, young adults, and adults)—A five-time winner of the Australian Children's Book of the Year Award, Southall has won international acclaim for books like *The Long Night Watch, Fly West,* and *Josh.* Memorable characters and compelling plots are the author's trademark.

Mary Stolz (young adult and children's novelist and short story writer)—Guided by a genuine understanding of her young protagonists (usually teenage girls), the author treats familiar themes—young love, peer acceptance, sibling rivalry, parental conflicts—with unusual depth and sensitivity. Never settling for a neatly contrived ending, she shows respect for her characters' integrity as well as her readers' intelligence in books like *Leap before You Look* and *Two by Two,* which speak eloquently to the emotional experiences of teenage readers.

Mildred Taylor (young adult novelist)—Winner of the Newbery Medal for *Roll of Thunder, Hear My Cry,* Taylor has been praised for her unsentimental treatment of the Black experience. Drawing from her ancestral past, Taylor attempts to refute history's image of Blacks in another of her award-winners, *Song of the Trees.*

SOMETHING ABOUT THE AUTHOR

AUTOBIOGRAPHY SERIES

Melvin Berger

1927-

"My mother (left), with her brother Sam and sister Dora, a few years after her arrival in America"

Mr. Berger," the high-school guidance counselor said to my father, "we've got the results of Melvin's vocational guidance tests. He shows two areas of strength—science and music. We would guess that he would do well in either career."

She then turned to me. "What are your feelings? What would you like to study in college?"

My main love and interest at the time was playing the viola (an instrument like the violin, but a little bigger and with a deeper tone), so it was easy for me to answer, "I'd like to be a musician."

"That's fine." she said. "But my advice to you is to get a degree in science first. Then go out and try to get a job in an orchestra. If you find one, that's fine. If not, you'll always have your science training to fall back on."

The suggestion struck me as very sensible. So while continuing to study and play the viola, I enrolled at the City College of New York, working for a degree in electrical engineering. From then on, until today, science and music, with the important addition of writing, have dominated my working life.

I was born on August 23, 1927, in Brooklyn, New York. Both my parents had emigrated from Russia to this country. My mother, Esther Hochman, arrived in New York from Minsk in the year 1897, at the age of ten. My father, Ben Berger, who grew up in a town near Odessa, came to the United States three years later, when he was twenty years old.

The third youngest of eight children, my mother had four sisters and three brothers. Her father and oldest sister had settled in America first, followed later by my grandmother and the rest of the children. The family settled on the Lower East Side of New York City, a center of Russian-Jewish immigrant life around the turn of the century. She advanced far enough in school to become a bookkeeper.

"My father's family in America around 1900. From right, my father, grandfather, Aunt Rose, and Uncle Louis"

"A 'walk' on the boardwalk in Coney Island when I was six months old"

My father's family, which was much smaller, included only a younger brother and sister. His brother, Louis, gave him the money for his passage to America. Louis had actually found it on the street of their town.

He wanted my father to leave Russia because he was about to be drafted into the Czar's army.

There was no one waiting on the dock to welcome my father to New York. My grandfather had emigrated earlier, but he was living in Providence, Rhode Island, at the time. Very soon after he came to this country, my father had the misfortune to slip on the ice and break his arm. Alone, and without money to live on, he had to stay in the hospital until his arm healed.

Although mother had been a bookkeeper before she and my father married, on August 24, 1926, she did not work outside the home while I was growing up. Mostly she looked after me, an only child, and helped Dad run his small upholstery business. The three of us lived in an apartment above the small shop in Brooklyn. While doing his errands, my father would sometimes let me ride next to him in his delivery truck, which he called a "Tin Lizzie." The smell of gasoline in the garage where he parked the "Tin Lizzie" is still a fondly recalled memory.

When I was four years old, my dad gave up his upholstery business and we moved to an apartment in Brighton Beach, also in Brooklyn, but very close to the ocean. By this time his brother Louis had come to America and become a furrier. He offered my father a chance to work for him. The job was to sew together small pieces and scraps of Persian lamb skins into big squares called "plates." The plates were then used to make collars and add decorative touches to coats. After a while, my father opened a similar business of his own.

For a whole year, starting in the spring, my father would sew together the fur plates. A few of them would be sold during the year. But most of them would be

"My father behind the wheel of his 'Tin Lizzie'"

"At age four, with my parents, just before we moved to Brighton Beach"

stored in a warehouse. The following spring he would take the whole year's work out of storage and sell the plates to buyers.

One spring evening, my father came home from work. He looked tired and worn, but entered without a word to either my mother or me. Walking to his favorite seat near the window he opened up the newspaper and started to read. Then suddenly, he put down the paper and began to cry.

In a choked voice he told us how, a few days earlier, he had received all the plates back from the warehouse. But overnight, his shop had been burglarized. Every single plate—his whole year's work—was gone. As though that was not enough of a tragedy, the exact same thing happened the following year!

In those Depression times, money was very scarce. To put bread on the table, my parents rented out one of the rooms in our three-room apartment. For several years, our family slept in one room. On weekends we either had company or visited one of my mother's brothers or sisters—Harry, Sam, Dora, Henrietta, Lena, Fanny, or Julius, or my father's brother Louis or sister Rose. Everyone usually sat around talking, eating, and laughing during those parties. While the adults socialized, I would fall asleep, usually on my mother's lap.

My neighborhood friends and classmates at the elementary school I attended also came from poor homes. But to my mind, we had less money than any of them. At a summer recreational program, an acting group was going to perform the Gilbert and Sullivan operetta, *Pirates of Penzance.* Admission was one nickel. Most of my friends were going and I wanted very much to be there, too. But I didn't feel it was right to ask for the five cents. Later, when I told my mother about missing the show, she was very upset.

Not long after starting school, I acquired a violin. My older cousin, Matty, who played already, gave me the small-sized instrument that he had outgrown. According to family lore, I pretended to play this violin, which had no strings, using a yardstick for the bow. Around second grade, my mother found a government-sponsored music school that gave free music lessons. After one month of studies my teacher put me on the stage to play "Lightly Row" in a school concert. Everyone agreed I was going to be a famous violinist one day.

A lot of the cultural interest I developed came from my cousin, Vivienne Hochman, who nurtured me during most of my growing-up years. Vivienne brought me wonderful leather pants from Switzerland and a beautiful school bag from England. She gave me stamps for my collection, took me to concerts and Broadway shows, introduced me to eating in restaurants, bought me books, and invited me to spend my summers at her sleep-away camp.

My years at Cunningham Junior High School went by very fast. A special program, called Rapid Advance, allowed me to complete two years of schooling in one year. Since I had also skipped a term in elementary school, I then entered Lincoln High School a year and a half ahead of my age.

Always an avid reader, I now decided to go through every book in the local library. Starting at the beginning of the fiction section, I methodically plowed through book after book. But after a few weeks I gave up this hopeless task and began to read only what I really enjoyed.

It was in high school that I first tried my hand at writing. I wrote a short story about a student (not very different from me) who was bored in school and always annoyed the teacher. The hero grew up and became a teacher himself. To his great dismay, though, he had a pupil who tormented him just as he had tormented his teacher. So proud was I of the story that I decided to publish it myself. I had once bought a copy of Poe's *Tales* on sale for twenty-five cents. At that rate, I figured out, publishing a small edition of my short story would cost very little. It was left to Uncle Herman, a practical man who was a printer by trade, to convince me how little I understood the publishing business.

On December 7, 1941, the Japanese bombed the American naval base at Pearl Harbor, drawing America into World War II. But that fateful day is seared in my memory for another reason. That is when we learned that my mother had cancer. Despite surgery and radiation treatment, the disease spread very rapidly. She died on July 5, 1943.

At about the same time, my father developed a terrible allergy to fur. He had difficulty breathing whenever he was near the skins, and the parts of his arms that actually touched the fur became red and painfully inflamed. In despair, he went back to his old upholstery work. But instead of renting a shop, he only took on small jobs that he could do in the customer's houses. Getting work meant leaving cards in mailboxes and then going door-to-door giving estimates. To do the job, he had to drag his tools and materials around, working on the heavy pieces of furniture in small, crowded apartments. The pay was a pittance.

My father and I lived a sad life without my mother. I graduated high school in January 1944 and entered City College as an electrical engineering student. But I was moving through life in a daze. The school work was extremely difficult. To add to the pressure, I was taking viola lessons and was playing three afternoons a week in a training orchestra for young musicians. The other two afternoons, I worked in my Uncle Lou's fur shop, soaking and stretching the Persian lamb paws before they were sewn together into plates. Between studying for school, practicing the viola, working and spending at least three hours a day on the subway, I was always exhausted. Any time I sat down I fell asleep. I even developed the ability to doze standing up in the subway!

By the start of 1945, I was close to the breaking point. I found it increasingly difficult to keep up the pace. The only activity that I really enjoyed was playing the viola. In May I heard about an opening for a violist in the New Orleans Philharmonic. After taking the audition, I was offered the job. Although it would not start until the following October, I dropped out of college, just weeks before the end of the semester. Needing a change of scenery and time to recuperate, I took a bus to Woodstock, New York, an artists' and musicians' colony in the Catskill Mountains just north of New York City. On my arrival I went to bed and slept for some forty-eight hours before venturing out of my room.

I loved being in New Orleans, devoting myself to the viola, and for the first time having a little money in my pocket. After a season in New Orleans, at $42.50 a week, I moved to the more prestigious orchestra in Columbus, Ohio, where I earned $60 a week. Finally I got a position in the outstanding Pittsburgh Symphony paying $85 a week. The salaries, although very low by today's standards, were considered high at that time—and seemed absolutely munificent to me.

Playing in orchestras was a splendid experience! Not only did I hear and play great music, see new parts of the country, meet interesting people, sleep in hotels, eat in fine restaurants, but I earned a good living at the same time. Yet, after three years, I felt something was missing. I began to regret the lack of a college education. There were too many things that I wanted to know about music and other subjects. I started to look for a way to return to college.

The Eastman School of Music of the University of Rochester in Rochester, New York, came to my rescue. Howard Hanson, director of the school, awarded me a full scholarship. And the Rochester Philharmonic, which rehearsed in the school's Eastman Theater, offered me a position in the viola section. Thus, I was able to carry a full program, while supporting myself by playing in the orchestra. In fact, from time to time I was able to send a few dollars home to help out my father. With the credits I had previously earned at City College, I received a bachelor's degree in three years.

Equipped with a college diploma, I returned to New York City and found a double position as Lecturer in the Music Department of City College and Fellow in the Music Department of Teacher's College of Columbia University. The latter appointment also enabled me to get a Master's degree in Music Education, although I had no intention at that time of ever teaching music.

Sometimes, as we all know, fate works in mysterious ways. While still teaching at City College I helped to found the Nassau School of Music at Hicksville, Long Island, a suburb of New York City. When asked to teach music in the nearby Plainview Public Schools a few mornings a week, I though it an ideal way to fill in the time when there was little to do at the music school. It seemed like a good idea for a year or two. By the following year, though, the Plainview job was offered to me full-time. It was a hard decision to make. But since I was already based on Long Island, I decided to leave City College and go into school music.

My duties at Plainview were mostly in the high school, teaching the string instruments and conducting the orchestra. Afternoons and on Saturdays, I taught at the music school. In between I performed as a freelance musician in New York City and on Long Island. To make matters a little more complicated, I "officially" lived with my father at home in Brooklyn, even though I also had a small apartment in the music-

"Conducting the high-school orchestra at Plainview, Long Island"

school building. While it was now in a car instead of on the subways, I still commuted several hours a day.

Life continued in this hectic way until the summer of 1957 when I was playing in the Symphony of the Air at the Empire State Music Festival in Ellenville, New York. One afternoon as I was sitting on the porch of the Arrowhead Lodge, the hotel at which I was staying, I saw a most attractive young woman arrive at the hotel for the July 4 weekend. Striking up a conversation, I discovered she was Gilda Shulman from the Bronx, up to attend the Music Festival. Throughout the season, we spent a lot of time together. When the Festival was over and I returned home, I added another stop—Gilda's home in the Bronx—to my Plainview-Hicksville-Brooklyn commute. In the middle of September, Gilda and I decided to get married.

Our wedding took place on December 22, 1957. The date was chosen because both of us were teaching and that was the beginning of our Christmas vacation. Although I foolishly cut short our honeymoon in upstate New York in order to play a concert in New York City, we made up for it by spending over two months in Europe the following summer. Just before leaving for Europe we bought our first house, a small one in Levittown, Long Island, a suburb of New York City. A little over a year later, we started our family with Eleanor, born January 29, 1959. Nancy arrived twenty months after that, on September 25, 1960.

S ome months before Nancy was born, an unexpected meeting turned my life around, although I was

hardly aware anything momentous was happening at the time. My cousin, Vivienne Hochman, introduced me to her friend, Julius Schwartz, science editor for the children's book division of the well-known publisher, McGraw-Hill. At the end of a very stimulating conversation about the relationship between science and music, Julius told me that there was a great demand for good children's books. In 1957 the Russians had launched *Sputnik*, the first step in the exploration of space. This made the Americans realize how badly

"Gilda and I drinking the first toast at our wedding, December 22, 1957"

they were falling behind in science and science education. To help us catch up, he said, schools and libraries needed books on science topics for young people.

Julius asked me to write a book that would explain to children the science of making music with instruments and recordings. Although the idea of writing children's books had never before occurred to me, I didn't even hesitate. The prospect of writing on two of my favorite subjects was irresistible. I immediately agreed to prepare an outline and description of the book, which I titled *Science and Music*.

Right from the start, Gilda worked with me—reading, suggesting, editing, typing, and helping in any number of ways. In fact, she often reminds me that I brought the proofs of *Science and Music* to her in the hospital right after Nancy's birth, saying that since she had nothing else to do she might as well proofread the manuscript!

Science and Music (1961) was very successful. It went into six printings and the editors at McGraw-Hill asked for another book. I suggested various topics. The one that caught their interest was a book on the effect of science, politics, and philosophy on contemporary music. But the more we discussed the concept the more it changed. Eventually it evolved into a book on the major scientific achievements of recent times and their effects on everyone's lives.

Entitled *Triumphs of Modern Science* (1964), the book sold many copies, mostly to libraries and schools. Most notable, perhaps, was the book's large number of foreign publications. It appeared in over twenty different translations, including Spanish, French, Portuguese, Vietnamese, and Hindi. One interesting version, printed in Japan, was to be used to teach English to Japanese students. In actual fact, *Triumphs of Modern Science* became the most-translated book published by McGraw-Hill.

Like a crusader, I hoped *Triumphs of Modern Science* would alert people to the amazing advances in all branches of science. The new research findings were clearly much too important to be left to the scientists alone. My goal was, and still is, to bring a knowledge and understanding of the latest scientific discoveries to young people in a readable and interesting way.

Having always closely followed news reports on science topics, I now kept up with the latest findings in nuclear energy, medicine, computers, space exploration, pollution, and the environment, with a view to working up these ideas into books for young people. In addition to being concerned about the latest advances in science, I also wanted to provide readers with a clear grasp of basic scientific principles. My chance to write a number of very fundamental science books also came about through a casual meeting with an editor.

Since 1961 we had been spending our summers on Cape Cod in Massachusetts, enjoying the beautiful scenery, swimming, and meeting some very interesting people who vacationed there. Through a friend who was also on the Cape, I met Margaret Farrington Bartlett, the editor of Coward-McCann's "Science Is What and Why" series of science books for very young children.

Margaret and I talked about a book that would explain atoms to six-to-ten-year-olds, *without* ever talking down to them. We agreed to include some of the latest discoveries about atoms. The book was to be forty-eight pages long with many illustrations, so that the typewritten manuscript could be no more than four or five pages.

Any ideas that I had about how easy it would be to write a four-page book were quickly dispelled. There was so much to say and so little space in which time to say it. Every word was essential to telling the story. It is possible that *Atoms* (1968) went through more revisions than any of my other books.

Margaret had a unique way of editing. Basically, she went through the manuscript with a fine-tooth comb. At every word or concept that bothered her, she inserted a large, bright red question mark. Rarely was she specific. She preferred to let me rethink the problem and find a new solution. Most often the changes necessitated a reworking of the entire text. But each revision brought us closer and closer together. When she was finally pleased, I felt extremely satisfied as well.

Atoms taught me a great deal about writing for very young readers. Among the things I discovered, for example, is that the writer and the illustrator rarely meet before the book is published. The only drawings that I was shown in advance for *Atoms* were those that I had to check for scientific accuracy. Otherwise, the artist worked from the text independently. It seemed odd to have no idea of the finished product until I saw the printed books.

In 1963, Gilda and I thought it would be wonderful to take a sabbatical from teaching and live for a year in England. I signed up to study for an advanced degree at London University. And for living accommodations we were able to exchange houses with an English family. In August 1964, we moved with Eleanor and Nancy, now aged five and three, along with thirteen fully loaded suitcases, to Great Bookham, a suburb south of London.

We had not even unpacked when a messenger brought us a telegram with the shocking news that my father had died on August 15, 1964. Although he had suffered a severe stroke the year before and been hospitalized, he seemed to be in stable condition when we sailed for England. The pain of learning that he had died, with us so far away, was nearly unbearable. Since it was impossible for all of us to return, I rushed by myself to the airport for the difficult flight home.

After this dreadful start, the rest of our year in Great Bookham was really quite wonderful. Gilda taught part-time in an English elementary school, enriching the children's regular classroom work by answering their many questions about life in America. Both girls attended school. Ellie was in the English equivalent of first grade at the Eastwick School; Nancy was at the Spinney Hill Nursery School. And I commuted to London each morning, taking courses for an advanced degree at London University, as well as practicing for a recital and two solo recordings with the English Chamber Orchestra.

In England I began my life-long fascination with old scientific instruments. Often bored while Gilda browsed in the English antique shops, I was one day unexpectedly attracted by an exquisite old brass microscope. Stunned by its beauty and amazed to think that researchers had used it for about two hundred years, I bought it. From then on I took a new interest in "antiquing." Now it is I who drag Gilda to musty shops, hoping to find microscopes, telescopes, scales, balances, medical kits, or other paraphernalia of years gone by. Among my collectibles are some extremely interesting and valuable "scopes," but my favorite piece is still a very old Chinese balance that was once used for weighing out opium!

While I did some literary research in England, most of my writing was for the thesis that was required by my studies at London University. A motoring trip through England, however, proved to be the inspiration for a whole series of children's books that I was to write some years later.

I had long known about Jodrell Bank, the largest movable radio telescope in the world, which was located in the Midland region of England. One day, when we were in the vicinity, we were able to arrange a visit to the world-famous observatory. As we approached the huge, white, gleaming dishlike antenna, we were startled to see it suddenly looming up over the calm, peaceful cow pasture. In a nearby laboratory, we met the scientists who worked there. They graciously shared with us some of their findings made possible by this astounding new tool of science.

The glimpse we had of Jodrell Bank was so intriguing that we thought of visiting other scientific sites in England such as the famous Greenwich Observatory and the Cavendish Laboratory at Cambridge University. From these trips came the idea of writing a series of books that would teach youngsters about modern

© 1964 The Advertiser, Croydon, England

"In 1964, with our two daughters, Nancy (left) and Ellie (right), after our arrival in England for a one-year stay"

science by taking them behind-the-scenes to a number of well-known laboratories.

Before returning to the United States, we spent a few weeks in France at the end of August 1965. Hardly had we settled back into our own home when I got a call from Edna Barth, my former editor at McGraw-Hill. Now working for another publisher, T. Y. Crowell, she invited me to write for her. The topic we agreed on was a collective biography of outstanding nineteenth- and twentieth-century biologists, focusing on their most important discoveries and their impact on our lives.

Entitled *Famous Men of Modern Biology* (1968), this was my first book to be based on actual contact with contemporary scientists. Of the fourteen important biologists that were discussed, I exchanged letters with the four who were still living. I learned many details of their lives and their research. Later, they were kind enough to check the individual chapters for factual accuracy.

Advances in the science of measurement were the subject of my next book. I chose the topic because there were few up-to-date books on this vital subject and the changeover to the metric system seemed imminent. Also, I was intrigued at the prospect of getting a close look at the National Bureau of Standards. During the several days I spent at their labs just outside of Washington, D.C., I met some of the leading figures in the science of measurement and saw the actual weights and rods used to set the official standards of ounce, pound, inch, and yard for the United States. The book, which I called *For Good Measure,* was published in 1969.

By 1970, Edna Barth had become editor-in-chief

"Nancy in front of our house in Great Neck, New York, bought just after our return from England in 1965"

at still another publishing house, Lothrop, Lee and Shepard. She again invited me to write for her. Knowing of my continuing interest in music, she and I came up with the idea of a biography of the contemporary composer Igor Stravinsky. I had already started researching Stravinsky's life when Edna learned that another publisher was preparing a similar book. After discussing whether to continue the project, drop it, or change its basic focus, we chose to expand the biography to cover fourteen outstanding composers, and named it *Masters of Modern Music* (1970).

Meanwhile, I continued to visit laboratories in the United States and to think about a series of books describing what I saw. Most young people's science books were concerned with the results of scientific research. I wanted to write about the process and methods of science by taking a close, firsthand look at the actual laboratory experiments. The proposal that I prepared for the "Scientists at Work" series described two books, *South Pole Station* and *National Weather Service.* I submitted the proposals to John Day publishers because I knew that they had put out a number of excellent science books. They were indeed interested, and under-

took to put out a whole series of "Scientists at Work" books over the years. In time, though, John Day was taken over by another publisher, T. Y. Crowell, and most of the books were put out by Crowell.

Since the scientific base located at the South Pole is administered by the Navy and the National Science Foundation from their offices in Washington, D.C., I did most of my research in the capital. Seeing my great interest, a Navy officer actually invited me to visit the South Pole station for a short stay. The idea was intriguing. But unfortunately, all flights to the South Pole occur during their summer, which is our winter, and I could not leave school for that period.

During the months I worked on the book, the public was very interested in the South Pole. Accounts of the life and the research at the Pole appeared frequently in newspapers and magazines. Yet, by the time the book was published, nobody seemed at all concerned about this fantastic outpost at one of the last frontiers on earth. As a result, this book never sold very well.

The research for *National Weather Service* (1971), the second title in the series, also began in Washington, at the National Meteorological Center. Weather reports flowed in here from all over America and the world. The walls were lined with weather maps and charts showing the conditions in every remote corner of the globe. The scientists kept very busy updating the maps and charts, preparing the forecasts and sending them out to pilots, ship captains, farmers, and others who depend on up-to-the-minute weather reports.

To get a full picture of the weather service, I was advised to visit three different types of weather stations: a big city station, an airport station, and a small-sized, average station.

Fortunately I live close to the very large New York City station at Rockefeller Center and to an airport station at New York's LaGuardia Airport. At La Guardia an official drove me around the field, pointing out the various pieces of weather equipment. We actually drove across the runways used by the planes. Each time, though, the driver had to radio the control tower to ask permission. A few times we had to stop and wait—at what felt like a hairbreadth distance from a plane landing or taking off.

The typical average-sized station I went to see is located at Albany, New York. I arranged to spend a full twelve hours, from 10:00 A.M. to 10:00 P.M., at the station to observe meteorologists at work around the clock. Since this book was to be illustrated by photographs, I packed my brand-new Miranda camera and several rolls of film. All day long, I scribbled notes and took pictures of the different meteorologists at work— releasing a weather balloon, receiving and reading the

"While Gilda takes notes, I photograph a scientist for a book in the 'Scientists at Work' series."

weather maps, preparing the forecasts, sending out reports to local radio and television stations, and so on.

When I returned home that evening I was tired, but also very pleased that I had received such a good idea of what goes on in an average-sized weather station. Early the next morning I brought the films, containing over one hundred pictures, to a custom photo lab for developing and printing. I planned to select about twenty or thirty shots to use in the book. Somewhat later I got a phone call from the lab with the awful message, "All of your film is ruined. It looks like your camera's meter was not working." Hearing the despair in my voice, the lab technician went on to explain that he could salvage some key pictures by printing them in a special way.

Still one more hurdle had to be overcome. Just before publication the government changed the agency's name from Weather Bureau to National Weather Service. Thousands of full-color covers had already been printed and the manuscript was being set into type with the old name. To throw out the covers and change the type would cost a lot of money. But otherwise, the book would be out of date right from the start.

Fortunately, the publisher agreed to print new covers and change the name throughout the manuscript. Although the book came out a little late, reviewers praised it for being very timely and the first with the agency's new name.

Enzymes in Action was also published in 1971. In a way, my experiences with this book were similar to those connected with *South Pole Station*. Enzymes were big news at the time I was writing the book, and people wanted to know what they are and how they work. Several big soap manufacturers advertised that enzymes boosted their products' ability to destroy dirt. The word was on everyone's lips as a "miracle cleaner." By the time the book came out, however, the excitement was over. Enzymes had not proven as effective as had been expected. While the book sold moderately well, it was hardly the smash success that the publisher and I hoped it would be.

Hard as it may be to believe, computers were scarcely known in the early 1970s. Few people knew what computers were, how they worked, and what they could do. Still carrying on my mission to inform young readers about the important advances of modern science, I undertook a really challenging assignment—to explain computers to six-to-ten-year-old readers of the Coward-McCann "Science Is What and Why" series. Simply entitled *Computers,* the book was selected as an outstanding trade book of the year by both the Children's Book Council and the National Science Teachers Association. First published in 1972, it is still in print—a remarkably long life for a science book.

That same year also saw the publication of my first book in a series on the various musical instruments for Lothrop, Lee and Shepard. These books were designed to meet the interests of youngsters who were just starting the study of an instrument. Having introduced many students to the instruments of the orchestra in my teaching, I was familiar with their questions and had a ready audience for testing my ideas. Over the next six years, I completed four such books—*The Violin Book* (1972), *The Flute Book* (1973), *The Clarinet and Saxophone Book* (1975), and *The Trumpet Book* (1978).

Coincidentally, our daughter Nancy was studying the violin at the time and Ellie was playing the flute. Since I was illustrating each book with photographs, I quite naturally used the girls as subjects to illustrate some of the points made in the text. Not long after *The Violin Book* was released, Nancy got an excited call from a girl in Jamestown, New York, whom she had met during the summer. The girl had received a copy of *The Violin Book* for her birthday and was surprised to come across the picture of Nancy. Our twelve-year-old daughter, on the other hand, having grown up with publishing, was rather blasé about the entire incident.

Ellie benefited a great deal more from my work on *The Flute Book.* As part of the research, I toured the William S. Haynes flute factory in Boston, Massachusetts. With camera in hand, I followed every step of the flute-making process, starting with the rough metal tubes through to the final adjustments. As a result I had a good chance to see the exacting standards to which each instrument was held. Since Ellie was a serious student, we decided to buy her a silver Haynes flute, a fine, professional-level instrument that she still cherishes.

To brighten the tone of my books and incidentally to shed some light on the topics, I often include humorous stories and anecdotes. Over the years I have been collecting and inventing jokes for this purpose. It seemed very natural, therefore, to assemble a number of these tidbits in a book others could enjoy. I titled it *The Funny Side of Science* (1973). My friend, J. B. Handelsman, an artist whose work frequently appears in *The New Yorker* magazine, supplied a number of original cartoons.

Three new "Scientists at Work" books—*Animal*

"Nancy, age eleven, as she appeared in The Violin Book*"*

"Ellie, age thirteen, as she appeared in The Flute Book*"*

Hospital, Oceanography Lab, and *Pollution Lab*—came out during 1973. Visiting the labs, watching the scientists doing their research, and getting to know them as human beings continued to be great fun. Not only did I get caught up with the scientists' triumphs, successes and achievements, but also with their problems, failures, and struggles. Their difficulties became my own. In fact, in my recurring fantasy, I was able to find solutions to problems that were stumping them!

One time, while I was researching *Oceanography Lab* at the Woods Hole Oceanographic Institution on Cape Cod, Massachusetts, I came close to getting more involved with the work than usual. A research ship was leaving for a three-month tour of the Indian Ocean—and there was room for one more, if I wanted to go. Unfortunately it was about two weeks before the start of the school year and it wasn't possible to leave on such short notice.

The many science books that were published in the early 1960s, right after *Sputnik,* covered most of the basic subject areas of science. They became the backbone of the science book collections in the school and public libraries. By the early 1970s, though, many of these books were out of date. There was a real need for fundamental science books that would include the latest findings.

In 1973 I began a series for T. Y. Crowell that grew to four titles over the next ten years: *The New Water Book* (1973), *The New Air Book* (1974), *The New Food Book* (1978), and *The New Earth Book* (1980). *The New Food Book* was different from the others in the series, since it was written as a collaboration with Gilda. Always well informed about food and nutrition, she made a major contribution in researching and writing the book. It therefore seemed only fair to acknowledge her participation by listing our two names as joint authors.

Around 1974, the U.S. Department of Health, Education, and Welfare was stressing career education in the school. Teachers and librarians were looking for materials that would inform young people about the opportunities in the various careers. Edna Barth, at Lothrop, Lee and Shepard, asked me to write two books in a career series they were publishing, *Jobs in the Fine Arts* and *Jobs That Help the Environment* (1974).

Perhaps the most personally gratifying book of my writing career was *Cancer Lab* (1975), another publication in the "Scientists at Work" series. As with the others, I focused the book on a leading research center, in this instance, the National Cancer Institute (NCI), just outside of Washington, D.C. And as was also usual, I got to know some of the researchers and staff members quite well. William S. Gray, Chief of the Education Branch, had been particularly helpful in introducing

me to the various researchers and in having each section of the manuscript checked for accuracy by an expert. Knowing of his great expertise and high position at the Institute, I invited him to write the Foreword.

Days and weeks went by, but Bill did not mail out the promised material. Nor did he reply to my notes or telephone calls. As the deadline for delivery of the manuscript approached, I made one last attempt to reach him on the telephone.

This time Bill explained the reason for the long delay. Some years ago, he had been a very successful writer on a national news magazine. Although still a very young man, he learned that he had a fatal form of cancer. The doctors who were treating him offered little hope. That is when he came to the NCI. The doctors there gave him some newly developed treatments that literally saved his life.

Bill was an excellent writer, but powerful memories of his illness evoked by my book were blocking his ability to put his story into words. He promised, however, to keep trying to write the Foreword.

On a Sunday morning, the day before the book was due, Bill called me long distance. He dictated the entire two-page introduction over the phone. In a very moving way, it told the story of his battle against cancer and encouraged the book's readers to work to conquer this dread disease.

Cancer Lab proved to be one of the most meaningful books to me personally. I was deeply touched by the powerful emotional effect it had on Bill. The brilliant scientists I observed doing research at the NCI gave me high hopes that we were on the way toward the conquest of cancer. And through all this time I was constantly reminded of my mother's untimely, cancer-caused death.

The three other books that came out in 1975 were quite different, one from the other, yet each one advanced a series I was writing. *Consumer Protection Lab* was the latest "Scientists at Work" book. Another volume in Coward-McCann's easy-to-read "Science Is What and Why" series was *Time after Time.* And *The Clarinet and Saxophone Book* was added to the Lothrop, Lee and Shepard series of musical instrument books.

By the end of 1975 I had written just under thirty books. Seemingly on a wide variety of subjects, the books fell into three basic categories. The main group dealt with the important topics of science, presented as clearly and accurately as possible, and in terms young people could easily understand. The second category had to do with the process of science, how and why modern researchers work as they do, and what they hope to achieve. And finally, the last group included the books on music, each one exploring some aspect of this wonderful art.

In 1976 I added three more books to the various series I was writing. *Medical Center Lab* and *Police Lab* were for "Scientists at Work." *Fitting In,* for the young "Science Is What and Why" series, was the first book on which both Gilda's and my name appeared as collaborators.

Until this point all of my writing had been for large, major publishing houses. Now a call came from Sidney Phillips, president of S. G. Phillips, a small company, for a book on folk music. Although I hesitated, he convinced me that his books got the same distribution as larger houses, but with more care and attention in editing, design, production, and marketing. Just as he said, *The Story of Folk Music* (1976) proved to be a best-seller. It also was named an outstanding book by the National Council for the Social Studies and the Children's Book Council.

A new challenge came from Franklin Watts around the same time. It was an offer to edit a series of books modeled on the "Scientists at Work" idea. The concept was to give readers close-up views of work in various occupations, so that they might become familiar with a variety of career and job opportunities. My editor at Franklin Watts, Wendy Barish (who had been at Crowell), suggested that I write some of the books myself, engage other authors to do the rest, and do the preliminary editing on all of the manuscripts.

Over the next two years we produced six books in the "Industry at Work" series. Unfortunately, librarians and teachers did not quite know how to use these books and they did not sell very well. The series was stopped after the six books were published.

The amazing accomplishments of the American space program spurred my interest in astronomy—a concern that continues to the present day. Fortunately, the publisher G. P. Putnam shares this fascination. In 1977 they published *Quasars, Pulsars, and Black Holes in Space,* the first of a "triple-header" series of astronomy books. This one was followed by *Planets, Stars, and Galaxies* (1978), *Comets, Meteoroids, and Asteroids* (1981), *Space Shots, Shuttles, and Satellites* (1983) and *Star Gazing, Comet Watching, and Sky Mapping* (1985). The books in this series have been particularly well received, having won awards from the Child Study Association, the Library of Congress, the National Science Teachers Association, and the Children's Book Council.

Throughout history the quest to understand the natural world has gone hand in glove with a curiosity about supernatural phenomena, such as ghosts, extrasensory perception (ESP), and unidentified flying objects (UFOs). Two personal encounters with the supernatural sparked my interest in the occult. The first occurred on Cape Cod, Massachusetts, where we spent our summers during the 1960s. At an art gallery one Sunday afternoon, I was approached by a stranger who introduced himself as a painter whose works were being exhibited.

"You grew up in Brooklyn, New York, didn't you?" he asked.

"That's right," I answered, trying hard to remember him from my youth. "Did you?"

"No," he said, and then went on. "You lived around Eleventh Street, didn't you?"

"Yes, but how did you know?" I answered, still struggling to recall his face.

"And you attended Public School 225."

"Yes, I did," I stammered, amazed that he could know so much about me when I did not know him at all.

"Your birthday is in August," he continued. "August 23 to be exact."

Now I was entirely confused. Only my closest friends and relations knew my birthday. When I insisted that he tell me how he happened to have this information he explained that he had a special ability to receive mental messages from certain people. From the moment I entered the room, he claimed, messages began to fly from me to him.

He kept on providing information. "Your father was an upholsterer. You own two cars; they are both black. One is an American product; the other is German—a Mercedes, I think."

I nodded my head in assent as I tried to figure out how this outsider could know so much about me. It was hard to believe that he was receiving messages from me. But it was even more difficult to explain it any other way.

My second brush with the supernatural came some years later when we were spending our summers at the Chautauqua Institution in upstate New York. One day we drove over to Lilydale, a nationally known spiritualist center that was located nearby. Passing through the gates of Lilydale was like taking a trip back in time and space. In the Victorian houses of this community lived spiritualists who did everything from read palms to communicate with the dead. They claimed to be able to see into the past and forecast the future. While no one succeeded in bringing me a message from loved ones who had "passed over," I was impressed by many others who claimed to have heard from spirits.

All this aroused my curiosity, and I decided to learn more about supernatural phenomena. I read widely and had long discussions with many people, from astrologers to psychics to witches. My studies also included interviews with scientists who do research on the occult. And I also looked into material on illusion and trickery written by professional magicians. From my research I learned that much that is called supernatural is really either coincidence, fraud, or human error. But I also came across many supernatural happenings that I could not explain in logical, scientific terms. I wrote up my findings in *The Supernatural: From ESP to UFOs* (1977). In the book I try to provide the facts and information as objectively as I can, allowing the readers to draw their own conclusions. Since the book came out, I am often asked whether or not I believe in the supernatural. It is a question that I go to great lengths to avoid answering.

The research for *FBI* (1977) was as different as could be from that on the supernatural. For a couple of days I visited the FBI Headquarters in Washington, D.C., spending time in each of the divisions, from the crime lab to the National Crime Information Center. Then, as with the National Weather Service, I was advised to go to a typical FBI office.

I chose the FBI office in Buffalo, New York. Two special agents took me out with them as they sought witnesses and suspects in a particular bank robbery case. I listened, sometimes uneasily, as they stopped, questioned, and spoke with people on the street and in their homes. At day's end, I accompanied them to the firing range where they practice their marksmanship.

They handed me a gun and let me take a few shots at the target. They said I did very well for a beginner, but I hope never to fire a gun again.

For my entire adult life, I had juggled three basic activities: writing books, playing viola, and teaching music. The writing, which had begun as an enjoyable sideline, was now occupying an increasing amount of time and represented a growing part of my income. I began to think of giving up teaching and devoting all of my time to writing and playing.

The problem was largely financial. Our two daughters were in college and our chief source of support had always come from my teaching job. Writing books and playing classical music are both notoriously low-paying occupations. Time after time, Gilda and I went over the figures to see how we could make ends meet if I gave up my teaching job. We asked each other "What if?" questions. "What if there is a bad depression, and no one buys books?" "What if libraries stop buying young people's science books?" "What if we get sick and cannot write?"

Gradually, however, I built up my confidence and resolve. I felt that we could probably succeed even under the worst scenario. Finally, in June 1979, after more than twenty-six years of teaching, I resigned from

"Gilda and I speaking to a scientist while researching Consumer Protection Labs*"*

the public school system.

The summer that followed my last days of teaching did not feel different in any way. We rented our house, and went up to Chautauqua, as usual. But when we returned at the end of August the full impact of what I had done hit me.

Any thoughts that I would be working less hard now that I wasn't teaching were soon put to rest. True, I didn't have to drive a half hour to school every day. Now I just walked downstairs to the writing studio in the basement to go to work. But while I had left school at three o'clock, finished for the day, now I'd work on the books morning, noon, and night. And as my own boss I was tougher on myself than the principal had ever been at school.

In part, these long hours were due to anxiety about making a living and the pressure to deliver manuscripts on time. But an even more important reason was that I really loved what I was doing, and I enjoyed all the time I spent working on the books.

For me, writing does not involve sitting at my desk all day long. Every book starts with a period of research, preferably from prime sources. Sometimes this means taking trips to scientific labs, offices, conferences, or other places. Here I meet with the people I

will be writing about and have actual hands-on experiences, where possible. Other times it entails visits to special libraries for hard-to-obtain materials. Almost always it requires checking out stacks of books from nearby public or college libraries. There is also correspondence with people who live in places I can't visit. In my letters I usually ask them questions and request specific reports or publications.

During the research period I immerse myself in the subject—talking, observing, reading. I collect information until I reach a point when I feel I could write the entire book without even looking at my notes. It is then that I start putting the book together.

The first step is usually to prepare an outline, a framework that organizes the material in an orderly, logical fashion. Often, this is the most difficult step of all. Then I start the actual writing. I always prepare the first draft in longhand. The manuscript then goes through a number of typed versions. My goal is to clarify the concepts, make the writing interesting and engaging, and see that the different ideas flow along in a clear, well-ordered way. Some manuscripts I revise as many as a half-dozen times before I am satisfied.

The task of revising the manuscript has been made much easier by the word processor that I got in

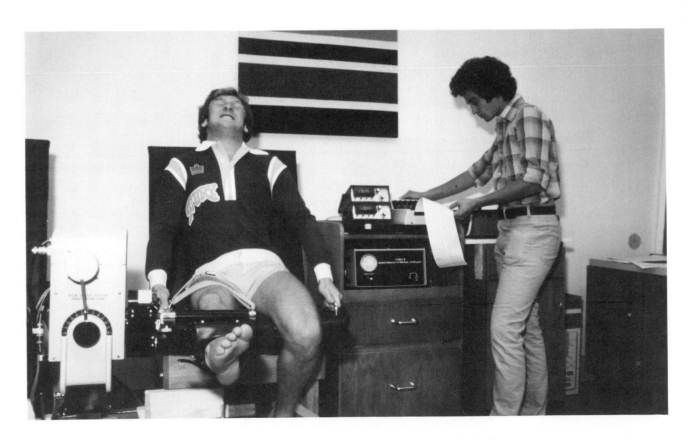

"Making firsthand observations for Sports Medicine*"*

1983. I can change or move anything from a single word to a whole paragraph by just pressing a few keys! A whole book can be automatically typed out by this amazing machine in less than a half hour. It takes longer than that for me to walk to the post office and mail it off to the publisher!

The Photo Dictionary of Football, which was published in 1980, caused me more problems and headaches than any other book. The original concept was to follow the adventures of one high-school football player through a whole season. I was going to write the text and take the photos. The very first day I was on the field with my camera I got knocked over trying to take a particularly exciting shot. I realized that I was not skilled enough with the camera for this type of assignment. Fortunately, I was able to hire Mel Finkelstein, a leading sports photographer from the *New York Daily News,* to take the action pictures.

Then, during the second game of the season, the hero of the book broke his leg. The doctor said he could not play for the rest of the year! This was a really tough situation. I had a contract to fulfill, and Mel Finkelstein had already taken dozens of pictures.

The solution that my editor and I hit on was to use a selection of the action photos to illustrate dictionary-like definitions of the terms, players, and plays of football. With the photos I already had, plus some more that I collected from various college and professional football teams, I was able to compile a complete dictionary of football. So attractive and successful was this book that the editor decided to do a similar book, *Photo Dictionary of the Orchestra* (1981). Here I was able to handle both the text *and* the photos.

A number of subsequent publications were heavily illustrated with photographs, some original, some borrowed from other sources. Among these were *Robots in Fact and Fiction* and *Mad Scientists in Fact and Fiction* (both 1980), as well as *Disastrous Floods* and *Disastrous Volcanoes* (both 1981).

One book has a way of leading to another. While working on the football dictionary, I became familiar with the fascinating world of sports medicine. This new area of medicine, the prevention and treatment of injuries to athletes, inspired *Sports Medicine* (1982), which won an award from the Children's Book Council and the National Science Teachers Association. The research took me into a number of leading sports-medicine centers in New York, Boston, and Philadelphia. I met the doctors and other professionals who treat everyone from the players on the New York Jets and Philadelphia 76ers to amateur joggers, tennis players, skiers, and school athletes.

Unfortunately, I required some medical assistance of my own at a sports-medicine clinic that I visited in

Massachusetts. The doctor suggested that I view a videotape of a special kind of knee operation that he performed before discussing the surgery with me. Forgetting for the moment that I become very queasy at the sight of blood, I watched the screen intently. Presently I felt myself growing light-headed and faint. After being revived by water and receiving some expert attention, I was able to go ahead with the interview.

A chance meeting with brain researcher Tom Carew led to the next book in the "Scientists at Work" series, *Exploring the Mind and Brain* (1983). While speaking to him I learned about his exciting field of study. Tom had discovered actual changes that occur in nerve cells during learning. Working with a big glob of a snail called *Aplysia,* he had found a chemical difference in these animals after they learned a simple type of behavior. I felt privileged to be present at this major scientific breakthrough. *Exploring the Mind and Brain* also covers nine other areas of brain research, ranging from a study on whether mental illness runs in families to tracing the specific action of various drugs in the brain.

From considering the scientific study of the brain I became interested in ways in which people control the brains and minds of others. In an age rife with drugs, cults, and therapies of all kinds, I was amazed to find the growing number of ways to change and direct other people's thoughts. *Mind Control* (1985) was a report on my voyage of discovery into this fascinating subject.

Two of the books I wrote around this time were additions to Crowell's delightful series for very young children, "Let's Read and Find Out." They are *Why I Cough, Sneeze, Shiver, Hiccup, and Yawn* and *Germs Make Me Sick!* (1983 and 1985).

Writers rarely have the chance to observe first-hand the spontaneous response of a child to a book they have written. One of the most heartwarming moments of my career came unexpectedly while on a holiday trip through upstate New York in August 1985. We had stopped in a bookstore in Corning, New York, to buy a gift for a friend. Having wandered into the children's section, however, I saw a young girl sitting cross-legged in a corner, completely absorbed in *Germs Make Me Sick!*

Lately publishers have expressed a need for reference books on many different subjects for young readers. I was asked to write four such books. They were divided between Franklin Watts, who issued *Energy* and *Sports* (1983), and Julian Messner, who published *Computer Talk* and *Space Talk* (1984 and 1985).

Gilda and I have long enjoyed reading and collecting accounts of the strangest and most notorious crimes. When we mentioned this hobby to our editor at

"The Berger family celebrating Nancy's graduation from law school, May 1985"

Messner she thought that many young people would be intrigued by these stories. So we retold the very best in two books, *Bizarre Murders* and *Bizarre Crimes* (1983 and 1984).

Around 1983 the interest in computers reached an all-time high. Everyone seemed to be involved with computer games and home computers. Since I had been writing about computers since 1972, I was asked to do several new books on this amazing tool of the twentieth century.

For Franklin Watts I wrote the basic texts, *Data Processing* and *Word Processing* (1983 and 1984). I also served as the consulting editor for their whole series of books on computer-related topics. The computer book I did for Crowell, on the other hand, presented a basic introduction to computers in the form of questions and answers. It had the obvious title *Computers: A Question and Answer Book* (1985).

At this moment, my last published book, *Guide to Chamber Music* (1985), is also my first adult publication. While it was enjoyable and challenging to write, I intend to continue writing books for young people. In fact, I am percolating with more ideas than ever. At an age when some of my friends are starting to talk about retirement, I am often asked about my own plans "to take it easy." My reaction is always the same. "I can't stop now. I've got too many more books I want to write!"

"On vacation in Assisi, Italy, June 1985"

BIBLIOGRAPHY

FOR CHILDREN

Nonfiction:

Atoms (illustrated by Arthur Schaffert). New York: Coward, 1968.

Gravity (illustrated by A. Schaffert). New York: Coward, 1969.

Storms (illustrated by Joseph Cellini). New York: Coward, 1970.

Stars (illustrated by Marilyn Miller). New York: Coward, 1971.

Computers (illustrated by A. Schaffert). New York: Coward, 1972.

Time after Time (illustrated by Richard Cuffari). New York: Coward, 1975.

Energy from the Sun (illustrated by Giulio Maestro). New York: Crowell, 1976.

Fitting In: Animals in Their Habitats, with wife, Gilda Berger (drawings by James Arnosky). New York: Coward, 1976.

Jigsaw Continents (illustrated by Bob Totten). New York: Coward, 1978.

Energy (drawings by Anne Canevari Green). New York: F. Watts, 1983.

Sports (drawings by A. C. Green). New York: F. Watts, 1983.

Why I Cough, Sneeze, Shiver, Hiccup, and Yawn (illustrated by Holly Keller). New York: Crowell, 1983.

Computer Talk (pictures by Geri Greinke). New York: Messner, 1984.

Space Talk. New York: Messner, 1984.

Germs Make Me Sick! (illustrated by Marilyn Hafner). New York: Crowell, 1985.

FOR YOUNG ADULTS

Nonfiction:

Science and Music, with Frank Clark (illustrated by Gustav Schrotter). New York: McGraw, 1961; London: Murray, 1965.

Music in Perspective, with F. Clark. New York: Sam Fox Music Publishers, 1962.

Choral Music in Perspective. New York: Sam Fox Music Publishers, 1964.

Triumphs of Modern Science (illustrated by John Kaufmann). New York: McGraw, 1964; London: Lutterworth, 1965.

Famous Men of Modern Biology. New York: Crowell, 1968.

For Good Measure (illustrated by Adolph E. Brotman). New York: McGraw, 1969.

Masters of Modern Music. New York: Lothrop, 1970.

Tools of Modern Biology (illustrated by Robert Smith). New York: Crowell, 1970.

Enzymes in Action. New York: Crowell, 1971.

The National Weather Service. New York: John Day, 1971.

South Pole Station. New York: John Day, 1971.

The Violin Book. New York: Lothrop, 1972.

Animal Hospital. New York: John Day, 1973.

Careers in Environmental Control. New York: Lothrop, 1973.

The Flute Book. New York: Lothrop, 1973.

The Funny Side of Science, with J. B. Handelsman. New York: Crowell, 1973.

Jobs That Save Our Environment (consultants Leo Eisel and Carl Tausig). New York: Lothrop, 1973.

The New Water Book (illustrated by Leonard Kessler). New York: Crowell, 1973.

Oceanography Lab. New York: John Day, 1973.

Those Amazing Computers! New York: John Day, 1973.

Jobs in Fine Arts and Humanities (consultants Arthur Kerr and C. Tausig). New York: Lothrop, 1974.

The New Air Book (illustrated by G. Maestro). New York: Crowell, 1974.

Pollution Lab. New York: John Day, 1974.

Cancer Lab. New York: John Day, 1975.

The Clarinet and Saxophone Book. New York: Lothrop, 1975.

Consumer Protection Labs. New York: Lothrop, 1975.

Medical Center Lab. New York: John Day, 1976.

Police Lab. New York: John Day, 1976.

The Story of Folk Music. New York: S. G. Phillips, 1976.

Automobile Factory. New York: F. Watts, 1977.

FBI. New York: F. Watts, 1977.

Food Processing. New York: F. Watts, 1977.

Quasars, Pulsars, and Black Holes in Space. New York: Putnam, 1977.

The Supernatural: From ESP to UFOs. New York: John Day, 1977.

Bionics. New York: F. Watts, 1978.

Building Construction. New York: F. Watts, 1978.

Disease Detectives. New York: Crowell, 1978.

The New Food Book, with wife, G. Berger (illustrated by Byron Barton). New York: Crowell, 1978.

Planets, Stars, and Galaxies. New York: Putnam, 1978.

Printing Plant. New York: F. Watts, 1978.

The Trumpet Book. New York: Lothrop, 1978.

The World of Dance. New York: S. G. Phillips, 1978.

The Stereo Hi-Fi Handbook (illustrated with diagrams by Lloyd Birmingham). New York: Lothrop, 1979.

Mad Scientists in Fact and Fiction. New York: F. Watts, 1980.

The New Earth Book: Our Changing Planet (illustrated by George DeGrazio). New York: Crowell, 1980.

The Photo Dictionary of Football (illustrated with photographs by Mel Finkelstein). New York: Methuen, 1980.

Putting on a Show. New York: F. Watts, 1980.

Robots in Fact and Fiction. New York: F. Watts, 1980.

Comets, Meteors, and Asteroids. New York: Putnam, 1981.

Computers in Your Life. New York: Crowell, 1981.

Disastrous Floods and Tidal Waves. New York: F. Watts, 1981.

Disastrous Volcanoes. New York: F. Watts, 1981.

The Photo Dictionary of the Orchestra. New York: Methuen, 1981.

Censorship. New York: F. Watts, 1982.

Sports Medicine. New York: Crowell, 1982.

The Whole World of Hands, with wife, G. Berger (illustrated by True Kelley). Boston: Houghton, 1982.

Bright Stars, Red Giants, and White Dwarfs. New York: Putnam, 1983.

Data Processing. New York: F. Watts, 1983.

Exploring the Mind and Brain. New York: Crowell, 1983.

Space Shots, Shuttles, and Satellites. New York: Putnam, 1983.

Bizarre Murders, with wife, G. Berger. New York: Messner, 1983.

Word Processing. New York: F. Watts, 1984.

Bizarre Crimes, with wife, G. Berger (illustrated by Cheryl Chalmers). New York: Messner, 1984.

Computers: A Question and Answer Book. New York: Crowell, 1985.

Mind Control. New York: Crowell, 1985.

Star Gazing, Comet Watching, and Sky Mapping. New York: Putnam, 1985.

Atoms, Molecules, and Quarks. New York: Putnam, 1986.

The Whole Book of Hazardous Substances. Hillside, N.J.: Enslow, 1986.

FOR ADULTS

Nonfiction:

Guide to Chamber Music. New York: Dodd, 1985.

Scott Corbett

1913–

The most serious fight I had in grade school involved writing.

A bully moved into our neighborhood, a beefy kid half-a-head taller than I was. I could sometimes sneak to school without meeting him, but there was no escaping him on the way home—and we walked home twice, the first time for lunch. There were no school cafeterias or school buses in those days, not at E.C. White School in Kansas City, Missouri, in the 1920s.

I would love to say we walked a mile to school, but I have seen the route with adult eyes, and I have to settle for half. With Bill bullying me, teasing, shoving, bumping, everything but actually belting me, though, it seemed like five. And I, a skinny little coward, cringed and took it.

Then one afternoon I was carrying home a paper with a good grade on it. For once I had managed to produce something that was neat and almost legible, and was eager to show it off. Well, Bill made a grab, and tore it, and—

That did it. The worm turned, reared up like a king cobra, and struck. In a red rage I began throwing roundhouse swings up at Bill's face so fast I hit him about six times before he got the idea that something unusual was going on. He *was* a slow learner.

We flailed away, toe to toe, for a brief spell, and fortunately Bill didn't seem to know much more about fighting than I did. Because of his size, maybe he'd never *had* to fight. Finally I came to my senses, realized with horror what I was doing, and turned tail to run for home, leaving him still standing there with a dumbfounded look on his face.

Nothing could have been worse than having to go to school the next morning. What would that hulking brute do to me, once he'd had a chance to think things over? But there was no escape. My father gave me a lecture and made me go. My father was a small, wiry man, but fearless, and nobody had ever pushed *him* around. There was something about him that made bullies decide not to try. So off I went to school, all atremble and wishing I had his courage, to face certain death.

Bill was not present. He wasn't there the next day, either. What had happened to him? A lucky punch, that's what had happened to him. Somehow I had

Scott Corbett

managed to give him the juiciest black eye of the season, and he refused to leave the house for two days.

When he returned, the rest of our story was a stereotype to be found in a hundred children's books, including one of my own. From that moment on, we were inseparable. Best friends. Fifty years later Bill and I met and fought again in *The Red Room Riddle,* a story in which almost everything is autobiographical—except for the ghosts.

My parents ruined my chances of ever being a great novelist by giving me a happy childhood. Everybody knows that's no way to become another Dickens.

My father's office was in Jenkins Music Company's warehouse, where he was in charge of drayage and shipping, a lot of which involved expensive things like Steinway grand pianos. He worked hard from eight in the morning till six at night, six days a week, for not

Corbett, about age six. "Note the high button shoes."

much money, yet we were envied by many of our friends and relatives simply because we seemed to get more fun out of life than they did.

When I was five, doctors gave my father a warning. If he wanted to stay alive, he would have to find a job that would keep him out-of-doors for a year. We were soon living in a tiny settlement in the Ozarks called Zincville, where he became manager of a zinc mine. I cannot remember the place, but family stories make it plain I had the time of my life there. The miners were a rough, tough lot who lived for Saturday night, which they spent in the local metropolis, Joplin, Missouri, drinking and fighting. Fighting was their recreation. They would beat the daylights out of each other, then come back Monday morning refreshed and ready to work side by side again. And every one of them was an honorary uncle of mine.

My favorite toys then were several wooden, jointed dolls dressed as circus clowns. One night my favorite one, Brownie (named after my special hero among the miners) was missing. I'd left him outside somewhere. I was stricken. Life could not go on without Brownie. The miners heard about it—heard *me*

wailing, no doubt—and organized a search party. I can still see them (from having heard the story so often) searching the ground around our cottage by the light of the candles in their miners' caps. And the best of it was, Brownie found Brownie.

After a year, we returned to Kansas City, but within three or four years my father was again ordered to live an outdoor life. This time we spent a year near Tacoma, Washington, on the small farm of my Swedish grandfather, Herman Emanuelson. No great amount of farming went on there; my grandfather was a candy salesman who spent the week on the road in his Model T Ford roadster, which he proudly claimed had the smallest steering wheel in the state of Washington. During the week my father found enough to do around the place to keep him in the open air, but both of us lived for my grandfather's return each weekend, because that was when he cleaned out his sample case, discarding the past week's sample candy bars. We were always on hand to help him.

Going to school in the olden days (during a school visit a third-grader once asked me, "What was it like in olden days?") was not much fun. E.C. White School in Kansas City was housed in a grim two-story brick box in which we were incarcerated from nine to four, with an hour off for lunch and fifteen-minute playground recesses in mid-morning and mid-afternoon. Life there was not unpleasant, but—especially during those long afternoons—grindingly boring. Our principal was a hatchet-faced lady named Miss Mack who knew how to maintain discipline. I am sure she never struck a child during her entire tenure, but the mere sight of her inspired icy terror in all of us. Her office was at the end of a long corridor that always seemed dark and gloomy. The sun might be shining outside, but it never shone *there*. If ever we were summoned to that dread place, we were sure it would be never to return.

So I was unprepared for my Washington school. At that time the State of Washington's school system ranked second in the land, just below Massachusetts'. For one idyllic year I attended school in a bright, cheerful building full of bright, cheerful teachers and children, the only time in the lower grades when I thoroughly enjoyed going to school. I walked to school and home through meadows and an enchanted pine forest, past huge anthills higher than my head, or so it seems now, just as it seems as if the weather was always perfect, though anyone who knows the rainy season in those parts knows there is something wrong with this memory picture. It doesn't matter; the happiness was there. In the end, it was harder to leave the friends I made in that school than any I'd ever known before.

My ancestry on my father's side is English, with a dash of Scotch-Irish. On my mother's side it is Swedish and French. In short, I'm a mongrel. In later years I loved to devil my half-Swedish mother with the joke preserved by Carl Sandburg in his poem *The People, Yes:* "What's dumber than a dumb Irishman? A smart Swede."

In one way, I had an unusual upbringing: not once did I hear either of my parents utter an ethnic, racial, or religious slur. No self-discipline in my presence was involved; they simply happened to be without that kind of prejudice. Some of this may have been accidental; before I was old enough to go to school, the upstairs neighbor who helped my young mother out in countless ways was Mrs. Schwartz; the apartment janitor who watched out for me in equally countless ways was James, a man then referred to as a colored man. Later there was Ida, also "colored," who cleaned house and washed clothes for us for most of my young life. She and I were great friends, but she was more than a friend to me, she was someone whose word was law. I would no more have thought of showing disrespect to Ida than I would have to my family. Her last act in our employ was a labor of love for me. By that time I was trying to become a writer—but at the same time I still had certain assigned chores around the house, such as taking out the garbage. One night when I was banging away hard at my first typewriter, Ida knew I was overdue on the garbage run. At that point, though we didn't know it, she was seriously ill. But rather than interrupt me, she talked my mother into letting her do my chore for me. I didn't know about this till too late, because she died the next day. By that time I had lost

Tolerant father, Edward Roy Corbett, watching son Scott's clowning around, 1944

a few relatives, but her funeral was the first one at which I wept, bitterly.

When I said my fight with Bill involved writing, I meant the physical act, not the creative one. At that time, I had no interest in doing any writing I could possibly avoid. On the other hand, I think I became a compulsive reader at about age six. Part of the reason for this may be that I shrewdly picked the right parents: both of them were readers. Once a week they made use of our splendid main public library. By the time I was old enough to read, they always took me with them. I spent my time trotting through the stacks reading book titles, and became quite an authority on the two lower shelves of the adult collection. I may be the only living person who knows that on one bottom shelf were sixteen copies of a novel by a popular magazine writer who must have tried to produce a "serious" work. His name was Clarence Budington Kelland, and the book was called *Dynasty.* I checked those copies week by week, and never once did I find a single *Dynasty* missing from the shelf.

"High fashions in the Twenties. An honorary aunt, my mother, and me." Inspiration Point, Denver, Colorado, 1926

"I n my four years in high school, I never once lost the annual essay contest," I have often told school audiences. I let them hate me for a minute, then add, "And the reason I never lost the essay contest is because I never entered it."

At Southwest High School in Kansas City there were six literary societies, and every senior had to belong to one of them, which meant that every senior had to write *something* for the annual literary contest—poetry, a short story, or an essay. I wrote my offering, *at* our final meeting, the day all entries were due. All the other Baconians (our society) had already turned in their masterpieces to our adviser, Mr. McKee, and gone their way. Mr. McKee was overdue at some central room where entries were to be turned in. I can still remember him standing in the doorway of the room, with smoke coming out of his ears, gritting his large teeth as he said, *"Finish that! I have to go!"* Meanwhile I was desperately scratching away, and finally lunged up at him with my paper, secure in the knowledge that nobody could decipher it enough to tell whether or not I had finished it, anyway. Mr. McKee snatched it and vanished. I'm sure that he, being a sensible man, crumpled my scrawl in his fist as he went down the hall.

Otherwise I had a fairly pleasant time in high school, and it was there I really established a lifelong love of walking, which has always been my principal form of exercise and which has helped keep me healthy ever since. Southwest High was two miles from home via streetcar. My allowance included a daily round trip, probably 5¢ each way, but if the weather was decent I preferred to walk home and save a nickel for less innocent pleasures, such as candy bars.

I picked a terrible time to go to college—1930, the year the Great Depression began. I was lucky Kansas City had a junior college which was, once again, only a streetcar ride away. I was also lucky that it had a faculty far superior to what I encountered at the University of Missouri during my final two years.

KCJC was housed in an ancient firetrap of a building just off Twelfth Street, an area of jazz bands, bars, and brothels that inspired the great jazz number "Twelfth-Street Rag." As the streetcar went by, the girls often waved at us college boys from their upstairs windows. But our junior college was a marvellous school, where each teacher was a sort of *prima donna* who did things his or her way, and did them unforgettably. In the meantime, I had drifted into a life of crime by reading every jokebook I could get my hands on—many of them in the public library, which stocked books with titles such as *3000 Jokes for All Occasions.* I plodded through every joke, good and bad, and in the course of doing so learned something about how jokes are constructed. My lowly beginning as a writer resulted.

In those days the lowest rung on the literary ladder was occupied by pulp magazines. Printed in black and white on the cheapest grade of wood-pulp paper, some featured Westerns, some crime, murder mysteries, and detective stories, and two of the smallest were a rough-and-tumble pair devoted to jokes and cartoons: *Captain Billy's Whiz Bang* and *Calgary Eye Opener.* In that relatively prim era, they were pretty racy stuff.

Fortunately, it only cost three cents to mail a letter way back then. If the rate had been what it is now, I couldn't have afforded to become a writer. Every time I stuffed an envelope with a batch of jokes I had to include a stamped and self-addressed envelope for their return, which ran the cost of each submission up to six cents. I spent a lot of six cents before the day came when *Whiz Bang* finally accepted one of my howlers and I found myself staring in ecstasy at a two-dollar check. That was the standard rate.

Another market I soon tapped, with different kinds of jokes—squeaky-clean ones—was the *Christian Science Monitor.* The jokes were different, but the pay was the same. A couple of years later at a sorority dinner party at the University of Missouri my girlfriend, Alice Hamilton, was sitting next to the dean of the university. He asked her how my joke-writing was going. "Oh, fine," said Alice. "He sends jokes to *Whiz Bang* and the *Christian Science Monitor,* and if he ever gets the envelopes switched you'll have to throw him out of college!"

By this time I had gone on to the university at Columbia, Missouri, for my second two years, majoring in journalism. My allowance for everything while there was $35 a month, which allowed me to get by modestly but perfectly well. Meals at the Dixie Cafe were 35¢, and the ambiance was delightful.

Early in my senior year, however, I broke into the big time—the humor page of the *Saturday Evening Post,* then the world's largest and most popular weekly magazine. I began selling short humor pieces to "Short Turns and Encores," as the humor page was called (later it became "Post Scripts") for an average of $30 per a couple of times a month. It is hard to explain what this dizzying rise in income meant to my lifestyle. I had a great senior year. To make it all better, I got the police beat on our journalism school's daily newspaper, the Columbia *Missourian.*

The setup at Missouri was unusual, and helped account for the fact that Missouri's journalism school was rated as the best in the country. Of course, Columbia University in New York City claimed that *its* school was the best, and this argument was never settled to anyone's satisfaction, but we knew better. The thing was, the *Missourian* was not just a college newspaper, it was a *real* newspaper that covered local news in direct competition with the town paper, and the town paper helped our education by pulling every trick in the book in an effort to beat us out. A scowling, growling old-time police reporter who wore a three-piece suit and a derby and had flat feet that hurt him was my arch-enemy, whom I have always remembered with deep affection. Without necessarily intending to, he taught me a lot.

My only trouble was that I spent so much of my time being an investigative reporter that I seldom showed up for another of my "classes," the copyediting desk, and was threatened with being flunked in that course. But then a break saved my neck. I got on the trail of a gambling den, and caught the chief of police and a few other officials on the scene. One of my happiest memories is of our city-editor professor standing alongside me while I banged out my story, ripping out each page as I finished it and rushing it to the copy-desk in order to beat that day's deadline. Some reshuffling in local government circles resulted, and I received a totally undeserved passing grade in copyediting.

My subsequent career, at least for the next twenty years, would make a good textbook example for aspiring young writers who want to learn how to succeed: my case history would tell them all they need to know about how *not* to go about it.

Instead of getting a job on a newspaper the minute I graduated, I decided I wanted to go right on living the most precarious existence possible, that of a free-lance writer. Actually, I didn't like the notion of working for anybody. The mere idea scared me. The only honest work I had ever done was as a page, or messenger, in a Kansas City branch public library during my junior-college years, in order to pile up some extra money for my next two years at the university. I didn't like having to be *anywhere* at certain hours. As a result, I spent the next twenty years working harder for less pay than almost any job would have provided.

Still and all, after three years, on the basis of my first and only sale of a short story to the *Saturday Evening Post* for the then staggering sum of $500, I did manage to take off for every young American writer's Mecca, New York City, where I lived *la vie de bohème* in a $35-a-month hole in Greenwich Village. And in 1940, incredibly enough, I married a beautiful girl who fortunately had a steady job as a social worker and an aunt who lived on Park Avenue. We began life in Elizabeth's aunt's apartment, and told people we lived on Park Avenue because we couldn't afford to live in the Village. Actually, within a few months we *did* move into our own apartment in the Village, and spent three happy years there, except for the moment when a terrible phone call came from Biltmore Forest in North Carolina, where Elizabeth's mother Sue lived.

Scott and Elizabeth Corbett, "off on our honeymoon to Havana on board the S.S. Oriente *(sister ship of the* Morro Castle, *which had recently burned off the New Jersey coast with great loss of life!)"*

As to mothers-in-law, I had an almost unheard-of experience: mine was one of my favorite people. I think I loved her almost as much as Elizabeth did. So, of course, instead of living forever the way hated mothers-in-law so often do, she died suddenly of a heart attack just two months before our daughter Florence was born. They would have been the greatest of buddies; we have always felt cheated by not having the chance to see the two of them go into action together.

About that same time, Uncle Sam decided the only way to bring Hitler to his knees was to put me in the Forty-second Infantry (Rainbow) Division. I remember it well, because I was called away from the table at my thirtieth birthday party to hear the news that I had received my call to the colors. As I told Elizabeth at the time, happiness carries a heavy price tag. I met many a man in the service for whom induction into the armed forces was a glorious release because it got him away from his wife and family.

I am lefthanded, and have always had a good deal of lefthanded luck. When I arrived at Camp Gruber, Oklahoma, for combat infantry training, the divi-

"Lithograph done at Camp Gruber, Oklahoma, by T/5 Don Freeman in 1943, before either of us had thought of writing any books for children"

sion's weekly newspaper was just being started. I became its reporter-editor, with the complete backing of our commanding general, and had as free a hand as was possible for someone who never rose above the rank of sergeant. I still had to sweat through the training, but then you can't have everything.

The free hand increased once we landed in France and joined the final big push through Germany (we took the southern, scenic route through Bavaria). We hauled along a mobile offset press, operated by a co-editor, and put out the newspaper on the move. Among other things, I wrote a column illustrated by Bill Newmark. Bill and I soon learned to stay as far forward as possible, beyond the reach of rear echelon brass back at Headquarters. We delivered the paper to guys in foxholes who would look up at us in scornful amazement and say, "What are *you* doing up here?" "Well, it's safer," we would tell them. "Have you ever tried at night to get past those trigger-happy sentries they have back at Headquarters?"

We went into Dachau the day the concentration camp was liberated. Newsreel pictures of the place were shown at home, but pictures never tell the whole story. For one thing, you can't *smell* pictures, and in Dachau the smell of death was everywhere. I wrote a letter to Elizabeth about it. When a sister-in-law read it, she said, "Well, I always thought all the stories about the concentration camps were just propaganda, but if Scott was there I guess they must be true." We Americans have a tendency to believe only what we want to believe.

Before our division could be shipped out to the Pacific Theater, the war ended. In October 1945 I was transferred to Paris to become the last editor of the Continental Edition of *Yank,* the Army magazine. Paris was grim, gray, and cold, but still managed to provide a few magical moments. One of the greatest was the chance to interview Gertrude Stein, who had written a book about the GIs she had known, and who was one of the best conversationalists that ever lived. I spent an afternoon with her in that famous apartment in the rue de Fleurus, where the walls were still covered with a treasure trove of modern paintings, including Picasso's portrait of her, now in the Metropolitan Museum in New York. At five o'clock her companion, Alice B. Toklas, came puttering in, pushing the teacart ahead of her. They were good and true friends of many an American soldier, especially us enlisted men.

In February 1946 I was on a troopship headed home. Meanwhile Elizabeth, who had been living in New Jersey with her brother Bill and his family, was scouring the Village for an apartment. Housing was very tight then in New York. Finally a real-estate agent said, "Why don't you buy an old brownstone in Chelsea?" (Chelsea being the district just above the Village.)

"Buy a brownstone? What with?" she wanted to know. Manhattan real estate was something the Astors and Rockefellers bought, not the Corbetts. But the agent meant it. "Don't worry, you'll rent out apartments on the top two floors, and keep the parlor and basement floors for yourselves, and the rents will cover your mortgage payments." So Elizabeth took the plunge, and I came home down West Nineteenth Street to find I was the landlord and janitor of an old four-story brick English basement house (I believe that is actually the correct description).

If you want to make a lot of money in this life, be greedy, but if you want to have a lot of fun, don't be, and you may even come out better in the long run, as we did. We made quite a few improvements in the place, which terrified our tenants in the floor-through apartment on the third floor and the two smaller apartments on the fourth floor; they were sure we would raise the rents. But we didn't. As a result, we all became good friends, and for five years ran a sort of commune, with everybody helping to make the place go. When I first showed up, by the way, on Saint Valentine's Day, I was, of course, still in uniform when Elizabeth and three-year-old daughter Florence greeted me with all the proper enthusiasm. The next morning I decked myself out in civilian clothes. When Florence woke up and came downstairs for breakfast, she took one look at me and ran away wailing, "That's not my daddy! My daddy is a soldier!"

I resumed my writing career, and I wish I could say I did so triumphantly, but the truth is I floundered. My literary agent, Willis Kingsley Wing, soon decided he would have to turn me loose and hope I could find myself (a wise decision: a few years later he asked me to come back, and we never parted again).

During those years I also made a few stabs at radio and television with various partners. We made some sales, but nothing of much consequence. Once Frank Reiley and I were called in and asked to write a sample script for a projected TV version of "The Henry Aldrich Show," which had been a blockbuster on radio for many years but had now petered out there.

Our sample script made us the fair-haired boys. We were summoned to the huge Madison Avenue advertising agency and rushed from office to office signing papers (probably signing our lives away) and getting everything set, after which the executive in charge of us, Baldy No. 2, rushed us over to a rehearsal of the show involving an initial script provided by the originator of Henry Aldrich, a man named Clifford Goldsmith. (To explain Baldy No. 2, by the way: both men we dealt with at the agency were bald, so we kept them straight between us by referring to them as Baldy No. 1 and Baldy No. 2.)

When we reached the studio and walked in at the back, the actors were already busy onstage. Baldy No. 2 muttered, "Oh, darn, rehearsal's already started," and I muttered back hopefully, "Well, I guess we haven't missed much," because I was eager to see a run-through from start to finish.

A couple of days later we got the bad news. The deal was off. We were out. Baldy No. 2 told Reiley, "I don't know why, but Goldsmith said, 'Get rid of Corbett. I don't want him on the show.'" What had I done? We couldn't figure it out. Years later, one morning on Cape Cod, I woke up laughing. Just as we sometimes dream the answer to problems we can't solve during our waking hours (my mother did this once with an arithmetic problem when she was a schoolgirl), I had dreamed the answer to the Goldsmith Riddle. I remembered how, when we entered the studio and

made our low-voiced remarks, he had turned around and looked at us with a hideous smile. Now, my voice happens to project with a force that might have made me a great orator, if I had anything to say (not that such a consideration has ever bothered most orators). If I come up behind someone and say something in what I think is a normal tone, that person often jumps straight up in the air. Even a muttered remark of mine is likely to carry quite a distance. My "Well, I guess we haven't missed much" must have carried to the sensitive ears of Mr. Goldsmith. Having been associated with the radio-TV jungle for so long, it naturally never occurred to him that I didn't mean the remark in a snide way, that I didn't mean we hadn't missed much because his script was probably a dog.

By that time I had long since recovered from any disappointment concerning the show, because it never got off the ground, anyway. But that and other such experiences have convinced me that a guardian angel looks after me and sees to it I never get involved in writing for anyone but myself. If I had, I might have made more money at the time, but I would have been unhappy, unfulfilled, and perhaps unmarried, because I doubt that even Elizabeth could have stood the kind of person I might have become.

Elizabeth and Florence (she hadn't changed her name yet) in front of the Reluctant Landlord's house in Manhattan, 1950

Toward the end of the decade, I sent the first few chapters of a terrible novel to a publisher. At the last moment, not wanting it to be thought I didn't have more than one idea in my head, I wrote in my covering letter, "I also have an idea for an account of my crazy experiences as the landlord and janitor of our old brownstone, which I would call *The Reluctant Landlord.*" The publisher handed me back my novel with understandable alacrity, but wrote, "We are, however, intrigued by your title, *The Reluctant Landlord,* and would like to hear more about it." On the strength of three words followed by a short sample, I signed my first book contract.

I had a wealth of crazy experiences to write about, many of which involved our tenants. Some of these were pretty intimate doings, like the time when, in order to deal with a phone-line crisis in Third Floor Rear, I needed to get into Third Floor Front. I thought the young couple who lived there were away. But when I unlocked the door, after knocking and calling out, they definitely were not. They were very much in bed. I rushed away downstairs so fast I left my keys in the door, and didn't show my face for two days. The morning after my terrible trespass, Elizabeth answered the door to find the young wife outside, holding up my keys. "I thought Scott might want these." While I cowered in a closet somewhere, the ladies had a giggling good time discussing my intrusion. "But why didn't you yell at him when he knocked?" Elizabeth finally asked. "Well, we thought if we kept quiet, he'd go away!"

Anecdotes such as this, once I had finished the book, made me begin to have second thoughts. After all, when the book came out we would not be safely out of the country, we would still be living with our tenants. How would they take it? Would a Lynch-the-Landlord movement swiftly get under way?

I decided to take my chances. When the book was published, I handed out copies and waited in fear and trembling.

They loved it!

It was then I learned an important lesson: people don't care what you write about them if you write it with affection. They were instantly my best publicity agents. They would go into bookstores, stealthily push a best-seller display aside, and put *The Reluctant Landlord* in its place.

In 1950, television was just beginning to come into its own, and the movie industry was running scared. The movie moguls, sure that TV was going to put them out of business, were cutting back drastically. Where as many as six-hundred properties had been bought by the movies each year in the past, that year only a handful, somewhere between a dozen and fifty,

were bought—but *The Reluctant Landlord* was one of them. (Later on, our tenants were indignant when they didn't hear from Central Casting. They saw no reason why they shouldn't play themselves in the movie.)

The sale was a modest one—we held out for and got $17,500 when my craven publisher, in for 10 percent, was ready to settle for $10,000—and with that small fortune in the offing we were ready to make a move we felt was becoming ever more necessary.

Our daughter Florence was seven years old, a New York City kid born and bred, growing up on the sidewalks of a tough neighborhood that was getting tougher. Every time brakes squealed when she was outside, our hearts skipped a beat. One of her friends was a little Puerto Rican kid named Pepe who lived down the block. One day she came home with news she found exciting: a body with a knife in it had been discovered in the basement at Pepe's house. Things like that influenced us, besides which we felt it was time we exposed her to such frills as grass and fresh air.

Scott, Elizabeth, and Jane (who had changed her name by now) on the beach at East Dennis on Cape Cod

At the same time, if we were going to move, we wanted to move beyond the nerve-ends of New York. Cape Cod, we decided, was where we wanted to be.

It was in February 1951—just the time any sensible person would choose to move to Cape Cod—when, with two suitcases and a bottle of champagne with which to celebrate our arrival, we set out in our small new Plymouth Suburban, the first all-metal-body station wagon, and the first car we had ever owned, for our new home in East Dennis, Massachusetts. In a raging blizzard, of course. We thought we would never make it. When we finally crawled into makeshift beds in an otherwise empty house, it was after midnight. Florence was one of those kids, however, who never forgets a rash promise. "Where's the champagne?" she wanted to know. "Go to sleep, or you'll find out!" I snarled. "I'll hit you over the head with it!"

We had been told that the salt air melted a snowstorm overnight on Cape Cod, and that time—the only time I can recall—it did. We cheered up, come morning, and began to look around us. So far we had not seen a sign of life anywhere, and we still didn't. We had moved from the biggest city in America to a village with a winter population of less than a hundred, and at first we thought that maybe *they* had left, too. But then, after a while a curtain began to flutter here and there as neighbors peeped at the new city folks, and presently they made themselves known. The school bus showed up and carted Florence off to her new second grade at Ezra Baker School on the south side of the township. That afternoon when she came running home from the bus, we asked her how she liked her new school. "Great! There's some kids who live right here in East Dennis, too!" The phone rang. I answered. A small boy's voice asked, "Can I talk to Janie?" "Janie?" I said. "You must have the wrong number." "No, no, Daddy—that's me!" cried Florence. She didn't like her name, and had become enamoured of the name Janie. When the teacher asked what her name was, she craftily saw her chance. "Janie Corbett," she replied, and that's the way she went into the books. When the principal heard about it later on, he chuckled tolerantly. "If that's what she wants, it's all right with us!" She was now Janie, and has remained Janie, or at least Jane, to this day, except to her parents.

Once again, before long, death put a damper on life; this time it was my father, who died just moments before we reached Kansas City. We spent some time with my mother, then left her facing her new life with the same kind of courage my father had always shown. She was destined to live nearly thirty years longer, and kept her upbeat outlook despite considerable ill health till the day she died at the age of ninety-two.

East Dennis was then still largely inhabited by genuine, crusty old Cape Codders, but after sniffing around us for a while they took us in. One of the secrets of getting along in a small town in New England is to be ready and willing to serve, instead of expecting to be waited on. At local affairs Elizabeth did her share of the cooking and I joined the men who waited table. By the time the summer people came down to their cottages, some of them complained to us, "We've been coming here summers for twenty years and we still haven't been able to make friends with all the Cape Codders *you* know!" They never learned the secret.

East Dennis was a glorious place to live then, uncrowded, unspoiled, simple. The largest outboard motor on any of the small boats in the harbor was ten-horsepower. The days of fancy folks with bloated power boats were still years away. Old D.H. Sears was still baking his fabulous bread and making his legendary ice cream in the village grocery store. The friends we made on the Cape have been among our closest friends as long as they lived, and some of them are still living.

Not long after we arrived, our movie showed up at the nearest theater, down in Orleans. In winter the Orleans Theater was only open Tuesday nights and weekends. *Love Nest,* which was the bizarre title Twentieth Century-Fox bestowed on it, appeared for one Tuesday night only. There were less than fifty people in the house; thirty-five were from East Dennis. We looked around at each other and said, "If we'd known this was going to happen, we could have brought a covered dish supper!"

Seeing so much of East Dennis there, I had a severe attack of nerves. What if the movie was a real dud? I pictured myself crawling up the aisle to a chorus of boos. Fortunately, though no Oscar contender, it was not too bad—not exactly faithful to the book, but not too bad. An actor named Bill Lundigan played my part; after which he was best known as a car salesman in TV commercials. June Haver played Elizabeth; after which she retired for a time into a nunnery, before giving up the religious life and emerging to marry Fred MacMurray. I kid you not, as Jack Paar used to say; he, too, had a small part as the boyfriend of a Wac. For plot purposes in the movie, I was suspected of having romanced her overseas. She was played by a then little-known actress named Marilyn Monroe. Where was she overseas when I needed her?

My second book, *Sauce for the Gander,* was also a personal experience story, and missed by a whisker being a Book-of-the-Month Club selection. It *was* an alternate selection, but there wasn't much money in that.

By then, we'd had enough harebrained experiences to give me ideas about writing an account of our life as newcomers to the Cape. This time, however, I was dealing with those crusty Cape Codders, so I felt I would have to be careful. I would create a bunch of composite characters, and in that way avoid being run out of East Dennis.

Well, I tried. I wrote a hundred pages of bilge that got blander and blander, duller and duller. One bleak winter morning I sat down at my typewriter and began a new chapter about a character I called Freddie Barr. As the pages suddenly came to life I realized that Freddie could be only one person, a hundred-percent Cape Codder named Billy Stone. I tore up everything but that chapter and began all over again, telling it like it was, with each character unmistakably one of my friends and neighbors. Would it work all right, the way it had with *The Reluctant Landlord?*

It did. The Old Cape Codder I wrote about the most outrageously was one of our most prominent ladies, a descendant of ship captains and a pillar of the village church. When she had caught her breath after reading the book, she said to a friend, "Well, I guess Scott wouldn't have written about us if he didn't like us," and she sent more copies to relatives all over the country than did anyone else. One dear old friend, Celia Crowell, came over to our car outside the post office just as one of my principal characters, Dean Sears, was going in to get his mail. She pointed to him and said, "Why didn't you put *me* in your book? I'm just as much of a character as *he* is!" Not once did any of them pull a sour face on me. Once again I had written with affection, and once again it worked.

We Chose Cape Cod did well, but neither it nor my next two books for adults provided us with a really good living. At one point, another chance to write for television came along. I was signed on as a writer for Bob & Ray, and after getting acquainted with their new TV show in New York, I would be able to send my material in from Cape Cod—and for this dream assignment I would be paid $100 a week! In the fifties, an extra hundred a week was the difference between penury and affluence. We planned trips. We planned improvements in the house.

For my money, Bob Elliott and Ray Goulding are two of the finest and funniest comedians in the business, but television is not their medium. Neither the show nor any jobs connected with it lasted very long. Our temporary affluence went a-glimmering. Again, it seemed I was destined never to write for anyone but myself.

Next a publisher suggested I write a story about taking a couple of kids on a cross-country trip. "Write it off the top of your head," the editor suggested, but I thought I knew better. No, we would actually make the trip, with Florence and a schoolmate as our guinea pigs.

A total disaster. First of all, twelve-year-olds don't want to sit in a car watching scenery go by: they want action. By the time we reached New York State, two days out, they were reclining in the back end of our small station wagon with their feet out the window. "Look, girls!" we cried at one point, "there's the Erie Canal! Look!" Florence yawned. "Why? We read all about it in Mrs. Howes' class." The best time they had during the first part of the trip was in New Orleans, when we went with friends to dinner at Galatoire's while the girls stayed home with poor-boy sandwiches and watched television.

After that, things got worse. Every few days, for some reason, a meal would lay me low. But then I would recover, and life would go on. We all had a great time with relatives in San Francisco, but when we drove on to Yosemite we entered a hellhole where the only way we could find shelter was by renting camping equipment and tenting for the night in a grimy, jam-packed campground.

As far as the girls were concerned, this was *the* best night of the trip.

By the time we reached Elizabeth's Uncle Ken's Massachusetts farm on the Mohawk Trail, I was obviously ill. When we finally got home, our doctor, Rene Murad, took one look at my yellow face and sent me straight to the pesthouse in Pocasset. What he saw was jaundice, the final symptom of hepatitis.

This was the only time to date I've been hospitalized, and I couldn't have picked a better hospital to spend sixteen days in.

The worst was yet to come, however. When I tried to write the book, to be called *Feet Out the Window,* I couldn't make it work, and it was never published.

But then I *did* finally try my hand at a book for children, little knowing I had at last found my salvation. The book's genesis came from a visit some years earlier by a niece who had never been near the shore before, and was called *Susie Sneakers,* because at first she was afraid to wade into Cape Cod's waters, which her mother had warned her were full of jellyfish and crabs and sharks (largely untrue!), without wearing her sneakers. Today the book reads like a historical novel: she arrived on the train!

The year after our cross-country debacle, Charlie Morton, the legendary associate editor of the *Atlantic Monthly,* got me packed on board a destroyer as a "guest of the Secretary of the Navy" to accompany the midshipmen's summer training cruise and write a story about it. For two months I was at sea in the North Atlantic with midshipmen from Annapolis and from various colleges' Naval Reserve Officers Training Corps programs. I returned with robust good health and the makings of a novel for boys I called *Midship-*

Corbett being highlined from the destroyer Turner *to the* N.K. Perry *off Cuba, 1956. "The captain of the* Turner *invited me to lunch the day we left Guantanamo Bay. When I asked how I'd get back to my ship, he said casually, 'Oh, we'll highline you back.' (As a rule only chaplains and doctors are ever highlined.) The ships, incidentally, were doing sixteen knots at the time."*

man Cruise.

Meanwhile, Florence was reaching another crossroads: she was ready for high school, and this was the period when the great college crunch began. Her elementary school was excellent, but kids who attended the regional high were not learning how to study, which was what they needed to do if they wanted to be accepted by a first-rate college. But she didn't want to go away to a prep school, and we couldn't have afforded it, anyway, so we decided we'd *all* move. For one thing, the handwriting was on the wall for our Cape Cod; it was being subdivided and "developed" to death. We began looking for schools in the Boston-Providence area, and found a girls' school in Providence that would take her on. As for me, I had decided I should have a second string to my bow—a paying one—so I looked for a part-time teaching job in another private school there, and by sheer good luck (just before the school year began; one of the new teachers they'd signed on was suddenly grabbed by the army) I

was taken on to teach two classes in English, having never taught a day before in my life.

For the next eight years I taught school mornings and wrote in the afternoons, a combination that proved to be a winner. My next two children's books were back-to-back Junior Literary Guild selections, and one of them, *The Lemonade Trick,* has sold the best part of a million copies in hardback and paper and is still going, after more than a quarter of a century.

Teaching, too, was a great experience. Teaching is closely akin to writing, anyway, because good teaching is a creative art. Like my junior college, Moses Brown School had a lot of first-rate teachers who were real characters—not quite crackpots, but in some instances close. Many times it was hard to keep a straight face—so I seldom tried—but my colleagues were wondrously tolerant, and many became friends I treasured long after I had left their professional company.

In 1963 the school even gave me a sabbatical—one semester off, that is, since I was a half-time teacher.

This brought on the beginning of what was to become a major influence on our lives: freighter travel. By now Florence was in college, at Middlebury. We went abroad for four months, two months in Italy and two in Greece, and to get there we booked passage on an Italian freighter.

As usual, we chose February for our travel month. When we boarded *Maria Costa* in Brooklyn, it was so cold the freshwater lines were frozen. Fortunately, the toilets operated on seawater. The first night out we ran into a storm that reduced us both to seasickness for the first and last time in our seagoing experience, and convinced us that our ship, an ungainly old 12,500-ton hulk, was going to break up at any moment. Anyone who has ever bellyflopped from a divingboard knows that water is a very heavy substance, and that hitting it is like hitting concrete. When *Maria* pointed her bow at the stars and then slapped it down on the waves, she shook and shuddered from stem to stern, and so did we.

The next morning when I staggered onto deck I found our captain taking a nonchalant morning stroll in shirtsleeves under balmy, sunny skies—which is the way things often work at sea, once you get clear of land and reach a decent latitude. Captain Sardi was amused at our concern; the night's acrobatics had been child's play.

From then on, though we still tossed around a bit, we all got our sea legs and began to live the magical kind of life that only seems possible at sea, in open waters, where the horizon is a perfect circle around you, with your own small, self-contained world in the center, the center of the universe. This is an illusion, of course, but illusions are absolute reality when they work.

A satisfactory freighter trip depends on two things: a good captain and a good chief steward, and on that trip we had both. As a bonus, we had ten exceptionally good fellow passengers. A freighter never carries more than twelve, because with fourteen or more an oceangoing vessel must carry a ship's doctor. A freighter *could* carry thirteen, but seamen are superstitious. At any rate, that first trip put the virus in our veins. *Maria* was the first of more than thirty freighters, on which we have spent a total of nearly three years at sea.

Within two more years it became apparent that I could no longer carry on two careers, besides which we had decided to take a really long trip. Florence had graduated and landed a job in an art gallery in San Francisco. Until our sabbatical trip, Elizabeth and I had never been able to go abroad together. Now we began to make up for lost time. We took a freighter trip around the world—and not the sort that would

"Itinerant bookseller visiting his public, 1978"

mean a mere hundred days on a single freighter. Ours involved six different freighters, with stops on the way in Hong Kong, Taiwan, Japan, Egypt, Greece, and Italy. Our rationale was that during the long runs freighters often make between ports I would be able to write my books, and this proved to be correct. I got as much work done at sea (no telephones, no chores, no unavoidable distractions, no set hours) as I would have at home. Even ashore—six weeks in Japan, a month each in Greece and Italy—I kept at it whenever I could. Looking back now, however, I can scarcely believe we actually traveled for eight and a half months. We even managed a gondola ride down the Grand Canal on our twenty-sixth wedding anniversary.

It had taken me an awfully long time to find my way to the kind of writing that suited me best, which was book-length stories, but once I did, that was it. It is estimated that as few as fifty and no more than two hundred authors in America make their living solely by writing books, and for the past twenty years I have been one of them. I don't write reviews or articles, I don't lecture, I don't teach creative writing, I've never been a writer-in-residence at a college—I just write books.

Well, of course, that—like so many things we all say about ourselves—that is not strictly true; I *do* occasionally write an article or a short story when some special situation moves me, but mainly for my own amusement. Some of them find their way into print. For example, not long ago two friends and I decided we needed to find out what it was like to go up in a hot-air balloon. We had a thrilling seventeen-mile trip, including an exciting landing (that's the hardest part, bouncing and tumbling your way back onto *terra firma*). Writing an account of our adventure was irresistible. Shrewdly, and successfully, my agent sent it to the senior-citizens' monthly, *Modern Maturity,* a magazine that likes to show us old gaffers doing things besides sitting in rocking chairs.

Besides not writing much other than books, another thing I don't do is sit down and grimly pound out my quota of words every day, as some writers feel compelled to do. At the same time, I can always get down to it when I need to. In college, and since then, I have known many people I felt were far more talented than I, people I felt could have been better writers; the only thing they lacked was the concentration and self-discipline to stick with it.

One reason I don't write every day is because I spend almost as much time thinking out a story as I do writing it. During that period I seldom make notes; I like to keep the working-out of a story as flexible as possible. Eventually I write most of a book in my head before I set it down on paper. It is the getting of ideas

Jane after trying out Gavin's skateboard down a West 79th Street hill in New York City. "Just before she fell off and broke her ankle, Gavin was shouting, 'Mom, you're going too fast!' "

in the first place I find the most agonizingly difficult part of the whole process. Seldom do they come unbidden. If I waited for a good idea to hit me obligingly on the head as I walked down the street, I would have starved long ago. I have to sit down day after day, sometimes for weeks, and grub around in my mind until that little glimmer finally appears—never a complete story idea, just something so crazy it's a challenge to build a story around it.

From then on, I like to mull over and develop an idea in the course of long walks. But where to walk, without being distracted by the passing scene or by friends and acquaintances who happen along? A few years ago I found the solution: a cemetery. Not only does the one I walk in offer a display of trees and bushes and flowers worthy of a botanical garden, it provides a chance to think without interruption; not one of the residents ever says a word to me. I owe the working-out of several stories to that cemetery, including one *about* it called *Here Lies the Body,* a ghost story full of Satanism and other strange doings. In this one a boy gets a summer job there cutting grass, and among other things he reads the names on the headstones and

*Marty Flusser, Gavin's pal and stepfather,
and wife Jane*

composes black-humor epitaphs such as:

> Here lies the body of Quentin Quigley,
> Done to death by something wriggly.

These caught the fancy of many young readers. Whenever I visited schools thereafter, I was usually greeted by a banner that almost invariably read:

> Here lies the body of Scott Corbett,
> Died on earth and went into orbit.

Only once did I get an idea painlessly. We were on a four-months' freighter run from San Francisco around South America, all the way down the west coast to the tip, through the Strait of Magellan, and up the east coast to Argentina and Brazil. Late one afternoon, bound for the port of Belém, we entered the mouth of the Amazon, a body of water so vast we could not see the other bank. Before we left on the trip, an editor had urged me to write a funny story for girls. Dinnertime was imminent, but I decided to go on deck for a few minutes just to start considering possibilities. And there in that exotic Brazilian setting, thousands of miles from home, I began to think about my own boyhood, and how as a Boy Scout I had been the world's worst cookie salesman (we Boy Scouts sold cookies in those days, once a year, door to door). I transferred my inept salesmanship to a Girl Scout, added a few insane touches, and within minutes had a good start on a story about a girl and her pet frog that became *Steady, Freddie!* Never again have I had that kind of luck.

Thinking back to my own boyhood, thinking what it was like to be a boy, has gotten me started on more than one story. Once another editor wanted a tough, funny story about city kids. A piece of cake! I thought. Two fruitless weeks later I was gloomily looking out of my top-story window at a Siberian scene that mirrored my mood. A heavy snowstorm had swept in suddenly. I watched a city bus picking its way painfully down a steep grade through the snow, and began to recall streetcar rides I took in my high-school days to a little outpost called Waldo, at the end of the line.

Waldo was the end of the line in more ways than one: a seedy collection of small shops and stores; strangely enough, what I liked about that scene was the desolation of it. I liked being there along toward dusk on a gray day, sniffing the melancholy atmosphere of the place for a few minutes, and then rattling away again on the streetcar toward the familiar cheeriness of home. I remembered all this and thought, eventually that bus would find its way to some drab little square at the end of *its* line. Now, what if a young punk, the last passenger left on the bus, decided to stick up the driver (they still made change in those days), and what if two boys, sons of a police sergeant, saw him doing it . . . A story called *Cop's Kid* took it from there.

For me, that "What if . . . ?" is what makes a story. I start with an everyday situation, and then think, "What if, instead of the expected, the unexpected happens?" The first two pages of *The Lemonade Trick* are straight out of my boyhood; then comes the zany "What if . . . ?", and before I was through exploring the possibilities of that question, not only *The Lemonade Trick* but eleven more Trick books resulted. The first section of *The Red Room Riddle* is strictly autobiographical (remember that fight with Bill?); the "What if . . . ?" part turns it into a ghost story. I'll never really understand where story ideas come from, but I've always been humbly thankful they come at all.

Time after time from New York through the Panama Canal to the Orient, time after time to

*On safari, Serengeti Plain, 1983: Grandpa, Gavin,
and Grandma*

Gavin's biggest moment, with noted young paleon-tologist Peter Jones in Olduvai Gorge, where in 1958 Louis and Mary Leakey discovered the skull of the hominid they named Zinjanthropus boisei. *Left to right: Gavin; Peter; Dr. Ben Page, Stanford geologist; and Grandpa.*

the Mediterranean, once to South Africa, around South America, around the world twice, once in each direction—it is fortunate we traveled when we did, because the best days of freighter travel seem to be over. Fewer and fewer freighters continue to take passengers. Often in recent years we have had to resort to the dullest but fastest means of getting places. We even had to fly to Singapore to reach an American President Lines freighter that spent a month in the Indian Ocean and Arabian Sea and ended up right back at Singapore.

A year or so before that trip, the month we spent in China was worth any amount of flying, and almost more so was East Africa, where we took our grandson Gavin on safari to the Serengeti Plain, Olduvai Gorge, and Ngorongoro Crater in Tanzania. With our penchant for choosing strange times to do things, we managed to be there at a time when Tanzania had closed its borders to Kenya. Planes were not allowed to make the forty-five-minute hop from Nairobi to Kilimanjaro Airport in Tanzania. Instead we had to fly to Addis Ababa, change to an Ethiopian Airlines plane, and fly in from there.

To nobody's surprise but the Tanzanian government's, their tourist trade dropped to—well, there were five in our party, and we met about seven or eight others here and there. We had the place to ourselves. It was an ideal way to see the magnificent animals and birds and landscapes. Of all the areas we have visited, East Africa draws us back the most. No other place on earth looks like East Africa or feels like East Africa. May it never be completely ruined.

When you get to be grandparents, you feel you

are entitled to a little entertainment from your grandchildren. Gavin is our only grandchild, but fortunately he's a one-man band. For example, I think of that time at the lodge above Ngorongoro Crater. We stayed in cottages that stood at some distance from the lodge. One night about dusk, after a day with the animals down in that vast, incredible caldera, as old volcano craters are called, we walked to the dining room ahead of Gavin, who was still dawdling in his shower. We had been warned that a Cape buffalo was fond of grazing in an area not far from the path, and were told to give him a wide berth, since these can be the most dangerous of African animals if aroused. We kept an eye out, but saw no sign of him.

Presently Gavin came walking in rather briskly. You might even say he was puffing. Saucer-eyed, he said, "You know that buffalo? Well, he was there, right there!"

"Say! How did you feel?"

"Well, I was nervous, but I didn't hesitate, I walked quietly by so he wouldn't get interested. I did a lot of tiptoeing—I mean, *fast* tiptoeing!"

As I've always maintained, if you're going to have daughters and grandsons, you might as well have amusing ones.

So time goes on, and I still write books. I don't work at it as hard as I once did, yet every so often another book or two add themselves to my list of over seventy books. The trouble is, only the kids can retire me, only they can put me out to pasture. Often they end their fan letters with, "Keep on writing books, and I'll keep on reading them!" I hope they'll do their part, and I'll probably keep on doing mine. It gets to be a habit.

Professor Charles Sullivan and Corbett (licking his dry lips just before the hot-air balloon went up). "With John Monaghan, managing editor of the Providence Journal, *and Paul Stumpf, balloonist, we floated seventeen miles and came down in a gravel pit."*

BIBLIOGRAPHY

FOR CHILDREN

Fiction:

Susie Sneakers (illustrated by Leonard Shortall). New York: Crowell, 1956.

Midshipman Cruise. Boston: Little, Brown, 1957.

Tree House Island (illustrated by Gordon Hansen). Boston: Little, Brown, 1959; London: Dent, 1959.

Dead Man's Light (illustrated by L. Shortall). Boston: Little, Brown, 1960.

"Trick" series (illustrated by Paul Galdone). Boston: Little, Brown, 1960–77. *The Lemonade Trick,* 1960; *The Mailbox Trick,* 1961; *The Disappearing Dog Trick,* 1963; *The Limerick Trick,* 1964; *The Baseball Trick,* 1965; *The Turnabout Trick,* 1967; *The Hairy Horror Trick,* 1969; *The Hateful Plateful Trick,* 1971; *The Home Run Trick,* 1973; *The Hockey Trick,* 1974; *The Black Mask Trick,* 1976; *The Hangman's Ghost Trick,* 1977.

Cutlass Island (illustrated by L. Shortall). Boston: Little, Brown, 1962; London: Dent, 1964.

Danger Point: The Wreck of the Birkenhead. Boston: Little, Brown, 1962.

The Cave above Delphi (illustrated by Gioia Fiammenghi). New York: Holt, 1965.

One by Sea (illustrated by Victor Mays). Boston: Little, Brown, 1965.

The Case of the Gone Goose (illustrated by Paul Frame). Boston: Little, Brown, 1966.

Pippa Passes (illustrated by Judith Gwyn Brown). New York: Holt, 1966.

Diamonds Are Trouble. New York: Holt, 1967; revised edition published as *The Trouble with Diamonds* (illustrated by Bert Dodson). New York: Dutton, 1985.

Cop's Kid (illustrated by Jo Polseno). Boston: Little, Brown, 1968.

The Case of the Fugitive Firebug (illustrated by P. Frame). Boston: Little, Brown, 1969.

Diamonds Are More Trouble. New York: Holt, 1969.

Ever Ride a Dinosaur? (illustrated by Mircea Vasiliu). New York: Holt, 1969.

The Baseball Bargain (illustrated by Wallace Tripp). Boston: Little, Brown, 1970.

The Mystery Man (illustrated by Nathan Goldstein). Boston: Little, Brown, 1970.

Steady, Freddie (illustrated by Lawrence Beall Smith). New York: Dutton, 1970.

The Case of the Ticklish Tooth (illustrated by P. Frame). Boston: Little, Brown, 1971.

The Big Joke Game (illustrated by M. Vasiliu). New York: Dutton, 1972.

Dead before Docking (illustrated by P. Frame). Boston: Little, Brown, 1972.

The Red Room Riddle (illustrated by Geff Gerlach). Boston: Little, Brown, 1972.

Dr. Merlin's Magic Shop (illustrated by Joe Mathieu). Boston: Little, Brown, 1973.

Run for the Money (illustrated by B. Dodson). Boston: Little, Brown, 1973.

The Case of the Silver Skull (illustrated by P. Frame). Boston: Little, Brown, 1974.

The Great Custard Pie Panic (illustrated by Joe Mathieu). Boston: Little, Brown, 1974.

Here Lies the Body (illustrated by G. Gerlach). Boston: Little, Brown, 1974.

Take a Number. New York: Dutton, 1974.

The Boy Who Walked on Air (illustrated by Ed Parker). Boston: Little, Brown, 1975.

The Case of the Burgled Blessing Box (illustrated by P. Frame). Boston: Little, Brown, 1975.

The Great McGoniggle's Gray Ghost (illustrated by Bill Ogden). Boston: Little, Brown, 1975.

Captain Butcher's Body (illustrated by G. Gerlach). Boston: Little, Brown, 1976.

The Great McGoniggle's Key Play (illustrated by B. Ogden). Boston: Little, Brown, 1976.

The Hockey Girls. New York: Dutton, 1976.

The Great McGoniggle Rides Shotgun (illustrated by B. Ogden). Boston: Little, Brown, 1977.

The Discontented Ghost. New York: Dutton, 1978.

The Foolish Dinosaur Fiasco (illustrated by Jon McIntosh). Boston: Little, Brown, 1978.

The Donkey Planet (illustrated by Troy Howell). New York: Dutton, 1979.

The Mysterious Zetabet (illustrated by Jon McIntosh). Boston: Little, Brown, 1979.

The Great McGoniggle Switches Pitches (illustrated by B. Ogden). Boston: Little, Brown, 1980.

The Deadly Hoax. New York: Dutton, 1981.

Grave Doubts. Boston: Little, Brown, 1982.

Down with Wimps! (illustrated by Larry Ross). New York: Dutton, 1984.

Witch Hunt. Boston: Little, Brown, 1985.

Nonfiction:

What Makes a Car Go? (illustrated by Len Darwin). Boston: Little, Brown, 1963; London: Muller, 1968.

What Makes TV Work? (illustrated by Len Darwin). Boston: Little, Brown, 1965; London: Muller, 1968.

What Makes a Light Go On? (illustrated by Len Darwin). Boston: Little, Brown, 1966; London: Muller, 1968.

What Makes a Plane Fly? (illustrated by Len Darwin). Boston: Little, Brown, 1967.

Rhode Island. New York: Coward, 1969.

What Makes a Boat Float? (illustrated by Victor Mays). Boston: Little, Brown, 1970.

What about the Wankel Engine? (illustrated by Jerome Kühl). New York: Four Winds, 1974.

Bridges (illustrated by Richard Rosenblum). New York: Four Winds, 1978.

Home Computers: A Simple and Informative Guide. Boston: Little, Brown, 1980.

Jokes to Read in the Dark (illustrated by Annie Gusman). New York: Dutton, 1980.

Jokes to Tell Your Worst Enemy (illustrated by A. Gusman). New York: Dutton, 1984.

FOR ADULTS

Nonfiction:

The Reluctant Landlord (illustrated by Paul Galdone). New York: Crowell, 1950.

Sauce for the Gander (illustrated by Don Freeman). New York: Crowell, 1951.

We Chose Cape Cod. New York: Crowell, 1953.

Cape Cod's Way: An Informal History. New York: Crowell, 1955.

The Sea Fox, with Manuel Zora. New York: Crowell, 1956; London: Hale, 1957.

Julia Cunningham

1916-

Julia Cunningham

playing in the city's parks (the giant stones were castles), kindergarten, myself the Empress of the classroom (a privilege not destined to endure), an awareness of stars on a single evening walk with my father, the coziness of after-supper with a story-telling, book-reading mother to lean against and listen to. And then the vision widened and the play acting began. Almost every evening the costume trunk was opened, the rugs transforming chairs into thrones, beds into pirate ships, rafts, islands (while the springs twanged). Kings and knights, queens and princesses, dragons and witches walked and fought and spoke, the knowledge of being children forgotten. Each Saturday I added a ring from Woolworth's to my jewel chest, those weekly dimes purchasing as much as pieces of eight.

A long velvet curtain separated the living room from the dining room and I knew that on bad days, my

Aunt, Mary Larabie

Sometimes when quietness enters my small house without knocking I sit in my desk chair and become a part of this near-silence. I seek nothing. I wish nothing. I wait.

I am waiting now. I am waiting for my self as I was and am so that I may speak as honestly as this self allows.

Slowly and clearly as a character emerging into a book I begin to collect the images.

The first is of a child of two in a New York City hospital. The long illness, the pain is shadowed but not that first memory of music. The aunt I loved, my mother's sister, was singing to me with the same gentleness that she held my hand through the terror of the nights. Music. The beginning of a river of music that would flow through and support whatever followed.

The next was a series: New York, two brothers,

Julia, age six, Atlantic City, New Jersey

own, the Devil stood behind it, regarding his prey. How piercingly real were these groups of unreality.

Is this where the writer begins before the writing starts? I believe so. The choice came later but the inner landscape was already formed.

At age six my memory holds the last true Christmas, the tall candlelit tree hovering over the magical, tiny model village, inhabited by inch-high people, the last gift of a father who was about to disappear, leaving me hooded by a darkness I couldn't understand.

His going was never mentioned, a subject prohibited by our mother. My nearest brother and I believed he was in some distant, romantic country, working, and during the next two Christmases, from the windows of rented houses, we watched the corner of the street for a return that never came. We never spoke as we watched. Our hope was too deeply understood and I believe now that we feared that words would have destroyed the thin chance of the waning miracle. And wasn't it somehow our fault that he left?

The year I was nine, living in my grandmother's great, brown house, I gave up, and became so ill danger dwelled in the bottomless, drowning nightmares. From wherever he was the vanished father sent me a crate of tangerines, then a luxury. I never touched one.

My spirit slowly consented to get well but I was not the same. I stepped over the line of nine into a role that later was to prove more than uneasy, but I remember the moment of decision. I would learn the rules that led to approval, acceptance, popularity and use them with success. I would become a pretender.

Is this when so many of the characters in my books were fated to be orphans? I believe so, unconsciously and inevitably. One's characters are oneselves and no escape is possible.

I tell all this, risking the "so what?" of the reader of this essay because I am convinced that many of us who turn to writing, who partially live in imagined worlds, have early come to feel the relief and release this offers. This is a kind of necessity and may provide the drive to continue.

As an adult, briefly passing by the brown house where this change took place, I met that nine-year-old again. We walked together the three blocks under the elms on the root-cracked sidewalk I had taken each morning to school and our minds conversed. Soundlessly she said, "I forgive you." Make of this what you will, but for me this reconciliation joined me, at last, to that long-ago self I had betrayed, now no longer lost. And if I still write about orphans she helps me make them true.

During the school years that followed, the disguise worked however hidden the real self. I learned as I

Julia, at age nine

attended a succession of public and private schools, the necessary devices and deceits to attain acceptance and even loyalty from my peers.

Writing of some sort was part of my days but the only existing evidence of this first period of eight and nine I found in my trunk and, just for fun, here it is, title unknown.

Once there was an author. Not the story book kind, a poor starving man who always makes a success but a wealthy landowner. In the public's eye he was a success but he himself was a failure.

Although he was a fine, grave and sincere old gentleman he had never filled his heart's desire to write a book made up of his own true thoughts. Ten years had passed and yet he had not written his book. He was never happy, not even when he was made a present of a wonderful jewel.

He hated the jangle of necklaces and the sparkle of jewels. He cared not for poverty or wealth. He disliked music and dancing. He approved not of drinking or smoking. Nor had he any desire but for his book and that was never written, poor gentleman, for he suddenly died midst all the things he despised.

The End

(I am pleased to be assured that I will end up happier than the fine old gentleman.)

There followed three-page novels about nuns who fled their convents in order to live in a New York garret, poor but extremely happy, to fairly tales that, though I was of course unaware of this fact, dragged their seven-league boots through much-too-long winding roads, lined with too many dragons, princesses who were traditionally helpless, knights without fault, and very usual plots. I had more faith in these. They were respectably long and sometimes so choked with dialogue the story line fainted midway for lack of action. Then came a valiant attempt at realism, which, as I remember, consisted mostly of as much innocent sordidness as I could summon from my small bag of experience.

I was twelve when I sent out my first manuscript, prompted by the same beloved aunt who had sung me that first song—a brief story about a duck who couldn't stop laughing. The editor of the magazine wrote a letter, a serious rejection letter, saying I had talent (perhaps he had children at home). I was very proud and this may well have set the mold of my goal to someday be published.

I must pause here because this is when I met the English teacher whose faith gave me the essential strength to create. The place was a school in Charlottesville, Virginia, where I went from eighth grade through high school. It had once been a mansion, columned, gracious, and peopled for me that first autumn by strangers. I was accustomed, after so many other schools, to stand back, sorting the losers from the leaders. I was both watchful and lonely and sometimes fearful but these never showed. My disguise was by now most skillfully tailored and I knew how to move forward and when.

The classrooms must once have been slave quarters, elevated as they were over storerooms and all leading out onto an L-shaped gallery. Only one was on a level with the courtyard, the English Room. This square space was somehow privileged, with its windows onto the green lawn, a magnolia tree and three oaks. And seated before us—we were only fifteen students—behind an antique table that was her desk, was the teacher.

I had no reason to hope or to expect it, but as she looked at us, one by one, I could tell she really saw us. We had identities for her and I hoped that she would sense the eagerness of that inner self that danced and

Mother, Sue Marshall Larabie, age thirteen

The author's mother at age twenty-five and in 1948

sang and wrote poems. She did. In all the five years I read and wrote and learned, I can't remember any personal conversations with her, but our friendship was real and I believe now that this reality grew from what her faith in my very unformed talent encouraged me to write. On paper, with words, the shield was down and I was freed to be original, often outrageous, and certainly trying for what can only be tried for.

Before the decision is made, either by choice or circumstance, of what we are to become, before we must face the actual doing, taking that first step onto the concrete, abandoning the grassy slope under the willow tree where all dreams seem possible, I believe that many future writers have desired to be something else. I know I did.

My earliest ambition was to be a violinist. This probably because my mother played the violin and I grew up hearing her practice—a sound I love today. Also she would tell me stories of her youth as a student in Paris. She gave me my first visions of France which never left me.

When I voiced my wish to learn, she took me to visit a class of my peers who had studied for two or more years. The off-pitch efforts that emerged from their instruments told me that my wish wouldn't be strong enough to survive so I chose the piano. This ended two years later when we left the southern town, the piano sold to pay a part of the back rent. The Depression also saw the loss of her beautiful violin.

Then came art lessons, given most generously by an artist who let me do the sweeping and brush-cleaning in exchange for instruction. My recognition that my talent was too small obliterated the drive to paint.

Acting was another lure but suddenly these somewhat nebulous aspirations were cut off by the necessity to earn a living.

I returned to the scene of my childhood, New York, and progressed from a deadly job in a bank to a music store where, failing accounting, I was made an editorial coordinator. I liked this contact with the musical world but after a time restlessness set in. Then I was sent by an agency to Dell Publishing and an interview with a very stylishly hatted lady editor (she was never without one) who thought I could successfully answer the fan mail of her movie-story magazine. Finally I was promoted to associate editor, perhaps because she was bored with doing the monthly editorials, and gave me the interesting problem of writing happy drivel above her signature. I was also given outside assignments for the magazine of making screen plays into short stories. My ultimate triumph was condensing *Great Expectations* into fifteen hundred words. Factual writing has never been my slot but it all helped, I am certain, to keep juggling words on my typewriter.

There were, of course, other jobs, a few part-time ones when I would essentially waste the free afternoons squeezing out meaningless fairy tales and inadequate short stories. But by this time my goal had solidified. I wanted to be a good writer. Poetry became a major occupation, although it had from very early days been a kind of therapy for having locked up my inner self. The burden of my submission to this false image had to be lightened somehow and poetry was one way.

One of the positions I liked the most was working in the book shop of the Metropolitan Museum. I am naming this place specifically because it provided an entire setting. It was a kind of homecoming. As children we had spent many adventurous hours in those galleries. Egyptian tombs and knights in armor, along with paintings and objects that we either adopted or didn't were part of our world. I still have silent friends there, the best loved a little, seated, twelfth-century stone monk from Chartres. His grave smile represents a comfort to me.

I also loved these years for another major reason. I was surrounded by people, not only friends, but that vast and fascinating grouping of everybodies called the Public. An immediate kinship was formed, though I am not forgetting as I write these words that one had always the protection of the Other Side of the Counter. The variety, as can be easily guessed, was myriad, from all sections of New York, the other States, and the farther world of Europe.

While the living continued—movies; long, into-the-morning discussions; experiments in the give-and-take and be-taken with friends and enemies—writing filled the margins of the days. One incident stays very clear.

One day, thanks really to the influence of Kenneth Grahame, I wrote a book about a fox. All I can recall of the fox is his name—Matthew—and his heroism in facing a pitiless world with honor. It was Matthew who led me into the Viking office of a very great lady, May Massee. She had rejected the story but wanted to see me.

In spite of my young maturity it was a very shaky, would-be writer who was introduced to a very stern silhouette, outlined in sunlight. She never smiled once but she talked and what she asked of me was a promise—that I go on writing. I felt glorified by such a show of confidence.

This rim of glory had to suffice for the next fourteen years—but I am getting ahead of myself.

After the first two years in a music club, where I was admitted thanks to a family connection, I shared apartments with friends who brought light and fun into my life. I required such friendships to keep me steady,

but gradually my disguises began to tatter at the sleeves, to wear thin, to show an all-too-vulnerable shape beneath.

The fabric ripped from head to heel, in an instant, during a Connecticut weekend at a party with intimate friends. In the middle of a sentence a rush of panic strangled me, the words blocked and I sat there undone, finished.

The next week I found a psychiatrist, the person and the friend (a three-fold treasure), who would help me to cast off my many-layered concealment. We travelled together, once a week, back to the beginning, to the scars of illness, to the loss of the father, and forward to the present. Many weeks passed before I realized that he was speaking to me in my own choices of language, using my own words and particular eccentricities of description. He was thus subtly showing me myself, my real self, and the moment came when I knew I was free, that *I* had come to be, but could only say, "I feel like new grass." He knew too. I had begun to grow, for better or worse, clothed however tentatively in my true colors.

The next scene, soon afterward, was a ship, a small ocean liner, the *De Grasse,* in the month of Octo-

Cunningham in front of the Institut de Touraine, Tours, France, 1951

Cunningham at the Cathedral of Chartres, France, 1956

ber, with me on board headed for France with very little money, French forgotten, and feeling of destiny. The storms of that passage seemed a kind of echoing of past darknesses but with a wonderful, if often frightening, difference. I shivered between "Oh, God, what am I doing?" and "Thank God I'm going."

When had the dream of France begun? With my mother's stories of her two radiant years in Paris? With the little Pierrot doll my artist-aunt had sent me when I was six? With the dedication to that most beautiful language in high school? All these and a presentiment that a part of me would recognize what up to then I had never seen or heard or loved?

What gifts would be mine! They were hard won but they came.

On the train from Paris to Tours, the city where I had chosen to study, I met a first kindness. A rotund Frenchman half my size, suited in brown cinnamon, ushered me off the train at the right station and lifted my two heavy bags down those perilous steps. I never saw him again in the following nine months, but his face has remained indelible.

The next day the language school gave me the name and address of a French family, consisting then of a war widow and her mother, who despite the cranky reluctance of the mother who had all the qualities of a bad witch, had decided to try taking in a boarder, a foreigner. They spoke no English. I knocked at the door of their apartment at the designated time and it was opened by someone who used those first few seconds to look not only at me but through me. I waited, not yet accustomed to this kind of intuitive scanning so usual in the French, and all the words I had to offer were "Je suis américaine." The person in the doorway smiled. My complete vulnerability needed that smile and the welcome that was immediate. So began the dream.

The beauty of the dream was there—is there—from the cobbled streets to the mansard rooftops, down through the lines of poplars leading to castles, up through the great skies, made majestic by the sun risings and settings and the noblest of clouds.

But although I gorged myself on the language with four hours of school and five of study each day, I was prey to all the uncertainties that a child must be prey to in the world of adults. I actually was a child again but with an adult's fear of seeming stupid and no way to show myself otherwise. I had to accept the role of utter helplessness. My defenses were gone. I could pretend nothing. I was a true stranger and I had to communicate with silent honesty. That was all I had.

In spite of the evident kindness of my hostess, a magic presence of sympathy and understanding, I was plummeted into a kind of rebirth that was excessively painful. I remember having a series of dreams in which I was encircled each night by gothic-featured judges in high seats (echoes of the trial of Jeanne d'Arc!) who could all speak French and did, vehemently, demanding answers of me to questions that were so much sound and no sense.

I've detailed this elected hell just to make reasonable the statement that within it I had forgotten that such a thing as laughter existed. The tension had eliminated even the chance of it. Until one evening, one blessed evening, a very small thing happened. I was rather wistfully standing just outside the kitchen door, watching the two ladies prepare supper. The younger, who had already accepted me as a person and a friend, was rinsing a bunch of parsley. She moved to the open window to shake the water from it when a gust of wind tore it out of her hands and it went scooting down the street. She looked at me, raised both hands in a very Gallic gesture, and said "God desired it." By some miracle I understood but also captured the comedy she intended and I collapsed into the relief of laughter. My first three weeks of dumbness were broken. I was myself again. No more nights of judgment. And from that time onward the clouds of non-comprehension scudded from my horizon so fast I was even able to reply to

At an outdoor market, Perigueux, France, 1985

questions like "Do you like flowers?" and "Last night did it not fall of the snow?" with appropriate one-syllable responses.

During that space of enforced silence I took solitary trips to see the great chateaux of the Loire, one every Saturday when the school left me free. Made sensitive by isolation, I found a direct appeal in the Middle Ages, a walking into them as simple as the feeling those long-dead people themselves felt toward their cathedrals and monasteries and stone stables and stained glass windows. It was alive for me, all of it, and the absence of the kings and peasants and troubadours and artisans was not a true absence. They were there as truly as I was. And this was not a ghostly happiness either. The winter rose I stole one snowy day from the gardens of Chenonceaux was mine just as certainly as another rose was once François the First's when he was around to pick it.

I would like to include that in opening my mind to a living appreciation and application of what is so beautiful in the French language I gained a new appreciation of my own, a new and largely unconscious awareness of how to use English words to more effectively carpenter a story. I believe I arrived at a sense of essence, for this was when, after many years of rejections, I began to write well enough to publish. In that same attic where I wrote on an orange crate beside a brass-bound trunk and a violin case I managed to construct my first-to-be-published book about a fox who was—naturally—French.

Then came a time of further testing. Although that first "new grass" had thickened and risen to the height at least of a violet, a shock cleaved my now-comfortable routine of school, private lessons, wondrous meals, talk (however limited, I was an eager listener), study, and writing. The daughter of my French family was coming home to have a baby. I had to go.

The pension I stepped into after Christmas might have been an ogre's dwelling. I have twice tried to use this background for a novel, a decayed manor house run by two mad sisters, the pitiful rations of food while they later feasted in the kitchen, the brown dreariness of the rooms and, last, my own serious illness. But both trials were without success. The terrible combat with the shadow of death, both physical and psychological, is perhaps still too much with me. An overdose of reality can spoil any attempt at distillation.

But during the long month it took me to recover, adding a block a day to my morning walk, even that small distance filled with the fear of collapse and no help coming was a victory. The dark side as well as the radiant was now mine and the experience of this balance made me strong.

The next fall I returned to my lovely attic room and my orange crate with a mysterious but very vivid confidence as a person and a writer.

One last anecdote about my beloved France. I had returned to New York and a new job at the Metropolitan Museum, both of which I liked, but whenever I looked at the skyline I felt the absences. Where was the line of poplars, the rise of the church steeple, the distant towers of the chateaux? And where was the vast and intimate Cathedral of our Lady of Chartres where my several pilgrimages had ended in awe and joy and a kind of glee that the enigmatic place was so much mine. The cathedral was built to please the Lady, and she is there to welcome anyone who comes. I had to pay tribute, to add my few dance steps as did the little juggler in his cathedral so many hundreds of years ago. So I wrote a story about Andrew, the rat, who came, as I did, to experience this new world of France. In the cathedral he tangles with gangster rats and the plot spins out from there. A reviewer called it a splendid spoof of the hard-boiled detective story. Little did he know that the laughter and love within the book were really a parade through my homesick self, the flag in the lead, the tricolor.

When the book was finally printed, years later, I had a friend, then going to Chartres, take a copy and leave it on one of the prayer chairs near the altar of the Lady, Andrew's and mine.

Now began the earnest sending, to one publisher after another, of what I had written in so far a country. After four years at the museum I moved to Santa Barbara, California, where I live now. I soon got a job in a bookstore and worked with the young owner, book by book, to restore the former prestige of the business. We did it and he allowed me to found a children's room, do all the buying and most of the selling. I stayed in this work until recently, and still miss being surrounded by walls and walls of books.

In these years an edifice of rejection slips and miles of typewriter ribbon built up around me, but there came a moment when this state of disappointment seemed no longer tolerable. I gave myself one last year of sending out manuscript after manuscript—even the postman confessed he hated to hand back those brown envelopes to me with such regularity. I vowed I would never buy another one and anything written would go directly into my trunk.

That year had almost turned into winter, mine and its own, when a letter arrived from Mary Cosgrave, the children's editor at Houghton Mifflin, saying she would like to meet me. No "yes," but no "no" either. She told me later that she had no notion as to whether I was eighteen or eighty and she had to find out if I had a reasonable future ahead, at least in years.

I just happened to be in New York and I phoned for an appointment. All that night I woke up smiling. Even if it was not a real acceptance at least I was to meet another editor, this one seeming a little more in my favor.

We met—this was a very warm and understanding person—and even if I was so trembly I couldn't manage the cup of tea she offered me, I sat there in that official office acting like a real writer.

We talked for ten minutes and then she pulled out the story I had sent (about my French fox), handed it to me, and asked if I would approve the changes. I would have agreed to any rearrangement short of destruction and I hurriedly scanned the pages. The only change was a deleted comma. We both laughed, were suddenly friends, and went out to lunch.

Now I had my own editor and my first three books were published with her assistance. Soon after moving to Pantheon she retired. The shock taught me something else—the absolute value of the mind and heart and patience that a fine editor offers to a willing writer. She was followed by Fabio Coen whose wisdom and daring and honesty increased the joy, however difficultly earned, I take in my profession.

In between, I worked with Emilie McLeod, who rescued two of my novels from a dusty death in my trunk, refusing to relinquish the challenge of the revisions that eventually resulted in publication on her list with Dutton.

When Fabio Coen left Pantheon, Patricia Ross saw my next book into print, and now I am truly fortunate to have Frances Foster of Knopf to steer me through the shoals and shadows.

I am naming names here as I have not done before in the more personal scenes for two reasons. First, I could not possibly include all the people I treasure, or evaluate their roles, not unless I wrote for ten hundred days, fast as the flight of a falcon; and, second, it would be an intrusion on their present privacy. But I herein salute them all, with love.

On a carousel in Avignon, France, 1985

I don't believe it would be appropriate to plunge into any lengthy discussion or description of my books, but I would like to pay a kind of secondhand tribute (secondhand because their existence is as real to me as my own) to some of the characters who inhabit them.

The tree house, the castle, the fetid cellar, the hut, the cave have no meaning without them. They are all a part of oneself but newly translated, transformed, given their own lives by the writer's invitation to them to come into being. They lead, follow, haunt, occasionally attack, keep one a hundred years in a dungeon. They love, hate, torment, and amuse. Most important of all, I belong to them, before all else and all others. And great friends that they are, they belong to me.

There exists a mutual seesaw of trust and friendship between them and me. And the keystone is sincerity. As the writer I must be as clear and honest as possible. Falsify the accent of a French mouse, carelessly describe the light-footedness of a heavyweight, forget that Emily Batsford gets indigestion from eating raw onions, and the characters will turn their backs, leave the writer very lonely indeed in front of a silent typewriter. The writer need not love the evil characters but must understand them. I am there to record, not to judge. All the time there will be a deep, almost subterranean bond between writer and characters. They will be loyal but only if I am. They will act with conviction and style and proceed convincingly to their natural or unnatural endings.

Some like Auguste, the mute boy, Little Cigarette, and Andrew, the rat, return, not to tell further stories about themselves but simply to visit. Often children ask me what they are doing now and I can answer without hesitation. Little Cigarette won first prize in a painting contest and will be going to Paris in September to receive her award. Auguste is touring England with his own mime company.

The children are believers in a very subtle sense and my quite frequent journeys to their schools, spring and autumn, are a kind of continuing reunion for me. I am neither higher nor lower then they. We think and feel on the same level. My first words must convince them of this because when they tell me how it is to invent stories, to capture ideas, to become a character, there are no differences between us except that I have had more time to develop my craft.

They understand and often they go beyond. An example: a child I recently met in a two-room country school outside of Eureka wanted to tell me how it felt to write. With his left hand he pointed to his head and said, "You wait a little while and then it starts in your mind, goes down through your ribs and then through your right arm to your hand and then into your pencil and then you write as fast as you can."

A visit to Washington School, Monterey, California

Children share easily and sometimes they confide their feelings of loneliness, betrayal, and hurt and all I can be is a listener, the only crust of comfort being able to tell them that experiencing these darknesses is not loss but the fabric that stories and poems are made from and to encourage them to use these feelings in this way.

Many already know this. I always come away from these intense sharings filled and refreshed.

Three years ago a writer friend and I started small classes for adult writers and I relearned, as I had with the younger people, how valuable this same encouragement and attention was to our shifting groups of aspiring writers and I began to wonder what this same interest might mean to junior high students of twelve and thirteen. What would happen if a professional writer, not a teacher, having been the victim of the punishment of rejections, the bouts of loss of confidence, the fear that what one is doing is slated for failure and also having known the vivid joy of acceptance, what would happen if this person led this middle-school group?

With the consent and approval of a school librarian and the principal I got what I wanted. The announcement of these weekly meetings was circulated in the English classes and anyone interested in writing as writers do would be welcome. The sessions were to take place after school with no scholastic credit given.

When that first Monday I was faced with my round table of four boys and six girls I made a startling discovery. They already knew all the guidelines to good writing. Their teachers had given them the fun-

Visiting a classroom in Salinas, California, 1985

Richard Green, Salinas Californian

damental theories that one finds in any good book on How to Write. Then what was I there for?

That evening I was desperate. What was I going to do? Then, suddenly, the firefly of an idea gleamed in my mental night. Why not write a novel?

The moment I threw out this suggestion to the group the response was electric. We decided together, or rather they decided and I agreed, on London, 1860, for the setting; the theme, murder (all but the villain ended up dead); the cast, to mention a few, Lady Angela, her poodle Bonbon, the ruthless Duke of Hempstead, a rather thready hero, Stephen Charleston, who didn't last long, a French maid, a butler, and, last, Lancelot, the archenemy. All the work, all the choices were theirs. My own role was almost always that of the listener. Every week a different boy or girl would be responsible for writing a chapter. Then I would type at home the latest installment and xerox a copy for each one so they could see what they had heard the week before, but I never changed anything except sometimes inventive spelling and an occasional misuse of quotation marks.

After the thirteen Mondays were over and each of us had been given a copy of the book, generously put together by a typing mother and the school bindery, I was asked to talk to the English department so that they could form an opinion as to the value of the experiment, although the school had in no way officially sponsored it.

I told them I wasn't sure of the project's value as a teaching tool. My young writers (mine only in fondness) didn't want to hear about "how" or "why." But in the sense of the actual doing, of writing as writers write with that mysterious urge to enter the country of the imagination and live there with the characters who soon took on a life of their own, it worked. They possessed several levels of talent but even in the less well-expressed chapters the writer was present in each one of them. Maybe only one or two will go forward later into writing as a profession, but the choice is available to each and I believe they realized this. Perhaps that was the gift I was able to give them.

To me the real success of the venture was that these ten people, destined, each in her and his way, to be different and to know the attendant pain that comes from this distinction, had during these Mondays found the approval and respect and friendship of their peers.

The publication party took place in an ice-cream parlor. I was only too happy to thank them with chocolate, vanilla, and strawberry sundaes. The party also bridged the good-byes that I would never have been able to say.

I briefly mentioned that a friend, Gayle Stone, and I had conducted weekly writing classes for adults. For three years, once a week at seven-thirty in the evening we met in my small living room that, to accommodate a maximum of twelve people, was lined with all the chairs in the house, plus a kitchen stool. The student writers were thus forced to sit shoulder to shoulder but they seemed to enjoy this closeness.

They all had projects in progress, straight novels, romances, young adult fiction, and some very original short stories.

Both Gayle and I were aware that writing cannot be taught. It must be practised. But we could point out weaknesses and strengths and stimulate discussion on dialogue, plot structure, viewpoint, characterization, and all the other elements of fiction, all the time conscious that what also needed to be encouraged during the reading aloud of two manuscripts a session was the individual writer's true voice.

We always ended up the two hours with a guided fantasy that each one responded to on paper entirely spontaneously and without thought. This exercise releases the unconscious and the results almost always surprised the writer.

This kind of surprise can also frighten. The outpouring of unexpected words acts as an unfamiliar mirror image that the writer may never have glimpsed before. But, more often, out of these inner journeys comes enlightenment and brings to the surface useable

Poetry group meeting in Julia's living room. Left to right, Bettina Barrett, Katy Peake, Meg Fraser, Perie Longo, Susan Gulbransen, Kit Tremaine, Julia Cunningham, Joan Fallert, and Kathleen Banks

material for stories. Some of our students told us that those unthinking paragraphs have actually served as the beginnings of stories.

I wish I could impart the spirit of kinship that filled that room. We were all related. The varying skills were never measured by anything more exact than the smiles and hums of approval that are the applause for the work recognized by all as well done. This was an uncommon generosity one to the other and often this ambiance of well-wishing was so potent there existed in this lamp-lit room a kind of invisible shining, binding us together.

But perhaps best of all, Gayle and I learned more than we attempted to teach, for no matter how advanced we may have been as writers we too are always at the beginning and, like the others, do the best we can at the moment of doing. We were both grateful for this experience of sharing what we knew and found ourselves encouraged.

A true source of joy for me for the last few years has been something I have done more or less secretly all through my life but never exposed to the trial of print—poetry.

Originally ignorant of the healing properties of this emotional outlet, I used it from the age of twelve onward. I was an adolescent tragedian (and who has not been one?). My first recorded poems dealt with

irony and death, tears and turmoil, but at the core was a desire to create music with words. I'm still trying with the support of added craft, skirting the whispers of a very familiar inner fiend that it can't be done.

But now I scratch out poems with a difference. I have found the pleasure of working together with other poets. Each Tuesday I attend a poetry workshop where one can, if it is wished, remain anonymous. Every week the poems submitted at our previous gathering are typed into a packet and read aloud by the instructor, a very gifted poet, who afterward opens the door for intelligent comment by all of us.

Among the thirty or more poets there are some whose first-class work catches the breath but the worst among us receive the same attention and respect. As in any other form of writing, the doing is paramount.

I know that, personally, this practice of condensing, of striving toward the essence of felt emotions has improved my journeys into prose. One is alert to the cadences of speech, the multitudinous voices of nature, trees and rivers, wind and sea, and even of silence; and much of this hearing weaves through what one writes in this form.

Out of this class evolved a much smaller group and there, too, although the anonymity is lost, we help one another with criticism and understanding. And how proud one is of that mutual sincerity of praise when it comes!

I recommend the practice of poetry to every writer. It seeps into the sought-for eloquence of any form of writing.

Now let me describe where and how I live. When the curtain goes up on my mornings in the small, ageing house I rent, I am immediately greeted by three and a half rooms, not counting the kitchen or the very narrow bathroom whose tub has claw feet. There are many windows, the largest in the living room where I often watch the passersby. Another is hung with three simple panels of stained glass I crafted myself and one ancient piece from some forgotten European church.

The walls of all the rooms, including the bath and kitchen, hold pictures (another kind of window)— prints, drawings, oils of landscapes and people and animals. The fireplace mantel and the tops of the adjoining bookcases show a parade of small objects: a desert fox skull, special stones, an Austrian orchestra no taller than a thumbnail, three tiny bears, several feathers, a book on Chartres, an Eskimo angel, a Haitian voodoo

painting on tin, a cobblestone found loose on the Pont d'Avignon, and many more. All of them speak in silent conversation with me and themselves. On the rim of the couch are two stuffed moles, a French boar, and a spotted wolf.

The second room is a bedroom of no particular interest except for a table that is mountained with books and papers; and the third room contains the TV set, a box of great fascination for me, a record player, a couch and two easy chairs and, of course, more pictures.

But it is that half-a-room where others before me may have eaten long ago breakfasts that contains a typewriter, a desk and chair, a window and my writer-self. It is the place where all the travels of far away begin.

I suppose this is the heart of the house but often I flee its waiting challenge and seek the world beyond it.

McDonald's in the center of downtown is one refuge. I take a tablet with me and sometimes write a poem but mostly I watch and listen. The regulars come and go. One is a woman, gallantly bereted, who has left the rational lanes of living. She talks to herself in a

Cunningham's family, 1984. Back row (left to right), nephew John; sister-in-law Vella; John's wife Robyn; nephew Richard holding son Chris; front row, niece Mary Howard holding John's daughter Ellen; brother John; Julia; Richard's wife Kathleen holding son Same; Mary's daughter Erica in foreground. "Only Robert, Mary's husband, is missing."

kind of desperate rush, her anger spat out in sudden gushes of unrelated words. Another is a man who carries—and on the street, plays—a battered trumpet and wears a variety of costumes, this day striped socks, short pants, and a shirt of six colors, brilliantly opposing each other. He usually has a vanilla ice-cream cone and licks it thoughtfully as though the flavor on his tongue is giving him messages. Just before Easter I listened to a young man, draped in a long gunnysack, who told his two friends that Christ came through his window almost every evening.

There are also the lonely and the laughing, the workers and the children. I have two other coffeehouses on my list, one a gathering place of retired men and women from several levels of financial security, from foreign homelands, as well as a few writers like myself who sit quietly puzzling over pages of manuscript.

Movies rate high in my adventuring. I see as many as I can and even the less excellent interest me. I can't claim reviewer status or judgment, although during my job on the movie magazine I did attend screenings and wrote two-inch reviews. My specialty is horror films from the early Lon Chaneys to the latest Dracula and I would dearly love to write horror stories and books. I've tried but never get beyond the first few pages, halted by a mounting fear of my subject, partially entrapped by the creatures of the dark. Maybe someday.

I am also devoted to my Honda and take to the road whenever possible. Farther has taken me, not often enough, across the Atlantic to Greece, Ireland, Scotland, Indonesia, China, and France. Every voyage, whether in Monaco for a week's international circus, a language school in Villefranche, meeting the gods on Crete, or hearing the mystical singing hills of Ireland, has been accompanied by good friends.

This brings me to the richest gift of all—the people who, from the beginning, have textured my life. I would not sacrifice the merest memory of any of them and most of what I am is owing to these interchanges of love. Should any of them read this account let them be certain of my gratitude and enduring kinship.

From here I would like to complete these pages with my feelings and convictions about writing.

I suppose there are as many definitions of what a writer is as there are writers but, aside from the instinctive drive, unconsciously present, to me a writer is a person of certain habits, and the first of these is the ability to listen. It's as though we had three ears instead of two. We may be crouched in grief or aching in the ribs with laughter but that third ear is recording the moment. And at the same time the mind is storing each detail in a vast attic where nothing is ever lost or forgotten but perhaps only unused.

Another habit is looking. All of this sounds so obvious—listening and looking—but the difference between the ordinary participation of all people and the writer is a matter of intensity. You see and hear not only for yourself but for your writer-self. In some ways this sounds like intrusive rag-picking, and maybe it is, but it remains irresistible.

Still another good habit is daydreaming. This may seem to some to be an alibi for laziness but it isn't. It is creating without recording.

Awareness of smell and taste is also on my list or worthwhile habits. I think that sometimes these two senses are neglected in books, especially books for children in middle grades. Yet these two senses are often the most evocative of mood and feeling. And a smell doesn't always have to evoke a rose. A stable, a cow pasture, acrid smoke from burning cloth, sweat—there are thousands of smells—can express what nothing else can. Someone once asked me what France smelled like. I happily rummaged in my memories of streets and alleys and churches and crowds and came up with three major sources: animal, architectural, and human, meaning drains, damp stones, and wine.

All these habits contribute to that fateful moment when the first sentence is put down on paper and maybe they can be headed by the word *attention*—attention of everything that passes, that happens, that makes for terror, joy, sorrow, humor—that same kind of intense attention that a very young child gives to whatever is suddenly new.

The last habit is discipline—sitting down and doing—which can make a very minor talent show results that an undisciplined near-genius will never know. Just plain grubbing has inchwormed many writers to success.

So one is at the beginning. Those first few steps are more often than not accompanied by a shadow—fear. The fear of failure. This fear opens and closes the accomplishment of a manuscript. It comes to each writer for perhaps different reasons. The weeds planted in childhood are varied and many, some of them poisonous, but essentially I believe it is the fear of commitment. You are giving of yourself and there you are, word by word, printed on a page for anyone to see and judge, fairly or unfairly. All your secrets, desires, feelings are in some way exposed, probably more clearly to yourself than to a possible reader, but there. In some writers this fear causes writer's block, a state of stillness so painful one risks even the mention of it.

The demons have many names, many shapes, many powers but however the writer sees them they are there, inside the mind or perched on the shoulders or even polluting the air around one's head like buzz flies. They are usually smaller than walnuts but their voices rival the thunder.

The demon dialogue attempts to shred self-confidence and when the hurt is felt they hop from leg to leg in glee.

"A writer? You think you are a writer? What gave you that idea?"

"I write." This is pretty feeble and the writer knows it.

"Who can't? A child of seven writes."

"That's absurd," the writer counters. "I've been at it for a long time."

"So? Go ahead. Sit there until your fingers fall off for all I care. The place where you're going is called Nowhere."

The writer gets up, goes to a window, opens it, and drinks draughts of fresh air, but is followed by three of the most persistent of the creatures.

"That's right. Find something else to do, something practical, something that just might buy you a sack of potatoes or a second cup of coffee."

This is the moment, or one of them, when the writer clenches her fists and with determined steps reseats herself in front of the blank paper in the typewriter. For five minutes the tapping out of words is constant and the demons are blessedly silent but ever vigilant, all of them ranged in rows, peering over the writer's shoulder.

She rereads what is written.

"Pleased with yourself?" asks one of them, now boldly astride the roller.

The writer stares in desperation at the blank wall in front of her. She might as well take up a crayon and scrawl in block letters: GIVE UP. YOU'LL NEVER MAKE IT. NEVER.

But something, something beyond the periphery of the demons flickers in the corner of her right eye. It, too, is small but now instead of pointed ears and a dragon's tail, this tiny being is encircled with light and has a hint of wings. It is followed by several more and a kind of musical humming seems to blunt the demon's buzz. For an instant the writer wonders if the demons and the angels (she gives the beings a name) will war with each other and if the white sheet of unfinished writing in her typewriter will have to be ripped out and scrapped.

Then she hears their voices.

"What a fine word choice you made in that paragraph!" says one and before the writer can even wish the angel would repeat those life-giving words, another speaks. "The idea you have for your novel is really original!"

Here a demon tries to crush this illumined creature but the angel escapes and sings in the writer's ear,

Cunningham, 1985: "Writer at work?"

"You know we are always here, too. You mustn't forget that when the demons appear. We are part of the self that looks forward to the new work, the part that finished the short story, the poem, the novel. We bring you words and phrases that fit like magic bits of a jigsaw. You can count on us. You can trust us."

So goes the day in the life of the writer. Call them what you will, the demons and the angels are always present, the struggle ongoing. But as long as the pages fill, as the writer writes, the angels are winning.

As an aside I would like to say that I believe it takes real courage to be any kind of an artist. Is anyone truly free of the fear of rejection? In the deepest part of me I admire this form of bravery in anyone who tries, no matter whether success ever attends the doing.

So you swallow hard, commanding the shadows to get behind you. At least if they must be present they can stand in the back of the room and let faith show a light, however faint. So much of creating is, to me, being able to float on self-trust.

This trust opens the gate of the unconscious, that mysterious realm of the magical, the unexpected, the country of dreams, the beckoner, the fathomless complexity of voices and images and, best of all, the helper and the friend of the writer.

William Maxwell wrote in the preface of one of his collections of short stories:

I didn't so much write them [the stories] as do my best to keep out of the way of their writing themselves. I would sit with my head bent over the typewriter waiting to see what was going to come out of it. The first sentence was usually a surprise to me. From the first sentence everything else followed. A person I didn't know anything about and had never known in real life stepped from the wings and began to act out something I must not interrupt or interfere with, but only be a witness to. I have sometimes believed that it was all merely the result of the initial waiting with an emptied mind—that this opened a door of some kind.

This happens in a concentration so focused it is like a half-trance. And it doesn't always happen. But when it doesn't, one simply has to wait it out, drone along for a few paragraphs or pages (that will probably end up in the wastebasket), trusting that the shepherd with the limp and an obsession to pick field flowers while his sheep stray over the mountain will come back, true and whole, and share his thoughts and perhaps his lunch with you.

And, there is the joy of writing. Far beyond and deeper than the anguish and disappointments is a feeling I have come to savor over and over again—gratitude. Just the act of creating is a gift whatever its motivation of loneliness, lack of confidence, escape (each reason is profoundly personal), a gift that gives me a place to be, a landscape to inhabit, innumerable character-friends, temporary freedom from the coercions of the outer life, and a curious reality that, being part illusion, gives me a reason for being. This is, to me, whatever the struggles in the dark, a true joy and I'm grateful.

Lastly, there is one essential element. Living in the world and listening to what speaks silently from between the lines of my books have taught me that all the words, all the work, all the talent are as nothing without the element of love.

BIBLIOGRAPHY

FOR CHILDREN

Fiction:

The Vision of Francois the Fox (illustrated by Nicholas Angelo). Boston: Houghton, 1960.

Dear Rat (illustrated by Walter Lorraine). Boston: Houghton, 1961.

Macaroon (illustrated by Evaline Ness). New York: Pantheon, 1962; London: Harrap, 1963.

Candle Tales (illustrated by E. Ness). New York: Pantheon, 1964.

Viollet (illustrated by Alan E. Cober). New York: Pantheon, 1966.

Onion Journey (illustrated by Lydia Cooley). New York: Pantheon, 1967.

Burnish Me Bright (illustrated by Don Freeman). New York: Pantheon, 1970; (illustrated by Shirley Hughes) London: Heinemann, 1971.

Wings of the Morning (photographs by Katy Peake). San Carlos, Calif.: Golden Gate, 1971.

Far in the Day (illustrated by Don Freeman). New York: Pantheon, 1972.

Maybe, a Mole (illustrated by Cyndy Szekeres). New York: Pantheon, 1974.

Come to the Edge. New York: Pantheon, 1977.

A Mouse Called Junction (illustrated by Michael Hague). New York: Pantheon, 1980.

Flight of the Sparrow. New York: Pantheon, 1980.

The Silent Voice. New York: Dutton, 1981.

Wolf Roland. New York: Pantheon, 1983.

Oaf. New York: Knopf, 1986.

FOR YOUNG ADULTS

Fiction:

Dorp Dead (illustrated by James Spanfeller). New York: Pantheon, 1965.

The Treasure Is the Rose (illustrated by Judy Graese). New York: Pantheon, 1973.

Tuppenny. New York: Dutton, 1978.

Lois Duncan

1934–

I can't remember a time when I did not think of myself as a writer. It's the only thing I ever wanted to be. When I was three years old I was dictating poems and stories to my parents, and as soon as I learned to print, I was writing them down myself. I shared a room with my younger brother, and at night I would lie in bed inventing tales to give him nightmares. I would pretend to be the "Moon Fairy," come to deliver the message that the moon was falling toward the earth.

"And what will happen to *me*?" Billy would ask in his quavering little voice.

"You'll be blown up into the sky," the Moon Fairy would tell him. "By the time you come down the world will be gone, and you'll just keep falling forever."

"With no breakfast?" poor Billy would scream hysterically. Eventually, our parents had the good sense to put us in separate rooms.

My first—and only—poetry recitation was given at age five, and it was a disaster. It was kindergarten show-and-tell time, and since I had forgotten to bring anything to show, I volunteered to recite a "made-up poem." It was a very dramatic ballad about a shipwreck.

My performance was greeted by a long silence,

Duncan, with brother Billy, celebrating her sixth birthday, 1940

Duncan, age two, being introduced to the joys of literature by her mother, Lois Foley Steinmetz, 1936

during which I waited patiently for the deluge of praise I was sure would come.

Instead my teacher said coldly, "You didn't make that up."

I was so surprised that I couldn't think of a thing to answer. I just stood there, staring at her.

"That's a well-known poem," my teacher said. "I've heard it many times. Go sit in the corner until you are ready to tell the truth."

I spent the rest of the day in the corner, and it was years before I trusted a teacher again.

Aside from tormenting Billy, I had few hobbies. A shy little girl, I was a bookworm and a dreamer. My parents, Joseph and Lois Steinmetz, were magazine photographers. They moved us from Philadelphia, Pennsylvania, soon after Billy was born, to settle us in Sarasota, Florida, from which they were in a good position to take photo assignments throughout the southeast United States and the Caribbean. They planned most of these trips for summer so Billy and I could go with them.

I grew up in Sarasota and spent a lot of time playing alone in the woods and on the beaches. I had a

Duncan's photographer parents, Joseph and Lois Steinmetz, in the Florida Keys on assignment for Holiday *magazine, 1949*

said that he appreciated my effort and that the story was a nice one, considering the age of the author, but that his particular publication was not currently in the market for fairy tales. The warmth of the letter cushioned its impact. I swallowed my disappointment and mailed the story off to another magazine. And I wrote another story and sent it to the *Journal.*

By the time that one came back, I had another ready to mail off, and so it continued. I now had a hobby, collecting rejection slips. It was painful, but exciting. Each day when other, better adjusted children were skipping rope and playing hopscotch and going over to play at each other's houses, I was rushing home to check the mail and see what stories had come back from what magazines.

My writing attempts became more and more ambitious. Tales of flaming romance, blood-spurting violence, pain and passion, lust and adventure flew back and forth to New York in a steady stream. My parents thought me cute and funny. My teachers thought me

secret hideaway in the middle of a bamboo clump. I would bend the bamboo until I could straddle it, and then it would spring up, and I would slide down into the hollow at its heart with green stalks all around me and leaves like lace against my face. I'd hide there and read.

Or I'd ride my bicycle. I would pedal for miles along the beach road with the wind blowing in my face and sun hot on my hair. There was a special point where I turned the bike off the road and walked it down a little path between the dunes. I parked it there and lay on my back in the sand and listened to the waves crash against the rocks and watched the clouds scud across the sky.

All of the thoughts that trickled through my mind during those long hours of dreaming found their way onto paper. I have today a whole drawerful of notebooks that I filled during those early years.

When I was ten, I submitted my first typed manuscript to *Ladies' Home Journal.* The story was about a little boy who enjoyed playing in the woods with fairies until he became six years old and decided to stop believing. The story was returned rather quickly, but it was accompanied by a kind letter from the editor. He

Joseph Steinmetz

Duncan's mentor, MacKinlay Kantor, long-time friend of the family who steered her into her first magazine sale when she was thirteen by advising her to "write from the heart about something you know." Kantor later won the Pulitzer Prize for his Civil War novel Andersonville. *This photo was taken by Duncan's father, Joseph Steinmetz, about 1950.*

horrid and precocious. As for myself, I was proud. I—plump, bespeckled, and unimpressive as I might seem—was plunging ahead to advance my glamorous career.

Three years passed, and I accumulated so many rejection slips that my mother made me stop saving them.

Then, one day, I came home from school to find a strange man occupying the living-room sofa. He was a new neighbor who had just moved in down the beach from us, and he was a writer. His name was MacKinlay Kantor.

"Lois," my father said after introductions had been made, "why don't you show Mr. Kantor that story that just came back from the *Saturday Evening Post?*"

He did not have to ask me twice. What an opportunity! I rushed to get the story and stood expectantly at his elbow as Mr. Kantor scanned the pages.

"My dear," he said finally, "I hate to tell you, but this is trash."

"Mack!" my mother exclaimed. "Lois is only thirteen!"

"I don't care how old she is," said Mr. Kantor. "If she is trying to sell her stories, she's old enough to be told what's wrong with them. What kind of subject matter is this for a kid? Lois has never had a love affair or seen a man get murdered. Good writing comes from the heart, not off the top of the head."

He turned to me and added more gently, "Throw this stuff away, child, and go write a story about something you know about. Write something that rings true."

I was crushed. I was also challenged. Later that week I did write a story about a fat, shy little girl with braces and glasses who covered her insecurity by writing stories about imaginary adventures. I submitted it to a teen publication called *Calling All Girls,* and by return mail I received a check for twenty-five dollars.

It was the most incredible moment of my life.

From then on my fate was decided. I wrote what I knew about, and could hardly wait to rush home from school each day to fling myself at the typewriter. The pain and joy of adolescence poured onto page after page. My first kiss, my first heartbreak, both became subjects for stories. When I wasn't invited to Carol Johnson's slumber party, I wiped away my tears and wrote about it. When I lost the lead in the class play to Barbara Werner, I wrote a story in which I *got* the lead. I flooded the teen magazines with manuscripts, and despite the unpolished writing, the gut reality of the material carried them over the line, and a surprising number of them sold.

Now that I was being published I had a decision

The Steinmetz family Christmas card, 1950: Lois, age sixteen; Bill, thirteen; Lois Sr.; and Joe

to make. My name was Lois Duncan Steinmetz, and I had been named after my mother. When my work appeared in print I didn't want everybody to think that Mother had written it.

We discussed the situation, and Mother wasn't too keen on the idea of changing her own name so it wouldn't be confused with mine. She suggested that I drop *Steinmetz* and use my first and middle names to write under. The idea pleased me. Duncan had been my grandmother's maiden name and it conjured up romantic visions of brightly kilted Scotsmen marching over rolling hills to the blare of bagpipes. So I wrote my editor and told her that I was going to publish under a pseudonym, *Lois Duncan.*

At sixteen I won second prize in *Seventeen* magazine's annual short-story contest. At seventeen I won third prize, and at eighteen I took first. My greatest triumph was the sale of my home economics report. I was the only girl in the class who flunked home ec. Lost in daydreams, I forgot to knot my thread and hemmed my skirt all semester long, working my way round and round the circle of material, drawing the thread smoothly along an endless path. When the end-of-the-year fashion show was held, I could not participate, but I wrote up the whole sad tale and sold it for fifty

Lois and Bill on the beach at Sarasota, Florida, 1951

dollars. With that, I bought a skirt that was perfectly beautiful. Whenever people asked me where I got it, I told them, "Home Ec."

My parents had always taken it for granted that both my brother and I would go to college. Daddy had graduated from Princeton, and Mother from Smith. Education was a tradition in our family, and I moved automatically from high school into Duke University, just as I had moved from grammar school into junior high.

It was a total surprise to discover that I was out of place there.

It wasn't the classes that created the problem. Those I found interesting, especially the English and history. What I missed was my own space. At home I had had my own room and a tremendous amount of privacy. At Duke, all our time was scheduled. Not only were there classes, there were dorm meetings, campus meetings, and religious services. There was constant togetherness. Girls flowed in and out of each other's rooms as though they were common territory, and each person's phone calls and callers were announced over a loudspeaker, so even those, in a manner, were shared. We ate together, studied together, exercised together, and brushed our teeth standing in a row in front of a line of basins. If you were noncommunicative, two dozen well-meaning dorm mates asked anxiously what the matter was. If you closed yourself in your room for twenty minutes, people rapped on the door to find out

if you were "all right in there."

Within weeks I was longing desperately for the ocean—the long stretch of empty beach, the whisper of waves and the cry of gulls—and solitude.

And I couldn't write! That was the most frustrating thing. Oh, I cranked out term papers at appropriate intervals, but I didn't consider that real writing. It wasn't communication, because no one got to read them except the graduate assistants who graded them. It seemed a waste of time and energy to spend days dredging up information and setting it on paper if nobody was going to publish it.

My own writing was impossible for me. My mind was numb, and my ears were ringing. In order to be creative, I needed time alone, and that was one thing college life did not provide. Neither did it provide freedom. I had thought somehow that leaving home would be a giant step toward independence, but I found myself under stricter chaperonage than my easygoing parents had ever provided.

When I went home at Christmas, I told my parents I thought one year of college might be all I wanted.

They regarded me blankly.

"But, if you drop out, what will you do?"

It was a question I could not answer. This was an era in which single women did not have their own apartments. They lived at home until they were married. Much as I loved my family, I had no desire to go back to being a child in their home. I wanted to be an adult in the adult world.

I returned to college, made the honor roll with my first semester grades, and started dating a senior prelaw student. Buzz was attractive, intelligent, and charming. He was also very persuasive, and I was at a point in life when I was vulnerable to persuasion. When he proposed, I said, "Yes." We were married in May, three weeks before his graduation and four days after my nineteenth birthday.

Our marriage lasted nine years. The first two, I was an air force wife, setting up housekeeping in one little service town after another. Our first daughter, Robin, was born in Seattle, Washington. When Buzz received his discharge from the service, he entered law school in St. Petersburg, Florida, and there our second daughter, Kerry, was born.

Back in school, in a class composed of mostly single young men, Buzz swung quickly into a single way of living. If he wasn't in the library studying, he was out playing tennis, or water-skiing, or chatting in bars, or attending parties. Since we couldn't afford a babysitter, I usually stayed home.

To fill the lonely hours, I began work on a novel. Since I was still so close to my own teen years, it

Duncan in the backyard of her home in St. Petersburg, Florida, with daughters Robin and Kerry, 1956. That year her first young adult novel, Debutante Hill, *won the Seventeenth Summer Literary Award.*

seemed natural that this—my first long project—would be a teenage love story. Its title was *Debutante Hill,* and it was sweet and sticky and pap, but in the 1950s that's the kind of book teenagers read.

When it was finished, I dedicated the novel to my mother and entered the manuscript in the "Seventeenth Summer Literary Contest," sponsored by Dodd, Mead and Company. It was returned for revisions because in it a young man of twenty drank a beer.

"We can't judge this," the editor told me. "You can't mention liquor in a book for young people. Clean it up and resubmit it, and then we'll read it."

I changed the beer to a Coke and resubmitted the manuscript. It won the contest, and the book was published. When the first bound copy arrived in the mail, and I lifted it out of its wrappings and held it in my hands, I felt almost as thrilled as I had been when I'd first held my newborn babies.

Meanwhile, my marriage was rapidly fading into nothing. Buzz graduated from law school, passed the bar, and became a lawyer. From then on, he was so busy that I never saw him. For the next seven years I continued to write books and to raise our children—a

little boy, Brett, had now joined the family—and to try to pretend to myself that I was happy.

What I wrote were romances, and they were pretty awful. I can't accept the total blame for this, however. Whenever I attempted something more interesting, publishers refused to accept it.

An example of this was my first attempt at an adventure novel. *Game of Danger* was the story of a girl and her brother, fourteen and twelve, who were engaged in a wild chase through New England in an effort to keep secret documents out of the hands of the "bad guys." Midway through the book, too exhausted to flee further, they stopped at an inn, rented a room, and slept for a couple of hours.

This chapter came back with exclamation marks in the margin.

"You have two people of opposite sexes sharing a room, and they're not married!"

"But they're brother and sister," I protested. "They're fully clothed, and they're lying on twin beds."

"That makes no difference," my editor said. "Librarians would never touch a book that included such a suggestive scene. You will have to have them rent separate rooms."

Since my characters had almost no money, I could not imagine their doing such a thing. Still, I didn't want to offend the nation's librarians. We finally reached a compromise with an L-shaped alcove in which the boy could nap out of sight of his sister.

When I was twenty-seven, the inevitable happened—Buzz fell in love with somebody else. We were divorced, and I was devastated. Those were days when marriages were expected to last forever. I had never known a divorced person. In a desperate effort to start my life over, I took the children and moved to Albuquerque, New Mexico, where my brother (now called "Bill," not "Billy") was living.

I had a half-dozen books in print by this time, but they were far from best sellers. If I remember right, they were earning me about $2,000 a year. I knew I couldn't support myself and the children on my tiny royalty check, so for the first time in my life I went out to find a "real job."

With nothing to recommend me—no college degree, no business training, no work experience—I was no prize as an employee. I was hired at last by a small advertising agency to answer the telephone, run errands, and write occasional copy. My monthly salary was $275, which I hoped to supplement by writing articles and stories in the evenings.

That was wishful thinking. By the time I left work and picked up Brett at his nursery, collected the girls at

The Steinmetzes visit Duncan and her children, Albuquerque, New Mexico, 1964: Bill; Kerry, age five; Lois Sr.; Joe; Robin, seven; Lois Duncan; and Brett, four

their after-school baby-sitter's, came home and cooked dinner and spent some time with the children, got them bathed and bedded down, cleaned up the apartment, did the laundry and got things into order for the next day, I was too exhausted to write a letter to my parents, much less something suitable for publication. I sat like a zombie in front of the typewriter and often ended up asleep with my head on the keyboard.

Because of this I was constantly looking for extra ways to earn money. On my lunch hour I entered contests. One was sponsored by the Florida Development Commission and was for "happy snapshots taken on vacation in Florida." Another was for "the most frightening experience of your life in one hundred words or less."

One day I came home from work after an especially tiring day, gave the mail a quick once-over and, finding nothing there but bills and ads, tossed it into a heap on the coffee table. The following evening I picked it up again to give it a second look before throwing it away. There was a letter I had thought was an ad because it started "Dear Reader." Now I saw that it was not an ad at all.

"Dear Reader," it said. "It is my pleasant duty to inform you that your 'frightening experience' has won first prize in *True Story*'s contest. Your check is enclosed."

Enclosed in what? Robin, whose job it was to take out the trash each day, had been conscientious. She had thrown away the envelope.

Our apartment was part of a huge, low-cost complex. There must have been fifty garbage cans lined up out back. The children and I got a flashlight and, starting at one end of the row, went rooting through all of them. Finally, halfway down about the fifteenth can, buried under somebody's leftover spaghetti, we found the envelope. Inside, there was a check for $500.

Five hundred dollars was almost twice what I was earning each month at the agency, and by working away from home I had the expenses of a nursery for Brett, an after-school sitter for the girls, commuting and panty hose for myself. I made my decision quickly. If there was this kind of money to be made by writing for the confessions, there was no sense spending my days writing advertising copy. One thing that made the decision easier was a phone call from the Florida

Development Commission informing me that my "happy snapshot" had won first prize: a live, trained porpoise from Marineland, Florida. At my strangled gasp of horror (I had a vision of the thing arriving in a crate of salt water and having to be kept in the bathtub) I was offered a chance to sell the porpoise back to Marineland for $1,000.

With this nest egg to draw upon while I taught myself the craft of confession writing, I quit my job, went to the newsstand, and bought every confession magazine on the rack. By the time that I'd read each one from cover to cover, I had a pretty good idea of how these stories were put together. They were sensational dramas of sin and suffering, written in first person as though they were true, but since they bore no by-lines, it was obvious they were really fakes.

I decided that I'd had enough practice writing fiction to be able to do these, so from then on, every morning, I got up, brushed my teeth, and sat down at the typewriter to confess. I wrote a story a week. Not every one sold, but most did, and not one editor ever asked me if my stories were true.

Soon the kids and I were living better than we had since the divorce. I gave up our awful apartment and bought a house. The little girls took dancing lessons and piano lessons and ice skating lessons, while Brett went to a private kindergarten. We ate steak at least once a week and sometimes more often. I got very good and very fast. I could start a confession Monday and have the final draft completed and in the mail by Wednesday. Among the titles of the stories of mine that were published (anonymously, thank God!) during those busy years were "We Killed Our Baby," "I Made My Son a Daughter," and "Twenty-nine and Mother of Two, I Wanted an Affair with a Teenage Boy." I won't elaborate upon their contents.

After two years on this schedule, however, I began to run out of sins to write about. Glued to my typewriter, I had had no time for doing research. One day Bill, who worked for the government, took pity on me.

"Get a babysitter," he told me, "and I'll take you out to the base and introduce you to some of the bachelor types who work in missile design. They'll tell you about sins you never dreamed of."

That evening I met Don Arquette, the man to whom I'm now married.

Don and I knew each other two years before he proposed. Each time he was ready to pop the question, another confession story would come out and he would panic. The week he did ask me to marry him, *Personal Romances* published "I Carry That Dreadful Disease," and he almost reneged. On our wedding day, out came "Can He Bear to Touch Me on Our Wed-

ding Night?" which made him think twice. But he did go through with the ceremony and adopted the children, and another stage of life began for us all.

As an electrical engineer with a Master's degree, Don earned a good living, and it was no longer necessary for me to be the family provider. Don expected (and I guess I did also) that I would now settle back to being what I had been once before, a full-time housewife who spent her idle hours writing gentle novels.

But sweet romances now bored me. I had grown used to marathon writing, and I'm a creature of habit; I automatically jumped up in the morning and sat down to confess. Story followed story, until one day I wrote "One of My Babies Must Die," about the operation to separate our Siamese twins. This story brought in mail from all over the country from readers who wanted information about the operation and the doctor who had performed it. It was evident, even to me, that I had gone too far.

"Don't you think it's time to move on a little?" Don said. "Why don't you stop this confession writing and start writing articles for nice wholesome magazines like *Good Housekeeping* and *Ladies' Home Journal?*"

"I could never sell to those," I told him. "I tried the *Journal* back when I was first starting out. They're not like the confessions; they use true material, and they publish your by-line."

"Then write something true," Don said reasonably. "Hasn't anything interesting ever happened to you?"

"Well—," a thought occurred to me. "I *did* once win a trained porpoise in a contest."

To please him, I wrote a two-page featurette called "The Year I Won the Contest" and mailed it off to *Good Housekeeping*. Back came a check for three times the amount I was used to receiving for a sixteen-page confession story. I was incredulous. Somehow, during those years of sitting down every day and forcing out words, I had learned the professional way of telling a story, and those story-telling techniques could evidently be transferred over into other forms of writing. From then on, I continued to write regularly for the national women's magazines, and to this day I have never written another confession story.

Now that the financial pressure was off, I also felt free to turn back to my non-lucrative, but immeasurably enjoyable, hobby of writing teenage novels. I immediately discovered that something had happened in the time that I had been away. The world had changed, and so had the books that were considered acceptable reading for young people. No longer did any writer have to worry about getting a manuscript back because someone in it drank a beer. When I browsed the young adult section of our local library, I found books on alcoholism, drug use, social and racial problems, premarital sex, parental divorce, mental illness, and homosexuality.

Thus began a whole new period of my writing career. The first novel I wrote under the new set of ground rules was *Ransom,* an adventure story about teenagers kidnapped by their school bus driver. Dodd, Mead wouldn't publish that book ("It's not your style of writing," the editor told me), but it was accepted by Doubleday, who published it in 1968.

Ransom was more successful than anyone expected, and the Dodd, Mead editor was very unhappy. It was runner-up for the Edgar Allan Poe Award which is presented by the Mystery Writers of America for each year's best mysteries. Suddenly librarians, who hadn't known before that I existed, began to notice me, and when my next book, *They Never Came Home,* appeared, they stocked it. That book, too, was runner-up for the Edgar. It also was taken by the Junior Literary Guild.

Duncan with son, Don Jr., Albuquerque, New Mexico, 1967

Meanwhile, at home, both good and bad things were happening. On the good side, my marriage to Don was a happy one, and within the next several years I gave birth to two children, Don Jr. and Kate. On the bad side, I lost my mother, who was my dearest friend, and for a long time I was so numbed by grief that I couldn't function. Family crises brought me back into motion—Robin broke her leg skiing, Kerry almost cut her thumb off carving a Halloween pumpkin, Brett slammed the car door on one of his fingers—but still I couldn't set words on paper. I was totally drained of all creativity.

Finally I came to the realization that I had to force myself to get back to work. If I didn't break this block, I might never write again. The book I had been

working on when Mother died had been a murder mystery. I took that manuscript now, and threw it in the trash can. There was no way that I could write about death, so I decided to do the opposite. I would write something light and humorous, aimed at a younger age group, and I would accept in advance the fact that it would not be publishable. It would simply serve as an exercise to get me moving.

The book was called *Hotel for Dogs,* and to my surprise, Houghton Mifflin published it in 1971. It did quite well, and is still in print in paperback. For the next thirteen years, this book served as my token attempt at humor. Then, in 1984, I wrote *The Terrible Tales of Happy Days School* which was published by Little, Brown. Each of these books was reviewed as having been written by a "new author, not to be confused with the Lois Duncan who writes teenage suspense novels." Because I was not known as a writer of humor, nobody realized that the two Lois Duncans were the same person.

Something else important happened in 1971. I was invited to teach a class in magazine writing at the University of New Mexico. The idea of doing this scared me to death. I wasn't a teacher, in fact, I wasn't even educated. I'd had only one year of college, and that had been long ago.

But Don, who knew how shy I was, thought the experience would be good for me.

Duncan with husband Don Arquette, enjoying a carefree hour between lecture sessions, when Duncan was on the faculty of the Cape Cod Writers' Conference, 1973

*Great excitement! Duncan, at forty-three, graduates from the
University of New Mexico, cum laude, with a B.A. in English, 1977.*

"Give it a try," he said encouragingly. "What's there to lose?"

And so I became a lecturer for the journalism department, a position I held for eleven years. I also became a student. I had always regretted my decision to drop out of college, and being back on a university campus was exciting. I began by taking just one or two classes—a literature course here—a psychology class there—and then I signed up for a course in news photography. I did well in this, for having been raised by photojournalist parents, I had absorbed a lot about photography without even knowing it. Even before the class was over, I was submitting photos to magazines, and Don had converted our extra bathroom into a darkroom. This hobby has been a source of lasting pleasure. In 1982, I had a book of juvenile verse called *From Spring to Spring* published by the Westminster Press, and the poems were illustrated by my own photographs.

Going back to school in middle age was a strange experience. In some of my classes, my own students were my fellow classmates. I would be lecturing them one hour as "Professor Duncan," and the next they would be nudging me and saying, "Lois, can I borrow your notes?" In 1977, I finally graduated, cum laude, with a B.A. degree in English, and we celebrated the event with a family party.

On the day of my graduation I was too excited to think about anything else, so I spent the morning at my desk, writing about it. The result was an article, "A Graduate in the Family," which subsequently sold to *Good Housekeeping.* The check they sent me covered the cost of my whole tuition.

So, the years passed. I'm not a person who has had many great adventures; most of my life has been centered around my family. Little League games, dance recitals, amateur theater productions, camping trips, ski vacations, and visits to grandparents filled our days. Robin grew up and became a professional singer; Kerry grew up and became an actress and then a television newswoman; Brett became a sound engineer with a rock band. My lonely father remarried. His second wife, Louise Palmer, is a talented artist, and MacKinlay Kantor, who had by this time reaped the Pulitzer Prize for his novel *Andersonville,* was best man at their wedding.

Another nice thing happened to my father in his later years. In 1979, an archive of work by early studio photographers was created at the Carpenter Center for the Visual Arts at Harvard University. My parents' photographic work during the thirties and forties was suddenly "discovered," and, overnight, my father leapt to fame. He was given a one-man show at Harvard in 1982, and a collection of his photographs was published in a catalog titled *Killing Time.* The show was

Duncan and daughter Kate horseback riding during a family vacation in the Pecos Mountains of New Mexico, 1973

The Arquette family, Albuquerque, New Mexico, 1974: seated, Don Sr. holding Don Jr., age six; Lois holding Kate, four; Robin, eighteen; standing, Kerry, sixteen; and Brett, thirteen

exhibited all around the country, and Daddy, now almost eighty, was heralded as "a social historian and an artist far ahead of his time."

My father accepted this notoriety with a complacent smile.

"I was just doing my job," he said, "and having fun."

For my own part, I continued, of course, to write books. I won't try to discuss them all in this short essay, but I will mention several that for one reason or another seem of special significance.

A Gift of Magic was my first book about psychic phenomena, and it was published by Little, Brown in 1971. During my year at Duke, back in 1952, the freshman class had served as subjects for ESP (extrasensory perception) experiments conducted by a Dr. Rhine. I became fascinated by the subject, and from that time on read everything about it that I could find. I decided that it would be fun to write a fiction story for eight-to-twelve-year-olds about a girl who had this gift, but it took me years to find someone willing to publish it. Every publisher I sent it to told me, "Kids aren't inter-ested in things like that." I didn't agree with this, I thought young readers would love it. When *A Gift of Magic* did finally make it into print, I was proven right. The book did well and established me as a forerunner in a genre that has since become hugely popular.

Down a Dark Hall taught me about the newest in taboos for youth novels. With all the freedom we writers now had in choice of subject matter, I had assumed I could write about almost anything I wanted to. *Down a Dark Hall* was a strange sort of Gothic about a girl who went off to boarding school and discovered too late that the head mistress was a medium. Ghosts of long dead artists, writers, and composers came flocking back to invade the minds and bodies of the unfortunate students.

This book was returned for revisions, not because the plot was so wild, but because the ghosts in the story were male and the victims were female. Like an echo from the past—"Librarians won't touch a book in which a sister and brother share a hotel room,"—I was now told "Librarians won't touch a book that portrays women as the weaker sex." When I changed the ghost

Joseph Steinmetz, with grandchildren Kate and Don, on a family vacation on the New England coast, 1979. This photo, taken by Duncan, was used to illustrate the poem "Grandfather Song" in Duncan's poem-photo book, From Spring to Spring.

of a male poet into the ghost of Emily Brontë, the book was accepted.

With *Summer of Fear,* a book about an Albuquerque family that was being intimidated by witchcraft, I learned something about the crazy world of film making. Retitled "Stranger in Our House," this story was televised as an NBC Movie of the Week, starring Linda Blair.

Kerry, who at that time was living in Hollywood, auditioned and won a small part in the picture. She called me often to tell me what was going on.

"You know the little dog in the book?" she asked me.

"Of course, I know him," I said. "After all, I created him."

"You wouldn't recognize him now," Kerry said. "Linda Blair likes horses, so the dog is now a horse."

That meant that all the scenes I had placed around an Albuquerque swimming pool were now laid at a California riding stable, and the handsome lifeguard my heroine Rachel was in love with was now her riding instructor. When the movie appeared on televi-

sion, there wasn't much about it that I recognized. Like most authors, I preferred the book.

Television has had an enormous effect upon youth books. Not only has it exposed young people to sophisticated subject matter at an early age, it has conditioned its viewers to expect instant entertainment. Few of today's readers are patient enough to wade through slow paced, introductory chapters as I did at their ages to see if a book is eventually going to get interesting. If their interest isn't caught immediately, they want to switch channels.

Because of this, writers have been forced into utilizing all sorts of TV techniques to hold their readers' attention. In *Killing Mr. Griffin,* I began with the sentence, "It was a wild, windy southwestern spring when the idea of killing Mr. Griffin occurred to them." I knew I was not going to have this man die until a third of the way into the book, and I was afraid that if I didn't give my readers an inkling that dramatic action lay ahead, they would not be willing to hang around that long.

With a family the size of ours, we've never had much room in which to spread out, and until recently my work area was a corner of the bedroom. This has now changed. As the older children left home, new rooms opened up, and I grabbed one of those for an office. I moved in my desk and filing cabinets, and then took a step into the Brave New Computer Age and replaced my ancient typewriter with a word processor.

This miraculous machine has made my work much easier. When writing *The Third Eye,* for instance, I originally envisioned the story as being laid in the autumn with high-school football games churning in the background and all the trees leafed out in gold. Then, a quarter of the way through, I realized that I was going to need to have a little girl drown in the Rio Grande. Since this is a river that runs fast and deep only in springtime, I would have to switch my autumn-based story to spring.

Formerly that simple change in season would have meant retyping sixty pages of manuscript. With the word processor, the changes took me ten minutes. All I had to do was go through the manuscript, locate the pages of description, and change gold leaves to green and football to softball. Then I scattered around a few daffodils. I pressed a button on the keyboard, and the printer went into action and ground out a nice, new, perfectly typed springtime manuscript.

I faced a similar situation with *Stranger with My Face.* In this book, I created a character named Jeff who was to be the love interest for my heroine, Laurie. I started out with Jeff a conventionally handsome teenage boy, and then, when I was partway into the novel,

I got an idea for a way to make him more interesting. I decided to give him a scarred face. This meant going back through the early chapters of the book and changing every section in which Jeff's looks were referred to. It also meant altering his personality to reflect the emotional damage that the physical disfigurement had caused. With the help of the word processor, I was able to make these changes quickly and easily and could also insert a full-page flashback detailing the accident that had produced the scarring.

Most of the books I've written have been fiction. There are two, however, that were a real change of pace for me. *Chapters: My Growth as a Writer,* published by Little, Brown in 1982, is an autobiographical how-to for young people who want to become writers. Some of the material in this essay has been drawn from it. This book contains samples of the stories and poems I was writing at various ages and describes what was happening in my life at the time I wrote them. My book for adults, *How to Write and Sell Your Personal Experiences*, published by Writer's Digest Books in 1979, takes up chronologically where *Chapters* ends and incorporates much of what I taught at the university.

This past year I turned fifty years old. I spend so much of my time submerged in the minds of the teenage characters in my novels that it comes as a shock when I look in the mirror and find I have gray in my hair. Don Jr. is now seventeen, and Kate is fourteen. Kerry is married and is soon to make me a grandmother.

Fifty seems a nice age to be, but then, so has every other age. I've enjoyed my life, and I expect to continue enjoying it. I look forward to travel and leisure time with Don after his retirement—to watching my children's adult lives unfold—to spoiling my grandchildren.

People ask, "Are you going to keep writing?" They might as well ask if I plan to continue breathing. I expect to do both just as long as I possibly can. Like my father, I'm "doing my job and having fun."

I'm working right now on a book called *Locked in Time*. It's the story of a family who have stopped the process of aging and are stuck forever as they are, unable to grow and change.

I find that a horrible concept, but I think the book will be a good one. As with every new book I write, I'm excited about it.

Lois Duncan, 1984

BIBLIOGRAPHY

FOR CHILDREN

Fiction:

The Littlest One in the Family (illustrated by Suzanne K. Larsen). New York: Dodd, 1960.

Silly Mother (illustrated by S.K. Larsen). New York: Dial, 1962.

Giving Away Suzanne (illustrated by Leonard Weisgard). New York: Dodd, 1963.

A Gift of Magic (illustrated by Arvis Stewart). Boston: Little, Brown, 1971.

Hotel for Dogs (illustrated by Leonard Shortall). Boston: Houghton, 1971.

Horses of Dreamland (illustrated by Donna Diamond). Boston: Little, Brown, 1985.

Poetry:

From Spring to Spring: Poems and Photographs (illustrated by the author). Philadelphia: Westminster, 1982.

The Terrible Tales of Happy Days School (illustrated by Friso Henstra). Boston: Little, Brown, 1983.

FOR YOUNG ADULTS

Fiction:

Debutante Hill. New York: Dodd, 1958.

Love Song for Joyce, as Lois Kerry. New York: Funk, 1958.

A Promise for Joyce, as Lois Kerry. New York: Funk, 1959.

The Middle Sister. New York: Dodd, 1960.

Game of Danger. New York: Dodd, 1962.

Season of the Two-Heart. New York: Dodd, 1964.

Ransom. Garden City, N.Y.: Doubleday, 1966.

They Never Came Home. Garden City, N.Y.: Doubleday, 1969.

Peggy. Boston: Little, Brown, 1970.

I Know What You Did Last Summer. Boston: Little, Brown, 1973; London: Hamilton, 1982.

Down a Dark Hall. Boston: Little, Brown, 1974.

Summer of Fear. Boston: Little, Brown, 1976; London: Hamilton, 1981.

Killing Mr. Griffin. Boston: Little, Brown, 1978; London: Hamilton, 1980.

Daughters of Eve. Boston: Little, Brown, 1979.

Stranger with My Face. Boston: Little, Brown, 1981; London: Hamilton, 1983.

The Third Eye. Boston: Little, Brown, 1984; published as *The Eyes of Karen Connors.* London: Hamilton, 1985.

Locked in Time. Boston: Little, Brown, 1985.

Recordings:

A Visit with Lois Duncan (videotape). Albuquerque, N.M.: RDA Enterprises, 1985.

Nonfiction:

Major André, Brave Enemy. New York: Putnam, 1969.

Chapters: My Growth as a Writer. Boston: Little, Brown, 1982.

FOR ADULTS

Fiction:

Point of Violence. Garden City, N.Y.: Doubleday, 1966; London: Hale, 1968.

When the Bough Breaks. Garden City, N.Y.: Doubleday, 1973.

Nonfiction:

How to Write and Sell Your Personal Experiences. Cincinnati, Ohio: Writer's Digest Books, 1979.

Portions of this essay are based in part on material from the author's books *How to Write and Sell Your Personal Experiences,* copyright © 1979 by Lois Duncan, published by Writer's Digest Books, 1979, and *Chapters: My Growth as a Writer,* copyright © 1982 by Lois Duncan, published by Little, Brown, 1982.

Henry Gregor Felsen

1916-

To A.S.

Why have you knocked
Upon my ancient door,
And filled with sound
My empty, silent rooms,
And caused my dust
So long content to rest
To swirl distressed?

There are more than four billion people on earth. In any given year the number of those requested to write an autobiography probably wouldn't fill a Greyhound bus. So I feel honored to be invited to board that bus. It is an honor, but the trip is not all joyride.

Going back through my life in memory, the landscape is not the same one I saw when I was younger, traveling through it for the first time in a different direction. The mountains are not as high, the gorges not as deep. Sweet and tender times recalled are painful; old wounds no longer bleed or hurt. The best and worst of life have been joined by time into a single creature of remembrance, like a two-headed calf with one set of vital organs.

I was born in Brooklyn, New York, on August 16, 1916, the third and last son of Harry and Sabina Felsen. Ahead of me were my brothers Sidney, six, and Milton, four. There were no sisters.

When I was three days old I contracted whooping cough. I couldn't breathe, turned a dark purple, and was seconds away from choking to death.

My father saved my life. He picked me up by the ankles, held me head down, and shook me vigorously. I coughed up the congestion, began to breathe again, and stayed alive.

I never thanked him.

When I was in high school I was taught—and had to agree to get a passing grade—that my parents came to this country around 1908 as part of "the wave of undesirable immigration." Both came from fairly well-to-do families. My mother could read, write, and speak six languages. My father was educated, a superb violinist, and an expert horseman.

What made my parents "undesirable" was not who they were, but *where* they came from. My mother lived in what was then part of the Austro-Hungarian Empire—a part called Poland. My father came from near Odessa in southern Russia. My mother's people were merchants and landowners. My father's family managed the forests on a large estate owned by some nobleman.

My father's family came from Germany. And I think they went to Germany from Spain about the time Columbus "proved" what learned people had known for a couple of thousand years—that the world was round. The family name was Wecker (pronounced Vecker). It was changed to Felsen when he came to this country. The Germans were noted for their skill in forestry management and were much in demand in other countries. My ancestors wound up in Russia. Had my parents come to America from Germany instead of Russia and Poland, they would have been regarded as "desirable," regardless of their character or lack of it. Or, being Jewish, perhaps not.

I weighed nine and a half pounds when I was born, and probably was programmed to be as husky and athletic as my big brothers. The whooping cough changed that. I came out of it with a strained heart and developed into a skin-and-bones little boy, constantly warned that I mustn't run or I would drop dead. My brothers tell me I whined and cried a lot.

When I was four my mother and we boys moved to the tiny mountain village of Wawarsing, New York, where the country air was supposed to be good for me. My father stayed in the city where he was an unsuccessful real-estate salesman and sent us a small check every week for support.

We lived in a large white house about a hundred years old, and one of the few in the village that had both electricity and running water. We had almost an acre of ground with beautiful maples and evergreens, a lawn, a summer kitchen to play in on rainy days, a big garden, an apple orchard, roses, grapes, berries, a chicken house. What more could a small boy ask for?

I was too young and puny to pal around with my big brothers, and the two boys my age in the village were seldom available as playmates. With my mother's help I became a reader before I was old enough to start school, and dreamed up adventures to make my solitary games more interesting. My mother's treadle sewing machine was my airplane, and the needle perforations in a sheet of paper were machine-gun bullet holes. I practiced throwing kitchen knives against the side of the woodshed, always as part of some battle against pirates or outlaws. So it may be that the whooping cough I suffered in the first week of my life was responsible for my becoming a writer instead of a policeman, a fireman, or a cowboy.

Although I wasn't supposed to run, I wasn't forbidden to walk. By the time I was in the second or third grade, I spent entire days roaming the woods alone, fishing along streams and in ponds and watching birds and small animals go about the never-ending work of finding food. I carried a forked stick for protection against the rattlesnakes and copperheads that were common in the area, but the few times I came upon a snake I fled without bothering to find out what brand it was.

Young Henry Felsen with his dog Wound, about 1923

The Felsen family: Sabina, Henry, Harry, Sidney, Milton, in Wawarsing, New York, about 1924

One of my favorite places was an old cemetery on a secluded hill. It was surrounded by a low stone wall and also bordered by huge, beautiful maple trees. The dates on some of the crumbling tombstones went back over 300 years. Most of the names were of early Dutch settlers, some of whose descendents still lived in the area. But there were others, mostly English-sounding, and even a few Indians.

Several of the mossy little headstones were for children my age. I resurrected them, imagining them as they probably roamed the same hills and fished the same streams I did, and felt the same joy of doing it. I took them with me, to live in my time, as I sometimes pretended it was 300 years earlier and I lived in theirs.

I read the faint, eroded epitaphs and tried to create boys and girls to fit the names. I didn't know it then, but I was teaching myself to create characters, and I was destined to spend most of my life dreaming up characters with names that fit them, or thinking up names first, then fitting characters to them.

The miracle was, and still is, that once these

made-up names and characters are put together, they become as real, if not more real, than living people. My grown children will bear witness that, when they were young and came to me with their questions and problems, or just looking for my company, I was often so involved with the problems of my "book children" that I didn't have the time or patience to pay attention to my own.

There was an old lady in her nineties named Mrs. Terwilliger who lived across the road from us. I used to visit her when I was little. She told me how, when she was a very little girl, she used to sit on her great-grandfather's knee while he told her about his adventures fighting in the American Revolution. She would let me wear his hat, and even wave his sword.

Even then I began to feel that what we call the past is only that part of the present that took place before we came along. When you have talked to someone who has talked with someone who saw George Washington, how can you think of those people and events as dead and gone forever?

That is why I read history in the same way I read the morning paper, to find out what *is* happening. It is all part of the same connected story. And no matter how far removed today's world *seems* from yesterday's, no present hour ever laid the egg from which it was hatched.

I attended the little country school in Wawarsing where one teacher taught all eight grades in one room. There were only about fifteen kids in the school, and most of the time I was the only one in my grade. The teacher let me go along at my own speed, taking the state regents' exams whenever I was ready. I finished in six years and started high school in Kerhonkson, four miles away. It was a new school, with fifty or sixty high-school students, and twenty or thirty in junior high.

When my children were young and attended schools only a few blocks from home, I thought they would be interested in hearing how I walked four miles to school every morning, and four miles back at night. They weren't. I will say only this about it to you: I couldn't feel sorry for myself making that walk in bitter winter weather, because the Townsend girls had to walk two and a half miles down a dirt road before they got as far as our house to walk the next four.

At the end of my freshman year the state bought our house. The house, the lovely maples in front were to be destroyed; the shaded, gently curving macadam road would be replaced by a straight, bare, ugly, sunbaked strip of concrete highway. The bulldozers wiped out everything—my home, the charm of the village,

my childhood. I went back a few years ago. Where our gracious old house stood there is a new dealership in farm implements and sporting goods. The surrounding ground is flat and bare.

We moved back to Brooklyn, to a small apartment. I hated the city. I went to Erasmus Hall High, with its enrollment of over five thousand students. I hated it, too. At Kerhonkson I was part of everything that went on in the school. The Erasmus horde was dominated by a group of apprentice big shots who wore suits, white shirts, and ties. No matter what activity you might be interested in, the club or group already had several hundred members and didn't want any more. I still have bad dreams about being lost in the huge school and not being able to find my classroom. During the summer I worked as an apprentice airplane mechanic at Floyd Bennett Field for no pay. Later I sold airplane rides on commission. I flew as often as I could, usually in old, open-cockpit biplanes being tested after servicing. I planned to become a pilot.

The winter I was fifteen, I had had all I could take of the city and the school. We were in the middle of the Great Depression, and living on the edge of poverty. I decided—not to run away from home—but to go to Florida by myself, find a good job, and then send for the family to join me, away from the dreary hardships of New York, in a place where the air was clean and the sun shone every day. One January day I took off without a word to anyone. I carried a small bundle of clothes, had a knife stuck in my boot, and thirty-seven cents in my pocket.

The first day I thumbed my way to Philadelphia and spent most of the night getting through the city to reach open highway again. In the morning I caught a ride in an ancient Chevy driven by two New York cabdrivers. They were on their way to Mobile, Alabama to find a better life. I went with them.

Their funds were limited, and I had to buy my own food (on what was left of my thirty-seven cents). By the time we reached Atlanta, I hadn't eaten for two days. The men went off to find a room and I stayed in the car. About midnight I went out to look for food. It was snowing. I found a small diner that was open and offered to work in exchange for something to eat. The man gave me a broom and I started sweeping. In a few minutes he had me stop to eat a large, hot beef stew he had prepared. I began eating, but I had been without food so long the hot, rich stew made me sick, and I had to stop. I returned to the car convinced that I was going to starve to death in a strange city. I lay down in the car shivering with the cold, fearful and lonely. I think I cried, but I wouldn't turn back.

We finally made it to Mobile, averaging about one flat tire every hundred miles for twelve hundred miles. So far the Sunny South had been nothing but cold rain, red mud, scraggly pine trees, falling-down shacks, and troubled people in shabby clothes. In Mobile I checked into a mission and was given a bowl of soup and a cot to sleep on, which I earned by listening to some preaching, praying and singing a few hymns along with the other drifters.

I left Mobile the next morning and hitchhiked toward Florida. Somewhere along the way I met a boy a few years older than I and we teamed up. Rides were hard to get, so we decided to find a more certain way of moving on. That night we sneaked into a railroad yard and waited for a freight train that was headed out and moving slow. When the right one came we ran for it and climbed aboard into a boxcar. To my surprise the car, like others on the train, was filled with men. Not hoboes, I discovered, but mostly small farmers in bib overalls who had lost their farms and had nowhere to go. They too were looking for a better place to settle down and bring their families.

It was their plight, not my own, that gave me my first feelings of social consciousness. It was wrong for these men to be driven off their land, to be riding freight trains, forced into humiliating flights from the railroad police, begging their bread, torn from their loved ones. It was wrong, and something had to be done! Certainly the seeds of my future radicalism were sown that night in the boxcar, surrounded by these dispossessed farmers who talked very little and stared at nothing with dull, shocked eyes.

Florida *was* sunny, the Gulf was blue and beautiful, and I was hungry. I was alone again, knocking on doors offering to trade work for food, but without success. I went back to the railroad tracks again, and tried the other side. The houses were small and unpainted, but neat. I knocked on a door. A black woman opened it and looked out suspiciously. I made my offer to work for food and the door began to close in my face.

"I'm from New York," I said. "I'm trying to . . . go home."

The door opened. The woman was smiling. "New York. My son works in New York. Come in."

I had a great meal of bacon and eggs, and when I left, she gave me a bagful of pecans. I walked along the railroad tracks, looking for a good place to hop a freight, when I saw a small black boy ahead of me. The full stomach had me feeling pretty good. As I neared the boy I smiled and held out the sack of nuts, offering him some. He looked at me with obvious fear in his eyes, turned, and ran off.

It was the first time in my life anyone had been afraid of me, and I didn't like the feeling. Why? I wasn't very big, or fierce-looking. I had offered to share and acted friendly. Why the fear? And it came to me there could be only one thing about me that would make him afraid. My color. He was afraid of my white skin, no matter who lived inside.

And that situation, that condition, was another wrong that had to be righted.

A few years ago someone asked me why I wrote about cars, and not about social problems like race prejudice.

"Go back forty years to my first books," I said. "Books like *Submarine Sailor* and *The Company Owns the Tools* and *Bertie Takes Care*. I was attacking race prejudice in my books twenty-five years before it was the popular thing to do."

I made my way to Pensacola, pretty well convinced that there was very little future in Florida for a fifteen-year-old vagrant. I went to the police station where the sheriff, a pleasant gray-haired man named Anderson, took charge of me. He saw that I was fed, wired my home for bus money, and saw me off when it arrived.

A few days later I walked into the apartment just as the family was at dinner. Nobody said a word about my being gone, my brothers didn't grin. My mother set a place for me as though I had just come in from playing ball in the street. I appreciated it. And I did thank Milt, who had paid my fare.

When I finished high school, Milt and I decided to go to the University of Iowa. It was a long way from New York, and it seemed the least expensive of any of the colleges we had written to. We had saved enough from our summer jobs to get started—or so we thought. Somehow we had misread the catalog, and all we had was half enough.

We managed. We worked at anything and everything we could find. At one time, I was working forty-eight hours a week just to pay for tuition and room and board. Although I planned to major in dramatic art and become an actor, necessity turned me into a "professional" writer. And I finally became a real professional because writing is the only thing I have ever been able to make a living at.

Writing was easy for me (in those days), and I traded short stories and essays for meals, guaranteeing no less than a B. There was a tavern called Don's that was popular with poor students because you could get a very large glass of beer for a dime. When I didn't have a dime (which was usually always), I could be hired to write a short poem on the spot for one beer. The purchaser could give me the desired theme, and it usually took longer to drink the beer than to write the poem. One night a musician friend, Dan Rodman, asked me to write a poem about dirty dishes. I still have a copy of it.

La Comida

A few pewter dishes
Lie gasping, exhausted,
Greasy faces upturned
And streaked where the
Bread brushed, sweeping away
The last remnants of a heavy meal.
The cups are there too,
Gaping dully around,
With the scattered gray ashes
Of a last cigarette
Smudging their white throats,
And the clean collars of their
Damp saucers.

Not the best poem ever written by a seventeen-year-old, but not too bad for a five-minute effort to earn a beer.

When I read a companion volume of this series, I was particularly interested in reading the autobiography of R. V. Cassill, who was a fellow student at Iowa, a friend of my brother Milt's, and an acquaintance of mine. He mentioned his artist friend, Dick Gates. Dick was my friend. In fact, we were arrested together one night by a couple of policemen reinforced by a posse of about a dozen inebriated civilian volunteers. We were hauled off to jail where we were charged with "committing communism on the public street." The policeman in charge drew his gun, laid it down in front of him, and said he would shoot us if we tried to escape.

Dick and I, along with my brother Milt and a mild little graduate student named Rob White, had been putting up posters around the campus announcing a coming rally "against war and fascism." As I recall, Dick had designed the poster. The four of us were in the room. We didn't try to escape. Rob White called the mayor, who gave the policeman hell and ordered him to release us at once.

At the time this happened I was on the staff of the ROTC news bulletin, and lived in a room provided by the military department. I was not only booted out of the room, but one of the instructors, an army captain, informed me that the colonel in charge "never wants to see you again."

"Sir," I said with a straight face, "does that mean I am not supposed to come to class, or did he just mean socially?"

The captain wasn't sure, but since basic ROTC was mandatory, he opined that I should continue com-

ing to classes and drill. I'm glad I did. When I went to Marine Corps boot camp, my knowledge of basic drill resulted in my becoming a squad leader, with a promotion to Pfc at the end of the training session.

A lot of people, when they find out I went to the University of Iowa, ask me if I studied with the famous Iowa Writer's Workshop. I didn't. First, it wasn't in existence when I was in school. Second, I wouldn't have gone if they did have one because I was not interested in becoming a writer.

Other than the usual English courses, I never studied writing in school. And today my opinion is that most writing workshops, including the Iowa, are nothing more than literary circle jerks. Workshops try to dangle famous writers as teachers, but famous writers are often so conscious of their fame that mostly what they teach is how famous they are. What you get is "portion control" literature with everybody trying to write the same way, like fast-food hamburgers.

I suppose there is an element of sour grapes here. I have never (with a few exceptions) been able to teach because I do not have a degree. And I have never achieved the literary fame that makes a degree unnecessary. Which is too bad, because I think I am a much better teacher than I am a writer. I know how to motivate students to write their heads off, and then to stay out of their creative way.

Two weeks into my junior year I ran out of money and decided to drop out of school. The dean of men, a wonderful old man named Rienow, offered me a college loan to get me all the way through, and I turned it down. It was still the Depression, and few college grads got jobs. I didn't know how I would ever be able to pay it back. I was eighteen, and should have been smart enough to realize that if the university lent me money to finish, it would also help me find a job so I could pay it back.

I returned to New York, and with the aid of some forged papers, I got a job as officers' messboy on the *Santa Barbara,* going to the west coast of South America. (Under another name, the ship was torpedoed and sunk in the early days of World War II.)

I had never been on a ship before, and didn't know its aft from my elbow. But I worked with two other messboys, a black and a Puerto Rican, who taught me how to do my job and helped me until I could do it alone. We went as far as Valparaíso, Chile, and I also went ashore in Callao, Peru, the port city for Lima. I loved the feeling of being the "dumb foreigner" who couldn't speak the language, and what I went through, trying to buy some English walnuts for one of the ship's Chinese cooks, was high (or low) comedy.

My best friend on the ship was Willy, a boy about my age, half black and half Irish, who had charge of the ship's table linen and silver. As a messboy, I had access to the food. I got along well with the Chinese cooks—they shared their own rice with me instead of giving me what they cooked for the passengers and crew—and I could have anything I wanted. Willy and I would set up a wooden crate in his storeroom, cover it with snowy linen, set it with sterling silver, and *dine*. I gained fifteen pounds on that trip.

Willy and I talked about a lot of serious things. One thing that troubled him was that when the ship was in South America, where there was no racial discrimination, the white crew members would be his friends ashore. But when the ship returned to the United States and he saw them ashore, they avoided his company.

Years later, when I was a Marine returning from the Pacific, there were two detachments waiting to board the ship. The armed forces were still segregated in those days, so one group consisted of white Marines, the other, of black.

When we were ordered aboard ship, we did not load according to group. We were told to alternate, one at a time. And when we got into our quarters, we were thoroughly integrated. I did not hear one complaint.

If, before boarding, we had been polled as to whether we wanted to share our sleeping quarters with blacks, I am sure there would have been a heavy vote against doing it. But when we were *ordered* to do so, it was done without a second thought. What I got out of the experience was the belief that segregation, discrimination, and other racist or sexist injustices exist where they are *permitted* to exist. And where those in authority do not allow these evils to exist, they disappear, or are without force.

I returned to Iowa with my South American tan but without a hat or gloves when it was thirty below zero. I holed up for weeks, living on the food my friends stole from the University Hospital. (I should not say "stole." More truthful to say they collected some of what was owed me.)

One summer—I think between my freshman and sophomore years at Iowa—I washed dishes at the hospital for nine hours a day, seven days a week. Each hour's work earned one meal, three of which were consumed then. The other six were put into a meal-credit account, that I would draw on in the fall. I worked a month or six weeks like that, and then went home for a rest. When I came back to school in the fall, a new rule had been made. Meal credits could not be piled up. I

had spent a couple of hundred hours slaving in that steamy dishwashing room for nothing.

I managed to get a job with the WPA Writers' Project in Iowa City, doing historical and other research for the *Iowa Guidebook*. I also began courting a slender blond girl I had met in the drama department, Isabel "Penny" Vincent. When my job ended I spent most of my time hanging around her, and interfering so much with her school work that her high scholastic standing hit bottom. She gave up school, and we were married in January 1937. We were both twenty.

My brother and friends collected ten dollars for us, and Penny's friends gave her a bouquet of flowers. One suitcase held all our worldly goods. We set off for Des Moines on a "honeymoon" trip to run down a rumor of a job. We went on the same train, but not exactly together.

Between the ages of fifteen and twenty, I had graduated from riding inside slow freight trains to riding on fast passenger trains. And I do mean *on*. Penny's father was a railroad conductor, and she had a pass. So my bride and our suitcase rode inside the train. I lurked in the bushes near the locomotive. When it started up I dashed forward and climbed into the "blinds," the open front platform of the baggage car, just behind the coal car. Instead of a shower of rice and confetti, I honeymooned alone under a shower of soot, sparks, and cinders. When we reached Des Moines I hit the ground at full speed in case there were any railroad police watching. There weren't, so I walked into the station and was reunited with my bride.

There were no jobs. We slept on newspapers on a friend's office floor and ate when and where we could. I worked for a few weeks in a furniture warehouse; Penny as a maid for a doctor. In time she got a job in the *Look* magazine picture library for fifteen or sixteen dollars a week. With no job for me in sight, I finally began trying to write for money. I sold a small bit of humor to the *Des Moines Register* for five dollars . . . I was on my way!

I also, at this time, was a "known communist." The Depression was still on, the air was thick with hopelessness, the sad unemployed were everywhere. The system wasn't working and there was no hope for the future. It was a time when any young person with any kind of feeling or guts ought to be speaking up for change. If necessary, by revolution. Although, to tell the truth, I hadn't the foggiest notion of how revolutions started or continued. The only one I really knew much about was the American. (Hadn't I waved the sword that helped fight for our freedom?)

An old college friend, Darrell Huff, was also working for *Look* as an editor. He knew I was interested in writing, and he had free-lanced successfully while in college. He suggested that we collaborate on writing "true" detective stories. I would do the research and write the first draft. Then, together, we would polish it and split what we made.

At first I scorned this idea of writing commercial trash, but since nobody wanted to buy my stories and articles about injustice in the world, I decided to give the detective stuff a try. I would get all the facts about a crime out of the newspaper, then write a heavy-breathing account loosely based on those facts. The case had to be baffling, the police work brilliant.

I found I had the knack of writing about mysterious footsteps and doors creaking in the night, but I didn't know how to write a story that had a logical beginning, middle and end. The sessions with Darrell taught me how to put a yarn together, how to create suspense, and how to keep the reader following false trails without actually telling him lies or misleading him unfairly.

The stories began to sell. The first was "The Slugging Slayer of South St. Paul." The second was "Serpent in Her Soul." I dredged up other nasty, dreary little murders and whipped them with vocabulary to make them appear mysterious, exciting, and dreadful. But I was learning that there are certain techniques that must be applied to almost every story, highbrow or lowbrow, to make it professional.

Once during this period I took time off to make a public speech in behalf of the presidential candidacy of Earl Browder, of the Communist Party. I spoke not as myself, but to fill in for Elizabeth Gurley Flynn, a well-known communist. I had to read her speech word for word, and feeling more than a little ridiculous, I began, "I am an Irish woman who has fought for the working class for forty years . . ."

About here, some men threw eggs at me. I ducked, and they hit a YWCA official who was just coming out of the library behind me. Two big detectives grabbed the egg throwers and roughed them up. I finished the short speech and returned to the crime story I was working on. (With brilliant, gentle detectives.)

There is a kind of funny wrap-up to my "communist period." In the early 1960s, Meredith Press of Des Moines retained me for a month on special assignment to California to work up some book projects. The publisher was very anxious to make a deal for the life story of an actor friend of his. The actor was Ronald Reagan.

I called Mr. Reagan when I got to Los Angeles, explained my mission, and he hopped in his car and drove down to see me. We sat on the balcony of my room at the Hilton and soon made the deal. Then Mr. Reagan asked me if I would write his book. I begged off, and he wanted to know why. Honesty, I decided, was the best policy.

"You are known for your extremely conservative political views," I said. "I have the reputation in Des Moines of being the Red Menace. If my name appeared on your book, it might be very embarrassing for you."

"Oh hell," Mr. Reagan replied airily, "I don't give a damn about that. I used to carry the pink flag all around Des Moines myself."

I held firm, and arranged to find another, more suitable writer. (After all, think what my name on his book would have done to *my* reputation as a commie.)

We parted with a friendly handshake and never met again. I returned to Des Moines to write more teenage books, and he went on to become governor of California and president of the United States. Unfortunately for all of us.

Darrell left *Look* to become editor-in-chief of the Sunday-school story papers published by the David C. Cook Company in Elgin, Illinois. They were the *Young People's Weekly,* the *Girls Companion,* and *Boys World.* He gave me a couple of articles to write, and when they were satisfactory he offered me a job as staff writer for the three publications at a starting salary of $32.50 a week. A fortune! I was twenty-four years old, and it was my first (and last) real job.

I wrote about everything except religion. That material was handled by religious specialists in another department. They wanted to fill the papers with biblical stuff, and we wanted more material about sports, jobs, grooming, dating, and so on. Every time we had more material than they did, there would be a solemn meeting with the company brass, which we referred to as "getting more Jesus in the story papers."

I did a little bit of everything, including the Aunt Polly advice-to-girls column in the *Girls Companion.* Not too long ago I actually met a gray-haired lady who admitted that she had written to Aunt Polly for advice about her romantic problems when I was doing the column, and she thought there was a real Aunt Polly.

I also, as an editor, bought fiction. So much of it was so bad that Darrell suggested I try my hand at some stories for the *Boys World.* I did, and they were better than the slush-pile stuff we were getting. I created Bertie and Bart Poddle in a number of funny stories. A few years later the stories were worked over and connected to make *Bertie Comes Through,* the first of three books about Bertie and Bart that were published by E. P. Dutton.

One day one of our steady contributors, Norman

Carlisle, told me he had read some of my stories, and I ought to try writing a book for teenagers. He had publishing-house contacts, and offered to act as my agent. I didn't know how to write a book; he said it was simple. A book should be about sixty thousand words, which could be broken up into twelve chapters of five thousand words each. We decided on a subject, the building of the Pan American Highway, and I wrote a story about two young American engineers on the project. Twelve chapters, each of five thousand words, complete with storms at sea, snakes, spiders, jungle vines, spies, and bulldozers.

The book was bought by Dutton, and I received a two hundred dollar advance. I immediately quit my job and moved to New York to become a book writer. I also had a deal to continue writing short stories for Darrell. Each story, whether it was about sports, adventure, flying—anything but religion—had to illustrate the Bible lesson for the week. I got fifteen dollars a story, and wrote three a week.

In the next eighteen months I wrote and sold nine books—*Navy Diver, Submarine Sailor, Some Follow the Sea, Pilots All, Struggle Is Our Brother,* and others—for four different book publishers. Advances were still a couple of hundred dollars a book, plus modest royalties—about twenty cents a book.

Penny and I moved out to the little town of Stony Brook, on Long Island. We rented a little furnished white house with a lot of yard, flowers, and a tennis court, for thirty-three dollars a month. We were out in the country, acquired a yellow cat, and began our family.

There was good news, and bad news. The good news was the arrival of our son Daniel. The bad news was about my brother Milt. During our college years he had gone to Spain to fight on the side of the Spanish Republic, where he was wounded. When we entered World War II, he joined the OSS (the ancestor of the CIA). He went through the most rigorous secret training that included low-level parachute jumps at night, learning to operate the military vehicles of friend and foe, and so on.

His unit was sent to North Africa, and got involved in an action supported by British artillery. A number of Italian tanks showed up, and the artillery departed, leaving Milt's unit trapped. He was hit seven times with machine-gun fire, and left for dead. But some Italian tank commander saw that he was still alive, picked him up, and brought him back to a hospital. When he healed he was sent to a prison camp in East Prussia and later survived one of the infamous death marches and came home. But all I knew at the time was that he was missing in action.

When I was working on *Navy Diver,* I wanted to describe the Navy physical exam. "Go ahead and take it," the Navy PR officer said to me. "Then walk away before you raise your hand."

I didn't get that far. As a volunteer, I didn't pass the physical on account of my overbite.

Dan was about six months old when I got a notice from the draft board that my classification was being called up, and to stand by for my call. I don't like being kept in doubt about anything, so I requested an immediate physical. After all, I had flunked it once. Why not get it over with. I went to New York City for my exam. When it was over, I called Penny. "Guess what," I said. "I'm in the Marines."

The physical for draftees must have been a little different from the one for volunteers. Anyway, I was ticketed for the Navy, but they did give you a choice. One of my best friends, an editorial writer named Bob Blakely, was a Marine. That was good enough for me. "It's pretty tough," the Marine officer warned me when I opted for that service. I smiled. "I'll survive." When I began my recruit training at Parris Island, South Carolina in the summer heat, I wasn't so sure.

I was twenty-six when I went in. One of the old men in the platoon. And all my exercise had been at the typewriter. It was more than tough in boot camp, it was brutal. If there was any weakness left in my heart, it had all the help it needed if it wanted to quit for good. But I survived.

When I was a small boy I used to borrow pulp magazines from a neighbor to read while I sat by the stove and ate apples. I liked stories about aerial combat in World War I airplanes, and one of my favorite authors was Major Arthur J. Burks.

One day when my platoon was at the rifle range, I was ordered to report to the training officer. I stood at attention in front of a heavyset man with a grim, square face. I looked at the plaque on his desk. It was Major Arthur J. . . . !

"I understand you're a writer," he growled.

"Yes sir."

"How many words do you write a day?"

"Up to five thousand, sir."

"I write ten thousand."

He looked at me, not very much impressed by my 140 pounds.

"Do you want to be a Drill Instructor?"

"No sir!!!"

"Dismissed."

Three weeks later I got my next assignment: Drill Instructor's school. I found out later this was often the first step toward officer training. Some solid experience training and handling troops, then off to higher rank.

I wasn't a very good DI. I could do the job all

right, but it was hard for me to glare at a platoon of men, each of whom outweighed me by a hundred pounds or so, and inspire terror.

About this time a station newspaper was started, the *Parris Island Boot.* I wanted to do some writing, so after I had put my platoon to bed at nine-thirty, I walked a mile or so to the newspaper shack, wrote until after midnight, walked back and slept to around four-thirty, when it was time to rise and look sharp before waking the platoon and starting the day's training.

One night I attended a basketball game between Parris Island and a Marine team from Cherry Point. The game ended in a tie, and the overtime became more of a gang fight than a game until our commandant, little General Moses, stepped in and restored order. We finally won the game.

I went back to the *Boot* office and wrote a funny piece called "Basketbrawl, Marine Corps Style." "The teams were evenly matched during the regulation period of play," I wrote, "but in the overtime Parris Island proved generally superior." For some reason or other I signed the piece as Pfc. Gunther Gherkin.

The morning the paper came out, I was in the office with the rest of the *Boot* staff, including our unit commander, a Captain Tim Sanders. Suddenly General Moses appeared in the doorway with a copy of the paper in his hand. He wanted to know who was responsible for the piece about the basketball game. As one man, my brave Marine companions raised their arms and pointed at me. General Moses smiled. "I thought it was very funny," he said. I would like to see more writing like that in the paper." He went away, and I was no longer a DI. The details of my transfer to the paper followed.

I began writing a regular weekly humor feature about the misadventures of Pfc. Gherkin, and also one short story a week. The Gherkin feature was picked up almost at once by all the other USMC publications and carried regularly. I wrote funny things about the gripes and discontents among Marines, and I was twice threatened with a court martial for poking fun at the Corps. But General Moses remained my fan, and I was safe.

I wrote my pieces for about a year. And you can imagine my feelings when a Colonel Barr, who had been at Guadalcanal, told me that my writing was "worth a battalion of men" to the Marine Corps.

I was transferred to the staff of *Leatherneck* magazine without warning. I returned from a furlough at eight in the morning as I was supposed to. When I checked in, the man on duty said, "You were transferred out of here as of seven this morning. You are already an hour late on your way to your new assignment."

Henry Gregor Felsen, USMC Combat Correspondent, Leatherneck-Pacific *staff, 1945*

Washington was a big city, so I hated it. After a few months I requested to be sent overseas, and I finally went in April of 1945, traveling as a team with Fred Rhoads, a gifted young cartoonist who has since also made a name for himself as a western artist.

Fred and I had fantastic orders. We carried papers addressed to the commanding generals of the various divisions and air wings requesting them to assist us in our mission as communicated to us orally by the Commandant of the Marine Corps. We could come and go whenever and wherever we felt like it.

We knocked around the various islands with me writing and Fred drawing. We went to Zamboanga in the Philippines to spend a month with a dive-bomber outfit. We volunteered to ride as rear gunners, and went off to bomb Japanese troops in Borneo.

The little SBD dive-bombers flew in tight formations of three planes each. Fred was only a few yards from me. Then we flew into some clouds. To my horror the planes moved closer together, with wingtips overlapping. I could almost reach out and shake Fred's hand. I asked the pilot—a twenty-year-old from Kansas—what was going on. He said that they had to stay close enough to keep visual contact. Losing the other planes in the mist could lead to crashing together. I was informed, but watching the wing of Fred's plane a few feet away from my nose, I was not comforted.

Over the target, I slid back my canopy and faced to the rear. It was cold. Anyway, I was shivering. The plane started down in a gentle dive. I began to breathe easier. Then the air brakes rolled out of the wing, the nose of the plane dropped, and my feet were at one o'clock while my head was at six. The machine guns broke loose and came back into my lap. If I had been facing forward, they would have knocked my head off. The rest of the dive was bucking, screaming, upside down blur. We started at ten thousand feet and pulled out at eight hundred. I don't know when the bomb was dropped, but I saw other planes coming down and disappearing into our dust before they bounced out again. At the time, I hoped we had hit some enemy soldiers. Today, I hope we didn't.

Fred and I made it to Japan a few weeks after the war ended. We sometimes had a photographer with us, and that, plus Fred's quick skill at doing portraits, gave us something to trade. And you survive in the military according to your bartering position. We traded pictures for good food, new uniforms, the use of jeeps, cigarettes.

When it was time to return to the United States we flew back to Hawaii to await orders and a ship. There was some delay. The Marine Corps had acquired several single-tail versions of the B-24 bomber, and was starting regular flights to China. It was suggested that while I was waiting to go home, I ought to take one of the China flights and write some funny stories about it. I had a photographer assigned to me and left.

We carried several colonels as passengers. As a buck sergeant, I was the lowest rated man on the plane. We were out over the Pacific when I was called to the cockpit. The pilot looked at me. "Where are we going?" he asked.

"Don't you know?"

He shrugged his shoulders. "Aren't you in charge of the airplane?"

I said I was only along for the ride, to pick up a few souvenirs to take home, and I'd be happy to go wherever he flew the plane. We went to Shanghai, Tientsin, and Peking. After I was out of the Corps I wrote a little account of an experience in Peking called "Li Chang's Million." It was rejected thirty-three times over a two-year period before *Woman's Day* bought it as an article. The following month, it was chosen for *Best American Short Stories of 1949*. It has been in many anthologies, and is still being bought.

To this day if you ask me what the difference is between a short story and an article, I'd have to say

Felsen, 1945. At 8,000 feet over the Pacific, on the way to China in a four-engine RY-3

that sometimes it depends on the editor who reads it.

After the war I returned to writing the teenage books I felt at home with, and tried free-lancing in the magazine field, usually trying to continue the humorous stuff I had done as Gunther Gherkin. I obtained an agent, a woman named Harriet Wolf. She was wonderful. She knew how to encourage me, to find new markets, and to send back the bad stories. When she gave up being an agent to become an analyst my writing world almost fell apart. I have never been able to replace her.

I bought an old stone house in the country near High Falls, New York. My nearest neighbor was half a mile away. There was no electricity or running water. When I worked at night I put a candle at each side of the typewriter, and that's how *Bertie Comes Through* was written. But we felt too isolated, and little Dan had no playmates, so we moved back to Iowa, where I continued working at my job of being a writer.

I always liked to write in a little office, as isolated as possible. I went to work in the morning just as to any other job, worked until noon, had lunch, and returned to the typewriter until five or six at night. (Sometimes until midnight). It was, seen from the outside, a very routine, dull life, but it helped produce as many as six books a year plus the magazine stories and articles.

I had to depend on heavy production to survive. Although my books were doing well, I was still only getting a few hundred dollars a book as an advance. It was publishing tradition I was told. Juvenile books got small advances. But I was making a living writing, and at that time there were only about a hundred writers in the country who were making their entire living as authors. And my royalties got better, which helped.

At this time I began to crack the big magazine market, with sales to *Redbook* and *Collier's* among others. I was also getting a hundred dollars each for my Allenby and Mirabeau stories—the old Bertie Poddle type humor with new characters—for the *Young Catholic Messenger*. And, for more than a year, I wrote the "Man Next Door" page for *Better Homes and Gardens* without a byline.

In 1948 I had an office across the hall from the Des Moines Safety Council. When the director, Bob Hassett, found out I wrote teenage books, he asked me to write one about driver training. I almost laughed out loud. What kind of a story could you write about *driver training?* I was writing *Davey Logan, Intern* then. With the help of a local hospital and an intern named Paul From, I wore a suit and posed as some kind of visiting doctor. I almost got into trouble a few times when a doctor, not in on what I was doing, asked my opinion of a diagnosis and invited me to examine a patient.

Bob Hassett continued to pester me, so to get him off my back I sat down and wrote a book about driver training. It took about fourteen working days to do, and I called it *Hot Rod.* The book was an immediate success. I actually got a thousand dollar advance for it. It was bought by Bantam books as a paperback experiment. They hoped it would sell two hundred thousand copies. They got it for two thousand dollars, half of which went to Dutton, and the book stayed in print for thirty-two years and sold around two million copies.

The *Hot Rod* sales picture changed my market value. For *Street Rod* Random House gave me five thousand, and Bantam offered ten—half of which went to Random House. A small step in the right direction. *Street Rod* proved to be another book headed for the hundred thousand sales mark in hard cover, and a million or more in paperback. As a result the advances for my next teen car novel were cut to thirty-five hundred from Random, and half of seventy-five hundred from Bantam!

Had I been writing adult books with these sales figures, I could have counted on very big advances. But writing juveniles. . . . Of course, a big advance means a big tax bill. And a book that makes its hundred thousand over a twenty year period puts most of the money in the writer's pocket. But it's hard not to feel put down when some writer whose book sells about a third or a fourth as many copies as yours gets advances that are ten or twenty times larger. And what the publisher loses on his book comes out of your hide.

I discovered you have to develop a thick skin when you write juveniles. Once in a while, on my visits

to New York from Iowa, I would be invited to a literary cocktail party. People would come up hoping I was an editor looking for new authors. When I said I was a writer they asked (hoping I'd turn out to be someone famous) what I wrote. When I said books for teenagers, they immediately—and contemptuously—turned their backs on me and walked away.

But then the *New York Herald-Tribune,* reviewing *Some Follow the Sea,* said, "Gregor Felsen writes books for boys that men can read without loss of dignity." What more could I ask?

When my father came to this country he was a fine enough violinist to be offered a place with a symphony orchestra. But one day he heard the great violinist Fritz Kreisler play. "If you can't play like that," my father said to my mother, "you have no right to pick up the violin." He put his down, and never played again until shortly before he died. Sick in body and mind, his fingers played a few simple tunes from his boyhood days. He seemed unaware that he was playing or hearing the music.

I am somewhat like my father in that respect. I have always loved to read, and like nothing better than to discover fine writers. But at the same time, I feel that if I can't write that well, I shouldn't be doing it at all.

Yet, unlike my father, I have learned that not everyone has to be a great artist. Not every violinist has to be the greatest classical performer in the world, and not every writer has to be Shakespeare. People like and need different kinds and levels of music or literature just as they need or like different kinds of food, clothing, or automobiles. The luxury sedan for one, the pickup truck for another.

When I began writing for teenagers, I thought it was just a step toward adult writing. Then, with *Hot Rod,* I began to get a different kind of fan letter, usually scrawled in pencil. "This is the first book I have ever read," the letter would begin, and then it would end with a request for the titles of other books I had written.

The teacher in me was elated. My car books were reaching young people who did not read, and were making readers of them. Now they would go on to look for other books about other interests. The more they read, the better writing they would demand. But I was the one who was starting them on the reading path.

And I asked myself this question: As a reader, is a person more important when an adult than when a teenager? Is a baby's need for milk inferior to an adult's craving for steak and potatoes? I realized that I had found my writing place, and it was a good one. My goal, not to be the greatest writer in the world, but to be the best in my field. Sometimes I reached it.

I sold a humorous western short story to *Collier's*, called *Why Rustlers Never Win*. Hal Kanter read it while flying from Los Angeles to New York, and bought the film rights. The movie he made was called *Once upon a Horse*, with Dan Rowan and Dick Martin.

A few years later, when I was in California, I met Hal. He had just become Chief of Comedy at 20th Century-Fox-TV, and we talked about the business of writing humor. Hal asked me if I had ever thought of writing for TV. I said I hadn't, but if anybody ever asked me to, I supposed I'd try it. And that was that.

A few days later I was swimming in a pool belonging to some friends. I was alone at the house, and when the phone rang I answered it. The call was for me. It was Ilse Lahn, a Hollywood agent who worked with Harriet Wolf. She spoke with a heavy German accent. "Hank, dear," she said, "vere haf you been? Hal Kanter has been looking for you all over. He vants to know vy you havn't come to vork."

Hal had hired me, and I was too dumb to know it.

I was given a two-room suite of offices in the old Writers' Building, and began work on a pilot script for a comedy western based on my magazine character The Curly Kid. My secretary was Helen Denver, whose brother Bob played the part of Maynard on the *Dobie Gillis* show, and who later moved on to become Gilligan of *Gilligan's Island*. I became good friends with the Denvers, and sometimes baby-sat for them.

Everybody loved The Curly Kid—the studio, the sponsor, the advertising agency. It was the one show that *couldn't* miss. I began to feel rich. Then some executive at CBS said you couldn't kid westerns, and The Curly Kid was shot down in his tracks.

I went back to Iowa and my books. With Hal, at long distance, the Curly Kid pilot was expanded to an hour show and ran on NBC as a *Bob Hope Comedy Hour* one-shot. Don Knotts played the Curly Kid. The script was nominated by the Writers Guild for best nonepisodic comedy of the year. It didn't win.

In Iowa, Heartland Productions bought film rights to my adult stock-car racing book, *Fever Heat*. I wrote the script. It wasn't a very good movie—or was it? It was the kind of film that was the last one shown when drive-in owners ran triple features, and went on at two or three in the morning. But there was an old automobile mechanic in Des Moines with terminal cancer who had his sons take him to the drive-in in the middle of the night so he could "see it one more time before he died."

I wrote my last teen car novel, *Boy Gets Car*, in 1960. It shocks me to realize it was the last book of any kind of fiction that I have written. I turned to nonfiction books, like *Letters to a Teenage Son; To My Son, the Teenage Driver;* and *Can You Do It until You Need Glasses? The Different Drug Book*. The drug book was published in 1977, and was my last published book. I am beginning to write again.

Daniel and Holly Felsen, West Des Moines, Iowa, about 1952

*Grandchildren John Henry Felsen and
Carly Welch, 1984*

To catch up on the personal: My father died just before I went into the Marine Corps. Milt came home from Germany when I was in the Philippines. My mother lived long enough to see him safely home, but she died suddenly while I was still in the Pacific.

Since that time Milt has been an official of the Screen Directors Guild for many years. Sid, whose formal education ended with little Kerhonkson High, and who spent most of his life in overalls, was "discovered" by Ryan Aviation and made what they call a nongraduate engineer. The way it happened is kind of funny. Sid had a job running tests on some instruments to be used on space vehicles, and they were failing the tests. A group of engineers came down to see what was wrong. "They're failing," Sid said, "because the design is wrong." One of the engineers said, sarcastically, "Well, if you know so much about it, why don't you design better ones?" Sid spent six months studying by himself, and came up with designs that worked. He was immediately promoted from the assembly line to a private office, and a new status.

When I was a little boy, my big brothers were my heroes. They still are.

My daughter Holly was born in Iowa in 1948. A little girl with dark curly hair and eyes like ripe olives, she wanted to be a teacher from the day she started kindergarten. She went through Drake University in three years, graduated with honors, and now teaches in Grand Island, Nebraska. She has a daughter, Carly, who is just turning one year old as I write this. With luck, I will see her for the first time this summer.

My son Dan followed my footsteps into the Ma-

rine Corps. When he returned he also graduated from Drake. He worked for the Iowa Crime Commission, then became a policeman for seven years, and now works for the state of Iowa. He has a lot of writing talent, and I think he might have become a writer if I hadn't been one. He preferred to hoe his own row. Some day, perhaps. . . . His son, fifteen-year-old John Henry, is my only grandson, and wants to become an outdoor writer.

Penny was a forty-eight-year-old social worker when she took a leave and returned to the State University of Iowa to earn her degree, and then continued in school until she earned her Master's. She became a very fine psychiatric social worker. For reasons that only concern the two of us, we were divorced in 1973.

I vowed that I would remain a bachelor for the rest of my days, but in 1975 I married Karen Louise Behrens, who was also divorced and the mother of two children, Joyce and David. They live in St. Louis. Joyce has two small children, Adam and Kimberly. David works for an architect.

Although I am twenty-six years older than Karen, we have been a good team. We have been together day and night for ten years, and are an affectionate and sharing couple.

Karen and I moved to Vermont in 1979, and I planned to continue my life as a writer with a lot of fishing in between books and stories, but it didn't work out that way. I had been feeling extremely tired for

Karen Felsen, in Arkansas, 1975

some time, too tired to write or even think about writing. I thought it was just a matter of getting old, and needing a long vacation after forty years at the typewriter. Oddly enough, I could row a boat all day without tiring, but I couldn't walk a hundred feet without having to stop and rest my aching legs. Karen insisted I see a doctor, and I discovered I had something called autoimmune hemolytic anemia. My spleen was devouring the red blood cells as fast as they were being manufactured. My blood had just about turned to water, and if I had waited a few more weeks to see a doctor, it would have been too late.

I was in a VA hospital for a month, had my spleen removed, and lost my immune system. Without that built-in protection, I began catching pneumonias, and had to be hauled to the hospital several times—usually in the middle of the night. I dragged around for a long time trying to recover my strength and my spirit. With no new book income, and old royalties dwindling, things began to look very grim. Karen came to our rescue.

Somewhat as a hobby, Karen had designed and made some elegant wool dog coats for a few neighbors. Then a friend, who had had two dogs shot in his back yard during the hunting season, asked her to create something to protect dogs. She got hold of some blaze orange Ten Mile Cloth and designed and trademarked a garment called a Safety Saddle Vest. We also gave her enterprise a name—Definitely Dogwear.

We hung a vest in a front window to attract customers. A man from the nearby prestigious Orvis Company drove by and saw it. He took several vests to test with bird dogs in the Georgia brush. When the tests were over, Orvis ordered five hundred. Karen—and Definitely Dogwear—were a business.

Today Karen's high visibility vests are being worn by dogs in every one of the continental United States. In addition to the thousands worn to protect sporting dogs and pets from hunting and road accidents, the vest has become a safety uniform for the Search and Rescue Dogs in several states, and for game warden and police K-9s. Since then, Karen has also designed and made half-a-dozen new items for dog safety, comfort, and control.

When the business began to grow I began to help out where I could. I wrote letters, dreamed up promotional copy, and thought up product names (The Lazy Dog Lounger, The Cozy Cat Napper, the K-9 Security Instant Activator). I also trimmed thread, turned bodies, packaged, and mailed. And even helped in working out the design of new products. Karen is a stickler for using only the best materials and providing the finest possible workmanship. And I learned that the satisfaction gained from turning out a top quality manufac-

tured product was not inferior to that of turning out an acceptable manuscript. Much to my surprise, business turned out to be rather exciting, and a genuine creative challenge.

I used to teach that once a manuscript was bound into a book and offered to the public for a price, it stopped being a personal work of art and became just as much a commodity as a loaf of bread, a shirt, or a stereo. And the first duty of the manufacturer (author) was to give the customer his money's worth of product (writing). (How many times have you said, or heard it said, about a book, a movie, or a record album, "It wasn't bad, but it wasn't worth the money"?) In a sense, the reader-customer is a partner in the work, and the only way you can give him his money's worth is with your very best effort—not only to please yourself, but to please him. If you are only writing to please yourself, give your work away. Don't ask someone else to buy the ticket for your private ego trip.

Although Karen and I have been together for ten years, I am constantly being amazed (and sometimes amused) by her creativity, her capabilities, and the variety of her interests and concerns. I realize that to particularize a person is to limit, and a list of the things one does is not the complete story of what one is. But I can't resist a few examples.

When she bought a couple of commercial sewing machines, she not only taught herself how to operate and adjust them, but also how to repair them. She rebuilt parts for one machine with liquid steel, and made a critical operating part for the other out of a paper clip.

When a lawyer she retained was willing to accept an unsatisfactory settlement from a large company in a business damage suit, Karen called the company lawyer, restated the case, and convinced him to almost double the offer.

When black flies bit me while I was fishing, and gave me viral encephalitis, Karen had it diagnosed correctly while two different doctors were still treating me for a strained back.

When we had car trouble, Karen (correctly) pinpointed the trouble as being with the fuel pump—while the garage mechanics and I were still trying to correct the difficulty with choke adjustments.

Above all, I think, she is a very caring person. When, with study and experience she became knowledgeable about the problems of starting and operating a small business, she was (and is) always ready to put aside her own work to advise some other woman with an idea who needed guidance in starting her own operation.

As a dedicated antinuclear person, she devised a

local program called "A First Strike For Peace And Freedom."

Recently, one of her suppliers said that because of foreign imports the American textile industry could be dead in as few as five years. Karen has a plan to save not only the textile people, but others who are similarly threatened. Don't discount her chances for success.

Obviously, my life revolves around my relationship with Karen, and there are no empty corners of existence. At home she is a great cook, has a beautiful singing voice, and is professionally knowledgeable about choral music. She is the complete fellow gypsy when the travel bug bites. She also likes to read a lot of heavy esoteric literature and considers me shallow because I fall asleep over it. A religious person in the broadest, most nonsectarian sense of the word, I can always get a rise out of her by pretending that my concept of God is of an old guy with a white beard who is so busy keeping His eye on the sparrow that He doesn't have time for people. I love her giggle.

But once a writer . . . When I felt ready to return to writing I began to contact publishers, but there was no welcome mat, no fatted calf waiting for the returned prodigal son. Bantam, which has sold millions of my books in paperback, made it plain that they were only interested in me as the author of teen car books, and they thought "car books have seen their day." I wrote to Random House, which sold several hundred thousand of my books in hard cover. I didn't even get an answer.

I began to take a hard look at myself. I was very popular in the fifties and sixties, described by one publication as "America's most popular author of books for boys." And in 1972 I was listed as one of the top twenty all-time best-selling paperback authors in the field of modern fiction.

But that was then, and this is now. Perhaps Bantam was right, and I have seen my day. It's a different world now than it was twenty or thirty or forty years ago, and it may have been going in one direction while I was going in another. It's something to think about.

My first love in writing was humor. I got into the teen car thing by accident, and became the prisoner of its popularity. Now I am free again, and it is an opportunity to find out if anything I write has a place in today's world.

So, for better or worse, I have begun writing again, starting from the beginning a second time. It would please me to be a successful writer once more, but my life and my happiness do not depend on it. After all those years sitting alone in a room with a typewriter, living with imaginary characters, it is a wonderful thing to have the affection and companion-

ship of a wife you love, and who loves you. The only accomplishment of Karen's that irritates me is her habit of having better luck when we go fishing together. (Or is it more skill?)

Anyway, if the writing doesn't pan out, Karen has promised me a real salaried job working for Definitely Dogwear. I suppose I will start at the bottom, but it could be a job with a great future. After all, being married to the boss ought to be a quicker way up the ladder than just being married to the boss's daughter.

When you have forty pages to tell the story of your life and work, and have lived almost seventy years, you have to leave out ten things for every one thing you put in. So you get a kind of hop, skip, and jump picture of how "I became me." I hope I have chosen the most informative incidents.

I would like to close with a word about my writing.

Every book I write is written for just one reader. The very first character I create is a boy or girl I think would be interested in the story, and I write it for him—or her.

When I decided to write *Hot Rod,* for example, I first created a boy about thirteen who lived in a small Midwest town and was more interested in cars than in reading. I saw him dressed in faded denims and a flannel shirt. I imagined him at a time when he'd had an argument with his parents and was feeling low. I saw him go into a drab little living room and sit at one end of a battered couch under a lamp with a scorched parchment shade. He picked up a book and began to read to forget his troubles. On the cover of the book was the title, *Hot Rod.*

"Now," I commanded myself, "write your book for that boy."

I do that with everything I write. I even created a reader-character for whom to write this autobiography.

You.

I wrote this little story of my life in May, 1985. In October a massive heart attack almost turned me into Henry Gregor Felsen, 1916-1985. I lay in a small hospital for twenty-one hours without seeing a doctor, and by the time I was transferred to Dartmouth College's Mary Hitchcock Hospital, I was more dead than alive.

Bypass surgery saved my life, but because the heart attack was not recognized or treated when it struck, my heart was too badly damaged to receive the full bypass it needed. Today is the first day of spring, 1986. I am still here personally, but my professional life may have come to an end. I was never the kind of writer who wrote a few pages every day. I stored a book up in my head until it was ready, then wrote it in

Henry Gregor Felsen, about 1967

anywhere from ten to thirty days, working up to eighteen hours a day. I can't do that any more, and I'm not sure this old dog has the time and energy left to learn new tricks.

BIBLIOGRAPHY

FOR YOUNG ADULTS

Fiction:

Jungle Highway. New York: Dutton, 1942.

Navy Diver. New York: Dutton, 1942.

Struggle Is Our Brother (illustrated by Woodi Ishmael). New York: Dutton, 1943.

Submarine Sailor. New York: Dutton, 1943.

Some Follow the Sea. New York: Dutton, 1944.

Bertie Comes Through (illustrated by Jane Toan). New York: Dutton, 1947.

Flying Correspondent (illustrated by W. Ishmael). New York: Dutton, 1947.

Bertie Takes Care (illustrated by J. Toan). New York: Dutton, 1948.

Bertie Makes a Break (illustrated by J. Toan). New York: Dutton, 1949.

Davey Logan, Intern. New York: Dutton, 1950.

Hot Rod. New York: Dutton, 1950.

Two and the Town. New York: Scribner, 1952.

Street Rod. New York: Random House, 1953.

The Cup of Fury. New York: Random House, 1954.

Fever Heat, under pseudonym Angus Vicker. New York: Dell, 1954.

Crash Club. New York: Random House, 1958.

Boy Gets Car. New York: Random House, 1960; published as *Road Rocket.* New York: Bantam, 1963.

Why Rustlers Never Win. New York: Scholastic Book Services, 1966.

Screenplays:

Fever Heat. Filmed by Paramount in 1968.

Nonfiction:

The Company Owns the Tools, under pseudonym Henry Vicar. Philadelphia: Westminster, 1942.

He's in Submarines Now. New York: McBride, 1942.

He's in the Coast Guard Now. New York: McBride, 1943.

Pilots All. New York: Harper, 1944.

Letters to a Teenage Son. New York: Dodd, 1962.

To My Son, the Teenage Driver. New York: Dodd, 1964.

A Teenager's First Car. New York: Dodd, 1966.

To My Son in Uniform. New York: Dodd, 1967.

Three Plus Three. Atlanta, Ga.: Scott, Foresman, 1970.

Living with Your First Motorcycle. New York: Putnam, 1976.

Can You Do It until You Need Glasses? The Different Drug Book. New York: Dodd, 1977.

FOR YOUNG ADULTS

Editor of:

Here Is Your Hobby: Car Customizing. New York: Putnam, 1965.

Other:

Doctor, It Tickles! (illustrated by Lawrence Lariar). New York: Prentice-Hall, 1953.

FOR CHILDREN

Fiction:

Cub Scout at Last! (illustrated by Robert Henneberger). New York: Scribner, 1952.

Anyone for Cub Scouts? (illustrated by Paul Galdone). New York: Scribner, 1954.

The Boy Who Discovered the Earth (illustrated by Leonard Shortall). New York: Scribner, 1955.

Jean Fritz

1915-

It was raining in Hankow, China, on the night of November 16, 1915, which complicated matters. For it was then I decided to make my appearance in the world and my mother, sick with dysentery, had to be carried to the hospital on a stretcher. The servants carried the stretcher; my father, walking beside my mother, held an umbrella over her. Had I heard this story as a child, I would not have been impressed that it was either unusual or picturesque. This was China, the only world I knew. A stretcher, if needed, was no more unlikely than any other mode of travel: rickshas mostly, horse-and-buggy on special occasions, sedan chairs, sampans, and always in summer donkeyback when we were in Peitaiho. Until the last few years of our stay in China, an automobile ride ranked among the high treats of life, along with ice cream, snowfalls, and rare visits to the movies (Jackie Coogan, Douglas Fairbanks, Rin Tin Tin).

I have chronicled my childhood years in China in *Homesick: My Own Story*, but in deference to the shape of the book, I had to omit (except for a brief reference) all my wonderful summers in Peitaiho, a resort for foreigners on the ocean north of Peking. When I was there, I didn't waste time being homesick for America. Indeed this was such a magical spot that later my children came to use it as a yardstick for measuring the relative merit of all ocean resorts. "Is this as good as Peitaiho, Mom?" they would ask.

And I would have to answer, No. In my eyes no place has ever been able to compete with Peitaiho. The ocean lay down a small slope at the end of a narrow goat path from our house. Our beach was bounded on one side by a peninsula which my father and I referred to as the "three-cornered island" and where at low tide we would chip oysters from the rocks. On the other side was Eagle Rock on top of which sat a house occupied by friends who every Sunday evening invited the American community to gather on their porch for a brief worship service. As we watched the sun sink into the sea, we sang "Day Is Dying in the West," a hymn of praise that I supposed had been written with that place specifically in mind.

The highlight of every summer was the day my parents and I and a few friends went for a picnic to Shanhaikuan where the Great Wall comes down to the sea. We started at five in the morning on donkeyback,

Young Jean Fritz on the downstairs veranda of her house in Hankow, China, about 1918

following the shore, crossing miles of mountainous dunes, carefully avoiding the areas of quicksand. We ate our breakfast on the dunes and our lunch on top of the Wall itself where I could look down at Mongolia on the other side. I loved being on the edge of Mongolia. It had a faraway, wild sound as if it were a place in a story and automatically that put me in the story too.

Compared to Hankow—a dull, gray industrial city—Peitaiho did indeed have a storybook quality. Hankow in the 1920s was for a while the seat of the new Communist party, the headquarters of Russian advisors, and a hotbed of antiforeign demonstrations. Several times I was in real danger. My mother and I were once stoned by angry peasants on a country road; we had a gang of union workers break into our living room and riot. Time and again, along with other foreign women and children, we had to evacuate Hankow on a moment's notice. Of course I was scared but it was nothing compared to the terror I felt one night in Peitaiho. My mother woke me in the middle of that night as I slept on my bed on the veranda. She hurried me into her bedroom, pushed me behind an upstanding wardrobe trunk, and told me to sit on the floor and not move. At the side of the house I could hear gunshots. The police, she told me, were shooting it out with a

Fritz at Peitaiho, China, 1920s

pirate who had landed on our beach.

A pirate! I suppose if I'd seen him, he would have looked like an ordinary Chinese fisherman but the word "pirate" flung me into the heart of a story and struck more terror in me than any mob of angry Chinese. After all, I was used to Chinese mobs. But a pirate!

Stories played a great part in my childhood. They existed on the other side of what was for the most part a lonely time, but the boundaries were not clear—not then and not now. Whenever my emotions run deep, whenever I am overtaken by surprise or confounded with wonder, I feel that I have slipped into Story. Cer-

tainly I felt like the central character when I stood at the prow of the ship which finally returned me to America and in keeping with the moment, I recited the lines which begin "Breathes there the man with soul so dead . . ." Is this me, I asked, sailing through the Golden Gate?

Sometimes I wonder if I would have been a writer if I'd not had so many stories to lean on, so many backdrops to my life, such a variety of characters weaving themselves through my days. I was surrounded by different cultures—not only the Chinese, but in the international settlement in which we lived, I had friends of all nationalities. I celebrated Christmas the German way with German children, the English way with English friends, played with the daughters of the Italian consul, lived for a while with a Russian family who had crossed Siberia to escape their revolution. My parents entertained American sailors, visiting evangelists, and once a Chinese warlord, but when it came to Bertrand Russell, my father drew the line. He didn't want a proponent of "free love" at his dinner table. So with such a cast of characters at hand, I began early wondering about people, recognizing more and more as time went on that everyone is a story waiting to be pieced together. I was alert to the conversation of adults which, I had discovered, might at any moment drop a clue to the mysteries of life, the incomprehensibility of adulthood. I kept up the habit of listening to everything within earshot and so over the years I have developed a talent for eavesdropping. My record in a restaurant is a conversation eight tables away.

We came to America in 1928 and I spent the first year in Washington, Pennsylvania, becoming acquainted with my relatives, discovering such marvels as the five-and-ten, summer circuses, vegetables that could be eaten raw, drinking water that came straight from the tap. The list of discoveries stretched on and on, for America seemed not only a different country but a different world—newer, cleaner, more homogenous, luckier. It was an additional, a second world, however, in no way replacing my first one. Most China-born Americans feel this double-love, double-loyalty; it is a kind of tie of mutual memory that binds us together in a unique way.

After a year in Pennsylvania, my father went to work for the YMCA in Hartford, Connecticut, and we moved into the first American house of our own. My mother hung yellow silk curtains at our dining room windows, put down our Chinese rugs (which are on our floors now in Dobbs Ferry), and for my room she bought a white bedroom set which included a vanity table with a long mirror in the center, drawers on ei-

Picnic on the Great Wall, China, about 1925: Fritz, upper left, with bottle of pop; father, Rev. Arthur Minton, lower right, with white hat; mother, Myrtle Minton, upper right, wearing necktie and riding pants

ther side, and a bench in front of it. I was old enough to know now that (at least in the 1930s) "sophistication" was the ultimate in feminine achievement but I was also smart enough to know that I could never acquire the assurance, the coolness, the chic bound up in the word. Yet when I sat at my vanity table and brushed my hair languorously before the long mirror, I experienced a glow of sophistication, so fleeting that I attributed it to a magical quality in the table itself.

During these high school years I had my first contact with teachers who were interested in stimulating their students rather than simply drilling them. Largely on my own, however, I discovered Amy Lowell, Walt Whitman, boys, Emerson's Journal, lipstick, Edna St. Vincent Millay, boys, Greta Garbo, and other vintage teenage enthusiasms. And thanks to my parents I became better acquainted with North America. Every year we vacationed in a new area—Maine, Nova Scotia, West Virginia, Cape Cod, Vermont. Generally when the local people heard of my father's background, they invited him to preach which, as far as I was concerned, cast a shadow over any holiday. Once he was in the pulpit, my father lost all sense of time and although my mother and I had secret signals we could give him from our pew, he never looked in our direction. His record was two hours at a vesper service in South New Fane, Vermont. I still suffer when I think of it.

After high school and in spite of a miserable record in mathematics, I was accepted at the college of my choice—Wheaton College in Norton, Massachusetts. A small women's college, it was just right for me. On the one hand, there was a close relation between faculty and students and on the other hand, sophistication was not as important a criterion for success as it had been in high school. I had always known I wanted to write, so of course I majored in English and never throughout my entire career have I felt more elated than when my first freshman composition was read aloud to the class. I acted in plays, wrote for the college newspaper, and headed up the Wheaton chapter of the Veterans of Future Wars, a satirical antiwar movement started at Princeton. I loved my college years—so much so that at times they assumed that old storybook quality. Is this really me, I would ask, walking across a college campus in the United States of America? Even so, I knew I was still experiencing life in the lower case. I wouldn't really live Life with a capital L until I was out in the world on my own. Preferably in Greenwich Village.

Graduating from college in 1937, however, I soon discovered that I wasn't prepared to do much of anything "on my own." My parents had moved to New York my senior year, so though I had to abandon dreams of Greenwhich Village, I did have a view of the Manhattan skyline from my bedroom window on Morningside Drive. The Depression may have been winding down but not enough for inexperienced college graduates to notice. I had no luck landing a newspaper or magazine job and when I tried writing advertising copy for coming movie attractions, I was told my adjectives were not sensational enough. So I went the way of most women college graduates of that day: I took a crash secretarial course. Before I was quite finished, I was interviewed for a job with a dramatic coach at Carnegie Hall. The woman had no interest in my educational background; all she wanted to know was the date of my birth. Then after lengthy mathematical calculations, she announced that our stars coincided; I could begin work the next day. Ah, this must be Life, I decided. Bohemian style.

Within two weeks, however, I was disillusioned. The woman was fearsome and tyrannical. Our stars, far from coinciding, clashed so irrevocably that I quit. Back to the Help Wanted pages, I found an advertisement for a secretary to fly to China with a man who was selling munitions to Chiang Kai-shek in Chungking. Better than Bohemia, this was Adventure and one which would take me back to China. I had never been up in a plane and if "flying over the front" sounded dangerous, it also sounded story-like. At the interview, I informed the munitions man that I could speak Chinese which I thought would surely clinch the matter, but the munitions man shook his head. No, he said, I wouldn't do.

"Why not?" I asked.

"You're too innocent."

Fritz, about 1938, "enjoying a beach"

Shattering as this was to a twenty-one-year-old ego, I had to admit later that whatever he had in mind, he was probably right.

I ended up working for a textbook company on Union Square, which didn't say much for my stars. Yet having had consistently unhappy school experiences as a child, I had developed strong ideas about education and looked forward to watching an organization experimenting with methods, working for improvement. I was, as the munitions man had pointed out, innocent. For as well-intentioned as textbook publishers may be, their primary thrust must be not toward innovation but toward sales. Textbook editors cannot be leaders; they must be followers and please as many segments of the public as they can. This insight into the textbook world would serve me well later when in my own way, and through a different route, I entered the field of education. At this time I also took a course in children's literature at Teachers College, Columbia University. I was, of course, delighted when my term paper, "Style in Children's Literature," was printed in a professional journal, but I still had no idea that this was the direction my own work would eventually take.

Life with a capital L suddenly took over and made all plans irrelevant and the future itself problematic. I was married to Michael Fritz on November 1, 1941, and six weeks later the Japanese bombed Pearl

Fritz, with her grandparents and her mother, after returning to the United States

A Loft Photo

Fritz, with husband Michael and son, David, after returning to New York at the end of World War II

Harbor. It seemed like the end of the world to me and yet, as it turned out, I was, as a war wife, lucky. Although Michael went into the army in early 1942 and served until December 1945, he was an officer in a radio intelligence unit, stationed first at the Presidio in San Francisco and then at Fort Lewis, Washington, and I was able to be with him all the time. Our son, David, was born in San Francisco and though being a mother without any of the amenities of washing machine, disposable diapers, or car was a time-consuming business, I felt I had somehow to keep my hand in the working world. I wrote stories for children as well as for adults and was disappointed but not surprised when all were rejected. I also talked the *San Francisco Chronicle* into letting me review new educational books and later in Tacoma, Washington, I managed to persuade the feature editor (a soft-hearted man) to abandon William Lyon Phelps and his syndicated column in favor of a weekly (and much cheaper) column by me.

After the war, we returned to New York. Our daughter, Andrea, was born in 1947, and I was able to make a fairly steady business of free-lance editing and ghostwriting for textbook houses. At the same time I continued to write; and I continued to be rejected.

It was after 1951 when we had moved to Dobbs Ferry, New York (where Michael took an administrative job with a Columbia University laboratory) that I began to channel my work more and more into writing trade books for children. When I found that the Dobbs Ferry Library had no children's room, no children's programs, and few children's books, I volunteered to conduct a weekly story hour. This proved so popular that I was asked to become the children's librarian, plan a separate room for children, and order books. For two years I immersed myself in children's books, reading ten to twenty books a week so that I would know not only how to order books but how to match books to children. This wide, continuous reading, along with reading aloud, gave me a strong feeling for plot, pacing, and for subject matter that appealed both to children and to me. In short, without being consciously aware of what I was doing, I developed a sense of story and in the process found my own voice. That children should be my audience is not surprising, for I held tight to the memories of my own childhood, always afraid that second world of mine would fade away.

I began sending out manuscripts again. A true account of a trip when my four-year-old son warmed up his baby sister's bottle on the engine of a train became a story in which the magazine *Humpty Dumpty* showed interest but, the editor said, I should "loosen up" my style. I was not averse to loosening, was grateful for the advice, and as a result, found myself at last in print. I graduated to Wonder Books and in 1954 sent out my first full-length picture book manuscript,

"Our house in Dobbs Ferry, New York"

Daughter Andrea and son David

Fish Head, about a "raggedy, scraggledy, patched-up, scratched-up cat" who quite by accident found himself at sea in a fishing boat. It seems logical to me that I settled on such a story for these were crowded years with a young family and a job, so of course there were times when I longed to find myself at sea just as Fish Head did.

Coward McCann accepted the book; Marc Simont illustrated it; and best of all I was now in the hands of Alice Torrey, a sensitive and demanding editor who made me feel excited about my potential and at the same time pushed me to try more difficult forms. My first full-length novel for children was a fanciful story of the children on our street in Dobbs Ferry which I renamed Pudding Street and which, in truth, had such an American, small-town look, it seemed ready-made for a story. The plot had the ups and downs that I knew now that plots must have but it was essentially a wish-fulfilling plot. By moving a retired sea captain into the neighborhood, I turned the street into a kind of dream street in which parents did not interfere and the children, with the help of this imaginative captain, had the time of their lives. I gave myself, however, a technical problem that would be difficult for experienced writers and was far beyond me at the time. The story revolved not around a central character but around multiple characters, a street full of children with equal story importance. Alice Torrey kept telling me to get farther *inside* my characters, so I rewrote and rewrote. In the end I think readers did

respond to the fun the characters had in *121 Pudding Street,* but it was, as Alice and I both agreed, a "learning" book, one which made me face technical problems, see alternatives, and most of all, one which convinced me that I could indeed sustain a long book with chapters.

My next book was much easier to write. I told the story through the voice of a single character, a girl with whom I identified so closely I had no trouble getting "inside" her. For years I had wanted to extend a story that had come down in our family into a book, but I had not been able to do it. The story was of my grandmother's grandmother, Ann Hamilton, a pioneer girl in western Pennsylvania in the 1790s, whose family one night entertained George Washington as he was traveling west to inspect land that he owned. It was a true story, but by itself, it was simply an anecdote. I would have to invent a plot to go with it. When I began looking inside Ann, I discovered that she was lonely, resentful of living in an out-of-the-way place where, she felt, nothing happened. I would use the George Washington episode as the climax. The book was *The Cabin Faced West.* It was not until after the book was in print that I realized I had in a roundabout way told my own story except that the location and circumstances were different. In a way I was carrying on a dialogue with myself. The adult me was asking why I couldn't have appreciated my own faraway experience while I was still a child. The child in me was answering: "But it was lonely."

Fritz and her father in the 1960s, "sitting on the one remaining original bench from the church Ann Hamilton and her family attended in the late 1700s"

It was while I was working on this book that I discovered the excitement of historical research—reading old newspapers, letters, church records, county histories filled with colorful bits and pieces of the past that never make it into textbook history. I had not thought of writing about America's past but after this experience, I was hooked. Just as I had been eavesdropping all my life in search of clues, so now I extended my arena to a new circle of people, those who had both lived and died and whose stories were complete.

I wrote three more historical novels (*Brady, I, Adam, Early Thunder*) but I became increasingly frustrated with the fictional framework into which I was fitting the history. I realized not only that life truly is stranger than fiction but that I wanted to gather all that strangeness together and put it down as it actually is and was. I rushed into writing biographies; indeed I felt as if I must have been preparing for this all along, for I knew this was where I belonged. I started with the Otis family of Massachusetts whom I had met while working on *Early Thunder*. I wanted to know more about them but this, I realized, would be a book for adults, not children.

I identified easily with Mercy Otis Warren, my central character, for she was a writer and unsure of herself and she was a mother who lay awake at night, worrying about her growing boys. My own children were teenagers now and I, too, was a worrier. And like many writers, I, too, needed reassurance. Yet there were others in Mercy's life whose stories I wanted to include: her brother, James Otis, one of the first revolutionaries who later became so divided in his loyalties that he lost his mind; Mercy's father; her sons; Abigail and John Adams, her best friends who became embittered as their politics differed. So my cast was large and although Mercy was at the center, I shifted voices. After I spent five years in research and writing, Houghton, Mifflin published *Cast for a Revolution*. Although it did not sell well, I have never been sorry that I wrote it. My attachment to Mercy was so strong, I felt compelled to bring her back to life, even if in a limited way.

The research for this book made me feel so much at home in Colonial and Revolutionary Massachusetts that when I went through the Granary Burying Ground in Boston, I kept running into familiar names, not of people who had played a big part in history but of those who had been on the sidelines and whom I had come across by chance. Again and again I would hear myself exclaim, "Why, there you are!" as if I'd suddenly met up with an old friend. Two Massachusetts figures made their way into short biographies I wrote for children—Paul Revere and Sam Adams. I wanted to tell their stories without any fictional embroidery, with humor, gusto, and with concrete bits of out-of-the-way information which, I thought, would help bring them to life. I had such fun writing these two books (*And Then What Happened, Paul Revere?* and *Why Don't*

Fritz in Ireland on a research trip for Brendan the Navigator

"Finding my childhood home in China"

You Get a Horse, Sam Adams?) that I went on to do more "question" books: *Where Was Patrick Henry on the 29th of May?*; *Will You Sign Here, John Hancock?*; *Can't You Make Them Behave, King George?*; *What's the Big Idea, Ben Franklin?*; *Who's That Stepping on Plymouth Rock?*; *Where Do You Think You're Going, Christopher Columbus?*

People often ask me if I am a "disciplined" writer. I tell them, No, I am a compulsive writer. The discipline comes when I have to go to the store, cook supper, vacuum, and perform other housekeeping chores. But I don't write all the time; I do other things too. For six years I conducted a writing workshop which was a happy experience for me in every way. Although some members dropped out, the core of the group remained the same. With a chance to write, rewrite, resubmit, rewrite again, most of the members had a long, ongoing experience that turned them into professional writers. Not only did I learn from the shared criticism of this group, but more important, the people in the workshop became and have remained my best friends.

When asked by children if I have a "hobby" (a word I dislike), I usually say, No, because I don't collect stamps or play golf or garden, which are acceptable avocations. I am not sure that children would ad-mit that reading and traveling are legitimate hobbies and I certainly would not care to trivialize them by using the word. Yet that is how I use my spare time. When our children were young, we used our vacations to explore new areas, just as I had done as a child with my parents. Our longest and most memorable trip was a five-week drive across the continent and back, cooking on a campstove, staying at motels within a fixed price range.

When the children were older, Michael and I were able to take occasional trips to Europe. By this time I had done enough traveling as part of research projects to realize that simply being a tourist was no longer enough for me. I wanted to travel with a *purpose*. I have always liked islands and I have, of course, liked far-away places with an end-of-the-world feeling, such as Mongolia had once been for me. When Mollie Hunter told me about the Orkney Islands, I knew that this was a place I had to go. In the North Sea between Scotland and Scandinavia, the Orkney Islands were historically the last stop explorers made when they were looking for the Northwest Passage. The *New York Times* expressed interest in a travel article on the Orkneys, so off we went.

Once there, I was carried away by the old sense of

Story. Was this me at the top of the world with the sun setting at midnight and rising at three in the morning? I lay down on the summer-warm ground in the center of a prehistoric ring of monolithic stones and dreamed myself into the beginnings of time. Yet time itself, like space, seemed undefined in this watercolor world where sea, land, and sky ran in and out of each other so that they seemed all of a piece, distinguishable only to the oyster-catchers, the cormorants, the guillemots with their summit view. The people went with the place: the man who could imitate the cry of seals and call them to the shore; the woman who went out on the rocks every night to talk with the homing gulls; the farm-woman who gave me a bottle of grottiebuckies (tiny Arctic sea-shells) to place on my kitchen windowsill in the same way all native Orkney islanders keep their grottie-buckies close at hand. On our last day we were on a dock, talking with a Scotswoman when a spectacular double rainbow suddenly arched over us. "Oh, I think John Knox must have sent us that rainbow," I said. "Because it's our last day here."

"Not John Knox," she replied tartly. "He wouldn't do anything for a foreigner."

I laughed both at John Knox and myself, for however far away I am from home, I never feel like a foreigner. Perhaps because I was a foreigner for so much of my childhood, the term has little meaning for me now.

There have been other memorable trips. Once to the Isle of Man for a travel piece and once to Ireland in preparation for my book, *Brendan the Navigator.* Sometimes people ask me if I need help with my research and I am always surprised. Help? The research is the most fun; I would stop writing before I would farm out any of the research.

Although from time to time I have written short books, retelling legends—*The Good Giants and the Bad Pukwudgies,* for example, and *The Man Who Loved Books*—I have also been interested in exploring characters at more depth than I was able to do in the "question" books. These books have been longer and designed for the upper elementary or junior high level: *Stonewall; Traitor: The Case of Benedict Arnold; The Double Life of Pocahontas;* and most recently *Make Way for Sam Houston.*

But throughout my writing career, I have wanted to capture the China-part of me and somehow shape it into a book. I did write several adult magazine stories (for the *New Yorker, Seventeen, McCall's*) based on China material but every time I tried to encompass my childhood in a book-length story for children, I felt at a loss. I didn't like the sound of my adult voice remembering nor did I feel comfortable putting myself directly into an invented plot set in China. Yet as time went on, I

Fritz visiting a school in Wuhan, China, 1983

felt increasingly the need to shorten my distance from this childhood by getting it into words. When my father died in 1981 at the age of ninety-six, I lost my last direct tie to the China years and the China memories, and then it seemed urgent to transcend the problems and repossess those years.

In the meantime China had opened up and Americans were going back. I longed to go too, but part of me was afraid. Would the strong, immediate experience of China today dull or confuse the memories? I concentrated again on trying to write the book I had so often attempted and so often abandoned. Somehow this time I did find my own voice as a child and by letting go of the real sequence of events, I was able to find a story shape where my China experience seemed to be at home. I called it fiction since I make such a point in my nonfiction of being able to document facts and dates, but emotionally the story, *Homesick,* was as true as I could tell it.

And when I had finished, I was really ready to go back, not just to validate memory but to make China part of my present life. The trip, which resulted in the book *China Homecoming,* was one of the most exhilarating experiences of my life. China is not just another

Fritz, 1985, "entertaining sugar birds on a Caribbean island"

country; it is another world and to rediscover and discover it at the same time stirred up emotions that kept me at fever pitch. Moreover, it was an additional joy not only to share China with Michael (who had been subjected to so much China talk throughout our marriage) but to see him take the experience and make it also his own.

Sometimes I feel like Columbus who went with such joy from place to place, planting his flag, taking possession. Perhaps because as a child I was made to feel that I was not "home," I have the habit now of claiming places as my own, once I have dug into the history, once I have made friends with the people both past and present. China is, of course, especially close to my heart and if luck is with us, we hope to go back. But as I have worked on my biographies, I have planted my private flag on many scattered bits of territory. And I have added islands to my personal map. For a number of winters now Michael and I have taken a few weeks vacation and gone to the island of Tortola in the Caribbean. During these vacations I have at last acquired a "hobby"; at least it serves as an answer when I am asked the question.

"Do you have a hobby, Mrs. Fritz?"

"Yes," I say, "I do. I snorkel."

"And how old are your children?" This is another common question and it indicates how defensive I have become when I hesitate to reveal to school audiences the age of my children. But now I have an answer to that too.

"I have a grandchild now," I say. "My first. Michael Scott Fritz. Born in April 1985."

"Will you keep on writing?"

"Of course. I don't expect to run out of ideas."

BIBLIOGRAPHY

FOR CHILDREN

Fiction:

Bunny Hopwell's First Spring (illustrated by Rachel Dixon). New York: Wonder Books, 1954.

Fish Head (illustrated by Marc Simont). New York: Coward, 1954; London: Faber, 1956.

Help Mr. Willy Nilly (illustrated by Jean Tamburine). New

York: Treasure Books, 1954.

Hurrah for Jonathan! (illustrated by Violet La Mont). Racine, Wis.: Whitman, 1955.

121 Pudding Street (illustrated by Sofia). New York: Coward, 1955.

The Late Spring (illustrated by Erik Blegvad). New York: Coward, 1957.

The Animals of Doctor Schweitzer (illustrated by Douglas Howland). New York: Coward, 1958; Edinburgh: Oliver & Boyd, 1962.

The Cabin Faced West (illustrated by Feodor Rojankovsky). New York: Coward, 1958.

Champion Dog, Prince Tom, with Tom Clute (illustrated by Ernest Hart). New York: Coward, 1958.

How to Read a Rabbit (illustrated by Leonard Shortall). New York: Coward, 1959.

Brady (illustrated by Lynd Ward). New York: Coward, 1960; London: Gollancz, 1966.

Tap, Tap, Lion--One, Two, Three (illustrated by L. Shortall). New York: Coward, 1962.

I, Adam (illustrated by Peter Burchard). New York: Coward, 1963; London: Gollancz, 1965.

Magic to Burn (illustrated by Beth and Joe Krush). New York: Coward, 1964.

Surprise Party (reader; illustrated by George Wiggins). New York: Initial Teaching Alphabet Publications, 1965.

The Train (reader; illustrated by Jean Simpson). New York: Grosset and Dunlap, 1965.

Early Thunder (illustrated by L. Ward). New York: Coward, 1967; London: Gollancz, 1969.

George Washington's Breakfast (illustrated by Paul Galdone). New York: Coward, 1969.

The Secret Diary of Jeb and Abigail: Growing Up in America 1776-1783 (illustrated by Kenneth Bald and Neil Boyle). Pleasantville, New York: Reader's Digest, 1976.

Brendan the Navigator (illustrated by Enrico Arno). New York: Coward, 1979.

Back to Early Cape Cod. Philadelphia: Eastern Acorn Press, 1981.

The Man Who Loved Books (folktale; illustrated by Trina Schart Hyman), New York: Putnam, 1981.

The Good Giants and the Bad Pukwudgies (folktale; illustrated by Tomie de Paola). New York: Putnam, 1982.

Homesick: My Own Story (illustrated by Margot Tomes). New York: Putnam, 1982.

China Homecoming. New York: Putnam, 1985.

Nonfiction:

Growing Up (illustrated by Elizabeth Webbe). Chicago: Rand McNally, 1956.

San Francisco (illustrated by Emil Weiss). Chicago: Rand McNally, 1962.

And Then What Happened, Paul Revere? (illustrated by M.

Tomes). New York: Coward, 1973.

Why Don't You Get a Horse, Sam Adams? (illustrated by T.S. Hyman). New York: Coward, 1974.

Where Was Patrick Henry on the 29th of May? (illustrated by M. Tomes). New York: Coward, 1975.

Who's That Stepping on Plymouth Rock? (illustrated by J.B. Handelsman). New York: Coward, 1975.

What's the Big Idea, Ben Franklin? (illustrated by M. Tomes). New York: Coward, 1976.

Will You Sign Here, John Hancock? (illustrated by T.S. Hyman). New York: Coward, 1976.

Can't You Make Them Behave, King George? (illustrated by T. de Paola). New York: Coward, 1977.

Where Do You Think You're Going, Christopher Columbus? (illustrated by M. Tomes). New York: Putnam, 1980.

FOR YOUNG ADULTS

Nonfiction:

Stonewall (illustrated by Stephen Gammell). New York: Putnam, 1979.

Traitor: The Case of Benedict Arnold. New York: Putnam, 1981.

The Double Life of Pocahontas (illustrated by Ed Young). New York: Putnam, 1983.

Make Way for Sam Houston. New York: Putnam, 1986.

FOR ADULTS

Fiction:

Cast for a Revolution: Some American Friends and Enemies, 1728-1814. Boston: Houghton, 1972.

Sound Recordings:

American History through Fiction. New York: Children's Book Council, 1977.

The Education of an American. Los Angeles: University of Southern California, 197-?

Six Revolutionary War Figures. Weston, Conn.: Weston Woods Studio.

And Then What Happened, Paul Revere?. Weston, Conn.: Weston Woods Studio.

Why Don't You Get a Horse, Sam Adams?. Weston Conn.: Weston Woods Studio.

Where Was Patrick Henry on the 29th of May?. Weston, Conn.: Weston Woods Studio.

What's the Big Idea, Ben Franklin?. Weston, Conn.: Weston Woods Studio.

Will You Sign Here, John Hancock?. Weston, Conn.: Weston Woods Studio.

Can't You Make Them Behave, King George?. Weston, Conn.: Weston Woods Studio.

The Double Life of Pocahontas. Weston, Conn.: Weston Woods Studio.

Homesick: My Own Story. Weston, Conn.: Weston Woods Studio.

Sonia Levitin

1934-

Sonia Levitin in Hawaii, 1979

Life is, among other things, strange and unpredictable. I begin writing this autobiography on the beach on the lush and beautiful island of Hawaii. It is my favorite place in all the world, warm and tropical, with pleasant people and gentle winds bringing a sense of peace. Here, my thoughts drift back to my parents and to my beginnings, so vastly different, for I was born in a severe time and into a way of life that was to end in destruction more savage and devastating than any before or since.

To be born a Jew in Germany in 1934 was to be born into crisis. From earliest childhood I knew that if Hitler had had his way, I would have been killed along with millions of other Jews. That knowledge has made me reverence life even more. I realize, too, that in many ways it has shaped my ideas about what is worthwhile, and how life is to be lived.

The actual story of my birth became one of my father's many humorous anecdotes. My father had a fine sense of drama, and told how he went to work as usual that morning, returning home to discover Frau Leuffelbein, the midwife, already in attendance. It was customary then to be born at home, and this midwife had performed her duties for my parents twice before. On that afternoon of August 18, 1934, Frau Leuffelbein met my father in the parlor, giggling and beaming, exclaiming, "Congratulations, Herr Wolff. This time you have a beautiful little boy!"

"I knew better," my father recounted. "What a sly one she was! I rushed into the bedroom to see for myself. Of course, it was a lie. Another girl. Three daughters! Ah, me. It would cost a fortune to get them all married off!"

Psychologists today might frown at the implication that is clear in this story. My father wanted a boy. Instead, he got another girl. Me.

So what? He told it with good humor, as a trick played on him by the fates. And while we were never really close, I suspect this was because of our particular personalities and also the culture of the times. Oh, he was proud of us, and in company he recited our accomplishments. Not the least of our so-called virtues was the fact that family friends all praised our looks. It was common in those days, at least among our crowd, for the grown-ups to talk about such things at length, and to speculate about which of us was the most attractive. Frankly, we loved it; we ate it up.

We three, like most siblings, were very different from each other. In many ways we still are, but time has a way of mellowing people, of grinding down the sharp edges of difference, so we get along despite them.

My oldest sister, Vera, is an intense person, devoted to work and system, orderly and emotionally sparing of herself. She is a nurse, presently an administrator; the job suits her.

My sister Eva, seven years my senior, played the role of "second mother" in those years when, as refugee strangers in America, my parents were forced to work nearly all day and night to support us. They left at dawn for jobs in the city, my father starting out as a peddler of neckties, my mother as a cleaning woman, and they returned after I was in bed, often using evening hours to learn English in adult school. (In later years I taught English to new waves of foreigners; I felt a great sense of continuity in this, and could sympathize with my adult students.) What a frightful change for my parents, just at middle age. They had grown accustomed to luxury and status in Berlin, considering themselves fortunate to be living in a cultured and sophisticated society. My parents had two hired servants, a housekeeper-cook and a "girl for the children." They took winter vacations in elegant resorts like Oberhof, and summers in Wiesbaden and Marienbad. I have photos of those idyllic times. In them my parents look young, radiant, and optimistic. How swiftly, and how crushingly it all ended!

When we left Germany (I should say "escaped," for we left in secret and had to steal away like thieves, clutching only a few possessions), Vera was thirteen, Eva eleven, and I was three. Even then, Eva was already a dancer. She had studied ballet in Germany, and as soon as my parents were able, they continued her training in the United States. Eva was graceful and lithe. She always loved fashion and expensive, pretty things. She actively sought (and tried to indoctrinate me with) ways to improve herself, to become acceptable among genteel people. I often frustrated her, being more of a tomboy in my youth.

I loved animals from the start, sought out stray cats and fed them. I still do. I rode horses, not for the ride, which actually terrified me, but to be near the smell and sight of their flesh, to see those noble heads and magnificent gleaming bodies. I climbed trees, loving both the climb and the vantage point, and I spent a great deal of time looking into other people's lives, going into their houses when I could, or imagining

their lives if actual entry was blocked.

In our early years in the United States, when I was five and six and seven, I spent a great deal of time just tagging after my big sisters. Vera was usually self-absorbed and did not like to be bothered playing nursemaid. But Eva enjoyed the role and was a fine playmate-parent; we played dolls, danced, sang in harmony, cooked (fudge and chocolate pudding were our specialities), and occasionally went to the movies. It cost a dime to get in, and sometimes we had an extra nickel for candy.

Like all siblings, Eva and I had our battles. It was a strong relationship, both of love and envy. When she scolded or criticized me, I was devastated. When she got married and left home, I cried for days, feeling utterly abandoned. Yet we had our differences. We fought, hit, kicked, and scratched. I look back on that with a smile and with some appreciation; sibling rivalry can help to toughen you up for life. And, heaven knows, we need to be tough.

Vera and I fought less, communicated less. She was a good student and a great reader and used to subscribe to a book club. This was a great boon to me as I eventually filched the books and read them in a quiet corner, until I was discovered with a shrill cry: "Mother! do you know what that *child* is reading?"

Eva, Sonia, and Vera in Los Angeles, 1941

Eva, Vera, and Sonia, 1975

Mother, weary from work and perhaps confident that words in books are more enlightening than dangerous, paid little heed. Nobody censored my reading, though sometimes it was suggested that I wait another year or so before getting into "that subject." Meaning, of course, sex or perversion. The admonition made me an even more avid reader.

I learned to read with the ease of a newly hatched fish taking to water. It was in first grade. One day, or so it seemed, the symbols suddenly *became* language. I was entranced and overjoyed. At six or seven I got my first library card and was amazed at the riches there for me, and all of it free. (I confess, however, that I never managed to avoid library fines for overdue books, always selecting more than I could possible finish in the allotted time. This weakness still persists.) Since then, I think there have always been books on my bedside table. I cannot imagine a day without reading.

I read all the Alcott books, all of "Nancy Drew," "Bobbsey Twins," Laura Ingalls Wilder, and the "Anne" books by L. M. Montgomery. I owned a few books, *A Girl of the Limberlost* and *Robinson Crusoe,* Kipling's *Tales, Jane Eyre,* and my all-time favorite, *Little Women,* which I read again and again and again. When I was eleven and had finished reading all the Laura Ingalls Wilder books, I was dismayed to learn that there were no more. A kind librarian suggested that I write a letter to the author. The idea would never have occurred to me: I had thought all authors were dead. I wrote the letter, and to my great joy, received a reply, which remains among my treasures to this day. In my letter I stated my desire to become an author, too. It was the first time I ever voiced that goal to anyone.

My father had preceded us to America without any savings, quite literally with only the clothes on his back. My mother arrived in New York with the three of us a year later, penniless. We were indeed poor. However, my parents bought me the things I really needed. Among them were books, paper, and art supplies. Eventually, too, we got an upright piano and I was given lessons. But at the beginning there was simply no money for extras.

We lived in New York City for a year, then moved to Los Angeles, to a neighborhood racially and ethnically mixed, all united by poverty and the desire to get ahead. In kindergarten I promptly fell in love with my teacher, Mrs. Stevens, and with the whole idea of school. Perhaps even then I already imagined myself as a teacher. By fourth grade that idea had crystallized. But between those years I had to face a minor disaster. After two years in Los Angeles, my parents, just having accumulated a little cash, decided to return to New York, largely because my aunt, uncle, and cousin had settled there. Back we went, from warm weather and casual atmosphere to the cold city with its crowds and clatter. I was always frightened on the city streets and, worse, found no friends on the cement school yard and no sense of accomplishment in the classroom.

In California I had been known as a bright student. In New York, with its educational system ahead of the west, I was immediately put back half a year and classified as a dullard in math. I got an F on my report card.

My mother was called to school. At that time my parents were the working partners in a five-and-dime store; someone else put up the money and my parents did all the work, weekends and nights included. We rarely saw them. Eventually the store failed and we were again reduced to utter poverty, my father having spent his savings on relocating us in New York. We returned to L.A., not by train, as we'd left, but by bus, a grueling, exhausting trip of four or five days and nights. But before that, Eva came to school in place of Mother, and I stood there while my ineptitude was paraded before me in the form of those disgraceful math papers.

"But Sonia knows how to add," my sister objected.

"Show me, then," said the teacher.

She wrote down strings of numbers. Deftly I added them up in my head, told her the answer, and she wrote it down, filling in the first column, carrying to the next.

I was astounded, It was so simple! In a twinkling

I learned the method, and to the teacher's amazement I completed an entire page of problems correctly then and there.

But it had taken many weeks of agony to reach this moment of recognition. And while I was known as the "dullard," something else happened. The effect of failure carried over to the other students, their opinion of me. I had no friends. Nor was I chosen for any other privileges, the small but exhilarating honors that can make a child's day at school a glory.

This experience served me well in later years when, as a teacher, I remembered that every child needs to be honored, singled out, respected. I took special care to rotate privileges and to give praise. I also realized that when a student fails the fault often lies equally with the teacher. It is the teacher's task to be meticulous about repeating step by step the method for any task, always soliciting questions from the students, always pausing to ask, "Do you understand?" and being able to recognize a look of puzzlement, then speedily to correct the dilemma. A teacher must be attuned to her students, not only what they say or ask, but what they need. All through my adult life, I have been engaged in some form of teaching. I have always loved it—but along with the joy of teaching I have always felt a heavy responsibility. I still teach, now in the Writer's Program for UCLA Extension.

Back in Los Angeles, I was deliciously happy with the sunshine, the lawns, and easy atmosphere. I returned to my old school and friends. But there were changes. World War Two had begun. The Japanese in our neighborhood all vanished abruptly, including my friend Setsu and her family. I learned that they had been sent to a Japanese internment camp, as all Japanese were considered potential spies. The cruelty of this act dawned on me much later; then, we children were only perplexed. Setsu's house was rented by a Latino family with six children. All of them routinely chased me home from school, throwing rocks and yelling, "Dirty Jew! Dirty Jew!"

I did not stop to fight. I ran. Six-to-one are impossible odds. I have always believed one must know when to fight and when to retreat with dignity. However, I did have a couple of fist fights in the yard, complete with cheering section and "seconds" who ascribed victory to each of us contenders.

The summer I was eight brought another experience which combined dread and joy. I was sent to a summer camp run by Quakers especially for refugee children. I suffered terribly from homesickness, which seized me the moment the bus rolled out of Los Angeles and was made more disturbing by a bout of nausea due to a two-hour truck ride into the mountains.

When we arrived at Quaker Meadow, however, I was enchanted by the landscape, and ever since I have found solace and the greatest pleasure in pine trees, little brooks, forest paths, and meadows. I love a campfire at night, and communal eating and singing in a log lodge. At Quaker Meadow I hovered between the pain of missing my mother and the joys of hiking, swimming in the icy lake, and acting in campfire plays. The counselors were uniformly kind and gentle people, taking us Jewish refugee children into their care with good humor and love. I have always respected the Friends since then. I read a great deal about their religion and might have adopted it, were I not so attuned to Judaism as I am.

After our escape from Germany, which became the subject of my first children's book, *Journey to America,* Mother and we three children waited in Switzerland for nearly a year until we could enter America. In Switzerland we were helped by many good people, non-Jews, who extended themselves through sheer kindness. To them I owe a great debt, not the least of which is my optimistic belief that despite evil in the world, there is goodness in great measure, and that goodness knows no boundaries of religion or race. At a time when both religious and racial hatred were deep and extreme, this was a vital lesson to learn. To this day I do not believe in either racial or religious exclusivity. I do not believe in a God who cares about form of worship or mere words, who accepts people by one label and rejects those of another.

I returned to the Quaker camp for four summers. I learned a great deal there. Later I took among my first paying jobs that of being camp counselor.

At camp, everything one knows becomes useful, so at various camps I have taught pottery, music, crafts, newspaper writing, nature studies. I have also, along with my husband, done less exalted tasks like digging latrines and hauling garbage to the dump.

When Lloyd and I first met he was twenty, I was eighteen, and we had each attended exciting camps that preceding summer. I had been to an interracial leadership camp, Anytown U.S.A., and he had been to Brandeis, featuring total Jewish experience. As we talked we shared those deeply emotional experiences and ideals. We dated almost exclusively from that first night and were married a little over a year later. First, however, our union also had to be blessed by two very special people in his life, Mom and Pop Walton, owners of the camp Lloyd had attended as a child. It became a lifelong friendship for all of us. The Waltons were the first visitors to see our infant son, Daniel. They remain as larger-than-life figures in our memories, Pop for his humor and common sense, Mom, still alive and active, filled with spunk, attested by her eightieth birthday photograph which shows her riding atop an elephant in Egypt. Such are the people I have been fortunate to find as role models.

At the age of nine or ten I met another person who was to have a profound influence on me. Mary Pollack, English by birth and breeding, the wife of an Austrian surgeon, came into our lives as my mother's employer. Mother, who had studied baby nursing in Europe, was hired first as the housemaid by Dr. and Mrs. Pollack, and soon was elevated to the position of "nurse" to baby Daphne and her older sister Serena. Soon the relationship became a deeper one. When the Pollacks traveled, Daphne, an adorable baby with red-golden curls, stayed at our house in my mother's devoted care. When my mother became ill and had to be hospitalized for a series of surgeries, the Pollacks reciprocated. I was invited to their house for several weeks at a time and often on weekends. For me, their home and way of life was a revelation.

They lived in the lovely Las Feliz district near Griffith Park in a home that was beautiful, immaculate, and spacious. Mary Pollack seemed the essence of serenity and gentle womanhood. Strong, composed, cultivated, and kind, she drew me into her orbit without fanfare, making me part of the daily activities that I found so gratifying. I was allowed to play the piano as long as I liked. (Later, after the doctor died a tragic, early death, and she and the girls moved to England, Mary gave that piano to me.) The doctor played accordion while we sang along. On weekends there were sometimes musicals in the living room, with friends playing various instruments. The Pollacks spoke both French and German, loved art, and owned a good-size library, the shelves lining an entire room. There I was left to browse and read to my heart's content, then to share my love of stories with Mary, who to this day maintains, "There is nothing more important in the world than art."

Now, Mary lives in London, where I visit her whenever I am abroad, and find her always vitally engrossed in books, theater, and art. When my son, Daniel, made her acquaintance, she was absolutely delighted to learn that he is a musician and questioned him at once about his opinion of the new David Bowie album. My son found in Mary, as I did, an attitude of acceptance and quiet grace. Where my family life was often erratic and highly charged with emotion, her home was serene, a haven. My parents had no time for the arts, nor money to pursue them. By the time they had established themselves in the United States, perhaps they had lost interest through the harsh demands of having to earn a living in a strange land. Whatever their reasons, I always felt a sad lack in my home. Books, paintings, classical music, drama were always important to me, but absent from my parents' lifestyle.

Fortunately, they respected my need and provided what they could and allowed me to find the rest on my own.

When I expressed an interest in painting, my parents encouraged me to work with a friend of the family, an old-timer who taught me something about color and perspective and had me painting in oils. Alas, he died soon after we began. It was the only art training I had until, as an adult, I took several classes in drawing and painting. But at the age of twelve I had made half-a-dozen oil paintings, and my parents were pleased and impressed when I actually sold one for thirty-five dollars. They were accustomed to my entrepreneurship. At the age of ten I had written and distributed a "neighborhood newspaper," filled mostly with escapades of the various pets in the Wolff household. We had two rabbits that almost daily escaped from their pen and hopped across the boulevard to graze in the produce section at Vons Market. At various times we also had numerous dogs and cats, all brought home by me. The best loved was Skippy, a brown terrier who slept on our beds, ran beside me for hours when I roller-skated on the streets of L.A., and learned various tricks, among them walking a narrow plank which I braced between two wooden benches. My father was

Sonia, age thirteen, with Skippy

delighted with the tricks and took home movies.

He was a showman, my father, with a natural gift for mimicry and the dramatic buildup. He played piano by ear, loudly and with exuberance. He sketched the coats and suits that he manufactured. He was the most artistic one in my family, yet it never occurred to him to devote any time to the fine arts or to write anything down. By the time my first book was published, he had already died. I know he would have been very pleased. He often claimed me as the "smartie" of the family, attributing this to his side, as his mother had had advanced schooling, a rare thing for a girl in those times. Mother, on the other hand, pointed out that one of *her* relatives had been a physician to the Kaiser, a remarkable feat for a humble Jew.

In several important ways, my parents were mismatched. This of course affected us children, not only in our youth, but when as adults we chose husbands and tried to make things right.

My father was brash and outgoing, impulsive and flirtatious, and at times he flew into thunderous rages. He also worked long and hard at his business of designing and manufacturing ladies' coats and suits. He rose

Helene Wolff, age twenty-five, with her mother in Berlin, 1923

at dawn and worked until six—a farmer's day. He toiled. And he was good at his work. He could create a design with a few swift strokes of a pencil, usually on the back of an old envelope, figure cost, profit, and sales potential in a matter of minutes, all without any formal higher education. Later, this was a source of some surprise to my young husband, with his numerous college degrees in business. My father had been apprenticed to a tailoring establishment at the age of fourteen. He told me often how desperately lonely he was in that town far away from home. My father's coats were stylish, warm (100 percent wool), moderately priced, and made to last. He was proud of his product and I, looking back, share that pride. At the time, however, there was nothing remarkable about his production line of garments filling our closets, hanging from door knobs and makeshift rods all over our small rented house in L.A. The detached garage was completely devoted to business. From there Father did all the wrapping and shipping. Boxes of buttons, labels, pins, bundles of swatches, piles of fur collars, and all the paraphernalia of the garment trade filled my growing-up years. We all learned to sew. Father bought me a huge old-fashioned factory machine. On it I constructed numerous outfits, often without using a pattern. Nobody thought it the least bit unusual to make a dress from "scratch." My family took it for granted that one must be inventive and capable.

Max Wolff, as a young man in Berlin

We were all paid by the piece for sewing satin linings into fur collars, and for hemstitching lapels or sewing the labels "Max Wolff - 100% wool" onto sleeves. Mother was already sewing when I got up in the morning. She would ask me to thread as many needles as I could before I left for school. She was fifty then, the same age I am now. Now I can appreciate her gratitude for ten threaded needles. She sewed efficiently and well, the way she did any manner of work.

Unlike Father, my mother was reticent and often too critical with people, puritanical in her outlook, and given to melancholy. She suffered terribly from guilt. Her mother was killed in a concentration camp. She had been unable to save her. Eva says Mother's depressions began then and changed her personality. I wouldn't know. I never knew her before the war took its toll in anxiety, suspicion, and fear. I do know that as a child she felt deprived and unloved, overshadowed by her brother and older sister. The brother was beaten to death by the Nazis in Belgium. His wife was shot in a forest as she tried to leap from a train packed with Jews being deported to a concentration camp. The grief and horror of those events cannot be fully described. From my earliest childhood I heard them being discussed by the grown-ups.

My mother, poor by American standards, still managed to send boxes of food and hand-knitted scarves to hapless friends and relatives left in Germany. When their letters of gratitude arrived many months later, tears streamed down my mother's face. She wept a great deal in those years.

Helene and Max Wolff, 1963

My father, on the other hand, took a stern and uncompromising attitude toward the Nazi regime. In his opinion, the entire German nation ought to have been pulverized.

The Holocaust experience left its deep mark on me. It is agonizing for me as a Jew to realize that our people were almost exterminated; it is equally agonizing, as a human being, to have to admit to the evil that humans can do to one another. I have returned to Germany several times as a tourist, always with trepidation and anxiety, and with some hostility. I cannot feel warm toward that nation; I cannot forget. I do not forgive. I believe strongly that some things are unforgivable, that we have to stand up and say "No! Never again."

When recently I visited Israel, and saw the memorial Yad Vashem, that overwhelming feeling struck through me: No. Never again. The truth is, that the Holocaust did not hurt only its obvious victims; it left a stain on all humanity, and all of us must join against the forces of evil, not only in the external world, but especially within ourselves. I believe that one of the greatest evils is not the active desire to do wrong, but apathy. Several books of mine have stressed this idea, especially my adult novel, *What They Did to Miss Lily,* and most recently, a young-adult novel still in the works, *Incident at Loring Groves.*

As to the effect of the Holocaust on my father, he vowed to enjoy life if ever he got back on his feet again, and he did. Enjoy! More than anything else, this was the legacy he left us. Life is short, he always said, shortening his own life with rich foods, cigarettes, and a frantic pace. He loved to dance, travel, fly, go to parties. He never drank, only coffee by the gallon, and a small glass of Passover wine. In the temple, which we attended infrequently, he sang loudly, more from a sense of showmanship, I suspect, than from religious fervor. I believe he believed in God and was perplexed by His inaction at the cries of the beleaguered Jews; but my father was also a pragmatist. It was man, not God, who stoked those ovens.

My mother spoke about God matter-of-factly. She taught us our prayers. Neither of my parents dwelt on philosophical matters, though both greatly admired teachers, philosophers, rabbis, and intellectuals.

Was it a happy childhood? Yes and no. My parents were strict and my life was often insecure, but I knew that they loved me, and their pride in me helped me to aim high.

Most of my aims centered around the arts and school activities. I took piano lessons until I was eighteen, and learned to play well enough to entertain my family, but could never get over the terrible nervousness that made recitals an agony. I wrote poems and short stories, tried various arts and crafts, working with clay, crushed glass, and fabrics. For sport, I roller-skated, walked, and played tennis, activities that I still enjoy, except that I have added jogging to the list.

The desire for physical fitness came to me relatively late. When I turned forty, I came to understand that life is limited, but that one does have choices about its quality. So I gave up smoking, the most difficult feat of self-discipline, and I took up yoga and running. Like many Californians, I am extremely body-conscious now, eating mostly vegetables and fruits, and taking exercise seriously.

As a child I was never good at team sports, but was often chosen as captain. My skills were people skills, I guess. I always craved leadership and participated in student government. I had a great interest in social concerns, and occasionally tried to put my ideas into action, as when I attempted to integrate my social club in high school. I failed. I discovered through many similar ventures since then that if you want something done, it's best to act without too much reliance on others.

As a young woman I joined many causes and volunteer organizations. The experience usually left me frustrated. I like to get things done quickly and efficiently; I have no tolerance for lengthy discussions on trivial matters. When at last I began to sell my writings, I considered it more important to make my con-

tribution in that way, and by taking a portion of my earnings and sending money to the causes I espoused.

While I tend to become impatient with organizations, because they often become unwieldy and stray from their purpose, still I have initiated several groups. In 1965 my husband and I founded the Moraga Historical Society. The group remains active; it won us many good friends, organizational experience, and fine memories. Some years later I founded and headed a nonprofit adult education organization in Palos Verdes, called STEP.

Most of my life is divided between family and friends or my work, writing. Being a writer, to me, is a continuous and full-time process. It means living fully, then trying to transcribe feelings into words. It is always very, very difficult. Every morning I must sternly put aside lazy or hedonistic inclinations and go down to my study and *sit there* for five to seven hours, and struggle to fill those pages with something that might be worth saving. Like every writer, I often fail, and my wastebasket is the only recipient of a day's labor. Or, worse, I send out a story in the mistaken belief that it is good, only to have it return to me like a homing pigeon. I still write and rewrite, laboring over some chapters as many as ten times. Others slide from mind to hand in a matter of hours; we all know those magical moments when the muse sits on our shoulder, whispering encouragement, and all our risks pay off, all our impulses work out. This has happened to me several times, once in a picture book, *Who Owns the Moon?*, which poured out of my mind in a single afternoon, and another time when I wrote a young-adult novel in only three weeks, *The Year of Sweet Senior Insanity*. Of course, that book had been brewing in my mind for two years before I ever set it down on paper—and much of it was grounded in life.

Young writers are often surprised to learn that "old-timers" still get rejections. They do. And every writer I know still has those bad days, those down-in-the-dumps periods when nothing works, and there is a lot of grumbling and growling and threatening to change careers, to do something else like editing, promotions, studying veterinary medicine, or working at the local bakery—anything but writing!

Then suddenly, sometimes after weeks of depression, a word, a phrase, or a mental image snaps into place, like a new clear vision suddenly emerging, and, presto! it's there again. Then the world is big and beautiful again, anything is possible again, writing is a joy, "success" for its own sake no longer matters; only the process, the feeling of creating, of being truly alive.

I am most alive when I have work to do, and when it is flowing. When the flow is there, I can work seven, eight, nine hours a day, and rise up in the morn-

Graduating from Los Angeles High School, 1952

ing eager and longing for more. The characters live with me then. The images and people that I created seem like another reality coexisting with my own daily life in a very real way. "They" are only waiting for me to get back to my typewriter, to share their lives, to give them flesh and a purpose. It is exhilarating. It is the real reason why I continue to write.

"But it must be so exciting to see your name in print," people say, thinking that is the main reason to write. It is exciting, but the *process* is the real prize and the reason why I will never stop. And the process includes discussions and exchanges with other writers, people whose lives are, like mine, devoted to discovery and to ideas. Most of my dearest friends are writers or artists, except for my husband. He and I are different in many ways, except those that count the most. We share the same values, and we adore and respect each other.

We met in college, at the University of California at Berkeley, where in a way my "real life" first began. Everything else seems like mere preparation. First of all, I was thrilled to be going away to school, to be living more or less on my own, to be spending all my time with my peers. I loved the idea of living in a boardinghouse, sharing my room, meals, study time, and social life. Group living has always had a certain appeal to me. The *kibbutz* lifestyle in Israel fascinates me; sometimes I think that in such an environment of cooperation and camaraderie I could flourish. Paradoxically, perhaps, I also greatly value my independence. My first taste of it came in college.

When classes began, I was completely dazzled and elated. I felt as if I had been hibernating all my life, and that the world was just now opening up before me. I had always been curious and eager to learn; now I encountered teachers who were just as eager to teach, to engage in endless discussion about everything, abstract or concrete, to speculate, delve, argue, go deeper. I studied psychology, sociology, anthropology, history, philosophy, religion, music, literature, economics, and education. Notably missing from this list were the sciences; I took only those required, stressing the humanities with emphasis on education. I had decided to become a teacher of English and social studies. The only other careers I had considered were journalism and veterinary medicine. I rejected the former because it seemed too insecure a profession. I rejected the latter because of my weakness in science and mathematics, and because I was afraid to commit to such an "unfeminine" line of work. I'm not proud of my reasoning, or of my lack of determination. However, teaching seemed a good choice for me, and one I have not regretted. I still teach, have always done so, and count

Sonia with Lloyd Levitin in San Francisco, 1952, the year they met

education among my strongest interests.

That first weekend at Berkeley, even before classes began, my friends and I went to a dance at Hillel House, and there I met Lloyd Levitin. I had smiled at him across the room in a way that must have suggested that I thought him quite the most attractive fellow there. We danced. We talked. After that we began dating just about every day, and by March we were engaged. I was eighteen. He was twenty. His parents urged us to wait before marrying, and we agreed.

That summer, instead of going back to Los Angeles, I remained in northern California, having convinced myself and my parents that I desperately needed to go to summer school. I did go to summer school, and so did Lloyd, during which time we lived with his parents in Marin County. It was a wonderful, beautiful summer. We took the ferry across the bay to Berkeley every morning. Afternoons we spent at his house in Fairfax, enjoying the beautiful garden, waiting for his father, Joe, to come home from his radiology practice in San Francisco. It was an idyllic time. My parents came to Fairfax to visit. They loved the place, as we all did, and my future in-laws and I came to know each other well. There was never any stiffness between us; they loved me and I loved them.

In many ways, Joe became a real father to me, granting me that parental closeness and guidance that my father was never able to give me. He was a brilliant man, well respected by his colleagues as by his family. He understood my need to make my own statement; he encouraged my involvement in the arts. However, he had a quite old-fashioned streak by which he insisted vehemently that I owed all my first efforts to husband and children. With any energy that remained, he said, I could indulge my interest in the arts.

Of course, I did agree with him: children cannot be left to a shabby upbringing by a mother so involved in her own needs that the youngsters are neglected. However, I did not like the emphasis he gave the matter, or the feeling that I had no choice. Through the years of my children's growth, I felt I was always playing the part of the juggler, trying desperately to meet their needs, to be there, to give close attention and concern—and yet to save something special and separate, something of myself, for myself.

It was not made easier by the fact that I behaved like a perfectionist. Years later my doctor pointed out his suspicion that this accounted for my occasional migraines. I wanted to be the perfect wife, the loving daughter, the wonderful mother, the active community leader, good entertainer, and so on and so on; I was no different from most caring and educated women of my generation. We all felt we had to be like some feature-film paragon, a combination Doris Day, Greer Garson,

Sonia with a gendarme on her first trip to Paris, 1954

and Katharine Hepburn—cheerful, continually courageous, and wise. The movies gave us a hard act to follow. I still wonder why we were so gullible, so ready to swallow the whole notion, hook, line, and sinker. I know I was, at least during my twenties and thirties.

Before that, during the summer I was eighteen, Lloyd and I went up to Walton's Grizzly Lodge, where we'd been hired as counselors. It was the first of several camp experiences, a subsequent one being two years later, when we worked at a camp for underprivileged children in New York, and learned a great deal about ourselves and about social dilemmas. At Walton's, I became quite ill, was briefly hospitalized, and Lloyd brought me back to his parents' house and took care of me for a week. The experience served to convince his parents that this was "really love" and not just a brief summer romance. We were married that December.

The first summer after our marriage, we took our delayed honeymoon trip, two months in Europe, his parents' gift to us. We left with one suitcase apiece, like two vagabonding kids, with no reservations and only the merest framework of an itinerary, based mainly upon the usual tourist sights, highlighting the art and architecture that Lloyd had studied in his Western Civilization course at Pomona College. That trip was the experience of a lifetime. It whetted my appetite for travel, an appetite which has never been sated.

Returning from Europe, we moved to Philadelphia, where my husband went to graduate school and I completed my education at the University of Pennsylvania. It was difficult being away from California; we resented the cold climate and the formality of the people. And we were living on a shoestring, in dilapidated furnished apartments, counting pennies for gasoline, sharing a single dessert not because of the calories but because we could not afford two pieces of cake.

A little poverty, I believe, never hurts, especially

Sonia with Lloyd's parents, Joseph and Helen Levitin, about 1967

when it is experienced at the start of your life. We learned to be very frugal and to summon our priorities.

Back in California, I took a teaching job and Lloyd worked as a public accountant. I loved my job in Mill Valley, a lovely town in Marin County, with bright, active students and cooperative parents. I taught seventh grade in a self-contained classroom that taxed all my powers; I even had to teach math.

By the end of that year I was pregnant with Daniel and decided instantly to give up full-time teaching. It never occurred to me not to stay home and raise the child myself. Lloyd decided to enroll in law school. He obtained a job as an assistant professor at San Francisco State College, and we embarked on four years of toil—he studying, teaching, attending classes at night, and I taking care of the home front, tutoring and teaching night school to earn some money on the side, and starting my new career, writing.

I began with a clear and conscious decision: it was time to write. All my life I had dreamed of becoming a writer. Now, with time at home and long, empty hours to fill, I would begin.

I plunged in, writing half-a-dozen short stories, submitting them to magazines, and getting them back with printed rejections. Amazed, I reconnoitered; something was obviously wrong. I had no idea what— after all, I'd been reading stories all my life. Why

should I have so much trouble writing them?

It was Lloyd who suggested that I go back to school. I received the idea with trepidation and excitement. At San Francisco College, one of the teachers in the writing department was the well-known Walter Van Tilburg Clark. (*The Ox-Bow Incident.*) Why not study with him? my husband suggested. I was awestruck at the idea. The next day I submitted several stories to Mr. Clark, as requisites for acceptance into the Directed Writing Program. A week later Mr. Clark telephoned me. Yes, he said, in that strong, deep voice, he would accept me into the program.

I remember weeping with joy.

Why had he accepted me? I asked him later, when we had become friends. Was my writing good? Not so much the writing style, he replied, but the subjects that I had chosen made him want me as a pupil. The subjects were thoughtful and serious, dealing with war, aging, love, sacrifice, freedom.

For the next two years the weekly meetings with Mr. Clark were my salvation. At a time when my husband was overwhelmed with his own commitments, and my only company was a small child, I was in desperate need of mental stimulation. We lived in Daly City, a stultifying suburb with its "little boxes" of homes, and while I tried to find outlets in volunteer work, and in visiting with other mothers of small children, what I really needed was meaningful work of my own, work that would help me to grow, to find approval and worth.

Mr. Clark arranged to meet with his directed writing students whenever they had a new manuscript to present. I made it my business to have a new manuscript ready every week, thus finding reason to request a meeting. Those meetings lasted two, sometimes three hours. During them, I truly lived. We talked about literature; he picked apart my stories, suggesting alternatives, always asking for realism, for motive, for detail, for artistic resolution. The first story I wrote under his tutelage was rewritten ten times. Upon the tenth submission, he wrote on the top in his small tortured hand, "Now you've got it!" No approval, whether in the form of money or words, ever meant more to me than that. That story was published in a literary magazine a few years later, my first fiction piece.

While I studied with Mr. Clark I read books about creative writing, scrutinized stories and novels, and looked for writing jobs, however insignificant or unremunerative. I began by offering my services as "publicity chairman" for various charitable and educational organizations. In this way I became familiar with newspaper work, writing publicity articles, getting them printed, meeting the editors. By the time we moved from Daly City to our new home in Moraga in

Sonia and Lloyd at a party in San Francisco, early 1960s

the East Bay, I had several published articles to my credit and was working on breaking into the slick magazine field. I produced many articles for *Parents' Magazine, San Francisco Magazine, Together,* and numerous smaller publications, and one long historical piece for *Smithsonian,* among others. In East Bay, I presented myself to the local newspaper and soon had two different columns with bylines; I was launched as a writer and decided to readapt my adult teaching career from social studies and English to creative writing. Correspondence courses gave me the necessary certification; the community of Moraga, with its host of potential students, gave me the impetus.

I taught creative writing at an old church, summoning sometimes as many as forty students. Those sessions became for all of us, I think, a joy and an education. Many of the group have remained together ever since as friends and associates; several eventually ended up publishing books and others found work in newspaper and magazine writing. It was a gratifying experience, and one that gained me several lifelong friends.

In 1962 our second child, Shari, was born. I had prayed for a daughter to round out the family. I was elated. By then, Lloyd had graduated from law school and was working for Kaiser Industries, and we were in every way the typical young couple with thoughts of upward mobility—except that I had an additional goal, now thoroughly defined and resolutely stated: I wanted to become a fiction writer.

I sold several stories to magazines, but none the big time that I hoped for. One day, on a lark, and with the intention of merely leaving my family memoirs for

Shari, almost two; Daniel, age six

my children, I began to write about my family's experiences in emigrating from Germany. I told the story from the viewpoint of twelve-year-old Lisa, a fictionalization of my sister Eva.

For several years I worked on the book, between other writing assignments, and eventually showed the half-finished copy to my niece, who was visiting. She loved the book, asked to see the rest. It gave me the encouragement I needed to finish the story.

I submitted it, cold, to an editor, and subsequently to eleven more, meanwhile rewriting, until *Journey to America* took on a tighter shape and moved from third to first person. After five entire rewrites, I sold the book to Atheneum, the publisher that had seen it first. Jean Karl became my editor for this and seven subsequent books for young people. When the book went to press, it was with only one editorial change! Never since have I been so lucky.

With *Journey to America* I felt that my career was launched, and that I had found my niche. I loved writing for young people. I felt that in this genre I could be both gentle and serious, idealistic and pragmatic. I realized that I happen to possess a wonderful memory for the details of my own childhood, for smells and sights and sounds, how faces looked, how feelings felt, and what childhood was really all about.

Journey to America won the Jewish Book Council of America award for best juvenile fiction of 1970. I went to New York to claim my prize and to bask in the glory of seeing a dream come true. It had taken me five years to write the book. Before that, it took seven years to come to grips with the mysteries of putting words on paper. Twelve years! And each night I had gone to bed with visions, mentally conjuring up the image of my little book standing on a library shelf, my words being read, my message being understood. I have heard, since then, that the way to success is just by such envisioning; I don't know. I only know that the reality of that first publication was more pure and more joyous than any since then.

Journey to America was followed by *Rita the Weekend Rat,* the middle-grade tale of a tomboy in love with a rodent, inspired by my daughter, Shari, and my son, Dan. I used all the homey, very ordinary events that can cause hilarity and distress in a family with two lively kids; I enjoyed writing it, and Shari loved reading it.

The next book, *Roanoke: A Novel of the Lost Colony,* was another labor of love and anguish. My fascination with the Lost Colony had begun when I was twelve years old and in sixth grade, challenged and irritated by the fact that this mystery of the disappearance of an entire colony had never been solved.

It was my mother-in-law's practice to take the

children to her house once a week when they were babies; it gave her full charge, and it gave me free time. Nearly always I used those free hours to browse in the University library. On one such afternoon, amid the dusty stacks, I came upon a large, darkly bound volume, titled *Raleigh's Roanoke Voyages*. From that moment I was hooked, and spent the next year researching the lives, the times, the possible fates of those colonists. I began by attempting to solve the mystery; I ended by deciding to write the most complete, exciting historical novel about that era that I possibly could.

It took ten years, about half-a-dozen rewrites, and a great deal of pleading on my part to get the book published. When it came out, however, it was nominated for three important state-wide prizes, and it held its own for many years as a book highly recommended in that genre. It is in many ways still my favorite book.

The next three books happened easily; two were picture books, *Who Owns the Moon* and *A Single Speckled Egg,* and one a middle-grade tale, about a boy named Jason, very similar to my Daniel in good sense, sensitivity, and derring-do. *Jason and the Money Tree,* written in six weeks, revised at leisure, was, for its author, a charmer.

Next came *The Mark of Conte,* also inspired by Daniel, older now and a good deal funnier and craftier. Conte is a high-school boy bent on outsmarting the high-school computer; his pranks and his frantic dealings spring from a mother's encouragement of tall tales (I listened each day to Dan's accounts of high-school chaos) combined with a writer's knack for exaggeration. There is no doubt in anybody's mind who Conte represents, and who his mom, a crazy artistic type, is intended to portray. I wrote that book for both of us. It won the Southern California Council of Literature for Children and Young People best fiction award for 1975, and was nominated for the California Young Readers Medal.

After *Conte* came a girls' book, a response to my interest in psychic phenomena. I have read widely on the subject, always with fascination guarded by a heavy dose of skepticism. In the story, a young girl discovers her own latent psychic abilities, and in the process she learns some hidden facts about her own past. I loved researching that book. It took me to the home of a professional medium in the San Fernando Valley, to dealings with a "past life reader," to lengthy discussions with a friend heavily involved in extrasensory perception and other psychic matters.

Many ideas opened up to me and many opportunities simply presented themselves in the progress of this book. I have always found this to be true; one receives that which one is ready to know. Everything we need is out there in the world; we have only to tap

it, to zero in, to concentrate, and utilize it. In no other book was this more apparent than in my work on *Beyond Another Door.*

On a brief vacation trip to the old Western town of Virginia City, I happened to spot a decrepit old covered wagon standing beside a road. I poked around. I felt the boards. I climbed up onto the seat. I was hooked.

I had always been fascinated by the saga of the California Trail; I had always marveled at the courage, foresight, and stamina of those who endured the westward migration. Somewhere in my reading I had come upon the name of Nancy Kelsey, one of the thousands of unsung heroines of the Trail, the first white woman ever to cross the plains into California, a young mother of seventeen who walked nearly all the way from Missouri to California.

The more I read about Nancy, the more I studied the diaries of that expedition, known as the Bidwell Bartleson Expedition of 1848, the more I was convinced that this was my story. Never mind that even cursory research into the card catalogue in the library showed a surfeit of pioneering books for young people. I was determined to write my story. And I did.

One of my severest critics, husband Lloyd, loved this book, *The No-Return Trail,* better than any other. He has amended his opinion only recently, with the publication of *Smile Like a Plastic Daisy.* For me, Nancy Kelsey came alive. I researched everything, from recipes for corn pone and johnnycakes, to how to build a log cabin, how babies were swaddled, fevers controlled, horses tended, and marriages performed out on the trail. *The No-Return Trail* won the Western Writers of America award for the best juvenile western of 1978, and the Lewis Carroll Shelf Award.

While I was away in Boulder, Colorado, to meet with my fellow writers and to accept my prize, my husband was promoting appointments for my subsequent project, an adult book that I had been wanting to write for years. Several newspaper items convinced me that the time was right, and that this was my book to write—the story of a teacher who is raped in her classroom, and whose lover is the cop charged with finding the rapist.

I knew nothing about rape or law enforcement or the psychology of the victim. It was frightening to imagine such trauma, to have to feel it along with my character. But I decided to plunge in and do research, this time with school officials, security guards, police, rape crisis center counselors, a district attorney, and gang kids.

That book, *What They Did to Miss Lily,* was published in 1981 under my maiden name, Sonia Wolff. In financial terms it was a dismal failure. I was heartsick when my potential "best-seller" garnered a few good reviews and promptly died. I was catapulted into the agonizing awareness that the adult market is a very different medium from the children's market, with its sanctuary in repeated sales to libraries, schools, and young readers eager for more of "their" discovered author. Perhaps it had been a mistake to use my maiden name. Perhaps none of that mattered; I was devastated, then briefly revitalized as several film prospects opened up, only to lead ultimately to disappointment. Now, I see that the book had its special value: it moved me into a new challenge, writing adult novels, and it gained me many friends who not only liked the book but considered it important and valuable as the story of a woman who is raped and who must discover how to overcome her trauma and to love again. Writing the book also got me personally involved in the problems of sexual assault, and prompted me to initiate a program for high-school students about rape awareness. With several new friends in the law enforcement field, I now do an annual program at the local high school, and I have encouraged various other districts to do likewise.

Between *The No-Return Trail* and *What They Did to Miss Lily,* I did three other projects. One was the light-hearted and loving account of our pets, two dogs and two adopted abandoned kittens, which I called *Reigning Cats and Dogs.* It is my only nonfiction book, a series of vignettes that makes gentle fun of us all, and which has brought a very important facet of my life into perspective, for I have always lived with animals and always loved them, believing that they enrich us and are true gifts from God. The kittens came into my life at a time when I was first feeling the "empty nest," Dan just having gone off to college. With two tiny kittens to nurture, I grew into my new phase, ready to meet the truly empty nest of a few years later, when Shari, too, went away to school.

Two other picture books, *A Sound to Remember,* and *Nobody Stole the Pie,* were published, and then two others, *The Fisherman and the Bird* and *All the Cats in the World.* Of course, it's not as easy as it sounds to write a picture book, which must have strict economy, poetry, and a good story. Mine are in the nature of folk tales, with a moral and twist; they are my present answer to my aborted career as a short-story writer.

My latest book due for publication is another young-adult novel, *A Season for Unicorns,* with a heroine who rides in a hot-air balloon in an effort to overcome her fears and take control of her life.

After my recent travels to Israel, I feel myself entering a new phase. For many years, I have wanted to write a novel about the Babylonian Captivity of ancient time, and I began this project two years ago. In the midst of it an event of such heroic proportions occurred that I dropped everything else to pursue it. It is the true story of the rescue of 10,000 Ethiopian Jews in a fabulous, secret airlift called Operation Moses, in late 1984 and 1985. I returned to Israel to see and interview many of those black Jews, a devout and courageous people. They inspired me to write *The Return,* a YA novel due out in spring 1987.

As things stand now, I have enough writing plans to keep busy for the next four to five years; meanwhile new ideas pop up continually. I tend to write quickly, and must moderate my own enthusiasm, write, rewrite, think, rethink, keeping in mind that my goal is quality.

In writing one's autobiography, pinpointing the highlights and major decisions of a life, it may appear that the road was smooth and purposeful, that all decisions led irrevocably to a well-defined goal. I am always bemused when reading other people's autobiographies or biographies at how organized and cohesive those lives seem, compared to the rather helter-skelter, fragmented times that I have experienced. Naturally, with the help of some distance, some introspection, things do seem to fall into orderly place. The emphasis on my life as a *writer* is a consequence of the fact that it is in this category that this autobiography has been solicited. However, I have worn many different hats and still do, and whether my life as a writer holds any

Shari and her grandmother Helene at home in Palos Verdes, California, 1978

special significance, only time will tell. I am also very much the teacher, the mentor, the wife, the mother.

From the moment my first baby was born, I took parenthood very seriously, and I still do. Children are our greatest responsibility, our wings to immortality. No relationship is quite so complex or so challenging.

When the children were little, I enjoyed playing with them. We went on outings to the park and the zoo and to every nearby attraction. We sang and played games and made projects. Shari was always interested in sports and got us involved in soccer league, softball, and horses. Dan was the tinkerer, the photographer, the fixer of anything broken. We were always planning things, making things, going places, it seems. We did Brownies and Boy Scouts, and got involved in all these activities, some entirely new to us, that the children discovered. On weekends, grandparents usually came to visit. We had some lovely garden parties, always a big birthday party, and family celebrations for Passover, Thanksgiving, and Chanukah.

In 1973 we moved from northern California to Los Angeles, which entailed a considerable adjustment for all of us. It was very hard to say goodbye to old friends and to a lovely, close-knit small town. In Moraga we had been very active in civic affairs; we had many friends and associates. Leaving meant sacrifice, which in turn led to new discoveries, friends, and opportunities. Once again I learned that there is no growth without pain.

Both the children went away to college, and both live away from home now. Dan is a musician; he composes, mixes, arranges, and plays. Nothing is more gratifying than hearing a tape that he has produced, knowing that this work comprises all his various talents and labors.

Shari now sells real estate, and we believe that sales is her innate talent. She relates wonderfully to people of all types, all ages. She is a terrific "idea" person, a born entrepreneur.

I take tremendous delight in my children's creativity, their kind and gentle manner toward others, their high degree of self-respect.

Our greatest pleasure, as parents, is the relatively recent discovery that our children are among the most interesting and exciting "friends" to spend time with. We try to vacation together at least once a year, away from home. I look forward to having the family grow; in my youth I always debated whether we ought to have only two children, or four, five, or six. I am very, very fond of children and count myself lucky to have several youngsters as personal friends. However, raising them has often filled me with anxiety and real terror; motherhood is among the hardest jobs on earth.

Marriage, too, in all its facets, is a relationship

Daniel and Lloyd at a Chanukah party, 1978

that makes great demands on both partners, and again, both Lloyd and I believe that a marriage must constantly be nurtured, and that the partnership it implies must continually be redefined and enriched.

We have been to several Marriage Encounter weekends, which we consider peak experiences and a great boon to our union. Many friends and acquaintances express astonishment that our marriage, begun so early, has lasted so long—thirty-two years. Our answer is that we both give it top priority; we never take it for granted. It has taken a lifetime together to learn to listen and to accept, to grow separately and yet not apart. Nor are we finished learning, I hope. Someday I would like to write a book about our marriage.

For me, the marriage is like a place, a shelter from which we can reach out to the world, take risks, make mistakes, and return with a feeling of confidence that love remains constant, independent of success or failure. Within the marriage relationship, we can be honest about our mistakes, our faults, our unmet goals, and still find love and acceptance.

All this is when the marriage is good, when the family relationship flows. A marriage and a family, like anything else, have their highs and lows. We've had our share of sorrows, strife, and of monotony. These we seem to have weathered. Nobody can expect to live on a constant high. I think work helps to moderate and organize one's daily life. I do not remember a time that our work lapsed, except temporarily, because of an emotional upheaval or a crisis.

Now, with only the two of us in a fairly large house, shared by two dogs, one cat, and various occasional strays (and guests!), we work every day that we

Lloyd and Sonia Levitin, 1985

are home, weekends included, saving time for long walks and talks in between, casual dinners with friends, and occasional weekends with one of the children. We travel frequently, both for business and pleasure, and a good part of our social life involves business connections, his or mine. We each have our role to play for the other—I as the "corporate wife," he as the "writer's husband." As I accompany Lloyd to many corporate functions, so, too, he appears with me at various author's events, banquets, and speeches.

Many writers hate public speaking. I suppose I am an anomaly. I love it. I have talked to many, many groups about writing and about particular areas of expertise involved in my various books. Best of all I like doing radio. Television is exciting, but I find that the camera is very critical and very perceptive. I do not like to see myself on camera; I enjoy hearing my voice on radio. One of my dreams is to do a weekly radio show about the creative person; I have thought of it for years. Typically, ideas like these will ruminate in my mind to emerge one day as if newly and completely hatched. Suddenly the time seems right. Then I plunge in all at once and with total involvement.

What I want to do with the rest of my life is to continue along this path: to write a truly wonderful book, to give and receive love, and to slowly and delectably unravel the meaning of it all.

BIBLIOGRAPHY

FOR CHILDREN

Fiction:

Journey to America (illustrated by Charles Robinson). New York: Atheneum, 1970.

Rita, the Weekend Rat (illustrated by Leonard Shortall). New York: Atheneum, 1971.

Who Owns the Moon? (picture book; illustrated by John Larrecq). Berkeley, Calif.: Parnassus, 1973.

Jason and the Money Tree (illustrated by Pat Grant Porter). New York and London: Harcourt, 1974.

A Single Speckled Egg (picture book; illustrated by J. Larrecq). Berkeley, Calif.: Parnassus, 1976.

A Sound to Remember (picture book; illustrated by Gabriel Lisowski). New York: Harcourt, 1979.

Nobody Stole the Pie (picture book; illustrated by Fernando Krahn). New York: Harcourt, 1980.

All the Cats in the World (picture book; illustrated by C. Robinson). New York: Harcourt, 1982.

The Fisherman and the Bird (picture book; illustrated by Francis Livingston). Boston: Houghton, 1982.

FOR YOUNG ADULTS

Fiction:

Roanoke: A Novel of the Lost Colony (illustrated by John Gretzer). New York: Atheneum, 1973.

The Mark of Conte (illustrated by Bill Negron). New York: Atheneum, 1976.

Beyond Another Door. New York: Atheneum, 1977.

The No-Return Trail. New York: Harcourt, 1978.

The Year of Sweet Senior Insanity. New York: Atheneum, 1982.

Smile Like a Plastic Daisy. New York: Atheneum, 1984.

A Season for Unicorns. New York: Atheneum, 1986.

The Return. New York: Atheneum, 1987.

Nonfiction:

Reigning Cats and Dogs (illustrated by Joan Berg Victor). New York: Atheneum, 1978.

FOR ADULTS

Fiction:

What They Did to Miss Lily, as Sonia Wolff. New York: Harper, 1981; London: New English Library, 1982.

Seon Manley

1921–

Seon Manley, 1985

My sisters and I spent our early teenage in a New England boarding school in Connecticut. It was modelled on the traditional British system with headmistresses and games mistresses, with a highly scheduled day, and with a group of children who were, very often, miserable at being away from home.

The thirties began to see divorces in many American families and the boarding school was the place to send children from broken homes. We three were not children of divorce but we did, indeed, have only our father, and he was planning to marry again. So, we fitted in perfectly to that curious world of childhood that is a boarding school. Perhaps in no other place on earth will you find a group of children so distinctly coming together for mutual support, for living by their own (often stringent) rules, and demanding a sense of order, a hierarchy, a different world in miniature, than that found in such schools.

We all associated ourselves, to a great extent, with children who had been sent away; like poor Dickens, sent away to work in the blacking factory as a young man and rejected by his father who—although he dearly loved his son—could not see the harm it would do the boy.

We were a very "reading" school with a good library and we all went through Dickensian-type books at a great rate. Reading was a great solace for homesickness, but school was not, of course, always a sorry place. We loved that school with the kind of strange affection that people have for some institutions. It was distinctly a refuge: a place of solace, with wonderful teachers, most of them sympathetic to the children— far more sympathetic than the administration.

There were long nights as each new group entered the school and those nights were spent the way children have traditionally spent their first nights at camp or their first nights of ever being away from home, if there is companionship: we told each other stories. We told each other ghost and supernatural stories more often than any other type of story. Perhaps it was because we were frightened, perhaps it was because we were in a new world, perhaps it was because we even believed them, perhaps it was because we told them well. All of us seemed to have dramatic, artistic, and literary possibilities. All of us, in some way or other, had been hurt. All of us loved books, words, libraries, the smell of old bindings, and, indeed, people, particularly those who were "a little different." How could other kids on the outside complain so much? We would never be complainers. We taught ourselves a real sense of values in that school. Fairness was terribly important. The right for everyone to be able to speak her mind at least within the group of children. The importance of coming together at a time of sorrow for another child and at the same time coming together when some great good luck befell a child, be it anything from a box of treats to new books.

We all lived in one enormous building and we knew the littlest children and how they would come to school with a kind of strange loneliness about them, and we told stories to them, too. Indeed, we began to feel more at home with words than we did with the outside world.

The school pets were of major importance and they, too, were remarkable and eccentric. The great twenty-five pound cat named Major, the one horse that was all bravery and no strength, and the other horse that was all strength and no bravery.

The school itself was on Long Island Sound. In our free time (very little) we were allowed to become beachcombers. We used to discover for ourselves all the joys of the marine world. We all had collections: bugs, shells, grasses, crabs, stones. But mostly we all had a great collection of tales. I had read, in our excellent library, some of the supernatural stories of Edith

Wharton and I was impressed by what she said: the teller of supernatural tales should be well frightened in the telling, for if he is, he may communicate to his readers that sense of the strange something undreamed of in the philosophy of Horatio.

Edith Wharton was a product of her time, when nannies used to tell stories in the night to frighten children. She was a teller of tales and she began to write very early. I began, myself, to put down bare outlines of stories I might tell, particularly to the younger children in the school. And it was then my sister Gogo and I acquired our affection for and ability in the world of the supernatural and the weird tale that we later showed in what we now call the Ghost Decades, a period of years when we regularly published a series of anthologies of supernatural tales.

It wasn't long before we discovered that women had a special gift for the ghost story, as they did for the supernatural story. And, by the time we were publishing our books, we decided to do several anthologies with stories published by the women of the nineteenth century and the early twentieth century, who had an extraordinary gift for ghost, mystery, and suspense tales. We pioneered, as those women did, in such anthologies of what Jane Austen declared was "a world of glorious frights." We tried to show how distinguished women writers of yesterday and today expressed their moods, their talents, their invention, and their sense of adventure into the world of the here and the beyond. Many of the writers had lost the popularity they once had. Even such writers as Dorothy Sayers were no longer available in book form, but all of them began once again to be as modern as the very years we were living in.

The books were very much applauded by librarians and enjoyed by young people. For over a decade we lectured and were known—at least to young people—as "those ghost-hunting sisters." It was a period that we enjoyed immensely.

When we were working over the dusty tomes that held so much of what I like to call lost-excitement, it was obvious that women writers, of which we were ones, had a strange kind of link with the nineteenth century in the fact that we did our literary work in more or less the same way that they did. The women writers, then and now, still have to fit their work in somewhere between the cleaning, the feeding of the children, and the dishes. They had always known obstacles and it was amazing to us that if you read such letters as those from the wonderful Brontë sisters—particularly Charlotte and Emily—you find how often they are filled with such comments as, "We must stop now and peel some potatoes." But most important, those women (and men writers, too, of course), despite

Seon Manley and her sister, Gogo Lewis, "when we first began our series of anthologies for young people. . . .We felt we grew up with our readers."

all the frustrations, tribulations, and irritations of life, had managed to preserve the two most important feelings that can give another dimension to life; first, is to be at peace with your own memories, (yes, even your worst can make you smile as you grow older) and the second, to preserve always your sense of wonder.

We did feel too—and still feel—that being a wife and a mother had given those women and ourselves a kind of structure and continuity in our lives and, indeed, that some of the enormous pleasures we had had in raising children extended into our delight in writing for them. It was rare for children to be such good friends as they were and are to another generation. We grew up creatively, with the children around us and they in turn grew up with a love of good books.

We did not just publish stories of the weird and the mysterious but we also published together many suspense and mystery books. They were very much appreciated by the young people to whom they were addressed, for adolescence itself is one of the greatest periods of suspense and mystery. It is a kind of limbo—that world between childhood and adulthood. It is a time when the young person can discover reading with a glorious sense of discovery. The various friends that we grew to know, Frederic Dannay and Manfred B. Lee—who were the famous Ellery Queen—said that they first discovered Sherlock Holmes—that master of the suspense—when they were adolescents. When they first opened a Conan Doyle book, they stood at the brink of

their fate, with no inkling, no premonition that in another minute their own life's work would be born.

Before boarding school, and after the death of our young mother, we had been raised by our maternal grandparents in New York. And it was Papa, as we called our grandfather, whose endless joy in talking still comes to me as I write, who taught me what helped to make me a writer. Papa had come from Scotland as a young man, his only baggage a collection of great stories (one of his ancestors had been the great collector of Celtic stories, Hector McLean, and his mother had been a traditional teller of tales); and our early years, charmed years, were rich with stories . . . and wonder. The stories helped with the painful reality of the early death of our young mother. We were, so to speak, outsiders in the household.

Papa taught me wonder. For the rest, my grandmother and Aunt Fiona saw that I was a well-instructed child. Theirs was the burden of raising another woman's children and, although they did it with love, they also did it with a thoroughness that was particularly alarming to a young child. As I look back now upon those painful years, I see that the raising of my sisters and me was a painful challenge to them. Where other children could fail in manners, morals, behavior, deportment; where other children, God forbid, could bite their nails, we had to learn to be superior to childish things, superior, one might almost say, to childhood itself. Only by our superiority in this way to the neighbors' children, to our young relatives, and to our childhood friends, could Fiona and Mama recognize that they had succeeded in their difficult task.

They were well-meaning but Fiona, perhaps, was one of those people who had never had a childhood of her own, and as a result, she buried her resentment in deportment, articulating carefully and warily as though even the words one used were not the coin of exchange between the people of the world but a sign, a sign of success or, horrors, failure. In all the years since, I have never heard anyone speak with the cautious lack of accent (she was born in New York) in which my aunt had trained herself, until I was introduced a year or two ago to a speech teacher who had carried the fetish through to a doctorate. She had that same bloodless modulation, the same wariness of error, the same eradication of a past which alerted my ears to the Bronx child she had been. My sympathy could not stomach the pretension, and when she turned to me and said she could not recognize my accent, I said with some satisfaction: "Second generation New York."

It was an unfair rejoinder—the kind that can be made only by a person insensitive to distress, who does not care to examine an old wound and resents the person who, merely by existing in a pleasant fall afternoon, has stirred up a deep conflict.

I was not second generation New York but third, and only that by a geographical stretch of the imagination. Still, there was a little difference between my aunt and me—that "little" that makes all the difference in the world. In that terrible cruelty that children have, that alert sensitivity to an adult's weak spot, I played upon Fiona's Achilles' heel like an old sneaker. I was justified, I said to myself, because I loved Papa and she did not; I was proud of Papa, and she was ashamed; I was delighted with his burr, and it grated on her ears. In short, I was jealous that she was his child and that I was another man's daughter and did not even bear my grandfather's name.

Papa had come from Scotland as a boy of seventeen. It had been a long, wearing trip for a young man, and if the streets of New York were not paved with gold, they were paved with something finer—achievement. One of his achievements was that he knew by name every person on his street, which to a New Yorker, perhaps, is a kind of reconciliation to the world which eludes all but the very few.

"Papa," Aunt Fiona used to say, "will talk to anyone. Anyone at all. You . . . ," and then she used to turn to me, speaking hollowly like the Delphic Oracle I thought later, ". . . you must learn to discriminate." Living with Fiona, I used to think, was like living with a dictionary. Off I went promptly to Fiona's Good

Book to look up *discriminate* and acquire at the same time a few new words which Fiona might *not* know. Our battles were the subtle ones of vocabulary and diction, but people who have experienced the strength of such devastating weapons will know that they were very effective. As I look back upon those battles now, it was a sorry victory when I won so many. I see now what Fiona meant when she raged out at Papa, because Papa, who spoke to everyone, did not, curiously enough, speak to her.

Somehow daughter and father had become alienated. And, although the old-fashioned word *background* is now much out of fashion, replaced by psychological and sociological terms which mean more and say less, Papa and Aunt Fiona differed in their backgrounds. Backgrounds means, at least to me, the physical grounds that people have covered in their past; the landscapes which will be familiar to one will terrorize another; home to one is horror to another, and, spiritually and physically, the landscapes with which we are familiar will be determining factors in our lives.

Papa's landscape was always Scotland. He remained a Scot until he died. Mama, however, was a woman with great pride in America; she felt completely at home in it, wearing the dignity of her country's years of independence, the independence which her ancestors had fought for and which she did everything to maintain, as gracefully as she wore her summer dresses. It is now fashionable to deride such organizations as the Daughters of the American Revolution, but if its body was often made up of Grant Wood's leathery battle-axes, it was made up generations ago by the many women similar to my grandmother, who married, made a home, and comforted the strangers to this country.

America was a big country, my grandmother often pointed out. When she had been a little girl, great areas of New Jersey were still unpopulated, and part of her family still cultivates great tracts of farmland. They were and are land poor, but my grandmother was bequeathed the richest heritage of all people: a love for the ground, the earth, the soil. She had married my grandfather as a young girl—barely eighteen. She had been a lonely child, and perhaps in my grandfather she expected too much. Old photographs (all now lost) showed him a dashing, blond hero (the Leslie Howard of my childhood), meticulously tailored. I was never able to discover how they met, the shy young girl isolated on a backwater New Jersey farm, and the young Scot chasing more successfully his dreams than his future. But meet they did and, out of necessity, she had come to New York. She always had a small income and it was desperately needed. They had four children: my mother, who died as I have mentioned when I was a child, my Aunt Caitlin, my gay, reckless Uncle Jamie, and poor Fiona. She was never called anything to my knowledge put poor Fiona, and it seemed to me she was pilloried between two cultures.

The rest of the family flourished on the rich meeting of two worlds, but somehow or other Fiona floundered. My grandmother's innate dignity, her tolerance for human foibles (providing, of course, they did not exhibit themselves in her own family) all became in Fiona calcified, undigested deposits. She was no copy of herself, and a poor copy of my grandmother; the faults intensified, a person grown up on the streets of New York, with no emotional moorings, with no love of place. She lived in a strange country of her own making and, for all her vocabulary, had never been able to use words to speak to people. These are the kind of people who never should be required to live in cities. The effort of communication comes too hard to them and where a bow of a head will suffice in a village or town, where some contact will be set up above flopping laundry in the backyard, in New York both flesh and spirit must be more than willing. My grandmother sensed this in herself and so made a pilgrimage to the country each year—more, I used to think, to renew herself in some way than to give us the advantage of playing in the open air. But Fiona, alienated, aloof, alone in New York, was equally bewildered by the country.

It was difficult for me to imagine that Fiona was Papa's child. I suppose, now, that his love was something I wished to reserve for myself but he had so much of it, there for the taking, so to speak, I could not see why Fiona did not greet him gaily when he came home, why she did not swoon with delight at his stories. So many exciting things happened to Papa every day. Looking back now, I'm sure that many of his stories were the routine happenings of every day, embroidered, enlarged, made poignant, illuminating, joyous, or pitifully sad. The world was Papa's oyster, and he was allergic to neither shell nor pearl. But, as with all people who experience deeply, he needed someone to share those experiences, to see them with his own eyes, forever touched with romance, forever shot through with reality and dream. As a child I felt my grandfather's isolation, so like my own, I thought, for despite our large household, I carried my loneliness as a reluctant burden, a horror almost, I could not shake off. I turned to my grandfather for comfort and conversation; I turned to him for the communication which is in an unshaved beard, the rough and ready reality of touch and sensation. In that curious fashion in which grandparent and grandchild transcend generations, with Papa I made peace with the world, and the world in turn gave me peace.

I had given my allegiance. Both Papa and I were then lumped together in Fiona's eyes. In some ways she was right. I was sitting around dreaming up stories of the wonders of the world instead of learning those secrets of success which Fiona, in some way or other, felt could be acquired along with accent and vocabulary. I know now, just as I do not know what Fiona meant by success, or even what Papa meant by achievement, or what my grandmother meant by love of country, that all their hopes, ambitions, and dreams are inextricably woven into my life—sometimes a gnarled thread, sometimes a taut and strong determining plumb line. But of all my teachers, Papa, bless him, let me wonder, and from that is made the kingdom of earth.

Raised as young children, in a generation away from our own, we sisters were siblings not only to each other, but to our aunts and uncle as well. It was our Uncle Jamie who taught us to enjoy the social history of our own time.

"In a real dark night of the soul," Scott Fitzgerald said, "it is always three o'clock in the morning." Those words, it seemed to me, must have been written for Uncle Jamie. There was a song that began, "It's three o'clock in the morning, we've danced the whole night through," and I thought it was a theme song for Jamie, the way "When the Moon Comes Over the Mountain" was a theme song for Kate Smith.

Some people belong completely to one decade of their own time. When that decade is over, they never quite adjust to the next or the next or the next. On the other hand, some of us are comfortable in one decade, then recoup our enthusiasm for another. But nearly all of us have some glorious period of years in which we are part and parcel of our times. The twenties, they said, was the age of the lost generation. Later I could not quite understand this when I read it, because Uncle Jamie was the prototype of that age. He never seemed to be lost at all, but always knew just how, where, and why he was going; and he was always going.

"He had," Papa once said, "more shoes than Jimmy Walker, more arguments than Clarence Darrow, more words than Sinclair Lewis, and more gall than Charles MacArthur in *The Front Page*." Jamie would often appear on those front pages, when I was a child, mostly because he was escorting some attractive woman on the fringe of some political crowd, where his good looks and, Papa said, "his gift of gab" saved him from working.

Conflict between generations, particularly between father and son, can be played out anywhere in the world—on the wide plains of the Midwest, the mountains of a far country—but, within the small framework of our little neighborhood it was realized with a terrible intensity. It was far more difficult for boys and men: I saw that it was easier to be a woman. A woman's continuity, even in a strange country, was as simple as recipes and children. Both endured. Children would always be children, food would always be food, homes would always be homes. As a girl I could see that I would always share in that continuity and permanence, and it made me feel warm and comfortable.

Although Jamie was twenty years older than I, he seemed to have none of that permanence. He had never liked his last name and even pronounced it differently—accenting it and anglicizing it in a way that shocked me. Many of the young men on the streets of our Scottish-Irish neighborhood had done the same. They had not changed their names, necessarily, but by a different inflection, they had raised or lowered their sights on language and life itself.

Life, said Jamie, was meant to be enjoyed. Certainly he appeared happy when he went out so late at night that he would never be able to get up in the morning. As a special treat I would look at some of the magazines he brought home. I could read very early. A secret happiness. Newspapers fascinated me with a world so very different than the world we knew. Clara Bow, perhaps, sitting on a jetty in the East River, lavishly ungarbed in a fashionable bathing suit and rubber slippers. I sharpened my vocabulary and my sensual appreciation of life on the rich language that Jamie so obviously admired.

"The vivacious, the orchidaceous Clara Bow. Feast your weary optics on the super-flapper of them all. The hyper-reality and the extra-ideality of a million or more filmgoers. In one person, in one pose, we have the genus American girl: refined, washed, manicured, permanent-waved, and exalted herewith."

I would read such a stupendous paragraph, retreat to the bathroom where I still had to stand on my toes to feast my weary optics upon my poor inadequate self, who obviously was no super-flapper of them all and probably, as much as I wanted to be, no true American girl. I used to sigh when I thought no matter how refined, washed, manicured, pedicured, permanent-waved I would ever be, I would never be Clara Bow. To Jamie, I would be no one.

Or perhaps that elegant, remarkable Texas Guinan. She was as Irish as the next street, Papa said, but in the newspapers she seemed to be even more bedecked and bedazzling than Clara Bow. Garbed in roses, gowned in calla lilies, bathed in pearls, her hair so marcelled it seemed to sink into the newsprint itself, her teeth and nose jutting somewhat aggressively out into the everyday world; I read that her battle cry was

"The curfew shall not ring tonight."

I begged Papa to buy a piano so that I could sit on top of it and sing. If I sang for Jamie, perhaps he would stay home one night; perhaps we could dance together. I'd put my patent leather shoes on, he'd stay home one evening and dance with me. I used to find, even as a very small child, his dancing pumps at the bottom of his closet. I pressed my cheek against their smooth polished edge on life.

One night, as Jamie was leaving, I said, "Curfew shall not ring tonight," having carefully thought it out all day, and I was waiting for him to smile or perhaps even to stay home.

"If you ever say that again," said Jamie, "I'll slap your mouth." What Texas could do and Clara Bow could do, I could not. I was not Norma Shearer or Edna Best, or even Ina Claire. Fortunately, I could afford to fail with Jamie because I was always successful with Papa. Just to be me was all that Papa wanted, so I could take great imaginative fliers to be interesting to Jamie. Florenze Ziegfeld had once roughly outlined the ideal woman in one of the magazines I found on Jamie's dressing table. I needed, that list said, native refinement: "Where this exists, education is not necessary."

I thought of abandoning school, but that seemed hardly worth it, not even for Jamie. And then there was a long list, some of which I passed, some of which I failed. Poise, symmetry. I was a little confused about just what symmetry was and felt a little sorry about my crooked tooth. One also needed spirit and style. I was in great doubt about my style and decided to abandon all plaid skirts; "personal magnetism" I thought I had, but I wasn't sure about Ziegfeld's warning, "You must have a quality of glory—that elusive something that is definite and yet intangible as the perfume of flowers."

"What is the quality of glory, Papa?"

"Glory," he said, "is the courage of history."

"Oh," I said, somewhat disappointed. "How would a girl go about getting glory?"

"No one should ever seek it," said Papa.

"Not even Amelia Earhart?" said I.

"The Lindberghs' sort of glory is ridiculous," said Papa.

"Did the Scots have glory, Papa?"

"Infinite glory," said Papa. "The Scots and the Irish had more glory than sense, nine times out of ten."

"Are there a lot of Scottish girls in the *Ziegfeld Follies*, Papa?"

"That's a piece of research I never undertook," said Papa.

"Well, that's real glory," I said. "Mr. Ziegfeld said so. It's real glory, and if you have it, you'd be in the *Ziegeld Follies*."

"I won't be," said Papa, "and I'll make pretty sure you won't be either."

"Why don't you stay up all night the way Jamie does?" I said to Papa.

"Because I work all day," said Papa, somewhat darkly.

"Does Jamie work?" I asked.

"There's all kinds of work in this world," said Papa, "even Auld Nick's, I suppose."

"What does he do, Papa, at three o'clock in the morning?" I said.

"I wish I knew," said Papa. "I wish I knew. I don't understand him at all."

"If Clara Bow lived here," I said, "He'd stay at home."

"If Clara Bow lived here, lass, I might stay at home myself."

"Would you say she had glory, Papa?"

"I think they call it 'It'," said Papa.

"I wonder if I'll ever have 'It'?" I said.

"I hope not," he answered. "Get your coat like a good girl."

"Where are we going?" I asked.

"We'll have a nice walk to the Museum of Natural History," said Papa.

"I don't much feel like it," I said.

"Why not?" he asked.

"Gogo and I aren't studying to be apes, you know, Papa. We're sick of all those apes at the Museum. I bet Clara Bow never went there. I'd rather have 'It.' 'It' and a little bit of glory."

"Ayc, lassie, and a wee bit sense wears longer than both."

And it was always Mama who taught us sense; and the need for structure in one's life.

Mama's sense was the home, the kitchen, kindness to friends and family, food, birds, cats, dogs, china, flowers, hooked rugs, warm quilts, the past, a sense of place, carpenter gothic houses, the seashore, shells, ghosts, sand, and love. Books did not overshadow her world, perhaps because in Papa's world, and later my own, they so often did. Papa knew every librarian, every bookseller, it seemed to me, in all of New York City. Being introduced to Mr. MacQueen, for example, was a high point in my life. I remembered it clearly and my first job (after college), was at the Gotham Book Mart, where I was trained by the extraordinary Frances Steloff; I was inspired by that meeting.

Mr. MacQueen's Pan-Celtic Bookstore was on a corner of Ninety-sixth Street in New York City. Ninety-sixth Street was a fascinating geographical entrance to the great wide world. From the street, you could look down into basement level of the shop and see the bookshelves that were built in such disarray that it appeared the whole shop might go tumbling down into the earth. Inside the shop the building seemed supported by the books. Touch one, take up a volume, perhaps without rearranging the surrounding titles, and all, like a house of cards, would come tumbling down around you.

"Life," said Mr. MacQueen, "has that tendency." It was not unlike Alice in Wonderland. He explained it to me when I first knew him. "We are all of us Alice," said Mr. MacQueen. "We are all of us the Red Queen. We are all of us the White Queen. We're all of us living, crazy-like, racing to the Mad Hatter's tea party."

"I've never liked Alice," I said.

"She was a weird, strange, curious individual," said Mr. MacQueen. "You'll find many of them here. These books are full of weird, strange, curious individuals who did one decent thing—a good book. A book is a good thing. It is the beginning and the end. It is a secure thing—see how you can bind it; see how you can sit on it; see how you can, well—hold it in your hand."

Over the years he put into my hand a strange collection of books. Some of the titles were as fascinating and as exciting as their subject matter. My favorite of all in those early years was Jane Porter's *Scottish Chiefs*.

"This is the original edition," he said, licking his lips. "Not a reprint, lass, for American children, all with pictures and large type, as though their eyes could not handle the decent print. You will never get the wonder of a book, lass, unless you have it in its own right way. You'll be hearing in years to come of first editions and the like of that. Never a bit of sense in the first edition, just a wee bit of money for those that sell them. Nonetheless, sometimes, just sometimes, you feel it's nearer the author. A warmer babe with the fresh breath of creation in it."

"There comes a voice that awakes my soul. It is a voice of years that are gone; they roll before me with their deeds." I read this comment from the title page of *The Scottish Chiefs* and was excited in a way that determined the profession I would follow. Surely books themselves were voices that awakened any soul. Surely everyone wanted to hear the voice of years—a voice, any voice, your voice, my voice, calling, rolling, ringing out through time itself. The author's name, Miss Jane Porter; it rang with importance and with history. Who was she, I wondered? Who was Miss Jane Porter?

"From the race of Douglass," Mr. MacQueen said. "There will never be the likes of that lady again."

"Does the book tell about the MacLeans?" I

asked.

"Now I don't recall properly. It might or it might not. But the strange thing about it, lass, is that Napoleon banned the book in France because it was dangerous to the state.

"Censorship is a weird thing," he reflected. "The right to speak up is every man's and woman's right, every child's right for that matter; providing his or her parents think so. Your grandfather is a good one for letting someone speak his mind."

I remember the book clearly. It had a rust binding, with intricate tooling, the "S" so entwirled with wisps and wasps of type, looking so eagerly like an illuminated letter stretching to eternity, that I thought it the most elegant and romantic of all books. It was surely romantic, but alas, quite a poor book that told nothing about the MacLeans (our grandfather's last name). But it confirmed what I knew about the Scots—their language rolled like the sand down to the Clyde.

In the corner of the room of Mr. MacQueen's top floor, there was the portrait of a great ship berthed on the Clyde itself. Whenever I walked down Riverside Drive to look at the Hudson, I compared it in my imagination to that Scottish river. The Clyde had spawned hope, shipped an entire culture. I disparaged the Hudson. The only time it was really interesting was when the shad went floating by and I used to watch to see if I could see them going painfully up the river in the spring. Why, I wondered, was the Clyde so exciting and the Hudson so dull? It was, I believed, because of Mr. MacQueen.

The ship in Mr. MacQueen's photograph, or rather old drawing, was called the *Lady Brisbane*. It was a great paddle-wheel steamer, and I thought it could stir up history the way the paddle wheelers had stirred up Mark Twain. Mr. MacQueen was my Mark Twain. He guided me around the eddies and flows of childhood literature; the Scottish Chiefs roared into battle, but the rest of literature was of a quieter kind.

On one shelf were little chapbooks. They were by a man who had shaken my hand warmly and treated me as quite grown up when I met him. His name was Jack Yeats. He was a great painter and he came from Ireland. He had illustrated all of the books himself, and the illustrations were particularly exciting for children.

Mr. MacQueen went to great difficulty locating a toy theater that was to accompany one of the books. It was about a sailor, a "tar" Mr. MacQueen called him, who found a comet and rode to heaven. Mr. Jack Yeats was the first author I ever met. I often heard Mr. Mac-Queen and my grandfather talking about another Yeats, or, for that matter, the whole Yeats family. The old man, J.B. Yeats, the father of William Yeats the poet and Jack Yeats the artist, was a permanent resident in New York. He ate regularly at a little French restaurant in the Thirties and there, upon occasion, one member or another of the Celtic groups that sprawled throughout our streets would stop and ask his advice about the state of the world.

Mr. MacQueen was most impressed by Jack Yeats, although he said, "Willie is a good man too."

"The truth, lass, is that we have nothing to compare with them in Scotland today. It's strange the way the Irish have not only the gift of the gab, but the gift of passing it down on paper for all to read and read again. Our jokes go up in the air; half of our talk dies before it is even uttered, but there is something lasting about the Irish words. We're better at deeds. We're a curious combination," he said, "and that's why we're such good engineers." (I myself married an engineer many years later.)

Mr. MacQueen had been an engineer. His grandfather had sailed on the Clyde paddleboats, and he had sailed on some of the first steam vessels to cross the Atlantic. He had an entire shelf of the store dedicated to Kipling.

"Kipling was the poet of steam," he said. "Kipling was part engineer and part bookman.

"When Kipling was dying in New York," said Mr. MacQueen, "I used to go every day to the hotel where he was staying. I was only one of the crowd, and I used to wonder how many of the ones who stood there went as I did, went in the same way as I did, because they knew that there lay a man who knew the taste of steam, the smell of steam, aye, lass, the way of the new world, as if he were recording the story of mankind itself."

"I like his stories," I said, "mostly I like the part about the great road in India in *Kim*."

I used to go to the front of the shop and look out on Ninety-sixth Street. It was the closest thing I knew to the great road. Buses went in both directions. Across the street they were building a great new building. People were rushing to and fro, always with the feeling of intensity; always with a feeling as if they knew where they were going. Some streets were like that, I thought. Some streets knew where they were going and where the people upon them were going. Some streets did not. You looked on the faces of some of the people who walked the streets, you would see that they did not know, they did not know who they were or what they were, or even what kind of a world it was.

So many things were happening all over the world. The world was opening up more and more. There was China, devastated now by a new Japanese terror. I would think of the little children who were left abandoned on the railroad tracks. Later there was a

Sara and Carol Lewis in Scotland: "My nieces, who have been a constant source of inspiration"

war in Spain, and children were smashed with bullets against the walls. I could not reconcile the pictures that appeared in the newspapers and the stories which I could now read about the world with much that I had learned in Sunday school.

There were very few people, very few writers to whom Mr. MacQueen would really give a license. He could list them on one hand. "Robert Louis Stevenson—it's a fine Edinburgh family; my parents knew his parents and they were all men of the good water. I think to sail the imagination of a lighthouse—they made fine lighthouses—is even harder than to curb the sea itself. And to sail a rough river of the imagination, because Stevenson did that, is a fierce, fierce voyage. Take his books, lass, take all of them and take these letters too. I don't need sniveling baby verses of gardens and swinging up into the sky; I mean the real words, I mean *Thrawn Janet* and *The Weir of Hermiston*.

"Take Robert Burns," he said, "take him and gather him up and never forget him. Take up that wild laughter and that wild understanding. In all lamp-black, gloomy life, in all our licensed living, in all these years of Prohibition, don't do this and don't do that, I hold onto Robert Burns. In every Scot," he said, "there is a Robbie Burns struggling to get out. Struggling to get out in wild and cheery laughter, and passion."

These were not his exact words but only the tone of his voice, and over the years his voice has crystallized into language. I can hear him speak to me as clearly as I hear my own voice repeating once more, "Robert Burns, or Robert Louis Stevenson. These are my friends."

"What about James Barrie?" I said.

"I don't think much of Barrie," said Mr. MacQueen. "He is a sniveling, snorting mama's boy. There

may be kail in the kailyards and there may be romance in every butt and ben in all of Scotland, and there may be beauty in every mother's soul, but I tell you one thing, lass, you cannot avoid everything uncomfortable and mean in life, and there's a great deal that is mean and uncomfortable, and pretty strange about Peter Pan. He's cold kail," said Mr. MacQueen, "very cold cabbage indeed."

But Kipling, oh, that was another story altogether. Kipling was a man among men and a writer among writers. Every Saturday afternoon, a group of Mr. MacQueen's cronies would gather on the top floor of his bookshop. Most of them were elderly gentlemen, as he was, most of them were there to discuss not literature, curiously enough, but the days of steam and the poet that they respected. The poet to whom they had given an individual license was Rudyard Kipling.

Words of the "MacAndrews Hymn" rang up and down the room. They bounced off the ceiling; bounced down the stairs to the cellar shop, echoed and reechoed through every nook and cranny. I listened, fascinated, while these men took the words of the poem apart and put them back together again, the way they would a machine. They oiled each one, turned it over in their hands, looking at it from every angle. They put it first in one place to see whether it would fit, they took it out again and then they put it back more securely in the place that Kipling had chosen for it.

These were my first literary critics, and I have never known any so astute or so remarkable again. They had the passion of understanding and they were seeking a voice.

Kipling, Stevenson, and Burns, to this triumvirate Mr. MacQueen added two more names: Mr. James Joyce (and Mr. MacQueen also referred to him always in that way, Mr. James Joyce) and Miss Jane Porter. I realized that there was something different about Mr. Joyce, just as there was something different about the lady who wrote *The Scottish Chiefs,* Miss Jane Porter.

These were not ordinary people, these were people set off from the ordinary course of events by honor, dignity, and title, Miss and Mr. All other authors could be called by their first names, even by their nicknames, look at Willie and look at Jack Yeats, but in these instances one must use their full names: Miss Jane Porter, Mr. James Joyce.

When Joyce began to creep into the conversation, Papa started to accompany me more and more to the bookstore. An element of censorship, perhaps, was already entering my life. The gay, wild abandon of words for the sake of words was now beginning to disappear. There was a great deal that I was putting behind me and, alas, some part of Mr. MacQueen was also being abandoned. He had led me to the rich, ripe, raucous cry of the imagination, and there, for awhile, I foundered, sometimes swimming, occasionally nearly drowning in the words of my own discoveries. Bit by bit I learned to swim, little by little, I read without support; my own independence creaked up a different stairway than the one that led to Mr. MacQueen.

And then suddenly our very brief childhood disappeared. Our grandparents died abruptly, followed almost immediately by our Aunt Fiona, and our Uncle Jamie.

Our father in Connecticut gathered us up, and the slow, regular life of a beautiful Connecticut farm began to heal us, and the private world of a boarding school began to let us understand our own generation. This close association, for some reason, resulted in our working and writing for young people, and others, years later.

But from Mr. MacQueen's bookshop, I still cull interests that I am working on today.

During those farm days of our adolescence, when we were not at boarding school, we lived in great freedom. One year we even took off and lived in the stables among the horses—a story that I'm still writing of those rather glorious years of our teenage. The horses, we felt, showed more intelligence than some of the human beings that we were around. We were not neglected, but my father and our consecutive stepmothers were often away and we did, indeed, live a bit wild.

It was during that period that all three of us read so much about the Brontës. All of their books, as I recall. And, we identified with the Brontë sisters.

When I came to write *Those Extraordinary Women*, so many of the women I had read as a teenager became very alive in my mind. Mary Shelley, for example. Motherless, still capable of that great and extraordinary story—the original of all science fiction—*Frankenstein* and those three sisters, Emily, Charlotte, and Anne Brontë, whose pictures I had once torn out of a British magazine showing all three of them in paintings by their brother that now hang in the National Portrait Gallery of London.

They kept diaries, so we kept diaries in that period. We found, as they had, that we were bound with a remarkable cord of dependence and fantasy. They made their own world, we would make our own world. If they had lived on the edge of a moor, we had lived on the edge of a great woods. They had a library to turn to, so had we. They had a housekeeper, Tabby. A rather delightful soul. We had a housekeeper, so cranky and red that we called her The Lobster. So, the identification was considerable.

They, too, had been shipped away from the moor that they had so loved, as we were shipped away from the farm we loved to boarding school. They suffered under the strictures of such a school, and so did we. They felt the pain of the younger children, the deprivation of all the children of not having a home, and so did we. And mostly, we read.

At school we had a strange, eclectic library. No book was ever thrown away. All books were precious. And at that point all three of us began to write.

My younger sister Cathy wrote less but sketched more. We wrote tiny books in those days when we weren't telling stories.

When I went to college (Wellesley) the campus, and students, were shocked in 1938 by the great hurricane that hit New England; it was just the first of a series of shocks: Hitler overrunning Poland, World War II, the atom bomb, the terrible disclosures of the Holocaust. I was still in love with the word (I still am) and I worked first in bookshops, then in publishing houses, and finally on my own books. I often collaborated with my sister Gogo Lewis, my husband Robert

Dame Edith Sitwell and her brother Sir Osbert Sitwell in the late forties. "I first read her mesmerizing poetry sitting in an apple tree when I was ten. . . . When she published her major poems in the terrible throes of World War II, I was working for the Vanguard Press which published these poems in the United States."

Paul Goodman, an old and dear friend, about 1945, "in a previously unpublished photograph by my sister, Gogo Lewis"

Manley, and my friend Susan Belcher, and I would like just the right book to do with my daughter, who is twenty-five, as I write this.

I have always written biographies with enormous pleasure. I wrote about that strange boy, Rudyard Kipling, whose life in India and his separation from his parents had so shaped and moulded his life. I wrote about Nathaniel Hawthorne writing by himself in the attic, lonely, dreamy, obsessed by his own family's history of the witch time in Salem. I wrote about Dorothy and William Wordsworth, sister and brother, who alone and together made themselves a world of flowers and poetry and strange walks into the natural world of England's nineteenth century. I went to all the places that these people had lived, where they had been born and where they had died, and my young daughter went with us because my husband, too, had joined us. Research is a wonderful field to work in because you can pack up your mind, the way you pack up your luggage, and carry it with you. So we had many walking trips in all parts of the world, with my daughter occasionally—at least when she was very young—making many suggestions which were sometimes very helpful.

I was always in touch with her friends because I liked them. I also worried—as so many contemporary young women do—as to whether I was giving her enough time, but because I carry my writing around with me, I was able to share those kind of secret times that mothers and daughters sometimes have that come unexpectedly and can never be captured if you deliberately seek them. I knew that there was a theory around that children had to have quality time with their mothers but I guessed—and I guessed correctly—that they also needed quantity time. They needed time to get angry, they needed time to get depressed, they needed time to be seen in all different kinds of ways and, fortunately, my writing was put in a desk and I could close the door on that and stand up and be a mother. It did not always work, of course. Small children want mothers twenty-four hours a day. All children can resent the very idea that mothers can have anything more interesting, more delightful, or more engrossing than a child twenty-four hours a day. But that, too, was something that in the learning I think my daughter found useful. As I write this, she too is in the media, but the news media, today; she deals with today's words in television. She is a person of her age as I was of mine, each of us being influenced by the world outside, eager to discover the world outside and eager to explain it and the problems of the world, their origins, and even their possible solutions.

I collaborated with my sister Gogo in many books that fit very much into the world of our time. We had moved from the age of anxiety to the age of the atom bomb, from the age of the Korean War to the age of Vietnam. All of it had been a terrible age of suspense. Then there had been the new age of outer space; the new world of marine technology; there were astronauts and aquanauts; the sea and the sky were getting to be neighborhoods. Our friend Marshall McLuhan said the world was beginning to be "a global village." All of these topics were subjects that interested us and all of them inspired anthologies or books that kept us busy.

I had always appreciated the remark of the Irish playwright J. M. Synge: "All art is collaboration." Truly, no one writes any book without observing and gaining help, conversations, background from the people around her. This is particularly true for anybody who writes books for young people, but it is often true of books for more mature readers when one is thrown together with people obsessed and delighted in some aspect of the world. That is particularly important, I think, when you are dealing with books of place. I collaborated with my husband, Robert Manley, on two books that have shown an obsessive interest in place: *Beaches: Their Lives, Legends, and Lore* and *Islands: Their Lives, Legends, and Lore.*

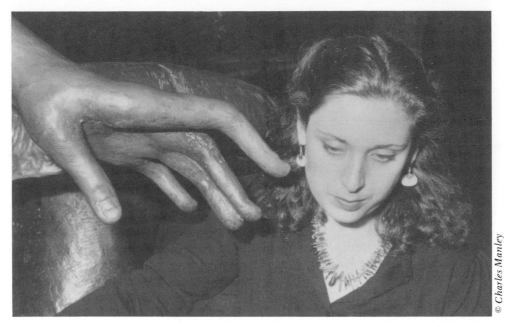

© Charles Manley

Shivaun Manley today, a writer and TV journalist, photographed in Central Park by Charles Manley, "the newest professional photographer in our family."

Books that appeal to an entire family are a great pleasure to write. After all, a writer would like to have as many people as possible read his or her project, and never deliberately writes for a very small group. If you're fortunate to love some aspect of history, or the world that interests (or should!) others, then you have a good chance of writing an enjoyable book and having it reach an audience that enjoys it. We never deliberately sought out the opportunity to write a book on beaches. But, for a long while, my husband and I had sought out beaches around the world that greatly appealed to us. We were collectors of beaches and when still a very young child, our daughter joined in the collecting. Beaches themselves, of course, appeal to that kind of ragpicker collecting instinct. There are always strange pieces of glass, magnificent shells, curious, dangerous looking jellyfish, beautiful pieces of seaweed. There are the changes that a beach sometimes suffers, sometimes enjoys, through all the seasons of the year. There are birds of all kinds, waves of all kinds, beach debris of all kinds and there are beach people throughout the world, all having the particular private rhythms of their lives going along with the rhythms of the ocean and the sand because, of course, beaches have a rhythm of their own.

You must have had a fascination of beaches when you were young if you are to love them when you grow up, but most young people have that fascination; from the youthful surfer to the mature beachcomber, there is wonder and mystery, unlike anything else, in the beach. If one scratches deep in the sands of the imagination, one remembers all the old stories of so many people who were inspired to write because they walked the sands: James Joyce walking the beaches outside Dublin; Wilbur and Orville Wright at Kitty Hawk thinking about the glories of not only the beach, but far more the glories of the air and preparing their first airplane; Nathaniel Hawthorne walking the beaches of Massachusetts; all of the great writers who left us memories of the beaches and waterways of the Great Lakes, the stories of the great resorts, and the animals of the beaches—such as the ponies of the eastern shore of Maryland; the wrecks of the beaches and yes, even the beaches of the times of war, from the bloody days of Normandy to the various beaches of the South Pacific.

We spent some 100,000 miles in the preparation of the book on beaches and then spent three or four years collecting from libraries around the world all the prints that would enhance it. My husband is an engineer and many of the trips were to gather scientific data on the tides, on the use of such things as isotopes which, when used properly, gave us an accurate picture of the tides, on the size and power of waves in various sections of the world. But always there was something additional: the pleasure of being beachcombers.

We began our book at the time when people were first beginning to understand that their environment was threatened. We had always been interested in the natural beauty and resources of the United States and had seen that others were taking a long time to realize

Seon and Robert Manley, about the time they began collaborating on books in the late 1960s

Manley with daughter Shivaun, age five, "during our summers on Long Island where our family interests in beaches, islands, oceans, and Long Island itself all turned into books."

that the tremendous beauty of our country was being endangered.

We concentrated on doing what we could to have people understand how beaches in themselves had to be preserved. Beaches, marshes, estuaries, and the birds and beasts of the beaches.

As the National Seashore beaches became established, we joined with our neighbors in an effort to make Fire Island in New York part of the National Park system. But other beaches were just as important to us. The beaches of the West Coast which, alas, are being threatened now more than they ever were before. A spot where everybody thought the beaches would remain just as they were. But beaches, of course, never remain just as they are. They are constantly changing. At times they build up, at other times they erode, and now, more frequently, alas, they are endangered by oil pollution; what they call in France, "The Black Sea of Oil."

We've all read stories of oil coming across the sands—we have seen them. Seen the disaster that's spread over beaches. Some oil has stained almost all the beaches in the world now, but fortunately scientists are developing materials to make beach cleanup easier. But, as scientists point out, beaches are not a permanent gift to us and it must take all our skill, ability, and own personal effort to make sure that the beaches will continue to exist for the generations after us.

It was then perhaps understandable that we would follow *Beaches* with a book on *Islands.* Islands

have always seemed to me wonderfully mysterious, filled with secret treasures; not only of hidden treasure that Robert Louis Stevenson created *Treasure Island* out of, but all kinds of other treasures. Of ways of life that might otherwise have disappeared, of the independence of people who have a particular love for their own islands.

The beginning of the seventies seemed to me to be a new start in the effort of women for equal rights. I was not alone but, as usual, I became so stirred up by the excitement of women looking at women, that I collaborated with a friend of mine, Susan Belcher, a young Canadian who I thought had a different slant from my own ideas, in a book entitled, *O, Those Extraordinary Women; or, The Joys of Literary Lib.* The subtitle was perhaps a little too humorous for those women so deadly serious that they could miss the high job status that literature has always given women.

My own experience in my working life was that one was always dealing with the word. I, myself, had met no prejudice working in the bookshops, no prejudice working in the publishing house—particularly in the Vanguard Press, then run by Mr. James Henle (one of the great editors of all time), and with its vice president, Evelyn Shrifte, later to be a pioneer as one of the first women to be the president of a publishing house.

Women, their opinions, their considerations, and

"Grip, whose story I wrote from historical letters and records, is the bird who inspired Edgar Allan Poe's 'The Raven.'" (Illustration from A Present for Charles Dickens *by Seon Manley. Copyright © 1983 by Seon Manley. Published by The Westminster Press.)*

the full worth of their minds, were very much appreciated by Jim Henle, as they had been by Frances Steloff of the famous Gotham Book Mart where I had also worked. So, I had no axe to grind, no feeling that I had enormously suffered, no "getting-back" at any man who had ever hurt me. I was very much captured by a character whose story I am working on today. An Irish woman who said, while in prison, "Nobody can ever really hurt me." It seemed to me when I first heard that remark—still the greatest form of freedom—we, ourselves, cannot be hurt if we do not allow it. We cannot be undervalued if we do not allow it. We cannot be abused if we do not allow it.

One of the countries I hold dear is Ireland and I have studied Irish history, written and edited material about Irish writers, and always identified with the Irish (although my own Celtic background is Scottish), in their valiant effort to seek their independence from the great British Empire before and during World War I. Southern Ireland became a free state in 1921— the year I was born—and its history, its people, and its landscape, all had personal meaning and identity for me. If I am away from Ireland too long, I miss the voices.

A very great psychoanalyst once told me that frequently we do not write about our lives as often as we write about the lives of our parents. It is those years

that are mysterious, unknown; that it is those people, as our parents—even as young as children, perhaps— who swamp our unconscious; make us want to recreate their lives and understanding. None of this, of course, is ever done in a conscious way. When we recreate history, it is often our own pasts that inspire such recreation. That is what I am presently working on: a moment in Irish history that had enormous significance to the rest of the world. This book will be a novel. I call it *Rising.* It is about the women and children in particular who supported a great movement for independence.

To sum up, I have enjoyed the writing game, as I call it. It is a hard game, and most of the rewards are internal. Samuel Butler said writing results from hard work; glue yourself to the seat of the chair; nine-tenths perspiration, Mark Twain insisted.

Everyone, man, woman, child, and adolescent has within him or her a writer struggling to get out. This desire to communicate is as primitive as the development of humanity and after all, don't we all have these essential ingredients? We learn to speak and to employ words. Writing is subtle communication and in a rather harrowing world it is desperately required.

I'm still struggling, and I hope the generations behind me take up the struggle—it's worth it.

BIBLIOGRAPHY

FOR YOUNG ADULTS

Nonfiction:

Adventures in Making: The Romance of Crafts around the World. New York: Vanguard, 1959.

Rudyard Kipling: Creative Adventurer. New York: Vanguard, 1965.

Long Island Discovery: An Adventure into the History, Manners, and Mores of America's Front Porch. Garden City, N.Y.: Doubleday, 1966.

Beaches: Their Lives, Legends, and Lore, with husband, Robert Manley. Philadelphia: Chilton, 1968.

My Heart's in the Heather (autobiographical). New York: Funk, 1968.

Nathaniel Hawthorne: Captain of the Imagination. New York: Vanguard, 1968.

My Heart's in Greenwich Village (autobiographical). New York: Funk, 1969.

Islands: Their Lives, Legends, and Lore, with R. Manley. Philadelphia: Chilton, 1970.

O Those Extraordinary Women; or, The Joys of Literary Lib, with Susan Belcher. Philadelphia: Chilton, 1972.

Dorothy and William Wordsworth: The Heart of a Circle of Friends. New York: Vanguard, 1974.

Editor of:

Teenage Treasury of Our Science World, with sister, Gogo Lewis. New York: Funk, 1961.

The Age of the Manager: A Treasury of Our Times, with R. Manley. New York: Macmillan, 1962.

Teenage Treasury of Imagination and Discovery, with G. Lewis. New York: Funk, 1962.

James Joyce: Two Decades of Criticism, with Eugene Jolas. New York: Vanguard, 1963.

Teenage Treasury of the Arts, with G. Lewis. New York: Funk, 1964.

Suspense: A Treasury for Young Adults, with G. Lewis. New York: Funk, 1966.

The Oceans: A Treasury of the Sea World, with G. Lewis. Garden City, N.Y.: Doubleday, 1967.

High Adventure: A Treasury for Young Adults, with G. Lewis. New York: Funk, 1968.

Polar Secrets: A Treasury of the Arctic and Antarctic, with G. Lewis. Garden City, N.Y.: Doubleday, 1968.

Shapes of the Supernatural, with G. Lewis. Garden City, N.Y.: Doubleday, 1969.

A Gathering of Ghosts: A Treasury, with G. Lewis. New York: Funk, 1970.

Ladies of Horror: Two Centuries of Supernatural Stories by the Gentle Sex, with G. Lewis. New York: Lothrop, 1971.

Grande Dames of Detection: Two Centuries of Sleuthing Stories by the Gentle Sex, with G. Lewis. New York: Lothrop, 1973.

Mistresses of Mystery: Two Centuries of Suspense Stories by the Gentle Sex, with G. Lewis. New York: Lothrop, 1973.

Baleful Beasts: Great Supernatural Stories of the Animal Kingdom, with G. Lewis. New York: Lothrop, 1974.

Bewitched Beings: Phantoms, Familiars, and the Possessed in Stories from Two Centuries, with G. Lewis. New York: Lothrop, 1974.

Ladies of Fantasy: Two Centuries of Sinister Stories by the Gentle Sex, with G. Lewis. New York: Lothrop, 1975.

Ladies of the Gothics: Tales of Romance and Terror by the Gentle Sex, with G. Lewis. New York: Lothrop, 1975.

Masters of the Macabre: An Anthology of Mystery, Horror, and Detection, with G. Lewis. Garden City, N.Y.: Doubleday, 1975.

Sisters of Sorcery: Two Centuries of Witchcraft Stories by the Gentle Sex, with G. Lewis. New York: Lothrop, 1976.

Women of the Weird: Eerie Stories by the Gentle Sex, with G. Lewis. New York: Lothrop, 1976.

Ghostly Gentlewomen: Two Centuries of Spectral Stories by the Gentle Sex, with G. Lewis. New York: Lothrop, 1977.

Cat Encounters: A Cat Lover's Anthology, with G. Lewis. New York: Lothrop, 1979.

The Haunted Dolls: An Anthology, with G. Lewis. Garden City, N.Y.: Doubleday, 1980.

FOR CHILDREN

Fiction:

The Ghost in the Far Garden, and Other Stories (illustrated by Emanuel Schongut). New York: Lothrop, 1977.

A Present for Charles Dickens. Philadelphia: Westminster, 1983.

Editor of:

Mystery! A Treasury for Younger Readers, with G. Lewis. New York: Funk, 1963.

Merriment! A Treasury for Young Readers, with G. Lewis. New York: Funk, 1965.

Magic: A Treasury for Young Readers, with G. Lewis. New York: Funk, 1967.

To You with Love: A Treasury of Great Romantic Literature, with G. Lewis (illustrated by Evelyn Copelman). Philadelphia: M. Smith, 1969.

Masters of Shades and Shadows, with G. Lewis. Garden City, N.Y.: Doubleday, 1978.

Christmas Ghosts: An Anthology, with G. Lewis. Garden City, N.Y.: Doubleday, 1978.

Nature's Revenge: Eerie Stories of Revolt Against the Human Race, with G. Lewis (illustrated by Jacqui Morgan). New York: Lothrop, 1978.

Fun Phantoms: Tales of Ghostly Entertainment, with G. Lewis. New York: Lothrop, 1979.

Walter Dean Myers

1937-

Where does life begin? I discount the idea that life has a strictly biological beginning. Sometime between the snatching of an unknown African from his native land and this writing, somewhere between the long forgotten past and the confusing present, the person that I perceive as Self came into being.

I don't remember being born in 1937 in Martinsburg, West Virginia. There are records that indicate that I was and I accept them. I sent for a birth certificate some years ago and I received a neat document which confirmed that I was, indeed, born. It is also noted under "race" that I am white. That amuses me. In a system that places so much importance on one's race, that error is a small gem of irony.

I don't remember anything about West Virginia. There have been family reunions in which I have sat, virtually an outsider, and listened to tales of long-past events which somehow define the existence of the Myers family.

My mother died during the birth of my sister Imogene. I have a picture of my mother, borrowed and copied from an older sister. In the picture I see a woman I never knew. I don't remember her ever holding me, or kissing me. She looks kindly, and I am told she was rather tall. I make a lot of this because my father was a short man. I assume, therefore, that physically I take after my mother's people who have been described to me as tall. I am over six feet.

My father, George Ambrose Myers, was also quite a bit darker than I am. My mother, Mary Green, was lighter in complexion. The Greens were known to be quick of temper and rather a mean lot. More than that I don't know.

My father managed to marry a number of quite attractive women. My mother was his second wife. He also managed to father quite a number of children, most of whom are still living. Three of my brothers have been killed—one in Vietnam, one hit by an ambulance, and one during a domestic dispute.

Hard times are common in West Virginia. When my mother died my father was left to care for Imogene, myself, my brothers Douglas and George, and my sisters Geraldine, Ethel, Viola, and Gertrude. Those old enough to go to school went to the "Colored" school in Martinsburg. There were few jobs to be had during

Mary Green Myers, in West Virginia, about 1933

that Depression era. There were some jobs in nearby mining towns but they hired few Blacks. And they paid mostly in "Scrip," which had to be spent at the company store. My father's parents helped as much as they could. My grandfather was a colorful character whom I met years later as a teenager. He was born on a Sunday just before the end of the Civil War. His mother, a slave, managed to keep a newspaper as a record of his birth. My grandfather, of course, didn't remember being a slave. He did remember stories of slavery that his mother related. I remember only that the stories, full of beatings and horrors, frightened me as a child.

Enter the Deans.

Extended families are common among poor people. If a family is experiencing difficulty it is not out of the ordinary for another family, faring only slightly better, to take in one or more of the first family's children. Herbert and Florence Dean took me to raise.

Florence Dean had been the daughter of a German mother and American Indian father. Herbert Dean was the son of a small businessman in Baltimore. His grandfather had been a slave in Virginia.

The Deans settled in Harlem. I am told that I left Martinsburg with them and two of my sisters when I was three, or thereabouts, arriving in New York's Harlem with a snotty nose and wearing a pair of my sister's socks. Harlem became my home and the place where my first impressions of the world were set.

We weren't poor in any way that I recognized—not that it would have mattered much. Being poor was not as important then as it has become. It had little to do with not having designer jeans, or the latest tapes, or other "things" that children connect with self-worth today. When I was a child there were two conditions that defined being poor. Were you hungry? Were you cold? With the Deans I was never hungry or cold.

I loved Harlem. I lived in an exciting corner of the renowned Black capital and in an exciting era. The people I met there, the things I did, have left a permanent impression on me. My earliest memories are of walking through the streets to Sunday school. The Sunday school teacher would pick up children from the neighborhood, and I would hold hands with my selected partner and sing "Yes, Jesus Loves Me," as we walked down St. Nicholas Avenue toward the church. Later, when we had moved to Morningside Avenue and I could go to Sunday school by myself, I would sing the words to the song to myself.

My foster parents were not educated people. They were, for the most part, unskilled. My father worked as a handyman and shipping clerk for the United States Radium Corporation. My mother was a factory worker. When she was not working she would keep me close by her side, or so I remember. My sisters, her natural daughters, suggested that she "marry" me because she had apparently loved me so much. This seemed to me a splendid idea and I was quite disappointed when I found that it wasn't at all possible.

Mama taught me to read when I was four and I remember reading to her as a five-year-old while she did housework. My father despaired that she would make a "mama's boy" out of me. Mama and I didn't care what he thought. She taught me to cook (her mother had been a cook in German restaurants around Chambersburg, Pennsylvania), and she would sneak food into my room at night when my father thought I was asleep. We would savor those stolen moments and talk about them later.

On the other hand, Herbert Dean, my foster father, was a different breed of person altogether. Usually he was working. He did all sorts of work besides his

Herbert and Florence Dean, 1944

job for U.S. Radium. Once he worked at the shipyards loading and unloading cargo. He would come home with this hair full of flour dust and I would hide from him. He worked in one of Dutch Schultz's legitimate businesses.

Herbert Julius Dean was born in Baltimore, Maryland. His father, William Dean, was a tall, straight-as-a-ramrod man who owned a hauling business in Baltimore. He was one of the first to realize that the horseless carriage was just a passing fancy and kept his teams of horses until the bitter end. My great grandfather was an ex-slave who owned land in Virginia, given to him by his former master in return for his services as a freeman after the Civil War. Herbert Dean left school during the third grade and didn't learn to read and write with any marked degree of competency until years later.

My foster father was good to me—except for the stories. What he liked to do, especially when Mama was out shopping, was to sit me on his knee and tell endless stories. There were stories of ghosts and of rabbits that came through walls and of strange creatures that rose from the sea (the sea being the Hudson River) in the still of night. I was never quite sure if I wanted Mama to leave me alone with Herbert. I didn't call him Dad because my older sisters didn't. I remember making him stop the stories and tell me that he loved me just before the scary parts came. Sometimes, when the stories were *really* scary, he would act as if he were scared himself. I remember one Saturday, Mama had gone to Fourteenth Street to shop, and my father told me a story about a huge bunny that escaped from a farm and went around looking for bad children. Apparently, this particular bunny had it in for children who cried when their mamas left them with nothing more tangible then the promise of a charlotte russe. This, of course, meant me. When Dad got to the part about the bunny coming up the fire escape (we lived on the fourth floor) he glanced toward the window, put on his best startled face, and took off running down the hallway of our apartment with me in close and screaming pursuit. We didn't stop until we reached Morningside Park. Years later, when my grandfather came to live with us after the hauling business failed, I discovered that the older man had even scarier stories not about huge bunnies but the very Wrath of God. At least God didn't come jumping through the walls.

Mama, on the other hand, told very nice stories. Her stories would sometimes include Shirley Temple, Bessie Smith, and an occasional princess whose man had done her wrong. Sometimes the handsome prince who saved them would be German. Clearly, the woman was civilized.

I went to school in the neighborhood. Most of the teachers were Irish, although a few were Jewish. The Irish had a reputation for not liking Colored children but for being eminently fair. My best friend turned out to be Eric Leonhardt, a German boy I met whose mother befriended my mother. Eric and I became fast friends for three reasons. First, he was as tall as I was and stood in line near me. Second, when I went to his father's bakery I was given chocolate chip cookies, a condition of friendship I still respect. The last reason for his friendship was that he taught me to masturbate. He was truly a wonderful kid.

My summers in Harlem, at least until I reached the age of thirteen, followed a pleasant, if somewhat rigid, pattern. Up in the morning at eight o'clock, breakfast, and off to Bible school from Monday to Friday and Sunday school on Sundays. Go home at noon and have lunch and then back to the street to play ball. We played stoopball for the championship of the entire world at least once a week. We didn't play stick-

Walter Myers, about age six

ball on our block but we played Chinese handball against the church wall.

As a child I learned to play basketball in the church basement. Everyone in the neighborhood had a flat jump shot because of the low ceiling in the church gym. I also went to dances in the gym where we were admonished to "leave enough room between you and the girl you are dancing with so that the Holy Ghost could pass through." When the lights were dimmed the Holy Ghost made quite a few detours.

We played sandlot ball on a lot on Morningside Avenue. A guy in our building, Mr. Reese, had a team called the Monarchs. They were a farm team of the Kansas City Monarchs of the old Negro League. Later Mr. Reese watched me pitch sandlot ball and asked if I wanted to try out for the team. I was big, and loved to play any kind of ball. The Negro League was in trouble, though; the majors were beginning to gobble up Black ballplayers.

We played basketball in the park. The younger kids would get to the park after Bible school (most of the kids in the neighborhood went to some kind of Bible school). If we got there before the big kids did and took all the courts, they would use a unique method of getting the courts back. They would simply walk onto the court, take our basketball, and throw it over the fence into the street. When we got big enough, we did the same thing. Basketball was serious, and rough. You weren't fouled unless you could prove it with *fresh* blood. Dried blood didn't count, you might have scratched yourself at home. If you were good you would visit other parks in lower West Harlem. Then, when you were really doing it, you'd go up to City College where they held the Rucker Tournament.

I never understood the source of my speech difficulty. I didn't hear anything unusual when I spoke. I knew what was in my mind but others apparently didn't understand what came out of my mouth. Other children used to laugh at the way I garbled my words. I used to fight children who laughed at me. As a result I found myself suspended from school a great deal. Although I enjoyed school, I found that I didn't always fit in.

But in the fifth grade a marvelous thing happened. I had been suspended for fighting in class and had to sit in the back of the class while I waited for my mother to appear. The teacher, known for her meanness, caught me reading a comic under the desk during a math lesson. The teacher decided that if I was going to read then I might as well have something decent to read. Later she brought to school a selection of books for younger people, and I was introduced to reading good books.

The teacher, Mrs. Conway, also instituted a new idea that appealed to me. She required that we read in front of the class. That was difficult with my speech problems. I would tense up badly, and my already poor speech would get even worse. Then she suggested that we could write something to read if we so desired. Oh, happy day! There were many words I could not, for the life of me, pronounce. Anything beginning with a *w* or an *r* gave me trouble, as did any word with an *sh* or *ch* sound in the middle. I began writing poems so that I could avoid the words that I could not pronounce.

When my friend Eric began going to parties to which I was not invited, I discovered that life was not as simple as had seemed. We had been friends for a long time. We had been noticing girls and he had taught me all I needed to know about the opposite sex. We had even selected girls that we were "in love" with. He picked a German girl and I picked a Black girl. It was Eric's suggestion that we not tell the girls so that they wouldn't get stuck on themselves, when they discovered their incredible luck.

But as Eric moved into social situations and I was not invited, it was awkward for both of us. For Eric it

meant either becoming a racial crusader or concealing his activities from me. For me it meant either accepting my role as his "colored" friend or rejection of his friendship altogether. Later in life I could have made other choices; at the time I chose to avoid Eric.

By that time I had been duly classified as a bright child, and had been through an accelerated junior high school program. I assumed I would go to college and eventually take my rightful place in the world of bright, influential people. But as I neared the end of my junior year in high school, I saw that going to college would be financially impossible. I also began to recognize that my "rightful place" might be defined more by my race than my abilities. I became depressed, disillusioned. What was the use of being bright if that "brightness" didn't lead me where I wanted to go. I stopped going to school, at least on a regular basis. I began to read even more than the several books a week I had been reading. The books became an escape from a world I felt had rejected me. I was just fifteen.

But if fifteen was bad sixteen was an absolute disaster. At sixteen I was writing poems about death, despair, and doom. I felt my life was falling apart, that I had no control over my destiny. I had won a minor prize in an essay contest; I also won a set of encyclopedias for a long narrative poem. But my family didn't seem to think it was a big deal. I was from a family of laborers, and the idea of writing stories or essays was far removed from their experience. Writing had no practical value for a Black child. These minor victories did not bolster my ego. Instead, they convinced me that even though I was bright, even though I might have some talent, I was still defined by factors other than my ability.

I imagine that every adolescent faces a similar problem. We exist in several worlds simultaneously. As young people we hear that there is a world in which all sorts of wonderful things are possible. In that world, we are told that we are limited only by our willingness to work hard. Somewhere in grammar school, I began to suspect that wasn't entirely true. The people in the "good world" of the movies and the books were all wealthy, attractive, and white. That was not my world. I was poor, considered myself quite homely, and I was Black. I remember going downtown, to Fifty-seventh Street, and looking at the people in wonder. Wasn't *this* the real world that people were talking about? But in the books I read there were no Blacks. And on television there were no Blacks that were not being ridiculed. Where was my place?

I saw that some people had a far better time of it than others. The handsome child, the gifted child, seemed to do better than others. To this list of "special" people I soon added the child favored by luck—who is liked by a teacher or whose parents were well-off.

We begin to compromise our ideals as we see that they exist in a more and more abstract plane. Sometimes, when the ideal seems completely unattainable, we abandon it altogether. That is a defense mechanism: we excuse ourselves from achieving what we once considered worthwhile for us as human beings. A youngster is not trained to want to be a gasoline station attendant or a clerk in some obscure office. We are taught to want to be lawyers and doctors and accountants—these professions that are given value. When the compromise comes, as it does early in Harlem to many children, it comes hard.

I said I wanted to be a lawyer. Not that I had any idea of what a lawyer did, but one had to become something. A friend of the family had the "kindness" to dismiss the idea of my ever being a lawyer because of my poor speech. I remember standing in my aunt's apartment next to an iron, marble-eyed alligator, and thanking this man for ruining my life. I'm sure that if it hadn't been for his conversation I would have taken up law, or at least made the attempt.

Having been dissuaded from law, I decided that I would become a scientist. However, New York's Stuyvesant High School convinced me that I did not want to be a scientist. I had no interest in chemistry, a mild interest at best in physics, and not more than a passing interest in math.

I worked part-time for a costume jewelry concern on Thirty-fourth Street. There was a girl who worked there named Lavinia, the same name as a girl in T. S. Eliot's *Cocktail Party*, which I read as I packed jewelry into small boxes to be mailed around the country. I fell in love with Eliot's girl. The real girl scared me to death. I fell in lust with her. What I remembered best about that job was imagining how Lavinia would look naked, and being humiliated when I took packages to the post office.

I ran into the real world at the post office.

"Man, what you got that book in your hands for?" This from a man with a handkerchief tied around his head, sweat dripping from muscular arms, the smell of wine on his breath. "You ain't nothin' but another nigger, just like me."

These were the people I most identified with, that I was forced to identify with, and it depressed me. I have always felt, since that time, that young Black people must have role models with which they can identify. And although I understood that the job was just an after-school, part-time position, I feared that it was a harbinger of things to come for me. I had been working to buy a typewriter. I quit as soon as I thought I

had sufficient money because I didn't want to associate with the people I was meeting at the post office. On the day I quit I bought a used book, Whit and Hallie Burnett's *World's Best*. The most interesting discovery I made in that book was Gabriela Mistral.

It turned out that I didn't have enough to buy the typewriter after all. My father interceded and bought me a used Royal office machine. I was bitterly disappointed. I soon reconciled myself to the use of the machine and began writing my stories on it. I kept it nearly ten years, pounding out hundreds of stories.

The idea of not going to college continued to bother me no end. Most of the Black men in my building, indeed, most of the Black men that I knew, had menial jobs. But even this traumatic realization took a backseat to my impending death.

I ran into trouble with one of the local street gangs. I had intervened in a fight between three gang members and a new kid in the neighborhood, chasing off the gang members. Then my brother, who had come to New York and lived around the corner from me, caught one of the gang members who had snatched a woman's pocketbook. The culprit received six months in a youth home and it was roundly announced in the neighborhood that the gang was going to kill me.

A short time after I quit the job on Thirty-fourth Street, I encountered one of the gang members. Thanks to a stiletto which I could open with the flick of a wrist, he found out quickly that I wouldn't be *that* easy to kill. I don't know that the gang would have actually killed me, but I did appreciate the possibility. I came close to finding out once when I let my attention wander. I was sitting in a tree in Morningside Park, across from the apartment building in which I lived, reading *Mourning Becomes Electra*, O'Neill's interesting play.

"Hey, there's that guy we gotta kill!" was the cry from below me.

I looked down and saw two members of the gang. I pulled out my stiletto, jumped to the ground, and took a swipe at one of them. He retreated just far enough for me to make a mad dash across Morningside Avenue. The other gang members, seeing what was going on, came flying across the street after me. Once I hit my building I knew I would be safe. No gang would go in the building after you. The logistics were just wrong. You could go up the narrow staircases and hold off an army unless they had a gun. Apparently, they didn't; I got away.

I "hung out" with a guy I'll call Tom. He was the son of a famous Black tap dancer. Tom was a good friend, a year older than me but shorter. He had the dubious distinction of being the only one I knew who had actually killed people. He had killed a bus driver in one incident, and two other people who had insulted his mother in another. Both of these were during periods in which Tom had "blacked out." Otherwise he was a pussycat. I used to read poetry to him while he drank beer in the park. Sometimes he would sing to me in what I remember now as a pretty good voice. Tom got involved in being a drug courier for a while and we both were involved in other activities that weren't exactly kosher.

My parents were quite troubled by my behavior. I had been a fairly good boy till then, but I changed quickly. I was steeped in the mystique of the semi-hoodlum. I think I imagined myself as François Villon, and actually looked forward to going to jail. Thank God I hadn't discovered Genet yet. My mother found out that I was skipping school when someone from the office called her. It was decided that I was "disturbed."

Around this time I thought about becoming a writer. Not as a profession; I still didn't know that people wrote for money. I was having doubts about everything in my life, including what had been till then a fairly deep religious conviction. When I discovered *Portrait of the Artist as a Young Man* I knew that I was not alone. If Joyce had these doubts, too, and he was a writer, well—I would also become a writer. I stumbled through *Ulysses,* and carried *Finnegans Wake* around for several weeks before surrendering. I read all the Balzac the George Bruce Branch of the New York Public Library had. I read Zola's *Nana* several times, usually under the covers.

I began to write short stories. A teacher in Stuyvesant, I remember her name as Bonnie Liebow, had called me aside and said that I was a gifted writer. Could that really mean something in my life? I wrote every day. When I was supposed to be in school I would go instead to Central Park, climb a tree, and write or read until it was time to go home.

Ms. Liebow made up a reading list for me. I still remember most of the titles—*Buddenbrooks, Père Goriot, Penguin Island,* and something by Zola. I fantasized about marrying her.

I read the poems of Rupert Brooke and suddenly it came to me what I had to do. I would hie myself off to some far-off battlefield and get killed. There, where I fell, would be a little piece of Harlem. At seventeen I joined the army. I didn't tell my parents that I had joined until the morning I left.

My mother cried. My father, at a complete loss to understand my actions, gave me his blessings.

In the army I went to radio-repair school and learned nothing about radio repair. I spent most of my

Myers, age seventeen, just home from basic training

time in the service playing basketball. I also learned several efficient ways of killing human beings. And, with images from poets like Byron and Brooke and Spender rather loosely in mind, I was ready to do battle with anyone. Oddly enough, I spent my three years in the army on a strictly vegetarian diet.

But the army did allow me some room to mature. A veteran at twenty, I returned to civilian life and to my parents, who were living by then in Morristown, New Jersey.

Whatever to do with myself in Morristown? Not much. I still didn't know who the hell I was supposed to be. I had a series of affairs with older women, trying to determine once and for all my masculinity (at least!). I found a job in a factory and I read a great deal. Gide's *Journals* come to mind, and Nietzsche, and Sartre. Camus was not as interesting as all that. Langston Hughes' translation of Gabriela Mistral was terrible. Morristown was dreadful; I decided to return to New York.

I remembered Harlem as a great place. Full of lively, warm people, most of whom meant you nothing but good. The gang that had chased me about just three years before was dissolved with most of its members in jail or dead. But something else happened in my absence. Drugs had come to Harlem in a big way.

I moved to the Cort Hotel on Forty-eighth Street in New York City. I shared a room with a lively family of cockroaches. I paid thirteen dollars a week for the room. I assumed the roaches had their own arrangement. That was my starving-artist period. I even went home to Morristown and got my copy of Schiller's life to make sure I was doing it well. I read Gide's *Immoralist,* Orwell's *Down and Out in London and Paris,* and others by Corydon, Juan Ramón Jiménez, and Lorca. I wrote bad poems.

I didn't start writing again in earnest—and by that I mean every day—until I was married and working in the post office, unloading the mail chute. I had married a wonderful, warm, beautiful, religious, caring woman named Joyce. She reminded me somewhat of Dylan Thomas's wife, Caitlin, because she felt my running about in the East Village was symptomatic of an evil neglect rather than an activity she chose not to participate in. It took me years to understand that there actually are people who don't share my passions.

I was fired from the Post Office. Then I worked for a while as an inter-office messenger and office boy, and later I was a clerk/interviewer in a factory.

Meanwhile, we had a daughter, Karen, and then a son, Michael Dean. When I had arguments with my wife, I'd take Karen to the bars.

Joyce liked music and I thought she would be happy when I began to play percussion instruments with friends. It was foolish of me, of course. She was home with the babies and I was off with my bongos. The "music" became more and more a matter of just plain noise as the drug usage in the group grew. Some of the people playing with us from time to time were "skin popping," injecting heroin just under the skin;

Michael Dean Myers, "a very tough one-year-old"

others were using cocaine in serious quantities. We told ourselves that we were heavy, though.

I tried writing jazz-based poetry, some of which was published in Canada. I felt that poetry was too personal, too restricting for me. Of course, it was my highly personalized poetry (which was then in vogue) that was the problem.

I was published in Black magazines such as *The Liberator,* and *Negro Digest.* I wrote for men's adventure and girlie magazines. I also drank too much and ran around too much.

I got a job as an interviewer with the State of New York.

I decided that what I wanted to do with myself was to become a writer and live what I imagined would be the life of the writer, whatever that might be. The marriage suffered and dissolved under the strain of my radically different life style.

I moved to the Lower East Side. I changed jobs as well, taking a position as a senior editor for the Bobbs-Merrill Publishing Company.

When I entered a contest for picture book writers it was more because I wanted to write *anything* than because I wanted to write a picture book. Somehow, I won the contest.

The book, *Where Does the Day Go?,* won the contest sponsored by the Council on Interracial Books for Chil-

Karen Elaine Myers, age three

dren. It was published by Parents Magazine Press. I had no particular interest in writing for young people. But I tried several more picture books and sold two of them for publication—*The Dancers,* and *Fly, Jimmy, Fly.* For the second book I changed my name from the one I was given, Walter Milton Myers, to one that would honor my foster parents, Walter Dean Myers.

I remarried, determined not to make the same mistakes I had during my first marital encounter. Joyce knew me as a person in the throes of emotional and artistic growth; Connie had the advantage of knowing me when I was much surer of who I was, both as a person and as a writer.

I was playing flute with street musicians in Marrakesh when Connie's sudden illness signalled the pending arrival of our son Christopher. Chris turned out to be very much like his older brother. They are both tall, Michael is six-four at twenty-two, and Chris is five-three at ten. They are both highly introspective, and both rather gentle. Karen, on the other hand, is outgoing and bolder than either of the boys. Perhaps I should have taken them to the bars, too. Chris now wants to travel to the same European cities I visited with Michael. Chris hasn't been to Rome or London yet but he has been up the Amazon, the Nile, and the canals of Thailand.

Christopher and a Quechua Indian, "somewhere up the Amazon"

Myers with Christopher, 1977

My mistakes with Connie have been absolutely new. She, however, is more forgiving of the mistakes. Middle age is also more forgiving. Or, perhaps, Connie is just biding her time. I understand women do that kind of thing.

I wrote for men's magazines until they gave themselves up to pornography. I also wrote for the *Sunday News Magazine, McCall's, Alfred Hitchcock,* and other magazines. Like other Black writers before me, I was faced with a dilemma: I had more successful writing for a white audience than writing for a Black audience.

At a party given by my agent, Harriet Wasserman, I met an editor named Linda Zuckerman. I wasn't particularly comfortable at the party—I'm never comfortable with strangers—but she looked as if she wouldn't hurt me, so I talked to her. She had read a story of mine that Harriet had given her and she had liked it very much. Then and there we made plans to publish, *Fast Sam, Cool Clyde, and Stuff.*

It was my first young adult novel and I wondered where my writing career was headed. I was writing humor in *Fast Sam. . .* something that comes to me

Myers with Michael at the Coliseum in Rome

fairly easily. I was also writing about the positive side of my Harlem experience, which most of it was.

In my next young adult novel, *Mojo and the Russians,* I wrote about my aunt, who had been a marriage broker. She once married off my cousin Sterling to a Black Brazilian woman. The relationship between my American cousin and this strange woman didn't last too long before Sterling's attentions began to meander. The woman put a pot on the stove, boiled up a blend of spices and herbs, and dropped his picture into it. He became ill and quickly mended his evil ways. Apparently, the only people interested in Mojo, or Voodoo, outside of the practitioners, are the Russians. They used to send their people to Harlem to talk to the shopkeepers who sold the multicolored candles, roots, and charms. I added them to the book.

Any career, if it is to be successful, demands constant reassessment. As a Black writer I had to assess not only *where* I was in my career, but *who* I was. What historical position was I meant to fill?

I recognized, as all writers must, that man is not a singular entity. We are all many people, depending on whom we are dealing with, and who we happen to be on a particular day and in a particular circumstance. At various times, we play the role of parent, boss, employee, child, martyr, or hero. But usually we are not called upon to identify ourselves at any given moment. As a writer, however, I am constantly asked to identify myself.

I learned something from the experience of other writers—like Frank Yerby, a superb Black writer. His early short stories are excellent examples of Black literature. Yerby soon discovered that his writing was boxed in by his race. He was expected to write of the Black condition (Write what you know!) but there were, and are, few market opportunities for the Black writer. Most of the popular magazines treat the Black story as a "special category." No one will announce this openly, but it is true nevertheless. A magazine with a predominantly White audience may well publish a story with Black characters, but will not consider another story with a Black theme or Black characters for the next year and a half. And there is no guarantee that a story will be published even if it is considered.

Furthermore, it is much easier for a White writer to publish a theme about a Black than it is for a Black to publish a story about a Black. The reason is simple enough. The story by the White writer is more likely to take a White point of view which coincides with that of the magazine's projected readership. This is also true in children's literature.

Where, then, did I fit in as a Black writer? How good a writer was I? If I wrote "what I knew best" and reached only a limited market, how could I progress as a writer? There are still no easy answers. Many young Black writers become discouraged and stop writing. I felt like quitting many times when I was younger.

A writer who has little hope of publication usually cannot put enough effort into the work to polish it sufficiently. I found myself dashing off stories and not working on them as much as I should have. There were a few Black magazines around and, more important, virtually no Black editors. For whom was I writing? Writing workshops helped a great deal. I joined John O. Killens' workshop at Columbia University. Nikki Giovanni was a member, as was Wesley Brown, author of *Tragic Magic,* George Davis, author of the fine Vietnam novel *Coming Home,* and the poet Askia Touré. I still yearned for more public success. A writer needs publication in the same way that a swimmer needs water. If you're not going to be published you might as well be a bad writer.

When Frank Yerby faced the same problem, he began to write romantic fiction which had nothing to do with the Black experience. He became an instant success. His books, like *The Golden Hawk,* were published with ships and bosomy ladies on the covers but no pictures of the author.

Was that to be my route? I had already published in the few Black magazines around. Hoyt Fuller, editor-in-chief of *Black World,* wrote that he liked my work very much but was limited in how much of it he could publish. I had also published a number of short stories in men's magazines which did not deal with the Black experience. On one level I could deal with both markets. But realistically I had to admit that the Black market was tiny compared to the huge White market. Furthermore, the need to publish was forcing my attention on the markets and away from my craft. The craft suffered.

Langston Hughes decided, in his later years, to write for White magazines under an assumed name. His agent felt compelled to discourage that. Although the agent claimed that Hughes was too good a writer to go that route, I suspect the agent hesitated to risk his business connections by palming off a Black author, no matter how good, on an unsuspecting magazine.

During the early sixties very few Black authors were being published. That changed in the mid- and late sixties. Blacks were in the news. There were riots in Watts and Detroit, speeches by Malcolm X and Martin Luther King, Jr., and a seemingly endless stream of tragic assassinations. Predictably, as our visibility increased, so did our marketability—tremendously. Less violent but equally newsworthy conditions had flourished during the twenties, the heyday of Black American literature.

The Harlem Renaissance of the twenties was marked by the formation of the NAACP, the flourishing of Marcus Garvey's back-to-Africa movement, and Black protests against lynchings in the South. It saw the emergence of such figures as Langston Hughes, Jean Toomer, Zora Neale Hurston, Richard Wright, Claude McKay, and Countee Cullen. The difference between that period and the Harlem Renaissance of the sixties and the seventies was that in the twenties Whites came to where the Blacks were and learned who was doing what. In the sixties and seventies Whites stayed downtown and waited for Blacks to come to them. Too many of the Blacks published during this period were simply people adept at self-promotion. That, too, should have been expected, since it wasn't the literature that attracted the publishers, but the marketability.

I still wanted to write about satin Black men who carried razors, and old men who carried dreams, and hard young girls in red dresses who tossed their wide hips as they pleased. But where would I publish?

I was hired as an editor—because the publisher, Bobbs-Merrill, wanted a Black editor. I had no experience editing and more than a little reluctance to take the job. I did take it, at Killens' prompting, and found myself in the heart of the publishing world at Fifty-seventh and Fifth Avenue.

I had this enormous desk, in this enormous office, and a blue-eyed, blonde secretary who kept popping into my office, asking me if I need anything.

"Would you like coffee?" she asked.

"No, thank you," I would respond.

She was very nice and told me as much as she could about the job. It was an interesting job, especially the lunches. I soon learned to take a writer or an agent to lunch and spend enough money to feed a family of four for an entire week. I also learned the book business from another viewpoint.

Publishing is a business. It is not a cultural institution. It has no pretensions of "fairness," or "equality." It is *talked* about as if it were a large cultural organization with several branches. One hears pronouncements like "Anything worthwhile will eventually be published." Nonsense, of course. Books are published for many reasons, the chief of which is profit. Occasionally an editor can slip in a book on "merit" alone, but the occasions are few and far between. As conglomerates eat up the book business, the occasions will be even farther apart.

Part of an editor's job is to recommend that the publisher buy a book, or commission an author to write a book. My first book contract was with Nikki Giovanni, the poet. I had met Nikki at Columbia and had liked her. *Gemini* was Giovanni's first book of prose. Later I published Ann Allen Shockley, Richard Perry, Jonathan Bramwell, and many other writers, White and Black. I learned that selecting books for publication was far from an exact process. There were fewer discussions concerning the relative quality of a particular book than how many copies a certain bookstore chain would accept. Works by Black authors were referred to by the sales force as "Black books," no matter what the subject, and sold accordingly.

My reading suffered during that period. It's hard to read anything more than the manuscripts you have to consider for publication when you're an editor. But I read a lot of Tillich, some Jaspers, some of the new radical theology. I recalled my feelings about religion when I was in Harlem. I seemed to be drifting back emotionally to those times. I had studied dance at the Church of the Master's afterschool program. Later, the church had become the home of the Dance Theater of Harlem. Once, when I was sitting in Geoffrey Holder's house trying to convince him to do a book on dance for Bobbs-Merrill, I realized that I wanted him to do it because dance took me back to another place and time. Later when, as an editor, I bought a book on the life of Josephine Baker, I remembered meeting her, too, at the church, many years before.

Generally, publishing was a good experience for me. After the initial disillusionment about the artistic aspects of the job, I realized how foolish I had been in not learning, as a writer, more about the business aspects of my craft.

Some friends had told me that I tended to intellectualize my characters when I was writing what I considered to be "serious" fiction. I discounted that until I saw, as an editor, that books with that tendency found a much smaller audience than books with more rounded characters. It didn't take me long to realize that I tended to compartmentalize social relationships according to neat intellectual concepts and my writing sometimes reflected that tendency. I examined my past work carefully and found this to be true, and that my most successful pieces involved a directly sensual approach. My writing improved.

I was also gaining an awareness of the Black image in literature, film, and television. The image was disturbing. Blacks were portrayed as nonserious people. Perhaps we were sports figures, or hustlers, or comedians, but we were still nonserious. Remembering my own childhood, I realized what an effect that had on the Black child. I hadn't been aware of feelings of inadequacy, or the derivation of those feelings, when I was a child. But I could see that I did feel inadequate as a Black person. Everyone presented to me when I was a child—presidents, inventors, writers, composers—had been White. The only Black people on television were Amos and Andy, uneducated buffoons. In the seventies the situation had changed very little. For the White child the heroes on the highest plane were astronauts, statesmen, and scientists. For the Black child it was still the popular musician and the athlete. We were still entertainers, still nonserious. There were also subtle messages which, though not racist in my opinion, still had a negative effect on Black children. The message was that even the best of the Blacks were somehow fatally flawed.

George Jefferson, a Black businessman, on TV's *The Jeffersons,* was portrayed as a clown despite the fact that he was supposed to be a very successful businessman, astute enough to have acquired seven stores. His business dealings on the show, however, rank in the same category as those of Amos and Andy. The successful Black in motion pictures was often the pimp or the dope pusher.

The same problem is evident in many books written for young people. Books like *Jake and Honeybunch Go to Heaven* show what are apparently good people—they do get to heaven. But the illustrations and the stories are reminiscent of a period long past when it was acceptable to portray Blacks as people interested mostly in playing music and having barbecues. The book only adds to the literature of Blacks as vaguely clownish people. Another book, *Words by Heart,* is the story of the poor Black girl who is "rescued" from the meanies by the intervention of the kindly White woman. Blacks suggested that there were Black characters in the story who would have taken more interest in the girl; the message was that it took a White woman to recognize and act upon the plight of the girl. Both of these books were met by protests from Blacks and both received awards from White organizations.

Racism? I think not. I believe that both these books were well intended; their authors presented the usual liberal views of Blacks. They suffered, however, from two circumstances. The first is that there are so few books about the lives of Blacks that every book published is asked to do too much, to be more representative than any one book should be. The second circumstance is that there has been so much negative material published about Blacks that anything that is not overwhelmingly positive in all areas can be viewed as negative. Thus it is often impossible to simply have fun with Black characters. A Black Laurel and Hardy simply wouldn't work.

And so I have come to understand one of my roles, newly found and cautiously approached, but there nevertheless. As my books for teenagers gained in popularity I sensed that my soul-searching for my place in the artistic world was taking on an added dimension. As a Black writer I had not only the personal desire to find myself, but the obligation to use my abilities to fill a void.

I was fired from my job as an editor in 1977. I was crushed. Being fired was terrible. No matter how impersonal they try to make it seem it still feels as if you're being singled out as the resident leper. The company was going through a number of changes and heads were rolling left and right. I had signed up a number of books by Black authors and on Black subjects. That, to some extent, I felt didn't help my cause very much. At least, sales figures on the books didn't help my cause any.

I was under contract to Viking to write a book at the time and that gave me some consolation. I finished the book and then went to Hong Kong to sulk. I'm good at sulking.

In Hong Kong my wife and I discussed the possibility of my not looking for another job. By the time we reached Bangkok I was a full-time writer. Nervous, but a full-time writer.

Back in New York we started looking for a larger place. I needed three bedrooms. A master bedroom, one for my two boys, and one to convert into an office. The rents in New York are absurdly high, so I considered moving out of the city. I also considered buying one of the old buildings put up for sale by the City of New York. I went to see some of the buildings and saw that some were little more than deserted shells, while others had tenants but were terribly run-down. The prices were cheap, some going for as little as twenty-five dollars. But what good was a building for twenty-five dollars if it would take fifty thousand dollars to make it livable?

I wondered what would happen, though, if teenagers bought such a building. This idea turned into my next book, *The Young Landlords.* The book turned out to be a humorous piece which found a paperback market, was optioned several times by Norman Lear, and eventually made into a film by Topol Productions.

I've been fortunate as a writer for young people. My books have done reasonably well, I've sold them at a great rate, and I've been able to support myself and my family on the proceeds. I'm not at all sure that I've hit upon my final destination, I suspect not.

I have a younger brother, Horace, who teaches in the New York City school system. When he asked me to come and speak to his class, I realized how few resources are available for Black youngsters to open the world to them. I feel the need to show them the possibilities that exist for them that were never revealed to me as a youngster; possibilities that did not even exist for me then. I've taught Black literature and creative writing and I enjoyed working with high-school kids in the classroom. As much time as I spend alone, as I've always spent alone, I enjoy being with people immensely.

"The Martinsburg Gang": from left, Gertrude, George, Imogene, Ethel, Gerry, and Viola,
"with Walter bringing up the rear. Missing from those of us born in Martinsburg
is Douglas."

Herbert, Chris, Michael, and Walter Dean, in Morristown, New Jersey

Two years ago I spent several months interviewing people who were or have been in state and federal prisons. I accumulated over five hundred pages of interviews with thieves, muggers, murderers, and addicts. I looked for the reasons that they had become what they were, while I had become a writer. Perhaps the ultimate reason was that I had acquired the strengths to turn away from disaster. Sometimes the turning away was a last minute decision, but nevertheless it worked. I was fascinated to see how similar my background was to some of the prisoners' to whom I talked. I'm still not sure what I will do with the interviews.

As a writer there are many issues I would like to tackle. I am interested in loneliness, in our attempts to escape reality through the use of drugs or through our own psychological machinations. I am interested in how we deal with each other, both sexually and in other ways, and the reasons we so often reject each other.

As a Black writer I want to talk about my people. I want to tell the reader about an old Black man I knew who told me he was God. I want to tell a reader how a blind man feels when he hears that he is not wanted because he is Black. I want to tell Black children about their humanity and about their history and how to grease their legs so the ash won't show and how to braid their hair so it's easy to comb on frosty winter mornings.

The books come. They pour from me at a great rate. I can't see how any writer can ever stop. There is always one more story to tell, one more person whose life needs to be held up to the sun.

I try not to make too much of my writing. My grandfather told stories, my father told stories, and that is what I do. Because I have published mine does not make me better than those who have gone before me. It makes the stories special that they are in print, and that is good.

I don't know if I have accomplished very much because I don't know yet what I want from life, or even what life has to offer. The older I get the more I think of being with people I love, and who love me, rather than recognition. But there are times when I see someone reading one of my books, or when I get a letter from some person who has read a story or book of mine, and it makes me feel so good it hurts.

I remember sitting on the floor in my parents' apartment in Harlem. I was about thirteen, maybe fourteen, at the time. We had a railroad apartment and there was linoleum on the floor in the living room. I remember sitting on the floor, the sunlight through the fire escape bars casting shadows across the *Sunday New York Times Book Review.* I read the reviews and had an idea that this writing, this talking about books and reading books was as much the stuff of life as anything. I think I was right.

BIBLIOGRAPHY

FOR CHILDREN

Fiction:

Where Does the Day Go? (illustrated by Leo Carty). New York: Parents Magazine Press, 1969.

The Dancers (illustrated by Anne Rockwell). New York: Parents Magazine Press, 1972.

The Dragon Takes a Wife (illustrated by Ann Grifalconi). Indianapolis, Ind.: Bobbs-Merrill, 1972.

Fly, Jimmy, Fly! (illustrated by Moneta Barnett). New York: Putnam, 1974.

Fast Sam, Cool Clyde, and Stuff. New York: Viking, 1975.

Brainstorm (photographs by Chuck Freedman). New York: F. Watts, 1977.

Mojo and the Russians. New York: Viking, 1977.

Victory for Jamie. New York: Scholastic Book Services, 1977.

It Ain't All for Nothin'. New York: Viking, 1978.

The Young Landlords. New York: Viking, 1979.

The Black Pearl and the Ghost; or, One Mystery after Another (illustrated by Robert Quackenbush). New York: Viking, 1980.

The Golden Serpent (illustrated by Alice and Martin Provensen). New York: Viking, 1980.

Hoops. New York: Delacorte, 1981.

The Legend of Tarik. New York: Viking, 1981.

Won't Know Till I Get There. New York: Viking, 1982.

The Nicholas Factor. New York: Viking, 1983.

Tales of a Dead King. New York: Morrow, 1983.

Motown and Didi: A Love Story. New York: Viking/Kestrel, 1984.

Mr. Monkey and the Gotcha Bird (illustrated by Leslie Morrill). New York: Delacorte, 1984.

The Outside Shot. New York: Delacorte, 1984.

Nonfiction

The World of Work: A Guide to Choosing a Career. Indianapolis, Ind.: Bobbs-Merrill, 1975.

Social Welfare. New York: F. Watts, 1976.

Emily Cheney Neville

1919–

Emily Cheney Neville

I started writing this autobiography in a little blue notebook in my lap on a packed train going through the People's Republic of China. That was in February 1985, and China was the farthest I had ever been from home, or from my birthplace in South Manchester, Connecticut, a silk-mill town. I am

sixty-five years old, a lawyer, the author of six novels for young people and a new book for small children to be published in 1986. I was born the youngest of seven children and grew up among many cousins, and I am the mother of five children. I cannot live without reading, and writing and walking around, sometimes quite a distance.

The occasion of my trip to China and Siberia was my son-in-law's one-year appointment as an exchange professor teaching English literature at Beijing (Peking) University, known as Beida for short. He and my daughter Tam and six-year-old granddaughter lived in Shao Yuan House, the foreign experts' apartments at Beida; and February was their vacation month, when they could travel to see more of China. Their presence in China provided a once in a lifetime opportunity for me to see China with friendly companions but no tour group.

My real reasons for making the trip go far back of the opportunity. Partly, the reasons are in books—the hours I spent in adolescence with Pearl Buck, as an adult with Barbara Tuchman's *Stilwell*, with Farley Mowat, George Kennan (the elder), and the Russians themselves, Tolstoy, Dostoevsky, and Chekhov. From reading, I cannot doubt that these people and Americans are made of the same bone and soul, and I want to see, hear, and touch for myself. I want to know from my own senses that the rantings are false that claim these people are not like us, hardly human, perverse peoples with no sense of good and evil.

On a much less lofty level, I took the trip because my life at home was in a rut. Most of the last twenty years, I have lived in Keene Valley, New York, a tiny summer-and-ski village in the Adirondacks. In the last ten years, my life had filled up with a law practice which seemed somewhat useless, inefficient, and unprofitable, and with the meetings and agenda of countless community groups. It was high time to shake loose, not for a quick vacation, but for a good long change of pace and place. I packed the essentials for about three months into two cases that I could carry myself, because all my life I've been pretty set on doing it all by myself. In China it turned out this was a very wise preparation—all Chinese trains, busses, and cities are crowded, and most everyone's carrying what they own. After six months of furious letter writing to China and to travel agents and dickering for visas and tickets, I arrived in Hong Kong and met my youngest son, Alec, who had got himself there on business.

Three days later, we made our first error, or stroke of genius—we failed to make reservations for the good through-train to Guangzhou (Canton). Reservations are needed for almost all Chinese trains. In sign language and Chinese the railway official indicated, Take local, walk over bridge to China. We agreed, happy that we didn't have to wait around all day. We couldn't have had a better introduction to China than that local and that bridge. Thousands of Chinese massed themselves in a series of funnels, first Emigration from Hong Kong Territory; then Immigration into China; then Health, Money, Tickets. Each was a separate assault by thousands of us, all carrying our burdens for a hundred yards or so between each gate and, midway, across a small arched bridge over a muddy creek. That was the border. The Chinese have extraordinary ability to push, to carry, and to be pushed without getting angry. For many of them the trip was long sought (only permitted in the last couple of years), perhaps a once in a lifetime project, to get back into mainland China to see lost families. They carried a few clothes, bedrolls, food, and maybe a flowering plant. Alec and I, the only English-speaking people I saw on that train, carried our tourist bags and thought, Are we really doing this? When we actually got tickets and could board the train, both the Chinese and we, the tourists, let out a whoop of joy. We'd made it!

I cannot detour this brief autobiography very far into a travel journal. Enough to say that China on your own, not in a tour group, is quite possible, but vigorous. We walked a lot or crammed ourselves onto the city busses, not too certain where they were going, through five cities and (best of all) one small village. We bicycled, boated, ate, drank beer, waited, and read. Sightseeing was included—the Great Wall, Summer Palace, Forbidden City—but what I wanted and got was just being there, seeing people. I saw none who were unfriendly to us. Among all those millions of people on crowded streets and vehicles, I only saw two family arguments, between either parents or children. I never saw a drunk, or a beggar, or anyone sleeping in a doorway. I saw very few who were frail or crippled or disabled. The air is terrible for breathing, from truck and bus exhaust and coal fires, and I coughed and breathed through my mouth for most of two months.

My best day in China (everyone who goes has one) was the day I spent finding and visiting the China Children's Publishing Company. I had written to them from back in Keene Valley and had got a reply, signed "Editor for Literary Works," with no name. There was an address written in Western letters. I got a student at Beida to put the address into Chinese characters, so that I could show it to people on my way as I searched. He also wrote down the proper avenues and bus numbers, but still I searched and bussed and walked for an hour or two. Finally a solid middle-aged Chinese interrupted his "sacred" lunch in his office to walk out to the sidewalk and draw me a little diagram, indicating one avenue and two lanes: Turn left, *there*. I did so, and followed the numbers down the lane from 82 till I came to 23, an apartment building. Three old men sat smoking their pipes in the gatehouse and were quite astonished to see a big Western woman. They directed me to the next gatekeeper, who offered me his chair and got on his phone for reinforcements.

A young woman appeared who spoke halting but correct English. She also was astonished to see me. After we'd talked a few minutes, she smiled widely and said, "I never speak English before. I never hear anyone speak English. Is first time!" I was a gift from beyond, an English speaker. She was also astonished because no one had ever arrived at that office before without exact arrangements being made through the proper offices. Chinese do not just drop in and certainly do not expect Westerners.

She led me up four flights in the apartment building, and there in two rooms was the China Children's Publishing Company, its editor, its Party representative, and an editor from next door who spoke fluent English. What, he asked politely and a little embarrassed, did I want? I said I just wanted to see what books they published for children and to talk about it. I didn't want to sell my book (which I showed them) or buy theirs. Soon the questions began to fly back and forth, theirs and mine, as we talked about authors and their royalties in America, and their salaries and the hard-to-enter writers' association in China, and I probed politely on the matter of the International Copyright. They said that would come, but they also said they sell their children's paperback novels for less than fifty cents, in order that children can buy them. We made some sly little jokes about how publishers can interfere with authors, and the Party functionary smiled, too.

My stomach rumbled—I had left Beida before eight, and it was now 2:00 P.M. Chinese never skip lunch, and magically the young lady appeared with a large enamel basin of *jiaozi*, dumplings stuffed with ginger and cabbage, to be dipped in hot soy sauce and accompanied by much tea. We felt very festive—it was an event in all our lives. On my way back down Dongsi Lane with its old one-story brick houses, I stopped at the community outhouse, where three old ladies were laughing and chattering. I went to put down my pocketbook, and a lady shook her hand (the Chinese sign for no) and indicated the hook on the wall. Theft is unthinkable, but in a toilet house you don't put things *down,* you put them *up,* where it's clean.

My best days in Siberia were several days on the Trans-Siberian train. Between Irkutsk and Novosibirsk, the friendly lady train-car attendant insisted on applying mustard plasters to my chest and wrapping me in blankets, to remedy my Chinese cough. Then we sat and "talked," passing back and forth the dictionary in the back of Berlitz's *Say It in Russian.* We found out all about each other's families and living places.

For the five days from Novosibirsk to Khabarovsk, I shared a compartment with a quiet Russian lady of about forty, who had one shopping bag for her food and one for her good clothes, to wear when she got off the train. On the train, we wore almost identical brown corduroys. She was on her way to the Far East because her brother had died. Generally we ate together in the compartment, from her well-chosen supplies, my few snacks, and what I bought at station stops or from the train attendants. She gave me a little history at different stops and was very worried when I dallied too long at a station and had to jump onto the slowly moving train. (People in both China and Russia seem to feel *responsible* for others, in a way that is unfamiliar to Americans.) We read our books together or dozed, companionably silent; she had a book of Russian poetry, a revolutionary novel, and a biography of a nineteenth-century philosopher.

Perhaps it is only on a train that a Russian and an American could spend five low-key, restful days together. Her English was self-taught and adequate. Her trip across Russia and Siberia cost her only about $40, since she was an employee of the railway newspaper. My ticket was about $200. She said she'd like to visit America, but she knew she could never do it—too expensive.

Siberians were well dressed and rather formal. Everyone wore overcoats, fur or fur-trimmed hats, knee boots, and women all wore skirts. The Chinese dressed in a variety of jackets and pants, some Mao style but more not. In both countries people make or have made most of their clothes; what I saw on the streets was consistently better than what was shown in department stores. Stores were crowded with both goods and people, but the people mostly looked, compared, and waited. A purchase is a big decision. Most of life goes on with what is already at home, in the way of dry goods, clothes, and staple groceries. The atmosphere of life is very different from America (or Japan) in that there is no continuous assault by advertising to buy this model, or that, or a dozen of these.

I don't know how to reset my cheap digital watch, so it stayed on New York time, and when I was in Novosibirsk that was again the right time (12 hours difference). The farthest I'll ever be from home, the other side of the globe—what a place to run out of books to read! It's hard to carry enough books in two bags that you're determined to carry yourself. I had wedged in four long ones: a Trollope, a Dreiser, a George Eliot, and Paul Scott's last volume of *The Raj Quartet;* and for my granddaughter, by request, two volumes of Laura Ingalls Wilder. My most vivid early memories tend to be pegged by what book was being read to me, and thereafter by the book I was reading myself. As I traveled through China and Siberia, musing about what Chinese and Russians thought was the right way to think and act and be, and how to manage the money, there on the seat beside me was Dreiser's *Financier* and George Eliot's *Felix Holt.* They were wondering about the same things, in nineteenth-century England and America. Especially the money.

I had almost finished both books and was looking at five days and nights on the train, when I found an oasis in Novosibirsk, a bookstore with a section of English books. Most were standard English and American classics for Russian students, but Progress Publishers also publishes some contemporary Soviet fiction. *Siberian Short Stories* was my favorite, together with *A Man in His Prime,* by Z. Skujins, a sort of Latvian-Soviet Man in the Gray Flannel Suit. Neither is an epic, but they're good reading, well written.

In wartime, or if trapped in any way, I have no doubt that we American democrats and Eastern communists will be capable of acting with unspeakable inhumanity. But as you read the literature, you cannot doubt that both our authors and theirs probe what it means to be human, how people love and hate, what honesty between people means in different circumstances, how self-worth grows out of work, and how money—which was perhaps intended as a mere measure—confuses and confounds human loyalties.

As detours will, this one got longer than I intended, but it was while I was on this trip that I started to look back at my own life and to put it on paper. There was the first day, December 28, 1919, and babyhood which I don't remember, followed by childhood and youth vividly remembered, and three years of newspaper work. That brought me up to age twenty-five and the final end of childhood. During the middle years, I was a mother, wife, and writer of children's books, and then for ten years a law student and lawyer. When you start to draw Social Security, you have to admit you're old; so here I am, living in a little town that my great grandfather, Horace Bushnell, one of the "climbing clerics" of the Adirondacks, discovered for my family back in the 1850s, and I can say I'm old.

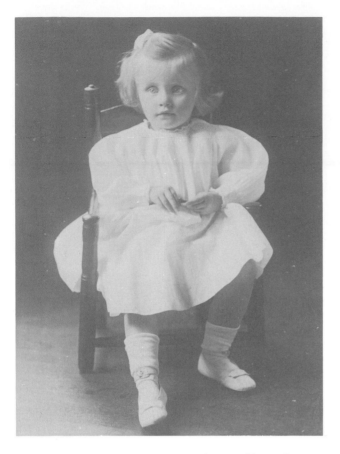

Emily, age two, holding Father's gold watch

Family home in South Manchester, Connecticut

When I was born, my mother, who was a Christian Scientist, did not go to a hospital, and the story goes that my father called a doctor friend who was a psychiatrist. His presence at my birth accounted for a lot, Father said. I hear the echoes: "Emily, sit *down!* Don't fidget so!" And at school: "Emily could be a good student, if she would learn to concentrate." The earliest picture I have shows me dressed in my best, about two years old, sitting quiet and prettily. But the only way they could get me to sit still was to let me hold Father's gold watch.

I was the ninth baby born at home to my mother. Seven of us grew to adulthood, and five of us are living still, ages sixty-five to eighty-three. Most of us were born in the brick house on the Cheney Place in South Manchester, Connecticut. The Place was like a golf course—green, mowed, fragrant or snow covered, and laced with curving red-dirt roads connecting a dozen or more Cheney houses. Father and Mother built theirs about 1899, soon after their marriage. Father had seven brothers, four sisters, and eleven first cousins, most of them living on the Place in Manchester, and

many working for the family Cheney Silk Mills. You can see now why it is natural for me to be family-centered, and why many of my good friends are cousins. That family childhood is almost a stronger bond than any later friendships from college or work.

My father worked at the mill, first as boss of the ribbon mill, later as head of a network of paternalistic labor relations and services. The mill whistle blew at seven o'clock, and we woke up. It blew at noon, and soon Father came home to lunch. He came home after the five o'clock whistle and soon he could read us a story. Uncle Remus was his favorite. My sister Mary and I liked the story too, but we liked especially the moment when Father's voice trailed off into a drone and he fell asleep, then jerked up his head and continued reading.

Superficially at least, the relationship between my parents and me was nothing like that of any of the family groups in my books. My father and mother were both forty-nine when I was born and so from the start they were almost in the position of grandparents. I wasn't conscious of this, as my best-friend cousins were also the youngest child of *their* middle-aged parents and, like me, had grown-up brothers or sisters. I assumed this was the ordinary family. We also all had nurses, cooks, or maids intervening between us and our parents.

I think of my father and mother as moving continuously through my childhood years, but mainly out of sight and out of my mind, reappearing as figures of authority, benign but absolute, and occasionally as providers of a treat. I picture my mother dressed always in pale gray-green dresses with white at the V-neck, cool and distant as a forest tree. She was slender and fairly tall, the same height as my father, who was pinkly roundfaced and chubby. I remember him coming to our nursery supper-table one afternoon, red-faced and sweating from playing golf, and putting down on the table a tiny turtle he had found on the course, kissing me wetly and departing with a grin but no words. I remember going quietly past the nurse's door and down the long, long dark hall to my mother's bed in the middle of the night, because of a leg cramp. I whimpered and pulled at her sheet, and she mistook me for the dog and said, "Down, Jump, get down."

On the one miraculous occasion when I alone went on a trip with my parents, to Charleston, South Carolina, there was another leg-cramp night, and Mother sat and rubbed off and on all night. In Keene Valley, where we went in the summer (again always in the same house), Mother and Father took us swimming in brooks, picnicked and climbed mountains with us. But we were returned to our keeper for early supper and bedtime. Evening family life could go on without us downstairs.

While I resented being shunted away, something more complex and important happened in those nurseries, Keene Valley or Manchester. I had a third parent, the pillar of my life between the ages of about five and nine, Mrs. Goodall, a governess. The word governess itself now seems as antique as the wimple, but Mrs. Goodall herself was solid. She was English, in her fifties at least, and she believed in authority. She also had a great need to love and be loved by children. She observed instantly that Mary and I had many shrewd forms of bad behavior which had routed a succession of prior governesses, and she let us know that such behavior was now at a stop. Right now. This established, she took us to ponds for skating, hills for sliding, lanes to pick fringed gentian; she helped me with my chickens and goats, and taught me to read and write and sew. She read aloud every evening or rainy day. The best were the books of E. Nesbit, especially *Oswald Bastable and Others,* coupled in my mind with *An Island Story: A Child's History of England,* by H. E. Marshall. The two kinds of books went together, humorous fiction and history, and I attained a second childhood home, in England. Many later inhabitants came into this world: *Children of the New Forest, Tom Brown's Schooldays, Bob, Son of Battle, Greyfriars' Bobby, Men of Iron, Otto of the Silver Hand, Little Lord Fauntleroy,* and *Merrylips.* The list could go on forever, most being books I eventually read to myself, but Mrs. Goodall always read, too. Mary and I often tried to grab the book she had been reading to read another chapter by flashlight under the covers. We had such harmless sins.

Perhaps next in importance to books in my childhood was food. I didn't like it. At lunch in the family dining room, I ate almost nothing. I hated all vegetables, except maybe beets; I hated potatoes, creamed codfish I positively could not swallow, and I didn't much like milk. Frequently, I could get Mother, Father, and Mrs. Goodall into a three-way scolding session which distressed all of them, and led to my being sent from the table. This was most satisfactory. I could snuggle in my bed, with or without a book, and I could always steal sugar lumps later when I got hungry. Mary and I ate supper upstairs while Mrs. Goodall had her tea, and that was a good meal—hot milk or cocoa, toast and jam, applesauce and friendly conversation. Jump, my dog, lay under the table, and crust

Family summer house in Keene Valley, New York as painted by a guest in 1902

corners could be sneaked to him. Breakfast was all right, too, once the amount of sugar for the cereal was settled. It was only dinner in the dining room that was full of bad flavors and bad vibrations. On my unhealthy diet, I had colds most of every winter. Cod liver oil in a thick molasses base was administered by Mother, and hot-mustard footbaths by Mrs. Goodall. I survived both the colds and the cures.

From the list of books, one can see that I liked dogs and boys. I didn't just like them—as a small child, I intended to *be* a dog; later, to *be* a boy. In my first written epic, of which four pages survive, I wrote in the first person the story of Jump and his arrival in Manchester:

> At last a little girl ran out with fair hair, blue eyes and a nose that turned up slightly. I didn't like the turn-up nose, but I thought she had a kindly eye. Her first question was, who did I belong to. She was to be my fucher Mistress.

I worked much harder on trying to become a boy. Whenever possible, I wore pants and insisted that they be real boy's pants, and I had my hair cut short. I wished to be not only a boy, but a knight or page. When I was decked out in a silk dress with a frilly

Mary and Emily Cheney, age ten and eight, with Emily "clutching her sword"

collar for my older sister's wedding and had to pose for the photographer, I clutched the side of my silk dress in a bunch. At least *I* knew that that was my sword, and that I was only in disguise as a girl. Of all my books, my favorite was Beulah Marie Dix's *Merrylips,* and I reread it every year until I was well into high school. Merrylips goes through the English Wars of the Roses—disguised as a boy.

Aside from books and avoiding food, a large part of my life was lived outdoors, in company with two boys who were cousins and our various animals. Teddy, who lived next door, had rabbits, so I got rabbits. Then I also got chickens and kept laborious notebooks of profit and loss, in pennies. On a long bicycle ride or a walk with Mrs. Goodall, I discovered a goat farm, and soon I got a baby goat. She was returned to the farm for the summer while we were in Keene Valley. Next winter, I noticed that she was rather fat, though I sometimes forgot to feed her. One winter night, she gave birth to a kid, which died, on one of those days that I had forgotten her. I felt very guilty. It was also the very first time that a birth had happened in my life, and at age ten I had no idea how it happened, or that it could be predicted.

My sister Mary had matured very early, when she was ten and I was eight. One day she was mysteriously kept in bed, in the little room down the hall, not our nursery double room. When she went in the bathroom, she locked the door. Mrs. Goodall was jealous and angry that Mary was removed from her care, and no one would explain to me what was going on. No adult ever did, as it turned out. I got an inkling that it was something to do with becoming a woman, and I simply

Emily, age eight, with Jump

Emily with goat, about 1927

became more determined to become a boy, so that it shouldn't happen to me. Probably because of my skimpy eating habits, nothing did happen till much later, when I was past thirteen. Other girls and an older cousin told me what to do about it, and it was years and years after that before I ever saw the word "menstruation" written in a book or magazine. I did wonder why no heroines in books were troubled by this problem.

I knew in the back of my head that governesses were not forever, and of course Mrs. Goodall knew it, too. However, a governess was supposed to nurture the child's first love and loyalty to the parents, never to act as if she wanted the child's love herself. As for me, I just avoided letting that question of whom I loved best, Mother or Mrs. Goodall, sneak into my head. Practically speaking, there could be little question: I was *with* Mrs. Goodall from first shoelace to last goodnight, with Mother only at intervals.

On a summer day, in the Pierce-Arrow driven by Joe, the chauffeur, we went to visit my oldest sister and her new baby, the first grandchild. On the way, Mother announced, "You're growing up now." This made me feel good, and I listened attentively. "When we go home," Mother went on, "Mrs. Goodall will be leaving. You're old enough to take care of yourselves, now." As the car rolled along, all was serene. Mother left no space for protests or tears. I knew something was terribly wrong, but I was not able to name it.

When we got home, Mrs. Goodall was at her most brisk and British. There were no little pats or smiles, and love did not seem to exist. We got through supper and baths, pretending life was normal. We got in our beds. I could hear the mumble of Mrs. Goodall's voice down the hall, saying goodnight to Mary. Finally she came into my room, swooped like an eagle to kiss me on the cheek, said goodnight in a voice tight with anger, and was gone. I no longer had a third parent.

The memory and the loss remain, but childhood does not stick in one bad hole, and my life went on after Mrs. Goodall's departure quite happily. Perhaps from this I assume that the preadolescent years are happy for most children. They were for me, because at last I was in charge of my child life. I could read, swim, bicycle all over town, and telephone or just wander out the door to meet the cousins who were my constant and only playmates. The older cousins were now the authorities, sometimes bossy, but still firmly part of the child world, a phalanx that did not ask help or tell tales to adults.

I had been to school with all of them for my first three years of schooling. Then, as the older cousins (and a few neighbors) went to high school or boarding schools, six of us younger ones went to school in, of all places, my house. My brother's piano was pushed into the corner, and the downstairs playroom became the school room for Mary and me, two boy cousins who had been my steady friends, and two other neighbors. With only one teacher, Mary and I did the same work, making me feel insufferably proud and bright.

The big school event occurred when I was ten and Mary twelve: we went to seventh grade in the public school. I was ecstatic, Mary was not. At last I could be one of a group of kids, I could have friends in the town. Until then, since my family owned the silk mills, we children were conspicuous. When I walked or bicycled down Main Street, I could feel or hear a whisper, "Cheneys." To complete my new identity, I insisted that Mother buy me some dresses at the local department store, not the made-to-order models she used to get from the Hartford dressmaker.

But I did wear dresses, and my new friends were all girls. That was revolutionary—at age ten, I had never before had a friend who was a girl. We bicycled together, I went home with them and they with me. We fired our slingshots, and I learned petty shoplifting. Before that, badness had consisted of stealing sugar lumps or ginger ale and reading under the covers at bedtime, but now chills of excitement ran down my back as I left a store with a stolen trinket, or as I fingered my cache of stolen goodies in a bottom drawer. Nothing I took was ever for actual use. After a few months, I stole a wooden necktie rack in the hardware store. It was too large to hide in a pocket, and I knew the hardware store men recognized me as I ran out of the store. I felt no more excitement, but real terror. What if they called Father? I couldn't think of it. I

The Cheney Family School: Emily (front row, second from left) and her sister Mary (second from right)

dropped the tie rack in the woods and gave up crime. (They never called Father.) I can still remember how my fingers yearned for that rack. At ten years old, and with friends who were girls, I was still working on becoming a boy.

There were two excursions with Mother, before she departed from my life. Though there are many things I remember about the trip to Charleston, South Carolina, the overwhelming one was simply that I, alone, was with my parents in a grown-up's place. Mary and I were both in bed with colds, when Mother came in and announced that I would go with them to the South. (Mary's cold was a single event, not a chronic condition, therefore not qualifying her for a trip.) I can't remember that I spent much time feeling sorry for Mary. I said I was sorry, and she did *not* say, That's all right. I've thought of it since, perhaps especially after my own children came and I realized how hard it is to do something with just one, how agonized a left-behind sibling feels. Off I went to the hotel country club in Charleston. There were no other children there, and I played backgammon with grown-ups. I ordered anything I wanted from the menu, everything with a French name, just to find out what it was, and no one nagged me to eat it all.

The last excursion with Mother took place in May when I was eleven. Of her own accord, Mother proposed that she would take us for a Saturday picnic at Marlborough Lake, where many Cheney families jointly owned a camp. The key was always kept in the black walnut desk in the living room with a brass tag on it that said Howell Cheney. Mary and I both liked to hold it as the car bumped up the dirt road to the camp. On this day in May, Mary asked first to hold the key.

Mother patted her pockets and said, "Oh, I must have forgotten it." We knew that was a joke. Mother didn't forget things. When we arrived at the camp, Joe waited for Mother to hand him the key. She went all through her handbag and pockets and finally admitted it—she really had forgotten the key. We walked over to a pasture with a brook and picnicked on the grass, and Mary and I built dams in the brook.

The next day, Mother was "not feeling well." It was the only day I ever remember her not coming down to breakfast. We went to her door and whispered good morning and goodnight that day, but I never really saw her again. She had pneumonia and refused for several days to have a doctor, or even to go to the hospital. She died at home within the week.

I did not grieve, and that worried me. Children in books were always devastated by the death of a parent. They moaned and sobbed and couldn't talk or eat. In our house, life went on, on the surface, as usual, and everyone talked about Mother all the time. It was my first inkling that some of my favorite books told untruths, emotionally speaking.

My mother's death occurred when I was eleven, and so that event marks a definitive end of childhood. The following years of adolescence would have had their distresses anyway, but I remember acutely the bewilderment and confusion of those first summers. We were supposed to be "good" and take care of ourselves, but there was nothing to do and no one in charge. The cook and maid and chauffeur, who had been our friends, were fighting among themselves. In Keene Valley I had no friends beside my sister, and no idea how to make any. There were kids around the swimming pool, but I didn't know how to become one of them. I had no idea how to call someone up and make a date.

I took refuge inside my head, where I was an entirely different person, living a whole other life. I remember people constantly wanting me to pay attention to something here, but I was walking around somewhere else, and the effort of jerking back to reality was wearisome. I lay around a lot, reading or doing nothing. I have no memory now of where those places were that I lived in my head, but they were concrete, and they were full of conversations. Long afterward, I found Jean Stafford's *Boston Adventure,* which described expertly what I remember, as the boy in her book kept having to switch back and forth between his two worlds, interrupting himself in mid-sentence. At the time, the stories in my head obsessed me, but I also knew there was something wrong with this, and I worried that I was not sane. I rushed to do something—swim, tennis, climb, anything—though activity didn't really help.

All this is associated in my mind almost entirely with summers, either in Keene Valley or Manchester. My ardent seventh-grade friendships faded away when, the following year, Father sent Mary and me to a girls' day school in Hartford. As the Depression came on, we spent more summers in Manchester, hot, bored, and lonely. Since we have all grown up, I've talked to my older brothers and sisters, and they share the same sense of a lack of friends in childhood. The Cheney cousin club was valuable, but it wasn't everything.

In 1931 when Mother died, the Depression closed tightly around Cheney Brothers, and most of its family executives had to leave the business. Father had never worked anywhere else. Without a job, and without Mother, his whole familiar world appeared to be vanishing. For one year, Mary and I traveled in and out to Hartford with cousins, and then Mary was sent off to boarding school. The next winter, for the first time in my life, I felt protective toward another human being, my father. We had our arguments, over when I could stay with new friends in Hartford, but in my bones I knew he shouldn't be left alone in the evening. Sometimes we sat, the two of us, eating dinner in the big dining room and saying nothing, but I knew I had to be there.

Father got a temporary job in Hartford, and slowly his world began to re-form. Our most cheerful and companionable times were spent in the car. Conservative, rational, and disciplined in all else, Father associated the automobile with adventure. He liked buying cars, driving them, and teaching his children to drive. He had taught me on the dirt road in Keene Valley as soon as I could reach the clutch and brake and see through (not over) the wheel. Now he let me drive occasionally on our commuting trips in and out to Hartford and on weekend excursions. He paid little attention to motor vehicle rules—he passed cars when *he* deemed it safe and convenient, and he let me drive when he felt sleepy. We had adventurous trips when the Connecticut River was in flood, and we went fifty miles upstream to find a high bridge. When Mary came home from boarding school on vacation and couldn't distinguish a Ford from a Chevy from a Buick, I was amazed. These were the important facts of life.

The bewildering double life of summer dropped away from me when school began. Before starting at Oxford in Hartford, I had my tonsils out and spent two nights in the hospital, a not wholly unpleasant event. School was totally satisfactory, full of sports, books, and friends. There were about ten new eighth graders that year, and we were in our own room; a tight group of comrades. At lunchtime, I observed that other girls ate, even with enthusiasm, and I began trying food. It wasn't bad, and nobody said I had to eat it. I got healthier. I had a minimum of trouble with clothes, manners, and boys (unlike my sister at boarding school, who was miserable because of all three). Other girls, who had grown up with radios in their homes, hummed popular tunes like "Night and Day" and sometimes talked about boys and parties. But I and my close friends were busy with field hockey, basketball, bicycling, learning to drive, reading books, and doing school work. I saw myself in print: two stories in the school magazine, one a fable about a camel, and the other about a girl who visited her strange old uncle. The girl in the story, who had gone out on a date, was sketched satirically, and the sympathetic character was the old man, immersed in his work and the thoughts inside his head.

Dates with boys were no part of my high-school life. I, who had spent childhood trying to become a boy, found young men daunting. I didn't know how to talk to them, and my first juicy kiss disgusted me and made me feel evil. I had no conscious desire in those years to be either feminine or masculine, just to be me. My body was not so easily satisfied, and it produced in my head masochistic fantasies involving either men or women. It wasn't until ten years later, when sex became a regular and satisfying part of my life, that the fantasies departed and I realized what had caused them.

As for the difficulty with talking to men, I made the discovery so many teenagers do, that talk came more easily after a couple of drinks. Rather surprisingly, in that New England background that sounds so staid and sheltered, my older brothers and sisters gave me cocktails from the time I was thirteen or so, and there was alcohol in the punch at our proper holiday dances in Hartford. Looking back, I wonder—how else could we have stood them? It was formal dancing, sweaty cheek-to-cheek, waiting desperately for a boy to cut in, so as not to be trapped forever with one partner. I knew none of the boys, never saw them at an easy, informal occasion.

At sixteen, I went off to Bryn Mawr College, both because I wanted to, and because there was nothing else I could possibly do. Teenage babysitting for pay hadn't been invented, and girls from good schools with good marks didn't waitress or work in the five-and-ten. My older sisters had gone to college, and all my family and my teachers headed me in that direction. What advice I got was to study broadly, to stretch my mind, and not to worry about a job. In fact, in those still-Depression days, we all rather assumed that a job would be enormously difficult to get.

College for me, in 1936, was definitely a step into a bigger and freer world than the Cheney Place or Hartford. (I think the reverse is now true for kids who go from high-flying suburban high-school life to a college dormitory. They find it unbearably confined, or so raucous that it's unlivable.) At last, I was living with a bunch of people my own age, with minimal adult interference, and on the whole I loved it. I majored in economics and history, and spent a good deal of time on the college magazine and newspaper. The extracurricular activity eventually turned into my first vocation, but the interest in history has continued—my current reading includes a book on medieval usury, a biography of Mao, as well as new fiction. The college friends have lasted all my life. Whether I see them or not, they are *there*, part of my life. In the final week of senior year, I wept openly because I thought I had failed an economics exam, and a few days later enjoyed myself enormously giving a hammed-up speech on the steps of Taylor Hall, an experience in public speaking that was not to be repeated for twenty-five years.

Emily, age sixteen, high school graduation

I graduated from college not knowing what I wanted to be. I knew I wanted to go to New York City and live without being directed by parent or teacher. I applied for jobs as an economic researcher and as a newspaper errand boy, and the latter came through first. I had a letter of introduction to the publisher of the *Daily News*, and he saw that the oncoming war would siphon off his copyboys, so he decided to be first in hiring a copy*girl*.

My first lodging in the Big City was a boarding house with bedbugs on East Thirty-sixth Street. About my third day at work, my fellow copyboys took a brotherly look at the welts on my forehead and told me how to check for bedbugs. I did, and set out to hunt an apartment. To hunt one's own place to live, what a revolutionary activity, for me who had always lived in the same family house! A series of apartments followed, with a series of girls as roommates. Rooming with the opposite sex would have been a highly unconventional activity. I had dates, but even if it was dawn, I came home. As World War II continued, my roommates disappeared one by one to get married, follow a husband to an Army camp, or to work in Washington.

I carried copy for a year at the *Daily News*, a vast private bureaucracy in which promotion was years away. I quit and got a job at the neighboring, and competing, *Daily Mirror*, a place of personalities, tempers, cliques, sex, and talent. Looking back, I'd have to say I got the job on the basis of sex—a young editor thought it would be fun to have the "blonde bomber" flying about the office. While the copyboys at the *News* had been brotherly, even protective, the boys at the *Mirror* were not. When I got a promotion ahead of another copyboy, he dropped the rumor that I was really a divorced countess. That did it—the wolves gathered. However, they also got drafted, and after a year or so I moved into writing the "Only Human" column, a daily profile. My life eddied back and forth between two shores: the excitement of learning to write (and photograph) and turn out a column every day, and the miseries of dealing with one or another pursuing male and thinking myself desperately in love with some. There is a myth that girls love the feeling of being pursued. It *is* a myth; they don't, or I didn't. Everyday I went out to lunch alone and thought of quitting. Then I had a beer and decided to go back to work.

Glenn later said that he saw me fleeing through the city room, where he was night city-editor, but it

Glenn T. Neville, editor of the Daily Mirror

cannot be said that I saw him until he came, as chief editorial writer, to the small feature room, 602B, where I worked. As I filed his name and address that first day, I thought regretfully, he's married. (It was well known that everyone who lived in Queens was married.) He walked up and down our long hall whistling and singing and bouncing on the balls of his feet, the way he walked all his life. He smiled at me, and it was a pleasant smile, not wolfish. Pretty soon he asked me to have a drink after work, and pretty soon that became a daily event. The drinks became a vehicle for talking, something we both needed. Since he was married, we both assumed nothing more was involved. After a few months, there came a Primary Day, and the bars were closed, and Glenn came home with me for the usual drinks, and he kissed me goodnight. It was most of a year after that before we slept together, and many months more before I was pregnant. Things ripened slowly, as I believe for many of us they have to.

I quit the *Mirror* in June 1944, and went to Colorado to stay with friends of Glenn's, Frank Mechau, an artist, and his wife and four children. The whole Mechau family, and the whole Rocky Mountains, seemed to support me and my swelling stomach. I loved being pregnant, then and four more times. It's the only work I've ever been able to do without effort, the only times at which the body needed no directions from the brain. I didn't even have colds when I was pregnant. I wrote pages and pages of letters to Glenn, and more pages of stories that never got published. I hadn't told my family that I was pregnant, just that I was taking a vacation. I luxuriated in being part of the Mechau family, so unlike my own. They were warm and openly affectionate, and we discussed love and war, sex and giving birth, music and art, all together, children and grownups. When I went back to that house in Redstone, Colorado, twenty years later, I felt as if it were a childhood home.

Glenn came out to Colorado in August, and we returned to New York City to live together in my little apartment, to have our baby, and to tell my father. The latter seemed to me the greater hazard. Characteristically, I wrote him a terse letter, telling him the essential facts without emotion. Glenn was rather appalled at my letter. Unrealistically, back in my bookish fantasies, I pictured my father being distraught at the news of an illegitimate child. I forgot all that I knew about my real life father, who in fact got on the phone and said he would come to New York the next day and see us at noon.

Then seventy-three, he came up our three flights of stairs, puffing a little. Glenn arrived, puffing a good deal more, having run the six blocks from the *Mirror* office. We all looked at each other and smiled and

Glenn H. Neville with his grandfather, Howell Cheney

kissed and said, Well. There wasn't a whole lot to talk about, except the practicalities of where and when the baby would be born, and where we would live. After lunch, Father winked at me and said he didn't intend to omit his traditional "look here a minute" with a prospective new family member, and he arranged to meet Glenn alone for lunch the following day. On that occasion he told Glenn, "If you don't love Emily, you can leave right now and don't worry, we'll take care of her." Glenn said he was staying, and from then on he and Father got along very well. They shared a love for me, for Keene Valley, and they both leaned to conservative politics and found my politics childish or incomprehensible. (Earlier in our relationship, Glenn had once declared that William Randolph Hearst was a great man, and I had burst into tears.)

Since that day some forty years ago, I have repeatedly found that children miscalculate their parents' ability to absorb bad news without falling apart. Most of the disasters have been pre-thought, lived through in imagination, in the dark hours of some worrying night. When the thing actually happens, it's something like hearing the second shoe drop, and the parent simply starts taking the appropriate actions. Father's only real concern, after making sure Glenn had an income and we had a place to live, was that there should be "no more false pride or secrecy about this

baby." So, when our baby Tam was a month or two old, he held a Cheney christening party. Several cousins whispered to me that they weren't sure whether to wear their wedding or their funeral faces and clothes, but they all came and all had a good time. It is probably worth noting, for those who grew up in the forties, that I never really encountered any embarrassment over my unmarried state. In December of 1948, a few months before our third child was born, Glenn and I were formally married. By then, Father said he realized it hardly mattered, as he knew we were committed to each other.

The main difference between my experiences as a mother and that of most of my earlier friends was that I always lived in the city. My babies started making friends as soon as they could walk, and I made at least two lifelong friends among other mothers, as we all sat in the parks day after day, first Beekman Place, then Stuyvesant Park, then Gramercy. We exchanged children each day it was too rainy or cold to go out, or if one of us was sick, and we fumbled and grumbled through the problems of children in the big public schools.

When I had three children below school age, I did indeed sometimes feel trapped, and there came into our lives a lady who had a name but was always known simply as Mademoiselle. She was sixty-five when I first knew her, and slowly she got older. She was instantly devoted to each baby in turn and jealous of me, the mother. It was evident to her that I knew nothing about raising children (true), that I had too few rules and too little patience, and that if she were not there to

The Neville children: from left, Tam, Glenn, Dessie, Marcy, and Alec

Neville (seated left), with Newbery Medal award, 1964. Ursula Nordstrom, her editor, is standing on the right. Seated in the center is that year's Caldecott Award winner, Maurice Sendak.

protect and direct them, my children would never survive. She was a very different person from Mrs. Goodall, and I was looking at her from a different perspective, but there was a reassuring continuity.

I started writing regularly about 1961, when my youngest child started school. Before that I had made erratic attempts at a story or an essay, but nothing was published. Fooling around one day on a cranky old typewriter with sticking keys and no return lever, I started being a boy arguing with his father. They argued about cats and dogs, or teenage music, or haircuts, or any other old thing. I had never written in the first person before, and it was fun, wonderfully freeing, just to *be* someone else, finally to *be* a boy in a way that came naturally, in writing. That experiment grew into a story, "Cat and I," which was published in the *Sunday Mirror*. (I sent it in without telling my husband or making any reference to him. I was still New England and stubborn, determined to do it all myself.)

I sent some picture-book stories to Harper and Row, and I met Ursula Nordstrom. The picture-book stories were never published, but Ursula looked at the cat story and said, "Why don't you try making this into a book? I'm so sick of manuscripts starting, 'Gold! the cry went up.'" At that time there were practically no contemporary books about boys in the city, and it

was well accepted that children didn't like books told in the first person. I didn't know that, so I went ahead. With Ursula's tender loving editing, her urging me to keep going, the story grew into *It's Like This, Cat.* The day I signed the contract and knew it was actually going to be a book was the big day of my life. Getting published is the difference between writing and being an author. When the book won the Newbery Medal for 1964, I went into a new excitement, which lasted into the American Library Association convention that summer. Glenn and I and our youngest son went, and Ursula held all our hands. I made my speech before the convention and discovered again that having a crowd respond to my words was heady stuff.

In order to write the book, I had taken its hero, Dave, and his cat to all the places in New York City that I had trudged around with my children. The details of the city are accurate, and so are the details of my characters' language, clothes, food, and friends, which pretty much came from my children and their friends. However, the emotions and characteristics of the people in my books are not my children's.

Young readers ask me where I get the ideas for my characters. Most of all, they come out of remembered childhood emotions and wants. Anyone who is reading this autobiography and has read my books will imme-

Neville speaking at the Manchester Library in Connecticut, with her husband and children looking on, 1964

diately say that the situations in my books are nothing at all like my own childhood. This is true. I probably write more often out of the felt lacks of my childhood than out of its actual events. But there are many bridges: when I described two boys fighting on the sidewalk in New York City, I remembered the tears of frustrations when I fought with my sister in our nursery room; Dave's attachment to his cat parallels my own attachment to my dog, and also grows out of the fact that my father hated cats and I never could have one. The funny portrait of Mary's beatnik mother in *Cat*, and of Sandra the girl-next-door in *Berries Goodman*, are both based directly on myself, parts of myself that I realize are absurd or unlikeable. The whole loving, argumentative but often silent, relationship between Dave and his father echoes my childhood with my father, and I have tried to create mothers who lasted and are *there*. The focus of all my books is how the child works out (or fails to work out) the relationship with the adults in his or her life.

As for me, I find it more difficult to write in this brief autobiography about my grown-up years. Perhaps that's why my books to date have been about children, and mainly for children.

The years between forty and forty-five were prob-

ably the most satisfactory years of my life. I had work I enjoyed and knew how to do; after that work, children to work or play with; food to cook and a husband to come home at night. Glenn didn't get home till seven or eight each evening, after the children had eaten their supper and were ready for bed. The two or three drinks we had started having each night at Benny's Bar near the *Mirror* continued as an every-evening event at home, virtually each night of our life together. Very occasionally, we had company or went out in the evening, but mainly our life was self-contained in the family.

They were very nearly ideal days, except for the fact that those evening drinks became almost our only idea for recreation and the goal of each day. We had many wonderful times together—writing, reading, fishing, having and sharing our children—but each event seemed to be aimed toward first-drink time. In 1963, Glenn had a mild stroke (in the summer, while reading *Little Women* for the first time) and was told to quit smoking and cut way back on drinking. For a year, I gave up drinking. I began to realize that we hardly knew how to talk to each other without that glass in the hand. The glass trap, even to those who do not become alcoholics, is that each drinker is two people, the original one, and the hazed-over one. What Glenn and I would have done and been with each other, if we had just been ourselves, I'll never know.

The easy days ended with Glenn's second stroke and death in June of 1965. The *Mirror* had gone out of business the year before, and after his first minor stroke we had spent the whole year in Keene Valley, hoping he would recover his strength. I didn't go back to New York City, because without a job to do there it seemed impractical and too expensive. I've missed it, and so at times have the children—they thought of it as home. The months of shock and grief at Glenn's death gradually moved into months of bewilderment. At my mother's death, I had had to establish an identity as a child. As an adult I hadn't really made decisions or thought who I was—certainly I never consciously planned to be a mother or a wife. Things had happened and carried me along. Now, without Glenn, I wasn't at all sure who I was, what I liked, or what I wanted to do. It went to things as trivial as wondering if I really wanted garlic in the stew. I'd always put it in, and it had seemed good, because he liked it. I'd loved going fishing, but it didn't seem worth doing alone. Why had we collected that set of Kipling, or all those stainless steel bowls? It was a long process, probably still going on, to find out who I was as a single middle-aged person.

I knew what I was doing writing books for children, and I didn't have to be "in the mood" to write. I've written best on some of the days when I felt worst. Each book seemed to take a little longer than the last, but I kept at it up until 1970. My books for young people are nothing like the books I read as a child. My own favorites were almost all heroic, and suspenseful. Courage and loyalty were their standard motifs. When I began to look at children's literature as an adult and an author, I began to see that heroes and villains are most useful in creating suspense, and also that teaching children to admire courage and loyalty teaches them to be obedient, a useful lesson from the adult perspective. (In real-life emergency situations, acts of courage are mainly performed by those who are trained: it is the skilled swimmer who saves the drowning child.) All of my own writing that I have liked has been rather loosely plotted, episodic rather than suspenseful; very conversational; and my characters tend to be individualists, not loyal team-players. A perceptive reader in St. Louis said he thought Cat was the character I admired most in that book.

A book I started, in about 1969, ground to a halt. My characters wouldn't talk properly, and the book would not go. In Keene Valley, I like the outdoors, the quiet, and the sparkling air, but sometimes humanity seems constricted. People look at the mountains and don't talk and wonder how to get out. I sprung myself out by talking the St. Louis city schools into hiring me

as "author in residence," since they already used *It's Like This, Cat* for eighth-grade reading. I worked in five or six different classrooms each day, getting children to write, and I enjoyed it enormously. I lived in a sparsely furnished apartment, the only place I've ever lived that I got just for me. I would have considered staying, but I knew of no other job I could get, I had a cold continuously, and it was too far from "home."

Out of that experience came my last book for young people, *Garden of Broken Glass*, not completed for several years. The plot, involving three black teenagers and one white, all of different families, gave me trouble, and so did the languages, black English and white English. When I came home from St. Louis, my workable house in the village was rented, and I prepared to live and work in the big old summer house, two rooms of which could be heated effectively. A young friend who was an artist needed a place for the winter also, and together we hauled wood and shoveled snow, and she painted and I worked on *Garden*. It didn't go well. I wondered what I'd do next winter—the friend would be moving out to get married. I couldn't live in this cold house alone, and I didn't know of anyone I wanted to live with. I looked at the pages in my typewriter, and there was Melvita, my strong, bouncing black girl, looking at the houses of the rich outside St. Louis and saying, "When I grow up, I goin to be there when they make the rules." It occurred to me that Dave's father in *Cat* was a lawyer, that my own father had had to leave law school because of illness, and that my hero in *Fogarty* was a law-school dropout. Personally, I hadn't thought of law school right after college, because I emphatically wanted no more schools right then. But what about now?

I didn't really make a decision. One blizzardy day, I sent for the LSAT application. I got a trial exam and did it for fun, the way one might do a puzzle. Just by a day or two, I was still in time for the February exam, the last date for those wanting admission in the fall of 1973. It'll never happen, I thought, and took the test. When it did happen, and Albany Law School admitted me, I went.

For three years I lived in Albany with an old college friend, and there I had a new identity: law student. It was hard for me to remember that, at fifty-three, I didn't look anything like the other members of the class. In a highly structured system, one assumes that all the pegs are alike. At the end of the first year, I had a grade point average of 64.54, which was just four-hundredths of a point from the flunk-out level. At the moment that I found that out, I was in New York City doing a final revision of *Garden*, which had been accepted by Delacorte. I kept writing.

I also went back to law school and, if for no other

reason, it was worth it as an experience in doing something I wasn't good at. I had never before come even close to flunking out of a school—I thought anyone could pass if they did the work. But in law school, I did the work, but I still didn't think like a lawyer. It gave me a whole new slant on the educational process, and a new real sympathy with children who can't hack school. By the strategy of electing courses that required a paper, not an exam, I managed to graduate. That thirteen-hour endurance test called the New York Bar exam consists mainly of written essay questions. My endurance was good, and way back at the *Mirror* I'd learned to write under pressure, and I passed.

Now, after eight years of law practice, I realize I will never really think like a lawyer. I think like a fiction writer. The actions and the conclusion emerge from the process of writing, of letting characters talk and seeing what they'll do. A lawyer must identify the goal at the start and plot strategies for reaching it through the complicated procedures of the law. I can do it, but not well. I've always made bread without measuring or keeping my finger in the reference book, but you can't practice law that way. I've always thought more about *why* people do things than *what* they do, but for a lawyer the whys are mostly irrelevant. It happened, and this is what you've got to do about it. Practicing law I have picked up many superficially interesting anecdotes and life stories, but few of them will ever appear in my fiction, because I didn't know any of those people well enough. I wasn't inside them, I was just trying to figure what they wanted from me. The writing that is associated with the law, motions and appeal briefs, also have nothing in common with fiction writing. A brief must be full of quoted

precedents; plagiarism is the soul of the law, and fresh new ways of saying something are not helpful.

The law has taught me something about how money, and rules, direct human activity. I didn't really know anything about that. Of course, I'd been short of money and altered plans to fit, but I'd never been aware of the pursuit of money as governing my activities. In my family-oriented life, including my life as a writer, I had seen the emotions of love, hate, vanity, jealousy, affection, protectiveness, and fear dominate people's actions. I had not realized that money is often the instrument, especially of vanity and fear, but of all emotions. In practicing law, I've seen how a minor change in a Social Services regulation (or even more, a Securities and Exchange rule) affects wave upon wave of human activity, far from the apparent sphere of that regulation.

More directly, however, money is the soul of the law. It is the substitute for brute force, the use of the fist or the gun to settle differences. Identify the difference, and measure it in dollars. In the lawyer's practice, money is the absolute measure of the value of what she does for clients, and for herself. As a lawyer, I don't have a product to sell like silk, or shoes, or carpentry skill; I sell my wits and the only measure of how good they are is money. I don't really like the hustle to get

Neville in Japan, 1985

Neville and friend, Hatsie Taylor, on a mountain top, 1985

good cases and to win them, and therefore I am easing out of the practice of law for a good lawyer's reason—I hardly more than break even. I enjoy talking to people about what might be called preventive law, how not to go to court, ever.

Meanwhile I'm writing again. I have two books for young children in the works now, some other things in the brewing stage. I realize there's no way I can live alone in a little rural village and have enough stirring in my head to write about. The trip to China was an eye opener, and I intend to leave home more often, though I certainly don't plan to become a continual tourist. My identity as a person is still growing, as whose isn't?

BIBLIOGRAPHY

FOR YOUNG ADULTS

Fiction:

It's Like This, Cat (illustrated by Emil Weiss). New York: Harper, 1963; London: Angus & Robertson, 1969.

Fogarty. New York: Harper, 1969.

Garden of Broken Glass. New York: Delacorte, 1975.

FOR CHILDREN

Fiction:

Berries Goodman. New York: Harper, 1965.

The Seventeenth-Street Gang (illustrated by Emily McCully). New York: Harper, 1966.

Traveller from a Small Kingdom (illustrated by George Mocniak). New York: Harper, 1968.

Richard Peck
1934–

Richard Peck, 1972

The neighborhood is any kid's first nation, and we lived on the border. It was the white frame house on the corner where Dennis Avenue ends at Fairview Park. I spent eighteen years growing up there.

To the north spread the park, a hundred and eighty-one acres of it. When it was laid out in the century before, it had been beyond the city limits of Decatur, Illinois, at the end of the tracks to give the streetcars a destination. Over the years it became a kind of catchall. Some of it was spiky with historic monuments and croquet courts. The rest was virgin timber threaded with dappled paths.

Early on, it had been the county fairgrounds with a race track where the Grand Army of the Republic, the national organization of Civil War veterans, was founded. Here my father's mother had been held up as a small child to be kissed by President Ulysses S. Grant. Over the years it was tamed to a city park. At some point a log cabin was dragged in and perched on a knoll. This was one of the original structures of the town, the first courthouse where Abraham Lincoln had served as a circuit-riding judge. It must have been much re-chinked, but it looked authentic, and the benches inside were rude and original. It smelled right too, with the cider-scent of old wood and early times.

Deeper into the park an amusement park had flourished briefly. This dwarf ancestor of Disney World featured a dance hall and a roller coaster descending into an artificial pond, called Dreamland Lake. We lived just over the hill from its smoothed-out remains, but my father who'd been a boy at the turn of the century remembered it in its glory days.

He recalled the strings of Japanese lanterns bobbing over Dreamland Lake and the swoop of the roller coaster. This alone confirmed me in what I already knew: that I'd been born after the party was over, that the present was no match for the past.

When we were eleven or twelve, my best friend, Chick Wolfe, and I set out to excavate the past. We figured we were too old to play, and so we became archeologists on a dig. The amusement park's old dance hall survived as a tennis clubhouse. The iron footbridge still arched over the little lake we called the duck pond. But where the roller coaster had risen was now brush and timber.

Chick and I went forth to find the pilings of the roller coaster, for proof. They were there. We didn't even have to dig, and so we sat on the crumbling concrete of these ancient monuments and tried to make our souls swoop. Since you couldn't go backward in time, I wondered if somewhere out beyond Decatur there was a world as exciting as a roller coaster.

Years later, out in the world, I wrote a novel called *Dreamland Lake.* In it two boys of a later generation, their minds fogged by the fantasies of television-watching, go excavating for the pilings of a vanished roller coaster. The story is a melodrama of being twelve, though no more my story than anybody else's. But the setting for it and the title are very real. I suppose that's what fiction is: what might be in settings that are.

In the other direction from our corner house, Dennis Avenue, a double row of bungalows and Dutch co-

lonial houses, stretched down to West Main Street. Chick Wolfe lived halfway down the block, so we were friends from our tricycle years because we didn't have to cross a major street to meet. Two doors down lived Jane Norris. She was older than I, and so she was my first adolescent.

Her youth culture was the one ahead of mine, a tremendous incentive for me to grow up in a hurry and achieve the complete maturity of a teenager. Jane, who was beautiful, wore cardigan sweaters back-to-front and carefully scuffed saddle shoes. The girls of her group came in teetering high heels to play bridge at parties in imitation of their mothers. The boys buzzed around the girls, driving vintage cars resurrected from the junkyard and restored as jalopies. All over their wire-wheeled Ford Model A's they wrote snappy sayings in howling colors, the forerunner of graffiti, but better spelled. Jane's generation drifted in a heady haze of jalopy fumes and Evening in Paris perfume as they paired off for dances at the Alhambra Ballroom and the country club. I sat in our yard, gaping at these terrific teens. Not only could they drive cars, they had someplace to go. They seemed like adults but better. Kinder than any adolescent can be expected to be, Jane put up with me. She had no pesky younger brother, and so I applied for the post.

Living next door between us were Mr. and Mrs. Daniels. They were country people retired to town. They sat on their porch swing, swinging, remembering old times and crowing over well-weathered jokes. Mr. Elmer Daniels was deaf, and so that made both of them clearly audible on the evening air. Through stifling summer nights I lay out on an old army cot on our front porch, listening to the Daniels reliving their past.

Except for my good companion, Chick, I couldn't get much interested in my own age group. They had neither the mobility of the jalopy-jockeying teenagers nor the mellow memories of the elders. It seemed to me that my generation didn't have much subject matter. With such a beginning, I might have been expected to grow up to write adolescent novels and historical fiction. I did.

In a neighborhood where other people's fathers went off to offices every morning in white collars and Plymouth sedans, my dad was apt to roar away astride a Harley-Davidson. Like the teenagers, he'd also gone scrounging in the junkyard and found an historic 1928 Packard coupe to drive to work. It was the size of a Sherman tank, but louder. It cornered like an aircraft carrier and had a rumble seat, and it loomed large among the Plymouth sedans.

Like any midwestern boy, my first romance was with the automobile. I sat on my dad's lap and pretended to steer the Packard while his hand rested on the lower rim of the wheel, the diamond in his Masonic ring glittering and giving him away. I learned words by naming the oncoming cars: DeSoto, Terraplane, Lincoln Zephyr, LaSalle, Oldsmobile Hydramatic—the streamlined poetry of progress.

Dad's Packard passed in time to the Tau Kappa Epsilon fraternity boys at the local college who were given to driving it along the railroad right-of-way. In the end, they were forced to abandon it on the Wabash tracks before an approaching locomotive. And so while the Packard by rights should be in a museum today, at least it died as it had lived.

My father, Wayne M. Peck, ran a Phillips 66 gas station in the other end of town. He conducted it like a club where elderly men—old truckers and farmers and railroaders—hung out, telling tales. Large, twelve-year-old boys rolled their newspapers at the station too, and so when I was way too young to be hearing it, I began to learn the uses of vocabulary.

The old-timers had honed their stories with years of retelling and flavored them with tobacco juice. The newspaper boys worked hard on their macho vocabulary and hoped to be believed. I was bombarded from both sides by the language of other generations, and from these rough tale-tellers I began to learn *style*.

My dad was easily the most identifiable man on Dennis Avenue. We weren't short of fathers either. There wasn't a broken home in sight, and a good many men came home for lunch. Elderly Mr. Daniels next door never left and spent the day swapping yarns with his wife. Still, my dad stood out.

He'd made his mark on the neighborhood early. When I was too young to know what was happening, he'd carved a jack-o'-lantern for me, or maybe for himself, one Halloween and planted it on the front porch.

It came to his attention that a couple of big, no-good boys were moving from shrub to shrub through our orderly neighborhood, knocking the pumpkins off porches. That gave my dad a splendid opportunity. In the kitchen he reached behind the refrigerator where he kept a twelve-gauge shotgun. Well armed, he crept quieter than any boy under the front porch behind a screen of spirea bushes.

Crashing through the underbrush, the two big louts approached. Just as they reached for the glowing pumpkin, my dad, six feet tall, rose up out of the spirea bush and squeezed off a round from the shotgun right over their heads. For years after, he wept with laughter at the memory of one of these galoots rocketing across the street and up a tree while the other remained frozen and whimpering, too certain he was killed to move.

My dad was a country boy beached in town. During the Second World War and the days of food ration-

Father, Wayne M. Peck, 1971

ing, he fattened calves and hogs on the farms of our rural relatives. After slaughtering day out on the farm, our back porch was full of steaming kettles of coiled sausage and long pans of scrapple. Cured hams hung in our garage throughout the war years to augment the meat ration, and there was enough to share with the neighborhood.

He brought chickens in from the farm, and they lived in a crate in the garage until the final, fatal day. Then the neighborhood kids with strong stomachs gathered at the edge of our backyard while Dad carried out two chickens, one to fry and one to freeze, and wrung their necks with good-natured zeal. It was a moment of profound theater, and it happened only in our backyard.

A long time later I began a novel called *Representing Super Doll* with just such a scene. A farmwoman wrings the necks of a couple of chickens because that's what chickens are for and she likes her meat fresh. This arresting opener gave my New York publishers much pain and continues to disturb my suburban readers. But it seems to me a useful antidote to a world steadily being engulfed by Chicken McNuggets.

When he could manage the time, my dad hunted and fished and brought home braces of pheasant and strings of croppie and blue gill and, the regional delicacy, catfish. My mother is a dietician by training and a famous cook in her circle. These two grass-roots gourmets worked hand-in-hand in the kitchen, preparing feasts. Mother created recipes and compiled them in volumes. Dad cleaned and cooked his own game, his

Masonic ring glittering in the pink water. Once at least, a dismembered turtle jiggled and seemed to do push-ups in the frying pan. Game I wasn't to see again for years, and then over-sauced and over-priced in restaurants, issued regularly from our kitchen.

From my father I learned nostalgia as an art form. I fell on Mark Twain's stories of middle-American boyhood because they merged with my dad's memories. He supped and drank for the rest of his life on his recollections of a boyhood full of hunting and fishing in the Sangamon River bottoms and staying out all night. He'd swapped seventh grade for the adventure of work. Wearing overalls over his serge suit, he hopped freights up to the Dakotas to work on a team running a steam threshing machine for the wheat harvest.

But like the boys of his generation, he was taken off the farm by World War I. When he came home from France on a hospital ship, partially disabled, his past wasn't where he'd left it. When he was well enough to work, he turned his face to town and lived there the rest of his life. But the fact that his country boyhood was a paradise lost to him only made it sweeter.

My mother, Virginia Gray, came from a prosperous farm family in Morgan County in western Illinois. They were old settlers for that part of the country. My great-grandfather William Gray had come from Ireland as a boy, acquired a sizable farm, and passed it intact to my grandfather, John Ewing Gray. Between them, this father and son farmed the same land from 1852 until 1964, for my grandfather lived to be ninety-one.

The Grays' place was called Walnut Grove Farm, a fine, high house with long, deep porches standing in a vast lawn of enormous trees and mounded flower beds. The views ran to the level line of the horizon. My grandfather gardened as his son-in-law hunted and fished. The weedless garden rows ran straight as a die from the fence line, burdened with bounty.

The house itself observed the formalities, with a long staircase rising out of the front hall and making a curve at the top. But the kitchen was the heart of it. My grandmother kept a bottled-gas stove to one side, but she cooked and warmed the room with a big iron range with a cob fire always glowing inside and a reservoir for hot water. This superior farmhouse boasted its own electric system run by Delco batteries. In time all the plumbing came indoors, though the outhouse and the pump continued to stand proudly out back on either side of the summer kitchen.

My Grandmother Gray, who was named Flossie Mae, had a whole gaggle of sisters, all with fine names: Pearl, Lura, Maude, Ozena. They'd been born in the 1870s and 1880s, and so they seemed historic to me,

and dignified. But once when I was still small enough to fit behind doors, I lingered outside the kitchen during a family reunion while they were fixing dinner.

Walnut Grove Farm was a place that mingled the present with the past anyway, but now as I eavesdropped, I heard their voices blending and bantering as they'd done back in their Victorian girlhood. I heard through the crack in the door the voices of another century and forgot for a moment they were old. They'd forgotten too.

A writer, early and late, does a lot of listening at doors, and those voices lingered in my mind. Long after these old ladies were gone, I went looking for the voice of a midwestern girl at the turn of the century to use in a book. I combined those real voices to give my character her speech. Her name is Blossom Culp, my most popular heroine through four books: *The Ghost Belonged to Me, Ghosts I Have Been, The Dreadful Future of Blossom Culp,* and *Blossom Culp and the Sleep of Death.*

Blossom speaks with a countrified precision and considerable emphasis. A vanishing rural Illinois accent isn't as familiar as a Southern accent or a Western drawl, and so Blossom's voice sounds all her own, but in fact it came right down out of my family tree.

I started out as an only child surrounded by elders of all ages. My mother was the middle of seven children, and my father's older sister and her husband served as an extra set of grandparents.

They were Uncle Tom and Aunt Geneva Kistler, farm folk too and old settlers, but only as dignified as they needed to be. In memory the card table is always set up in the front yard, and the ice-cream freezer is already packed with rock salt and waiting in the cellar to be cranked. Rural electrification had not found them, and so they trimmed wicks and filled lamps and lit their world with mellow coal-oil flame and laughter.

Little wonder that old folks stalk through my novels about being young. Madame Malevich, the wise, disillusioned drama teacher in the smug suburb of *Are You in the House Alone?* Uncle Miles, the rapscallion great-uncle of *The Ghost Belonged to Me* who derived from my own great-uncle, Miles Peck. Miss Gertrude Dabney, the eccentric recluse with a ghost in her pantry of *Ghosts I Have Been.* Polly Prior in her wheelchair, the third oldest woman in the township of *Remembering the Good Times.*

When you write to young readers, you need the wisdom of those people at the other end of life. I came to writing with an entire crew of seasoned elders on my side.

I marched into kindergarten on the day Germany marched into Poland. I too was fortified. My mother had read to me, making me hungry for books and school and the world. Because of this, I wanted to be a writer before I could read. Luckily, I was born too early to have to learn my first language from *Sesame Street*, from a large crepe-paper bird speaking out of a small box. I heard my first book-stories in my mother's voice. A satisfactory substitute for this has yet to be found.

By hearing books and listening to my elders and the radio, I'd avoided baby talk. At home three adults sat at the dinner table, talking over my head. My Aunt Rozella, my mother's younger sister, lived with us for the first fifteen years of my life before she married and had sons of her own.

In time, the conversation turned to the war, World War II. Four thousand miles behind the nearest front line we were thoroughly mobilized. We had air-raid drills, and my dad in a white tin helmet went off into the night as an auxiliary policeman to direct traffic in the blackout. My aunt carried bedpans at the hospital through long evenings as a nurse's aide. My mother, the dietician, went to nutrition classes to find us balanced diets amid the shortages.

Posters stared down at us grade-schoolers from the halls of Dennis School, warning us not to discuss military secrets because LOOSE LIPS SINK SHIPS. We Cub Scouts conducted marathon scrap-paper drives and collected flattened tin cans. We recycled everything we could lift, and we never walked when we could march.

Children are the natural militants anyway, and so we gladly joined up in this khaki-colored world. Small boys trooped off voluntarily to the barber for haircuts in imitation of grown GI's. At recess we formed air-force squadrons and thundered in formation across the school yard with arms out like wings, bombing Berlin. The girls sat in the swings, presumably discussing shortages.

As the war ground on, a captured JAP SUICIDE SUBMARINE went on display in Central Park downtown. We could peer down the hatch to see realistic dummies of suicidal Japanese sailors inside, and our flesh crawled. This far behind the lines, the war was very nearly heaven.

It was clearly heaven-sent to our teachers who invoked military discipline. Any little infraction of the rules was called unpatriotic, and even correct spelling was somehow connected with winning the war. It may have had something to do with never having to erase anything because rubber was rationed.

Maps festooned the schoolroom with pins to denote the advancing front (we never retreated.) It was Us-Against-Them on a global scale, the *Them* being three cartoon characters: Hitler, Tojo, and Mussolini in that order.

The young will play Us-Against-Them even without a war, and so we sped home from school pretty exhilarated by this high drama. But at home, I sensed a difference. My dad wasn't buying all this drum-beating. Alone of all the fathers, he'd been old enough to fight in the First World War. I knew the wounds he'd suffered then pained him still. Now I saw him in another kind of pain. His generation had been promised that their sacrifice would end all war for all time. He didn't believe in the entangling alliances our country was in, and he thought we'd been maneuvered into the war to boost the economy and for more ominous reasons still. In short, at home the enemy was Franklin D. Roosevelt, the very hero whose picture hung in our classroom.

Nothing interests a child more than adults disagreeing. It didn't even divide my loyalties. On the sly I cast my lot with my dad who'd paid more for his beliefs in the trenches than my teachers had by watching newsreels at the Lincoln Square Theater.

I awoke to the interesting point that adults don't provide a united front. This alerted me to viewpoint, which is a novelist's stock-in-trade. Writers aren't nearly as interested in what happens as in their characters' various and conflicting points of view. My dad could make his viewpoint crystal clear.

On the whole, the war suited me pretty well. Apparently nobody remembered the Great Depression. People looked back upon the golden prewar years with nostalgia. I could go along with that. I'd been born nostalgic. The war opened up the world too, with all that map-reading. That suited me too, for I'd been homesick all along for places I'd never been. If the whole world wasn't to be bombed back into the Dark Ages, I began laying early plans to get out there and see it.

From the war I'd acquired another new vocabulary: a kamikaze/blitzkrieg vocabulary of melodrama and long distance. I acquired a sister too. My sister Cheryl was born in the darkest days of the war. Now she looked up in astonishment as the technicolor postwar era came roaring in with unrationed chocolate, toy balloons, and new cars toothy with chrome.

Not long after, it was time to swap the certainties of Dennis Grade School for the rigors of Woodrow Wilson Junior High and the hormonal horrors of puberty.

Nobody remembers more about puberty than he can help, but in junior high we began to catch glimpses of the future: of high school, the big time, and even college. Miss Swenson, our seventh-grade homeroom teacher, informed us that every detention slip we received would go right on our record to be looked at by any college unwise enough to consider us. We believed her.

Every kid from the west end of Decatur had to sign up for Miss Van Dyke's Fortnightly Dancing Class. This was held in a club downtown where Miss Van Dyke, a miniature woman in a black dress, with a castanet stuck to one hand, introduced us to the mysteries of the waltz, the foxtrot, and for a change of pace, the rhumba. We went willingly even though the girls tended to be a head taller than the boys, because we knew that if you couldn't dance by high school, you were on the social ash heap.

From this world being run by powerful women, my friend Chick and I went daily to the after-school paper route we shared. Our turf extended over a large area dominated by a mysterious mansion on the corner of Pine and Main left over from the Gilded Age. It had been built by an early financier in the "Tuscan" style with turrets against the sky and a brick barn behind, standing in an acre of lawn. By then it served as the town art museum. It served me later as the home of Alexander Armsworth in the series of weird adventures he shares with Blossom Culp.

When it was time for high school, we all ganged together in a crumbling red brick structure downtown, like a factory with pillars. Its only recent addition was a luxurious gymnasium for the sole and sacred use of the starting five of the varsity basketball team.

Though I didn't know it at the time, Decatur High School was the least provincial setting I was ever to inhabit with the possible exception of the army. It was racially integrated long before that was fashionable, and the children of every walk of life were thrust together, two thousand of us. Somehow, it seemed bigger than the town it served.

Even the most privileged and prominent people in town sent their children to the public schools because private schools were considered undemocratic. The almost invisible children of the very poor were there too, kids like Carol Patterson, the heroine of my first novel, *Don't Look and It Won't Hurt*. There was even a splinter group who climbed down out of yellow buses straight from the farm, a blending of worlds that crops up in *Representing Super Doll*.

In high school my friendship with Chick Wolfe had expanded to include Don Baer. In a place where everybody seemed to be majoring in cliques, we three provided a united front. Chick was showing evidence of genius, either in engineering or music, we weren't sure which. Born too soon to be a computer whiz, he seemed to have a computer in his head. I'd scraped through algebra in ninth grade as a charity case, and he got me through plane geometry and surged ahead to trigonometry by himself.

With math behind me, I was aiming myself at the National Honor Society in the idea that I'd need a full-tuition scholarship if I was going to go to a private college. Don provided comic relief and a cherry-red Chevrolet ragtop.

Most of our mutual stunts remain shrouded in history, but Don had a fake gorilla head and a convincing, long-haired fur coat, and was known to drive around town as an escaped ape driving a convertible. This gave a number of courting couples parked along dark lanes occasional moments of sudden terror. The gorilla gear surfaced again briefly in a recent novel of mine called, significantly, *Remembering the Good Times*.

We seem to have been the last youthful generation who were kept really busy. It was the final moment before television blanketed the earth, and I for one was afraid to go to school without my homework done. On Saturdays I bagged groceries at the A&P for the wage of $7.45 which went farther then. A good deal of it went for wrist corsages since our social life revolved entirely around dancing, the more formal the better. By junior year I'd achieved a shawl-collared white dinner jacket worn over a maroon cummerbund. Spiffy.

I wasn't falling for high school though. I was scanning the horizon for college and farther fields than that. By the summer I was sixteen I went to visit a distant relative who'd married a dignitary assigned to the United Nations and lived in the mythic city of New York. I raked yards and shoveled snow for a chair-car ticket on the Pennsylvania Railroad and was on my way.

It came as quite a relief to me that the outside world was really there and somewhat better than the movies. I began to explore the streets of New York and plumb the depths of the subway system all the way to Coney Island. It occurred to me that this was the place I'd been homesick for all along, this place and London. That first trek into the Great World ended on June 25, 1950, the day the Korean War began. The postwar era we'd waited for all through grade school had turned out to run less than five years, and the 1950s had truly begun.

High-school courses were taught at that time very much on the level of college courses today. But I managed to squeak into the National Honor Society. Then on the first day of senior year, I encountered the terrible Miss F. She taught senior English to the College Bound. We'd all heard about her, but if you aspired to college, there was no avoiding her.

"I can get all of you in this room into the colleges of your choices," she remarked on the first day of class, "*or I can keep you out!*"

There wasn't a nonbeliever in the bunch, certainly not me. But I had more to learn from Miss F. I'd fallen into bad habits as a student. I'd grown accustomed to receiving A's on my English compositions, and you don't learn much from an A.

When I got my first paper back from Miss F., it had no grade on it of any sort. Instead, written across the page were these memorable words: "NEVER EXPRESS YOURSELF AGAIN ON MY TIME. FIND A MORE INTERESTING TOPIC."

Well, I was seventeen. I didn't know what a more interesting topic than me would be. I actually went to the woman and asked, "What would a more interesting topic be?"

"Almost anything," she replied.

That led me to the library, a place I'd successfully avoided up until then, in search of subject matter that wasn't me. All these years later, I'm still searching for it. Miss F. taught us that writing isn't self-expression. Writing is communication, and you'd better have your reader far better in mind than yourself. Miss F. didn't teach Creative Writing, of course. She knew the danger of inspiration coming before grammar. She knew that without the framework for sharing, ideas are nothing.

I wasn't slated to write a line of fiction until I was thirty-seven years old, but it was Miss F. who made it possible. In the boot camp atmosphere of her classroom she taught us that the only real writing is rewriting. She taught us that deadlines are meant to be met, not extended. She taught us how to gather material more interesting than ourselves and to pin it on a page. By the time I got to college the next year, I was already praising her name.

I won the scholarship I'd been chasing and went to DePauw University in Greencastle, Indiana. Both my parents encouraged me to go to college, my mother because she was a college graduate, my father because he wasn't.

The great authority figure for a boy in the 1950s was neither parent nor teacher. It was the head of the local draft board. On our eighteenth birthdays we registered for the draft, to be inducted for a two-year stint after high school unless we were allowed college deferments, renewed annually. After graduation, we were marched off.

Moreover if a boy didn't maintain a college grade point average in the upper half of his class, the university informed his local draft board, and he soon found himself in Korea. When I was a freshman, one of the seniors in the fraternity house allowed his grades to slip and was drafted out of school in mid-semester. This had an electrifying effect on the rest of us, and we all became a lot more scholarly than we'd meant to be. Silent study hours were invoked and homework seminars were set up in the dining room. It was far from an animal-house environment.

In fact the entirety of college life then is hard to describe now. At DePauw no student was allowed to have a car, and drinking led directly to expulsion. Strangely, the college had a widespread reputation for its brisk social life. It was the high-water mark of the fraternity/sorority system. Girls dazzling to behold descended long curving staircases to claim their wrist corsages, and we danced away to formal evenings, cheek to cheek and sober as judges.

I entered college with the full complement of late-adolescent complexes. For one thing I had this secret itch to be a writer, though I wouldn't have admitted any such long shot. Instead, I planned to be a teacher, which seemed to be my nearest approach to the written word. But here I had another problem. Though I was training to be a teacher, I couldn't stand up in front of a group of people, any people, and speak. My knees buckled and my tongue went dead. I should have headed straight for the Speech and Drama Department in search of a cure, but I dealt with the problem in the usual adolescent way. I avoided it. In the single course in Speech I had to take, I collected a C and went back to my desk at the far end of the room on wobbly knees.

I was hung up too between literature and history. On the faculty was the celebrated Dr. Andrew Crandall who taught the Civil War as if he'd taken part. But the unborn novelist in me edged me nearer the English Department, and at last to England.

I took my junior year and most of my literature courses at Exeter University in the southwest of England. Though I'd never seen the open sea until I crossed it, I sailed away in the fall of 1954 aboard the now vanished liner, *Ile de France,* an ocean-going Art Deco fantasy flowing with red wine even in Third Class. But I was drunk enough on the adventure of it all. The ship pitched through the gray waves while we passengers danced the nights away on slanting floors under swaying chandeliers. I'd raised the fare, a hundred and sixty-five dollars, by running the dishwasher at George Williams College Camp on Lake Geneva in Wisconsin. And I'd obtained a dispensation from my draft board to leave the country for a year. Then, any undrafted twenty-year-old was regarded as a potential fugitive.

But it was all worth the effort. Every late adolescent should be cut out of the pack to find out who he is.

Exeter, the County Town of Devon, is a medieval city grown around a famous cathedral set among the folded green hills. Early in the war the town had been half flattened in an air raid, and there were more parking lots, laid over rubble, than cars to fill them. Food rationing had just ended, but the college dorm kitchens still seemed mobilized for war. Whole meals were built around mashed potatoes and brussel sprouts, both gray.

I'd expected the English to be as austere as their dinners. After all, we undergraduates trooped into the dining room of Mardon Hall wearing black academic gowns over several layers of tweed, and the teachers looked even more professorial than their American counterparts. But the English turned out to be far too sociable and welcoming to let their image get in the way.

At Mardon Hall, which was run very like an American fraternity house, I fell in with three friends. One of them was Henry Woolf, by far the most brilliant student at the university. He was of a Jewish family hounded out of Eastern Europe by Hitler, and attended the university, like almost everyone else, on a government scholarship. He'd had to start over in life more than once as a displaced child, and was going to be the first of his family to be an Englishman. David Wheatley, of a colonial family, had grown up in Africa and India in the dwindling days of Empire and trailed its glory in his speech and manner. Arthur Dark was the scholarly son of a retired sailor from the port of Plymouth. For these friends a wartime childhood had been a real experience. Bombs had rained on them, and so they seemed older to me. They'd been rigorously prepared for university study and hand-picked. They were walking encyclopediae, and yet, amazingly, they knew nothing about America.

For the first time, I myself began to wonder who Americans were. I'd grown up thinking that the world had its eye on us, was even hanging on our every word. Now I was among people who were getting along very well without our inspiration.

Through the tutorial system and the social life, British students mingled with their professors. At a party I dared approach my sharp-tongued literature instructor, Professor P. Unwisely, I tried to drum up some conversation. "In the United States," I said, drymouthed, "we study British literature, but here there's no course in American literature."

"Ah," he said, pale eyebrows high, "when America writes something, we will be glad to read it."

Trying again, I said, "At home we study T. S. Eliot and Henry James as American writers. Here they're regarded as British."

Professor P.'s eyebrows were still high. "From humble beginnings come many great men," he remarked.

I gave up, but it was another lesson in viewpoint.

An English family took me under their wing and gave me a second home. They lived in the north Devon market town of Barnstaple below the heights of Lorna Doone's Exmoor. They were Mr. and Mrs. Arthur Jones and their beautiful, elegant daughter, Mair, pro-

viding a friendship that mellows down the years to a new generation of the family.

I returned to DePauw University in Indiana, heavily tweeded and with midwestern accent blurred, for senior year and all the grim courses needed for a teaching credential. But among the suave and sociable British, I'd been cured of my stage fright. In a country where anybody was liable to have to stand up at a public dinner and propose a toast, even I wasn't exempt. I could now speak in public without my knees buckling. Fortunately I overcame this disability before I encountered my own students in a classroom.

Graduation day came, and not long after I was marched off, on cue, to the army. Everybody who was ever in the army remembers the day he went in and the day he got out. I was to catch a 3:00 A.M. train for the induction center in St. Louis, and I well remember sitting in the station, bent over *Moby Dick,* which I'd never gotten around to reading. I had the idea that I was about to spend two years without anybody to talk to, and so the least I could do was catch up on my reading. This overlooked the fact that virtually every able-bodied member of my sex and generation was going where I was going, and it was a place where you made friends because you needed them, and you kept them for life.

As it turned out, I learned at least as much from the two years of army as from two years in college, and it even took me back to Europe. Better yet, it was my first, unexpected chance to put my new college education to work.

This was the peacetime army in that interval between the end of the Korean War and the beginning of Vietnam. A tremendously swollen force, fueled by cheap and threatened draftee labor, occupied the American sector of West Germany. This army ran on neither guns nor its stomach. It ran on paper work. It didn't take long to learn that anybody who could type, spell, and write what can only be described as self-protective prose came in handy working as a company clerk in an office being run by functional illiterates. A major goal in the army is to find yourself a sitting-down job in a dry room next to a warm stove. Literacy helps.

This post was housed in former Nazi barracks above Ansbach, a town picturesque almost beyond belief. It had castle walls and a palace and windowboxes burgeoning with red geranium. Farmers and their wives came to market on flatbed wagons drawn by tractors through a countryside of storybook barnyards and pillowed wheatfields. Here was the enemy territory, and the enemy, we'd been taught to dread in grade school.

In the long run I proved too useful to the army to

get more than a single three-day pass in two years. From writing up convincing reports as company clerk, I branched out into an entirely new field by ghost-writing sermons for the chaplains (all denominations.) Having grown up in the Methodist church and studying at a Methodist college, I knew the Bible. I'd heard my share of sermons too, which are like novels because they must recognize their listeners. I began to polish my craft, slipping my first sermons under a chaplain's door until I had him on the hook. The next step was to get myself qualified as a bona fide Chaplain's Assistant and to be posted to the stimulating metropolis of Stuttgart.

As it turned out, I found myself writing for a livelihood in the army. I garnered good, human material too in the lives of my fellow soldiers who turned up at the chaplain's door because I was on duty and hearing confessions far longer hours than the chaplain was.

From the army I entered graduate school at Southern Illinois University in Carbondale, Illinois, where I put myself through as a teaching assistant in the English Department. Graduate assistants were assigned the teaching of freshman composition. On the first night of my teaching career, I entered the classroom in a new civilian suit to find myself the youngest person in the room. My students were of all ages, beginning college work in a night-school class.

This wasn't quite how I'd pictured teaching. I'd thought the problem would be to establish my authority before a room full of rambunctious eighteen-year-olds. Instead, the room was a worried mass of grownups who weren't sure they should be there. From that first evening, I saw a teacher's job is to reassure, to convince people that their abilities and their experiences count for something. From the first night, I fell for teaching and managed to keep too busy for years to feel sorry for myself that I wasn't a writer. Without knowing it, I was learning to be a writer in every class I taught.

After receiving my degree and spending two more years in college teaching, I turned to high-school teaching, my original plan. It was at Glenbrook North High School in Northbrook, Illinois, an affluent suburb of Chicago. Here was my first glimpse of adolescents. They weren't so much younger than I was, but they looked like a whole new species. They were growing up over-indulged in a superior subdivision with neither sidewalks nor roots. I'd spent my youth dreaming of big cities, but they seemed unaware of Chicago, the city just down the highway.

It was a school system built on the error that all of its students were college material. Only a minority of people should go to college. Most people have potential skills and talents that need other kinds of training.

But in suburbia it seemed that parents needed college-bound children to maintain their own social standing. This created a lot of young casualties, and many of them were already happening in high school.

The whole country seemed to be suburbanizing, and years later so many letters from young readers bore suburban postmarks that I was to place several of my novels in suburban settings to respond to my readers' lives: the Glenburnie of *Close Enough to Touch,* the suburbanizing of Slocum Township in *Remembering the Good Times,* the Oldfield Village of *Are You in the House Alone?* and most notably as far as my readers are concerned, *Secrets of the Shopping Mall.* I wrote it to ask the suburban young why they want to spend all their waking hours (and all their sleeping hours too, in the novel) in a place as crass and artificial as a shopping mall. I'm not sure if this questioning of their value system comes across. I have an idea they like the novel because it's about their favorite place. After all, the mall is the only place to be in many suburbs.

I came to the end of my teaching years at a school for academically gifted girls on Park Avenue in New York City, far from the suburbs. The world of the young, and their teachers, was changing fast. For the first time I was teaching junior-high level students and looking high and low for books that reflected their realities, books that were "relevant," the battle cry of the age. It was a time when students were excused from school to march on Washington in masses to protest the war in Vietnam, a war they couldn't find on the map.

One day in the midst of life I quit teaching. I wasn't being allowed to teach as I'd been taught. I turned in my gradebook and my pension plan one May day in 1971 and went home to write a novel. I didn't dare think too far ahead, and I didn't dare stop writing. It was, as the saying goes, the first day of the rest of my life.

As a teacher I'd been in on the beginnings of a lot of other people's lives. I knew things about the young that their parents will never know. Best of all, I had an identifiable group of readers in mind before I ever started my first novel: two groups, in fact: junior high and high school, the puberty people and the adolescents. And what did I know about them? Not enough certainly. The writer can never really know all he needs to know about the lives of his readers.

It was junior-high students, the puberty people, who taught me how to be a writer. They taught me what I hadn't learned elsewhere: that people don't read fiction to be educated. They read fiction to be reassured, to be given hope. As a novelist I wasn't going to give them happy endings every time. They have television for that. But I knew never to leave the reader without hope for the future and a new beginning. My students reminded me that puberty, the time of life when you're too old for a Care Bear and too young for a driver's license, is a rough passage. From books such readers want fictional friends as companions and role models.

The first novel I wrote for them was *Don't Look and It Won't Hurt*. It was based on the experiences of my close friends, Jean and Richard Hughes, who took into their home in suburban Chicago girls from a local home for unwed mothers. In the end, I wrote the story not from the viewpoint of the unwed teenaged mother-to-be, but from the viewpoint of her younger sister. I cared more about the young person who wasn't already in the kind of trouble that adults can no longer overlook. I identified Carol with the quiet students who'd always sat at the back of the classroom, wondering what life had to offer for them, and what they had to contribute.

I hand-carried this first manuscript to George Nicholson who was Juveniles Editor-in-Chief of Holt, Rinehart and Winston. On the following day, after I had a restless night, he called me up and said, "You can start your second novel." And so I did.

In all the years before I became a writer, I'd heard how hopeless the whole business is: how nearly impossible to get a first novel published, how unlikely to make a living from writing. But every writer's career, like his books, is different. I believe my first novel was accepted by the first editor who read it because it was written directly to an identifiable readership, young people, and it was told from the viewpoint of one of them.

The hardest part of being a writer wasn't the uncertainty of it; it was the solitude. I'd been a teacher, and so I was used to being surrounded by students and other teachers from dawn on. Life had been divided into segments by ringing bells and interrupted by fire drills. I was used to being besieged by voices, activity.

Instead, I was sitting alone in a room, staring into a typewriter, trying to make a blank page speak. This lonely interlude didn't last long. A writer can't afford to sit very long alone. He has to get out among readers, researching their worlds. When you write for young people, the problem deepens. At your typewriter you're aging every minute while, mysteriously, your readers remain the same age. Worse yet, they change their protective coloring, their fads in clothes and speech and music, every semester. And they live different lives in different parts of the country.

As a writer I spend almost a quarter of my time visiting readers and their teachers and librarians. I go where I'm invited, in school visits and as a speaker to conventions of librarians and educators. I've looked in

on the lives of young people coming of age on a raft in a logging camp outside Ketchikan, Alaska. And of young people growing up in a sheep station called Ridgway, high in the Colorado Rockies. And of young people in inner-city Cleveland and along the Mexican border at Calexico, California. I need to know their differences and what all young people have in common. What they all have in common forms the backgrounds of my novels. Their differences, individual ones, inspire the characters.

I see the world, just as I'd hoped to do when I was a kid. I look for readers for books I've already written and ideas from those readers for books I haven't written yet. To write *Secrets of the Shopping Mall,* I haunted malls all across the country. In visiting schools where most of the students are from broken homes, I got the idea for *Father Figure,* the story of a boy who only thinks he's adjusted to growing up without a father. In real life, he might never have encountered his dad again, but in my book they're reunited. The story turns on the conflicts they try to resolve. I wouldn't have thought of that novel by looking around my own life. I found it by looking into the lives of readers.

One day in a book store I was forced to notice that young adult novels were losing ground and shelf space to romances. I simmered a while until I could think of a romance story with a difference. It came to me. I'd write a love story from the viewpoint of a boy because boys have emotions too. The novel became *Close Enough to Touch*.

From reading newspapers wherever I go, including suburban newspapers, I was alerted to the epidemic of adolescent suicides now raging. I wrote *Remembering the Good Times* from this starting point, about a privileged suburban boy who's driven to despair because he doesn't believe his long adolescence is preparing him for the future.

Junior-high readers advised me to write supernatural stories. I was happy with realism, but they wanted the weird.

As it happened, I was already writing a novel at the time. My novel was about a young boy's association with his aged great-uncle, Miles. Because of reader-pressure, I introduced a ghost into this novel: a girl-ghost, glamorous rather than ghastly. The minute she entered the story, I didn't know what I'd done without her. For balance, a live girl entered the novel, and she became Blossom Culp. The novel was called *The Ghost Belonged to Me*. The first thing that happened to it was a filming by Walt Disney Productions. I decided to listen more carefully to the advice of young readers.

I've had advice from my publishers too. Though I was having a full life among the young, I was commis-

Peck, his sister, Cheryl, their mother, Virginia Gray Peck, 1985

sioned to write one and then three novels for my fellow adults. The idea for the first one, however, came from young people: junior-high boys, in fact. Because they all seem to be experts on the sinking of the steamship *Titanic,* I built my novel, *Amanda/Miranda,* around this popular disaster.

The second novel was *New York Time,* inspired by the midlife crises of my own contemporaries. The third was *This Family of Women,* a generational novel that deals mainly with coming-of-age in various eras. Coming-of-age remains the topic that interests me most. After all, I grew up reading *Huckleberry Finn,* and while he can't be matched, he can inspire.

There's a saying (or there should be one) that goes: "Be careful what you wish for. You're liable to get it." When I was a kid, I dreamed privately of being a writer and living in New York and traveling everywhere. I got it all.

There are days when I have to remember to be grateful. There are days when living in New York isn't quite worth what it costs in several ways. There are days when I'm hung up between racing across the country to talk about books and staying home to write one. There are days, plenty of them, when the typewriter won't talk back to me, and I'm in the room alone.

Nobody promises rose gardens to writers. We have to get along without pensions and paid vacations and negotiated coffee breaks. There are days when we're high and dry in a world that appears to be full of people going off to less demanding, more secure jobs. And there are evenings when we suspect that everybody else is out having a good time while we're looking at deadlines. There are long nights when I worry about where the next readers are coming from in an age rendered blind and verbally anorexic by television, slack schooling, and loss of language.

But then dawn breaks, and the mail arrives, and there's a young reader writing back from some town where I've never been. On a very good day, that young reader says, "I'm the one you were writing about. Do you live around here?"

I try.

BIBLIOGRAPHY

FOR YOUNG ADULTS

Fiction:

Don't Look and It Won't Hurt. New York: Holt, 1972.

Dreamland Lake. New York: Holt, 1973.

Through a Brief Darkness. New York: Viking, 1973; London: Collins, 1976.

Representing Super Doll. New York: Viking, 1974.

The Ghost Belonged to Me. New York: Viking, 1975; London: Collins, 1977.

Are You in the House Alone? New York: Viking, 1976; London: Pan Books, 1986.

Ghosts I Have Been. New York: Viking, 1977.

Father Figure. New York: Viking, 1978.

Secrets of the Shopping Mall. New York: Delacorte, 1979.

Close Enough to Touch. New York: Delacorte, 1981.

The Dreadful Future of Blossom Culp. New York: Delacorte, 1983.

Remembering the Good Times. New York: Delacorte, 1985.

Blossom Culp and the Sleep of Death. New York: Delacorte, 1986.

FOR CHILDREN

Fiction:

Monster Night at Grandma's House (illustrated by Don Freeman). New York: Viking, 1977.

FOR ADULTS

Fiction:

Amanda/Miranda. New York: Viking, 1980; London: Gollancz, 1980.

New York Time. New York: Delacorte, 1981; London: Gollancz, 1981.

This Family of Women. New York: Delacorte, 1983; London: Gollancz, 1983.

Nonfiction:

Old Town: A Complete Guide, with Norman Strasma. Chicago, 1965.

A Consumer's Guide to Educational Innovations, with Mortimer Smith and George Weber. Washington, D.C.: Council for Basic Education, 1972.

Editor of:

Edge of Awareness: Twenty-five Contemporary Essays, with Ned E. Hoopes. New York: Dell, 1966.

Sounds and Silences: Poetry for Now. New York: Delacorte, 1970.

Mindscapes: Poems for the Real World. New York: Delacorte, 1971.

The Creative Word 2, with Stephen N. Judy. New York: Random House, 1973.

Leap into Reality: Essays for Now. New York: Dell, 1973.

Transitions: A Literary Paper Casebook. New York: Random House, 1974.

Urban Studies: A Research Paper Casebook. New York: Random House, 1974.

Josephine Poole

1933-

Josephine Poole in the garden at Poundisford, 1984

I seem to look back into an attic full of jumble, a miscellany of people and places and happenings and things, and perhaps the very first thing lying in the doorway is the woolly lamb my grandmother gave me when I was born. I called him Lamby, and I clearly remember pulling out his beautiful glass eyes, in those days before safe toys. I did not want to blind my favourite toy, but I could not resist the shiny, black-pupilled glass. He had to make do with button eyes after that; I still have him put away. He lies on the threshold of my experience.

My father is the only person to stand full in the sunlight that streams into this "attic." There he is, bathed in gold, entirely loved, in no way dreaded. Perhaps because he had four daughters and no sons, he had a unique, unrivalled place in our family. For me, he calmed everything: if he was there, the end was safe and assured. Yet he was a very modest person, he conveyed strength without advertising.

He was not tall, and had a humped back from bending anxiously over his desk. He was dark, and thin—he wore the suit he was married in to each of our weddings. He had a large, bony nose, and thick black eyebrows overhanging his little eyes, which were brown and kind. He wasn't a talkative man, but when he spoke, everyone listened, and he had a keen, somewhat caustic sense of humour: he could be extremely funny in a few, perfectly chosen words. His hands were square with blunt fingers, the sort of hands that are good with tools; he could make or repair most things.

Every year we went to the seaside. This was a great excitement from the first appearance of the trunk, which had wooden supports and a striped lining. On one occasion my father swam out with me on his back. The water round his pale, slow-moving limbs was deeper than I could see, dark, mysterious, perilously cold. I clung to him, screaming with terror. Perhaps this was the year that Chris, my older sister, put pebbles (which had to be extricated with tweezers by a doctor) into my ear. Another time I was stung on the mouth by a bee which got into my sandwich. Once I made a mess in my yellow bathing costume, something I would have liked to forget, but Chris remembered. A foreground of regrettable incidents against the wide sands, the hushing sea.

The war separated our parents, because my father worked in London, while my mother evacuated to the north country with us, to stay with his aunt. I was six when this happened. I remember it very clearly. I remember stopping on the journey, on the moors between Lancashire and the Lake District. At first, everything seemed perfectly silent, and then I became aware of the sound of a rushing stream, an urgent voice that had been there all the time. And then a curlew called, long and long—not sadly, not mournfully, but expressing the desolation of that place. My experience was immediately wrenched open: there were depths, there were distances. I thrilled with expectation. Nothing would be the same again.

My father's aunt had never married. She had been a nurse during the First World War. Now she was ready for the Second, running the household on a minimum of rations, dismissing servants so that they could participate more fully in the war effort. The house was very big, and cold, and dark—lit only by oil lamps. A wood pressed close, catching the wind which moaned as it tried to escape from the branches. There was the gentle talk of pigeons, loathed and shot at by the remaining gardener who had been the family coachman in the old days. And he trapped mice in the greenhouses. So to pay him out, to show Aunt Ellen how wickedly he behaved, I arranged their floppy, silky corpses on her dressing table. Even so, she became my friend. We went for walks together, usually to the local rubbish tip, a source of hidden treasures, which she prodded out with her stick.

Aunt Ellen was a formidable character, not to be trifled with: even Pelo, the youngest of the four of us, met her match. The most devastating thing about her, from a child's point of view, was her sweeping acceptance of our shortcomings. She expected us to be a nuisance. She was prepared for it, she did not blame us, we were children no different from all children. She loathed any kind of humbug. She preferred, on the whole, the company of her social "inferiors" and was very involved in the village, particularly its amateur theatricals. She spoke Spanish and Italian fluently, also German and French, and began learning Russian when she was over eighty. She had travelled extensively with her sister through Europe, and the house was full of their pictures, Spanish interiors in sombre colours, towns and castles and pastoral scenes. She had loved her sister, who had died of tuberculosis of the spine. We always assumed that her lover had been killed in the First War, but no one knew for certain that this was so. It was generous of her to take us in, because our grandmother had made trouble in the family, and they had been estranged for many years.

The house was run on the lines of a hospital. I discovered that there is nothing so comforting as a fire in the bedroom; nothing so dark as a lamp which has just been put out, when night crammed round my palpitating frame; nothing so demoralising as fear; nothing so miserable as incipient flu, before one is ill enough to be put to bed; nothing so breathtaking as beauty, striking through any of the senses directly to the heart. Is it fanciful to put these impressions into myself as a child? I don't think so; they are present in all children, one way or another: each of us includes an "attic," almost empty in childhood, into which the events of life are hurled.

And nothing was so important as my mother. For before the war we had had nannies, barriers between our parents and ourselves. It is an odd thing that I always felt very close to my father, although during my first years I only knew him from his kiss at night, from the time he was cross with Chris and me because we

escaped from nanny and much worried our mother, from his magical ability with a primus stove if we went on a picnic, and from those summer seaside holidays when he was the purchaser of the coloured tin buckets and wooden spades for the glory of the sands. But my relationship with my mother was much more wary. She loved us most devotedly and was amazingly proud of us, but she was totally committed to our proper upbringing and good behaviour. This carried with it, for me, an onus of guilt in case I let her down, and a dread of her disapproval, because I knew—oh, very early on!—that I must follow my own way all the same, and work out my own fulfillment.

Where is my mother in my "attic"? Everywhere! She influences the whole of my understanding. But she does not rule it: in the end we became free and happy companions. Before that could happen, however, there were difficult, at times very bitter stages in our relationship.

She was marvellously encouraging. We all painted pictures and wrote stories—no television in those days! She wasn't uncritical, but she understood so quickly and so perfectly what any of us tried to express, and found so much to praise in it. She was an artist: when she left college to marry, her teacher wept because she was very talented and he did not see how she could fully develop her artistic gifts in a domestic environment. My father's sisters were at the same college and she met him through them. They were artists of a different sort: very careful, conscientious during their training and in their later work. My mother had lightning perception, great flair, a wonderful gift for pinning down character on paper. Her caricatures of her friends as animals or allegorical figures were very witty, never unkind. On a little canvas with subjects so well-known and loved, she was brilliant. She became a successful illustrator of children's books. She might deplore a vapid story, but she put all her thought and energy into these pictures. She had complete artistic integrity, and no one contemplating a career in any of the arts could have had a better example.

She was a natural actress, and when she read aloud to us, as she loved to do, the whole book came to life. *David Copperfield, Nicholas Nickleby, Vanity Fair, Dombey and Son*—all four of us cheered when Nicholas beat Squeers, and burst into tears together when George Osborne lay dead, with a bullet through his heart. By this time I was myself a voracious reader. I can remember hiding behind the curtains to finish *Treasure Island*, when I was six or seven. The cesspit at the far end of the garden had a special fascination for me, as a possible source of the same disease that had killed most of the school in *Jane Eyre*. And I loved historical romance—in my fantasy life, I was usually Bonny Prince

Charlie.

Chris and I began our education before the war, in London. Down the road from our house there had been a little school kept by three old ladies, the Misses Wedd. Miss Edith and her sister, too good fairies of incredible age and wizardry, taught the alphabet and numbers, and French nursery rhymes; Miss Mabel, silent and mad, did the garden in a lacy hat like a shower cap. When I left I had been given as present, or perhaps prize, a copy of Nathaniel Hawthorne's *Wonder Book* and *Tanglewood Tales*. I had loved hearing these stories read aloud in summer, in the warm security of Miss Mabel's garden.

Now we had a governess—a person of whalebone and taut springs who issued bone-dry information. Out came, and in went mathematical tables, history dates—and poetry. I adored poetry and memorised it quickly and forever. Our governess had taught richer, cleverer, in every way more elevated children, and sickened us with stories of them.

The first winter of the war was deeply, terribly cold. Snow fell until we couldn't open the front door; it reached halfway up the ground-floor windows. The yellow sky made one's eyes ache. The lake froze, right across, and somebody bicycled down it, from Patterdale to Pooley Bridge. Our mother's help, who was slightly odd in the head, and moved on from us to work eventually in a nuclear research station, taking, she said, the temperature of the atomic bomb, fell into a snow-covered dustbin on her way across the fields, and cut her leg on a bully beef tin.

Away from the semicircles of warmth round the fires, the house was as cold and damp as a vault. I can remember the sheets crackling with ice from our frozen breath when we woke in the morning. There was never enough to eat; Aunt Ellen thought that children could be reared on boiled nettles and barley. Pelo was very ill, with croup. That winter must have been a nightmare for our mother. When at last the snow began to thaw, zebra stripes appeared on the mighty shoulders of the mountains, where the swollen becks ran down towards the lake. Our wet macks slapped our knees scarlet and sore as we went on our obligatory walks. As soon as the roads were passable, the doctor, an immensely tall Scot, came out to see Pelo; to amuse her he crept into the nursery on hands and knees, and unwittingly threw her almost into hysterics of terror. I had already half-killed her with toadstools. Our mother had always lived in a town, and now she was overcome by the beauty of nature. I found some puff balls in the wood, and arranged them to please her. Pelo found and ate them, and had to be dangled by the heels and given salt to make her sick. This was typical

Sister, Chris, the day before she married in 1954

of her: years later, when playing croquet, I tapped her playfully on the head with my mallet, and she went to bed for three days with a concussion. The sister between us, Rosemary, was a more ordinary, stout, and smiling child. The only harm she ever suffered, as I recall, was that we painted rings round her eyes with red ink. We wanted her to look ill for a hospital game, but the ink was indelible, and did not wear off for some months. It was difficult to play with Chris, as she was the eldest, responsible and conscientious, and in a way an extension of the grown-ups. The little ones were different, I felt that they admired me and I led the games. They were always kind to me and never told tales, though even so I was often in trouble.

My mother now found a cottage to rent in the heart of the country. We moved into it, with chickens and ducklings and a cat, and a pony and trap for transport. The nearest telephone was at the mill, over a mile away across the fields, but there was a neighbouring farm, and now that I am a farmer's wife, I can endorse my childhood estimation that there never was a kinder man than Mr. Hodgson, who worked it. We were always welcome, never in the way. I was even allowed to milk Pansy, the easiest of the cows, which took me an hour by hand. We rode the cart-horses, rocked home on the hay, slid down the rick, collected eggs, fed calves—he had the drudgery, we the pleasure. He had no children of his own, so perhaps that was why he put up with us. In return, we loved him whole-heartedly. I don't know whether he really was a re-markably good-looking man, but he seemed like a god to me. I remember we told him our Christian names—we each had three—in order to find out what his names were. "Ronald Cavendish Harrington Martin Robinson Hodgson," he said, but we never discovered whether it was true.

As I remember, all the work was done by the horses, Daisy and Dan. The fields were small, the hedges thick and thorny, the farm buildings low, dark, and nicely smelly. The fields of wispy hay were full of flowers. I remember lying on my face in the long grass, beside a tiny stream than ran across a field. The sun warmed my back, the stream smelt of mint, and I could hear the whine of insects, and watch the labori-ous beetles among the stems. I was perfectly happy then. I did not mind being alone, if you could call it alone, in that world.

There were dramas. Chris had appendicitis in the middle of the night, and Bertha, the mother's help of the time, had to pick her way to the telephone. Then the ambulance came at dawn, and Chris was whisked interestingly to hospital, wrapped in a red blanket. In the books I was reading at the time, children did not recover from such sicknesses. An early death was the crown of a spotless life in *Jessica's First Prayer, Pete the Pilgrim, Granny's Treasures*—improving books I bor-rowed from Mrs. Hodgson and devoured with fascina-tion.

The bull was a perpetual drama, an ongoing situ-ation of terror and excitement. He would stay on the side of the fell with his cows, until out of the blue he felt the urge to return to the farm. Then he would trot home, head low, bellowing softly—growling better de-scribes the noise he made. If you saw him, you took cover—there was nothing else to do. Mr. Hodgson and Dick, the farmhand, took pitchforks and managed with skill and courage to manoeuvre him into a loose box. There he was triumphantly imprisoned, and I remem-ber putting my eye to the keyhole of the stout wooden door and breathlessly making out, in the tight dark-ness, his massive, malevolent force.

As our part of the country was so wild and empty, it was often chosen as a route for heavy armoured vehi-cles on manoeuvres. This was another, hideous drama, ever lurking like the bull. We would set out in the trap on some innocent spree, my mother bravely holding the reins with Chris at her elbow. The pony had once pulled a milk cart, and still stopped at every gate. Then we would hear the dread thud of a motor bike,

and a soldier would appear and warn us that a convoy was coming. The pony immediately understood, and became tiresome to control. Having managed to turn him without going into the ditch, my mother then had to remember a place where we could wait safely for the convoy to pass. Before she found it, the rumble of ap-proaching tanks would madden the pony. He would fly up the road, mane and tail streaming, the wheels of the trap spinning, its occupants clutching each other. Only Chris was enjoying herself: she loved horses, and snatched the reins, thrilled by this display of spirit.

We had so few neighbours, that they stood out as characters, with the space and the freedom to behave oddly. Old Emma and old Harry, who lived at the top of the farm drive, kept all their animals inside the cot-tage with them at night. These were not mere dogs and cats. At dusk old Emma (or old Harry, or on occasions both) would open the front door and call, and all the ducks and hens and lambs and the house cow trooped in. Every morning they were let out again. Then there was the Major. None of us had ever seen him, but we knew where he lived, and reckoned that he was a spy. (Spies had actually been caught near Aunt Ellen's house, so we took them in our stride.) Then there was the fey author who wanted my mother to illustrate her book. When she visited us, she spread a plaid over the bonnet of her car, explaining: "It feels the cold like a little, little child." Then she turned to us children and said to the stout and smiling Rosemary: "Don't tell me your name—let me guess. You must be Deirdre—Deirdre of the Seven Sorrows!"

In winter we were snowed up again. All the pipes froze, but we were warm and well-fed, and my mother had the chance to try a bath in milk, an experiment I suspect she had always longed for, but would not re-peat. Everything was strange and beautiful, clothed in snow. The whole proportion of the landscape was al-tered, and the night visitors to our house were betrayed by their little tracks in the morning. Mr. Roper came to thaw out the pipes. He smelt of putty, and he used wonderful words, like "galloway" for horse. Two of his fingers were back to front, cut off in an accident and stuck on by himself too hastily, the wrong way round. There was so much to look at and listen to, so many things to do—we resented having to submit to formal education.

But the whalebone governess had followed us here. I can see now how long-suffering she must have been, putting up with a tiny room in a country cottage after the marbled halls of her earlier experience, for which her soul longed. But at the time we hated her. She used to pinch us secretly under the table if she thought we weren't behaving properly, and I can still see her thin and angry figure at the top of the field, and hear the screech—"Chriss-ie!"—when we had escaped to the farm. But she was better than what came next: boarding school.

We were weekly boarders, and I think that Chris enjoyed most of it, though we sat on the floor of the taxi together every Sunday evening, in floods of tears. (The taxi driver kept a local pub. He had a strawberry nose—a huge, blobbish, pitted, scarlet feature, from which it was difficult to shift one's eyes.) Chris was cheerful, sociable, and hardworking, made friends quickly, and was popular with her teachers. I feared most of them, and most of my contemporaries as well. I remember an old-fashioned w.c. where there was a lavatory with a polished mahogany seat. I used to lock myself in there, sit on it, and read. I remember crying every morning in prayers (to the crimson embarrassment of poor Chris) because our mother had health problems, and the hymns made me afraid that she would die. The most frightening pupils in the school were boys who had been taken in with shell shock, from cities in the north. One of them used to stand banging his head against the wall; another suddenly went berserk, tore the lilies and fish out of the ornamental pond in the garden, and was actually expelled (it was said, in a padded van). But the maths master

Father, Charles Graham, about 1955

was the worst; it was rumoured that he had broken a hockey stick on a boy. He was very tall and thin, with an irascible temper. People said that he was desperately in love with the headmistress's daughter, but this unhappy passion did not humanise him.

All this time my father was working in his engineering business in London. But infrequently, gloriously, magic of magic, he would visit us, materialise in the early morning, be discovered sleeping across two armchairs, having travelled overnight in a blacked-out train full of troops, using the luggage rack as a hammock. And on one of these nights, when he was already safely on his way, our London house was blown up.

Our parents must have been dreadfully upset. There were so many treasures that we hadn't brought with us to the north: my mother's books, for instance; the remains of them were pitted and scored with the effects of the blast, and had an earthy smell. As far as I was concerned, it was the toys that mattered—not the German doll, Lobelia, who was far too beautiful to be played with—but the dear company of stuffed animals, and worst of all the bear, as tall as I was myself, for whom there had been no room in the car. Bizarre details reached us from friends. The glass chandelier had been blown out of the window, and landed unscathed on the lawn, the rocking horse having accompanied it on its flight.

Now my father went to live with his mother and two unmarried sisters. My maternal grandmother had died when my mother was only fourteen; from the stories we heard she was alluring, exotic; a beautiful, careless creature who lived on oysters and champagne for digestive reasons, and loved parties. My mother had a marvellous way of describing people, that turned the spotlight full on them; she brought them, particularly her own family, to superhuman life. Certainly in photographs her magnolia mother was beautiful. My living grandmother was very different. She was tall, blonde, and beautiful in a static, Germanic way. She dressed darkly, her skirts almost ankle length; always wore a dark velvet ribbon fastened round her throat with a brooch, and a hat when she went out. She had a devastating way of producing a loaded question, or statement, just when one was happy to be with her and trying to please her. I was afraid of her, but she was undoubtedly good to us. She wrote regularly to each of us, and often enclosed a present, a postal order with the letter. Her writing was foreign, very exact and sloping; her mother had been Prussian, her father Czech. She had great courage, my mother said. We saw it whenever she crossed a road: she would walk straight across without deigning to look to right or left, while the traffic screamed swearing to a halt on either side.

I remember I loved having visitors to the house,

especially my father's sisters, the unmarried artist aunts, and my mother's cousin Pip. He was a scholarly man, a schoolmaster with a ready wit and good sense of humour. He had a charming and pretty wife, and they came at least once during the summer. The aunts always visited separately. They rode bicycles, walked for miles, handled the pony bravely. Our mother needed people to talk to, beyond her local friends who were mostly older than she was, and her young family. That, I think, was one of the reasons why I so much liked these grown-up visitors: they, so to speak, "earthed" my mother.

Our own friends were mostly the children of the local gentry, as they used to be called: now the word is "landowners," I suppose, a somewhat opprobrious term. Yet on the whole they provided fair employment, reasonable housing, environmental beauty, and security for many people. Without the envy fostered by a succession of what Aunt Ellen would have called "lamentable parliaments," English social evolution in my lifetime might have been less destructive. In those days most families had an aged nanny still living in, a respected person who did such small jobs about the house as her health permitted. Now she would live alone, or in a Home. Has independence through the State made her any happier? I doubt it, but this is no place to pursue the subject.

So the war came to an end, and so does this chapter of recollections, this dusty peepshow in a corner of my "attic" that still contains its sequence of magical pictures, their brilliance undimmed. Nothing can spoil them, although with my adult mind I know that Mrs. Hodgson died young, of cancer; that the wicked bull ripped up her husband, but Mr. Hodgson recovered, and went to live in Spain; that the last time I passed our remote cottage, the owners were keeping lions which they hoped to sell to the local wildlife park. But it looks so small when one returns. The toiling hills are so easily skimmed in a car.

Our family returned to London, and everything changed completely. Particularly for my mother, things must have been different; from seeing my father only sometimes, now they were reunited. But for me, a new school became of paramount importance. It was certainly pleasanter than the one I had endured for the last four years, and with several of the girls I became friends for life. Within this routine, writing mattered more than anything to me. It was flowery—words, marvellous, cornucopia words! My poetry changed from the excruciatingly banal to the flowing blank verse which I found suspiciously easy to do (how blank was my verse). In my last year, I wrote a comic play for my class and we performed it in front of the assembled teachers and parents. It was a skit on the sort of plot so much used in opera, including an unhappy love affair, tragical mistaken poisonings, and people discovering that they are unexpectedly related in the last act. I myself took the part of the villain, the wicked Duke. Vanessa Redgrave was not in it: she was two years younger, and as a prefect I was supposed to keep her in order, a difficult task as she was much taller than I.

When I left school, I spent four months in Portugal with my mother's father, who lived there, and his second wife. He was a benevolent but not particularly long-suffering gentleman who was happiest in his study surrounded by books, including *The Last Days of Pompeii* and *The Decline and Fall of the Roman Empire.* He had perfected his Latin and Greek on bus journeys to and from his work when he was a young man. He wrote good poetry. While I was there, I went to French classes, given for some reason by a Portuguese lady, and I was asked to several dances and parties. In those days things were very formal, but I had only two long dresses. One was a hideous blue taffeta with puffed sleeves and a net overskirt, which had been worn by my uncle's sister-in-law when she was his bridesmaid. It was well and truly out-of-date and I loathed it. The other was black and white, cut very low at the back. It was definitely glamourous, although it had belonged to my mother. My grandfather was shocked when he saw me in it, and forbade me to wear it. He was even more upset when I protested that my mother, his daughter, had.

I can't say that my social life in and around Lisbon was a great success, or that I enjoyed it much. I expect it was fairly normal in those days for girls to feel unhappy in the things their parents expected them to wear, and this has changed for the better. I have five daughters, and none of them have ever taken much notice of my fashion suggestions, though they are all pleased when I admire them. One's taste in clothes, as in food, is a personal matter, and should be as free as possible. One of my worst afternoons was a swimming party. I hate bathing suits, I can hardly swim, and I sat in acute misery while my bronzed "friends" plunged in and out of the waves. So far, I had no physical assurance.

Perhaps I should have gone to university, but even now, I don't regret the fact that I didn't. I was afraid of becoming an academic. I wanted to preserve my tiny originality, and I was afraid this would be swamped by better-informed opinions. I still think that this is a fair excuse, provided one is dedicated enough to continue one's own education. I took an au pair job in Belgium for six months, at the end of which I could read French fluently, even if I spoke it with a Belgian accent. When I came home, I did a three months' concentrated secretarial course, and then got a humble job with a firm of Jewish solicitors in the City, whose clients tended to be on the wrong side of the law. I loved listening to cases in court, and I enjoyed the seamy side of life, which carried the illusion of being more "real." My boss was the junior partner, an extremely handsome bachelor who, when drunk at the office party, danced with the brilliance of an African. He was kind, too, when I accidentally upset a cup of tea into his homburg, and he was understanding enough to give me an afternoon's solitary filing to do, when I was suffering from the effects of unhappy love.

Love! It dominated my horizon. I was always in it, from the days of Ronald Cavendish Harrington Martin Robinson Hodgson. Even the thin and irascible maths master had made my heart beat faster, because he was never unkind to me. If one of my star-spangled heroes was actually *kind*—I became scarlet and speechless. About this time my mother, who had been an agnostic, became a member of the Church of England. Pelo was christened—this had never been done—and my mother pressed me to be confirmed. I agreed to take confirmation classes, against certain sneaking doubts in my own mind, and so for half an hour every week, I basked in the personal magnetism of the vicar of St. Jude's, who though elderly was still strikingly handsome, and full of Pentecostal enthusiasm.

But I was becoming obsessed with the idea that my "real" life couldn't begin until I had mutual love—a husband, and above all, babies. The husband, the love were still fantasy, but I felt more and more that I needed my own children. My desires, my imagination were very strong. I had various boyfriends, and my mother worried, which made trouble at home. But I was determined to find the right partner for the rest of my life—now, before I got too old—I was twenty.

How clearly I can see my childhood; and once I grew up, that time too, with all its mistakes, is clear. But adolescence is confused by passion, I was torn between the heights and depths. The futility of everything would suddenly open in front of me, devastating what should have been "a nice time." Often I hated my mother, hated and feared her. I spent as much time as I could in the elegant home of the girl who had been my best friend at school. She was a musician, her sister a dancer, her eldest brother was my most regular boyfriend. The house was always full of music and people, attractive relations, talented friends. I would have liked to belong to them. I don't remember that I spoke much, but I glowed in the artistic ambiance. They had parquet in their hall, we had lino. So mean are our judgements when we are young!

My father went to Spain on a business trip, and took me with him. Even then, with him who was dearer to me than anyone in the world, I had to go off on my own. I went away before dinner, along the darkening beach, walked through the noise of the crickets that starts at sundown—and found myself in a scene of ancient Greece, with columns and ruins strangely silhouetted in the night. I discovered later that it was an old film set; it was odd to find myself there among the bizarre outlines, with my turbulent spirit. My father meanwhile was anxiously waiting at the hotel, not knowing where to search. He was furious with me when I returned, it was the only proper row I ever had from him.

My mother's religious awakening led her steadily beyond the Church of England, along the path to Rome. She became a Catholic, an all-important step for her. Rosemary and Pelo followed; I dithered on the brink. Historically it was appealing; I liked the universal Latin, the uncompromising attitudes. At the same time I feared organised religion. It made me feel overemotional, also guilty. I didn't think that it was right that it affected me like this, but it always had. I could never see myself with the white-robed on the heavenly side of the all-dividing river. Even when I was a child, I was afraid that I had no place there. My mother and I talked about it a great deal. I could see that she was deeply excited and happy. I knew that she longed for me to join her. A lot of the time I did not enjoy being myself, I did not admire myself. Would this be a solution? If Grace could do anything, why not?

I began to receive instruction from Father Vernon Johnson, best and holiest of priests. Too holy for me, too good—too attractive. Of course he joined the star-spangled heroes. That was not in any way his fault, but I might have been more truthful with a down-to-earth, didactic, plain priest. But then, the very word priest, with its suggestion of candles, incense, the sacraments, carried an esoteric glamour. Somewhere in my heart of hearts I knew, and still believe, that I am most truthful before God on an open patch under the sky—in fact, I am what Father Vernon used to call "a blue domer." I can't help it: religiously, I am too easily rocked, and I mistrust my own emotions.

At the last moment I tried to back out. It was too late. My mother's reasoning was irrefutable, and I was received on the Feast of the Sacred Heart. I was twenty-two.

That autumn I went to Rome with a friend, and on the second day of the visit I met an Iraqi in a café, and we fell in love. Far beyond his broken English, we seemed to talk the same language. He was a sculptor, a very good artist. Although he was not a Christian, he promised to become one to marry me. He travelled through Italy with Elizabeth and me, was our guide in

Rome and Florence, and Siena. For me he was a revelation, he shed light into the world. He radiated force, intense humanity. We said good-bye at Pisa. Neither of us had much money. I gave him a silver cross and pencil that had belonged to my mother's mother, and a brooch from Scotland, a relic of my Prince Charlie days. He gave me a bracelet of tiny coloured stones.

My parents were shattered. My mother particularly was appalled that I should enter the Church one day and fall for a Mohammedan the next. She could not understand how I could do this. I did not have the courage (or the money) to leave home and go back to Italy. In many ways I was afraid. So I wrote, and put an end to it. Now, so many years later, I can't deny that among all the phantom heroes, he alone is real. It was the first time I fell in love, and it would happen once more, but not for twenty years.

There followed the most curious coincidence. I had married, I had four children, I was on a train, and I had in fact chosen a seat near a very dark young man because instinctively I liked the look of him. The train was held up for some reason, and we got into conversation. It turned out that he was my sculptor's nephew—had in fact been almost brought up by him!

Now I was working at the BBC. I had moved from the Engineering Department to Features (long since absorbed by Drama and Talks). Louis Macneice was in the same department; Alan Burgess, Douglas Cleverdon—I worked for Marjorie and Eddie Ward and later, for Christopher Sykes. I enjoyed it, and I had already taken the first steps that would transform me, I hoped, from secretary to studio manager, and eventually producer, when I met Timothy Poole at a Catholic club.

We were married that summer, and Theodora, the first of our four daughters, was born within a year. We had hardly any money: Tim was not qualified for any career, and as far as mine was concerned, that appeared to be that. But we were very happy to begin with. Our house was full of purpose, and there was always the hope that our impecunious circumstances would change. We lived in a suburb in South London, and I became a model of thrift and efficiency. After the housework was done and the shopping achieved on a shoestring, I read seriously, or whirled Theo out in the pram for miles down streets that all looked the same, driven by the contrary spirit that would not allow me to relax with other mothers and subside into a routine of coffee mornings and children's teas. I started a Catholic Discussion Group. I longed for the commendation of priests at this time, but never felt I got it. Soon we had a second child, Emily. She was the greatest pleasure, although my routine was so efficient that

Poole, about 1960

her arrival hardly interrupted it. She was still a baby when I began writing my first children's story, *A Dream in the House.*

As soon as I became aware of books, I had known that I was going to be a writer. I clearly remember my first attempt: I must have been very small, because it was before the war, and I remember how painful it was to get the letters right. I printed: "Why don't you come and look at me, for I'm the queen you know," and above I drew a picture of a girl who was feeling very proud because she was wearing a dress with a sash that did up in a bow in front. Bows always tied at the back when I was small, and it seemed to me a waste.

When the manuscript was finished I sent it to the literary agent A. P. Watt, and eventually heard that Hutchinson wanted to publish it. They paid me forty pounds. The book came out while I was in hospital giving birth to my dear Kate. Tim had already moved to Taunton, having found work as a driving instructor. We followed him into the country, where we had a beautiful old house. All the things I had longed for were happening: the devoted husband, the children, the country place—yet now I was attacked by postnatal depression which lasted for months. It was a very grim time. Tim's aunt came to tea, a stout and cheerful lady. I managed to tell her that I felt rather miserable most of the time. "Do you?" she asked briskly. "Why don't you write another book?" So I did. It was called *Moon Eyes,* and Dorothy Tomlinson had taken over the children's department at Hutchinson: as excellent an editor as one could have. Soon after I finished it, Isabel was born.

My next book was *The Lilywhite Boys,* an adult novel set in the flat countryside around our home. It was published by Hart-Davis. In 1970 *Yokeham* appeared, the result of much thought, and revision under the guidance of Simon Young at John Murray. *Catch as Catch Can* and *Billy Buck* were published by Hutchinson Junior Books.

For me it has always been places, particularly houses, that are the catalysts that crystallise my ideas into books. The chapter house in *Catch as Catch Can,* and the family house which is burnt down in *Billy Buck,* both exist in Lancashire, where we spent summer holidays every year with Tim's uncle, the kindest and funniest of men. I loved him. The devil-beset house in *Moon Eyes* is our home near Taunton; nearby, Yokeham still stands, there is a farm machinery sale in its grounds every year. My characters were carefully worked upon; perhaps in those days I was a bit like Rabbit, the friend of Winnie-the-Pooh, who "never let anything come to him, but always went and fetched it."

My father died of cancer before *Yokeham* was published.

My mother left London, and returned to the house in the Lake District which my father had inherited from Aunt Ellen, and where we had spent many holidays. In the summer Tim and the children came too, but now every winter, I visited her for a few days on my own. We would sit together talking about books mostly, or the Faith—hers continued to illumine her life until she died. These winter visits when we were alone together were very happy. I never said that my marriage was going wrong—I didn't know that it was. I was acting happy marriage. But something broke when my father died.

When I met Vincent Helyar, my marriage to Tim did not end, because in a sense it had never really existed. We had lived side by side in a harmonious way. We hardly ever had an argument. But we could not share, because, pretend as I might, there was a whole dimension in my life where he could not follow. Vincent was already there. He had the force, the human intensity that I had known once before.

I went north, and told Tim's uncle what had happened. I did not dare to tell my mother. Chris was

Vincent Helyar, 1985

going to stay with her, and she told her. I was expecting Vincent's child, and we moved into his family house with Emily, Kate, and Isabel. Theodora stayed with Tim. She was very unsettled for a time. No one who has been through a divorce will deny that it is an agonising situation, regardless of which side you are on. Tim was upheld by the knowledge that he was guiltless, and so he was—after all, he couldn't help his nature. I suffered horribly, but I was strengthened by the certainty that I would do it again—for me it had been total necessity. Enough said: those three faithful daughters have become very fond of Vincent, who was the first committed father they had had, and therefore sometimes something of a shock. Theo has accepted him, and she is fond of him too. And we have two children: Charlotte and Vincent.

I haven't written any more adult novels, though I have worked hard since I came to Poundisford. It is a very old house, and Vincent's family has lived here for hundreds of years. I don't need to hunt any longer for a catalyst for my ideas.

I am still writing children's thrillers. The latest, *Three for Luck*, has just been published. *Touch and Go* became a television serial. *Hannah Chance* (my own favourite) and *Diamond Jack* were written here, and I have also contributed several plays to the television series *West Country Tales*. Of these, "The Harbourer" and "Miss Constantine" are the ones I like best. Vincent and I found the locations for "The Harbourer" when we first met: it is about stags, and was filmed on Exmoor. "Miss Constantine" is a perfectly terrifying, true modern ghost story, which was told to me by the clergyman involved in it, and was filmed in Poundisford. Charlotte acted as a child spirit in "The Sabbatical," and again, with her brother, in "With Love, Belinda."

Recently, Caroline Roberts, Hutchinson's children's editor, commissioned me to write a collection of short stories about animals. I have loved doing them. We chose rooks, red deer, frogs, bees, fell ponies, voles, foxes, badgers, and swallows. It was like going back into childhood, the timeless observance of brothers and friends—certainly not specimens. Vincent has the key to the places where I was happiest as a child. Through him I have discovered that none of the magic has been lost.

My last work, just completed, is the script including lyrics of a musical which will be performed by Vincent Junior's prep school in the new year, and will go on into the local theatre after that. Very exciting, and the greatest fun! Another musical commission is in the air. I have had a lovely summer collaborating with the composer, Michael Dyer, who lives nearby. Vincent does most of the research for these projects. He is an avid historian. He is also a truthful critic, and always hopeful and encouraging.

My mother's distress over my broken marriage was terrible. She never cut me off, but for a long time she could not accept Vincent. But in the end, thank God, she did. In the end we were true and loving friends, and happier together than we had ever been.

The river dividing the righteous and the unrighteous has run dry, all can be seen as children of God.

BIBLIOGRAPHY

FOR YOUNG ADULTS

Fiction:

A Dream in the House (illustrated by Peggy Fortnum). London: Hutchinson, 1961.

Moon Eyes. London: Hutchinson, 1965; (illustrated by Trina Schart Hyman) Boston: Little, Brown, 1967.

Catch as Catch Can. London: Hutchinson, 1969; (illustrated by Kiyo Komoda) New York: Harper, 1970.

Billy Buck. London: Hutchinson, 1972; published in America as *The Visitor.* New York: Harper, 1972.

Touch and Go. London: Hutchinson, 1976; New York: Harper, 1976.

When Fishes Flew: A Selection of Legends and Old Wives' Tales from the West Country (illustrated by Barbara Swiderska). London: Benn, 1978; published as *Kings, Ghosts, and Highwaymen.* London: Carousel, 1981.

The Forbidden Room (illustrated by Tony Kerins). London: Benn, 1979.

The Open Grave (illustrated by T. Kerins). London: Benn, 1979.

Hannah Chance. London: Hutchinson, 1980.

Diamond Jack. London: Methuen Children's Books, 1983.

Three for Luck (illustrated by Barrie Thorpe). London: Hutchinson, 1985.

Wildlife Tales. London: Hutchinson, 1986.

Television:

West Country Tales. British Broadcasting Corp., 1975-82. "The Harbourer," 1975; "The Sabbatical," 1981; "The Breakdown," 1981; "Miss Constantine," 1981; "Ring a Ring a Rosie," 1982; "With Love, Belinda," 1982; "The Wit to Woo," 1982.

FOR ADULTS

Fiction:

The Lilywhite Boys. London: Hart-Davis, 1968.

Yokeham. London: Murray, 1970.

Nonfiction:

The Country Diary Companion (photographs by Simon McBride). Exeter: Webb & Bower, 1984.

Charlotte and Vincent, Jr., 1985

Marilyn Sachs
1927-

My story really begins when I was four years old and my family moved to Jennings Street in the east Bronx, a borough of New York City. At first we lived in an apartment on the fourth floor of 741 Jennings Street. It was a long, dark apartment with a piano that a former tenant had left in one of the smallest, darkest rooms. Here I began my first attempts at composing, playing the most beautiful, harmonious music ever heard. Unfortunately, nobody else in the family recognized my talent and I was usually encouraged to go outside and get some fresh air.

Grown-ups really believed in fresh air when I was a child, and my older sister, Jeannie, and I were outnumbered by the grown-ups in our lives, all of whom believed in fresh air for the two of us. Not only did we have a mother and a father at 741 Jennings Street but we also had a widowed aunt—Aunt Bertha—living with us, and for a time, another widowed aunt—Aunt Amelia—who stayed, I think, in the room with the piano.

Aunt Amelia was never a favorite, but when she left to go and live somewhere else, she hid pennies all over the place—under the sofa cushions, inside the radio cabinet, between the bedsprings of various beds, and probably behind the piano.

It was a lovely way to say good-bye because in those days a penny could buy much more than it can today. Across the street, and it was never a busy street because it dead-ended at the corner, stood the neighborhood candy store where Mr. and Mrs. Eckman presided. For a penny, you could stand in front of a large glass case containing so many possibilities, it was never easy making a simple decision. You could buy an assortment of small, colorful gumdrops with your penny, or a chewy apricot candy we called shoeleather, caramels, chocolate kisses, papers of pink and white candy "buttons," hard candies in pretty, rustly papers, chocolate marshmallows or pretzels either circular or straight. There were many other choices, and Mr. and Mrs. Eckman from time to time grew impatient if the deliberations went on for too long.

On one side of Jennings Street stood the apartment houses—red brick, five stories high, each one smack up against the next, with a "super" who lived in the basement. At an earlier time, more-prosperous tenants probably lived in the houses since each of them

Mother, Anna Smith Stickle

boasted fancy stonework over the doors and windows, and gleaming brass mailboxes in the vestibules as well as shapely brass handles on the outside doors.

You can see the door handles in a photo taken of me when I was about eight years old. Don't be deceived by the real leopard fur on my hat, collar, and muff. My family was poor, like everybody else on Jennings Street, but I did have an uncle who was a furrier and who always managed to save scraps of fur for his nieces. For many years I dreamed of owning a whole leopard-skin coat, but that was before I realized there was a living animal under the beautiful fur.

By the time this photo was taken, we had moved to 745 Jennings Street, right next door to 741. We

Marilyn, age eight

moved because my mother had been in an accident and spent many months in the hospital. When she recovered she walked with a limp and was no longer able to manage the four flights up to the apartment at 741.

Apartment 745 was on the ground floor. You can see our living room window in this photo of my sister and me with our dolls and our father. My sister is the tall, beautiful girl with the large doll. I am the one in the middle with the small doll. Her name was Buttercup, and she was one of childhood's big disappointments.

Our favorite aunt had given my sister her doll some years earlier on her birthday, and before my eighth birthday, I knew she was planning to buy me a doll too. Of course, like most younger sisters, I wanted the exact same doll my sister had, but my aunt bought me one of the newer and, she said, more expensive dolls. (But who cared about that!) My sister's doll had a sawdust body, but Buttercup was made entirely of rubber and could even wet her diapers. As you can see from the photo, she did not look anything at all like my sister's doll, and I never grew to love her.

Across the street was Junior High School 40 and

its large schoolyard. During the week, the schoolyard gate was left open after school so that children could play inside. On the weekends, the gates were locked and no kids were supposed to enter. This ruling was not universally accepted, however, and there were always two bars stretched apart so that small bodies could get into the schoolyard at any time. Every so often, the bars would be straightened out, but they never remained straightened out for very long.

Next to the schoolyard stood three small houses from an earlier time, the candy store, a large apartment house, and a grocery store at the corner.

Jennings Street had no trees, birds, or flowers. But it had kids. Every day after school and all day on the weekends, holidays, and during the summer vacation, the kids poured out of the apartment houses and filled the sidewalks, the playground, and the street itself. Hardly any cars ever came through so that the street served as a field for stickball or a rink for roller skaters. Other games like "Potsy" (known as Hopscotch in other less-civilized parts of the world), Red Light-Green Light, Jump Rope, Old Mother Witch, Time, A My Name Is, Mother May I, and Hide-and-Seek were generally played on the sidewalks while punchball, handball, and basketball were played in the schoolyard.

After a certain age, the sexes separated out. Boys did *not* play Potsy, Time, A My Name Is, nor did they jump rope. Girls did *not* play stickball or basketball. Both sexes could play stoopball, handball or Hide-and-Seek, but seldom together.

For intimate conversations, the stone stoops in front of each house were preferred places. My sister and I are sitting on our stoop in the photo. Sometimes the super, if he was cranky, might chase you away or, even worse, some older boys might use other forms of persuasion to gain possession of the stoop. Once, after some huge, savage boys (about twelve or thirteen years old at least) had driven us off, my sister emptied a bucket of water on them from our window which, as you can see, had certain strategic advantages.

We lived on Jennings Street from the time I was four until I was fourteen. Franklin Delano Roosevelt or, FDR as most of us thought of him, was president forever. Everybody was poor and nobody I knew owned a car.

I started kindergarten when I was four. My mother said I was five. Either she thought I was amazingly mature for my age or she wanted to get rid of me. I prefer the former reason.

All was well in the beginning. I drew large crayon pictures, played happily with the pegboards, enjoyed the circle games like Blue Bird, Blue Bird through My Window, and didn't even mind ending up as the cheese

Marilyn (center), with her sister and father, about 1935

in The Farmer in the Dell. But one terrible day, when I raised my hand and asked my teacher if I could go to the girls' room, she told me I would have to wait until somebody else needed to go as well. Evidently nobody else needed to go and my desperation grew. My teacher suggested we play The Farmer in the Dell and as the game progressed, my self-control failed me.

"Look!" cried one of my classmates. "Look!"

Everybody looked. It was one of the most humiliating moments of my life. But humiliating moments are mother's milk to writers, and the episode ended up forty-five years later in the first chapter of my book *Class Pictures.*

In the first grade, my teacher divided us all up by smart rows and dumb rows. We read stories in our reader about a boy named Dickie Dare. You had to have a clean handkerchief pinned to your dress every day, and if you were caught wiping your nose on your sleeve you were banished to the dumb row for the rest of the day.

Somewhere in the course of that year, my teacher asked us to write a composition about what we wanted to be when we grew up. It is the earliest piece of writing that I have. In it, I said that I wanted to be a nurse when I grew up, and that in order to be a nurse, I needed to go out into the street, find a dead tramp, and cut him up into thousands of little pieces. If I could put all the pieces back together again in the right places, then I could be a nurse and my mother would be very proud of me.

My teacher wrote on the top of the paper, "Start all your sentences with capitals." She didn't say, "No, no, that is *not* the way to become a nurse." Maybe she also thought it was the way. New Yorkers often have strange ideas.

Deciding what to put down in this autobiography is like standing in front of Mr. and Mrs. Eckman's glass cases filled with candies and trying to make a selection. Writers generally have good memories and mine hovers helplessly over coloring books of the Dionne Quintuplets, my first pair of roller skates, learning how to jump Double Dutch and breaking my two front teeth in a fall . . . Which memories to pick? I wish I could take all of you back in time with me to some glorious days of high adventure scaling Indian Rock in Crotona Park or sucking lemon ices out of little paper cups on hot summer evenings when we could stay up almost as late as we wanted. Bits and pieces of my childhood have ended up in many of my books. *Amy Moves In,* my first book, probably comes closer to describing my life on Jennings Street than any of my other books.

My mother was ill during the summer I was six, and my father shipped my sister and me off to summer camp in order to provide her with the peace and quiet she required. Over the following summers, we were to be sent to other camps, all charity camps for poor city children who needed to learn the beauty of the countryside. Some of those camps were so awful—one in particular right out of *Jane Eyre*—that my sister and I have been confirmed city lovers ever since.

Marilyn (third row, right) and kindergarten class, 1932

But that first camp my father sent us to was really the best of the bunch. It was called Camp Edalia on Lake Tiorati in New York State and I believe it may still be there. It had log cabins, patient counselors, a wonderful lake to swim in, arts and crafts, and great freedom for the campers. The only problem was that the minimum age was eight and I was only six. My father had added on two years in order to get rid of me. Or perhaps he too considered me extremely mature for my age.

The truth did not come out until the first roll call when my age was revealed. A few of the counselors were for sending me home but my sister, aged nine at the time, stepped forward and said, "This child is bright for her age." Since my sister was not given to compliments on my behalf, I was extremely elated at the time and have remembered her statement to this day.

I became the pet of the camp, and I never had to make my bed, sweep the floor, or participate in K.P. Everybody wanted me as a mascot. Many nights, as I remember, various bunks tried to kidnap me, and furious pillow fights were waged on my behalf. Lucky me!

Unlucky me! In one of the bunks, some older girls, around nine or ten, told ghost stories. And even worse—stories about vampires who sneak up to you while you are sleeping and suck the blood out of your throat.

After that I always kept the covers over my chin and made a special point of sleeping as far away from the door as possible. At future camps, I always made sure there were other bodies between myself and the door so that the vampire would be sated before he reached me.

I grew afraid of the dark and always needed to sleep with a light on. Grown-ups assured me I would outgrow it, but I never really did. It's hard for me to admit that at fifty-seven years old, I still am afraid of the dark and still like to sleep as far as possible away from any given door.

Some of our other camp experiences were so unpleasant that my sister vowed when she grew up and had children, she would never make them go to camp. She kept her word too, and neither of her children ever went to camp. My kids, on the other hand, relished the camps they went to but I never made them go.

My second book *Laura's Luck* was supposed to be an anticamp book. Only parts of it are based on my experiences. I'm afraid it turned out much more positive than I had planned because I keep receiving letters from kids who want to go to "Camp Tiorati" as it is called in the story.

When I was in the third grade at P.S. 63, my mother ended up in the hospital, and I spent a lot of time crying. This is the time for me to make a painful confession about myself as a child. I was, in many respects, a real loser. Of course, I didn't think of myself that way then. Like most of us, I regarded myself as delightful and unique if frequently misunderstood.

In actuality, I was a little, skinny, cowardly kid. I was also a liar and a crybaby. All the neighborhood bullies used to line up waiting for me after school—hundreds and hundreds of them—at least that's the way it seemed to me then. I used to look carefully up and down the block almost every afternoon before I went out to play. My older sister, who always seemed to me a glorious figure of righteousness and revenge, frequently had to fight my battles for me. My father gave me boxing lessons but to no avail.

I couldn't help the lying. My own rearrangement of reality always seemed much more appealing than what everybody else considered the truth. One of the best and most charming children's books to deal with this dilemma, incidentally, is Dr. Seuss' *And To Think That I Saw It on Mulberry Street.* My own mother read articles in the women's magazines and lectured me very severely on my lack of truthfulness. My sister said I disgusted her. It was humiliating.

Nowadays, whenever I speak to groups of kids, I make a special point of telling them what a liar I was as a child. I tell them—those of them that get into trouble for not interpreting the truth more precisely—not to despair. I tell them that lying might even be a good qualification for fiction writers. Basically, the child who lies and the writer who weaves stories out of her own experiences, are each doing the same thing. They are rearranging the bare, boring facts into a more harmonious, meaningful pattern. The child, of course, gets scolded for lying while the writer is praised for her imagination.

In the third grade, my teacher, a lovely, young woman named Mrs. Powers, announced that she would be leaving at the end of the year. She didn't say why. I suspect she was pregnant, but words like that weren't bandied around in front of children at that time. Some years earlier, Mrs. Powers' husband had made a doll's house for her class. It was supposed to be a replica of the house that the three bears lived in. I loved it. All the children loved it, even the boys. There were three wooden bears coming up the front stairs, on their way home from their famous walk in the forest. In the back, completely opened up, were two floors filled with wonderful handmade furniture. Downstairs was the kitchen with a pantry full of delectable dollhouse food—corn on the cob, strawberry shortcake, a huge Swiss cheese, a loaf of bread, roast turkey. In the dining room stood the dining room table, covered with a red-and-white checked tablecloth. Three chairs were grouped around it—a great big one for the Papa bear, a middle-sized one for the Mama bear, and a little, tiny one for the Baby bear.

Upstairs were the beds, each one with its own sheets, pillows, and blankets. In the smallest one lay a tiny, golden-haired doll with eyes that opened and shut. Goldilocks.

The children in Mrs. Powers' class were permitted to play with the Bears' House, and none of us looked forward to the last day of school. Because Mrs. Powers had said that on the last day of school, she was going to give the Bears' House to "the best child" in the class.

Teachers spoke like that then. There was always a "best child" and invariably a "worst child." Everybody knew who was who in those days, and if there was any doubt, the matter could be settled conclusively by the number of gold stars any given child had received in the course of the term. If you were very well-behaved—which meant sitting quietly at your desk, hands folded in front of you—you might receive a gold star for behavior at the end of the day. If you were very smart, got 100% in spelling or math, you might also receive a gold star for your work. Some people got stars for both.

Not me! I spent too much time crying. Now, I was a crybaby even in the best of times. I still cry easily. But in the third grade, with my mother in the hospital, I outdid myself. And you don't get gold stars for crying.

But on the last day of school, to everybody's amazement, Mrs. Powers gave me the Bears' House. It certainly didn't have anything to do with gold stars or being the best at anything except maybe crying. Probably she was just so tired of seeing me cry that she thought wouldn't it be nice if I could get this kid to laugh at least once before I leave.

I laughed all right. But my classmates didn't. It took the combined powers of my sister and some other sixth graders to convey me and my Bears' House home safely.

Later, when I became a writer, I tried to tell the story as it had happened to me but I couldn't. One thing you learn as a writer is that you must distance yourself from your own life or nobody will want to read what you write. It's necessary to start off with something that matters to you, but you must learn how to open it up for your readers as well. I made three attempts before I finally wrote *The Bears' House* in its present form. Fran Ellen's family and circumstances were different from mine, but her joy over her bears' house comes very close to the joy I felt over mine.

Back to Mr. and Mrs. Eckman's candy counter. I want to share with you birthday parties, Halloween, and all the stray cats and dogs we kept bringing home and were never allowed to keep. I want you to come swimming with me summers in Crotona Park Pool or jump the waves at Rockaway Beach where more affluent relatives had a bungalow and where we, the poor relations, were invited for two glorious weeks. I want you to be with me in the winter when we made forts out of the mountains of snow pushed to one side by the snow removal trucks and sometimes roasted potatoes in snowy fireplaces that tasted much better than anything we ever ate in our warm kitchens.

And I want you to come with me to the Morrisania Branch of the New York Public Library where my life as a writer began.

A large, brick, forbidding-looking building with a children's room upstairs. It was no easy matter getting inside especially on Fridays in the wintertime. You had to stand on a long line with other kids that usually stretched outside into the street. It took forever before you got into the building and began the ascent on the stairs leading up to the children's room. You were expected to be quiet once you got inside. "Children should be seen but not heard" was a favorite expression of adults. An evil looking, frog-faced man who we believed owned the library patrolled the stairs, and any child caught talking above a whisper was thrown out. You had to get past him before you made it up to the desk. There, a couple of severe-looking women clerks inspected your books for torn pages, smudges, or greasy finger prints (Never mine), and collected overdue fines (generally paid on the installment plan), before permitting you to pass.

But your troubles weren't over. You had to deal with the librarian—a smiling, soft-faced woman who always tried to give me books she said I would enjoy.

Usually they had to do with girls my own age crossing America in covered wagons. It took a combination of good manners and deceit to thank her gracefully for her suggestions and then, later, when she wasn't looking, to sneak the books back on the shelf and pick out the ones I really liked.

Years later when I worked as a children's librarian myself, I made sure never to interfere with children who wanted to pick out books for themselves, and never, never to recommend any books about girls in covered wagons—except maybe for the ones by Laura Ingalls Wilder.

You were only allowed to take out two books then and to keep them no longer than two weeks. This meant frequent trips to the library on my part. Some days, on school holidays particularly, I might spend the whole day there, being eased out when the library closed, my eyes blinking and my head filled with the glories of other times and places.

Books can close doors as well as open them. When I read, I was no longer a little, skinny, cowardly crybaby who lived in the Bronx. I could travel anywhere I wanted, like the little lame prince whose magic carpet took him anywhere he wanted to go. In the beginning, I read only fairy tales in which the youngest usually turned out to be the best—a vast improvement over my real life in which my older sister was not only more truthful than I but stronger, braver, and smarter as well.

After the fairy tales, I moved on to the epics and then, with occasional lapses, to historical fiction that took place before 1600. My favorite authors were Caroline Dale Snedeker, Howard Pyle, Jefferey Farnol—whose heroines could outride and outduel any man—Sir Walter Scott, and later, Alexandre Dumas.

I read other things as well—comic books, magazines, The Bobbsey Twin series, and any books my sister recommended. She was one of the strongest influences in my life when I was a child, and I always respected her judgment beyond that of anybody else.

Books brought me such comfort then, and still do, that after I gave up my dreams of nursing, I determined to become a writer.

Our family didn't own many books, and the ones we had came in sets. The only time children's books were ever bought were for birthdays. When I was ten, I asked for and received *Uncle Tom's Cabin*. On my ninth birthday, *Grimm's Fairy Tales*, and on my eighth—I'm saving this one for last which is why I'm going backward—*Rebecca of Sunnybrook Farm* by Kate Douglas Wiggin. Now, Rebecca was not a book I would have chosen for myself, but my mother had read it and loved it as a child and she picked it out for me, certain that I would love it too.

And I did. Probably because it was the only book she ever read to me. I could read very well by myself at that time, but it didn't matter. She would read me a chapter every day, usually in the afternoon. I would hurry home from school and carry a small chair into the living room. She sat on the sofa and I sat below, looking up at the book and her face above it. She loved that book. Sometimes she'd stop to laugh at parts she thought were very funny, and I'd laugh too even though I didn't always understand what was so funny. It's still very sharp in my mind—sitting there with my mother, sharing that special book that I didn't quite understand, but knowing that my mother and I were doing something together that belonged to nobody else.

Everybody told stories in my family, and everybody's stories were different. Aunt Bertha, so prim and proper ordinarily, told the most delicious stories about her brothers and sisters—my father was the youngest of eight—who grew up on the lower East Side of New York City at the turn of the century, and whose lively, squabbling antics delighted me. I had a great-grandmother who hid fugitive slaves before the Civil War, and I loved to hear about her.

My father's stories tended to deal with the epic and heroic. He favored history and the Bible, changing any details that stood between him and a more dra-

Grandmother, Sarah Smith, about 1900

Vote for

AMERICAN LABOR PARTY — CITY FUSION PARTY

Candidate for

A S S E M B L Y

Fourth Assembly District

Nominated
by
City Fusion
Party

Nominated
by
American
Labor Party

Endorsed by
Progressive
Party

Endorsed by
Progressive
Party

SAMUEL STICKLE

The Citizens Union has stated that "our present Assemblyman (see 1937 report) has an average record."

Conditions in our district warrant more than an average record.

Elect a Labor candidate who will fight for a program fitting the needs of the Fourth Assembly District.

Vote Straight American Labor Party—Row C
266

Father, Samuel Stickle, 1938

matic telling. Like myself, my father often embroidered reality and was the one member of my family not disturbed about my lack of truthfulness. He liked telling ghost stories too, particularly delighting in doing "The Golden Arm" at my Halloween parties where he could scare the daylights out of my friends.

Some of the best stories came from my mother's mother who had come to this country from Russia around 1900 with my mother and oldest uncle. She was the inspiration for the mother in my book *Call Me Ruth.* It took me many years to find this picture which I have hanging up in my home and love looking at. My grandmother became one of my favorite people although I didn't care much for her when I was a child. She had a funny accent for one thing, and I thought at the time that the best Americans spoke perfect English. She also frequently grew impatient with

my sister and myself, referring to us once as the "boiled rats"—meaning spoiled brats. Her stories of "The Old Country" were full of darkness, curses, and magic—the kinds of things I loved to read about in fairy tales but didn't necessarily want to meet up with on Jennings Street.

I told stories too. According to my mother, I told them even when I wasn't supposed to. Soon I began writing some of mine down.

In 1938 my father ran for the New York State Assembly, and lost. It was my introduction to politics and although I'm afraid my contribution to his campaign consisted of tearing down the posters of his opponent, it began an involvement and interest that has never left me.

My mother died in 1940 when I was twelve, and it wasn't easy for our family to do without her. She brought order and stability to our lives that we never regained after her death. In 1941 I graduated from Junior High School 40 in a long white dress that my sister had worn a few years earlier. My father bought me a corsage of red roses which I still have, all dried out and pressed inside my autograph album. Inside the front cover I charted my future. "High School, College, Career (Writer) and Marriage (?)"

You asked me to write
What shall it be?
Two little words
Remember me.

wrote one of my friends. And yes, I do remember her. I also remember missing my mother very much. I used to look at her autograph album, circa 1913, and try to think of her when she was young. There was a funny jingle in her album that I wrote in the albums of some of my friends.

If you want to be blessed
With more heavenly joys
Think more of the Lord
And less of the boys.

Boys!

I always liked boys. Even in junior high school when boys and girls were separated into different classes, one of my closest friends was a boy. His name was Seymour and, like myself, he was a small, skinny kid with curly hair and blue eyes. I had known him since fourth grade, and our friendship was to last until we were both married—to other people. Over the years, we roller-skated all over the city, and I was thinking of him when I wrote *Peter and Veronica.*

I really fell in love for the first time when I was nearly fourteen in the third term of high school. There was a boy in my class who was a talented pianist. Everybody thought he was funny looking except me. We sat next to each other in our homeroom class and I, who ordinarily never had a problem talking, was almost speechless in his presence. Finally, we began speaking to each other and occasionally we walked to school together. Once I went with him to Carnegie Hall for a concert. Gallantly, he offered to pay my train fare, but somehow we managed to get on the wrong train so I had to pay his way back. I kept hoping he would invite me to other concerts even though I didn't understand much about music. He never did. Towards the end of the term, he developed a crush on a pretty, empty-headed girl named Lorraine. Boys always seemed to like girls like that when I was a teenager. Maybe they still do.

I'm not finished with the subject of boys, but I need to pause here to say good-bye to Jennings Street. We moved away in 1943, when my father married again. Our new neighborhood was in the west Bronx which was a step up on the social ladder. I could have transferred to another high school, but I loved Morris High School and wanted to finish there. Every morning, I had to take a couple of buses across the city in order to get to school. One day, I picked up a conversation with a boy—a very nice boy, as a matter of fact. The only problem was that he had a crush on a friend of mine, a girl very much like pretty, empty-headed Lorraine. Then, I felt only self-pity but a few years ago, when I wrote *Bus Ride,* I could only be grateful.

Although there were many disappointments during my teen years—my skin (pimples), my hair (too curly—I wanted straight, shiny hair), and my inevitable crushes on boys who liked other girls—my high-school years were very happy ones for me. I had many friends, belonged to everything, and had established myself as a writer. I wrote stories for the school magazine, "The Tower," and was an editor of the school paper, "The Piper."

I even won a prize for a story I submitted to a contest sponsored by "The Tower." It was called "The Icicle and the Leaf," and was inspired by the fairy tales of Oscar Wilde.

This might be a good place to offer some advice to future writers. Read! As much and as widely as you can. Read for pleasure and without realizing it, you will learn the craft of writing. You will absorb from those writers you admire the ability to put words together, to tell a story, to pace, to highlight, to beguile. Sometimes when I write, I can almost trace some of the scenes in my books back to other sources. When Mrs. Firestone—an old, eccentric woman in my book *Underdog*—says, "You see, Izzy . . . it's like this" I remember Joe Gargery, the kindly blacksmith, in *Great Expecta-*

tions by Charles Dickens when he says to Pip, "Why you see, old chap . . . " When Tanta Sadie, a Jewish immigrant in 1909, in my book *Call Me Ruth* says, "Well, girls, we had a very nice visit," she is a descendant of Mrs. Bennet, an English lady one hundred years earlier in Jane Austen's *Pride and Prejudice,* exulting over her dinner party. "Well girls . . . what say you to the day?"

I had luck with my teachers too in Morris High School. One or two were sadistic, and it has been my pleasure over the years to put them into my stories. (I should tell you that revenge is one of the joys of being a writer. You literally have the last word.) Many of my teachers were excellent and one in particular gave me the push I needed to become a serious writer.

She gave me an 86 as a final mark in her English class. Most of the other kids in the class got 90 or above. Everybody knew she was an easy marker, and I considered myself one of the stars of her class. So why the 86?

I asked her but she didn't tell me then. Instead, she invited me to spend a summer with her, her husband and their two young boys in their summer house in the country. There were to be some other kids as well—seven in all—and I would act as a counselor. I've already told you what I thought of camps and the country, so in the beginning I was suspicious. Finally, I decided to go. She said I could bring a girlfriend too.

It ended up as one of the most glorious summers of my life. It gave me glimpses of other possible ways to live and to think. I was fifteen then and the kids ranged in age from six to twelve. We swam, played punchball, fingerpainted, and gave plays and variety shows on weekends for visiting parents. We picked blackberries, daydreamed, fought, hiked, and watched the mists rise on the mountains. There was tragedy too when the youngest child, a six-year-old girl, died suddenly of a brain tumor.

All summer long I plagued my teacher with the question of that 86. She said she thought I knew why she had given it to me. I protested that I did not. Finally, months later, she wrote me a letter which I've kept to this day. She said she thought I was very talented but also very lazy, which, she said, would stand in my way as a writer unless I got the better of it. The 86, she wrote, was a compliment in that she was telling me the work I did in her class did not measure up to what I could do.

Now that was a teacher! I think of the 86 many times when I don't want to go to the trouble of making changes in a story that needs to be revised, and I'm grateful to her. In 1979 I dedicated a book to her called *A Summer's Lease.* The book is very loosely based on my experiences that summer, and none of the characters are like their real-life prototypes. I hunted my teacher down, found her after all these years, and sent her a copy of the book.

I haven't mentioned the Second World War which was being waged while I was in high school. We had no young men in our family off fighting and no close relatives in any of the occupied countries. There were shortages of sugar, meat, shoes, and all of us had to use ration cards. But for myself as a teenager, not knowing until years later the true horror of war and that war in particular, the war was kind of fun. I volunteered as a messenger in the Civil Defense and wore a special arm band with a lightning insignia. I was the war stamp rep. in my homeroom class, president of the Victory Corps, and I knitted scarves for the Red Cross. What I enjoyed the most when I was fifteen and sixteen was lying about my age in order to work as a hostess in a canteen for soldiers. Most of them were terribly homesick and showed me pictures of their wives or girl-friends. Many years later, I made friends with a woman my age who had lived in France during the German occupation. While I was dancing and laughing in the American canteens, her parents and little sister were being dragged off to Auschwitz by the Germans just because they were Jews, and she was in hiding. I wrote a book based on her experiences called *A Pocket Full of Seeds,* and the two of us went around to

Senior class writer, Morris High School, 1944

speak in different schools, contrasting our experiences during the Second World War.

I was class writer when I graduated from high school. You can see me in this drawing from my year book. Seymour was class actor. We went together to our prom, which was held in the school gym because of the war.

That summer, in between working in a day camp and reading *An American Tragedy* by Theodore Dreiser, I had one of my happiest teen romances. It happened on Orchard Beach in the Bronx when I met Lou, a friend of a friend of a friend. He was a tall, thin boy with dark gold hair and eyes (In two of my books, characters have gold hair and eyes) and a golden suntan to match. He was an engineering student at City College, and I would start at Hunter College in the fall. We were surrounded by romance. My sister met her husband-to-be on Orchard Beach at the same time and one of my friends also paired-off with a boy she met there. Other couples joined us as we met each Saturday during the summer to hike, swim, ride the Staten Island Ferry (only five cents then), and generally enjoy being young and in love.

In the fall, I entered Hunter College and found it much harder than high school. Even though Hunter was a free school and I was living at home, my father expected me to pay all my expenses and contribute something to the household. I worked at many different kinds of jobs including teaching foreigners English at a private school, and acting as secretary to a French lady emigrée who employed me mainly to write angry letters to her husband's former mistress. My French, after four years at Morris High School, had not equipped me to deal with the kind of language she wanted me to use, and I found the various French dictionaries I consulted also rather limited in that respect.

Sometimes a little adversity is a good thing. In my first term at college, I ended up with two D's and began to wonder if a budding writer really needed to go to college. Thank goodness for my father! Instead of encouraging me and urging me to stay in school, my father kept insisting that I leave school and go to work. It had nothing to do with the two D's. He said girls didn't need to go to college since they would end up as wives and mothers anyway. Much better, he insisted, for girls to work, make money, and contribute generously to their families.

Yes, indeed—a classic sexist! Then, I argued with him fiercely and angrily. But now I think if he had been the kind, encouraging parent he should have been, maybe I would have dropped out of school since I wasn't enjoying myself anyway. But spite, I have always found, is a powerful motivating force. It turned me into an ardent feminist, and I moved out of my father's house at seventeen, determined to finish college.

And I did. It wasn't easy. I had to support myself and overcome my natural laziness. It was hard juggling all the various part-time jobs I worked at and buckling down to the kind of scholarship Hunter College demanded of its students. Some nights I hardly slept, but my marks rose; and if I didn't enjoy all of my courses, I learned to endure them.

My English literature courses were revelations. Chaucer. Milton. Blake. Shakespeare. Wordsworth. What company for a young writer to keep! Many of the teachers at Hunter were outstanding scholars and inspiring teachers. Often, I'm asked if I think it absolutely necessary for future writers to go to college. No, I suppose it's not absolutely necessary if you can come to these great writers on your own. For me, reading is an indispensable part of a writer's education. A good college should force you out of the complacency you might feel when you don't understand what the competition is doing. By being exposed to some of the greats, you begin, painfully, to develop critical judgment about your own work.

I majored in English literature and took many writing classes as well. Do writing classes help? I don't know. They force you to write, but maybe you would be writing anyway.

College wasn't all work and no play, however. Hunter College was an all-girls' school, and I made many friends. When I could, I joined them down in the cafeteria where passionate discussions raged over art, literature, politics, and, of course, boys. I belonged to a "house plan" which meant that we could have parties and invite boys from City College or N.Y.U. Hunter was fortunate in having a beautiful, historic house— Roosevelt House—in which we could hold our parties.

By this time, my romance with Lou had faded just as his sun tan had faded. There were some others who came and went, one of whom wrote a poem to me. It was a takeoff on Joyce Kilmer's poem "Trees" which begins

> I think that I shall never see
> A poem as lovely as a tree

My friend's poem, written after a date when I had a heavy cold, went

> I think that I shall never see
> A nose like yours that runs so free

It isn't every girl who has a poem written to her, and I never forgot it. Years later, I used one like it in my book *Fourteen*.

The photo here shows me and some of the girls in my house plan, around 1945, cavorting on the beach. I

A day at the beach, 1945. Marilyn is second from left.

am the second one in from the left, wearing the loud two-piece bathing suit.

When I was eighteen, I met my husband, Morris Sachs. Both of us belonged to a left-wing youth organization, AYD, which stood for American Youth for Democracy. (Another reason to be grateful to my father. When I left home in the Bronx, I moved to Brooklyn, which was where I met my husband.) The first night I met him, after the meeting, all of us went out onto a crowded street to raise money from passersby in order to help us in our struggle to get Black players into the major league baseball teams. It's hard to believe that even in 1946, talented Black players could not play on any of the big-name teams. I was never good at asking people for money, and everybody passed me by as I mumbled out my plea. But Morris—with charm and confidence—intercepted many of the passersby, explained our cause eloquently, and collected as much as twenty-five cents from one person.

That's when I fell in love with him.

Our courtship was largely spent on picket lines, demonstrations, rallies, and mailings. The causes were all good, and the candidates we supported, like Henry Wallace in the 1948 presidential campaign, were invariably noble and inevitably lost.

My husband was an "older" man. He was twenty-three, a veteran of the Second World War, and to me, he seemed possessed of incredible *savoir-faire*. For one thing, he knew how much to tip waiters. Most of the boys I went out with, who were close to my age, were awkward and uncertain on this question. I admired his confidence, his maturity, and his good looks. We were married on January 26, 1947, at my father's house. My father and I had made up by this time and, of course,

Morris and Marilyn Sachs on their wedding day, 1947

he approved of my getting married.

If you look carefully at us in this wedding picture, you will notice that one of my false fingernails had fallen off and rests on my husband's hand. I've been a nail biter since I can remember and still am with occasional attempts at reform.

Shortly after our marriage, we moved to North Brother's Island in the East River. Originally a hospital where Typhoid Mary had finally been quarantined, it had been turned after the war into a student-veterans' housing development. My husband and I were both in college—he supporting himself on the GI Bill, and I on my usual part-time jobs. Most of the young people on the island, like ourselves, were broke a good deal of the time, but the island was beautiful, the ferry ride fun, and it was really amazing how many people one small chicken and a large pot of spaghetti could feed.

What about my writing? I knew I would be a writer. Wasn't I turning out poems and short stories all through college? But when I graduated from Hunter in 1949, I didn't know what to write about. As a stop gap, until I could pull some literary ideas together, I took a job with the Brooklyn Public Library as a library trainee, never thinking I would stay for very long. We had moved to Brooklyn again and were to remain there until we left for San Francisco in 1961. "Do you like children?" one of my interviewers at the library asked when I applied for the job. "Oh, yes!" I replied fervently, and was initiated as a beginning children's librarian. I stayed in the Brooklyn Public Li-

brary for ten years. I went to Columbia, and got my Master's in Library Science. I worked in branches, on a bookmobile, and in hospitals. I told stories in parks, playgrounds, and housing projects. In the photo, I am telling a story to a bunch of kids in Tompkins Park, Brooklyn. The library is the pretty, little brick building behind us which, sadly, has been torn down since. I loved my job, most of the kids, and the books. I read and read and read and somewhere along the line, I realized what kind of books I wanted to write and who I wanted to write for.

In the meantime, my husband had given up his job as a teacher in the New York City school system in order to be a sculptor. He had begun working at various part-time jobs and used the front end of our Brooklyn apartment as his studio. I realized that I would need to take time off from my absorbing, demanding job in order to write. My husband and I saved five hundred dollars, a goodly sum in 1954, and I arranged for a six-months' leave of absence in order to complete my book.

The first thing we did was to buy a painting for two hundred dollars which meant that I was going to have to write faster. It was lovely—my husband banging away at his statues in one end of the apartment, and I happily pecking away at my typewriter in the other.

I finished the book in four months, entitled it *Amy Moves In,* sent it to somebody I knew at Knopf, went back to work at the Brooklyn Public Library, and waited impatiently for my book to be accepted. I considered it a masterpiece, which is exactly how every new writer should feel about a first book. Nobody wanted it. For nearly ten years, nobody wanted it.

Ten years is a long time to wait to get a book published, and I don't recommend it. The only comfort you can have is believing that your book is ahead of its time. And in a way, *Amy Moves In* was. By today's standards, it is a quiet, noncontroversial book, but by the standards of the fifties, it was a real shocker.

At that time, there was no such thing as realistic children's books. Most contemporary stories dealt with white, middle-class families who lived in the suburbs. Nobody died in children's books, nobody was poor (You could be poor at the beginning but not at the end), nobody was sick (unless you got better), and parents were always wise and never divorced. Very seldom did a children's book concern minorities, and if it did, the particular minority had to be exotic—i.e., Chinese wore pig tails, Indians feathers, and Jews celebrated Jewish holidays all the time. And all problems had to be solved by the end of the story. No loose ends. Maybe in life there were loose ends, but never in children's books.

Bernard M. Jaffee

Sachs telling stories in Tompkins Park, Brooklyn, New York, about 1953

My book, based on my own childhood, had as its main character a girl named Amy who told lies. Her family was poor, Jewish, lived in the city, and didn't celebrate any Jewish holidays in the course of the story. The father had trouble keeping a job and the mother, hurt in an accident, was still in the hospital by the end of the book.

No! No! No! said most editors. Get the father a job, bring the mother home by the end of the story, improve Amy—and how about a few Jewish holidays?

I was anxious to get my book published but not like that. So I stopped sending it around, settled down to working again, and having babies. Two—a daughter, Anne, in 1957, and a son, Paul, in 1960.

In 1961, we moved out to San Francisco where we still live. People out here say "awrange" instead of "ah-range," "chahcolate" instead of "chawclate," "mother" instead of "mothah," and make fun of the way I "tawk." But it is a beautiful city and we never regret living here.

From 1961 to 1963, I was busy working part-time for the San Francisco Public Library and being a full-time mother. My kids were totally enthralling and absorbing to me, and frequently maddening as well. As a younger woman, I hadn't even been sure I wanted kids, but after they were born I was sure. And when my son, at thirteen months, contracted meningitis and nearly died, I was 101 percent positive.

In 1963, a woman I had worked with in the Brooklyn Public Library wrote to me. She had become an editor at Doubleday, had heard about my old manuscript, and asked to see it. I pulled it out of its hiding place in the closet, read it over again, and no longer thought it a masterpiece. To me it seemed full of weaknesses. But I sent it off to her, knowing I would have to wait months before she rejected it. New writers, and often old as well, need to know that publishers *always* keep you waiting. It is a very cruel form of torture causing nervous anxiety and an unhealthy preoccupation with the mail.

I didn't wait very long. Two weeks later, a letter arrived. I wasn't expecting it, and had been too busy scolding my kids. We were on our way out for an airing, and I had been reading the riot act to the two of them—Anne, aged five and Paul, aged two-and-a-half. The letter was in the mail box. It said, simply, that they liked my book and wanted to publish it. By the sixties, realism in children's books had become acceptable.

"I'm going to be an author," I shouted to my daughter.

"You don't have time for that," she responded.

Well, she was wrong about that even though her judgment about so many other things has been right on the mark. I did have time, in between working twenty hours for the San Francisco Public Library and taking

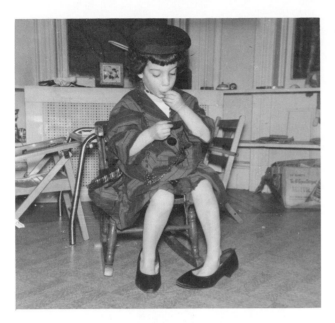

Anne Sachs, age four

Paul Sachs, age five, in his father's studio

care of my kids. My husband, sculpting and working part-time as well, divided up all household chores and child care with me. He has always been totally supportive of me and my work, as I hope I have been of him.

Still, life was often a circus in those days. We never had much money—artists usually don't—and I never had a room of my own then, as Virginia Woolf prescribes for serious artists. But I wrote—in between childhood sicknesses, peace marches, flooded toilets, and all the other demands life made on my time. It was hectic and it was good.

I wrote about a book a year. First, there were the Amy/Laura books which came out of my own childhood. Then *Veronica Ganz* which I always considered one of my best books. Veronica was a composite of all the bullies who terrorized me as a child. One of the pleasures of writing is that what you couldn't do in your own life, you can do in your books. You have a second chance. *Veronica Ganz* gave me an opportunity to take revenge on all the bullies I cowered helplessly before as a child.

"I am going to write a book about a bully named Veronica Ganz," I informed my daughter, aged nine at the time, "and I will kill her at the end of the story."

"If you kill Veronica Ganz," warned my daughter, "I will never speak to you again as long as I live."

So I took her advice as I have on other books she has critiqued for me. She has always been my most savage and incisive critic. When she was a child, she kept me humble by reminding me that I wasn't Laura Ingalls Wilder, Beverly Cleary, or any of her other fa-

vorites. She usually also told me that she liked my last book better, and when she was in junior high she insisted that my language was not up-to-date. She advised me to spend a few days in her school, and I did, relearning the English language. She has prevented me from being overly sentimental and unnecessarily vicious. Not only did she save Veronica Ganz's life but another character as well in *Class Pictures*.

When Anne was a high-school senior, we collaborated on a book, *Dorrie's Book*. The story is supposedly written by an eleven-year-old, so we needed drawings that looked as if an eleven-year-old had done them. My daughter, aged seventeen at the time, always drew like an eleven-year-old so she got the job. I wish I could tell you that we enjoyed working together, but I'm afraid we did not. Anne was too busy with millions of school and social activities to respect things like deadlines. I followed her around wringing my hands (and, well, yes, shouting too from time to time) and pleading with her to finish the drawings. Finally, she came down with a heavy cold, stayed home for a few days, and did the drawings. It was the first book she had ever illustrated and after working with me, she said at the time, it would be the last.

My daughter, a college instructor, now lives in New York, but I always ask her to read any new book I'm working on. When she likes a book, I am hopeful that it might not be as bad as I feared. I tend to hate a book once I finish it and see only its shortcomings. This, I understand, is a very common characteristic of many writers.

As a child, my son never seemed interested in any

Sachs and daughter Anne

Sachs and son Paul

of my books. "What would it take," I asked him finally, "to get you to read something I've written?" "When you write something interesting," he said, "I'll read it." To him, the only interesting thing was baseball, so two of my stories, *Matt's Mitt* and *Fleet Footed Florence* are about baseball. He also always loved animals and would never, never read a story in which a dog died. One of my most recent books, *Underdog,* is dedicated to him. A number of people die in that story but not the dog, so I know he will read it. Now, he also reads my manuscripts and gives me the benefit of his opinions. He lives in Berkeley, California, and his field is transportation planning.

My husband also reads my manuscripts, but he is too eager to give me the support he knows I crave to be entirely trustworthy. He wants to like everything I do, but I can always tell when he doesn't. He is the one who is stuck with me when I go into my periods of deep despair and self-doubt about my work.

Except for *Amy Moves In,* all my other books were written in San Francisco. The first six all took place in the Bronx during the forties. I was tempted during that time to return to Jennings Street in order to refresh my memories but wisely refrained from doing so. It would have been painful and confusing for me to sift through the changes that inevitably had occurred, and my own "mind's eye" was certainly a more accurate chronicler of that time and place. My illustrator for *Amy Moves In,* Judith Gwyn Brown, did go, on her own, and as you can see from this copy of the title page, drew an apartment building very similar to the one I lived in on Jennings Street.

When I first began to write, childhood was inevitably tied in with my own. One of the important things I had to learn was how to keep a distance without losing the emotional power of shared memory. André Gide, the famous French writer, states it perfectly:

> By localizing and specifying one restricts. It is true there is no psychological truth unless it be particular, but on the other hand there is no art unless it be general. The whole problem lies in that—how to express the general by the particular—how to make the particular express the general.

I have never lost my sympathy for losers, and my books are peopled with losers—liars (*Amy Moves In*), awkward bookworms (*Laura's Luck*), bullies (*Veronica Ganz*), cowardly thumbsuckers (*The Bears' House*), fat girls (*The Fat Girl*) . . . culminating in a book about a neglected orphan and a neglected dog (*Underdog*).

I am coming to an end, and realize that I have left out much more than I have included. I have said nothing about daydreaming which is indispensable for writers. Daydream! And if people accuse you of not listening to them, or criticize you for wasting your time when you could be playing with your computer, tell them you are gathering material for your next book. And you are.

I haven't told you about our travels to Europe and all the camping trips we've taken to different parts of the United States, but I hate hearing about people's

by MARILYN SACHS

illustrated by JUDITH GWYN BROWN

AMY

MOVES

IN

DOUBLEDAY & COMPANY, INC., GARDEN CITY, NEW YORK

Illustration by Judith Gwyn Brown from Amy Moves In *by Marilyn Sachs.
(Copyright © 1964 by Marilyn Sachs. Reprinted by permission of
Doubleday & Company, Inc.)*

trips and looking at travel slides and I suspect you may too.

I haven't told you about all the losing candidates I have supported since Henry Wallace in 1948. My children say they grew up on peace marches, integrated schools, demonstrations favoring trees rather than freeways, and boycotts of grapes and South Africa. I am happy to say both of my children are continuing in the family tradition of believing in and working for a better world.

I feel very lucky in my life and my work. My husband and I, for over thirty-eight years now, have worked, played, argued, laughed, cried, and stayed together. What would I do without him! I have had editors that pushed and shoved me into doing the kinds of books I do both at Doubleday and at Dutton. My kids are wonderful, and so are my friends. For every bad day I have, there are twenty good ones. I have written twenty-five books at this point and hope to write many

more. Each book I write is new territory for me, new research, new thoughts, new daydreams.

And I write for the choicest group of readers possible. They send me letters. Sometimes they don't like my books and they let me know why. Often they tell me their problems and identify with a character in one of my stories. It makes me feel proud that a book of mine can comfort someone as books have always comforted me. Here is a letter I received not too long ago.

I am writing to compliment you on . . . *Bus Ride.* This book really "hit home" with me as I have a few too many pimples and will not exactly receive the "most popular" award in my class. Now I have a small sense of hope . . . There are many girls in my freshman class who resemble Karen Shepherd and I envy them just as Judy envied her.

Your book fit me in every way and as

Morris and Marilyn Sachs, Keams Canyon, Hopi Indian Reservation, Arizona, 1979

I read I realized that I was Judy Koppelmacker.

Lucky me!

BIBLIOGRAPHY

FOR CHILDREN

Fiction:

Amy Moves In (illustrated by Judith Gwyn Brown). Garden City, N.Y.: Doubleday, 1964.

Laura's Luck (illustrated by Ib Ohlsson). Garden City, N.Y.: Doubleday, 1965.

Amy and Laura (illustrated by Tracy Sugarman). Garden City, N.Y.: Doubleday, 1966.

Veronica Ganz (illustrated by Louis Glanzman). Garden City, N.Y.: Doubleday, 1968.

Peter and Veronica (illustrated by L. Glanzman). Garden City, N.Y.: Doubleday, 1969.

Marv (illustrated by L. Glanzman). Garden City, N.Y.: Doubleday, 1970.

The Bears' House (illustrated by L. Glanzman). Garden City, N.Y.: Doubleday, 1971.

Marilyn Sachs, 1985

A Pocket Full of Seeds (illustrated by Ben Stahl). Garden City, N.Y.: Doubleday, 1973; London: Macdonald & Jane's, 1978.

The Truth about Mary Rose (illustrated by L. Glanzman). Garden City, N.Y.: Doubleday, 1973; (illustrated by William Stobbs) London: Macdonald, 1973.

Dorrie's Book (illustrated by Anne Sachs). Garden City, N.Y.: Doubleday, 1975; London: Macdonald & Jane's, 1976.

Matt's Mitt (picture book; illustrated by Hilary Knight). Garden City, N.Y.: Doubleday, 1975.

A December Tale. Garden City, N.Y.: Doubleday, 1976.

A Secret Friend. Garden City, N.Y.: Doubleday, 1978.

Class Pictures. New York: Dutton, 1980.

Fleet-Footed Florence (picture book; illustrated by Charles Robinson). Garden City, N.Y.: Doubleday, 1981.

Call Me Ruth. Garden City, N.Y.: Doubleday, 1982.

Underdog. Garden City, N.Y.: Doubleday, 1985.

FOR YOUNG ADULTS

Fiction:

A Summer's Lease. New York: Dutton, 1979.

Bus Ride (illustrated by Amy Rowen). New York: Dutton, 1980.

Hello . . . Wrong Number (illustrated by Pamela Johnson). New York: Dutton, 1981.

Beach Towels (illustrated by Jim Spence). New York: Dutton, 1982.

Fourteen. New York: Dutton, 1983.

The Fat Girl. New York: Dutton, 1984; Oxford: Oxford University Press, 1985.

Thunderbird (illustrated by Jim Spence). New York: Dutton, 1985.

Baby Sitter. New York: Dutton, 1986.

Plays:

Reading between the Lines, first produced in New York, 1971. New York: Children's Book Council, 1971.

Zilpha Keatley Snyder

1927-

Zilpha (right) with her parents, Dessa J. and William S. Keatley, and her sister, Elisabeth, about 1930

When I look back to the beginning, at least as far back as memory will take me, I see most vividly animals and games and books. People are there, too, my mother and father and older sister, but in those earliest memories they are much less distinct. I don't know what this says about my priorities at the time, but there it is.

There were lots of animals. Although my father worked for Shell Oil, he had grown up on cattle ranches, and by dream and desire he was always a rancher. So we lived in the country where he had room for a garden and as many animals as possible. Among my earliest acquaintances were cows, goats, ducks, chickens, rabbits, dogs, cats and, a little later on, horses. I can recall in some detail the day we acquired a collie puppy and a young kitten. I was three years old. The kitten was nominally mine and from the mysterious depths of a three-year-old's mind I produced a name—Maryland. I can remember some of the ensuing argument—no one else thought it was a sensible name—but I can't remember the reason for my choice.

Neither the kitten nor I had ever been to Maryland, nor had either of us, as far as I know, ancestors from there. But Maryland she was, and she and her offspring play a prominent part in many of my early memories.

And then there were games. Some were secret, some less so, and most of them grew out of a compulsion to endow everything animal, vegetable and mineral with human characteristics. I suspect that all very young children are naturally given to anthropomorphism, but with me it must have been almost a full-time occupation. Not only animals, but also trees, plants, toys, and many other inanimate objects had personalities, and sometimes complicated life histories. Often these creatures seemed to have been in need of a helping hand. I built leafy shelters for homeless insects, doctored ailing toys, and every morning I saved Orphan Annie from drowning.

Glazed on the bottom of my cereal bowl, Orphan Annie was daily threatened by a sea of milk and gummy oatmeal. It was necessary for me to eat the disgusting mess quickly to save her from drowning. But once her face was uncovered, and the milk dammed behind a dike of oatmeal, my duty was done. My mother may have wondered why I began so eagerly and then left that thick dam of oatmeal around the center of the bowl.

Other inhabitants of my world of secret games were not so helpless, or so innocuous. Knives and hammers could be intentionally cruel; wagons and roller skates and all their ilk were often sneakily vindictive; and at the foot of my bed there lived a permanent settlement of little black demons with pitchforks just waiting for me to carelessly straighten out my legs. But I fooled them. For years I slept curled in a ball.

There were many other demons, most of whom haunted closets and the dark corners of rooms. Although they really frightened me, I don't think I would have wanted to be talked out of them. They were *my* demons and we had a working relationship.

Books and reading must have had a beginning somewhere but it is beyond memory. I seemed to have been born reading. Actually my mother claimed I taught myself after eavesdropping on lessons she was giving my older sister. Then one day when she was sick and I was four years old, I offered to read to her. When

"Princess" Zilpha in the wagon, about 1933

I proceeded to do so she thought I had memorized the book until she began to ask me individual words. Later when I became, briefly, a kind of neighborhood oddity—I had not yet been to school and I could read the newspaper and was sometimes called into neighbors' homes to demonstrate to sceptical guests—my mother claimed to have had nothing to do with it. Actually I think she used two methods which are almost certain to produce an early reader. First of all, she read to us—a lot. And then, when I tried to horn in on my sister's reading lessons, she told me I was too young—a challenge that no self-respecting four-year-old is going to take lying down.

Of course the games and the reading merged. Little Orphan Annie and the demons were soon joined by the likes of Heidi, Dorothy and Dr. Dolittle, not to mention some of the more intriguing characters I met in the pages of a very fat book called *Hurlbut's Story of the Bible.* My favorites were the ones whose lives included episodes that played well, such as Noah, Daniel and Jonah. Jonah, in particular, was a role that adapted well when one had, as I often did, tonsillitis. Being forced to stay in bed was less of a handicap when the scene being enacted took place in a whale's stomach.

But something should be said about the real people who were an important part of those early years. My father, William Solon Keatley, was a tall slow-moving man, the memory of whose kindness, patient devotion and unfailing sense of humor is, to me, proof that it is possible to surmount the effects of an appalling childhood.

The first child of John William Keatley, a young Englishman who immigrated to America in the 1870's, and Zilpha Johnson his Nebraskan bride—my father's first few years of life were happy ones. But when he was five years old his mother died. Putting my father and his two younger brothers in an orphanage, my grandfather went to California, promising to send for the boys as soon as he was able. But for some reason the summons to a new life never came. The orphanage, losing patience, allowed the two younger boys to be adopted. But by then my father was too old to interest adoptive parents, and old enough to be of temporary interest to various people, some of them relatives of his mother, who needed an extra ranch hand. Forced to do a man's work at the age of eight, often beaten, punished by being sent out mittenless in freezing weather, so that his frozen hands very nearly had to be amputated, he survived to become a gentle man with crooked hands, who loved people almost as much as he loved horses, and who treated both with unfailing kindness.

As a young man he worked as a cowboy, in the

days when many ranges were still unfenced; and in later years he told wonderful stories about bronco-busting, roundups and stampedes and above all—HORSES. He sometimes said that he might forget a man but never a horse, and I'm sure it was true. As a child I knew all his horses through his stories including Old Washboard who had an iron mouth and a penchant for hunting wild horses and who, on spotting a herd of wild ones, took off, completely ignoring the desires of his helpless rider who willy-nilly accompanied him on a mad chase, leaping gulleys and plunging down almost vertical cliffs with wild abandon. Fearing that someday Old Washboard would tackle a cliff he couldn't handle—"the only horse that ever scared me spitless," my father would say—he chickened out and sold him to a gullible passerby; just as innumerable owners had surely done before.

It was not until my father was in his forties and the owner of a small horse ranch in Wyoming that he was contacted by his father. Warmly received by his father's second family in California, he decided to relocate there. And it was there that he met Dessa Jepson, a thirty-five-year-old spinster schoolteacher, a cousin of his stepmother.

The Jepsons were Quakers. They had lived for many generations in Maine, the first Jepson arriving there in 1720, but in the 1870s several branches of the family moved west. My mother was born in California, the youngest of six children. Several years younger than her nearest sibling, she was born when her parents were middle-aged, and on the death of her mother she became her father's housekeeper and companion.

I never knew my grandfather, Isaiah Clarkson Jepson, but he must have been a complicated and determined man. A farmer who had tried photography and teaching and who loved poetry, he doted on Dessa, his youngest daughter, and effectively discouraged her early suitors. She became a schoolteacher, attending UCLA when it was still Los Angeles Normal School, and devoted herself to teaching and to her father. His death when she was in her early thirties left her rudderless and she suffered what she later referred to as a nervous breakdown. On recovering she returned to work and was teaching in Yorba Linda, California when she met my father. It was a romance right out of Zane Grey—the bachelor rancher meets the lonely schoolteacher.

My parents were living in Lemoore, California when my older sister, Elisabeth, and I were born, my father having accepted what he thought of as a temporary job until he could get back to ranching. But the Depression deepened and, to support his growing family, he continued at a job he hated. It was after he was transferred to Ventura, California that my younger sis-

ter, Ruth, was born.

Like my father, my mother was a storyteller. Like his, her stories were true accounts of past events. Mother's childhood was always very close to her and she had a tremendous memory for detail. She made the people and events of rural California at the turn of the century as real to me as were those of my own childhood in the 1930s.

So I came by my storytelling instincts honestly but, as it soon became apparent, their acquisition was all that was honest about them. It wasn't exactly that I was a liar. I don't think I told any more of the usual lies of childhood—those meant to get you out of trouble or get someone else into it—than most children. It was just that when I had something to tell I had an irresistible urge to make it worth telling, and without the rich and rather lengthy past that my parents had to draw on, I was forced to rely on the one commodity of which I had an adequate supply—imagination. Sometimes when I began an account of something I had heard or witnessed my mother would sigh deeply and say, "Just tell it. Don't embroider it."

At the age of eight I became, in my own eyes at least, a writer. I sometimes say that I decided on a writing career as soon as it dawned on me that there were people whose life's work consisted of making up stories. Up until then my tendency to "make things up" was one of the things that came to mind when I repeated that phrase about "trespasses" in our nightly prayers. The idea that there were people who were paid, even praised, for such activities was intriguing. I began as most children do with poems and very short stories, and I was fortunate to have a fourth-grade teacher who took an interest in what I was doing. She collected my works, typed them, and bound them into a book. I loved it—and her.

This early opus, while showing no great originality of thought or unique turns of phrase, does seem to exhibit a certain feeling for the rhythm and flow of words. The following excerpt owed its subject matter to a "social studies project" on China.

The Water Buffalo

Did you ever see a water buffalo,
Slowly around a rice field go,
Dragging a plow at every step?
To plow a rice field takes lots of pep,
So when the buffalo's work is done
He goes down to the river to have some fun.
He wallows down where the mud is deep,
And shuts his eyes and goes to sleep.

My memories of my first five years of school are

pleasant ones. I was a good student, although my abilities were decidedly lopsided. I could memorize a poem in a flash, but the result of multiplying seven times eight eluded me for months, until my mother printed this slippery bit of information on a card and pinned it to the wall in front of the kitchen sink where I was forced to stare at it every evening while doing the dishes. It worked, I guess. I'm not sure whether my hatred of doing dishes spilled over onto the multiplication tables or vice versa, but I'm still not particularly fond of either.

Although there were times when I would have gladly traded my proficiency in reading and writing for a little skill at something that really mattered to my contemporaries such as running races or catching fly balls, I had few problems in the small country schools I attended until the end of sixth grade. But then came the seventh grade in the big city of Ventura. Too young for my grade, having been advanced by a first-grade teacher who didn't know what to do with me while she was teaching reading, and further handicapped by being raised by a mother who hadn't really faced up to the twentieth century, I was suddenly a terrible misfit. Still wearing long curls and playing secret games, I was too intimidated to make an effort to relate to girls who wore makeup and danced with boys. So I retreated further into books and daydreams.

Books! Books were the window from which I looked out of a rather meager and decidedly narrow room, onto a rich and wonderful universe. I loved the look and feel of them, even the smell. I'm still a book sniffer. That evocative mixture of paper and ink and glue and dust never fails to bring back the twinge of excitement that came with the opening of a new book. Libraries were treasure houses. I always entered them with a slight thrill of disbelief that all their endless riches were mine for the borrowing. And librarians I approached with reverent awe—guardians of the temple, keepers of the golden treasure.

It has occurred to me to wonder if I might not have faced up to life sooner if I had been deprived of books. (I know my father worried sometimes about the amount of time I spent reading. My father, not my mother. Her first priority was that we were safely and virtuously at home, with a book or without one.) Lacking a refuge in books, would I have been forced to confront my social inadequacies and set myself to learning the skills that would have made me acceptable to my peers? Perhaps. But then I wonder if it would really have been a fair trade. Would dances and parties and inexpert kisses by pimply contemporaries have made me happier than did Mr. Rochester, Heathcliff, the Knights of the Round Table and the many other heroes and heroic villains with whom I was

intermittently in love? Who's to say? In any event, I went on reading—and suffering the daily agony of the preteen outcast.

Beyond my personal world of home and school and books and dreams, the Depression deepened. Although my father never lost his job, his salary was cut and cut again until he was finally unable to cover the mortgage payments and it was only the New Deal's mortgage relief legislation that enabled us to keep our home. Like so many other families, we lived constantly under that sword of Damocles called the "pink slip." My sisters and I, as well as many of our friends, knew about the slip of pink paper which might at any time be included in our father's pay envelope, and we knew that the result would be the disgrace of "relief lines" and perhaps actual hunger. Sometimes as I walked past the "Okie Camp" that had sprung up on a neighbor's vacant land—trying to pretend I wasn't staring at the cardboard shanties, broken down cars and ragged dirty children—I fantasized that I belonged there; that I would turn in on the dirt road and as I approached the first crumbling shanty I would see my mother in the doorway. It was a game that both intrigued and terrified me.

As the first decade of my life ended the times slowly began to get better. The Okie camps disappeared, people who had been laid off went back to work and salaries began to rise. And then one day when we turned into our driveway after a Sunday morning at church, a neighbor ran to meet us. The Japanese, she said, had attacked Pearl Harbor.

I was in my early teens during the war and I would *like* to report that I thought deeply about the issues involved and the terrible suffering that was going on around the world—but it wouldn't be true. In spite of the fact that a Japanese sub once shelled an empty field not far from where we lived, and we had occasional air raid drills in our class-rooms, the war seemed distant and almost unreal. I wrote a few sentimental war poems and went on reading and dreaming. Years later when I visited Anne Frank's apartment in Amsterdam and saw the pictures of movie stars on her bedroom walls, familiar Hollywood faces of the forties, treasured by teenage girls in California as well as those in hiding in Amsterdam, I was deeply shaken. I cried not only with grief for Anne but with shame that I had known and cared so little.

By the time I was in high school my social skills had begun to improve, and I became a little less afraid of my peers. I had some good teachers and made some exciting new friends, such as Shakespeare and Emily Dickinson.

And college was wonderful. At Whittier College, a small private liberal arts school in Southern California,

Zilpha at Whittier College, about 1947

originally established by Quakers, I grew physically and socially as well as intellectually. I discovered contemporary authors, politics, social injustice, psychology—and boys; men, actually, as the time was the late forties and campuses were full of returned servicemen. It was a good time to be in college. I learned a lot at Whittier: facts, ideas, and essences. Many of the facts have faded, as elusive as seven times eight, but I remember that Whittier taught me how little I knew; a startling concept to any new high school graduate. And even more important—how little anyone knew. Until then I had been satisfied that all possible knowledge was pretty much in hand, and as a student my only job would be to commit it to memory. What a thrill to realize that a lot of so-called facts were actually still up for grabs, and that decision-making was a part of learning.

And one more thing I owe to Whittier—my husband, Larry Snyder. We met first in the Campus Inn where we both waited on tables, and when I first saw him he was playing the piano. Six-foot-five with curly black hair and blue eyes, Larry was a music major who was also an athlete, a charismatic extrovert who was—and still is—a natural scholar, and a small-town boy who was born with a Ulysses-like yearning for new horizons. I liked him a lot. I still do.

But I was planning to be a writer. I wanted to live in New York City, in an attic apartment, and write serious novels for serious people. It's a good thing I

didn't try it. At barely twenty-one with a new college degree, I had a sketchy instinct for self-preservation and all the sophistication of a cocker spaniel puppy. New York City would have eaten me alive, and that's without even trying to guess what New York editors would have done to me. The pages that have survived from the period suggest that as a writer I still had the lively imagination of my childhood, and some feeling for the sound and sweep of a sentence. But style, theme, subject matter, and even handwriting (I still didn't own a typewriter) have a pronounced aura of puppy.

Facing up to the fact that I didn't even have the money for a ticket to New York City, I decided to be practical. So, "temporarily until I got back to ranching," I took another job—I decided to teach school. Only I was more fortunate than my poor dear father. I didn't hate my temporary job. In fact, I liked it a lot. After the first year, which was a bit traumatic until I stopped being surprised when I told the class to do something and they did it, I developed into what must have been a pretty good teacher. I taught in the upper elementary grades for a total of nine years, three of them as a master teacher for the University of California at Berkeley, during which time my classroom was almost constantly being observed by teachers in train-

Larry A. and Zilpha K. Snyder, June 18, 1950

ing. I found teaching to be as rewarding as it was demanding, and I would probably still be at it if I hadn't been lucky enough to have my dream-ranch become a reality when my first book was published—but that was later. And I also decided to accept Larry's offer of marriage, which was probably the best decision I ever made.

Larry and I were married in June of 1950, and the next ten years flew by. They were happy years for the most part, although I sometimes think that if they hadn't been I might not have had time to notice. During that time Larry was in graduate school at Eastman School of Music; taught for one year at Eastern Washington College in Cheney, Washington; and then, because of the Korean War, was in the air force in Texas, New York and Alaska, before returning to graduate school at UC Berkeley. In the period we moved fifteen times, I taught school in New York, Washington, Alaska and California, and we had three children. Our first child was born by emergency caesarian section in 1952 and died two days after his birth. Our daughter, Susan Melissa, was born in 1954 in Rome, New York and our son Douglas in Alaska in 1956. There were no further additions to our family until 1966 when our foster son, Ben, came to live with us. Ben was born in Kowloon, China and when he became a part of our family he was eleven years old and spoke no English, and three years later he was the valedictorian of his eighth-grade class. Ben is like that.

In the early sixties the dust began to settle a bit. Larry was out of school and teaching at the College of Marin north of San Francisco, and the children were in school, Doug, the youngest, in kindergarten. I was still teaching but there seemed to be a bit more time and I caught my breath and thought about writing. Writing for children hadn't occurred to me when I was younger, but nine years of teaching in the upper elementary grades had given me a deep appreciation of the gifts and graces that are specific to individuals with ten or eleven years of experience as human beings. It is, I think, a magical time—when so much has been learned, but not yet enough to entirely extinguish the magical reach and freedom of early childhood. Remembering a dream I'd had when I was twelve years old about some strange and wonderful horses, I sat down and began to write.

Now comes the hard part. I've always maintained that I would never write an autobiography. To me, writing anything other than fiction is a chore. Take away the marvelous incentive of a world yours-for-the-making, and the joy dies. Thus, I once answered when asked if I would write an autobiography, by saying, "Not unless they'd let me make it up as I went along."

But then I weakened and accepted the invitation to participate in the *Something about the Author Autobiography Series,* and up to this point I've found, to my surprise, that I've enjoyed it a great deal. But from here on it won't be so easy.

My husband says that all authors' autobiographies should be entitled *And Then I Wrote.* This, of course, has put me on my mettle to avoid, not only that phrase, but also anything even remotely resembling it while, at the same time, covering twenty-one books and a computer game. After considerable thought I've decided to rely on the appended bibliography to provide chronology, while I deal with my years as a writer in a less structured way.

One of the questions most often asked of a writer concerns how he or she managed the giant step between being "would be" and "published." Everyone has heard about the difficulties involved in selling a first book; the closets full of unpublished manuscripts, and walls papered with rejection slips. I've been known to answer such questions by blandly announcing that I sold my first manuscript to the first publisher I sent it to. It's the truth, but not unfortunately, the whole truth; and I always go on to explain the less glorious particulars. But once when I made the initial pronouncement in a gathering of writers and before I could qualify it, someone said quite justifiably, "Stand back, everyone. I'm going to shoot her."

The truth is that I did send my first attempt to write for young people to Atheneum and it was, indeed, published there some time later. The other part of the story is what happened in between.

I was still teaching school that year and I began to write at night after a day in the classroom. I was a lousy typist and at that time I was completely unable to compose at the typewriter, so I wrote on a tablet, and my husband, whose fingers move almost as well on a typewriter as they do on the piano, typed it for me. Later, when the book was accepted, he bought me an electric typewriter and told me to get busy and learn to type as he didn't intend to make a profession of typing manuscripts.

I didn't exactly pick Atheneum because it was at the beginning of the alphabet, but it was nearly that arbitrary. It was recommended to me by our school librarian as a house that had recently published some good fantasies. But what I received when I mailed in my manuscript—"over the transom," no agent, no introduction—was neither the rejection slip I fully expected, nor the enthusiastic acceptance of which I'd occasionally allowed myself to daydream. What I received was a long letter, two full pages, telling me what was wrong with my story. It was only at the very end that the editor, Jean Karl, stated that if I were going to be working on it some more she would like to see it again. I remember telling my husband that either she was slightly interested or I had just received the world's longest rejection slip.

Of course I was going to be working on it some more. It never occurred to me to reply, "Who the hell are you?" as one well-known author is reported to have done when an editor asked for changes in his first manuscript. It was my first attempt to write for young people, and almost the only writing I had done for ten years. I knew I had lots to learn and I was delighted that someone was willing to help.

My first version of *Season of Ponies* was, among other failings, much too short to be a book for the age level towards which it was aimed. Jean liked the ending but wanted me to lengthen and strengthen the body of the story. I did, and she liked it better, but still there were problems. It was after the third complete rewriting that the book was accepted, and I became a published writer.

Being published, I found, makes a difference. It makes a difference to all writers, but there are, I think, differences specific to the writer who is also a wife and mother. Almost no one feels called upon to honor the working hours of an unpublished wife and mother who insists on wasting large chunks of time in front of a typewriter. But once she is published, friends are somewhat more hesitant about calling up for long mid-morning chats, and recruiters for the United Fund, the PTA and Faculty Wives are a little less inclined to put her on the "readily available" list.

Within my own family, however, being published made very little difference. Larry had always been encouraging and supportive, and he continued to be.

Ben and Doug (and Wotan), about 1966

And my mother, who often lived with us, continued to bring her reading or mending into my room. "Just for the company, I won't say a word." She would say, "Go right on with your writing." And I would try to, knowing that she was lonely and watching for the slightest sign that my attention was wavering and that I was, therefore, fair game. And, of course, published or unpublished, I was always fair game to the children. Rules concerning an off-limits area in the general vicinity of my typewriter during certain hours of the day were impossible to enforce in the face of such major crises as the need for financing an ice cream purchasing expedition, or the mysterious and momentous disappearance of a baseball, rollerskate, sneaker, or any one of numerous pets, including cats, dogs, hamsters, rats, snakes and one very large, very green iguana. The demand for my expertise as a pet finder was especially pressing when the snakes or iguana were involved, since grandmothers and other guests objected to coming across them suddenly in unexpected places.

But children do go to school, and after I stopped teaching there were the blessedly quiet hours of the school day in which to write, and the list of my published books began to grow, usually at the rate of one a year.

My second book evolved from the remains of a manuscript written when I was nineteen years old, a novel for adults set in a fictional town in Ventura County during the Depression. The story, lustily begun, had run into plotting problems and had dwindled off in midsentence on about the forty-fifth page, but the setting and a few of the characters still intrigued me. Knocking a dozen years off the ages of the central

Melissa and Douglas Snyder, about 1960

characters I began the book again and the result was *The Velvet Room.*

I had not been a published writer for long when I discovered a new threat to my precious time at the typewriter, one which I had not counted on. I began to get invitations to speak or lecture. Many were requests that I speak in classrooms, and these, except for the loss of writing time involved, were never any problem. I was accustomed to the classroom situation, I enjoy interacting with children, and it was a thrill to learn about their reactions to my books. But a request that I speak to an adult group was a different matter. I accepted the first one because I was asked eight months ahead of time and I didn't think they'd believe me if I said I'd already booked the date. And then it was such a long time away—perhaps the world would come to an end, or some other fortuitous circumstance would prevent me from having to face up to my commitment. But the day did arrive, preceded by many sleepless nights during which I lay awake wondering what my hosts would do when I collapsed in a dead faint at the podium. But both I and my audience of several hundred librarians managed to survive that one, the requests continued to come, and my terror when facing large bodies of librarians, teachers or writers, gradually diminished.

The Egypt Game was my fourth book, and a good one to look at as an example of the complexity of the only possible answer to a simple, and very commonly asked question; "Where do you get your ideas?" Children ask it poised on tiptoe, ready to run off and get some of their own, and adults suspiciously, as if expecting one to either: 1) Admit to having personally experienced every event described in one's body of work, or 2) Own up to hereditary insanity. The only answer to the question is "everywhere," and without meaning to be facetious, because in any one book the idea roots are many and varied; some of them easily followed while others are fainter and more mysterious.

For example the beginning seeds of *The Egypt Game* were sown during my early childhood, as is true of a great many of my books. A fifth-grade project on ancient Egypt started me on my "Egyptian period," a school year in which I read, dreamed and played Egyptian. But my dream of Egypt was private and it was my daughter, many years later, who actually played a game very like the one in the story, after I had turned her on to the fascinating game possibilities of a culture that includes pyramids, mummies, hieroglyphic writing and an intriguing array of gods and goddesses. However the actual setting and all six of the main characters came from my years as a teacher in Berkeley. The neighborhood described in the story, the ethnic mix in the classroom, as well as the murder, were all taken from realities of our years in Berkeley. So, as I tell children who ask me if I ever write "true" stories, all of my stories have bits-and-pieces of truth—true events, true people, true facts, as well as true memories and even true dreams (the real sound-asleep kind). But the fun comes from what goes on in-between and around and over the bits-and-pieces, tying them together and making them into a story. The inbetween substance is woven of imagination and that is what makes fiction fascinating, to write as well as to read.

And then there is another element, a mysterious idea source which, it seems, many writers tap from time to time, and its unexpected and unpredictable gifts provide some of the most exciting and rewarding moments in writing. One might call such exciting moments a lateral thinking breakthrough, serendipity, the light-bulb syndrome, or just sudden inspiration; an inspiration that seems to come from nowhere and to have no known roots. Whatever you call it, it's the kind of thing that makes you look up from the keyboard and say, "Hey. Thanks a lot."

The Egypt Game came out in 1967. We were still living in Marin County while across the bay to the east, Berkeley was leading the way in a world-wide explosion of protest. To the south, in San Francisco, the Flower Children were painting gracious old Haight-Ashbury Victorians purple and living on love and LSD. And in our own neighborhood Ken Kesey's psychedelic bus was parked not three blocks away, and Janis Joplin's west coast hangout was just up the street. Larry and I marched in anti-war parades but otherwise mostly watched in wonder from the sidelines while lifestyles changed, traditions crumbled, and protest, drugs and violence became a part of American life— and our children entered their teenage years. It was not an easy time to be a parent or a writer of books for young people. *Eyes in the Fishbowl, The Changeling, The Headless Cupid,* and *The Witches of Worm* came from those years.

Also during those years Larry became the dean at the San Francisco Conservatory of Music, and we began to make almost yearly trips to Europe. In 1970 we spent a month touring France with our three children, who were sixteen, fifteen and thirteen at the time. Melissa chose the day we arrived in France to announce that she had just become a strict vegetarian; Ben, who had been working hard at being a typical American teenager, perfected an admirably authentic teenage griping technique; and Doug showed little interest in French culture other than *pâtisseries,* pigeons and stray cats. With the five of us cooped up together daily in a small rental car Larry and I came to the conclusion that early teenagers, like fine wines, do not travel well.

Zilpha in France, 1968

Larry and Zilpha at a party celebrating the 100th year of their house, The Gables, 1977

It was not until some years later that all three of them began to tell us how much they enjoyed that summer in France and how much it had meant to them.

In 1971 Larry took a position at Sonoma State University in Sonoma County and we moved to a one-hundred-year-old-farmhouse in the country near Santa Rosa, California. Larry was anxious to get out of administration and back into music and teaching and we wanted to get our children into a quieter, more rural atmosphere. We were also eager to own horses, a goal that was quickly accomplished after the move. I was out horse shopping almost before we were unpacked.

In our old house, mysteriously like the one I'd described in *The Headless Cupid,* I finished *The Witches of Worm, The Princess and the Giants, The Truth about Stone Hollow* and the three books of the Green-sky Trilogy.

Like so many of my books the trilogy's deepest root goes back to my early childhood when I played a game that involved crossing a grove of oak trees by climbing from tree to tree, because something incredibly dangerous lived "below the root." Years later when I was writing *The Changeling* I recalled the game, and in the course of embellishing it for that story, became intrigued with the idea of returning to the world of Green-sky for a longer stay. The return trip took three years and produced three more books. Initially published in 1975, 1976, and 1978, the trilogy has recently (1985) been reincarnated as a computer game, as well as in a new paperback edition by Tor Books.

The computer game transpired when I was contacted by a young computer programmer named Dale Disharoon. After Dale introduced me to the world of computer games, I wrote and charted, Dale programmed, and a young artist named Bill Groetzinger made marvelous graphics for a game that takes off

from where the third book of the trilogy ends.

In 1977–78, with our children grown and away from home, Larry and I spent his first sabbatical year in Europe. Larry, who is quite fluent in Russian and had done much of his graduate work on Russian music, had for some years been leading a UC Berkeley Extension tour to the Soviet Union during the summers. For his sabbatical project we traveled for seven weeks in Russia, the Baltic Republics, Poland and Czechoslovakia while he did research on contemporary music. It was an incredible trip, sometimes uncomfortable and often a bit dismaying, but never less than fascinating, and very productive in terms of Larry's project.

When we finally reached Italy we were ready to settle down, which we did for four months in a lovely villa in the Tuscan countryside between Florence and Siena. During that time we alternated trips around Italy with long days of work, in which Larry compiled his collected data and practiced the piano, and I finished a novel for adults, *Heirs of Darkness,* and began a children's book set in Italy (a sequel to *The Headless Cupid* entitled *The Famous Stanley Kidnapping Case*). "Just like Chopin and Georges Sand," Alton Raible, who has illustrated many of my books, wrote, and then added, "Without all the coughing and spitting, I hope." Our villa was part of a complex of rental units constructed from a country manor house and outlying farm buildings, and among the residents were writers, artists and academics from various countries. It was an environment *molto simpatico* and friendships we made there have been important and lasting.

On returning to Sonoma County I began work on a novel for young adults. It was a story concerning a teenage boy and a magnificent buck deer, and when I began to write I had in mind a fantasy about mythical animals. But *A Fabulous Creature* turned out to be one of those novels that seem to take over and direct their own development and I soon found I was writing a story that was quite realistic and that had a bit to say about one of my pet antipathies—the whole mystique of hunting. As had happened many times before, I suddenly said, "Oh, so *that's* what I'm writing about."

That backdoor approach to themes or "messages" has been a part of the scene for me since my first book, when I thought I was basing my story's antagonist on Greek mythology and only discovered after-the-fact that I'd been writing about someone I once knew—and feared; and my unconscious theme concerned the evil that arises when selfish and insensitive use is made of a naturally dominant personality.

It worried me for a while, this rather haphazard approach to thematic material, and now and then I tried it the other way, starting a few stories with the intention of addressing a given problem. But it never turned out well. Plots went lame and characters turned into caricatures. After a while I decided that, for me at least, "messages" were best left to their own devices. I would mind my own business, which was to tell a good story and let "messages" take care of themselves. They could, and would, I found, and in more subtle and interesting ways than when marshalled by my conscious mind. A case in point were some books of mine that were endorsed by NOW (National Organization for Women). The stories in question had been written before my own consciousness had risen very far, and I'd not set out to say anything in particular about liberation or equality. But the message—that little girls can be vital and original and courageous people—found an appropriate opening, and there it was. Or when *Heirs of Darkness*, which I'd set out to write as a straightforward, one-dimensional Gothic horror story (not for children) turned into an exploration of guilt, and its relationship to the passive/masochistic personality.

As the eighties began we were still living in Sonoma County. Larry had been lured back into administration serving as Dean of Humanities and then of the School of Performing Arts at Sonoma State Univer-

Larry and Zilpha and a camel named Moses, 1985

sity—and the pendulum of American Youth Culture had begun a dramatic swing. Liberal arts departments were shrinking, while business management and computer sciences burgeoned. Watching this new breed of hard working, practical young people, it suddenly occurred to me that some of the present teenagers, were undoubtedly the offspring of the flower-child generation. And the next step was to wonder where teenage rebellion might take a child who had grown up in the "hippie" milieu. The result was another young adult novel called, *The Birds of Summer.*

Blair's Nightmare, a third book about the Stanley family of *The Headless Cupid,* and *The Changing Maze,* a picture-book fantasy illustrated by Charles Mikolaycak, brings me up to the present, the spring of 1985—a present set in a garden flat near the Porta Romana in Florence, Italy, where Larry and I are again living, this time for a year in which he is serving as director of the California State Universities' Foreign Study Program in Italy. Having transported a word processor to Italy, with no little difficulty, I am still writing while Larry deals with the Italian bureaucracy and sixty-nine California students of art, literature and architecture. Among the side trips we've been able to make this year was a nine-day exploration of Egypt, a destination that has been high on my must-see list since I used to walk to school as Queen Nefertiti when I was ten years old. In the fall, after another trip to the Soviet Union for UC Berkeley, we plan to return to the San Francisco Bay area.

So there it is, the story of my life and work, and while sticking to the facts wasn't easy, or nearly as much fun as fiction, I've faithfully done so. "See Mom, no embroidering." But before I sign off there's just one more question I'd like to address. And that is *why?*

Once, some years ago during the question and answer period after a lecture, a man asked me why I wrote for children. "Do you do it for the pocket book, or just for the ego?" was the way he put it. He didn't give me any other choices, but there is another answer. The ego and the pocket book are affected, of course, at least minimally; much of the time only too minimally. But the maximum reward is simply—joy; the storyteller's joy in creating a story and sharing it with an audience.

So I write for joy, my own and my imagined audience's—but why for children? Unlike many writers who say that they are not aware of a particular audience as they write, I know that I am very conscious of mine. Sometimes I can almost see them, and they look very much like the classes I taught, and often read to. And, like those classes when the story was going well, they are wide-eyed and open-mouthed, rapt in the story and carried out of the constraining walls of reality into the spacious joys of the imagination.

I began to write for children by accident, through the fortunate accident of nine years in the classroom. But I've continued to do so because over the years I've come to realize that it's where I'm happiest. It is, I think, a matter of personal development (or lack of it, as the case may be). There are several peculiarities that I share with children which, like having no front teeth, are perhaps more acceptable in the very young, but which, for better or worse, seem to be a part of my makeup.

First of all, there is optimism. Since growth and hope are almost synonymous no one begrudges a child's natural optimism, but a writer's is another matter. It's not fashionable to write optimistically for adults, nor I must admit, even very sensible, given the world we live in today. But my own optimism seems to be organic, perhaps due to "a bad memory and a good digestion" (a quote that I can't attribute due to the aforementioned failing).

Secondly, there is curiosity. Mine is as intense as a three-year-old's, but where a three-year-old's most obnoxious trait might be asking "Why" several hundred times a day, I am given to eavesdropping on conversations, peering into backyards and lighted windows, and even reading other people's mail if I get a chance.

And thirdly there is a certain lack of reverence for factual limitations and a tendency to launch out into the far reaches of possibility.

So I enjoy writing for an audience that shares my optimism, curiosity and freewheeling imagination. I intend to go on writing for some time, and though I may occasionally try something for adults, I will always come back to children's books, where I am happiest and most at home.

BIBLIOGRAPHY

FOR CHILDREN

Fiction:

Season of Ponies (illustrated by Alton Raible). New York:

Zilpha Snyder and friends, 1983

Atheneum, 1964.

The Velvet Room (illustrated by A. Raible). New York: Atheneum, 1965.

Black and Blue Magic (illustrated by Gene Holtan). New York: Atheneum, 1966.

The Egypt Game (illustrated by A. Raible). New York: Atheneum, 1967.

Eyes in the Fishbowl (illustrated by A. Raible). New York: Atheneum, 1968.

The Changeling (illustrated by A. Raible). New York: Atheneum, 1970; Guildford, Surrey: Lutterworth Press, 1976.

The Headless Cupid (illustrated by A. Raible). New York: Atheneum, 1971; Guildford, Surrey: Lutterworth Press, 1973.

The Witches of Worm (illustrated by A. Raible). New York: Atheneum, 1972.

The Princess and the Giants (picture book; illustrated by Beatrice Darwin). New York: Atheneum, 1973.

The Truth about Stone Hollow (illustrated by A. Raible). New York: Atheneum, 1974; published in England as *The Ghosts of Stone Hollow.* Guildford, Surrey: Lutterworth Press, 1978.

Below the Root (first book of "Green-Sky" trilogy; illustrated by A. Raible). New York: Atheneum, 1975.

And All Between (second book of "Green-Sky" trilogy; illustrated by A. Raible). New York: Atheneum, 1976.

Until the Celebration (third book of "Green-Sky" trilogy; illustrated by A. Raible). New York: Atheneum, 1977.

The Famous Stanley Kidnapping Case. New York: Atheneum, 1979.

Come on, Patsy (picture book; illustrated by Margot Zemach). New York: Atheneum, 1982.

Blair's Nightmare. New York: Atheneum, 1984.

The Changing Maze (picture book; illustrated by Charles Mikolaycak). New York: Macmillan, 1985.

Poetry:

Today Is Saturday (photographs by John Arms). New York: Atheneum, 1969.

FOR YOUNG ADULTS

Fiction:

A Fabulous Creature. New York: Atheneum, 1981.

The Birds of Summer. New York: Atheneum, 1983.

FOR ADULTS

Fiction:

Heirs of Darkness. New York: Atheneum, 1978; London: Magnum, 1980.

Dorothy Sterling

1913-

Ibecame a writer because I couldn't draw and because my dog had puppies. There was also a dream my father had, and a third-grade teacher who wore a squirrel coat. Perhaps I had better begin at the beginning.

I was born in New York City, born at home as most babies were in 1913. My father, Joseph Dannenberg, was twenty-five; my mother, whose maiden name was Elsie May Darmstadter, twenty-three. Both were German Jews whose grandparents (my great-grandparents) had come to the United States as immigrants in the 1850s. A photograph of Great-Grandmother Bertha Falk, who landed at Ellis Island in New York harbor when she was twenty-five, shows the stern, unsmiling face of a woman equipped to fight for survival in a strange land, to learn a new language and new ways. Celia, the third of Bertha's eight children, was my father's mother. She bore a strong resemblance to Bertha, except that she smiled more frequently. She

Grandmother Celia Dannenberg with Aunt Alma Dannenberg and cousin Edgar, about 1912

Bertha Falk in 1907 when she was seventy-six

was short, fat, and good-natured. In her dresses, always ankle-length, always black, she was shaped like a pyramid. When we were small, my cousin Edgar and I used to climb up to her capacious bosom to play a game called "sliding down grandma." When we were older, she used to take us to the movies and tell us the stories of films she had seen.

Celia's husband, Moses Dannenberg, was born in New York in 1856. He owned a dressmakers' supply store in New York's garment district. He and grandma lived across the street from us and each morning before going to work he stopped by to say hello. I remember

Grandpa Moses Dannenberg with Edgar, about 1911

synagogue.

My family's desire to forget its German ancestry was sharpened during World War I when Germany was at war with the Allies. When the movie theater a few blocks away showed newsreels of the war, everyone hissed Kaiser Wilhelm, the German emperor, and his goose-stepping troops. At the same time that I learned "Jack and Jill" and "There Was an Old Woman Who Lived in a Shoe," I gleefully chanted:

> Down by the river,
> Down by the lake.
> The Kaiser's got a bellyache.

We lived at 65 Fort Washington Avenue in the neighborhood known as Washington Heights where the battle of Fort Washington had been fought in 1776. The fort had long ago given way to apartment houses, but the Heights were still there, with long steep streets leading to Fort Washington Park and the Hudson River. We rode sleds at dizzying downhill speeds in winter; in the spring we picked violets and had picnics in the park. Even more interesting was our "mountain," a rocky, wooded area with a stream running through it where I hunted for frogs and snakes. On

him as short and dapper, with a carnation in his buttonhole and a brown derby hat. I have always thought that he looked like Al Smith, the Irish Catholic governor of New York who ran for President in 1928.

Grandpa died when I was four, but grandma lived until after I was graduated from college so that there would have been ample time for her to tell me about her childhood during the Civil War and what she remembered of the old days—or even to teach me some German. But nobody wanted to talk about the old days or the old country, and I didn't think of asking them. The only German I recall hearing in our home was *nicht für Kinder*, which my sister Alice and I quickly understood to mean "not to be talked about in front of the children." The fact is that grandma and grandpa and mother's parents who lived in Philadelphia were determinedly American. They were proud of the fact that they spoke unaccented English, unlike their fellow Jews who had come to the United States later, and they passed along nothing of German culture and very little of Jewish history or religion either. We had Christmas trees instead of Chanukah candles, Easter eggs along with Passover matzos, and seldom went to a

Joseph Dannenberg in the 1890s

Saturday mornings, my cousin Eddie, two years older, and I set out with a bag of peanut-butter-and-jelly sandwiches and spent the day exploring. One spring when I had whooping cough and couldn't go to school, we even planted a garden there. Nothing grew, however.

If you had to be a city child, Washington Heights was a good place to start. Fort Washington Avenue had sidewalks broad enough for games of hide-and-seek and hopscotch, for jumping rope and bouncing balls. Horse-drawn wagons delivered milk and ice (no electric refrigerators in those days), and only a few cars drove sedately by. From her window on the second floor, mother could keep an eye on Alice and me and call us when it was time to come in. With her permission, we walked a block east to Broadway where there were stores and movie theaters, or turned west for the trees and flowers of Fort Washington Park—both places safe for small children. Sixty-five Fort Washington Avenue is still standing, shabby and dirty now, but our "mountain" was long ago transformed into the Columbia Presbyterian Medical Center, and our park along the Hudson is a crowded, smog-filled highway.

Life wasn't all play. Dad, the first member of his family to go to college, was a lawyer. Mother had graduated from normal school and had taught for a year before getting married. The youngest of four sisters, with an invalid mother, an overworked father,

Elsie and Joseph Dannenberg, 1912

"Mother and her three sisters": Claire, Elsie, Helen, and Bertie Darmstadter

and a much younger brother, she had been responsible for the work of their large household after her older sisters found jobs or married. Alice and I saw her as Cinderella, prettier and brighter than her sisters, but condemned to be the household drudge until the prince (Dad) came along and carried her off to New York. It was always accepted in our household that New York was better than Philadelphia and the Dannenbergs a cut above the Darmstadters, at least in their ability to earn a living.

Mother was not only pretty and bright; she was an excellent cook, a capable seamstress (she made many of our dresses), and an energetic and efficient housekeeper. But she refrained from passing along these skills to her daughters. Even when we were teenagers we neither cooked nor cleaned, sewed nor ironed, nor made our beds. Some of these chores were performed by a succession of "green girls"—newly arrived Polish or Irish immigrants who slept in a tiny bedroom off the kitchen and worked for little pay while learning the language and American ways of housekeeping. On Thursday nights—maid's night out—we were required to dry the dishes while mother washed them. This was our only household responsibility.

Puzzling over this later, as I lamented my lack of household skills, I concluded that mother, subconsciously at least, had thought that if we didn't know how to do housework, we would never have to do it. How did she think we were to escape the chores which were every woman's fate? One obvious answer was to marry men rich enough to employ servants—and not "green girls" either. The other was to "be somebody" ourselves. This was a novel idea. Careers for women were frowned upon in the 1920s. A few exceptional women were doctors or lawyers; the small number of others who earned their own living were teachers, typists, or—heaven forbid!—factory and domestic workers. What we were to "be" was never spelled out, but mother, frustrated in her own ambitions by her family and her marriage, was determined that her daughters be exceptional. Not just in some way either, but in every way.

We were not only expected to excel in school; we were also to be pretty, popular, fine athletes, good dancers, and to have all of the feminine graces that would attract a successful man. Mother ran into trouble with me right away. I had blonde, tightly curled hair which she was determined to transform into the long golden ringlets of storybook children. She brushed and brushed. My hair and I resisted until finally I cut it off one day and ran away to my aunt's house to escape a spanking. Mother should have suspected early that I wasn't going to turn into a conventional all-American princess when I ignored the dolls I was given for Christmas and instead of playing "house" with the neighborhood girls trailed after Eddie and his friends. I joined them in shooting immies (marbles) in the street, and retrieved paper matchbooks from the gutter for his collection. I read early and endlessly, but preferred *Tom Swift and His Motorcycle* and the exploits of the Rover boys to *Bunny Brown and his Sister Sue* or the series about Elsie Dinsmore, an unspeakably pious child who was a model of female virtue.

As if to make up for the advantages that she had missed, mother saw that we had elocution and French lessons, and piano lessons, too, after we moved to an apartment large enough to house a baby grand. The lessons failed as far as I was concerned. Alice, three years my junior, brought tears to the eyes of visitors with her rendition of " 'She's somebody's mother, boys,' he said, 'For all she's old and gray.' " and willingly showed off her French phrases. Nothing could make me perform in public. And I was clumsy too. I fell and scraped my shins when I roller-skated, turned my ankles as soon as I buckled on ice skates. I pedalled a tricycle down Fort Washington Avenue, but never learned to ride a two-wheeler. Nor was I good at jumping rope or playing "One-two-three-O'Leary" with a ball.

These failures bothered me less than they did my parents. I was happy wandering by myself along the river and scrambling over the rocks on our "mountain," picking flowers, gathering leaves, watching butterflies and caterpillars. I even devised a trap to catch a sparrow, a cardboard shoebox baited with bread crumbs which I placed on the fire escape outside of the living-room window. The birds ate the bait, but easily pushed up the lid of the box and flew off. My parents paid little attention to my absorbing interests. They were city people and had never known anyone who cared about plants or small living creatures, except for Uncle Herbert Darmstadter who lived in Philadelphia. He was a doctor as well as an accomplished naturalist, but they considered him antisocial, without the proper get-up-and-go that a New Yorker would have. On our monthly visits to the Darmstadters he would take me to the backyard to see his garden and tell me the Latin names of the flowers. I loved the garden and his attention to me, but I was put off by the fact that my parents thought him odd.

"My sister Alice and I, about 1920, wearing dresses and bloomers that mother made"

School was the only area in which I was successful. I learned to read when I was five, painstakingly spelling out the words in the box on the front page of my father's *New York Times*: "All the News That's Fit to Print." Kindergarten that same year was dismal because I couldn't master scissors, crayons, and paste, but from first grade on, I took off. P.S. 46, the neighborhood public school, was big, dark, dirty, and overcrowded. Probably that's why they had a system called Rapid Advance for any students who showed ability. I advanced at breathtaking speed, covering first and second grades the first year, third and fourth the second year, and so on.

P.S. 46 was a blur with only two events that stand out. The first was in third grade when I wrote a composition titled "My Teacher." Miss Tunney who had a squirrel coat that I greatly admired, corrected my spelling of "squirrel," but said, "This is very good. You're going to be a writer." A writer. Hmm. That was something to think about. The second occurred in sixth grade when the teacher, reading the roll in the morning, found that two of us had birthdays that day. We stood while the class sang "Happy Birthday" and I still remember my dismay when I looked at Edward who was three years older and more than a foot taller. Suddenly I realized that a gulf separated me from my classmates. For the first time I discovered that the path of a loner is sometimes lonely.

Fortunately, the moment of loneliness didn't last long. My mother had heard that a group of psychologists at Teachers College, a part of Columbia University, were selecting "intellectually gifted children" from the public schools of the city for an experimental class. Before long I was riding a double-decker bus down Broadway every morning to P.S. 165 where the Special Opportunity Class was housed. There were some fifty boys and girls in Spec. Op., as we called it, and we remained together for three years. All of us had been loners or freaks in the schools we came from. Many were younger and smaller than I—and some were brighter.

It was believed then that the IQs determined by intelligence tests were an accurate measurement of intelligence, that they remained the same throughout people's lives, and were largely determined by heredity. To confirm this, and to check on the value of newly devised tests, we were given different ones every few months. Even our parents, sisters, brothers, and grandparents were tested. And we were told the results of the tests so that we knew whose IQ was 190, the highest in the class, and whose was 135, the lowest.

I no longer believe that IQs are an infallible test of intelligence or that people should be told their scores, but Spec. Op. was a dramatic rescue operation for a group of girls and boys who had been caught in the toils of Rapid Advance. Instead of sitting quietly and copying what the teacher wrote on the blackboard, we waved hands wildly, begging to be called on, desks sliding across the floor as a debate grew warm. We argued about everything, accepting neither teacher nor textbook at face value. The brightest boy in the class (IQ 190) regularly insisted that the South should have won the Civil War and was regularly pummeled for his partisanship.

We learned almost as much from each other as from our teachers. A special cabinet was provided for the display of our collections: carefully mounted butterflies, rocks, shells, even a snake skin. The shelves below were for books we brought in. In this library, run by a class committee, I first encountered the Oz books, Ernest Thompson Seton's *Two Little Savages,* the novels of Jules Verne, as well as *Little Women* and *Oliver Twist.* Best of all, a boy whose uncle had just started a crazy mail-order book business called the Book-of-the-Month Club gave me as a birthday present one of the club's first premiums—four illustrated books on flowers, trees, birds, and butterflies. Other people, it seemed, were interested in natural history too.

In addition to using us as guinea pigs for their tests, our fairy godmothers at Teachers College arranged for us to take trips all over New York: to the Museum of Natural History, the Metropolitan Museum of Art, the Academy of Medicine, to a bakery, a brick factory, a laundry. We attended concerts, saw films and plays, and teachers came from Columbia to give us courses in French, algebra, social studies and— the one I liked best—biography. For the latter we researched the lives of people of the past in whom we were interested and wrote biographies which we then read to the class. I wrote about George Eliot, Mark Twain, and John Muir, the naturalist who crusaded for national parks.

It was during the Spec. Op. years that my father had a dream that he told me about. I had become a writer—famous, of course—using the pen name of Dorothy Dee. Now when people asked, "What are you going to be when you grow up?" I answered, "A writer." So, I note from a tattered Spec. Op. memory book, did four other girls in the class. None of us planned to be housewives and mothers.

The trips and special courses were unheard of in the public school system of the day, but even our enterprising psychologists could not break fully with tradition. In our third year in Spec. Op., the boys were given special instruction in science and shop, while the girls were taught sewing. Indignant, I drew up a petition which all the girls signed, asking that we too be permitted to study science. To our astonishment, our

long-suffering classroom teacher was so angry at us
that she refused to speak to us, or even call on us in
class, until our mothers came to school to apologize.
Perhaps it was my chagrin at this failure that led to my
first venture into politics. Class officers were elected
twice a year. Because boys were in the majority, they
always won all the offices except for a token girl as
secretary. But, as I pointed out in the privacy of sewing
class, if we selected an all-girl slate and stuck to it instead of scattering our votes, we could win. For the last
semester of Spec. Op. the class was governed by a girl
president, vice president, secretary, and treasurer.

From the time I was eight I spent summers in
camps in Maine where, my parents hoped, I would
improve in sports, make friends and, not incidentally,
give my mother two months respite from the continuing struggle between us. The first camp was a somewhat ramshackle affair on a low-lying peninsula jutting out into a lake. It was an unusually rainy summer
and we sloshed from bunk to dining hall, trailed by
clouds of mosquitoes. The baseball field and tennis
courts were under water, a relief to me because I could
spend most of my time in the woods where, thanks to
the rains, there was an unusually luxuriant growth of
mosses, ferns, and mushrooms of every conceivable
shape and color. The mushrooms—strange, unflower-

*On a trip to Mount Washington, summer 1928. "The
dark green wool shirt was heavier than the white middy
blouse, hence okay for trips."*

*Dorothy in camp costume, about 1922, "not a Camp
Fernwood outfit—how sloppily the tie is tied"*

like growths—particularly fascinated me. Did they
have names? How did they grow? It would be more
than twenty years before I found out.

In contrast, Camp Fernwood, which I attended
from 1924 to 1928, was shipshape in every way: lake
and docks, well-tended playing fields, well-mowed
lawns, forests of fir and pine, and a garden which supplied the camp with fresh vegetables and raspberries
free for the picking. The bunks, housing ten campers
and a counsellor, were rainproof, mosquito-proof, and
as neat as an army barracks. Ten toothbrushes, ten
washcloths, and towels were lined up in the bathroom;
ten beds covered with Camp Fernwood green and
white blankets; floors swept clean for daily inspection.
At last I learned to make a bed with hospital corners
and to use a mop and broom.

The campers were as neat as the bunks: white
middy blouses, folded green ties, pleated green bloomers, black stockings, and high white sneakers. So strict
was the dress code that if a player had an air space
between bloomers and stocking tops, the game would
be halted until she corrected the error. The schedule
was rigid too. A bugler played "Reveille" at seven.
Then came setting-up exercises and a dip in the lake.
After breakfast, bunk cleanup and inspection were fol-

lowed by sports and swimming. More sports in the afternoon, plus arts and crafts and nature study. In the evening there were hot-dog and marshmallow roasts around the campfire with everyone joining in singing camp songs. "Taps," blown at nine, meant lights out, no whispering.

I was fair in baseball, poor in basketball, hopeless in track. I learned to swim well enough to earn a Junior Red Cross badge and to paddle a canoe. I hiked, went on canoe trips and, one memorable summer, climbed to the top of Mt. Washington, the highest peak in the White Mountains. And then there was nature study. The nature counsellor wasn't as popular as the counsellors who taught baseball and track. She was quiet and studious rather than "peppy," the approved adjective then. But I took all the walks she offered, absorbing the names of trees, flowers, birds, berries, and the nature lore that went with them. I discovered a humming bird's thimble-sized nest (the only one I have ever seen), found wild orchids in a marsh, wild strawberries at the edge of the woods. No other camper shared my interest; in fact it was thought a bit queer, but my moment of glory came during the last two weeks of camp when there was fierce competition between the Green team and the White team for an annual award. I sat on the sidelines during the sports, but nature counted ten points just as baseball did, and my team always won the nature contest.

My five years at Fernwood confirmed that I was still a maverick, not unpopular, but not "peppy" either. I found a few oddballs like myself who defied the rules by reading under the covers by flashlight after "Taps" and joined in "midnight" feasts (9:30 P.M.) with food saved from the dining hall. On the last night of camp when green "F's" were given out for sportsmanship and camp spirit, I always felt a twinge of regret because I knew I would not win one.

In 1924 we had moved downtown to West Seventy-ninth Street, two blocks from Central Park and the Museum of Natural History, both favorite haunts of mine. After graduating from Spec. Op., I went to Dalton High School on Seventy-third Street, where my sister and I received partial scholarships. Dalton was a progressive school, more experimental than Spec. Op. had been. The Dalton Plan (which has been considerably modified since my day) called for monthly contracts in each subject which a student completed at her own pace. That is, we were assigned poems or plays in English, lessons in French, math problems, and so forth. When we had done them, we handed in written work or were quizzed by the teacher. Helen Parkhurst, the originator of the plan, believed that "if you make a child study things that he doesn't care for . . . his brain

will be impaired forever." That might have been all right for people who didn't plan to go to college, but for those of us who planned to take College Boards, specific subject matter had to be covered whether we cared for it or not. The gaps in the plan were so obvious that a conventional math teacher was imported to drill us in algebra and geometry in my senior year. During most of my four years at Dalton, however, I completed my assignments in three weeks and spent the fourth reading in the English room. Once again I missed out on science because the only course given in our all-girls high school was a general survey with a smattering of biology, physics, and chemistry.

As in Spec. Op., I learned from my classmates too, although it was a different kind of learning. Most of their ancestors had also been Jews from Germany, but they had come to the United States earlier than mine and had founded department stores like Saks, Gimbels, Namms, or bought seats on the Stock Exchange. They came to school in chauffeured cars, some with governesses accompanying them, and spent their weekends at dances or speakeasies where bootleg whiskey was served. A constitutional amendment prohibiting the manufacture and sale of alcoholic beverages had gone into effect in 1919; by 1928 it was openly violated by millions of people and drinking was the thing to do even among high-school students.

My classmates were friendly in school, but they never invited me to their parties nor did I expect them to. I was two or three years younger than they were, still short, curly haired, freckled, and ignorant in the ways of the opposite sex. In Spec. Op. I had competed with the boys in class, teased and fought with them in recess, and been teased and roughed up in return. Now the most popular girl in my class explained, "All you have to do is to look up at them and say, 'I think you're wonderful.' " There was no way I could do that. I still lacked those feminine graces that my mother had hoped I would learn. Once, on a rare occasion when I did have a date, I strode purposefully from the apartment-house elevator and pulled open the heavy vestibule door before my companion reached it. "You're not supposed to do that," he scolded. "You must wait until *I* open the door." He never called again.

In my Dalton years, my father walked us to school in the morning on his way to his office downtown. Perhaps because he had no sons and I was his oldest daughter, he would tell me about his business triumphs and troubles. At first, the triumphs dominated our conversations. His law practice was moderately successful but, more important, he and everyone else he knew was buying stocks. In 1928, the stock market made front-page headlines as it went up, up, up each day. Not only lawyers, doctors, businessmen, but barbers, shoeshine boys, and speakeasy waiters were using savings and borrowing money to buy stocks which would surely make them rich. After Herbert Hoover moved into the White House there were warning signs. Stock prices went down as well as up. The day I graduated from Dalton, my uncle could not come to hear my valedictory address because he was in his broker's office watching the stock ticker. But stocks went up again that summer and my parents were able to send me on a trip across the United States, to see Pike's Peak, the Grand Canyon, California, and Oregon. While I was away the chairman of General Motors wrote an article for *Ladies' Home Journal* titled, "Everyone Ought to be Rich."

The crash came in October 1929. Front-page headlines reported tumbling prices, billions of dollars of paper profits vanishing overnight. My father lost his life's savings; my uncle had to give up his chauffeured car and move to a smaller apartment. Millions of people—bankers, auto executives, barbers, and waiters were broke.

I was accepted at Wellesley College but because I was only fifteen I elected to stay out of school for a year. For a few months I worked at Dalton, sorting papers in the mimeograph office (no copying machines then) and running the telephone switchboard when the regular operator was at lunch. After I twice disconnected Miss Parkhurst's calls, I was fired. For the rest of the year, I wandered around New York. Because mother couldn't bear to see me sitting around doing nothing, I left the apartment early each morning, sometimes meeting my cousin Eddie who had dropped out of college after the stock-market crash and had not yet found a job. Usually we went to the Metropolitan Museum of Art, although occasionally we traveled downtown to explore Greenwich Village. Other days I went to the public library at Forty-second Street, checked out an armload of books, and read then across the street in a department store's ladies' room. I wish I could report that as a would-be writer I used these leisure months to write stories or poems but the fact is that I wrote nothing except an occasional letter.

When I entered Wellesley in September 1930, it was as part of a 10 percent Jewish quota; that is, out of every one hundred students admitted, only ten could be Jews. Wellesley was not unique in this; probably every private college in the country had a similar quota. Nor did I find it particularly disturbing. Anti-Semitism was simply something one lived with. Once when I was small my family had gone on a picnic in the country and some farm children had run up to us to shout, "Dirty Jews! Dirty Jews!" I was puzzled rather than upset. How did they know we were Jewish? And why did they care? I knew that in parts of New York landlords refused to rent to Jews. There were clubs my parents couldn't join and restaurants where they were unwelcome. When my father had dreamed that I would write under the pen name Dorothy Dee, it was because writers with Jewish-sounding or foreign names changed them for publication. If one were to glance through the magazines and books of the 1920s, one might think that only descendants of the Pilgrims were authors.

Anti-Semitism was just one aspect of the deep divisions in American society. First, there was a pecking order among the Jews themselves. Once when I became friendly with a girl whose parents had recently come from eastern Europe, my father took me aside to warn, "She's not our kind." On another occasion we walked along Central Park West and stopped to admire the synagogue built by Spanish and Portuguese Jews in 1655, the oldest Jewish congregation in America. "*They* are better than we are," he said.

But if some people were better, my generation was taught in a hundred different ways that others were inferior. Chinese were always the villains in movies and mystery stories; as a child I had recurrent nightmares of Chinese escaping from ships in New York harbor and kidnapping me for the white-slave trade. In *The Keeper of the Bees* by Gene Stratton Porter— who had written such favorites of mine as *Freckles* and *A Girl of the Limberlost*—I discovered that Japanese were sneaky and clever. In Booth Tarkington's popular *Penrod and Sam*, and in stories in the *Saturday Evening Post*, blacks were comic figures, lazy and ignorant. I was still in Spec. Op. when Congress confirmed these prejudices by passing a law severely restricting immigration from all but Anglo-Saxon countries. Only 100 Chinese and 100 Africans were permitted to settle in the U.S. each year while the quota for Germany was 51,000 and for England, 34,000. In high school I followed newspaper accounts of the case of Sacco and Vanzetti, Italian anarchists accused of a holdup and murder in Massachusetts. People from all over the world who protested their execution charged that the judge and jury had been prejudiced not only because the two men were anarchists, but because they were Italians.

Although no one had ever spelled it out for me, I expected my college mates—largely white, Anglo-Saxon Protestants—to be superior beings, wise, witty, cultured—serious intellectuals, in short. Everyone was cordial to me, although they shunned the lone black girl in our dormitory. Intellectuals, however, they were not. Their conversation was limited to dates, marks, movies, popular songs, with rarely a concern for books and ideas. I was particularly surprised because by 1930-31, the Great Depression had begun. As the only girl in the dorm who subscribed to the *New York Times*,

I read of bank failures, farm holidays, and thousands, then millions of unemployed. These events were scarcely noted on Wellesley's serene and beautiful campus. By sophomore year, when there were hunger marchers in Washington and people lining up for handouts at soup kitchens, Wellesley girls began knitting for "the poor." With the country tumbling down about our ears, this response did not seem adequate to me.

My courses were a disappointment too, although this was largely my fault. When my parents' friends, few of whose daughters were college-bound, had asked why I was going, I would explain that I was not going to learn a profession, but to become a well-rounded, cultured human being. Then I would pompously quote John Keats:

> Beauty is truth, truth beauty,—that is all
> Ye know on earth, and all ye need to know.

It took me some years to discover that this was not all *I* needed to know. Meanwhile I concentrated in the liberal arts: English and French literature, philosophy, art history, music. Although I had done well in the math College Boards, it never occurred to me to study mathematics or economics. To fulfill the science requirements, I took two years of botany. Botany classes, where I learned plant structure and classification, worked with a microscope, and grew seedlings in the department's fragrant greenhouse, offered me a different kind of truth and beauty. But when I considered a botany major, the professor discouraged me. "The only job open for a woman botanist is as a landscape gardener, and you draw too poorly for that," she said. Actually, there were a handful of women biologists and geneticists then, but I, a scientific illiterate, had never heard of them and was easily convinced to turn back to liberal arts. It was a decision I still regret.

In my sophomore year I joined the College Press Board, an undergraduate group that publicized Wellesley activities in newspapers across the country. When an article of mine was published in the *New York Sun*, the paper sent me a check for two dollars. My father photocopied the check, framed it, and hung it on his office wall. He remembered his dream even if I showed signs of forgetting it.

Disappointed in Wellesley, I transferred to Barnard College in New York for my last two years and commuted to school by subway. Back in the city, I saw the Depression at first hand: unemployed men selling apples at every street corner, people begging for a nickel for subway fare, Hoovervilles—cardboard and tar-paper shacks built by the homeless—on Riverside Drive and in Central Park. Barnard's tiny urban campus couldn't compare to Wellesley's tree-shaded lawns and lake, but there was an excitement there, and across the street at Columbia University, that I had missed. Franklin Delano Roosevelt was elected President that fall. The day after he took office he declared a bank moratorium and every bank in the country closed its doors. The nation had hit rock bottom. Promising "action and action now," Roosevelt brought a group of college professors to Washington to advise him. One member of this Brain Trust, as it was called, was Raymond Moley who taught at Barnard. Once a week Moley returned to New York and most of Barnard jammed into his classroom to hear the latest news. I continued to major in philosophy, but I never missed one of Moley's lectures.

Payment for Dorothy's first published article

After my graduation from Barnard in June 1934, my sister and I went to Europe, having saved enough from our allowances to finance the trip. Our family was certainly not rich, but looking back now I realize how privileged we were to be able to go abroad that grim summer when millions of other young people were unemployed and on relief. Alice was an art history major at Vassar and we toured museums, churches and galleries. However, we also saw Mussolini's *carabinieri* strutting through the streets of Rome, only a year away from their invasion of Ethiopia. And we were in Milan, close to the border, when the Austrian chancellor was assassinated by native Nazis, and in Paris when Hitler proclaimed himself Fuehrer and *Heil Hitler* became Germany's obligatory greeting.

So there I was in the fall of 1934 with a brand-new Bachelor of Arts degree and a head crammed with information about literature and art. My philosophy professors had taught me about Plato and Aristotle, but they had never mentioned Karl Marx whose economic theories were beginning to seem pertinent. There were no longer apple-sellers on street corners or Hoovervilles in the parks, but millions were either employed on government work projects or had no jobs at all. I thought of becoming an editor at a publishing house, but publishers weren't hiring. I tried for a job on a newspaper and was given an occasional book to review. I did volunteer cataloguing at the Frick Collection which opened as an art museum that year. Total earnings for twelve months' work: $90.

In the fall of 1935 I got my first job on *The Art News*, a weekly magazine. As the youngest of three editors, all women, I reviewed the minor art exhibits and wrote a weekly column of "Paris Notes," gathering the information from French newspapers, for a salary of $12 a week, later raised to $15. After three or four months, a new owner purchased the magazine and the women were all replaced by men. Then someone told me that the New York offices of motion picture companies gave out novels to be summarized so that story department executives could decide whether they were worth considering for moviemaking. With every unemployed writer in the city applying for this work, I was lucky to receive two books a month to synopsize.

I was still living at home, discouraged and bored, when I heard that there were job openings on the Federal Writers Project. As part of its attempt to pull the nation out of the Depression, the New Deal had instituted work relief programs. At first these were pick-and-shovel jobs but by 1935 some money was channeled into the Works Progress Administration's art program: the Federal Art, Music, Theater, and Writers Projects. Unemployed artists painted murals in public buildings or gave art lessons to children, actors and

Dorothy, about 1936. "I was having my hair straightened by this time."

directors put on plays, musicians gave concerts, and writers researched and wrote. Any unemployed writer—novelist, poet, journalist, even inexperienced college graduates like me—was eligible. I worked on the Writers Project from February 1936 to the following November. It was one of the major learning experiences of my life.

For the first time I met people who did not share my sheltered, middle-class background. There were aging Greenwich Village poets, elderly Yiddish playwrights, experienced journalists whose books I had read, aspiring black novelists, and scores of talented young people who would later make names for themselves. Almost all had been on relief and were now supporting grandparents, parents, children on the $23.86 that Uncle Sam paid us each week. Some were Communists, others Socialists, Trotskyites, Zionists, Democrats, Republicans, and the old loft building on Lexington Avenue where we worked rocked with political debate. The excitement was electric as we followed the CIO's union-organizing drives in the auto, steel, and coal industries, and cheered the signing of the National Labor Relations Act. That summer Spain was in the headlines because conservative army officers, with military assistance from Hitler and Mussolini, led a rebellion against the country's republican government. Liberals and radicals the world over, seeing the war as a struggle between fascism and democracy, took up the cause of the Spanish republic. While we attended rallies to raise money for ambulances and medical supplies, some fellow-writers joined the Abraham Lincoln Brigade and went abroad to fight. Two young poets I had worked with on the project lost their lives in the fighting outside of Madrid.

There were struggles at home, too. Periodically, Congress would cut funds for the arts projects or threaten to disband them. For people who were receiving paychecks for the first time in many years, the threats were frightening. On May Day I joined a march to Union Square where thousands chanted, "WPA must go on!" and carried banners reading "No Cuts!" and "More Jobs." Later, when mass layoffs were ordered, we traveled to Washington to parade around the White House shouting:

> Give the bankers Home Relief.
> We want jobs!

That time the cuts were rescinded and it seemed to me that if people joined together to make known their wishes, they could actually influence the government.

The comradeship, the working together toward shared goals was, for me, the most important experience of the Writers Project. No longer was I a loner or a member of an elite group. I was sharing "the action and passion" of my time, to borrow a phrase from Supreme Court Justice Oliver Wendell Holmes. Everyone argued—often bitterly—over politics, but there were no divisions between black and white, Christian and Jew. Most of the Jews on the project boasted that their parents had been "1905ers" who had come to the United States after taking part in a revolution against the Russian Czar that year. I learned enough history to claim that my ancestors had been "1848ers" who had left Europe after an earlier revolution.

We worked too. The Federal Writers Project's major work was the production of more than fifty state and city guidebooks that are still standard reference works. In seventeen states, workers interviewed ex-slaves to record their recollections of the slave experience. More than thirty volumes of these valuable reminiscences have been published in the last decade. Folklorists collected songs and stories from different ethnic groups; a Historical Records project surveyed significant records stored in town halls and municipal buildings. The staff of a Motion Picture Bibliography project summarized every book and article on films, from the 1890s to 1935. The first massive volume of *The Film Index* was published in 1941; a second volume, *The Film*

Philip Sterling, about 1936, "when we first met"

as Industry appeared in 1985, with an introduction by Philip Sterling; and a third volume is soon to be published.

Assigned initially to Historical Records, I soon engineered a transfer to the Motion Picture Bibliography where Philip Sterling was an associate editor. Phil was a newspaperman who had lost his job early in the Depression. His parents were "1905ers," his father a house painter, his mother a former garment worker. When I told my mother and father that we were going to get married neither said "He's not our sort." Hitler's persecution of the Jews had broken down the old caste divisions.

Before we could marry, however, one of us had to get a job in "private industry" because WPA regulations forbade the employment of two members of the same family. On November 23, 1936 I went to work as a secretary on *The Architectural Forum*, a monthly magazine published by Time Inc. I remember the date so precisely because (1) it was my twenty-third birthday and (2) the first issue of *Life*, Time's big new picture-magazine came out that day. My secretarial skills were slight, but the three editors I worked for overlooked my typing errors largely, I think, because they liked to talk and I was a willing listener. As on the Writers Project, we discussed the plight of republican Spain, the growing menace of Hitler, and a new spurt of unemployment in the U.S. which encouraged unionism and influenced Congress to pass a law establishing a forty-hour week and a minimum wage. We also put out a magazine each month, usually late, which included articles and pictures on the best of modern architecture, reports on new building products and methods of construction. I did proofreading as well as typing, carried layouts from the art department and occasionally—very occasionally—wrote a paragraph about a new product.

Phil and I were married on May 14, 1937. After a three-day honeymoon we set up housekeeping in a small, pleasant apartment in Sunnyside, Queens, a half-hour bus ride from the *Forum* office. My cooking was no better than my typing and Phil had to teach me how to run a vacuum cleaner, but somehow we managed. On our combined income of $50 a week, we saved enough in a year to buy a second-hand car, a roadster with a rumble seat and red leather upholstery, in which we traveled to the country on weekends. A writer on the project had told us about Wellfleet on Cape Cod where there were magnificent beaches, dunes, and tidal flats, and not many people. We were vacationing there on September 1, 1939 when the radio brought us news of Hitler's invasion of Poland. World War II had begun.

While we followed the frightening progress of Hitler's armies in Europe and Japan's in Asia, we had personal preoccupations as well. Soon after I went to work for *The Forum*, I joined the Time Inc. unit of the American Newspaper Guild. I received a raise and a cut in hours when, after long negotiations, the first union contract was signed, but the clause I was most interested in was the one promising a six-month maternity leave and a guarantee of rehiring. The Depression was by no means over and although Phil, too, worked in "private industry" by then, we were afraid to start a family without the assurance of two incomes. After the union contract gave us this we could go ahead with our plans. Our son Peter was born in June 1940—and my life changed radically.

We moved to a tiny two-story row house in Sunnyside, the first time I had ever lived in a house rather than an apartment, the first time I had had a backyard—and the first time I had a baby. There were no maternity courses in those days, no disposable diapers, snaps, or zippers, no washing machines and dry-

ers. Most important there were no day-care centers. The nursery school Peter went to when he was two closed for every conceivable holiday. When I protested the school's celebration of Valentine's Day right after Lincoln's Birthday, a teacher said, "We don't believe in mothers working." My friends felt the same way. "Poor little Peter," a neighbor used to say. "He stands out on the street just waiting for you to come home." Poor me! At the end of each day I hopped off the bus and ran down that street with my heart pounding. Determined not to shortchange him, I gave him breakfast before I left in the morning; supper, bath, and a storybook at night. On weekends I pushed him in a stroller to the library and then for a visit to the firehouse or railroad yards where he could see the engines depicted in his books. Long before he was ready, I'm afraid, we took the bus to Manhattan for trips to the Museum of Natural History or one of the art museums.

My job, too, had become more demanding. The week that Japan attacked our fleet at Pearl Harbor and the United States declared war, I transferred to *Life*, at first as a secretary and then a researcher. The pace on a weekly magazine was far more hectic than on *The Forum*. Schedules were tight and if you were working on a late-breaking story you worked late too, even if a child was waiting at home. The magazine had a hierarchy of managing editor, senior editors, and department heads, but the basic working structure was the writer-researcher team. Some story ideas came from the top, but most originated with the writers and researchers. The writer had to produce stories and get them into the magazine or *he* was soon looking for another job. *He.* All writers were *he.* All researchers were *she*, and the pressure to produce that started with the managing editor was transmitted by the writer to the researcher. *He* usually came up with the idea for a story. *She* investigated it and drew up a list of picture possibilities. *He* okayed her picture script and arranged to have a photographer assigned to the story. *She* went with the photographer, holding his lights, telling him what to shoot, and taking notes which were turned over to the writer. After the story was written, it was returned to the researcher to be checked for accuracy. *She* went over it, word by word, putting a pencil dot above each word to show that it had been verified. After a story was published, if a reader pointed out an error, the researcher was blamed, not the writer.

The training was valuable. A researcher had to be able to gather information on any conceivable subject quickly. Within a short period, I worked on stories about helicopters and spring peepers, ballet dancers and transatlantic planes. One day I might have to find out the color of the eyes of the Speaker of the House, on another, the height of the Washington Cathedral. You couldn't say "I don't know" or "I can't find out." You picked up the telephone or searched in the library until you had the answer.

On long picture essays, the researcher did her own legwork. For a story on the Waldorf-Astoria Hotel, I spent a month interviewing managers, chefs, chambermaids, and poking around in supply closets. My fifty-or-so pages of research even included statistics on the number of cakes of soap and rolls of toilet paper used each day. After the picture script was written I went back to the hotel with photographer Alfred Eisenstaedt and his assistants for the actual picture-taking.

In many ways it was a fun job. You could telephone or wire to any place in the world. When people, including generals, senators, movie stars, heard that you were from *Life*, they would eagerly cooperate. There was also the feeling that you were on top of the news—ahead of it, really, because the teletype and *Life*'s correspondents brought it to you before it appeared in the newspapers. And sometimes, particularly during the war, when news was censored, you often saw CONFIDENTIAL NOT FOR ATTRIBUTION memos from Washington or unexpurgated reports on the scandalous behavior of public figures which never appeared in print.

But there were bad things about *Life* too. Time Inc.'s conservative bias distorted much of its reporting of national and international news. I avoided the news departments as best I could, usually teaming up with a writer who specialized in nature, aviation, and cultural events. And the fact that writers were men and researchers women took its psychological toll. The line between writer-male and researcher-female was so hard and fast, the conditioning so strong, that I came to believe that I couldn't write. Once when the magazine was going to press, my harried writer tossed the "Letters" pages to me and asked me to write the brief editorial comment which accompanied each letter. I sat for hours with a prize case of writer's block and a blank sheet of paper in my typewriter. Finally, he wrote the comments himself.

After the birth of our daughter, Anne, in July 1944, I moved up the ladder a step to become assistant chief of *Life*'s News Bureau, the department that kept in touch with correspondents across the country. The job brought a raise and some prestige, but more important it promised regular hours and a guarantee that I would not have to go on out-of-town assignments. These trips with a photographer were more interesting than most New York stories, but I did not want to be away from my children.

As a family, the war touched us lightly. We sold our car when gasoline rationing was instituted, conscientiously saved coupons for sugar and shoes rations,

Peter and Anne Sterling, in Rye, New York, 1948

and kept tight blackout curtains on our window. During the first year, when air raids seemed imminent, I worked at a Civil Defense message center at night, ready to spread the alarm if enemy planes were sighted. We worried about Phil's brother in the Navy, Alice's husband in the Army, and friends overseas, but Phil, as the father of two, was deferred by the draft.

I was vacationing in Wellfleet with Peter and Anne when U.S. planes dropped the first atom bombs on Hiroshima and Nagasaki. None of us understood the dire consequences they would present in the future. When Japan surrendered a week later, we rejoiced. For the first time in our adult lives, my generation was optimistic. We foresaw a lasting peace, guaranteed by the new United Nations, and full employment for all. In the words of Vice President Henry Wallace, we were entering "a people's century." In this optimistic mood, a group of us, mostly friends from Sunnyside, decided to buy land in the suburbs and build homes cooperatively. We found nineteen acres of hilly land—big trees, rock outcroppings—in Rye, New York, only thirty-eight minutes from the city by train. Shortages of building materials delayed the project; postwar inflation doubled costs; but on a rainy day in April 1948 we moved into our new home, a house of modern design with big picture windows and space for everyone. Peter could walk to school by himself and a nursery school called for Anne each day in a station wagon. That summer I started my first garden.

At *Life,* as men returned from the army, women who had moved up into executive jobs began losing them. When the head of the News Bureau was fired and a man put in her place, I decided it was time to move on. The job which had been exciting during the war when every foreign correspondent who came back stopped at my desk now seemed dull. Phil had been working as a press representative at CBS for several years and his job, plus the severance pay and profit sharing I would receive from Time Inc. gave me the courage to make the break.

But what would I do? I thought of seeking work as a researcher, but before I did that I had some business to finish. Whenever *Life* writers and researchers got together, we would swap tales about the sometimes outrageous, sometimes funny things that happened, principally the way stories were slanted or rewritten to make them conform to Time Inc.'s editorial policies. As we talked, someone was sure to say, "That's one for the book"—the book about Time Inc. that someone, some day, would produce. I had taken this seriously enough to make notes of many of these conversations, and to save company memos and "inside" reports from the Washington office. Sure that I was incapable of writing "the book," I set out to find a writer—male—who could. A competent but overworked journalist agreed to take on the assignment if I would complete and organize the research. For the better part of a year I read back issues of *Time, Fortune,* and *Life;* interviewed correspondents and staff people; and put all the information together, chapter by chapter. My collaborator was still too busy to work on it, but when he saw my manuscript, titled "It's about Time," he said "There's your book." I didn't believe him until a prominent literary agent read it and asked if she could submit it to publishers.

Then strange things began to happen. It was 1950. Instead of the lasting peace we had dreamed of, a cold war was being waged against the Soviet Union and against anyone in a position of authority in the United States who had ever shown sympathy toward socialism. Intimidated by Senator Joseph McCarthy, who claimed that the government had been infiltrated by Communists, people were afraid to speak out on any issue. It was at the beginning of this period of fear and repression that my agent set out to sell "It's about Time." Several publishing houses were enthusiastic about the manuscript. Again and again she telephoned to say "I think it's sold," only to have it turned down the following day. Wise though she was in the ways of the publishing world, she couldn't understand what had gone wrong. Nor could I until, many years later, I learned that at least one publisher had telephoned the FBI. He said he had "an excellent manuscript . . . a very fascinating and readable document" by Dorothy Sterling, but what was her background? After checking

the files, the FBI official told him to "stop, look, and listen, and be very careful" in dealing with me because fourteen years earlier I had signed a nominating petition for a Communist candidate for public office. It would have been consoling to know this at the time when other books were being suppressed because of their authors' politics. As it was, my agent gave up after a while and I saw the rejections as one more proof that I was not a writer.

During these unpleasant months I had not been idle. Our dog, Sophie, a handsome dachshund, had a litter of puppies on Anne's bed. The picture possibilities were obvious. Our neighbor Myron Ehrenberg, a professional photographer, started photographing them while I improvised a shooting script, as I had done on *Life.* He followed the puppies from birth until they were half-grown—with Anne and Peter, his own children, and other neighborhood youngsters observing them. Puppies and children were so attractive that it was easy to weave a little story about them, including

Anne with one of Sophie's puppies, 1949

Sterling with Billy Wright, hero of Billy Goes
Exploring, *examining a cocoon*

information about Sophie's pregnancy and the puppies' birth and development. Mike and I enjoyed this project so much that we then took a young neighbor, Billy, on a tour of the local woods, ponds, and farms to look for signs of the coming of spring. We helped him find birds' nests, a newly hatched butterfly, a turtle, and so forth, and I again organized the pictures in the form of a story.

So there we were with two books—maybe. I had met the editor of Doubleday's Books for Young Readers whose office was then in the Time and Life Building. With considerable trepidation I brought the books to her. Many months later she wrote to tell me that *Sophie and Her Puppies* and *Billy Goes Exploring* were both accepted for publication and would be selections of the Junior Literary Guild. Did we have ideas for further books, she wanted to know.

We did—and so did she. By the time Mike and I had completed *Trees and Their Story,* a straightforward nature book without the sugarcoating of a story, Doubleday asked us to do a book on the United Nations. I researched *United Nations, N.Y.* exactly as I had done the *Life* story on the Waldorf-Astoria Hotel, spending weeks at U.N. headquarters before writing a picture script and bringing Mike in to take the pictures. In between the photographic books, I wrote *The Cub Scout Mystery,* a story which grew out of Peter's experiences as a Cub Scout and which was set in a community resembling Rye.

By 1953 I had five books in print, but I still didn't think of myself as a writer. For the most part I was doing just what I had done on *Life* except that I was having more fun—and earning less money. Almost every morning when I faced my typewriter I had to tell myself, "You're writing research for your writer." Only after I had addressed a few sentences to this mythical superior being could I get going. During one of these daily struggles my mind wandered back to Spec. Op., to biography class and the hateful sewing class which had deprived me of science. I decided to write a biography of a woman, a heroic figure who would say to girls, "You are as strong and capable as boys."

Then came the problem of choosing a subject. Someone suggested Harriet Tubman, the leader of the Underground Railroad before the Civil War. I found a biography in the library and was tremendously moved by her courage, ingenuity, and dedication. To gather further information, I went to the Schomburg Collection in New York, a major research center for black history, and for the first time learned about the crusade to end slavery and its black and white supporters. I was excited, but also bewildered and angry. Why had I never heard of Harriet Tubman or Sojourner Truth, Frederick Douglass or William Lloyd Garrison? Here was a wealth of information, dozens of inspiring stories to tell young readers. I wrote *Freedom Train: The Story of Harriet Tubman* quickly and with confidence. I had found a subject about which I cared deeply. At the age of forty, I had finally become a writer.

After *Freedom Train* I decided to write a biography of Robert Smalls, a slave who captured a Confederate gunboat, the *Planter,* during the Civil War, and turned it over to the Union. Afterwards he was elected to Congress and remained a popular spokesman for his people until his death in 1915. It was an adventure tale, the story of a poor boy succeeding in the face of great odds, that seemed a natural for young readers. After reading about Smalls and interviewing his son, Phil and I made a trip to Beaufort, South Carolina, Smalls' home town.

It was our first trip to the South and we were typical tourists, stopping the car to gaze at fields of cotton in bloom and sampling roadside barbecues. Beaufort, in the Sea Islands, was a beautiful old town, its well-preserved houses built before the Civil War, its streets lined with magnolias and live oaks dripping with Spanish moss. But it was segregated. We had read about the South's Jim Crow laws which kept whites and blacks apart, but we had never encountered them before. Black people whose parents had known Robert Smalls entertained us in their homes; we could not repay their hospitality by inviting them to our hotel or buying them a cup of coffee in a restaurant. I read old newspapers on microfilm in Beaufort's public library,

Ernest Crichlow, illustrator of Captain of the Planter,
*Dorothy Sterling, and William Robert Smalls,
about 1957*

but the principal of the black elementary school was not permitted to enter the building. As a special favor, she could borrow books if she asked for them at the back door. The half-filled shelves of the black library down the street were stocked with tattered discards from the white library. Schools were separate and blacks sat in the rear of buses and the gallery of the local movie theater. As a U.S. Congressman and, later, Collector of Customs in Beaufort, Smalls had worked with white people. Some were still alive, but they all refused to talk to me.

Our experiences in Beaufort made me see Smalls' life as more than a simple adventure story. After doing a considerable amount of historical research, I wrote *Captain of the Planter: The Story of Robert Smalls* as an account of a significant period in U.S. history when the ex-slaves' dream of freedom and equality was betrayed.

As I wrote it was becoming increasingly apparent that the growth of segregation which began in Smalls' lifetime was threatening to destroy American democracy. In 1954, the Supreme Court had declared that separation of children in public schools by race was unconstitutional, and had ordered schools to "make a prompt and reasonable start" toward integration. The response from the deep South was "Never!" White Citizens Councils and a host of other racist groups organized in the states of the old Confederacy, and were ready to resist any attempt at integration with threats, boycotts, and organized terror. By the fall of 1956,

when schools in the mid-South—Kentucky, Tennessee, Virginia—began to integrate, dynamite blasts shattered black homes and stores and schools were bombed. The small number of black children who attempted to enter the "white" schools were met by crowds of white men and women who screamed threats and taunts, spat in their faces, and sometimes roughed them up.

Reading newspaper accounts of these courageous children, I proposed to my editor that Mike and I go South to do a book about them. Doubleday had been willing although unenthusiastic about publishing biographies of Harriet Tubman and Robert Smalls, figures from the past, but the company had no desire to take sides in what threatened to become a second Civil War. However, Hill and Wang, a small publishing firm, agreed to gamble on the idea, and Mike and I set out on a tour of the mid-South in the spring of 1957. Armed with introductions to black leaders and the few whites sympathetic to integration, we interviewed scores of black children and parents as well as some of their white classmates and teachers. The weeks we spent on this assignment were weeks of revelation.

In Clay, Kentucky, we talked with the mother of the only two black children to enter the "white" school. After ten-year-old James had heard about school integration on the radio, he had said, "Mommy, why can't we go to the school in Clay?" "If you've got the guts to go, I've got the guts to take you," she had replied. On the first day of school, a crowd attacked their car, almost overturning it. By Day Three a hundred National Guardsmen were needed to escort them safely. "I died a thousand deaths every day until three o'clock," their mother recalled, "but I couldn't take their courage from them." In Clinton, Tennessee, we walked down the hill from the black section of town with nine teenagers who had been beaten outside of school and tormented in classrooms and study hall. Tight-lipped, tense, but with heads held high, they ignored the name-calling by fellow students and went inside to their classes. The walk to school, one of them told me, was "the longest journey in our lives." In Virginia, Maryland, Delaware, other children said, "I'm not going to school to socialize. I just want to get an education." Or "I hope what I'm going through will help those who come after me." Or "I wanted to show that I could do the same work they did. And I can."

Tender Warriors, our text-and-picture report on these embattled children did not cause much of a stir when it was published in 1958, but I was so emotionally involved that I wrote a fictional account of a black girl's first year in an integrated school. Ordinarily, I am a slow writer, completing a page or two a day, but I wrote *Mary Jane* at top speed, with my legs so tightly wrapped around my typewriter table that they ached at the end of the day. Doubleday held the manuscript for some months before deciding to publish it. It was boycotted in the South and in some northern cities when it was first issued, but by the 1960s, after sit-ins and freedom rides had focussed national attention on segregation, it became a best-seller and was reprinted in nine foreign countries.

Meanwhile, I was moving in several directions as a writer. I continued with mystery stories, drawing on my children and their friends, but the plots always had a hidden message: if children used their eyes and brains and worked together, they could solve problems that baffled adults. *The Brownie Scout Mystery* and *The Silver Spoon Mystery* were a little different. In these I set out to show that if *girls* used their brains and worked together, they could solve problems that baffled *boys*.

As Peter and Anne grew older, my mystery-story mine petered out, but I still continued my interest in science. When the first polio vaccine was introduced, Phil and I wrote *Polio Pioneers,* which was even translated into Japanese. *Insects and the Homes They Build* and *The Story of Mosses, Ferns, and Mushrooms* were illustrated with photographs by Myron Ehrenberg; for *Caterpillars, Creatures of the Night* and *The Story of Caves* I worked with an artist friend, Winifred Lubell. When people asked why I chose these subjects, I would blame them on Peter and Anne's curiosity about insects and plants and the difficulty of finding answers to their questions. The fact is, of course, that it was my own childhood curiosity I was satisfying. I had never forgotten the mushrooms and mosses I had seen at my first summer camp. At last I had a chance to identify some of them and learn their place in the plant kingdom. And don't think my father, who followed my career with proprietary interest didn't ask, "Who would want to read about mushrooms?" I was glad to be able to tell him, on the basis of sales figures, that there were enough oddball young people in the country to make the book's publication worthwhile.

Besides, the books gave me an excuse for doing all sorts of things that I had always wanted to do without seeming eccentric. For *Insects and the Homes They Build* I kept a praying mantis egg case on the kitchen window sill until the baby mantises hatched, dug up a bumblebee's nest, and watched honeybees repair their hives. When I was writing *Caterpillars,* I was the only housewife in town who planted parsley in order to attract parsley caterpillars which later spun cocoons and became black swallowtail butterflies.

Peter and Anne shared many of these activities with me. When we were first married Phil and I mourned the fact that we were "semi-skilled intellectuals." Our children, we promised ourselves, would have skills, a trade or profession which would enable them to find work even during a depression. Because we were both interested in science, the books and games we bought and the walks we took with them encouraged them to notice the living world around them. In a notebook tacked to the kitchen bulletin board we jotted down the names of flowers, birds, and insects we saw at different seasons of the year, keeping lists which were useful when I later wrote *Spring Is Here!* and *Fall Is Here!* And during one Easter vacation, Winnie Lubell took her two children and I mine on a tour of caves which gave us the background for *The Story of Caves.*

In the late 1950s when Peter had gone off to Cornell—to major in biology—and Anne was beginning to leaf through college catalogs, Phil and I became active in the local NAACP. As chairman of the Housing Committee, Phil's major problem was finding safe and affordable housing. Rye and the neighboring town of Port Chester were not as segregated as Beaufort, South Carolina, but there were white and black neighborhoods with clearly defined boundaries. How firm these boundaries were I discovered when Orial Redd, president of the branch, asked me to help her find an apartment. She and her husband were living in three rooms, in an apartment so small that her four-year-old daughter had to sleep in a crib because there was no room for another bed. Now she was pregnant again and feeling desperate. Together we began to check out homes and apartments. If I went to real estate agents, they had places to show me; if she went, she was told, "So sorry. No vacancies." After months of proving to ourselves that, yes, there was discrimination in Rye, we decided to act. When she learned by telephone that there was a vacancy in a nearby garden apartment, but was told it was "no longer available" when she showed up in person, I looked at the apartment, signed an application for a lease, and gave a check for a month's rent. Next, a group of us, including a minister and several tenants of the apartment house, called on the owner of the building who lived in New York. We asked him to rent to the Redds. He was a friend of black people, he said, but he returned my check the next day. Some months later, after the passage of a state law against discrimination in housing, we began again. I was offered apartments all over town; the Redds were always turned down. When my name and face became familiar to renting agents, my sister and others took over the checking. We organized a Rye Council for Human Rights, hired a lawyer, and brought two cases to the State Commission Against Discrimination before the Redds obtained an apartment. Their second child was fifteen months old when they moved in.

Our struggle in Rye was only a pale reflection of events in the South where a broad fight against segregation was under way. Black people were sitting-in at lunch counters, churches, libraries. Blacks and whites were traveling together and using hitherto-segregated restaurants and waiting rooms in bus terminals. In May 1961 a bus carrying Freedom Riders, as they were called, was ambushed and set afire. As the riders left the burning bus, they were savagely beaten. When photographs of the incident were published, others flocked to join them, and there were more ambushes, more mob attacks.

Late that month Peter telephoned from college. "I'm going on a Freedom Ride," he said. My heart sank. "Must you?" I asked, but I knew the answer. A few nights later, we saw his picture on television. He was in New Orleans being trained in non-violent tactics before his group, black and white, took a train to Jackson, Mississippi. The next day, the *New York Times* reported that eight Freedom Riders had been arrested in Jackson. Peter telephoned from jail to assure us that he was all right. Cornell students and friends in Rye raised money to pay his fine for "breach of the peace" and he was released. So the story ended happily—almost.

Between my attempts to find an apartment for the Redds and the Freedom Ride, the Sterlings were often in the local paper. A fortnight after Peter's return home, Phil and I were awakened by a sharp noise. A gunshot? We looked out the window to see a seven-foot cross burning in the front yard. The police came quickly; the fire was doused without damage and the paper published an editorial calling the cross-burning "despicable and cowardly." Dozens of people, strangers as well as friends, called and wrote to offer sympathy. There were nasty calls too—a woman telephoning to scream "Bastard!"—and anonymous anti-Semitic postcards.

After a few weeks, the excitement simmered down. Phil and Peter seemed to forget about the burning cross, writing if off as a college-student prank. I didn't. The incident had punctured a romantic illusion. When we moved to Rye thirteen years earlier I thought we were settling there for life. Rye would be my children's hometown, if not mine; the place they would return to all their lives. But the hometown feeling was never complete. Our modern house was too unconventional—"a chicken coop" some neighbors called it. I worked, wore blue jeans, went hatless, while the other mothers in the PTA wore long skirts, exchanged recipes, and hooked rugs. We were Jews in a predominantly Christian community; left-of-center politically amid conservative Republicans. Now the cross-burning

Phil and Dorothy Sterling inspecting the cross burned in front of their home, June, 1961

seemed to tell me that I was never going to be the popular all-American girl that my mother had once dreamed about. Once the hurt faded—for I was surprised to discover that I had shared mother's dream to an extent too—I somehow felt free, with renewed courage to speak out.

In the 1960s there was plenty to speak about. Blacks were battling segregation in Alabama and Mississippi, Tennessee and Washington, D.C., and more and more whites were joining their cause. At the beginning of the decade I wrote *Lucretia Mott: Gentle Warrior,* a biography of a white woman who, working with black people, had been a leader in the fight against slavery. I was trying to say to white readers, "This is your struggle too." In *Tear Down the Walls!* I wrote a history of the civil rights movement from the first slave revolts in the seventeenth century to the present day. The book had just gone to press when Martin Luther King was assassinated. After his death, the freedom movement took a new turn. Blacks who had been singing "Black and white together/We shall overcome" began to talk about "Black power" and to insist on being their own spokesmen. It was then that I wrote *The Making of an Afro-American: Martin Robison Delany,* a biography of a black nationalist of the nineteenth century.

In addition to writing, I had a brief career as a public speaker and editor during those years. In an article on *The All-White World of Children's Books,* a librarian had pointed out that less than 7 percent of the books published for young people included mention of blacks. The statistics were even more dismal when history textbooks were examined. Since I was one of the very few to write on black subjects, I was suddenly transformed into an expert. Congressman Adam Clayton Powell invited me to come to Washington to testify before the House Committee on Education and Labor which was investigating the treatment of minority groups in text and library books. After publishing-house executives and school administrators were taken over the coals for their racial bias, I spoke about the "truth gap" in children's literature that prevented both black and white youngsters from learning the real facts of American history and life. When my statement was published, I received invitations to speak to the National Council of Teachers of English and other gatherings of teachers and librarians. Two of my speeches, "The Soul of Learning" and "What's Black and White and Read All Over?" were published in the *English Journal* and were widely reprinted.

As a result of the Powell hearings and the civil rights revolution which was still underway, Congress appropriated large sums of money for school libraries, particularly in black neighborhoods. When publishers

responded with a rash of books on black history and life, I found myself editing two series of biographies of blacks for young people as well as scholarly books on black history for Beacon Press. We lined up black writers and historians for most of these books, giving some of the younger people their first opportunity to work with commercial publishers. During this period, I put in ten-hour-days and, for the first and only time in my life, made a considerable amount of money. Once a publisher paid me $1,250 for attending a one-day conference to discuss an anthology of black poetry. Had he only known it, I would have conferred for nothing.

Then, as abruptly as black books had become acceptable, they were "out." Congressional funds were cut, book sales plummeted, and my editing jobs came to an end. By 1970 I was working on a collection of letters, diaries, and other writings by black Americans. The first of these, *Speak Out in Thunder Tones,* was published in 1973, the second, *The Trouble They Seen: Black People Tell the Story of Reconstruction,* appeared two years later.

Meanwhile, there had been major changes in my personal life. Phil had left CBS to do writing of his own: an anthology of black humor, an award-winning biography of Rachel Carson, a collection of interviews with teachers in urban schools, and several young people's books on black figures. After completing college and graduate school, Peter and Anne had indeed become scientists, teaching and doing research at the University of Pennsylvania and Brown Univer-

Grandchildren Daniel and Emily Sterling, on the road to the Wellfleet beach in the 1970s

Nelson Fausto, Anne's husband, a professor at Brown University

sity, respectively. Both were married and Peter had two children, Emily and Daniel. Our closest friends had left Rye. The house seemed big and empty, and we were tired of coping with roofers and plumbers. It was time to move on. For three years we lived in an efficient apartment development in Greenwich, Connecticut, where we had ample space for desks and bookshelves and no worries about a leaky roof or sink. But we had gotten out of the habit of hearing strangers' voices through apartment walls. Our windows looked out on an incinerator smokestack, and there was no space for our dog, a poodle named Jake, to run.

In the spring of 1973, we moved to Cape Cod. More than a decade earlier we had built a summer house in Wellfleet, winterizing it and adding guest rooms as we had the money—"a grandchildren trap," Phil called it. During the busy sixties I had taken time off from politics to write *The Outer Lands: A Natural History of Cape Cod, Martha's Vineyard, Nantucket, Block Island, and Long Island,* illustrated by Winifred Lubell. *The Outer Lands* gave me a chance to learn about the Cape—its special history and geology, and the plants and animals of the woods and marshes, dunes and tidal flats. Winnie and I snorkeled in a marsh creek to look at shrimp and baby flounder. We found an orchid growing in a boggy spot between two dune peaks and walked the tidal flats to watch whelks and moon snails construct their egg cases. Of all the Cape's varying environments, my favorite is the bay at low tide where one can see crabs and worms, snails and clams, and, of course, the famous Wellfleet oysters. Our house is only a two-minute walk from the bay and Jake and I have a choice of tidal flats or pine woods for our morning walks.

Nevertheless, after living in or near New York City all my life, it was a wrench to move to a town with a population of two thousand, which swells to thirty thousand in July and August when vacationers arrive. I would not have wanted to make the move when I was younger or if I had not been able to bring work along with me. As it was, we moved with a substantial library, three typewriters and a microfilm reader. Black books were "out" by the time we settled in Wellfleet, but books about women were suddenly in demand. We had scarcely unpacked when Feminist Press asked me for a book about black women. I replied enthusiastically with a proposal for a historical study which would start in slavery days, a project that I had been collecting information on ever since my encounter with Harriet Tubman more than twenty years earlier. But Feminist Press wanted a book for high-school readers, as part of a series on women's lives and work. Selecting three women from the thousands whose stories I wanted to tell, I wrote *Black Foremothers,* a book which only whetted my appetite for the larger project. I knew that there was a rich supply of letters, interviews, diaries, autobiographies, but to collect them would take time and money, and my royalty income had dropped precipitately. I spent a month applying for fellowships

Phil with Jake II, Christmas, 1982

Peter and Dorothy at her seventieth birthday party

friends. But I like living in a small town where clerks in the stores call me by my first name and the plumber once refused pay for his repairs, asking for an autographed copy of a book instead.

Wellfleet is an offbeat town where people wear blue jeans and denim jackets, and artists, writers, and retired professors get along well with the native population of fishermen, carpenters, and mechanics. Sometimes there are fights about enviromental issues and partisans shout at town meeting and write angry letters to the papers. But I feel much less of an oddball here than I did in Rye. However, it will never be my home town, or my children's. No matter how long we live here we will always be "wash-a-shores," as the "born heres" call the city folk. They like to tell about a town meeting at which a speaker insisted that he was a Cape Codder. "I've lived here for forty years," he said. "My children were born here." A voice from the back of the auditorium interrupted. "If a cat has kittens in the oven, that don't make them biscuits." End of discussion.

Looking back over more than seventy years, I am somewhat surprised to find that I am an accidental writer, an accidental naturalist, an accidental historian. Living at a different time, I might have become a botanist, an archaeologist, or, possibly, an investigative reporter. I would still like to visit Africa and China and see the statues on the Easter Islands. I wish I had learned how to ski and play tennis and listen to music.

and grants until I realized that no foundation was going to assist an aging writer who claimed to be a historian but had no graduate degrees. About this time an aunt died, leaving her small estate to Alice and me. Part of the money went to build the greenhouse that I had coveted since I had studied botany at Wellesley, the balance became my foundation grant.

For more than five years I collected black women's papers. I made trips to Washington, Boston, and New York, but most of the material came by mail in the form of photocopies and microfilm which I could read at my desk overlooking Wellfleet Bay. File cabinets were overflowing when I reluctantly called a halt and began to organize and annotate the material. A bulky 800-page manuscript was edited down to a 500-page book. *We Are Your Sisters: Black Women in the Nineteenth Century* was published by W. W. Norton shortly after my seventieth birthday. Now I am working on a biography of Abby Kelley, a white New Englander who devoted her life to the struggle against slavery and for women's rights.

I have cut my working day in half, allowing time for walking, swimming, gardening, and taking naps. Our children visit often, particularly in summer when they can swim and windsurf in the bay. Anne has just published her first book, *Myths of Gender: Biological Theories about Women and Men,* and our granddaughter is a freshman in college. I still read the *New York Times* and miss the theaters and museums of the city, as well as dinners with my sister and brother-in-law and old

Anne Fausto-Sterling, 1985

Dorothy Sterling at her desk in Wellfleet, 1984. "I no longer straighten my hair!"

Maybe I'll do some of those things in the future, but whatever happens I intend to keep on writing as long as I have something to say.

BIBLIOGRAPHY

FOR CHILDREN

Fiction:

Sophie and Her Puppies (photographs by Myron Ehrenberg). Garden City, N.Y.: Doubleday, 1951.

The Cub Scout Mystery (illustrated by Paul Galdone). Garden City, N.Y.: Doubleday, 1952.

Billy Goes Exploring (photographs by M. Ehrenberg). Garden City, N.Y.: Doubleday, 1953.

The Brownie Scout Mystery (illustrated by Reisie Lonette). Garden City, N.Y.: Doubleday, 1955.

The Silver Spoon Mystery (illustrated by Grace Paull). Garden City, N.Y.: Doubleday, 1958.

Secret of the Old Post-Box (illustrated by G. Paull). Garden City, N.Y.: Doubleday, 1960.

Ellen's Blue Jays (illustrated by Winifred Lubell). Garden City, N.Y.: Doubleday, 1961.

Nonfiction:

Trees and Their Story (photographs by M. Ehrenberg). Garden City, N.Y.: Doubleday, 1953.

Insects and the Homes They Build (photographs by M. Ehrenberg). Garden City, N.Y.: Doubleday, 1954.

Polio Pioneers: The Story of the Fight against Polio, with Philip Sterling (photographs by M. Ehrenberg). Garden City, N.Y.: Doubleday, 1955.

The Story of Mosses, Ferns, and Mushrooms (photographs by M. Ehrenberg). Garden City, N.Y.: Doubleday, 1955.

Wall Street: The Story of the Stock Exchange (photographs by M. Ehrenberg). Garden City, N.Y.: Doubleday, 1955.

The Story of Caves (illustrated by W. Lubell). Garden City, N.Y.: Doubleday, 1956.

Creatures of the Night (illustrated by W. Lubell). Garden City, N.Y.: Doubleday, 1960.

Caterpillars (illustrated by W. Lubell). Garden City, N.Y.: Doubleday, 1961.

Forever Free: The Story of the Emancipation Proclamation (illustrated by Ernest Crichlow). Garden City, N.Y.: Doubleday, 1963.

Spring Is Here! (illustrated by W. Lubell). Garden City, N.Y.: Doubleday, 1964.

Fall Is Here! (illustrated by W. Lubell). Garden City, N.Y.: Natural History Press, 1966.

It Started in Montgomery: A Picture History of the Civil Rights Movement. New York: Scholastic Book Services, 1972.

FOR YOUNG ADULTS

Nonfiction:

United Nations, N.Y. (photographs by M. Ehrenberg). Garden City, N.Y.: Doubleday, 1953.

Freedom Train: The Story of Harriet Tubman (illustrated by E. Crichlow). Garden City, N.Y.: Doubleday, 1954.

Captain of the Planter: The Story of Robert Smalls (illustrated by E. Crichlow). Garden City, N.Y.: Doubleday, 1958.

Lucretia Mott: Gentle Warrior. Garden City, N.Y.: Doubleday, 1964.

Lift Every Voice: The Lives of Booker T. Washington, W.E.B. Du Bois, Mary Church Terrell, and James Weldon Johnson, with Benjamin Quarles (illustrated by E. Crichlow). Garden City, N.Y.: Doubleday, 1965.

The Outer Lands: A Natural History Guide to Cape Cod, Martha's Vineyard, Nantucket, Block Island, and Long Island (illustrated by W. Lubell). Garden City, N.Y.: Natural History Press, 1967.

Tear Down the Walls! A History of the American Civil Rights Movement. Garden City, N.Y.: Doubleday, 1968.

The Making of an Afro-American: Martin Robison Delany, 1812-1885. Garden City, N.Y.: Doubleday, 1971.

Black Foremothers: Three Lives (illustrated by Judith Eloise Hooper). Old Westbury, N.Y.: Feminist Press, 1979.

Fiction:

Mary Jane (illustrated by E. Crichlow). Garden City, N.Y.: Doubleday, 1959.

FOR ADULTS

Nonfiction:

Tender Warriors, with Donald Gross (photographs by M. Ehrenberg). New York: Hill & Wang, 1958.

We Are Your Sisters: Black Women in the Nineteenth Century. New York: Norton, 1984.

Editor of:

I Have Seen War: Twenty-Five Stories from World War II. New York: Hill & Wang, 1960.

Speak Out in Thunder Tones: Letters and Other Writings by Black Northerners, 1787-1865. Garden City, N.Y.: Doubleday, 1973.

The Trouble They Seen: Black People Tell the Story of Reconstruction. Garden City, N.Y.: Doubleday, 1976.

Colin Thiele

1920-

Colin Thiele

As I remember it, the world of my childhood was brown and golden. All round our farmhouse the waves of wheatland rolled to the edges of the hills, rising and falling gently as if the land itself were breathing. In summer the stooked hay stood in a thousand shining cones, the ripening awns swayed and rustled, the stubble gleamed in the hard bright light. I was a barefoot boy of four or five, walking round and round the paddocks following the harvesters all day long like a devoted blue-heeler. It was 1925, in a place called the Hundred of Julia Creek in South Australia.

My father had taken up land there about twenty years earlier and had married my mother in 1910. He and his brothers had had a hard life before that, for which they blamed my grandfather who had migrated from Germany to South Australia in 1855 on a ship called the *La Rochelle*. It had sunk with all hands on the return voyage. My uncles kept telling me that if it had sunk on the outward journey they and I would never have existed. That possibility seemed to fascinate them.

My father and mother both spoke German rather than English. So did most of the other farmers and the storekeepers and workers in the little country towns of our district. Their legacy from Germany was intense in spirit and all-embracing in scope. Food, religion, dress, speech, and attitudes were fundamentally German. My mother had been Amalie Anna Wittwer. She claimed that the Wittwers had sharp wits and skillful hands. She may well have been right.

Religion was central to their lives—Bible-readings round the tea-table every night, church on Sundays, Sunday school on Saturdays. If that sounds Irish it is explained by the daunting distances the pastor had to travel in his buggy or his Model T Ford.

The Lutheran pastor was a commanding figure in his flowing robes. He was usually a thunderous preacher who liked to crash his fist on the pulpit and roar out in German to make his points. It was hard to go to sleep during his sermons. The little churches with their steep spires and lovely mellow bells dotted the countryside and provided him with ample opportunities for firing off his salvoes. Some churches even had their pulpits half way up the front wall near the altar so that he could appear dramatically through an opening behind it like a cuckoo from a clock.

The hymns were German too, the music created by German composers. My father was an organist in the Julia Lutheran Church for almost forty years. The bare pinewood pews accorded well with German convictions about rigour and discipline. Luckily many of them were dotted with pine knots that small boys could press and lever surreptitiously during sermons until they popped out like corks. It was challenging work. Stubborn knots could take years to loosen, and some—twisted and bent infuriatingly like Chinese puzzles—wouldn't come out at all even though they were as loose as granny's teeth.

I had three sisters and a brother. We all had our jobs to do, young as we were—milking cows, separating cream, making butter, cutting firewood, and feeding a great array of horses, calves, fowls, pigs, and turkeys. We also had to pitch in on special occasions when the whole family was embroiled in a common enter-

Father, Carl Wilhelm Thiele, about 1905

direction, avoiding obvious dangers near deep wells, angry bulls, or poisonous snakes. It was a wonderful world to grow up in with its space and solitude, its wild life, its summer heat, winter mists, and the miraculous rebirth of spring. Much later I wrote about my response to this natural environment in pieces such as *The Quality of Experience* and *Sunrise and Starshine: A Boyhood Revisited.*

Apart from farm and church the third important influence in our early lives was school. I first went to the Julia Primary School when I was four. It was a tiny rectangular building, just big enough to hold twenty children. It had stone walls, brick facings at the windows and door, and a galvanised iron roof. There was a lean-to shelter shed on the leeward side and an iron tank full of rainwater in which birds, snakes, and possums periodically committed suicide. There were more than eight-hundred such little Bush schools in South Australia at that time.

The school affected me profoundly. My mother always claimed that I left home on my first morning speaking nothing but German and returned that eve-

prise such as making jam, bottling sauce, preserving fruit, or killing a pig.

We made jam in twelve-gallon batches in the copper and stored it in big vats or tins in the cellar. Beside them stood drums full of dill cucumbers, rows of preserves, earthenware jars of lard, and bottles of ginger beer or hop brew. From the cellar rafters overhead hung rows of smoked hams and bacon flitches, and a forest of dangling sausages—*Bratwurst, Mettwurst, Leberwurst,* and the rest.

I slept in a little room above the cellar some distance from the house, aware not only of the rich smells of the earth's fruitfulness, but periodically shaken by exploding bottles or the squizzling and sizzling of pent-up forces culminating in a cannonade of corks against the floor under my bed. This was especially so whenever my older brother became a little overenthusiastic in dealing out the hops or yeast for his home brew.

Beyond my responsibilities in the farmyard I had great freedom—the kind of freedom that is only possible where frontiers are wide and the world is still young. In the hills beyond our farm I roamed at will, usually alone. Country parents in those days had no choice but to let their children develop self-reliance in their own way—carrying firearms, acquiring a sense of

Mother, Amalie Anna Wittwer, about 1905

ning speaking nothing but English. While the transition could hardly have been as cliff-edged as that, I do recall plunging into English with gusto and being fascinated by the nature and variety of words in both languages.

I remember causing my mother excruciating embarrassment after the Bible-reading session one night by asking what the word *Hurerei* meant because it seemed to keep recurring with unreasonable frequency in certain passages of the Bible. She flushed and flustered and finally told me that I would find out when I grew up. Needless to say I went hotfoot to the nearest source of information on such matters—the worldly-wise boys at school. Later I was able to confirm my research with a German dictionary.

Our teacher was always a young woman, euphemistically called a "missioner" by the Department of Education, and paid a pittance for trying to civilise us. I realise now how critically important these women were to our small communities, slaving unremittingly at their task until they finally retreated to the city or were carried off and wed by some local Caliban.

The one-teacher schools were the agents of literacy and social growth. They were really extended families where we developed responsibility, where the older child helped the younger, where we shared daily tasks together. We knew the other boys and girls as thoroughly as we knew our own brothers and sisters. They all had their nicknames: Blinkers and Pigtails, Fritzie and Mettwurst, Lardy and Bismarck. We studied plays by Waggle Dagger and a poem by Dunny Wentworth—an early Australian rhymster with the initials W.C. I was Tealeaves.

Before the local hall was built the school even doubled as a social centre for meetings and dances—the desks piled up against the back wall in craggy cliffs, the floor laced with candle grease or Fuller's Earth. The shelter shed with its bench-seat along one wall was an attractive retreat for courting couples. It was our delight to reveal them there with the sudden shaft of a flashlight and to watch them disengage like bursting furzepods.

Even more spectacular were the antics of suddenly exposed lovers on the wheat stacks at the railway siding. In the days before bulk handling of grain the wheat was carted in three-bushel bags and built up into gigantic stacks. Three sides were as sheer as walls, but the fourth was sloped and stepped to ground level for easy access. On mild summer nights romantic men liked to take their girls up to the nooks and hollows on the top of the stacks, and small boys—as sure-footed as Barbary sheep—liked to creep up silently, pinpont the lovers momentarily in a dazzling beam of light, and flee away into the darkness. One outraged lover, leaping after his tormentor, was said to have gone right over the side of the stack and fractured the bones in his shins—the only man in Australia known to have broken his legs while making love.

In school we wrote with a penholder and a fiercely pointed steel nib that had to be dipped into a small earthenware inkwell after every word. Apart from anaemic, duck-egg-blue fluid the inkwells also contained bits of chalk, chips of wood, hair from the girls' pigtails, and drowned flies which we impaled on our nibs. They were capable of causing spectacular blots on clean white pages.

In 1927 or 1928 our long cumbersome desks, each seating six children, were replaced by small dual desks where we sat in pairs. Most of us called them "jewel" desks, just as children have always called the equator a "menagerie lion" running around the world. I have a deep affection for the small Bush school. I guess that is obvious enough from some of my later essays such as *Once Upon a Year* and *Childhood and Change*.

One of our teachers was a particularly engaging woman who read us long stories from her personal collection of books, especially on stormy days when only three or four children succeeded in making it to school. There were times like that when we sat in front of the log fire all day while she read whole sections of *The Arabian Nights* (somewhat bowdlerised, I now realise) or *Robinson Crusoe* or *Treasure Island*.

Our school library consisted of about twenty-five books standing in a box against the wall. Most of them were stories about pirates or American Indians, and I had read all of them by the time I was ten. Apart from the Bible, some magazines, and a few German novels at home, there was really nothing else to read. This shortage of material, and the influence of our story-telling teacher, must have induced me to try to add to the supply because when I was eleven I wrote a massive pirate novel called *Blackbeard*. It was an ambitious work, over two inches thick and illustrated with ink drawings and red pencil—for the pirate blood which I spilt prodigally. I wrote it at night by candlelight in my cellar room on the farm, periodically burning off my left eyebrow in the candleflame as I bent over the manuscript with intense concentration. No doubt the world experienced a sense of loss some years later when I thought so poorly of it at high school that I burnt it.

In the morning before lessons began, or during recess and lunch, we often sat on the fence in front of the school like a row of starlings watching the big wagons going by to the railway station a few miles off. They were a magnificent sight, loaded high with bales of wool or bags of wheat and pulled by ten or twelve powerful draught horses. A canvas waterbag usually swung from the rear axle between the giant wheels, and the wagoner's dog plodded along beside it, tonguing in the heat.

Over the rise we could see the smoke of the steam trains hauling their loads to Adelaide, seventy miles away. They were huge locos—"mountain types" we called them—because they were modelled on the famous engines used in the Rocky Mountains of America. And on the rough roads of the district the first cars—"Tin Lizzies" from Henry Ford—were beginning to appear, sending the horses berserk in the paddocks and frightening the cows out of milk.

There were other signs of intruding technology too, especially the "wireless." My brother built himself a crystal set over which we sat hunched like a couple of gurus while he twiddled the cat's whisker and coaxed discordant sounds out of the air. In our headphones it all sounded so miraculous that we shouted our astonishment at each other even though we were sitting only two feet apart.

The end of my elementary schooling at Julia coincided with the Great Depression. It presented my family with a crisis and shaped the course of my life. For there was no place for me on the farm. My father, when he could sell his crops at all, was being forced to accept prices way below the cost of production. My brother, six years older than I was, had already taken his place beside him. At the best of times there wasn't enough land to support another son. So I had to go. I was acutely aware of the impending upheaval in my life. I loved the farm and its environment, and I wanted to stay. My heart was raw at the thought of being torn from the warmth of my own family and thrust out into a world I regarded as alien and threatening. But it had to be.

As nobody knew what to do with me, I was told to continue on at school. That in itself was rare enough in those days, especially for country children from the backblocks, and it needed prodigies of improvisation. Secondary schools didn't grow on trees.

Luckily, two of my eccentric bachelor uncles had recently sold their farm and retired into the town of Eudunda, so I stayed with them and went to the Eudunda Higher Primary School. It was really nothing more than one room tacked on to the normal elementary school where about twenty children could prolong their education for a further two years.

Nevertheless Eudunda affected me deeply. For the first time I had to rub shoulders with children from different places, different backgrounds, different social classes. School life was much more competitive and rigorous. And there were more books. One of these, *While the Billy Boils* by Henry Lawson, startled me with its reality. Instead of the unreal heroes of the adventure fiction in our *Boys' Own Annual,* or the quaint British schoolboys surrounded by a world of "fagging" and "rugger"—words as distant and incomprehensible to me as the outer planets—here were living Australians I could recognise.

Here were the wheat lumpers and carters, the shearers and labourers, and "used-up-looking" women I knew. And here was the adolescent boy milking a cow—softening sore teats, dodging kicking hocks, drowning dungy debris in the bucket, squirting at a calf, and milking into his mouth—exactly as I did. With a shock of recognition I saw myself writ large. This, I thought, was how writers should bring their characters to life.

At the end of my two years at Eudunda there was another crisis. I had run out of schools, so to speak, and I still needed another year or two to qualify for entry to higher education at the teachers' college or university in Adelaide. This time my parents were extraordinarily innovative. There was a real high school at Kapunda, about twenty miles from our farm, and a daily train that lumbered through the nearest siding at six in the morning and huffed back at eight o'clock at night. By riding my old bicycle to intercept the railway I could make the daily journey to and from school in a series of sorties. I later described it, and its effect on me:

> I went to Kapunda. Every day. Up at 5:30 in the morning, my mother and breakfast waiting in the kitchen, three miles on my bike to the railway siding, train to Kapunda, long walk to the high school on the hill, lessons all day, homework after school until train time again, walk to the station at seven o'clock, slow haul up the line to the local siding, ride home through the darkness, steaming dinner and mother both waiting in the kitchen at half past eight, bed time at nine. A rigorous, perpetual cycle. And I loved it.

> When the wind blew gales and the rain flung serpents and fish fins in my face I didn't much notice their buffet and sting. I stood on the pedals of the cranky old bike and felt like Conrad's Marlow. I rode through frost in the winter with my fingers unfeeling on the handle-bars, scattered limestones over the unmade roads in the dark, plunged as sodden as kelp through downpours and cloudbursts. And it was splendid. Exhilarating.

> The daily trundle up and down in the train served many purposes. It gave me time to read. Most of Hardy I read that way, a twice daily transformation that took me into Wes-

sex and the superb isolation of Egdon Heath. Much of Dickens I read too, and Conrad, and Mark Twain. I could readily have been Tom Sawyer. And I read a good deal of poetry, and all kinds of many-splendoured things.

The train also gave me a new view of the ebb and flow of life. It was like a hundred vantage points all in one, a moving crow's nest. The run of colour in the landscape, the subtle daily change of green, yellow, rust or brown, new furrows on the slopes, crops sprouting in myriad green wicks, ears of barley and wheat bursting out as suddenly as bells, sunlight sharper than quince-juice, hills changing day by day like time-lapse photographs. At one moment clouds lowering around the carriage and rain lunging diagonally down the window, at the next the dust blowing off the fallow and the mud in the dry dams crazing in the heat.

And the train gave me people. Not many, but enough to teach me a good many things about humanity.

By the time I had spent two years at Kapunda High School I was sixteen and ready to sidle shyly into the academic life of Adelaide. That was at the end of 1936. Again my parents made plans. I was to be a boarder at the Lutheran Seminary in North Adelaide, within easy walking distance of the university. It was a fortunate arrangement. I had a bed-sitter with ideal study conditions, meals and laundry provided, access to a good library, and daily debate with students from the seminary and the university. And it was cheap. By working during the vacations, or trapping rabbits, or getting a little help from my parents I eked out a student's existence.

By now I knew that the writing virus was in my blood. Throughout my high school days I had been serving a kind of apprenticeship, writing endlessly in many forms—poems, stories, essays, schoolboy plays. Some were published in school magazines or local papers. Some unbelievably won prizes in Agricultural Shows where they were displayed before the public, squeezed between rashers of bacon and award-winning watermelons. And when I left Kapunda High School in 1936 I was given a dictionary inscribed "For Literary Ability."

At the university my interest in writing quickened, but naturally enough the things I did came under closer scrutiny and harsher judgment. I wrote a story based on my own experience and was told that it was

Thiele as a student at the University of Adelaide, 1938

"too autobiographical to be any good." To salve my pride I won faint praise for two entries in the annual university poetry award.

More important, I met other writers. Some, such as Paul Pfeiffer and Donald Kerr, were soon to be destroyed by the Second World War. Some, Rex Ingamells in particular, were fervently nationalistic, convinced that Australian writing had to find a distinctive voice of its own. To that end Ingamells had just founded the Jindyworobak movement. Others, led by Max Harris, were avant-garde and experimental. Harris himself was later to be embroiled in the Ern Malley affair. But they were all passionate young men who, like young men of all eras, were keen to revolutionise the universe. Though they didn't exactly want to blow up the world (Hitler was shaping to do that effectively enough), they nevertheless wanted to move it somewhere else. As usual, their problem was to find a place to stand on.

Many of them used to meet in Paul Pfeiffer's room at St. Marks—a residential college of the university—where they read poetry aloud with gusto and daring late into the night. Some also drank inferior claret with equal gusto and daring until they were beyond the reach of poetry.

By the end of 1938 it was essential for me to get a job. Times were still tough. I couldn't expect my parents to keep subsidising me, even though my board was only a pound a week—the equivalent of two dollars. So I applied for admission to the Education Department as a junior teacher—an antiquated system whereby teenagers learnt to teach by teaching. The Department regarded it as training on the job, the Teachers' Union as slave labour. I had applied twice previously but had been rejected because I was said to be under-qualified at the first attempt and over-qualified at the second. Third time lucky, I was appointed to the primary school in a little town called Robertstown.

I enjoyed 1939 despite the gathering war clouds that finally broke during the year. Teaching seemed to come naturally to me, and the children—about twenty of them spread through the first three grades—were mainly from farms that I knew. I think we related well to each other. We shared stories together, learned to read, worked out our sums, and sang tunes untunefully. I played football with the local team and spoke German with the oldtimers on market day.

In those days a year of junior teaching experience was an entrance ticket to the teachers college, so in 1940 I was back in Adelaide again, picking up the thread of academic life. It was a lovely city of about 350,000 people with wide parks and gardens and plenty of space. I graduated at the end of that year and was earmarked for high-school teaching. The war worsened and some of my colleagues went off to confront it. I still wrote spasmodically and published poetry in the Jindyworobak anthologies and other journals.

In February 1941 I met my future wife. She was in the library on her own one day, a kind of maverick

Rhonda ("Rhonnie") Gill, 1942

because she had been in hospital and had missed the normal pre-term programme. She was small and petite and pretty. It took a long time to find out what her name was but I managed it in the end and asked her out. She refused. She apparently needed a week to check my credentials before she finally relented. It was the beginning of a relationship that still endures. Her name was Rhonda Gill—"Gilly" to her friends at that time, and "Rhonnie" to everyone now.

I think her father had deep misgivings about me. He was a practical man, an engineer and a mathematician, who had served with distinction in the Australian Army during the First World War. His ancestry was English. With Hitler's forces devastating Europe it wasn't hard to imagine what he thought of a fellow of German descent who wrote poetry! Clearly his daughter was making the mistake of her life.

The gloom of the war deepened still further. And then, quite suddenly, came the attack on Pearl Harbor and the fall of the Philippines and Singapore. Almost before anyone realised what was happening, bombs were raining on northern Australia and Darwin had been destroyed. The consequences were galvanic and inevitable. Within a few months we were all in the armed services. I joined the Royal Australian Air Force and served in New Guinea and the islands north of Australia until the end of the war.

It was still possible to write during the war, despite the difficulties. Piecemeal, in tents, bark shelters, and prefabricated huts, I produced a novel, sending the handwritten sections of the manuscript south for Rhonnie to type. It was a pubescent piece—groping, tentative, and unsure. I called it *Of Few Days,* a pretentious title taken from the Book of Job: "Man that is born of a woman is of few days . . ." It sought to catch the spirit of the land I had known in my boyhood—the fallow and harvest, the brown furrows and straw-gold slopes, the rhythms of the seasons and the cycle of human life. And above all the passing of time, inexorably, relentlessly. But the writing was self-conscious and wooden, the plot contrived, the characterisation inept. I was mildly ashamed of it. The nuances I had sought to catch had proved uncatchable. After the war I put it away unpublished. I don't think anyone except Rhonnie ever read it.

I continued to write poetry too, contributing irregularly to service magazines and such civilian journals as still existed. One of these was *Angry Penguins,* edited by Max Harris, who was now even more avant-garde than he had been earlier. I remember having two poems in the notorious Ern Malley issue in the autumn of 1944. When I heard that Harris was being prosecuted for publishing indecent material—ludicrous as the charge was—I wondered vaguely whether some

Colin and Rhonnie Thiele at the time of their wedding, March 17, 1945

wowser detective was likely to come looking for me in the jungle, or whether I would be discharged dishonourably from the Air Force for consorting with obscene and outrageous authors.

In the same year a long poem which I called *Progress to Denial* was awarded the Miles Poetry Prize and published as a slim volume. This encouraged me to gather some of the pieces I had written during the war and to have them published in a little collection under the Jindyworobak imprint. The title was *Splinters and Shards.* Both publications were inconsequential and are best forgotten.

Rhonnie and I were married in March 1945—on St. Patrick's Day. This may have seemed a quaintly ironic date for someone with my background, but the choice was dictated by the war, which rarely respected human sensibilities. We had to seize the opportunity while I was on leave. I returned to New Guinea, but only briefly, for hostilities ended suddenly and in October I was at last a civilian again.

I could have gone back to the university to read for a higher degree—something I had eagerly wanted to do back in 1941. But a week on the campus disillusioned me. The war had changed my attitudes. I found the place cloistered and claustrophobic. A few weeks later I accepted an immediate appointment to the staff of Port Lincoln High School. Rhonnie and I bought all our household furniture in two hours and set off on a

bucketing voyage in a little ship called the *Minnipa.* We were to stay in Port Lincoln for ten years.

In those days it was a place for dreams. A tiny town of 4,000 people, it nestled at the foot of the hills and looked out on one of the finest harbours in the world. It was a blessedly simple, unhurried place. I felt at home in it at once. Many of the areas south of the harbour were still virtually inaccessible, without roads or walking tracks. Along the coast the cliffs reared into ramparts against the Southern Ocean that came sweeping up unchecked all the way from Antarctica. It was a wild region, essentially unchanged from the day of its discovery by Matthew Flinders in 1802.

It was also a place for fishermen. Because many of the boats had been commandeered during the war, the fish had bred unchecked until they were so plentiful that they jumped at a sneeze. I became an enthusiastic amateur. At the same time the commercial tuna fishery and the sporting Big Game competitions began to develop, giving me first hand insights that, many years later, grew into *Blue Fin* and *Maneater Man.*

We worked hard and lived energetically, sharing household tasks at the weekend. I taught at the high school, Rhonnie at the infant school. She stopped for a time when our two daughters were born—Janne in 1948 and Sandra in 1954—but she achieved various distinctions nevertheless. The shortage of teachers was so acute that she was even persuaded to return when

*Colin, Rhonnie, and their first daughter, Janne,
with Penny the cat, 1951, following the announcement
that Colin had won two first prizes in the
Commonwealth Literary Competitions*

she was pregnant—something that was unheard of and almost scandalous. At another time she taught at three levels in three different schools—infant, primary, and secondary—all in the same year, which was also seen to be something of a record.

Meanwhile late at night, after marking exercises from various classes of fifty, I was writing for radio. A chance meeting with a couple of producers from the Australian Broadcasting Commission had encouraged me to submit material to them. The link blossomed. I liked radio; it was receptive to words and to evocative writing.

During my ten years at Port Lincoln I poured scripts of all kinds into the medium—plays, documentary features, essays, stories, poetry, school broadcasts, magazine cameos, even accounts of personal experiences. A good deal of this was produced Australia-wide and gave me a national audience. In 1951, during the Jubilee Celebrations commemorating the federation of the Australian States, I was awarded two first prizes in the radio drama and features section. The money enabled us to buy our first car and to drive back to Ade-

laide during vacations via the overland route—much of it over unsealed roads so jarringly primitive that we suffered from what was popularly called "numb-bum neuralgia." And whenever we stopped, the bush-flies were so thick that we also developed the "windscreen-wiper wave" common to most Australians.

In the meantime I had also gone into the business of publishing school texts. I fell into it by default. Soon after our arrival in Port Lincoln, when I was thrown hugger-mugger into the turmoil of classroom teaching, I became dissatisfied with one of the prescribed textbooks on South Australia. It was palpably beyond the scope of junior high school students. As no alternative seemed to be available I sat down and wrote my own, printed it on the school duplicating machine, and distributed it to our classes.

Soon teachers from other schools wanted copies. Before long I had so many orders that I had to spend part of the long summer holidays sending shipments to other parts of the state. In the end I couldn't cope with it so I handed everything over to a publishing house, Rigby Limited, who turned it into a minor best seller. It was the beginning of an association with Rigbys that has lasted through hazards and vicissitudes to the present day. In 1951 I also published another small collection of poetry, *The Golden Lightning*, and two years later produced the annual Jindyworobak Anthology as guest editor for Rex Ingamells.

At the end of 1955 we left Port Lincoln and bought a house of our own at Seacombe Gardens in Adelaide—a new two-storey place in a former vineyard. It had a big backyard with lawns, twenty fruit trees, a vegetable garden, a long shed, a rabbit hutch, an aviary that doubled as a possum cage, and a white picket fence. My study was upstairs and we built a nice studio for Rhonnie where she could sketch and paint, because her real love was art. We lived there happily for the next twelve years.

The house was not far from Brighton High School where I had been appointed Senior Master in English, but within twelve months I was offered a lectureship at the new Wattle Park Teachers College, and thereafter faced a long daily trek across the city to the eastern foothills. I remained at Wattle Park in one guise or another for almost twenty-five years, until my retirement in 1981.

B y the time of our return to Adelaide from Port Lincoln I had been writing part-time since my early days at the university—a diffuse twenty-year period of trial and error, patience and practice. I had just celebrated my thirty-fifth birthday. There were all kinds of projects in my head which hadn't been able to get out and which were becoming insistent. Somewhere

I had read a statement by John Galsworthy claiming that nobody could expect to write good prose under the age of thirty-five because writing needed maturity, patience, and experience of life. If I had therefore been procrastinating I had now even run out of that excuse.

I still had the country of my boyhood at heart, and I still held on to the belief that someday I would be able to catch its spirit in words. To that end I wrote a couple of short stories about a German farming household like the ones I had known. They were comic pieces, tentative testings of the water where the sharks of literary criticism swam. I sent them off to the famous literary section of the Sydney *Bulletin*, known universally as "The Red Page." It was edited at that time by Douglas Stewart, a New Zealand-born poet. He was an outstanding critic and I knew I would get an honest response from him. To my delight he liked them, praising them as deftly written and "authentic." I liked that word. Perhaps I was beginning to find the right voice at last.

For several years I was busy developing new courses and adapting to faculty life in a tertiary college. Then, unexpectedly, I was awarded a scholarship to study teacher education in the United States. I travelled by sea from Sydney to San Francisco in July 1958 in an old passenger liner, the *Himalaya*. An hour or two out of Sydney Harbour we lost sight of land, and from then on the world consisted of nothing but sea and sky. I have never been one for wasting time, especially on quoits, deck tennis, or pool parties, so I rejected the jollying exuberance of the purser's assistant whose job it was to keep us entertained, and "retired to my cabin," as they say. I saw this as a god-given chance to write all day and all night without interruption. At last I could try to create that book about the German-Australian communities in the Hundred of Julia Creek.

I decided that it was to be episodic in form—a series of related pictures and incidents held together by a simple plot with a boy in the centre. I thought this would be the best way of catching the flavour of the place and the people. Dialogue, of course, was a problem because it was hard to reproduce the heavy German accent of the local farmers in English prose. In real life they couldn't pronounce the "th" or "wh" sounds, and so "this," "that," "then," and "there" became "dis," "dat," "den," and "dere," just as "what" became "vot" and "third" became "tird."

Obviously there were pitfalls and embarrassments in many of these pronunciations, just as there were risks of impatience and boredom on the part of readers if the mangled speech were reproduced in too much detail. So I compromised by suggesting the tone of it from time to time rather than setting down every sound slavishly.

The book flowed easily. Once I had caught the feeling of it—and once the purser ceased pestering me to play deck games and gave me up as antisocial—I wrote fluently and joyously. I incorporated two of the *Bulletin* stories as discrete chapters and wove a series of boyhood antics into the plot. By the time the ship docked in San Francisco three weeks later the book was finished.

One of my assignments in America took me to Arizona State University at Tempe. Those were heady days on the campus because Arizona State had just been granted university status. I felt at home there, and in the state as a whole—its light and heat and craggy desert landscape. I boarded with a warm-hearted landlady, shared a room with a Burmese educator who was Nature's gentleman, and attended classes by day. At night I borrowed an old typewriter and typed, corrected, and bound the manuscript of my novel. I called it *The Sun on the Stubble*.

The following year, when I was on my way home through Sydney, I called on Angus and Robertson, Australia's old and reputable publishing house, and asked whether they might be interested in the sort of thing I had written. Douglas Stewart, who coincidentally was now an editor there, was complimentary about it, and so were some of his colleagues, but they considered that it wasn't their kind of book. I wasn't sure about it myself. Perhaps it fell between two stools, between the worlds of adults and juveniles.

Back in Adelaide I eventually showed it to Ian Mudie, another poet, who was then managing editor at Rigbys. He was blessedly enthusiastic. When I said that perhaps it was partly a book of boyhood, partly of adulthood, he answered, "Of course it is. It'll be read by kids aged eight to eighty."

Happily he was right. The book came out in 1961 and has never been out of print since. It has sold hundreds of thousands of copies. I am now getting letters from the second generation of readers: "My Dad says that when he first read *The Sun on the Stubble* twenty years ago he wet his pants laughing."

I was asked to write a sequel—as I have been asked often enough with other books since then—but I refused absolutely. I can't help believing that sequels are written with leftovers. Their motivation is usually money. In any case I was off on an entirely different tack—a children's book set in the wilderness region of the Coorong. At that time the area was still virtually untouched—a world of sandhills and scrub, of waterbirds, untrodden beaches, and vast lagoons. I had always loved it, especially in my university days when we had camped on its shores, fished in its reaches, and walked along the ocean beach that stretched away from the mouth of the River Murray into seemingly endless distance. One could live there for weeks without seeing a human being. It was an elemental landscape, a place of wind and water, driftwood and tussock, reeds and pelicans, a place of high skies and sunglades where the summer light glinted so brightly that we winced; a place where solitude was so complete, so intense, that we could imagine ancient prophets walking from it as they had from the desert. Here, surely, humanity could sense universal truths.

Early in 1962 Rhonnie and I and our two daugh-

went home and wrote *Storm Boy* in a few weeks, and John Baily illustrated it just as he had wished.

It was not only about a unique place. It was a story about growing up, about tragedy and loss, about human cruelty and the savage intrusion of the world into vulnerable lives, about the impossibility of escape even in the most remote of retreats.

Ian Mudie at Rigbys liked it very much, but he said it was too short. It needed 'filling out a bit.' So I sat on my high horse and wagged my finger at him like

At the gathering of writers for "Writers' Week," the Adelaide Festival of Arts, 1962: from left,
Flexmore Hudson, Kenneth Slessor, and Colin Thiele

ters spent a lovely holiday in the nearby town of Port Elliot. We shared a house with the artist John Baily and his family. John painted watercolours near the Murray Mouth and I watched the pelicans. One day he told me he was keen to illustrate a story about the Coorong, a story he could visualise about a solitary boy in that vast environment. He saw him as "the storm boy."

I had had similar ideas myself although I had tended to push them into the background because I wanted to give the German farming communities of my boyhood precedence in any writing I could manage. But now that *The Sun on the Stubble* was on the bookshelves I was free to look in other directions. I

a judge, saying, "A story is as long as it has to be" and threatening to walk out with the manuscript under my arm if he fiddled with it. I cited some of the best pieces of writing I could think of that would probably have been branded "too short." I remember that Hemingway's *Old Man and the Sea* was one of them.

In the end Ian surrendered and said, "Okay, okay, we'll publish the damn thing as it is." The incident revealed one of the few advantages held by part-time writers who earn their living by other means. They are in a position of strength; they don't have to compromise. They can literally walk out with their manuscripts because they don't depend on them for bread and butter.

Storm Boy was unbelievably successful, again because it was supposedly accepted by readers aged eight to eighty. It went through many reprints, new editions, and foreign translations, and in 1976 was made into a wonderfully successful film by the South Australian Film Corporation. I can never remember figures, but I believe that, world-wide, it has sold a million copies. Inevitably I was asked to write a sequel, and to provide material for a second film. I refused both requests.

I think *Storm Boy* helped to typecast me as an "environmental" writer. Yet it would be hard to imagine two books more fundamentally different than *The Sun on the Stubble* and *Storm Boy*—the one a series of comic sketches or vignettes about German-Australian farm life with its emphasis on humour of situation, dialogue, and characterisation, the other an attempt at a poetic evocation of a unique region and of a child's tragic encounter with human heartlessness and stupidity.

A year or two later some members of the Bushfire Research Council approached me with a request. They believed that a story like *Storm Boy* could influence children powerfully against the wanton destruction of wildlife. (This was soon borne out by the thousands of letters I received from children, epitomised by one that consisted of a single sentence: "Dear Mr. Thiele, I will never, never, NEVER kill a pelican, Yours sincerely . . .") The members of the Council believed that a harrowing story about bushfires could likewise help to prevent the summer devastation that regularly swept parts of Australia.

I agreed to try, provided I had a completely free hand. The result was *February Dragon,* published in 1965. That, too, has remained in print ever since. Unhappily, its theme is only too relevant today and will always remain so. Indeed, after the horrifying destruction and the loss of seventy-seven lives on Wednesday, 16 February 1983—now known universally as "Ash Wednesday"—I had many letters from young readers of *February Dragon* asking me how I knew about Ash Wednesday in advance. Sadly I had to reply that there are other such days still to come.

If, in fact, the tone and detail of the book are true to life the reason is probably close at hand. I knew farm life from personal experience, and I had fought bushfires. The morning of Ash Wednesday was exactly like the morning I had described in my story twenty years earlier: people going about their daily business oblivious of the coming cataclysm, the countryside tinder dry at the end of a long summer, a north wind raging at fifty miles an hour like the breath of a furnace, temperatures of 43°C (110°F), the carelessness of human beings—all were parts of the scenario for the holocaust to follow.

February Dragon affected some young readers deeply. A girl who owned a horse just like the one that was burned to death in the story couldn't bring herself to face the horror of it, even though she knew that such things really did happen.

Meanwhile, I was publishing other things as well. I produced seven or eight anthologies of prose, verse, and drama for use in schools, acting as coeditor with some of my colleagues and sometimes supplying notes, annotations, and teachers' handbooks to go with them. In 1960 I had also published another book of my own verse, *Man in a Landscape,* which was reviewed nicely and awarded the Grace Leven Poetry Prize.

It was a busy time. I had been appointed deputy principal of the teachers college in 1964 and had barely accustomed myself to that role when the principal died suddenly in May 1965 and I was appointed to take his place. Overnight, or so it seemed, I was pitched into directing an overcrowded and rapidly growing college. The demands were intense.

Fortunately by now I had accustomed myself to

Colin and Rhonnie Thiele, about 1965

writing late at night. The daily pattern I had evolved over many years seemed to have become second nature to me: work at the college from eight in the morning to five or six in the evening, an hour for dinner with my family, three hours of college work out of my brief case while the girls did their homework, and then another two or three hours when I could write in a quiet and uninterrupted environment. Often, of course, there were evening meetings or lectures or bureaucratic bunfights to attend so I was lucky to average three writing nights a week. I had to make the most of them. I couldn't afford to wait for divine inspiration, astrologically propitious signs, or productive surges of temperament. I had to sit down and get on with it.

It was Rhonnie who carried the burden. Just when she was ready to relax, to talk about the day's events, to enjoy another person's company after her solitary stint at home, I disappeared into my study. She said she suffered a double deprivation—hers was both an academic and a literary widowhood. Fortunately she was able to go back to work, simultaneously studying at the School of Art and completing a second diploma.

The girls were growing up and becoming more self-reliant. Janne was about to finish at high school, Sandy about to begin. Sandy had developed a passion for horse riding that took us to riding schools or horse shows almost every weekend. Even today, married and living more than a thousand miles away in Queensland, she still loves her horses as only a horse rider can. I have promised never to write a book about horses!

In 1966 I published a collection of short stories called *The Rim of the Morning*. The title came from one of my own statements and was designed to suggest the march of the generations—how adults grow old and fall behind, but the young push on until they reach the rim of their own particular morning and look out on their own new world. It was a popular book and has also remained in print. In the same year I published a further collection of verse, *In Charcoal and Conté,* the title indicating that many of the poems were sketches, verse portraits of humanity.

At about this time I was asked whether I would be prepared to write a biography of the artist Sir Hans Heysen. While the idea appealed to me I knew that it would be impossible to attempt a project of such magnitude on a piecemeal part-time basis. I therefore applied for a grant from the Commonwealth Literary Fund, took a year's leave from the college, and settled down to an intense routine of writing and research. It was the first time I had ever done this all day long, seven days a week, and I revelled in it. History had been one of my majors at the university, and I had always liked biography, although now the responsibilities of the biographer—in accuracy, ethics, interpretation, inference—daunted me.

I need not have worried. Sir Hans was a superb subject, utterly honest and totally cooperative. He helped to make the task a joy and enabled me to finish it on time at the end of 1967, happily approving the result. It was a big book, and barely done soon enough. Six months later he was dead.

For ten years I had been mulling over the seeds of a story based on the tuna fishery at Port Lincoln. I had known some of the skippers there and I had taught their sons at the high school. I had a deep admiration for many of the boys. Although their teachers may have considered them hopeless at Latin or mathematics, it was a different matter out on the fishing boats. I had actually seen two boys from my own classes helping to handle a ketch in wild weather and I knew how capable and self-assured they were. It was a tough world, pole-fishing for tuna out on those exposed waters, and the boys had to face it with the men. It was my belief that they rose to it splendidly, as they did to many other demands, even though their success at school was minimal.

I therefore wrote the story round a boy who was seen to be a "no-hoper" and a misfit by almost everyone, even his own father, but who proved his resourcefulness and courage when the chips were down. As a teacher I had often been distressed to see boys and girls humiliated because they "weren't any good" at algebra or French or athletics, when, in fact, they had admirable attributes in other directions. They were said to have "failed" and were even called "failures." After a while they believed it themselves; the system convinced them of it. Their courses were so narrow that they had no chance of demonstrating other skills. My story was going to be a counter-stroke, a vindication of the latent abilities of youth.

I called it *Blue Fin,* and it was published in 1969. Readers liked it, whether they knew tuna fishing or not. It was highly commended by the Children's Book Council of Australia, awarded a Certificate of Honour by the International Board on Books for Young People, and published in many countries, both in the English language and in foreign translations. In 1978 it was made into a feature film by the South Australian Film Corporation.

Rhonnie and I enjoyed travelling, especially under the wide horizons of inland Australia. We still do. By 1970 we were able to indulge ourselves a little more often because our daughters had grown up. Janne had graduated as a teacher and Sandy had started her science course at the university. Janne had married at the end of 1969.

I took every opportunity, official and unofficial, to

The Thiele family, about 1970: from right, Sandy, Colin, Rhonnie, Janne and her husband, Jeff Minge

visit distant schools where our students were undertaking field work and teaching practice, and in that way managed to spend a little time on the opal fields at Coober Pedy. It was an amazing environment. The dugouts of the miners ranged from mere holes in the ground to underground homes of great opulence. Above ground the countryside looked like a moon landscape—dusty, waterless, and pock-marked with mines and mullock heaps. I had flown over it and looked down on it during the war, but now I could actually walk over it or drive about on its gouged surface.

The community was a polyglot mixture of humanity from many races and nations, ranging in status from outcast and renegade to policeman and parish priest. And there were undercurrents of secrecy and mistrust and, one suspected, of violence. It was one of the last frontiers, a stranger-than-fiction setting for a story.

Out of all this came *The Fire in the Stone*—the struggle of a boy in that harsh locality, again suffering hurts and buffetings as he grew up, but this time with a feckless father. I had to write it during one of the busiest periods of my life. Profound changes were taking place in the world of my daily work. The college was becoming an autonomous organization under its own council with new financial, administrative, and academic procedures. At the same time we were developing a new campus to supersede the overcrowded one at Wattle Park. It was called Murray Park—a beautiful

thirty-acre site about a mile north of the old college, equipped with large new buildings and playing fields.

I therefore had endless meetings with architects, treasurers, government officers, planners, builders, academics, librarians, landscape gardeners, staff members, and students. I was on call from breakfast time to midnight. Under these conditions *The Fire in the Stone* suffered. It became a neglected child. Often I could devote no more than an hour a week to it, picking it up and putting it down in fits and starts.

Paradoxically it grew to be too long. There is a yarn—probably apocryphal—telling how Bernard Shaw is supposed to have begun a hasty letter to a friend by saying, "I'm writing you a long letter tonight because I haven't the time to write you a short one." It's a point well made. Spare, succinct writing needs time and thought. Sloppy verbiage can be splurged across the page very quickly. I think *The Fire in the Stone* would have been a better book if I'd had the time to make it shorter.

Nevertheless, it was nicely successful in Australia, was runner-up for an Edgar Allan Poe Award from the Mystery Writers of America in 1974, and was made into a film in 1983.

At about the time I was writing *The Fire in the Stone* I also faced one of the most important decisions of my life, not on literary or academic grounds, but on medical ones. For fifteen years I had been suffering more and more acutely from rheumatoid arthritis. It had started during our transfer from Port Lincoln to Adelaide in 1955 with cruelly painful knuckles and inflamed and swollen joints. I ignored it for a while but finally went to a doctor and then to various specialists. After the diagnosis I began a range of treatments and I've been doing so ever since: gold injections, drugs of every kind from analgesics to steroids, acupuncture, surgery, physiotherapy, and mechanical aids.

It must be hard for anyone who has never experienced rheumatoid arthritis to understand or even imagine the disease. It is relentless, frustrating, crippling. Medical science does not know the cause, let alone the cure. Its trademark is pain, unremitting pain. It burns in the body, sometimes like slow-moving acid from joint to joint, sometimes like a bushfire raging over the whole body. The pain is excruciating. When joints are burning with inflammation it is impossible to use them without agony. One cannot move them, cannot stand or put pressure on them, cannot lift things, cannot even lie in bed without pain. When at last compelled to use them it is necessary for sufferers to brace themselves beforehand knowing what is to come.

If all this sounds overly dramatic I can only direct the sceptic to speak to any one of the millions of arthritis victims in the world. Perhaps the proof of their suffering lies in the billions of dollars they are willing to pay in their search for relief, and the incredible remedies that quite rational men and women will be induced to try: cooper bracelets, seaweed, mineral water, utterly contradictory diets, faith healing, grass, herbs, and immersion up to their necks in warm camel dung. They will even keep three nutmegs in their pockets and hang seahorses round their necks—any talisman or superstition or quack remedy that promises hope.

It isn't easy to catch the essence of such pain in words. For pain is an intensely personal thing. It can't be shed onto anyone else, can't be transmitted like electricity by holding hands. It is therefore the great isolator. I tried to say this in one of my poems. It was published in the national paper the *Australian* in 1974 and led to a series of poems on pain which perhaps identify me as one of the most painful poets in the country:

Pain is the lonely ice to be lost upon,
The personal blizzard,
The ultimate isolation.

A landscape stripped of sharing—
There is only one inhabitant where the white plain
Burns in its own glaring.

Pain puts up its icy palisades
Enormously apart, alone;

Shrinking, we know the sign: No Visitors.
Each man's prison is his own.

Pain is the final purity,
The axiom beyond rejection;
Pain has its own perfection.

By 1972 it was palpably clear that I could no longer cope with the physical demands of a new college. Even simple tasks like climbing flights of stairs or walking about on the thirty-acre campus were beyond me. I was warned that stress and excessive bodily strain would exacerbate things and force me towards a wheelchair. Fortunately at that moment it was decided to convert the old college at Wattle Park into an inservice research and conference centre for teachers in the field, and applications were called for a director to establish and develop it. It was largely a sedentary job, the sort of thing I thought I could still do. Within a few months I had resigned my position at Murray Park and started as director of Wattle Park Teachers Centre.

During the preceding years I had been producing a variety of books—children's stories for very young readers (*Mrs. Munch and Puffing Billy, Yellow Jacket Jock, Flash Flood* and *Flip Flop and Tiger Snake*), as well as the first of my factual books on South Australian history and aspects of the local environment (*Barossa Valley Sketchbook* and *Coorong*). In 1970 I had also published a novel for adults, *Labourers in the Vineyard,* set among the descendants of the original German settlers in the Barossa Valley. It was another march-of-time book. I intended it to be the first volume of a trilogy that would take the central characters through to the present day, but I didn't ever get round to finishing it. I don't suppose I ever will.

Thiele (right) with historian Ron Gibbs, 1974, during the writing of Grains of Mustard Seed, *the history of state education in South Australia*

© *Fritz Kern*

*At the Austrian Book Award ceremony, Vienna, 1979. Award winners: Christine Nöstlinger
(second from left), Kath Recheis, and Colin Thiele.*

I continued to write as vigorously as I could during the remainder of the 1970s, often alternating history with fiction, and adult books with children's books. It was a productive period. I found that I had more time at night and at weekends, and I had much less administrative trivia to cope with. Between 1974 and 1980 I published more than a dozen books. Some, as the titles suggest, were attempts to catch the flavour of certain distinctive places that I loved, and to evoke their spirit: the northern Flinders Ranges (*Range without Man*), the misnamed "desert" near the border of South Australia and Victoria (*The Little Desert*), the vast loneliness of the Great Australian Bight (*The Bight*), and the unique quality of an old farm (*Lincoln's Place*). Some, again, were stories or fantasies for very young readers (*Ballander Boy, Tanya and Trixie,* and *The Sknuks*—which was awarded the Austrian State Prize in 1979.) One was a biography (*Maneater Man*), another a large work of educational history commissioned by the Minister of Education to commemorate the centenary of state education in South Australia. I was seconded from my normal duties for a time and I had the assistance of a professional researcher. As with the biography of Heysen it was a case of working day and night seven days a week to meet the deadline for the book. I called it *Grains of Mustard Seed,* an appropriately biblical title.

Rhonnie and I had taken a trip round the world in 1977 and I felt that perhaps I'd done quite enough travelling, considering the state of my bones. Rhonnie had pushed me about in a wheelchair in the Louvre in Paris and the Tate in London. However when the Austrian success of *The Sknuks* was announced, we decided to fly to Vienna to receive the award. We had a ball. I gave the main address—in German—and obviously surprised the audience with my antipodean German accent.

Other books of the seventies were novels for children of varying ages. *Albatross Two* openly stressed the dilemma inherent in offshore oil drilling—the world's thirst for oil measured against the threat of ecological disaster. It was not a good book but it was popular among high-school classes studying modern social issues. *The Hammerhead Light* explored the relationship between youth and old age, characterized by a young girl and an old seaman. And *River Murray Mary* tried to recreate a special era in Australian history—the establishment of irrigation settlements along the River by soldiers returning from the First World War.

Three books of this period—*Uncle Gustav's Ghosts* (1974), *The Shadow on the Hills* (1977), and *The Valley Between* (1981)—were once again based on the German-Australian background of my boyhood, but they were not sequels to *The Sun on the Stubble.* They used different characters and sometimes different localities. Instead of presenting a sequential view of life in a continuing narrative from one book to the next, they were ranged rather like the spokes of a wheel around a common hub. The view varied from story to story but the centre remained the same.

The Shadow on the Hills, for example, was much more sombre in tone than *The Sun on the Stubble*—as the titles suggest. In place of lighthearted escapades and happy adventurousness (even though examples of these were preserved) there was emphasis on greed, malice, and overtones of madness.

The four books together, spanning exactly twenty years of my writing life, have been immensely satisfying. It was a lovely postscript when *The Valley Between* was named Book of the Year by the Children's Book Council of Australia in 1982.

In fact, many nice things had been happening in my life, not the least of them being the award of a high honour in the National Honours List in 1977—Companion of the Order of Australia—"for services to literature and education."

One other book of this period, *Magpie Island* (1974), perhaps warrants comment. It is really an allegory, a form of writing that I like. But instead of anthropomorphising the magpie I leave him as he is—a bird—even though I am saying things about human beings. He is a castaway on a lonely island in an infinite ocean, rejected and living among strangers: "A dot on a tree, that was a twig on a hill, that was a hump on an island, that was a barrow load of rock." It is a story about strength of character and spiritual resilience, a story about resolution and heroic endurance, a story that seeks to lift the human spirit: "He would become a legend as big as a mountain. He would be a Crusoe for modern men. He would stir the hearts of lonely people and make stale dreams come alive and fresh again."

I have often been called a didactic writer. If that means that I see stories as a teaching instrument I make no apologies for it. I have often argued that all writers for children are teachers whether they are aware of it or not. They influence attitudes and affect values. But if I teach when I write I sincerely hope that I don't also preach. I am greatly heartened by the fact that although *Magpie Island* has been called didactic it has also been one of the most popular and most generously reviewed of all the books I have written.

Chadwick's Chimney, published in London by Methuens in 1980, was also labelled didactic, although utterly different in every way. Its setting is the sinkhole country of south-eastern Australia where tragedies con-

tinue to happen when scuba divers descend too far into those dark, water-filled caverns. My story dealt with the horror of being trapped in that tomb-like world, with no apparent hope of rescue. It was a successful story. The German edition (*Die Höhle*) has even been awarded a "bookworms prize" (*Preis der Leseratten*) by a young readers' jury in West Germany, being considered *"ein sehr gutes und spannendes Buch."*

The time for my retirement came at the end of 1980—technically on 31 January 1981. It was a memorable moment, not only because forty years is a large slice of one's life to devote to children and teachers, but because of the quite unexpected response that came from schools all over the state. At a large farewell function organized by the Schools Libraries Branch of South Australia, the crowd suddenly parted and a dozen children came up the laneway formed by the adults. They were lugging two enormous rolls of something. I couldn't make out what they were—each one more than six feet long and two feet in diameter. They were presented to me with much dignity and decorum, and then unrolled. I couldn't believe what I saw. They were patchwork quilts, covered with more than six hundred squares, each one representing a scene or character or an artefact from one or other of my books. The thought that hundreds, perhaps thousands, of children had been bending over their stitching and embroidery for my sake moved me deeply, especially when I heard of a little girl of seven who confessed that she'd needed "a bit of help from Mum."

A day or two later I was given an equally stunning gift from the English Teachers' Association. This time I was presented with four magnificent volumes of handwritten or personally typed contributions from the

Thiele with author Max Fatchen on November 6, 1980, when Thiele gave a program of readings from his works to mark his retirement

children of the state—letters, poems, stories, good wishes, private thoughts, aphorisms, and pieces of advise, as well as sketches and paintings. The four books were beautifully bound in red leather, gold-blocked and handcrafted. They sit on my bookshelves at this moment, ever ready to be dipped into for laughter or reminiscence, new ideas, gratitude or reflection.

Since my retirement I have continued to write. Obviously. Once the compulsion—or addiction—is in the blood it is harder to cure than hepatitis. But I write by daylight rather than under a midnight lamp. And at the end of the day Rhonnie and I can sit down in a civilised way in each other's company. She has retired too after an energetic career and is busy with her own interests.

Arthritis, of course, has continued to tighten its grip on my body but I have been able to keep on top of it psychologically. One of its greatest banes has been its inhibiting effect on physical activity. Many of the things I have always enjoyed doing since my boyhood—gardening, hobby farming, using hand tools, pottering, recreation, even walking—have become difficult or impossible. As always, Rhonnie is affected too because I can no longer accompany her on trips overseas, or on the walks and outings she enjoys.

During the past decade Rigbys have negotiated further contracts in many parts of the world—with Harper and Row in America and Collins in England for English language editions in those countries, and with a multitude of publishers in Russia, Germany, Austria, Finland, Sweden, Norway, Denmark, Holland, France, Italy, China, Japan, and sundry other countries. A book is a kind of pebble dropped into a sea of thought; eventually its ripples wash the outermost shores of the world.

Thiele with children in the City Library at Rockhampton, Queensland, Australia, 1983

My most recent book is *Pinquo,* about human involvement in natural calamities, and about the way ancient legends concerning the earth's wild creatures have their roots in long-forgotten events. It is a strongly environmental book. Many readers have found it sad, but it has been encouraging to receive letters from children and adults alike saying that it has pride of place on their bookshelves. There are two or three other books with the publishers at present, so it seems that I am as busy in retirement as I was in employment.

For more than twenty-five years I have been visiting schools and colleges by invitation, as well as clubs, parent groups, and conferences, speaking to audiences of all ages from five-year-olds in Kindy to university students, teachers, librarians, booksellers, and administrators. Even today Rhonnie and I often pack up and set off, sometimes for a month at a time, and undertake a long safari of such visits in the other states of Australia.

We enjoy it. The children sit and listen to stories, show us their own work, ask searching questions, and give us morning tea with biscuits and party cakes of their own making. Together we can all share the magic of words and the strange power of stories that leave us wide-eyed with wonder. I try to tell them that life is indeed magical, that their own body is a miracle, that the earth we live on is astonishing and unique, that

© *Advertiser Newspapers, Adelaide, S. Australia*

Sandy Thiele on Canadian Bay, winning an important show-jumping event at the Adelaide Royal Show, 1981

nothing is boring unless we ourselves invest it with boredom. It is the theme I have often emphasized with adults too, as in *Childhood and Change:*

> I believe that life is an ineffable boon and that it should be savoured richly from earliest childhood. No matter what the crises of day-to-day living or the burdens of bodily sickness there is always something to lift the human spirit. George Borrow's gypsy sums it up better than I can: "There's night and day, brother, both sweet things; sun, moon and stars, brother, all sweet things . . . There's the wind on the heath, brother; if I could only feel that, I would gladly live forever."

The children, in turn, tell me what they think about the world, what they like doing, what makes them happy or hurt or sad. They do the same in their letters—hundreds, indeed thousands, every year from all parts of Australia and even from England, America, Sweden, Germany, and other places beyond. I try to answer every letter personally unless it comes as one of a class set of thirty, or a school set of three hundred, in which case I preserve my time and sanity by writing a single letter in reply.

There are many adults too, of course, who are avid readers, or who are preparing theses for higher degrees, arranging conferences, or undertaking research, who have requests to make by telephone or post. And there are young writers who drop in to discuss their manuscripts and to ask questions about the craft of writing. As if anyone has the answers! But I enjoy talking with them, listening to their points of view, hearing details of their struggles with intractable artistic problems, encouraging them to go on trying to catch the uncatchable.

I have also gone back to radio in recent years, broadcasting hundreds of little historical cameos that again set the telephone ringing with requests from listeners who have become absorbed in this issue or that. I continue to be amazed at the diversity of human concerns.

I am often asked whether I consider that some of my books are better—or worse—than others. Well, of course. There are things I have written during the past forty years that could have been done better. I guess all writers feel that way. The vain ones defend themselves by saying, with Somerset Maugham, that "only a mediocre writer is always at his best."

There are still a few unwritten books jostling about inside my head. I don't know whether they'll ever get out. If I keep on being busier and busier as I grow older there may be a bit of a logjam up there in the river of my imagination.

As it is, you'll notice that this is a long autobiography because I didn't have the time to write a short one.

Colin and Rhonnie Thiele at the Hillvue Primary School, Tamworth, New South Wales,
1983, with a pelican made by one of the children for Colin's collection of pelicans

BIBLIOGRAPHY

FOR CHILDREN

Fiction:

The Sun on the Stubble. Adelaide, Australia: Rigby, 1961; London: White Lion, 1974.

Storm Boy (illustrated by John Baily). Adelaide, Australia: Rigby, 1963; London: Angus & Robertson, 1964; Chicago: Rand McNally, 1966.

February Dragon. Adelaide, Australia: Rigby, 1965; London: Angus & Robertson, 1966; New York: Harper, 1976.

The Rim of the Morning: Six Stories. Adelaide, Australia: Rigby, 1966.

Mrs. Munch and Puffing Billy (illustrated by Nyorie Bungey). Adelaide, Australia: Rigby, 1967; San Francisco: Tri-Ocean, 1968.

Yellow-Jacket Jock (illustrated by Clifton Pugh). Melbourne, Australia: Cheshire, 1969.

Blue Fin (illustrated by Roger Haldane). Adelaide, Australia: Rigby, 1969; New York: Harper, 1974; London: Collins, 1976.

Flash Flood (illustrated by Jean Elder). Adelaide, Australia: Rigby, 1970.

Flip-Flop and Tiger Snake (illustrated by J. Elder). Adelaide, Australia: Rigby, 1970; London: Angus & Robertson, 1971.

The Fire in the Stone. Adelaide, Australia: Rigby, 1973; New York: Harper, 1974; Harmondsworth: Puffin, 1981.

Albatross Two. Adelaide, Australia: Rigby, 1974; London: Collins, 1975; published as *Fight Against Albatross Two*. New York: Harper, 1976.

Magpie Island (illustrated by R. Haldane). Adelaide, Australia: Rigby, 1974; London: Collins, 1974.

Uncle Gustav's Ghosts. Adelaide, Australia: Rigby, 1974.

The Hammerhead Light. Adelaide, Australia: Rigby, 1976; New York: Harper, 1977; Harmondsworth: Puffin, 1983.

Storm Boy Picture Book (photographs by David Kynoch). Adelaide, Australia: Rigby, 1976.

The Shadow on the Hills. Adelaide, Australia: Rigby, 1977; New York: Harper, 1978.

The Sknuks (illustrated by Mary Milton). Adelaide, Australia: Rigby, 1977.

River Murray Mary (illustrated by R. Ingpen). Adelaide, Australia: Rigby, 1979.

Ballander Boy (photographs by David Simpson). Adelaide, Australia: Rigby, 1979.

The Best of Colin Thiele. Adelaide, Australia: Rigby, 1980.

Chadwick's Chimney (illustrated by Robert Ingpen). London: Methuen, 1980.

Tanya and Trixie (photographs by D. Simpson). Adelaide, Australia: Rigby, 1980.

Thiele Tales. Adelaide, Australia: Rigby, 1980.

Little Tom Little (photographs by D. Simpson). Adelaide, Australia: Rigby, 1981.

The Valley Between. Adelaide, Australia: Rigby, 1981.

The Undercover Secret. Adelaide, Australia: Rigby, 1982.

Patch Comes Home. Adelaide, Australia: Reading Rigby, 1983.

Pinquo. Adelaide, Australia: Rigby, 1983.

Pitch the Pony. Adelaide, Australia: Reading Rigby, 1984.

Potch Goes down the Drain. Adelaide, Australia: Reading Rigby, 1984.

Coorong Captive. Adelaide, Australia: Rigby, 1985.

Seashores and Shadows. Sydney, Australia: Walter McVitty Books, 1985.

Poetry:

Gloop the Gloomy Bunyip (illustrated by John Baily). Brisbane, Queensland, Australia: Jacaranda Press, 1962.

Gloop the Bunyip (illustrated by Helen Sallis). Adelaide, Australia: Rigby, 1970.

Songs for My Thongs (illustrated by Sandy Burrows). Adelaide, Australia: Rigby, 1982.

Nonfiction:

The State of Our State. Adelaide, Australia: Rigby, 1952.

Looking at Poetry. London: Longman, 1960.

Editor of:

One-Act Plays for Secondary Schools, with Greg Branson. Adelaide, Australia: Rigby. Books I-II, 1962; Book III, 1964; revised edition of Book I published as *Setting the Stage,* 1969; revised edition of Book II published as *The Living Stage,* 1970.

Beginners Please, with G. Branson. Adelaide, Australia: Rigby, 1964.

Plays for Young Players, with G. Branson. Adelaide, Australia: Rigby, 1970.

FOR ADULTS

Fiction:

Labourers in the Vineyard. Adelaide, Australia: Rigby, 1970; London: Hale, 1970.

Nonfiction:

Barossa Valley Sketchbook. Adelaide, Australia: Rigby, 1968; San Francisco: Tri-Ocean, 1968.

Heysen of Hahndorf (biography). Adelaide, Australia: Rigby, 1968; San Francisco: Tri-Ocean, 1969.

Coorong. Adelaide, Australia: Rigby, 1972; London: Hale, 1972.

Range without Man: The North Flinders. Adelaide, Australia: Rigby, 1974.

The Little Desert. Adelaide, Australia: Rigby, 1975.

Grains of Mustard Seed (on state education). Adelaide: South Australia Education Department, 1975.

Heysen's Early Hahndorf. Adelaide, Australia: Rigby, 1976.

The Bight. Adelaide, Australia: Rigby, 1976.

Lincoln's Place. Adelaide, Australia: Rigby, 1978.

Maneater Man: The Story of Alf Dean, the World's Greatest Shark Hunter. Adelaide, Australia: Rigby, 1979.

Poetry:

Progress to Denial. Adelaide, Australia: Jindyworobak, 1945.

Splinters and Shards. Adelaide, Australia: Jindyworobak, 1945.

The Golden Lightning. Adelaide, Australia: Jindyworobak, 1951.

Man in a Landscape. Adelaide, Australia: Rigby, 1960.

In Charcoal and Conté. Adelaide, Australia: Rigby, 1966.

Selected Verse, 1940–1970. Adelaide, Australia: Rigby, 1970.

Plays:

Burke and Wills (verse), first produced at Adelaide Radio Drama Festival, 1949; published in *On the Air.* London: Angus & Robertson, 1959.

Edge of Ice (verse), first produced on radio, 1952.

The Shark Fishers (prose), first produced, 1954.

Edward John Eyre (verse), first produced at Adelaide Radio Drama Festival, 1962.

Editor of:

Jindyworobak Anthology (verse). Adelaide, Australia: Jindyworobak, 1953.

Australian Poets Speak, with Ian Mudie. Adelaide, Australia: Rigby, 1961.

Favourite Australian Stories. Adelaide, Australia: Rigby, 1963.

Handbook to Favourite Australian Stories. Adelaide, Australia: Rigby, 1964.

John Rowe Townsend

1922-

John Rowe Townsend, Beacon Hill, Boston, 1985

I wrote my first novel when I was eight and my second when I was thirty-eight. The second was published, and has sold about half a million copies. The manuscript of the first, unfortunately, has long been lost. If I could put my hands on it now, I would have high hopes of finding a publisher for it. It was good gripping stuff, though I say so myself.

It filled five red-backed penny notebooks. (In England, in those far-off days, you could buy a notebook for a penny.) It was written in pencil and illustrated in colored crayon. It had two readers, my mother and myself, and we both thought it was terrific. I resolved to write several more novels, and listed about a dozen forthcoming titles. But I must have run out of pennies, or pencils, or patience—or found something more fascinating to do—for the subsequent books were never written.

The book that was completed had more than two hundred pages. It was called *The Crew's Boat*, and was about the adventures of a family of twelve children, six boys and six girls. This family was more remarkable than I realized, for all the children were aged between nine and twelve, and none of them were twins. The eldest boy was called John, like me, and was brave, strong, and endlessly resourceful. The others did as John told them.

There was a big tree growing in the back yard, and one day, under John's direction, the children took an axe to it, hollowed it out to make a boat, carried it down to the ocean, and launched it. So far as I can recall, the book didn't say how long this took. It was probably all of twenty minutes. The Crew then rowed around the world, having adventures all the way.

One episode recurred, with variations, several

times. The Crew would arrive, in their hollowed-out tree, at a faraway island in the Caribbean, the Pacific, or some other convenient ocean. The island would be inhabited by fierce, painted savages, seven feet high, armed with sticks, stones, spears, clubs, bows-and-arrows, and any other weapons I could think of. But John and his siblings were undaunted. They would row ashore through a hail of flying arrows, all of which would, fortunately, miss. John would knock the savage chief flat with a straight left to the jaw, whereupon the savages would instantly surrender. What chance, after all, has a tribe of fierce, painted savages against a family of English children? Our heroes would then hoist the Union Jack on the nearest palm tree and proclaim the island part of the British Empire. (On second thoughts, even if I did find this masterpiece, it might be better not to publish it. It would be justly condemned as imperialist and racist.)

John would then give instructions to the savages on how to run a democracy, British-style, and how eating people was wrong. He would teach them to sing "God Save the King." The savages would promise to behave themselves in future. Our heroes would then re-embark in their hollowed-out tree and row on to the next island, though delayed perhaps by an encounter with pirates, whom they would compel to walk their own plank, or with a shark, whose jaws they would wedge apart with a stout stick. They returned home at the end of Volume Five, laden with presents for their parents, who were proud of them all, especially John.

John, Christmas 1923

I wrote *The Crew's Boat* with great speed and confidence. It was, I may say, the most purely literary work I have ever produced, for the adventures of the Crew were based entirely on stories I had read. My actual experience of life had been about as different as it could be. I was born in an inner district of Leeds, an industrial city in Yorkshire, in the North of England.

The real world I knew as a child would seem to many people to be a grim one. It was a small, urban world—a maze of narrow streets and alleyways, a world of little cramped dwellings and corner shops. It was a sloping world, for our district was built on what had once been a living hillside, though it was buried now under bricks and mortar. Through the middle of it ran a main road, and along the main road journeyed the tall, two-deck streetcar, known as the Tram. The Tram groaned painfully uphill toward the higher, and superior, suburbs; then came wailing and clanging back down its tracks into town at twice the speed.

Though the world was a brick world, there were living things in it. There were grimy grasses and riotous dandelions on empty sites where houses had been pulled down. There were cats and dogs around the garbage-bins, and budgerigars in cages that hung in windows. Children played, and in summer almost lived, on the street. On a sunny summer day the pavement was hot to your bare feet and the doorstep hot to your bottom. On freezing winter mornings, men slipped and skidded in their booted, before-dawn descent to the clothing factory or engineering works. There was laughter and singing, shouting and swearing and quarreling outside the pubs on a Saturday night, and on fine Mondays the clotheslines were hung across the streets and blossomed with washing. (Anyone who has read my novel *Dan Alone,* published in 1983, will recognize some of this description.)

I wrote a great deal as a child and as a teenager, but I never dreamed of setting a story in such a district. I preferred distant oceans and exotic islands. I didn't realize that a writer's inspiration lies around and within him. I recognize now that at the deepest roots I am, and shall be until I die, a child from Leeds. The seas of humble rooftops that used to stretch in great waves around the city are to me as the "blue remembered hills" of Shropshire were to the poet A.E. Housman.

Four generations: infant John with mother Gladys, grandfather Hedley Page, and great-grandfather Reuben Page

We lived in Lucas Place, and my Grandpa Page—my mother's father—was round the corner in Hartley Avenue. These streets were at the upper, more desirable end of the district. My mother, who had herself been left motherless when in her teens, had been married young; and she and Grandpa Page were child and parent still. When I was small, Mother went round to Grandpa's every day, leading me by the hand and pushing my baby sister in her trolley. She told Grandpa her problems, and Grandpa told her what to do about them. And Grandpa always had something for me, if I'd behaved myself.

"Has he been a good boy, Gladys?" Grandpa would ask. Usually Mother would say "Yes," although sometimes she'd squeeze my fingers as she said it, meaning that I hadn't been as good as I might have been but she wasn't going to give me away. Then Grandpa would give me something: an orange or a handful of dates or a biscuit; never money. Occasionally, but very rarely, I was in disgrace when we arrived at Grandpa's, and Mother told him I hadn't been good. Then I got nothing.

Grandpa Page was severe in moral and religious matters, but in everything else he was a mild, kind, helpful man. He was round-faced with a fringe of white hair, and I think of his appearance as saintly, though this may be because my idea of saintliness is derived from Grandpa Page. A neighbor once told me, "Your Grandpa's a saint." I didn't doubt the truth of this, but was not altogether delighted by it. Saintliness took a lot of living up to.

Like Grandpa Purvis in *Dan Alone*, Grandpa Page had on his sitting-room wall a Lord's Prayer, cut out of satinwood with a fine saw, mounted on dark blue plush, and framed like a picture. It was two feet wide and three feet deep, and had taken the leisure time of three years to make. It was in elaborate Gothic lettering, surrounded by marvelously convoluted scrolls and flourishes. But as he neared the end of his task, Grandpa's saw had slipped and taken the middle out of the final "e" of "for ever and ever." He was not dismayed, and often pointed to this flaw as demonstrating the imperfection of all human achievement. "Only that which God does is perfect," he used to say.

Grandpa Page's father, Great-Grandpa Page, died when I was very small. I have only one memory of him—a large old man with a bushy gray moustache who was propped up on a brass-railed bed and had a moustache-cup at his bedside. I was fascinated by the moustache-cup, which had a little shelf to keep his whiskers out of the water.

There was once a Great-Grandma Page, but I don't remember her at all. She had been a bonneted Salvation Army lass and had kept up her connection with the Army; and when she was dying at over eighty, my mother told me, she sang hymns at all hours of the day and night in a voice that was still strong and confident. The Army gave her a slap-up funeral, and a brass band led the procession and played the Dead March all the way down Woodhouse Lane.

Grandpa Page's first wife—my mother's mother—was born Ada Pinder, and was a volunteer nurse in a hospital for wounded soldiers in World War I. She died soon after it ended. Great-Grandpa Pinder was a tanner, and I have a magnificent sepia photograph, taken in Leeds about 1890, of him with his handsome, bombazine-dressed wife and their family of five children, of whom Ada was the youngest.

The Pages and Pinders and their numerous kin were solid, rooted Leeds folk of the lower middle or upper working class. They were not "the poor," of whom there were plenty in the Leeds of the 1920s when I was born, but they were far from well-to-do. They saved from modest earnings so that in their old age they would not be a burden on their children or the public purse. They went to Chapel on Sundays. "Respectable" was a key word in their vocabulary. They were honest, truthful, plain-spoken, down-to-earth, and totally unimaginative. None of them had the slightest interest in the arts, or would have encouraged writing aspirations in their children. It was not through any expectations of theirs that, from the age of five or perhaps before, I was always sure I was going to be a writer.

In childhood, I didn't see much of my father's family. The Townsends had their roots in Dorset, an agricultural county almost at the other end of England.

Though England is a small country, its regions and the people who live in them are very different. Dorset and Yorkshire people in my childhood were as far apart as Californians and New Englanders now are.

My father, George Townsend, born in 1886, was the eldest of eight children. He was the son of another George Townsend, said to have been "a great man with horses." Grandad Townsend had been a coachman and a head stableman, but in his later years, when I knew him, he had become a small farmer who kept a few cows and had a milk round. Grandfather and Grandmother Townsend were referred to by my parents, when speaking to my sister or me, as Grandad and Granny, to distinguish them from Grandfather and Step-Grandmother Page, who were Grandpa and Grandma. As a small boy, on my rare visits to the farm, I would often drive around with Grandad in his high horse-drawn trap, in which stood a couple of galvanized milk-churns. He sold his milk by the pint or half-pint, measured out in long-handled ladles to customers who brought their own jugs.

"You're a stubborn lot, you Townsends," my mother used to complain to my father from time to time, and she was quite right. Three hundred years of closeness to the soil had bred an earthy peasant rigidity in them. Grandad and Granny were a match for each other in stubbornness. Granny would not let Grandad into the main part of the farmhouse, which had gaslight, unless he first took off his heavy boots. Grandad refused to take off his boots, and sat reading his newspaper by candlelight in the lean-to kitchen until bed-

John with Granny Townsend, about 1924

time, when he would at last remove the boots and pad in his stockinged feet to bed.

Granny tried several times to persuade him to wear slippers, but he would have no truck with such effeminacy. He had worn boots all his life, as a man should, and had no intention of wearing anything else on his feet. He had a refuge in the shape of a little room above the cowshed, perilously heated by a coke stove, to which he would retire at lunchtime and in any period of leisure during the day. Granny visited him there once, and was distressed to find him brewing tea over the stove in a rusty old tin can. She bought him a kettle, a china teapot, and a matching cup and saucer. Grandad hid them under the eaves, and went on using his old tin can.

The Townsends had come down in the world. They were kinsfolk of a former Bishop of Salisbury and Chaplain to the King. But their heyday was a long time ago. For three centuries they had been ordinary villagers at Upwey, near Dorchester. I know a lot about them now, because of some genealogical research I once did at the request of an American cousin.

But as a child I knew nothing of the ups and

George Townsend and Gladys Page, about the time of their wedding, 1921

downs of the Townsend family. Apart from Grandad and Granny, I hardly knew the Townsends existed. Leeds, my mother's city, was my home and my horizon. My parents met in Leeds, were married in Leeds, and lived in or near Leeds for the rest of their lives. My father came to the city as chief clerk with an outfit called the Yorkshire Copper Works; my mother was a secretary there. He was thirty-four and she was just twenty-one when they married, and I was born a week before my mother's twenty-second birthday.

Of my earliest memories, the most vivid is of the day when my step-grandmother, Grandpa Page's second wife, who was not an amiable woman, sat on a piece of purple Glitterwax which I had left in an armchair. Glitterwax was an easily melted material which, when warm, could be molded by a child into any desired shape. Overheated by Grandma's posterior, it spread itself greasily over a large area of her dress, causing allegedly irreparable damage. After more than half a century, I can still quake at the recollection of her fury and my disgrace.

I have an equally vivid memory which must unfortunately be rejected as spurious. This is of the arrival of the family doctor, Dr. North, who told me, "I have a lovely surprise for you, John. I've brought you a little sister." Whereupon he opened his gladstone bag and produced my only sibling, Lois, who is four years younger than I am. I recall perfectly his appearance, the size and shape of the bag, and his putting it on the sitting-room table, which was covered with a dark green plush cloth. Even now, I can hardly believe that this didn't happen.

I was an early reader; and my earliest reading seems, in retrospect, to have been done on Sunday afternoons at Grandpa Page's house. It was the gathering-place of perhaps a dozen relatives, who would sit around and talk in immense detail of everything that had happened in the past week to themselves and their friends, relations, neighbors, friends of neighbors, neighbors of relations, friends of neighbors of relations, and so on in an endless network. I would not be allowed to go out and play, since Grandpa Page was a strict sabbatarian, and I would lie on the carpet, as the hours of adult small-talk droned over my head, reading a children's book from Grandpa's shelves.

The books all dated from Grandpa's own, Victorian, childhood. They were unbelievably moral and pious. Wicked children—that is, children who did almost any of the things that children would normally want to do—were duly punished and warned where their sins would ultimately lead them. Goody-goodies were praised and rewarded. It was all rather alarming.

I never went into a bookstore in my childhood,

Out for a stroll in Leeds, 1925: John with his father, George Townsend

but when I started at elementary school I soon began borrowing from the school library. The books were battered in condition and mostly not very good, but they were a great deal more enjoyable than Grandpa's. I was ahead of my age in reading skills, though not in judgment, and at seven and eight I read numbers of school and adventure stories. By the time I wrote *The Crew's Boat,* I had certainly read *Treasure Island* and *The Coral Island,* as well as a great deal of inferior stuff in the same mode.

My father was a handsome man, bright and promising, and his job was quite a good one. For a while we were modestly prosperous. We even had a maidservant, a young girl called Mabel. But two or three years after my sister was born, my father was afflicted with Parkinson's disease, the "shaking palsy." The rest of his life, to borrow a phrase from Arnold Bennett, was a tragedy in ten thousand acts. His illness killed him in the end, but took thirty years to do it.

His condition deteriorated very slowly over the decades. Gradually his hands trembled more and more; his strange, skating gait degenerated to a perilous totter; he had ever greater difficulty in eating and in washing and dressing himself. He was a constantly increasing burden on my mother. For some years he managed to go to work, in successively humbler capacities, but this became too difficult for him and he retired early on a very small pension. After that we were desperately hard up.

My later childhood and adolescence were, in fact, heavily shadowed by my father's illness. At elementary school, where the competition was not very strong, I was something of a star pupil, and when I was eleven I won a scholarship to Leeds Grammar School, an academically orientated high school. My six years there coincided with the years of deepest difficulty at home.

The school was an ancient foundation, dating from 1552, at which most of the pupils were fee-paying. It was assumed that students came from fairly well-to-do homes. A good deal of expenditure was required on books, school uniform, sports kit, and outings of one sort or another.

My scholarship paid for my books but didn't cover the other expenses. Though not particularly sensitive, I could see that every demand for the purchase or replacement of some item of school or sportswear presented my parents with a crisis. I would go to considerable pains to avoid telling them of such needs. I destroyed the notifications of school or class outings, and never went on any of them. My friendships were heavily restricted by a fear of becoming involved with freespending families from the plushy suburbs which were the habitat of most of my fellow students.

I fell, I think, between two stools. I was gradually being separated by education from those around me. The Page and Pinder relations and their friends were awed by my learning and at the same time slightly contemptuous of it, because it came from books. If I'd been outstanding at a major sport I might, for better or worse, have moved upward socially in spite of my parents' lack of money, since at our school as elsewhere everyone wanted the friendship of the brilliant sportsmen. But the only sport at which I excelled was cross-country running—I had a certain dogged determination that kept me going when the rest had got bored with the whole thing—and this was not highly regarded.

At Leeds Grammar School, I was no longer the star pupil, for the competition was now much fiercer, but I was still among the little cluster at the top of the class. It didn't do me much good at the time. I was unaware of any such concept as the love of learning. So far as I was concerned, education was a matter of passing examinations at the right level and obtaining the right certificates. I saw this as a duty I owed to my

John with a cricket bat, 1935

parents, who were making great sacrifices to keep me at school. Oddly, I was still a would-be writer. How it was possible to wish to write and yet have no interest in English literature, except as examination fodder, I do not know. I would not have dreamed of reading for pleasure the books I had to read to fulfil my class assignments. For enjoyment I turned to such popular writers as P.G. Wodehouse and Agatha Christie.

The one thing I did in school hours that was creative was something I'd have been punished for if the school authorities had known. This was to construct, together with half a dozen of my contemporaries, an elaborate system of Ruritanian states. Its moving spirit was Richard Beck—still a friend today—and it was based for some unknown reason on the old Germany before the unification of that country, when it consisted of a large number of little principalities and Grand Duchies. Dick Beck was the ruler of Mecklenburg; I was the Grand-Duke of Thurn-Taxis; others of our contemporaries reigned over Brandenburg, Württemberg, Alsace-Lorraine, and Lausitz-Altenburg. We had our (bizarre) political and legal systems, our imaginary statesmen, our newspapers and popular entertainers;

we formed alliances and made war on one another.

The affairs of Mecklenburg and Thurn-Taxis were conducted by means of announcements, drawings, and news bulletins, surreptitiously passed around the classroom when the teacher was not looking. They were an escape from what I saw as the necessary drudgery of schoolwork and from the hard times that afflicted my home. Many years later I was able to turn them to advantage, for they gave me the idea of writing my novel *Kate and the Revolution*, set in the imaginary principality of Essenheim. Of all my writings, this book probably gave me the purest and most self-indulgent pleasure.

My parents didn't want me to go to university. Even if I'd won another scholarship, they couldn't have afforded to have me dependent on them in any way. I had to earn. They took me from school and put me, at the age of just seventeen, into the lowest ranks of the civil service. All my Page and Pinder relatives approved of that. As people who kept with some difficulty above the poverty line and had lived through the Depression, they were profoundly conscious of the benefits of security. The civil service was a Safe Job. I could not be fired for any offense less serious than running amok among my superiors with an axe. I would never be hungry. At sixty—forty-three years hence—I would retire with a pension and be in no danger of ending my life in the workhouse.

Besides, the Second World War was looming. I don't know whether my parents and the relations thought it would really come, and there is no one still alive whom I can ask. But they got me into the Inland Revenue just in time, for no permanent appointments were made during the war.

I stuck at the Inland Revenue (the income-tax department) for three years. Looking back, I think I could have done worse. Contrary to what might be supposed, work in the Revenue gave one remarkable insights into people's histories, ways of life and private secrets, as well as their finances. I used to read the files with eager interest while eating my lunchtime sandwiches. They were an education in the ways of the world.

But the war was on, and Government offices were frustratingly far away from where the action was. We did have a roster for "firewatching," which required us to sleep on camp-beds in the office once a week. If the Luftwaffe had dropped firebombs on the Inland Revenue offices in Leeds, we should have been there with hand-pumps and buckets of sand to put them out. This, however, showed no sign of happening.

At the age of twenty, I left the Revenue for ever and joined the Royal Air Force. I was realistic enough

Townsend as a recruit in the Royal Air Force, 1942

to know I could never be a pilot; my eyesight wasn't good enough; but I thought I might just scrape by as a radio-navigator, a new species of airman required for night-flying bombers. Fortunately for my conscience, which would later have had a hard time of it (if, of course, I had survived), I failed the vision test for that as well, and finished up fairly safe on the ground, among the complexities of codes and cyphers.

And so to the main turning point of my life. In the spring of 1944, after brief spells in Egypt and Palestine, I arrived in Italy with the Mediterranean Allied Air Force. I was posted to Number One Field Intelligence Unit, one of a number of small maverick units operating on the Italian front. We were supposed to follow the troops into newly captured territory and report on the materials that the enemy would carelessly have left behind in his flight. My personal rôle was merely to encode the reports. But soon after the unit was formed, the front came to a prolonged halt between Florence and Bologna, and Number One Field Intelligence Unit came to a similar halt, rather elegantly ensconced in requisitioned premises in the heart of Florence. There my education began.

I had left school an ignorant youth with a heap of

certificates. I had carried my ignorance intact through the Inland Revenue and two years of the RAF. Now I suddenly found myself aware of art and architecture, and, arising rapidly out of this awareness, literature. It was the Enlightenment; it was the Brave New World.

During the long days and weeks in which there were no enemy materials to report on, and consequently no cypher messages to be sent, I wandered around Florence until I felt I knew every street and square and statue; I made Italian friends and learned rather good Italian; I studied French and Italian language and literature. My bewildered parents found themselves mailing art books and books of poetry out to me.

It was a voyage of discovery. I found that certain poems and paintings did more for me, or less for me, than others; I wondered why. I found that one thing led me on to another, and that to another. I found that people had written about poems that I read and paintings that I looked at; I wanted to know what they had said and how their experience compared with mine. I wanted to go to university to extend my discoveries.

Townsend at Emmanuel College, Cambridge University, 1947

Back in England in 1946, I took a train from Leeds to Cambridge, and a bus from Cambridge station to the city center. I knew that the University of Cambridge was divided into about twenty colleges; that was all I did know about it. From the bus I saw on my right a building that looked as if it might be a college. I got off the bus. The building was indeed a college. I walked in and said I wanted to become a student. Somebody from the college office took me to see the Senior Tutor. He talked to me for three hours, at the end of which he offered me a place. I thanked him politely, and took a train back to Leeds.

I didn't know that by luck rather than judgment I had achieved the almost-impossible. Cambridge colleges were beset at that time by thousands of bright, highly qualified young people competing for admission. Colleges didn't admit provincial nobodies who just walked in off the street. But I had had the good fortune to encounter Edward Welbourne, Senior Tutor and afterward Master of Emmanuel College, a remarkable and unorthodox figure. I was one of his minor unorthodoxies. The following year, at the age of twenty-five, I became a student. And soon after becoming a student I got married.

I haven't said anything so far about affairs of the heart. Actually I'd been in love throughout my childhood and adolescence with a succession first of little girls, then of young girls, then of young women older than myself. These love affairs were conducted almost entirely inside my head, and only the earliest of my passions were declared. (I proposed to a little girl at the age of five, and was promptly rejected.) In later adolescence there were more serious connections.

I met my wife, born Vera Lancaster, at a time in my Inland Revenue days when we were both members of a walking club that rambled the Yorkshire hills and dales. We were married for a quarter of a century and had three children; she died in 1973 after a long illness. As I write, her death was nearly twelve years ago. I have never quite come out from its shadow, and I think I never shall; but the worst times do pass, and I am now able to look back and be thankful for the good years we had together.

Postwar Cambridge, in spite of some lingering austerity, was an idyll. There were a great many veterans, ranging from ex-privates to ex-colonels, among the undergraduates, and Vera and I were among some hundreds of married couples. We didn't need anything for happiness beyond the modest grant made by His Majesty's Government, a pair of bicycles to get around on, time out for an occasional visit to the Arts Theatre or afternoon on the river, some friends, and of course

John and Vera Townsend on their honeymoon in Alassio, Italy, 1945

each other. We lived in Cambridge all year, and could welcome the rush of activity with the start of each new term and the pleasant peace that descended when term was over.

My major was in English. The English faculty was dominated by the austere, impressive figure of Dr. F. R. Leavis, whose stringent critical methods were not to everybody's taste but served to concentrate all minds. My tutor gave me two pieces of advice at the outset of my career as a student: "Read books, not books about books" and "Don't spend time discussing Dr. Leavis." The former of these two pieces of advice holds good, I believe, today. Dr. Leavis has died, but when Cambridge English graduates who are old enough to remember him get together they still discuss him. He was one of those teachers who leave a deep and lasting mark on all who encounter them.

While at Cambridge, I developed, for better or worse, an infatuation with journalism. There was an excellent student newspaper in those days, printed on the presses of the local daily, and selling over 5,000 copies of each issue, though the student population was only about 7,000. I joined it. Promotion in student organizations is rapid, and from a reporter I soon became news editor and then chief editor. The cost to my aca-

demic work was high, and I paid it gladly.

We had enormous fun with the paper. We wrote slashing editorials, telling the authorities how a university should be run. (They'd been doing it for about 600 years, but we all felt we could teach them a thing or two.) We turned out features, columns, "profiles," diary paragraphs, the lot. We had photographers, who included the young man later to be Lord Snowdon and husband of Princess Margaret; he was fired from the student newspaper by the picture editor. We had sports writers and we had would-be political correspondents who wrote about the university's would-be politicians. We designed elaborate layouts, and each week we saw our paper through the press, learning and nonchalantly using as many of the technical terms of printing as we could absorb. I never enjoyed journalism so much again.

It was still my ambition to be an author, but when the time came for me to leave the university I was under the powerful spell of journalism. My immediate aim, I decided, was to be a newspaperman on a serious paper; then, in the fullness of time, the ultimate objective would be achieved and I would modulate from journalism to authorship. The paper for which, above all others, I wanted to work was the *Manchester Guardian*, whose editor was then the late A. P. Wadsworth—a brilliant, infuriating, and lovable man. I wrote to him, offering my services. He didn't reply. I wrote to him again, two weeks later, reminding him of my offer. He still didn't reply.

Then came the day when I, a married student, was threatened with court proceedings by the local Gas Board for nonpayment of a bill which in fact had, with much effort, been paid. I sat at the typewriter, rolled up my sleeves, and wrote a scorching letter to the chairman of the Gas Board. By the time I'd finished it, I was thoroughly warmed up, and in the mood to compose more scorchers. I remembered the editor of the *Manchester Guardian*, and wrote him an angry letter which concluded, as nearly as I can remember: "Kindly regard my application as cancelled. I would prefer to work for an editor who has the courtesy to answer his correspondence." Back by return of post came a letter from Wadsworth inviting me to Manchester for an interview, after which he offered me a job.

Once again, as had been the case when I got into Cambridge, I didn't realize how lucky I was. Wadsworth received scores of applications from bright young people just leaving Oxford or Cambridge who wanted to work for the *Manchester Guardian*. He hardly ever accepted any of them. But he liked outspoken and cussed people; and in the succeeding years I sometimes thought I disappointed him—not, I hope, professionally, but by being, as a rule, fairly even-tempered and amenable. I think he'd have liked a bit more devilment.

I believe that Wadsworth was influenced in deciding to hire me by my interest in newspaper design and production. These matters had little appeal for most of the bright young people who wanted to work for the *Guardian*. He set me to work as a sub-editor, headlining other people's copy and specifying column widths and type sizes; and he kept me at it for the next three years. From time to time I would tell him that (like all the rest) I wanted to be a reporter or editorial-writer, to which he would invariably reply that reporters and editorial-writers were ten a penny and that the best prospects in journalism lay with the backroom people who put the paper together.

After three years of this, he made me picture editor of the *Guardian*. I had to arrange for pictures, mostly of news or sporting events, to be taken by our own photographers, and I also had to choose from among the photographs sent in by free-lancers and picture agencies. And, having got the pictures I wanted, I had

Guardian *days: Townsend in his office, about 1954. Drawing by Françoise Taylor.*

to bargain for space in the paper to display them, and I had to cut them to the right sizes and shapes. Many years later I made use of this experience in my novel *Cloudy-Bright*, whose hero is trying to get a job as a photographer on the local evening paper.

From being picture editor I graduated to the editorship of the *Guardian's* weekly international edition. This was, and is, mainly but not entirely a selection of the best material from a week's issues of the daily paper. It circulates largely overseas, and in my day it sold far more copies in North America than any other British publication.

I liked this job of selection, and it allowed me to make up my own paper just as I wished, with the satisfying feeling when the week's work was over that there was something to show for it: a brand new crisp clean issue. It also brought me my first trip to the United States, in 1956. I was invited by a certain Dr. Henry Kissinger to take part in the Harvard International Seminar. This seminar, which was Dr. Kissinger's brainchild, brought together each year some forty young or youngish people from a variety of countries, offered them a program of lectures, seminars, and visits, and exposed them for six weeks to the American way of life, or at any rate the American way of life as seen from Harvard. The program was excellent, but I would say without disrespect to Dr. Kissinger that the main benefit to me lay in getting around and meeting people off campus.

Editing the *Guardian Weekly*, in spite of its advantages, was out of the mainstream and didn't involve much writing. I used to think I could do any job on a newspaper except that of music critic or sports reporter, and that if really pushed I'd have had a good shot at those. Wadsworth, I believe, would have brought me back to the main paper; but a year or two after I took over the weekly edition he died, and I stayed where I was.

A year or two later came another turning-point. One day the book review editor came to me and suggested that I might like to write about children's books for the daily paper. My only apparent qualifications were my own two small children, and I had no special knowledge of children's literature. The Victorian books on Grandpa Page's shelves and the adventure stories I had so indiscriminately gobbled were the whole of my own childhood reading. I accepted the suggestion mainly because I was glad to contribute to the daily *Guardian*. I had no inkling that within a very short time I would be deeply interested and excited; that I would see children's books as a new field of discovery, a new and unique stimulus.

Inside myself, down at the deepest roots, I was still

the boy from industrial northern England. My blue remembered hills were still in Leeds. And whereas my experience of the arts, of higher education, of journalism with the *Guardian,* had taken me back no farther than to my own awakening at the age of twenty, here was something that led me back into the profound depths of childhood. My involvement in books for children, my attempts to read as a child would read, brought my two selves together in what turned out to be a complicated creative tangle. Before long, either the Leeds child in John Townsend was writing a book, or John Townsend was writing a book for the Leeds child alive in himself.

This was *Gumble's Yard* (American title *Trouble in the Jungle*): a story about poor children in a district not unlike the one I'd lived in, fending for themselves after they'd been abandoned by the grown-ups who were supposed to be looking after them.

I had four immediate reasons for writing *Gumble's Yard.* As a reviewer of books for children I'd come to the conclusion, rightly or wrongly, that British children's books of that time were altogether too harmless, hygienic, and middle-class, with little in them of the flavor of life as it was known to a large part of the population. I had been writing some articles for a magazine on the work of the National Society for the Prevention of Cruelty to Children, and for this purpose had had to go out on the beat with some of the NSPCC inspectors in poor districts of London and Manchester. This had brought it sharply home to me that many children were poorer than I had thought possible, and that the most desperate form of poverty was not financial but was the lack of loving care.

About this time there was a report in our evening paper, the *Manchester Evening News,* about a family of children whose mother had walked out on them, and who had attempted to look after themselves because they were afraid of being "taken into care" and split up among different homes. And finally, I started going to work in Manchester on the train; and the train seemed to stop every day on top of a viaduct overlooking a canal basin. This basin was part of an industrial landscape which at first one would dismiss as ugly and dismal, but which, seeing it every day, I eventually perceived to be extraordinarily beautiful in its own strange way. I wandered around it in my lunch-hour; I found myself putting people into it, especially the four abandoned children as I imagined them to look; and from this it all grew. At long last, thirty years after my childhood epic, I was writing a book.

I didn't think it would be published, and referred to it in conversation as Townsend's Folly. But newspapermen hate to write anything and not see it in print. I thought I would at least try to find a publisher, and sent it to three leading houses. Two of them turned it down. The first liked the characters and background but not the story; the second liked the story but not the characters and background.

The third was the London firm of Hutchinson, whose adviser on books for children in those days was the poet James Reeves. He recommended publication, and they published it. It ran into a certain amount of flak. A young lady who interviewed me accused me of writing a sordid book for children. I can't remember exactly what I replied; I hope I said I didn't see it as a sordid book but in its way as an inspiring one, since it showed children winning through in very adverse circumstances, and if they'd won through once they could win through again.

While I was working on *Gumble's Yard,* I thought I was trying to write a book that would say something to, and about, and on behalf of, ordinary poor city children. It was years before I realized that this was not the heart of the matter. I wrote *Gumble's Yard* because it was there inside me, wanting to come out; and it was there inside me because of the child I had once been.

Writing and publishing *Gumble's Yard* changed my life, though I didn't at first realize that it would do so. In its first year after publication it earned a little over two hundred pounds. One couldn't support a young family on that kind of money. I saw it as an interesting and worthwhile venture, but not one that I could afford to repeat very often. Essentially I was still a journalist with a full-time job to hold down.

In the long run, *Gumble's Yard* did well. It was broadcast and televised; it was published in hard and softcovers in half a dozen countries; it is still in print after twenty-three years. But at the time I didn't foresee any of this.

A side effect of publication which I also underestimated at the time was in changing the name I was known by. I had always been plain John Townsend. Soon after the book was accepted, my editor called to tell me there was another John Townsend already writing. He had published a book called *The Young Devils,* about his experiences as a teacher in a tough inner-city school. He had also written two children's novels. If I started publishing under the same name, my editor said, there would be hopeless confusion.

"Do you have a middle name?" she went on.

"Yes," I said. "It's Rowe."

"That's fine. We'll use that. You can be John Rowe Townsend, okay?"

I'd never before given the name Rowe a moment's thought. It was the maiden name of Grandad Townsend's mother, who died before I was born. I didn't

Robert Smithies, The Guardian ©

Townsend, 1962

give it a moment's thought now.

"Okay," I said. "After all, it's my name." And that was that. For twenty-three years now I've been John Rowe Townsend. What happened to the other John Townsend I don't know. I've never heard of him since. Occasionally I curse him. Having three names instead of two is a great nuisance.

Americans don't get me wrong. They take it for granted that my surname is Townsend, and they index me correctly under T. But the British are hopelessly at sea. I am frequently given a hyphen; I am introduced, as often as not, as "Mr. Rowe-Townsend"; I am as likely to be indexed under R as under T. People who look under the wrong letter think that I'm not on the telephone or my books are not in print.

Maybe that's only a minor nuisance; and the extra time taken to sign a three-name autograph is also not important, although there are occasions when, signing my name 100 times at a school, I wish it were Bill Hill. A more important drawback, for a person who like myself has written about poor people in poor

city districts, is that to have three names is considered in Britain to be upper or at any rate upper middle class. Nobody with three names, it's thought, could possibly know what it is to be poor or to live in an industrial city. So, for instance, a British commentator has accused me of writing "outside-looking-in" books, based on "observation rather than experience." He hadn't bothered to find out the facts.

The involvement with children's books took over my professional life by stealth. *Gumble's Yard* was some fifteen months in the press, and by the time it came out, in 1961, I had found I was again with book. As with *Gumble's Yard,* I had a sense of what wasn't being produced in Britain, though it was already common in the U.S.A. This was the teenage, or "young-adult," novel. In Britain, it seemed to be assumed that young people suddenly grew up overnight at around the age of thirteen, and moved straight from children's to adult fiction.

It was plain to me—but was not then a commonplace in my own country—that there were subjects which were of special interest to adolescents but which were not being written about for young people: such matters as leaving school and starting work, or not leaving school and not starting work when all your friends are doing so; arriving at new relationships with parents and authority and the other sex; and above all finding out who you are and what you have it in you to be and to do. It also seemed to me, as a convinced feminist since long before the women's movement took off, that there was a fictional dearth of spirited, enterprising girls who were not merely "tomboys"; since there are after all real and valuable differences between the sexes other than the obvious physical ones.

Hence my second book, *Hell's Edge,* in which a girl from a superior private school in the South of England is thrown together with a rough, tough, gruff boy from the North, and they strike quite a few sparks from each other before they can come to terms. This book is set in the hill country of western industrial Yorkshire, a few miles from Leeds—a land that, as somebody says in the book, is ugly on the surface but beautiful in the bone. *Hell's Edge* is not as well-known a book as *Gumble's Yard,* and not a particularly good one, but in Britain it has stayed in print for twenty-one years so far, and I have a soft spot for it myself.

Meanwhile Irene Slade, my editor at Hutchinson, had left to take charge of the list of a small publisher, Garnet Miller; and it was her suggestion that I should write a brief historical outline of English children's literature. There was one accredited history, written in 1932 by F. J. Harvey Darton, and taking the story only up to about the year 1900. Irene thought it was time for another. In between doing my job as editor of the *Manchester Guardian Weekly* and writing a third novel, I managed somehow to fit in the reading and research required for this project.

The first edition of *Written for Children* came out in 1965 and, along with the reviewing I'd been doing in the daily *Guardian,* helped to establish me as a writer about children's books as well as a writer of them. It was this new reputation that took me on my second trip to the United States, and was to take me on most of the subsequent thirteen. It was this second trip also that found me an American publisher.

America has been of great and increasing importance to me. I am immensely pro-American, and one of my favorite and most firmly held beliefs is that there is nobody in the world as nice as nice Americans. I seem to have met a great many of them.

In 1965, I was invited to teach for a semester at the University of Pennsylvania, in Philadelphia. I had a dual appointment—to run a seminar at the Annenberg School of Communications on the comparative merits and demerits of American and British newspapers, and to teach a course in the Graduate School of Education on children's literature. In the four months I was there I grew fond of Philadelphia and made good friends. The key encounter, professionally, was with Hugh Johnson, then a vice president of the fine old publishing house of Lippincott.

Hugh and I met for the first time in the house of friends, and talked the sun down the sky on the subjects, naturally, of people and books. My own third novel, a sequel to *Gumble's Yard,* was just out in the U.K. Hugh showed great interest, and had me send a copy to Lippincott's children's editor, who was then Jeanne Vestal. She accepted it. Its British title was *Widdershins Crescent.* Joseph Lippincott, Jr. declared—correctly, I am sure—that such a title would never do for the American market, and it was changed for the United States to *Good-Bye to the Jungle,* the "Jungle" being the slummy area in which my fictional family lived.

The timing was right. It was the era of the Great Society and of Title II. *Good-Bye to the Jungle* got excellent notices; it sold, and went on selling. Lippincott published my next book, *Pirate's Island,* which in spite of its exotic title had the same industrial-city setting. Among other reviews was a long, favorable one in the *New Yorker.* Lippincott then went back and picked up *Gumble's Yard,* soon to be retitled *Trouble in the Jungle.* The three books were A.L.A. notables, and together became known as the Jungle Trilogy.

It was the beginning of the end of my career as a journalist. In 1969, *Gumble's Yard* was published in Brit-

ain as a Puffin paperback. This, combined with American publication of all three books and the sale of subsidiary rights, pushed my earnings as a book writer to a higher figure than my salary. There was of course no certainty that this situation would last. Writing is a notoriously chancy business. But I was in deep time trouble. To do my job properly, write my books, and see anything like enough of my wife and children was clearly impossible, failing the introduction of the fifty-hour day, the ten-day week, and the hundred-week year.

Meanwhile, my old Government department, the Inland Revenue, was taking large bites out of my earnings. For a long time I complained bitterly to all who would listen that the Revenue made financial nonsense of my efforts as a fiction writer. Then one day the simple, beautiful, and liberating thought occurred to me that I could put this complaint the other way round. What if I were to regard my writing income as basic? In that case, the Revenue was making nonsense of my salary and I was working for peanuts. I should leave the *Guardian.*

In spite of the financial logic, it wasn't an easy decision to make. I was giving up an appointment of some standing. I had three children, all in school, and a large mortgage. I suffered a good deal from financial cold feet. But it was now or never. Naturally, I talked it over with my wife.

"If it's what you want to do," she said, "do it." In June 1969, I handed over the reins of the *Guardian Weekly* to John Perkin, and left next day for Seattle to teach summer school in the University of Washington. Knowing that ex-editors always disapprove of the direction taken by their successors, I never again opened a copy of the paper. I did however retain for the next nine years a small part-time connection with the daily *Guardian* as children's book review editor.

As these words are written, I've been a full-time professional writer for sixteen years, and I do not expect or wish to be anything else. America has continued to be important to me. The visit I make this year will be my fifteenth. After the semester at Penn and the summer school at Seattle, I taught a second time at Washington and made three lecture tours, incorporating the May Hill Arbuthnot lecture, the Whittall lecture at the Library of Congress, and the Anne Carroll Moore lecture in the New York Public Library. Since 1978 I have been, with Jill Paton Walsh, a visiting faculty member at the Center for Children's Literature in Simmons College, Boston. I have also spent a month on tour in Australia and a few—too few—days in Japan. When my wife died in 1973, I didn't want to go on living in the home we had built together at Knuts-

Townsend at the tiller of a 60-foot canalboat, jointly owned with Jill Paton Walsh, 1975

dead ends arrived at, the despair.

There's a period of sheer, dogged slog, when only willpower keeps me going. Then, with luck, comes the recovery—the realization that it can be made to work out after all, the returning enthusiasm, the completion of the first rough draft. That first draft is the hardest part, accomplished by what Arnold Bennett called "brute force of brain." Then there's a second, and sometimes a third draft; the book must be shaped and reshaped, improved and polished. It's hard, craftsman's work, and it takes a lot of time. For me, completing the final revision is like coming into port at the end of a long voyage. But somehow the book is never *quite* as good as I'd hoped when setting out. Perhaps next time will be different. At least it will be a different voyage. I don't ever want to make the same one twice.

Looking back, I can see that certain themes have recurred in my work, although it was never a deliberate intention that they should do so. One is a theme that a great many writers for children and young people have explored in different ways—the theme of youngsters taking on responsibility for their own and other lives when the adults cannot or will not do so. Other themes are more individual to myself. I am endlessly fascinated by human relationships which have to grow and flower in a brief period of time, like those (in my own books) of Graham and Lynn in *Goodnight, Prof, Dear;* of Philip and Ann in *The Summer People;* of Ben and Katherine in *The Visitors.*

I am intrigued by moral problems to which there is no easy answer, as in *Noah's Castle,* set in a future time when millions are starving. The central character is a father who saw what was going to happen and stocked the basement of his big old Victorian house with everything needed to withstand a siege—which is what he has to do in the end. He doesn't care what happens to anyone else, so long as his own family survives. Is he a terrible man, or is he only doing what a father ought to do, namely protect his own young at all costs? I don't know the answer; if I'd known it, I probably wouldn't have wanted to write the book. I am interested in asking moral questions; I'm not interested in laying down a moral line.

Places inspire me—in particular strange, remote places that in some sense are the end of the world, whether it be the row of derelict cottages on the canal bank in *Gumble's Yard* or the village that is crumbling into the sea in *The Summer People.* I love dens and refuges of all kinds; and I love, especially, islands. Islands seem as if they were specially made for adventure; and for a writer they have the advantage that you can concentrate a great deal of human passion and conflict into a small space.

The mystery of time intrigues me, too, and I have

ford, near Manchester, and I moved back to Cambridge, which I had always loved. Here I have stayed, through twelve years and as many books. My children have grown up and my first grandchild has been born.

Professionally, I'm one of the world's lucky ones. I am what I always wanted to be, a writer. People ask me often if I don't want to write for adults. Actually *Written for Children* is a book for adults, and I have written a great deal of journalism for adults; but they mean fiction, of course. I have always said that if I were captivated by an idea which could only be realized in an adult novel, then I would write an adult novel. In the meantime I am very happy to write for children and young people, who seem to me to be an ideal audience, receptive, and constantly renewed.

The writing of each successive book is a new and different enterprise. It never becomes a routine. Yet there are stages to be gone through every time. There's the initial fascination with an idea, the excitement of planning and starting work, the first fine careless rapture of writing. Then come the problems: the tendency of every narrative to go its own way and of every character to do what he or she is not supposed to do; the falling apart of plots, the wrong directions taken, the a feeling that I may well explore it further. I like to show events in the distant past still working themselves out today, as in my recent book *Tom Tiddler's Ground;* and there's the impossible but ever-appealing notion of time travel, which I have handled only once. This was in *The Visitors.* In contrast to fairly numerous books in which people from the present have traveled into the past or the future, *The Visitors* has people from the future arriving in the present. It's a situation which allows the writer to take a look from outside at our own society.

And then there have been the books that were sheer fun: the Ruritanian extravaganza of *Kate and the Revolution,* and two which are published only in England and probably wouldn't travel to the States— *Clever Dick,* the diary of a thoroughly obnoxious child, and *Gone to the Dogs,* in which a family of dogs keep two children as pets.

My sustained critical writings have been *Written for Children* and two books of essays on contemporary children's writers, *A Sense of Story* and *A Sounding of Storytellers.* The criticism of children's literature has been something of a minefield in recent years; one is under heavy pressure to judge books from nonliterary points of view, in terms of social, psychological, or educational desirability.

I have always declined to do this, though I wouldn't deny the right of others to do it. I have never understood why it should be supposed that there is only one correct critical stance and all others must be wrong. There is room, in my view, for different kinds of critic. For myself, I have no wish to construct abstract critical theories or to engage in the kind of criticism that lays works of art out on the slab and dissects them. That way, it is all too easy to finish up with the dead remnants rather than with the living body, the thing that breathes and moves.

My personal leaning is toward appreciative criticism. I try to approach every new book in a spirit of hope and excitement, though not without discrimination. One thing I believe most passionately is that a good book for young people must be a good book, period.

My present way of life is quiet, and pleasant enough. I still live in Cambridge, and have no thought at present of moving. I have a half-share in a country cottage in the riverside village of Hemingford Grey with Jill Paton Walsh, and we work there together for three days in every week. Thanks to our yearly visit to Simmons, we've discovered the joys not only of Boston itself but of Maine and New Hampshire and Vermont; of Cape Cod and the islands. It's been a good life.

And Leeds? Oddly enough, my younger daughter, Penny, went of her own choice to Leeds University,

Townsend with Paul and Ethel Heins, then of the Horn Book,
at Pemaquid Point, Maine, 1984

lived and started work there, and married a young man from Pudsey (a township between Leeds and the neighboring city of Bradford). She is now teaching in that part of the world, and shows every sign of staying. So a connection is maintained.

I find as I grow older that my heroes in the arts are those who continue working with undiminished powers in ripe old age. In an eightieth birthday interview a year or two ago, the famous novelist Graham Greene was asked whether he had any remaining ambitions.

"Yes," said Greene. "To write a good book."

We can't all be Graham Greene, but, while ever we have the health and strength to push a pen or pound a typewriter, we can all keep trying to fulfil that aim as far as our talents allow. That is what writers are for.

BIBLIOGRAPHY

FOR YOUNG ADULTS

Fiction:

Hell's Edge. London: Hutchinson, 1963; New York: Lothrop, 1969.

The Hallersage Sound. London: Hutchinson, 1966.

The Intruder (illustrated by Graham Humphreys). London: Oxford University Press, 1969; Philadelphia: Lippincott, 1970.

Goodnight, Prof, Love (illustrated by Peter Farmer). London: Oxford University Press, 1970; published in America as *Goodnight, Prof, Dear.* Philadelphia: Lippincott, 1971.

The Summer People (illustrated by Robert Micklewright). London: Oxford University Press, 1972; Philadelphia: Lippincott, 1972.

Forest of the Night. London: Oxford University Press, 1974; (illustrated by Beverly Brodsky McDermott). Philadelphia: Lippincott, 1975.

Noah's Castle. London: Oxford University Press, 1975; Philadelphia: Lippincott, 1975.

The Xanadu Manuscript (illustrated by Paul Ritchie). London: Oxford University Press, 1977; published in America as *The Visitors.* Philadelphia: Lippincott, 1977.

The Islanders. London: Oxford University Press, 1981; New York: Lippincott, 1981.

King Creature, Come. London: Oxford University Press, 1981; published in America as *The Creatures.* New York: Lippincott, 1980.

A Foreign Affair. London: Kestrel, 1982; published in America as *Kate and the Revolution.* New York: Lippincott, 1982.

Cloudy-Bright. Harmondsworth: Kestrel, 1984; New York: Lippincott, 1984.

FOR CHILDREN

Fiction:

Gumble's Yard (illustrated by Dick Hart). London: Hutchinson, 1961; illustrated by W. T. Mars) published in America as *Trouble in the Jungle.* Philadelphia: Lippincott, 1969.

Widdershins Crescent. London: Hutchinson, 1965; published in America as *Good-Bye to the Jungle.* Philadelphia: Lippincott, 1967; revised edition published in London as *Good-Bye to Gumble's Yard.* London: Penguin, 1981.

Pirate's Island (illustrated by Douglas Hall). London: Oxford University Press, 1968; Philadelphia: Lippincott, 1968.

A Wish for Wings (illustrated by Philip Gough). London: Heinemann, 1972.

Top of the World (illustrated by Nikki Jones). London: Oxford University Press, 1976; (illustrated by John Wallner) Philadelphia: Lippincott, 1977.

Clever Dick. London: Oxford University Press, 1982.

Dan Alone. Harmondsworth: Kestrel, 1983; New York: Lippincott, 1983.

Gone to the Dogs. London: Oxford University Press, 1984.

Tom Tiddler's Ground. Harmondsworth: Kestrel, 1985; New York: Lippincott, 1986.

FOR ADULTS

Nonfiction:

Written for Children: An Outline of English-Language Children's Literature. London: J. Garnet Miller, 1965; New York: Lothrop, 1967; revised editions, Harmondsworth: Kestrel, 1974; Philadelphia: Lippincott, 1974; Harmondsworth: Kestrel, 1983; New York: Lippincott, 1983.

Modern Poetry. London: Oxford University Press, 1971; (photographs by Barbara Pfeffer). Philadelphia: Lippincott, 1974.

A Sense of Story: Essays on Contemporary Writers for Children. London: Longman, 1971; Philadelphia: Lippincott, 1971; revised edition published in England and America as *A Sounding of Storytellers: New and Revised Essays on Contemporary Writers for Children.* London: Kestrel, 1979; New York: Lippincott, 1979.

Twenty-Five Years of British Children's Books. London: National Book League, 1977.

P. L. Travers
1906-

P. L. Travers, 1984

I find it difficult to write autobiographical notes. To me, all that matters, in any instance, is the story of a soul and one can't put that down on paper or wear it on one's sleeve for the world to pore over. It is a private matter. Why must we always want to know "what porridge John Keats ate"? It is just lucky for us that he was alive and wrote his poems.

In any case, it is all, like life, so chancy. Did this or

that episode really happen as one remembers it or was it something that imagination got to work on? One thing I am certain of—I was born; an event important enough for me and my parents, little though it mattered to the rest of the world. It was in a small township in Queensland, Australia, set in sugarcane country and wild bush. My Father came of an old Irish family and my Mother was of Scottish descent, a product of English and French finishing schools. Both were articulate by nature and full of the legend and poetry of their native backgrounds. A child could absorb a great deal of lore simply by living in their atmosphere.

I think that atmosphere was the most fruitful part of my education. There were few books, the classics in my father's library and an array of novels—probably from some lending library that sent books by post—and on these, except for Beatrix Potter, *Alice in Wonderland,* and a prolific and gifted Australian writer called Ethel Turner, the children, especially myself, had inevitably to feed their thirst for knowledge and information.

No, I'm wrong! As well as the classics and the novels, one could buy at one of those small country shops—everything from toothpaste to reels of cotton—one could buy what no child of today could even dream of—one could buy penny books. It was an exquisite agony to stand before the bookshelf, penny hot in the hand, and try to decide whether to have a single Fairy Tale (green cover) or a Buffalo Bill (blue and red). Thinking of them recently, for the purposes of this article, I found myself wondering if I had invented them—the lovely Walter Crane fairies in frothing gowns, and the Buffalo Bill shotgun you could get for nineteen shillings and eleven pence if you could ever save up so much? "Were they true?" I tentatively asked a friend, a famous English novelist.

"Of course we had penny books," she replied, with an ardour equal to my own, and we brooded together on those long-gone scraps of tattered paper—for tattered they were in a very short time—and congratulated ourselves on our good fortune.

For what could you buy for a penny today? Not even a stamp!

And now I remember another treasure, a small housewifely periodical (was it four pence, I forget!) called *Home Chat* that had, amid the recipes and knitting patterns and what to do when a baby had colic, an early version of the serialised modern comic with a hero by the name of Tiger Tim who, oddly enough, I remember as a bear!

With all this—and Shakespeare—what more could you want? You had everything.

For me, however, there was something more, one thing, but writ large in my mind and heart, and continually there all my growing years. I wanted to go where there were, I was sure, other books, as well as a whole different scene. I wanted to go to the land of my fathers, for something told me, very early in life, that that was where I belonged.

And eventually, with the dew still on me, I got there, fully expecting and prepared to sweep crossings for a living, like Little Joe in *Bleak House.*

I had been fortunate enough, while still of school-age to meet people in Australia—editors and the like—who encouraged me to go on writing the poems that seemed then to spill out of me. Some of them were, astonishingly, willing to print and give me money for them and the stray pieces of—doubtless naive—prose that sometimes fell off my pen.

It was inevitable that I should earn my living eventually; that had always been made clear to me. But I never set out to be a writer. And what, if one thinks about it honestly, is a writer, anyway? Just a human being who takes pen or typewriter and makes certain marks on paper. The work of a weaver or a carpenter is just as useful. I read, later in life, the words of Ananda Coomaraswamy who said: "It is not that the artist is a special kind of man but that every man is a special kind of artist." And, though I could not have put it so well, that is how I had always thought.

Well, there I was, at last, where I had always wanted to be. There were no crossings to sweep. The streets of London were paved, though not, of course, with gold. I was not living in one of my beloved fairy tales. But there were many small highbrow magazines—when one is young one's brow tends to be particularly high—that to my surprise said Yes to me. And then one day, which turned out to be a central point in

A. E. (George Russell), Irish sage, poet, and mystic

my life, I ventured to send a poem to A. E. (George Russell) the Irish poet and mystic, who was then editing the *Irish Statesman* in Dublin. With all the hauteur of youth I sent no covering explanatory letter, merely enclosed a stamped addressed envelope for return.

And back the envelope duly came with, wonder of wonders, a cheque in it. And in addition there was a letter from A. E. saying that nobody but an Irish person could have written the poem, that he was publishing it immediately, and that if ever I was coming to Dublin would I step into his office and see him?

This from A. E. on whose poems and prose writings, along with those of Yeats, I had nurtured my growing years!

Of course I was coming to Dublin, as a natural course, to see my father's people, but now I had a more important reason. I was coming to see the man who, I found eventually, was to be my friend and mentor—as Zeus might be to a page in his court—for the rest of that man's life. No—more! For when he had gone his teaching remained alive in me, and I pray it may continue to do so for the rest of my life.

Through him I came to know all the poets that were then thronging Dublin—Yeats, James Stephens, Oliver Gogarty, Padraic Colum, and a host of others. There was a poet on every corner.

My relatives, however, when I came to know them, were by no means enthusiastic over my new congregation of friends. Poets were all very well in books but out of place on street corners. And they professed not to like the idea of me consorting with "men who

saw fairies." "It's your father coming out in you," they said. "He was spouting poetry in his cradle." Well, I was only too pleased to have my father come out in me, and happily set myself to learn all I could of his world.

So I grew, moving back and forth between England and Ireland, constantly under the instructive eye of A. E., who saw to it that I had introductions to editors, making me known to famous people so that I could interview them for the papers, encouraging me in my lifelong study of myth, legend, and fairy tale, subjects in which he, too, rejoiced. "When you write a book," he would say, "these will all come out in it."

A book! I had never thought of such a thing in relation to myself. It seemed to me aiming too high. Nevertheless, when I was convalescing from an illness in an old house in the country in England—the date 1610 was carved on an oak beam over a fireplace as big as a bedstead, but the local people insisted that it was mentioned in the Domesday Book—I began for my own amusement to put together certain ideas that came filtering into my mind—from where, I do not know—does anyone? When asked if *Mary Poppins* was a book written for children, I have to say that it was not consciously so. It was for anybody who would read it, grandfather or grandchild.

C. S. Lewis, of the *Narnia* books, is reported to have said something to the effect that a book written solely for children was by definition a bad book. He had ideas to present and those ideas sorted best with the kind of book that children as well as others could

Pound Cottage, Sussex, England, where Mary Poppins *was written*

read. He described the process of this kind of writing as "bird-watching." Myself, I would be inclined to say "listening." You do not invent. You just set yourself to listen for what, with luck, may be told you. Well, luck brought me *Mary Poppins,* which was now a bundle of typewritten papers. A friend read it, took it to a publisher and, at once—or so it seemed to me—it was a book, standing firmly on booksellers' shelves in England and the United States and a little later it appeared in about thirty translations.

And presently, a year later, for I had grown stronger, there was more to say in a sequel called *Mary Poppins Comes Back.*

Then came the war which found me in New York where Katharine Cornell and her husband, Guthrie McClintic, the stage director, wanted to have the books made into a play. But the project came to nothing. I did not then see it in dramatic terms.

And anyway, longing for home and my nearest and dearest and unable to cross the U-boat-infested Atlantic, I had not the heart for magic. And yet a kind of magic happened. The then-Minister for Indian affairs, a friend of A. E., seeing my homesickness, suggested as a cure that he invite me to spend some time on an Indian Reservation. It seemed an unlikely antidote but I did indeed find it a healing process, living among the Navahos, riding among the women, wearing wide flowery skirts like theirs, speaking little but hearing much, folding myself away as much as possible so that I should not seem to be listening to their stories, present at their dances and songs, sharing at other times their silence. Myth and legend were all about me in the sagebrush, renewing in me the vital wish to work. I was able to write *I Go by Sea, I Go by Land,* half-story, half-diary about children sent to the States to save them from the London bombs; also a bibelot called *The Fox at the Manger,* a story built on an old French carol; and then a game with the alphabet called *Mary Poppins from A to Z.* And when I went back to New York I was ready for a third sojourn with the Banks family which I wanted to call *Goodbye, Mary Poppins,* for it seemed to me that I had now said all there was to say about her. But my publisher begged me not to do so. "You never know what will happen!" he said.

So the title became *Mary Poppins Opens the Door.* And, in the event, my publisher turned out to be more of a prophet than I. For when I had returned to England, after the war and all its living-and-dying, gradually, chapter by chapter, as time went by, *Mary Poppins in the Park* began to appear on my typewriter. New translations of the series seemed to appear in many places. Russia purloined it and the translator, the same man who translated *Winnie-the-Pooh* and made him ap-

P. L. Travers, about the time she wrote Mary Poppins

pear in peaked cap, bandolier, and jack boots, wrote to me and said that it was selling in the millions. Well, a million in Russia is a mere nothing. No mention of roubles came with the letter but I was happy to think of Russian children, with the wealth of fairy tales from the past running in their blood, reading about Mary Poppins—who appeared in the illustrations as a wispy little girl with matchstick legs—never mind the roubles.

And after that came *Friend Monkey,* based on a character from the great Hindu epic *The Ramayana.* I think *Friend Monkey* is the favorite of all my books, it is so steeped in myth. Besides, it was a book that very nearly failed to exist. When I was about halfway through it, the manuscript was mislaid. Dowsers came to my house and searched for it with their pendulums. Not a sign. It was like losing a child and it was not until I had again spent some years in the States, being Writer-in-Residence at Radcliffe-Harvard, Smith College, and Scripps College at Claremont, that the thought came to me that if Carlyle could rewrite *The French Revolution* and T. E. Lawrence *The Seven Pillars of Wisdom,* I could at least try to resuscitate something as fragile as *Monkey.* And it came back to me almost word for word, when I was staying with friends in Virginia.

Then came *About the Sleeping Beauty,* in which I

tried to collect as many versions as I could of my favourite fairy tale, including, perhaps immodestly, one of my own and after that—don't ask me about times or dates, I can never remember—there was *Two Pairs of Shoes,* one pair culled from a collection older than the *Arabian Nights,* the other from the *Mathnawi* of the Sufi poet, Jalal ud-Din Rumi.

As for the rest—one is a human being before one is a writer—there was living to do, articles for the New York magazine *Parabola* which has given ten years of devoted service to Myth and the Quest for Meaning and is now moving into its eleventh. Those are the things that have meant most to me, not the articles, but the Quest and the Myth. I agree with A. E. who said that Mary Poppins came straight out of myth. Where else could I have found her or she me? She was even seen making a fifth visitation a year and a half ago in *Mary Poppins in Cherry Tree Lane.* So you see, I have a lot to be thankful for. Most of all for being given life, no matter what the cost of living it.

BIBLIOGRAPHY

FOR CHILDREN

Fiction:

Mary Poppins (illustrated by Mary Shepard). New York: Reynal & Hitchcock, 1934; London: Howe, 1934.

Mary Poppins Comes Back (illustrated by M. Shepard). New York: Reynal & Hitchcock, 1935; London: Dickson & Thompson, 1935.

Happy Ever After (illustrated by M. Shepard). New York: Reynal & Hitchcock, 1940.

I Go by Sea, I Go by Land (illustrated by Gertrude Hermes). New York: Harper, 1941; London: Davies, 1941.

Mary Poppins Opens the Door (illustrated by M. Shepard and Agnes Sims). New York: Reynal & Hitchcock, 1943; London: Davies, 1944.

Mary Poppins in the Park (illustrated by M. Shepard). New York: Harcourt, 1952; London: Davies, 1952.

Stories taken from *Mary Poppins* (illustrated by Gertrude Elliott). New York: Simon & Shuster, 1952-53. *The Gingerbread Shop,* 1952; *Mr. Wigg's Birthday Party,* 1952; *Stories from Mary Poppins,* 1952; *The Magic Compass,* 1953.

The Fox at the Manger (wood engravings from Thomas Bewick). New York: Norton, 1962; London: Collins, 1963.

Mary Poppins from A to Z (illustrated by M. Shepard). New York: Harcourt, 1962; London: Collins, 1963.

Friend Monkey. New York: Harcourt, 1971; London: Collins, 1972.

Two Pairs of Shoes (folktales; illustrated by Leo and Diane Dillon). New York: Viking, 1980.

Mary Poppins in Cherry Tree Lane (illustrated by M. Shepard). New York: Delacorte, 1982; London: Collins, 1982.

Other:

About the Sleeping Beauty (illustrated by Charles Keeping). New York: McGraw, 1975; London: Collins, 1977.

Mary Poppins in the Kitchen (culinary consultant, Maurice Moore-Betty; illustrated by M. Shepard). New York: Harcourt, 1975; London: Collins, 1977.

FOR ADULTS

Nonfiction:

Moscow Excursion. New York: Reynal & Hitchcock, 1935; London: Dickson & Thompson, 1935.

Aunt Sass (biographical sketch). New York: Reynal & Hitchcock, 1941.

Ah Wong. Privately printed, 1943.

Johnny Delaney. Privately printed, 1944.

George Ivanovitch Gurdjieff. Toronto: Traditional Studies Press, 1973.

Translator of:

The Way of Transformation: Daily Life as a Spiritual Exercise, by Karlfried Dürckheim Montmartin. Translated from the German with Ruth Lewinnek. London: Allen & Unwin, 1971.

Barbara Wersba

1932–

Barbara Wersba, 1932

Wersba, age five

I was born in 1932, to a father whose parents were Russian-Jewish, and to a mother who was a Kentucky Baptist. The only child of this stormy marriage, I grew up in almost total solitude. I thought I was lonely when I was simply a loner—and spent much of my childhood daydreaming, writing poems, and creating dramas for my dolls. We lived in California, in a suburb, on a hilltop, and I would spend hours sitting in an almond tree in the back yard—gazing at the glittering city of San Francisco, miles away. I wanted to be a musician, or a dancer, or a poet— anything that would lift me out of what I considered to be a sad life. At night, lying in bed, I would hear the sound of trains passing in the valley, and imagine that I was on one of them. Get away, get away, said the wheels of the trains. Get away, get away, I echoed.

I was, in the words of James Agee, "disguised to myself as a child," and did most of the things that children are supposed to do—attending the local grammar school, joining the Girl Scouts, selling war bonds (for this was World War II), and spending every Saturday afternoon at the movies. To my mind, World War II was a heroic effort undertaken by people like Tyrone Power, Van Johnson, and Betty Grable. Movie stars swam through my mind day and night, and I papered the walls of my bedroom with their pictures.

Family photos show me, as a young child, happy and obviously loved. But around the age of seven or eight there was a change, and I became a somber person whom people were always telling to *smile*. Grammar school was a quiet, unspoken torture. Children's parties were a torture, too. In those days little girls were supposed to look like Shirley Temple, with tight curls and starched dresses. For reasons that I have never understood, I looked more like a German refugee—my mother choosing to dress me in knee socks,

Oxfords, and dark wools. My long hair was skinned back into two tight, unforgiving braids.

I remember a blue bicycle with balloon tires, which I rode like a fury up and down the California hills. I remember the wonderful scrape of new roller skates on smooth pavements. The fields of wildflowers were being turned into developments, and there was always the skeleton of a house to climb. Heady with the smell of wood sap and fresh nails, I would climb to the top and gaze out over the fields, the church steeples, to the bright blue bay. There was a longing in me for other places and other times, but I could not put it into words.

Then the evening came when a grownup, a friend of my parents, turned to me at the dinner table and asked the inevitable question. "What do you want to be when you grow up?" "An actress," I said without blinking, and the minute the words were out of my mouth, they had the ring of truth. I would be an actress. Like Bette Davis and Joan Crawford. Or even— like Greta Garbo.

There was a community theatre in the town where I lived, and it seemed the logical place to begin. So one Saturday I walked through the door and asked them for a job. Running errands, going for coffee, handing out programs. I would work for nothing, I said, as long as I could watch rehearsals. Unable to turn down such a sweeping offer, the directors gave me the job and my heart soared. I was now a part of the American theatre and had a place in the world. I was eleven years old.

Within six months the theatre had given me a part in a play, and from that day on I was stagestruck. No matter that I did not like to act, that it frightened me, and made me almost sick. I had a purpose in life

Josephine Quarles Wersba

and no longer felt alone. "I am going to be a great actress," I would say to myself over and over, as though words could make truth. I memorized my lines until I could say them in my sleep. I went to the library and did research, for the play was set in Russia, and learned how to use stage makeup. Was I any good on opening night? I cannot say. Like many of the important moments in my life, this one is shrouded.

That year my mother told me that she and my father were getting a divorce. Without knowing what had gone wrong, I watched like a distant observer as my father departed, the house and furniture were sold, and my two cats were taken away to be put to sleep. I loved animals more than people in those days (and still do) so that the loss of the cats was worse than the loss of my father. On the day they were taken away, I crawled into a little space under the house, near the furnace room, and wept.

The next thing I remember is my mother and me on a train heading East—sitting in a small compartment playing gin rummy. My father's relatives, to whom she was still close, lived in New York City. We would start over there.

The older one grows, the more interesting the past becomes—but to this day I know very little about my background. There are remnants of stories, told to me

Wersba, age eleven, in Listen, Professor, *Burlingame, Calif.*

Robert Wersba

by various people, but the remnants do not make a fabric. I know that my Jewish grandfather met my grandmother in Riga, Latvia, when he stepped into a bakery shop and fell in love with the girl behind the counter. In the classic American tradition, he came to New York, made his fortune, and brought his young wife and her relatives over one by one. On the other side of the family, I know that my great-great-grandmother once stood in the door of her Kentucky farm with a rifle, in the midst of the Civil War, to keep Yankee soldiers away—but that is all. I wish I knew more, but most of the people are gone now, and all that remain are the fragments of tales that become more and more mysterious to me.

My mother and I set up housekeeping in a hotel near the Broadway theatre district, and the first thing I did in New York was to go out and buy a ticket to a play. I had never heard of the playwright or the star, but when the matinee was over, I sat in my seat paralyzed by emotion. Ushers were picking up discarded programs, the work-light on stage had gone on, but I could not move. Finally, an usher led me from the theatre and deposited me on the sidewalk outside. The play was *The Glass Menagerie* by Tennessee Williams, and the star was Laurette Taylor.

What I could not have known was that backstage,

attending Miss Taylor, was a woman who would many years later become my friend when I myself became a playwright. These coincidences, which are not really coincidences at all, have shaped my life entirely. I no longer find them strange, choosing to believe that there is a synchronicity to life, a merging of inner and outer events, that involves us all.

I forgot about movie stars and concentrated my attention upon Broadway actresses. Lynn Fontanne, Katharine Cornell, Eva Le Gallienne. I sat in the last row of theatre balconies, holding a small flashlight and writing in a notebook, and watched these women act. I was in love with all of them, but one, Eva Le Gallienne, captured my heart with her steady pursuit of excellence in the theatre—classics, repertory. Thirty years later I would write a play for Eva Le Gallienne called *The Dream Watcher.*

For me, having come out of a small California town, New York was a revelation. There were museums, and opera and ballet, and more book stores than I knew existed in the world. From nine to three each day I went to private school, but after three o'clock the city was mine. By age fifteen, I was taking acting classes at the Neighborhood Playhouse. By sixteen, I was studying dance with Martha Graham.

I look back on these days with a kind of sadness, for I, on my way to becoming an actress, did not like to act. What I really liked was being alone, reading and writing, and collecting books. A loner from birth, I felt uneasy in the social atmosphere of the theatre, and suffered from stagefright so severely that I once went to a hypnotist to be cured. Every spare moment I had was spent writing stories and poems, but I did not take this seriously. My writing seemed terrible to me, awkward, imitative, trite.

I was now disguised to myself as an adolescent, and did all of the things that young girls in the late 1940s did. Wore blazers and bobby socks, stuck new pennies in my loafers, swooned over Frank Sinatra, sat by the phone waiting for boys to call. I wore taffeta formals to proms and received gardenia corsages, fought with my mother over curfews, wore pale lipstick and nylons, went away on my first overnight date to West Point. But the person who did these things was not real to herself. It was as though I felt an obligation to be a "teenager" for a certain number of years. After prep school, this obligation was over.

My father insisted that I go to college, his choice being Vassar. Instead, I boarded a train one day and traveled up the Hudson to apply at a small liberal-arts college called Bard. To my surprise, my entrance exam was an audition on stage. I did a scene from Shaw's *Saint Joan* and was accepted. My father was furious when he found out, via the mails, but I persisted, and

Wersba in her mother's apartment, New York City, about 1947

at the age of eighteen packed my trunks and went off to school. Save for brief vacations, I never returned home.

If each life has a pattern, and if the meshing of inner and outer events—synchronicity—does exist, then I was fated to go to Bard College. From my first day there until my last, I was happy and fulfilled. I acted in all the plays and took all the English courses. I played the piano far into the night in a little glass observatory on a hill. I kept stray cats in my room, ran a donuts and coffee enterprise that traveled from dorm to dorm, made friends, got crushes on professors, fell in love. Applying for a Fulbright Scholarship to England, to study acting, I suddenly developed cold feet and wrote a letter to Eva Le Gallienne, asking her advice. Amazingly, she wrote back—suggesting that I study in my own country rather than abroad. I took her advice and did not go.

Bard College was small in those days, just three hundred students, and the teachers taught on a one-to-one basis. They were young and vital—each a professional in his field—and I was like a sponge, trying to absorb it all, acting, directing, stagecraft, dance. In the summers, I went off to act in small summer stock companies. In the winter field periods, I worked at off-Broadway theatres in New York. My friends were actors, my mentors were actors—but I did not like to act. Rehearsals over, homework done, I would hole up in my dormitory room around midnight and write stories. I could not stop writing, and yet my writing caused me anguish. It wasn't any good. I never finished anything.

A few years ago I went back to Bard to accept an honorary degree, and the friend who went with me says that I wept the entire day. I do not remember the day clearly, but I suppose I did weep, for everywhere I turned, everywhere I walked, the ghost of my young self was just ahead of me. I saw her running across the lawn in jeans and bare feet, emerging from the library, sitting in the coffee shop. Thin, blonde, intense, that girl was more real to me than she had been to herself, and as I accepted the degree I felt her by my side.

I graduated from college one June, and a week later was in rehearsal in Princeton, New Jersey. The stock company was a good one, and it was said that producers and directors from New York would be coming down to see the plays. I had the lead in every one of these plays—long, difficult parts. I was exhausted from the last year of college. And my stagefright was now chronic. The first production was *Camino Real* by Tennessee Williams. I played Marguerite Gautier, the legendary "Camille," and on opening night, after the curtain had come down, a famous director came back-

College student and aspiring actress, age twenty

Wersba as Marquerite Gautier in Camino Real, *Princeton University, 1954*

stage and said that he had a part for me on Broadway. After he left the dressing room, my fellow actors crowded round me, but where my happiness should have been was an empty space. I knew that I would never call the man, but did not know why. As far as my acting career was concerned, the journey downward had begun.

That autumn, independent for the first time in my life, I took a coldwater flat in the East Village, got a series of part-time jobs, and began to make what in those days were called "the rounds." These rounds consisted of going to numerous theatrical offices, trying to see someone important, never being allowed to see someone important, and departing in anger—leaving behind a photo and resumé that always ended up in the wastebasket. The tenement building I lived in on Ninth Street was crowded with young actresses, and since among us there was only one good coat—a fur— we would take turns wearing it. If Monday was my day for making rounds, I got the fur coat. If Tuesday was someone else's day for the coat, I stayed home. I worked in book shops and department stores, ran a projector for a film company, typed in offices. My oddest job was making seed-mosaics in an empty studio where I never once met my employer. He would leave instructions and money, and I would laboriously construct huge mosaic pictures, made of colored seeds, that were sold as decorative objects to hospitals. I became

governess to the young son of a television personality, lived in her West Side apartment for a few months, and departed when I realized that the women was insane. My worst job was waiting tables at Schrafft's, where I dropped a poached egg into a woman's bodice and was promptly fired. My best job was as the head of the correspondence department at a government housing agency. A secret acting student, I worked there by day, getting more and more promotions, while I went to acting school at night.

The house on East Ninth Street has figured in several of my books, most recently in *The Carnival in My Mind,* because the building and its inhabitants were themselves like a character in a novel. In the basement lived Dennis, who was five feet tall and wanted to be an opera singer. On the top floor lived Samantha, who was a harpist, but whose room was too small for her harp. She kept the harp in the hallway. Next door to my apartment, on the second floor, was Beryl, a shady type who had a stream of gentlemen callers. In the winters all of us froze in our rooms—in the summers we roasted. Rats and roaches were common, but what I remember most from those days was the sunlight on my windowsill and the straw chair in which I would sit reading. I had painted the floors brick red, had built bookcases from floor to ceiling, and played Bach and Mozart on a dilapidated phonograph. The bathtub resided in the tiny kitchen—which meant that it was possible to bathe and cook at the same time.

After college I had attended acting school for three years, under the guidance of a brilliant, temperamental teacher. His insistence that his students provide themselves with employment by forming their own companies was so strong, and so believable, that upon graduating seven of us did just that. Putting together a staged reading of famous stories about childhood, we hired a booking agent and went on the road. It was my job to adapt the stories into acting form, as well as act in them, and though I did not know it at the time, this work was my first real work as a writer. The stories were wonderful—by people like Dylan Thomas and Virginia Woolf—and as I shaped and cut them, and turned narrative into dialogue, I knew the first pleasure in working at a typewriter that I had ever known. The program was called *When I Was a Child,* and one day in winter, in a rented Volkswagen bus, the seven of us headed West.

The first thing that happened was that we got lost and wound up at Niagara Falls—and the second thing that happened was that one of our members began to go out of his mind from LSD. Stuffed into the little bus with our suitcases and guitars, stage lights and costumes, we spent three wild months traveling across America, playing in college auditoriums and sleeping in run-down motels. By the time we returned, all of us worse for wear, plans were afoot to put the show on Broadway. But I had fallen ill.

The diagnosis was hepatitis—and so, leaving the company behind, I went to a friend's house on Martha's Vineyard to recuperate. Lying there in bed day after day, staring at the ocean, free of responsibility for the first time in years, I knew that I would never return to the theatre. Something had broken in me that could no longer be repaired, and I was glad. No more part-time jobs and making rounds, no more despair over the lack of jobs in the theatre, the cruelty of the theatre. I did not know where I was going, but after fifteen years of struggle I was free. It was then that my hostess said, "Barbara, why don't you write something?"

I asked her what she thought I could possibly write, and by way of answering she brought a pad of paper and a pen to my room and left me alone. I looked at the pad of paper, and then I looked at the sea and began to write. A few weeks later I had completed a story called *The Boy Who Loved the Sea.* I didn't know it was a children's story because I knew nothing about children's literature. All I knew was that this was the first piece I had ever been able to finish. It was a fantasy about a child who goes to live in the sea, and I was rather proud of it. Beyond that, I thought nothing.

A few nights later, the chief copy editor of a New York publishing house came to dinner, and without telling me, my friend and hostess put my manuscript into the editor's purse. The editor read the manuscript, and took it to the children's book editor at the firm where she worked. "If you don't publish this, I'm quitting," she told the woman. She was joking, of course, but her friend did not know this. She read the story, liked it, and dropped me a note saying that she would publish it. All of this happened without any effort on my part.

Suddenly I was about to have a book published, and it gave me pause for thought. What was life all

Wersba, a published author, about 1959

about, when fifteen years in the theatre bore no fruit, but one small manuscript did? What was fate trying to tell me? I was not a good writer, but something told me that I had the temperament of a writer, that I could teach myself to write, and have more joy in doing so than I had ever had acting. Thus, at the age of twenty-six, I began a new career.

The second book, a fantasy about ballooning in the eighteenth century, was harder to do, but I stuck at it. And now the copy editor who had seen to it that my first book was published introduced me to a fine agent, who took me on as a client. This editor, Connie Campbell, is dead now, and so I can never ask her why she went to so much trouble for me. I did not know her well, and we were never close. But every time I help a young writer, a new writer—I think of her.

It was clear to me that the form in which I wanted to work was the children's book, and so I began to read children's books by the dozens, trying to understand the difference between picture books and story books, story books and novels. I worked as hard as I had ever worked in my life, sat at the typewriter for eight hours a day, and produced a third book—this time a fantasy about mythical animals. I moved to Rockland County, in New York, and rented a small house. The fourth book appeared, and then the fifth, as I worked steadily to improve what I was doing, to clarify what I wanted to say. I knew so little about story-telling, and yet in some ways story-telling had been the basis of my life. Reading and writing and collecting books had been my occupations since childhood.

From the beginning, people said to me, "Why write for children when you could be writing for adults?" and they are still saying it. Implicit in the question, of course, is the notion that children's literature is second-class, that lesser talents create it, and that it should be used as a stepping-stone towards something else. I never agreed with these notions, always proud to be working in a genre that has attracted geniuses. Why write for children? Because the form is tantalizingly short, and thus tantalizingly difficult. Because the form implies hope. Because those of us who use this form still experience our childhood in strong and passionate ways. There is no chalk line on the sidewalk with childhood on one side and maturity on the other. It is all the same life, it is all one, and the best children's writers know that they are writing for the child in the adult, and the adult in the child.

In 1967, I was working on an historical novel set in eighteenth-century London when a voice came into my head. This voice, that of a young boy, was so strong and insistent that I put the historical novel away, sat down at the typewriter, and did not get up again for seven months. The voice which would not stop speaking belonged to a boy named Albert Scully, and the book in which he told the story of his life was *The Dream Watcher*. On the day that I finished this book I burst into tears, for I knew it to be a milestone in my life. Little did I realize, however, the paths down which Albert Scully and I would walk.

The Dream Watcher, published by Atheneum, was the first of my books to have any length and develop any real characters. Told in the first person, it is the story of a fourteen-year-old boy, a misfit and a loner, who meets a beautiful old woman who tells him that she has been a famous actress. Taking him into her home and her life, Mrs. Orpha Woodfin develops such a sense of integrity in Albert that by the time she dies, he has come into his own. No matter that she lied to him about having been an actress. What she has given him is himself.

From the day it was published, *The Dream Watcher* changed my life. To begin with, the book sold well and received fine reviews. People all over the country began to write me about their identification with the characters, about an older person who had changed their direction in life. And it was only then that I realized that this theme of older person helping younger person had been the underlying theme of my own life. Unable to relate to my parents, I had sought parent substitutes everywhere. In teachers, theatre directors, college professors, and in my wonderful agent Pat Schartle. In friends who were always older than I, and who gave of themselves generously.

During the next few years I wrote several picture books, became a book reviewer for the *New York Times*, and began to write articles for magazines. I taught fiction writing at New York University. But *The Dream Watcher* would not go away. People connected with the movies came to see me, to inquire if the book couldn't be turned into a film. Others suggested that I do a sequel. I was well into my second novel for young people, a story set in the drug culture of the sixties called *Run Softly, Go Fast*—but *The Dream Watcher* persisted.

The book went into paperback and kept bringing in mail. Again and again I was told that the story should be turned into a play or a film, but those possibilities seemed remote. What I wanted was to move on, to leave the book behind me and do something different.

It was not to be—for in the early 1970s a friend of mine gave *The Dream Watcher* to Eva Le Gallienne to read, and one evening this friend called to say that Miss Le Gallienne wanted to play the part of the old woman. Although I was only forty, I felt that my life had come full circle.

The next five years were a kind of detour, as Eva Le Gallienne and I struggled to make *The Dream Watcher* a reality. I had been so moved by meeting this actress that I had been rather mute, but when she turned to me in front of the fireplace of her Connecticut home, an old woman now, not the actress I remembered, but the personality I remembered—the vibrancy, the vitality, the beautiful voice—when she turned to me and said, "Why don't you write me a play?" I was done for. All plans for children's books and children's novels were swept from my mind as by a great invisible broom. "I don't know how to write a play," I said to her. "Learn," she advised.

For the next eight months I read two plays in the morning and two in the evening—to learn this difficult form—and in between I struggled to dramatize my book. As each act was completed, I would take it over to Miss LeG's house, she would give criticism, and then I would head back to my typewriter in Rockland County. What I wrote, she kept telling me, was *literary*. What she needed was something to act.

Within a year I had turned *The Dream Watcher* into a play. I had also become friends with one of the great stars of the twenties and thirties. To my surprise, the glamorous woman I had admired in my childhood was herself a loner—a person who fed animals from the woods every night from her kitchen door, whose main interest in life was her garden, and whose library was the finest I'd ever seen. When I realized that Miss LeG's companion and secretary, Eloise, had been backstage working for Laurette Taylor on the same day that I—age twelve—had sat stunned by *The Glass Menagerie,* unable to leave the theatre, I knew that synchronicity was at work again.

We opened at the White Barn Theatre in Connecticut, in 1975, and that night I had a sudden understanding of why people write plays, of why in the midst of so much difficulty and pain, playwrights persist. For

Eva Le Gallienne in The Dream Watcher, *Westport, Connecticut*

at the evening's end, as the curtain calls began, and as Miss LeG was led onto the stage by the young actor who played opposite her, a kind of thunderstorm broke. People cheered, and wept, and applauded, and stamped their feet, as she took curtain call after curtain call. As the applause continued, I ran into the lobby where refreshments were being served, grabbed a glass of champagne, and, without spilling a drop, ran up the back stairs of the theatre and handed the glass to Miss LeG when she came offstage. It was one of the happiest moments of my life.

The production at the White Barn Theatre had been a summer tryout, a preparation for what we hoped would be a Broadway production. And in the summer of 1977 that production materialized. The play was re-cast, re-designed, and a large group of us flew out to Seattle, where the play would be produced in partnership with the Seattle Repertory Theatre. This out-of-town tryout would continue on to Boston and Philadelphia, until eventually we reached Broadway. But just as the White Barn production had been destined to succeed, so this new version was destined to fail. A boy who was much too old had been cast in the part of Albert. An insecure young director had been hired. Ornate, revolving sets had been designed—sets that almost swallowed up the play—and I had been asked to do countless rewrites, none of which I believed in. Opening night was a disaster, and the following day Miss LeG gathered the cast together in the theatre's green room. "We have failed," she told them. "Our butterfly has been cloaked in iron."

I came home to Rockland County, went to bed with my two cats, and slept. For some years home had been a nineteenth-century country store, with stained glass windows, marble counters, and gas lamps—and so I walked through the house for days, staring at the books in my library and watching the sunset turn the stained glass into something evangelical. In the early 1960s, a partner and I had bought this building and restored it to its former beauty. And since it had always been a country store, we decided to operate it as one again—selling penny candy and tobacco, Vermont cheese, homebaked goods, jams and jellies, housewares, toys. It was a marvelous store, and though it never earned a penny, it received constant publicity. NBC television did a feature on it for their evening news. Theatrical people from New York drove out to sample its wares—Noel Coward, Katharine Cornell, Mary Martin, Ginger Rogers. During the seven years that we ran the store, I was a writer in the mornings and a storekeeper in the afternoons. It was a good combination.

In order to do something after Seattle, in order to heal myself, I took a step that surprised me—I opened

The Palisades Country Store

a school. A small school. Ten students. All women. I called it The Women's Writing Workshop, held the classes in my home, and found a new door opening. More and more women joined the workshop, soon there were two sessions going, then three, and I found myself functioning again, but in a different way. There is an old saying to the effect that the only way to learn something is to teach it—so that now, after many years of writing, I was beginning to understand writing for the first time. Guiding the students away from any need to prove themselves, to be good, to shine, I also guided myself away from these goals—and soon I was doing the assignments with them, learning to write naturally, from feeling rather than expectation. The students' work amazed me. My own amazed me too—and the following year I began to give classes at a local cultural center. The women I taught were housewives, secretaries, nurses, and very few had a chance of being published. But it was not publication we were aiming at. It was truth.

I did not marry and I did not have children. Instead, I had animals. Stray dogs, stray cats—and once even a stray parrot—all passing through my house as though it were an underground railway. I loved every one and found every one a home—but there were years in which I thought my life would be consumed by the attraction animals have for me, and I for them. I have found cats and dogs in shopping centers, along highways, on city streets, and in the deserts of the Southwest. Not one has ever been turned away, and all have given me joy. One, in fact, gave me a book.

On a hot summer day in 1979 I was walking up Fifth Avenue, in New York, on my way to meet two friends in front of the Metropolitan Museum. I had come into town with them that morning, and was about to return to Rockland County in their car. Then I saw the man. Disheveled and crazy, he was trying to sell a starved Irish setter to anyone who would buy it. The young, emaciated dog had collapsed on the sidewalk from the heat, and though a crowd had gathered round, no one—in typical New York fashion—was willing to get involved. Giving the man twenty dollars, I half pulled, half carried the dog into my friends' car and took it back to the country. The setter, whom I named Bridie, was around six months old, of show quality, and it was likely that she had been stolen. Within a week, she was beginning to return to health.

There were several things about Bridie that I had not considered. The first was that she would grow. The second was that she would need training, which I never gave her, innocently believing that I would locate her owner. As I searched the back issues of the *New York Times,* trying to find a "lost" notice for a young Irish setter, Bridie became more and more energetic. Walking her through the neighborhood three times a day was like a battle, as I struggled to keep her on the leash. I began to read books about Irish setters, only to learn that they are a manic breed, that they belong in the field. Through a grapevine of dog people, and animal rescue people, I became involved with the Irish Setter Rescue League of America, an organization whose president was also its only member. This woman tried to help me, as did many others, but Bridie's original owners could not be found. I began to advertise her in the local papers, trying to find her a home.

Bridie, whom I loved, became an enormous, undisciplined, wildly affectionate dog. Greeting a newcomer, she would stand up, put her front feet on the visitor's shoulders, kiss the visitor, and then knock him down. There was no way of controlling her, and one day in late summer the inevitable happened. Bridie knocked me down. Seeing another dog, she became so wildly excited that she pulled me down in the driveway. I felt my right foot crunch, and for a moment the world went black. The next day I was on crutches with a badly sprained foot and a dog to walk.

By the grace of God, Bridie found a home with a strapping man who wanted a large dog to jog with, a large dog to be his friend. One day she was gone, and instead of being relieved I was inconsolable. Vacationing for one week on the island of Martha's Vineyard, I began to write a book called *The Carnival in My Mind.* It was about a neglected boy whose mother raises Irish setters.

From the day I began writing professionally, I have worked at the same desk—a large craftsman's table that I bought for ten dollars. And after ruining dozens of typewriters with my pounding, I now type on a solid, indestructible IBM. I begin work around five in the morning, when I know it will be quiet, work for six hours, and return to work in the afternoon if I am deep in a book. For every manuscript that succeeds there are five that fail, but I can never bring myself to throw the failures away, and they are all kept in a trunk labeled *In Progress.* I have had my share of rejections and disappointments, and a certain number of calamities—like the play—but the impulse to write persists. What keeps it alive is simple curiosity. There is no literary form

that cannot be explored more deeply, whether it be novel, short story, or poem, and this is what interests me.

The first thing that comes when I am about to write a book is the title. Indeed, titles often appear far in advance of the book itself, so that I write the title on a piece of paper, paste it up over my desk, and wait. One of my favorite titles, *Let Me Fall before I Fly,* arrived so many months before the actual story that I found myself repeating the words over and over, as though they were a mantra or a prayer. Let me fall before I fly, let me fall before I fly . . . Then, suddenly, I knew what the words meant and began to write a story about a little boy who owns an imaginary circus. Of all the books, this one is my favorite. It says what I believe, and it reflects my life.

I have been blessed with many things. With awards and honors, with books published abroad, and, since 1980, with the friendship of my fine editor Charlotte Zolotow. I have spent the last twenty-five years doing what I like to do, leading the kind of life I think is right for me—and for these things, I am grateful. My

Carson McCullers

career has allowed me to meet people whose talents have influenced me profoundly. Eva Le Gallienne, Janet Flanner, Irwin Shaw, Carson McCullers. Carson, in particular.

In 1966, a friend asked me if I would be willing to read to an invalid twice a week in the neighboring town of Nyack. *Very* reluctantly, I said yes, and the invalid turned out to be Carson McCullers, the great Southern writer. My journal records our meeting this way. "In the midst of a large bed is a tiny person with enormous brown eyes and short ragged hair. She is so frail that there hardly seems to be a body under the covers. One hand is doubled up and stunted, like a little paw. I shake the other. She stares at me with her huge eyes, and suddenly none of the amenities are possible. She has had strokes, heart attacks, and cancer. She is almost completely paralyzed. I feel that I am not meeting a person at all, but a soul. She is exactly like her books."

For the next two years, I visited Carson McCullers every day—read aloud to her, went shopping for her, ate meals with her, and loved her deeply. She was not easy to love, but before me always, in my mind, were her books. Her great books. Unable now to write physically, she dictated stories to me, phoned in the middle of the night with ideas for novels or with fragments of poems. She had written her last book, *Clock without Hands,* by typing it with one finger, one page a day. Now she was beyond typing, but the stories and the poems kept surging through her frail body.

Carson always wrote about herself, and the things she had to say were said over and over, like voices on a lazy summer day repeating the same words. She wrote about freaks because she felt like one. She was lonely and wrote about loneliness. Her characters survive through illusion, as she did, and hope to be redeemed by love—and never are. The things that obsessed her as a child were to obsess her all her life—imaginary friends, snow, the glamor of distant places, the loneliness of being too tall, too thin, too boyish, a freak.

I think of Carson and remember that her left hand was crippled, but that the right was as thin and elegant as a hand in a Pre-Raphaelite painting. Morning and evening, it held a silver goblet filled with bourbon. And if her world was one of alcohol and dreams, we knew, all of us who loved her, that she would be leaving books behind whose beauty was beyond price. Until the moment she died, at age fifty, she was the epitome of the word Writer.

The country store was sold in 1983, and I now live on the eastern end of Long Island, on a narrow peninsula. In front of my house is a large cove, in back of it are deep woods—and I am surrounded by wildlife.

My cats and dogs have been replaced with herons, egrets, white-tailed deer. And it was no accident that upon moving here I bought a camera and began to photograph these creatures. My days are spent half at the typewriter and half in the woods, or at the beach, learning a new art, a new patience.

The camera does not always see what the eye sees, and I am terribly slow in capturing the fleeting life of wild animals. Yet one in fifty frames is a revelation. That dawn-shot which I was certain required more light, when developed reveals a black silhouetted swan on a pond trembling with gold. That great white egret who soared over a marsh one day, and who so thrilled me that I shot continuously, not even knowing if he was in the viewfinder, is now frozen in a picture of pure spirit, wings uplifted as he takes off from the water. The background is a blurred bottle-green. The feet of the huge bird, as it leaves the water, have made a silver splash.

I look back on my life and ask myself questions. When have I been the happiest? Walking in the Swiss Alps, all worldly cares left behind, all values altered by the enormity of nature. When have I been the most sad? During those moments when human cruelty has been apparent to me, especially if the cruelty is directed towards animals. What do I hope for now? In a conventional sense, very little.

I have loved being on this earth and feel grief at the thought of leaving it some day. I have been moved to the depths by the natural world, by the passionate desire of plants and animals to reproduce themselves and carry their genes into the future. A flock of Canada geese passing over my house, their honking almost like the barking of dogs, a lone male bird leading the formation—this sight can reduce me to tears. And only yesterday a great swan flew over my head on a passage unknown, its wings making a humming sound on the winter air.

The journey continues.

BIBLIOGRAPHY

FOR CHILDREN

Fiction:

The Boy Who Loved the Sea (illustrated by Margot Tomes). New York: Coward, 1961.

The Brave Balloon of Benjamin Buckley (illustrated by M. Tomes). New York: Atheneum, 1963.

The Land of Forgotten Beasts (illustrated by M. Tomes). New York: Atheneum, 1964; London: Gollancz, 1965.

A Song for Clowns (illustrated by Mario Rivoli). New York: Atheneum, 1965; London: Gollancz, 1966.

Let Me Fall before I Fly. New York: Atheneum, 1971.

Amanda, Dreaming (illustrated by Mercer Mayer). New York: Atheneum, 1973.

The Crystal Child (illustrated by Donna Diamond). New York: Harper & Row, 1982.

Poetry:

Do Tigers Ever Bite Kings? (illustrated by M. Rivoli). New York: Atheneum, 1966.

Twenty-Six Starlings Will Fly through Your Mind (illustrated by David Palladini). New York: Harper & Row, 1980.

FOR YOUNG ADULTS

Fiction:

The Dream Watcher. New York: Atheneum, 1968; London: Longmans Young, 1969.

Run Softly, Go Fast. New York: Atheneum, 1970.

The Country of the Heart. New York: Atheneum, 1975.

Tunes for a Small Harmonica. New York: Harper & Row, 1976; London: Bodley Head, 1979.

The Carnival in My Mind. New York: Harper & Row, 1982.

Robert Westall

1929-

The beginning is a dream; a dream of invincible happiness.

It persisted right through my childhood till I was a young man. It always came as I was dropping off to sleep, and it was always exactly the same. It differed from my other dreams and nightmares, because nobody else ever came into it.

It was simply an experience of falling head over heels through endless blackness. It should have brought terror, except that I was falling very slowly, turning over and over as in a slowed-down movie; and the darkness was deliciously warm. And I had no fear of hitting the bottom, because I knew the bottom was a warm soft trampoline that would send me spinning upwards again in an exhilarating way. There were sounds, huge watery sounds like the running of streams and the roaring of the sea. And my happiness was total and invincible. . . .

I have never told anybody before, because I later worked out that the dream was a memory of how it was before birth, and I thought if I told people they would think I was mad. But now some psychologists hold that having memories of before birth is a quite tenable proposition.

Because I have known total invincible happiness, I am always on the lookout for it again. I certainly don't have it now; and I often shudder to think that my paradise was only my mother's vulnerable body that might have been ended in a flash by a fall or an automobile accident. But the reality of it remains real; I look for it again; it makes it easy for me to believe in my Christian heaven; death, at most, will be a slow retreat back into that endless joyful twisting and turning. . . . This affects my whole stand as a writer. It makes me an optimist. I don't think I shall ever plumb the hideous depths that Dostoevsky plumbed. Optimists are very limited writers, though popular.

It limits me in other ways, too. At heart, I am a loner. I make forays out from fortress-me and grab at my heart's desires and drag them back inside to brood over them. I drag my hurts inside and brood over them, too. Ask me how I have fun, and I would say people. . . . Ask me how I recharge myself and I would say alone, with a cat on my knee and Bach's Double Violin Concerto and a single glass of whisky. I don't mind someone else being in the room providing they don't get too noisy—like asking whether I'd like a coffee every two hours or so. All my working days are a cheerful journey towards being alone. If I don't get a evening alone every second day, my engine starts to run rough. If I were sent to prison, I'd choose solitary, with books.

This means there is so much about people I can never understand. Sibling rivalry seems like madness. I have no desire to keep up with any possible Joneses. I do not need the approval of a peer group. I shun fellow writers; I'd rather sit in a cafe in a strange town, an ignored stranger while the old ladies come in with their shopping and get on with their chat, treating me as of no more significance than a hat stand. Old ladies' talk, anybody's talk, is totally fascinating. I love talking to strangers on a train, providing it's only an hour's journey.

My books tend to have lone heroes—heroes who *choose* to go off by themselves. My heroes are not outcasts—they're quite popular, as I think I am quite popular. When you have no strong needs, no strong demands to make on other people, it is not difficult to be polite, pleasant and amusing. . . .

In my second dream-memory, I am buried inside the foundations of a house, and struggling to get out into the light of day. The foundations are of a deep red brick. There is a tunnel through them, a kind of maze, full of right-angled corners that are narrow and hard to wriggle round. I get very near to panic, but I manage to contain it and keep on wriggling. In the end, I get my head and shoulders out and just lie there, gawping at the blinding light and breathing gratefully, with my body and legs still inside the foundations.

I think this is a memory of birth; this theory too is now quite respectable in psychology circles. Again, it left its mark on me, as a child, as an adult, as a writer. As a child, I could never bear to be hugged tightly. I used to kick and yell and shout "Don't *struggle* me!—don't *struggle* me!" In my writing, situations of close physical context are always of combat, struggle, horror. When I write, I feel I am still in that dream. I once told Leon Garfield that to write a novel I have to wriggle my hero into a dense maze and then have him fight to get out. While he is fighting to get out, I am writing very fast, in a near-total panic; I exhaust myself. But the second half of my books is always the best—my first halves tend to be slow. Leon told me he had to use exactly the same technique—the cat wriggling into a sack and then struggling to get out. I wonder how many other writers use the same technique?

And now to my first *waking* memory. I am sitting on a sandy beach; I have wriggled my bottom into a hole and sit as secure as an egg in an egg-cup. I know I am less than eighteen months old because I cannot walk. That makes it the summer of 1931.

I can see and hear the sea; it delights me. It makes the same watery rhythmic swoosh, swoosh that I used to hear in my paradise. The infinite blue of space delights me too.

But near at hand, I am in trouble. All my relatives are playing with a huge beachball, tossing it to and fro over my head. I can hardly see my beloved sea for a forest of sandy sunburnt legs, tall as trees. Only these trees are in violent motion. At any moment they may bang into me hard, hurt and knock me over. I watch the ball warily, but as it crosses the blazing sun it blinds me and sends dry sand scything down into my eyes.

I think about escape. Shall I yell my head off? But it seems inappropriate. My great sunburnt gods mean me no harm; they are gay, laughing. I really don't want to spoil their fun, for I am genuinely fond of them.

Shall I try wriggling out through the forest of legs? But I'm pretty sure the gods know where I am; while I sit still they will make sure not to harm me or bounce the huge ball on my defenceless head. If I start to move, I shall throw out their calculations and anything

Robert Westall at nine months. "The offending beach ball is now firmly under control."

might happen. I sit still, and silent; I endure by great effort of will. Soon they drift away down the beach. . .

My God still seems the same today. I cannot believe in a wrathful punishing, avenging God. Again, the agonies and inner lives of people like Dostoevsky's people, like John Wesley the great evangelical preacher, are closed to me as a writer. If I go to a revivalist tent-meeting, I am seized with a terrible urge to giggle. Nor can I believe in a God that wishes me evil; I have no time for dualism.

My God is joyful and, when he remembers, loving. But he is so big and I am so small; he may trample on me in a fit of joyous abstraction and wipe out my life and regret it bitterly afterwards. When the earthquake hit Mexico City in 1985 I screamed at him, "Did you have to be so bloody clumsy?" And then it seems to me that he is in all the people too, all the marvellous people who have rushed in to help. He is sorry; he wants to make amends; but it is too late in one way; the babies in the hospital and the mothers are nearly all dead. Perhaps the babies and their mothers are all happy in Heaven; but it's damned hard luck on the fathers. I am pretty rude to my God most of the time; sometimes he is so blunt in return he shuts me up for weeks.

That's why my books are full of religion and empty of piety.

I was always a word-child. I learnt to talk nine months before I learnt to walk (though I was an incredibly fast crawler who only realised that crawling was impractical when I got outside and found stony ground hurt my hands. If I'd been issued shoes for my hands, I'd probably be crawling still).

Crawling was safe, fast, and practical and gave me everything I wanted. Walking was ridiculous, impractical and mainly consisted in bumping into things painfully. Talking was a miracle; I could throw my voice, my ideas, like lightning, right across the room, and adults who had ignored me before suddenly not only expressed amazed delight and profound interest, but actually answered my questions by throwing their ideas back. No wonder I relegated walking to the scrapyard. . . .

My father taught me to read by accident before I was four. Being a kindly man, he used to take me on his knee when he got home from work, and read to me aloud from a comic called *Puck*. Only, being a board-school boy who left school at twelve, he used to run his finger along the words as he read aloud, as they were taught to in board-school in those days.

One day he found I was reading on ahead, four paragraphs in front of him. It seemed to my parents, who were very ordinary people, a total and incomprehensible miracle. (I really think it happened because my father was so un-tense; he was never at all a tense man at home; he flopped completely. And so I wasn't tense either. He wasn't trying to teach me to read, to force me. And so conditions were relaxed, perfect for learning.)

And so I got my reputation as wonder-child, miracle-worker. This was the most marvellous freedom. My parents expected nothing from me; they expected anything from me; they gave up trying to shape me, and just sat back like a rapt audience, expectant for the next amazing thing I would do. . . . As I got older, my mother would often say, "You're one on your own; you're like nobody but yourself." Sometimes she said it wistfully; sometimes even angrily; but a permission to be like nobody but myself was beyond the price of rubies. I was *free*. I like to think I lived up to their expectations. They didn't quibble when I went for twenty-mile walks on my own, on wild and stormy nights, as an adolescent; they didn't quibble when at university I became an abstract sculptor and dragged home huge, wild, misshapen lumps of plaster. Later, when my books arrived, they got the first copy. One evening my mother tuned in early for her favourite soap opera, to see my face on the screen instead, describing the Nazi bombings of my childhood. She took it all in calm and joyous tranquillity, merely telling the admiring neighbours that I had always been like nobody but myself. . . . I am glad that in a modest way, I was able to amaze them to the end.

If you asked me why I write, I could truly say it's not for the money (though the money is very nice). And I don't think it's for the fame, for I now lurk in the backwoods of Cheshire and have a great reluctance to take part in any 'famous' activities. No, I think I still do it in an attempt to amaze; amazing an audience, whether you leave them thoughtfully stunned or wildly laughing, is for me the greatest feeling on earth.

The talking-walking thing has crippled me as a writer, of course. I have never expressed myself with physical movement; I was always a lousy ballroom-dancer, and ballet, unless it is the utter tops, just sends me to sleep. I never express rage physically either. I have never broken a bone in my life (neither did either of my parents, to the end) I have never thrown or broken an object in wrath (neither did either of my parents—my mother died at eighty-two, leaving a tea set she got when she married, and which she used, in an absolutely perfect condition). So the whole world of physical achievement and physical violence is a closed book. I am capable of the most appalling verbal violence and cruelty—my tongue can cut with a knife-edge, though I have long trained myself to curtail it. So, I could write a dialogue between a couple having a row as easy as eating pie. But let the husband lay a hand on the wife (or vice versa) and I am as much at sea as the famous Ouida was about the Boat Race between Oxford and Cambridge.

A growing boy gets his image of masculinity from his father. Some fathers seem to prove their masculinity by shooting a lot of small and harmless wild creatures; some by how much they can drink without falling down; some by how many women they can lay. My father did none of these things, thank God. For him, a man was one who could make things, and put things right.

He was a foreman-fitter at the local gasworks, but to me he was the Oily Wizard. When he came home from work, he smelt of strange and terrible magic—benzine and sulphur hung around his overalls and a cap, so filthy you could see no pattern on it. His dreadful black boots, which he never cleaned (though his recreation shoes always shone like diamonds), lay sooty and caked beside my mother's gas stove. He washed regularly, yet he could never quite get rid of the oil and soot he was caked in every day; even dressed to go out he had the swarthy good looks of Valentino in *The Sheik*. His thumbnail grew out in five separate segments, where he had hit it with a hammer as an ap-

Mother, Maggie Alexandra (Leggett) Westall, age twenty

Father, Robert Atkinson Westall, Sr., age twenty-eight, "The Oily Wizard"

prentice. I thought it should hurt desperately, but when I pressed on it with all my might, he just grinned. He never had a cold; he said the air of the gasworks was so full of chemicals it killed off the germs; the little school that cowered beneath the gasworks' walls was similarly immune to colds.

But his wizardry lay in more than that. I would watch him looking at an ailing engine, with his finger held lightly against it, feeling for vibration and his head cocked on one side, listening for the one tiny sound among so many that would mean trouble. I have never since seen such concentration.

At home, too, it was make, make, make. Radios; elaborately decorated cabinets for radios; model galleons. Some troublesome relative spilled something on the velvet-covered seats of our fireside fender. My father poured some strange-smelling liquid on to remove it. The liquid caught fire with pale blue flames—pale

blue flames everywhere. My father put them out with a laugh and a careless sweep of his hand. And ten minutes later the velvet seats were not only unharmed, but free of the troublesome stain. Pure magic!

He made me the confederate of all his schemes. I glued hatches and lifeboats for him, before he stuck them on the galleons. I helped to unload the pile of plain wood that, before my very eyes, became a greenhouse. He installed central-heating pipes in the greenhouse, shaping the pipes with his own hands, and I kept the boiler stoked while he was at work. If any of my toys got broken, he mended them without fail. He would only buy me British toys, and German toys. British was best; but the Germans, he allowed, were good engineers in spite of Adolf Hitler. Everything else was foreign rubbish; worst of all was Japanese rubbish. He was once talked into buying a Japanese lighter for two shillings. It looked just as beautiful as a British lighter, but worked twice and then broke. I shall never forget the snarl of disgust with which he threw it on the fire. He could never understand the Japanese war-successes of 1942; he remained convinced that their ships would sink in the first storm, the wings peel off their fighter-planes in the first dive.

Among his other talents, he had a gift for drawing. When he was left alone with me, for an evening, and I grew demanding, he would take me on his knee with a sketchbook and draw anything I named. Horses, dogs, my mother, grew miraculously from his pencil. But he loved to draw ships best. When he wasn't there, I learnt to draw by copying his drawings. I thought everybody could draw; my father never thought anything of his gift; it was simply a way of keeping the child amused. When I got to school and found most people couldn't draw, I was most surprised.

Best of all, though, were the stupendous toys he made for me in his spare time at work, in the summer when things were slack in the gas business. A full-size model of a Vickers heavy machine gun; a three-foot model of a battle cruiser. He would simply walk in some evening, his face full of glee, say "Shut your eyes" and when I opened them, there was something wonderful. I think I got my need to amaze people from him.

But best of all was my trips to his magic kingdom. Sometimes he would forget his "bait" or packed meal (sandwiches done up in the regulation spotted red "bait-hankie" and the tea tin full of an execrable gelatinous mix of thick condensed milk, sugar, and black tea leaves, to which he would add scalding water spurting out of a tap on one of his huge steam boilers). I, at age four, would be sent to give it to him.

The only thing I have read since that equals my approaching view of that gasworks is Tolkien's description of Mordor. The massive red-brick walls were twenty feet high, with broken glass set in concrete on top. Behind, two red chimneys reared a mile into the sky, belching a pall of black fume. The very air turned brown, like an old sepia print.

My purpose was to avoid the gate keeper, whom I hated with a deep, undying hatred. For one thing, he wasn't a proper man; he had a clean face and clean hands and a collar and tie, and did nothing all day but push sheets of paper about. For another thing, he would intercept me if he could, and take my precious burden from me and send me home, saying he would see to it . . . I crept under his window on tiptoe, doubled up. A short sprint, and I was in my father's kingdom. To Tolkien, it would have been a vision of hell. The cobbled road was half-flooded, and in the pools, films of oil and benzine swirled and cracked, all the sick colours of the rainbow. Pipes in blackened walls belched steam and choking smoke, or dribbled nameless black poison. Every cavernous doorway showed a different scene. Men stoking retorts, turned to black skeletons by the terrifying red glare of the fires; a blacksmith hammering with ringing strokes that ran in one ear and out the other and were like an iron spike ringing in your brain; showers of red and white sparks leaping all over his arms, his face, his scarred leather apron. And, oddly pastoral, one cavern was a stable in which two huge shire-horses stood, chewing hay in the darkness. My father said that at night the rats came out and nibbled away the horses' hoofs. . . .

I would wander as far as I could; Hell to Tolkien but Heaven to me, because the Dark Lord of Mordor was my father. Oh, there *was* a manager; but he was only there to do the paperwork for my father. Father hated paper; his favourite saying was "It's all right on *paper*, but it'll never work in practice." He abused and crumpled paper at work, scrumpled it up, and put his black fingerprints all over it.

Anyway, I wandered, sometimes for half an hour, entranced, until a real man with blackened face and shining white eyes and teeth asked me what I wanted.

And then I found I was a sort of crown prince. "It's Bobby's lad!" they would shout above the screaming racket. "Anybody know where Bobby's working?" "He's in the retort-house!" "He's up on the conveyor!" "He was in the coke-crusher ten minutes ago!" It seemed that my father, like God, was everywhere at once. A crowd of his black-faced subjects would gather, getting bigger and bigger. And at last my father, black-and-white-teethed as the rest, scarcely recognisable as my father, would appear, with a couple of men trotting alongside asking what to do about the clogging in number five retort. He was always in a hurry but never flustered; rather like a little black tramp-

steamer, steaming fast through a stormy sea of endless problems.

He would take his bait and see me to the gateway, pointing out the grimy sparrows that survived by pecking the horse manure from the great carthorses, or the tiny bright-green weeds that somehow flourished in crannies in the burnt-black brick. At his coming, the hated timekeeper would be silenced, and slink away to the back of his time-office.

Only once did my oily wizard cause me grief. I was watching him start a thirty-foot steam engine, by pushing with his shoulder against a seven-foot flywheel, when I noticed a subsidiary engine, in one corner. It was only three feet long, but a perfect gleaming miniature of the big one.

"Would you like that one?" asked my father. I stared at it. It was fixed to the floor with massive bolts, but with my father everything is possible.

"I'll fetch it home for you when I come off shift, then!" He was laughing. I ran home in a dream of joy. I met him as he came home expecting he would have it under his arm; just like the cruiser or the machine-gun . . . I burst into my worst-ever hurricane of tears and was inconsolable for three days. It is hard being a wizard's son sometimes; the boundaries between the possible and the miraculous have been a bit blurred for me ever since.

Only in one thing did he maim me. I was always clumsy with my hands. I wanted to make things, like him, but they never came out right. Years later at school, I was set to plane a block of wood square; the sides curved irredeemably; the more I planed, the more they curved. In the end the woodwork master said, "What are you making, Westall, a Viking ship?"

At home, when I tried to make something and it went wrong, and I asked my father for help, he would put right the mistake quickly and competently, and then leave me with a sniff of disgust. He would never show me *how* to do it. This attitude turned my incompetence into a deep conviction of my own total buffoonery. By the time I left school, even putting a screw into a wall filled me with sweating terror. This was backed up by his often-repeated statement that when I started work I would *never* get my hands dirty. I could do anything in the world except dirty my hands. When I got my degree, the only thing he said was, "Well you'll never have to get your hands dirty now!" All the kingdoms of the world were open to me, and he would help me on my way; all except one, *his* kingdom.

I got my sweet revenge though. In my thirties, I became, at my son's urging, a pioneer in the design of three-foot model sailing catamarans. There was no preceding design research I could find. Plenty of monohull model yacht design; plenty of full-size catamaran design. I worked from first principles, learnt maths again, and built first a model that sailed, then one that sailed very fast. I found that with wood, as opposed to metal, that although I was panicky and wore myself to a sweating flick-haired frazzle; to my amazement, with sweat and blood I found I *could* do it.

When he came to visit, I had the gleaming model on the table. He looked at it. He said, disbelief covering his face, "You *didn't* make *that*?" When I convinced him, he had to go and sit down. But he came and watched me sail it. After all, wood wasn't really his province, but metal.

And I still can't even change the wheel of a car. When we get a puncture, I go for a walk while my wife rings the RAC for help. If I try to undo a screw, I know deep down that first the screw won't shift, then the spanner will slip, and then my hand will come into violent contact with a sharp filthy metal surface and the blood will flow. I had mastered the theory of how a car works from a book by the time I was eight. But as my father would have said, that was only on paper; I wouldn't work in practice. My son became an engineer, like my father. They used to sit and talk about cranks and cams and thousandths-of-an-inch for hours, and look at me, pityingly as the odd one out. . . .

My father's effect on my writing was huge. He is the father of *The Machine-Gunners* and *Fathom Five*. But more than that, he is the source of wizardry in my books; he showed me a world in which things could be transformed beyond belief; he made the miraculous possible in my writing. And of course, he moulded my picture of God. I am happy with the God who created all things, the Great Engineer who got the Milky Way ticking over just right. But, like my father, this God is very busy, with an incredible number of things to see to, and sometimes he is almost impossible to find. Always benevolent, but sometimes just too busy. The one thing I cannot understand is when the earth goes wrong as in Mexico, and kills people. I sometimes think that Dad would never have let that happen; and it worries me . . . .

I found when I finally got to school, aged five, that the wonder-child was on an upward spiral of achievement and confidence. Word of my being able to read had gone before me. My first teacher immediately tested me. The book she used was absurdly simple; I galloped through it at a breathless pace, drunk with my power. She then set me on to drawing, and thanks to Dad, my drawings immediately began to go up on the wall. I was set cards of sums to do, and I whipped through them like eating cookies. I moved into my comfortable slot of wonder-child again. I wonder my classmates didn't beat me to a pulp, but children were quieter in those days.

Nonetheless, I became a problem; always first finished; hard to keep occupied. In the end the teacher uttered the marvellous words, "Go and find yourself something to do." And she waved her hand towards the little shelf of teaching reference books that stood behind her desk, and which no other child had ever touched.

My first library. Dad only had engineering books full of indecipherable formulas, and diagrams only fit for a magician. But now, at five, I became a tiny scholar, self-feeding. Of course, I only read what interested me, and especially those things that could be turned into drawings. Mainly Romans. I can still draw a mean Roman centurion in full armour. But there were also biremes, with two banks of oars, and triremes with three. And prehistoric dinosaurs to model in bread dough, bake and eat. I casually knocked off the ordinary schoolwork in between, anxious to get back to my real work.

Now I am not boasting; I am really telling you how very lucky I was to have this wizard for a father. I realise now that the children round me, labouring painfully over their work with their tongues out, were already starting to be crushed by the system. They were becoming panicky about being too slow; with every mistake they made, their confidence went down. Work became depressing for them, something to be endured, something imposed by a cruel ultimate authority. They were already learning to accept being failures, and comforting themselves with surreptitious sweets under cover of the desk, or too-frequent trips to the toilet. I honestly don't think I started off brighter than other people; I was simply not crushed and maimed in my confidence in myself. I worked on smoothly, without any of their burdens. No teacher made any attempt to crush me until the physics master in high school, and by then I was fourteen and it was too late. I stared at him in slightly hurt amazement, wondering what I had done wrong. Then I realised what it was. He was a *scientist*, and I regarded all scientists as being inferior to the arts side. Then I caught him out with a couple of sharp questions, and I knew that for all his years and degree, I was basically brighter than he was. We lived in an uneasy truce after that, and when he got the PE teacher pregnant and had to leave, my judgement of him was delightfully confirmed.

But the culmination of this upward academic spiral had come years before, at infant school. I have a grotesque memory, a memory so grotesque I sometimes wonder if it's another, and for once, lying dream. I seem to remember my beloved infant-school headmistress walking round the school with me, and telling everyone we met how highly intelligent I was. It struck me then it was a dicey thing to do, calculated to give me an enormous swollen head and make me pretty unpopular with my schoolmates. But it didn't make me an obnoxious bighead; contented and satisfied within, I hugged my genius to myself secretly and gleefully, and outwardly went very quiet, cooperative and willing to be nice and help other people. But then I've always found that success doesn't spoil people; *true* success makes the people I know nicer. It is failure that embitters. . . .

I write two kinds of books: realistic, earthy, comical books; and spooky books. And they really have no relationship to each other. Between Mrs. Spalding in *The Machine-Gunners* hopping to the shelter with her knickers round her ankles because a bomb has blown her off the toilet, and the extremely nasty monster of *The Creatures in the House* is a great and unbridgeable gulf fixed.

Grandfather Westall, age thirty-six, in Highland dress

And this gulf was created by the gulf between my two sets of grandparents. The Westalls were earthy; grandfather Westall was a wondrous and fabulous monster; a man of gigantic strength and passion. When his sixth child was born dead (as all the others were except my father—grandmother was rhesus negative in the days before anybody understood about such matters), he tore the massive cast-iron cooking stove from its mountings and threw it downstairs in his grief. He had volunteered to fight in the Great War although he was well over-age, and had been shell-shocked at Caparetto. My grandmother always kept a kettle of water heating on her kitchen range, and she had to be careful not to let it come to the boil, because then the steam would make the lid gently rattle, a noise exactly like that of a distant machine gun. This would be enough to set Granda off into one of his nightmares. At the end of his life, he always wore a black beret with two army badges, rather in the manner of the famous Field Marshall Montgomery. One badge was his own regiment's lamb-and-flag; the other he had taken from the body of an Austrian soldier he had killed in a bayonet fight. The nightmare consisted of the dead Austrian coming back and demanding his badge. But Granda was a jovial sociable man, when the nightmares weren't on him. He was often drunk, but held his drink like a gentleman. The only signs of drink were a tendency to sing old marching songs, a tendency to give me large and unsuitable presents of money (which were instantly confiscated and later returned to him by the rest of the family), and to burst out with self-invented rhymes like:

> The boy stood on the burning deck
> His feet were full of blisters
> His father stood in Guthrie's bar
> With the beer flowing down his whiskers

I stood in terror of him; but it was the enthralled, delighted terror of the giant in *Jack and the Beanstalk*. His love of German military bands, which played what he called "German music," the way that during the war, he every morning raised the Union Jack on his flagpole, in defiance of the German bombers, saluting it standing rigidly to attention . . . never a dull moment with Granda Westall.

His wife, my *beloved* grandmother about whom I am still constantly telling stories *ad nauseam* to this day, was a fitly Olympian mate. She was built like a tank, and would carry me about for miles till I was over three years old. In the First World War, she had tended the gasworks' engines that my father was later to repair so lovingly. She did everything with a fabulous definiteness. My mother's custard was disappointingly sloppy and runny; my grandmother's was so

Grandmother Westall, age thirty, in Highland dress

thick and solid you could have carved it with a knife and put it in sandwiches. She was the matron of a girls' school. The headmistress was a dragon, who sent her teachers about in fear and trembling and frequently reduced them to tears. When they were so reduced, they fled to Nana's kitchen, and she gave them a cup of tea and heard out their woes. Then she would take up arms on their behalf with the dragon-headmistress. These rows would usually end with Nana threatening to resign, which always somehow brought the dragon to heel. In the evening, Nana would announce with satisfaction, "I handed in my notice again today, but Tempy came off it." She had started life as a cook in a large house, and there was something of "Upstairs Downstairs" and Mrs. Bridges about Nana. She knew her place; but God help anybody who crossed her in that place. Had she been male, she would have been the kind of sergeant major that has held the British Army together for several hundred years.

And yet she was delightfully feminine. I have her photograph, taken when she was nineteen, and I am

more than half in love with it. Even in youth her body was muscular and powerful, but her face was beautiful. High broad cheekbones, almost Slavic; huge, bold, and utterly candid blue eyes, without a shadow of doubt or thought of deceit. I would have married her; any man in his senses would have married her; in her depth of strength, endurance, warmth and love, she was the ultimate earth-mother. She loved her wayward drunken giant with an invincible love. Once, coming home from drinking, he slipped up a back alley to relieve himself (a common habit in those crude Victorian days). A woman, coming out of her backyard gate, saw him, and instead of, as usual, turning her head away, she reported Granda to the police and had him arrested for indecent exposure. The moment my Nana heard this, she went to the woman's house and after a noisy episode reported by the neighbors, frogmarched the woman by the scruff of her neck down to the police station, where the good lady recanted and Granda was released without a stain on his character. All Nana said was, "Silly bitch—I was at school with her and she was a silly bitch then."

He led her a terrible dance, but when he died, she came to within an inch of dying from grief. Then she married again (a widowed Methodist lay-preacher who had admired her from a distance since girlhood) and lived on for another healthy twenty-eight years. I often

George Leggett, age fifty, "Ghost Grandfather in his days of prosperity, the master builder"

wonder what she made of her pious piano-playing, tee-totaling second husband—when he died, she grieved, but only in moderation.

She was always on my side; to be near her was perfect safety. She appears in several of my books.

So much for the earthy side. My other grandparents were the spooky side. Grandfather Leggett was dead before I was born; but his long sad face, with drooping moustache, balding head, and mournful blue eyes stared down from almost every wall of my aunt's house. He looked a little like a triste version of King Edward VII, and he had wined and dined the late King, as Master of the Freemasons of East Anglia, in the days of his prosperity.

Grandfather suffered the kind of Great Fall that seems to have happened far more often in Victorian times than it does now. He was a very prosperous master builder, who was foolish enough to guarantee a bond for a friend to the tune of £20,000 (about two million pounds in today's money). The faithless friend scarpered with the money, leaving grandfather penniless.

He was popular in Yarmouth where he lived; he had done a lot of good. Plenty of people offered to set him up in business again and tide him through the crisis. An earthier man would have accepted with thanks, and gone on to repair his fortune. But too-honourable grandfather saw his misfortune as a Disgrace. He packed his bags like Moses, and travelled to the foreign land of Tyneside, two hundred miles up the coast, where he took work as a humble carpenter. There, however, he was regarded as an objectionable foreigner. His tools were stolen and thrown in the river; they were recovered at low tide, rusting and useless. When my grandmother hung out her washing, the sheets were torn by the neighbours, smeared with unmentionable matter or simply stolen. Had the family been black, they could not have been treated worse. Heartbroken and demoralised, he remained a humble carpenter for the rest of his life.

My mother was born in the years of his exile; his consolation; his favourite. She would get up early to breakfast with him in the garden in summer, before he went to work; she adored him and—highly intelligent man that he was, and highly intelligent girl that she was—he became her university. She would often wish out loud that he had lived long enough to teach me his wisdom. (He died three years before I was born.)

I, on the other hand, little grabby brat that I was, had no desire to learn the lessons that this grandfather had to teach. This grandfather with his quixotic and unbelievable gift for snatching failure from the jaws of success had nothing I wanted to imbibe. I hated his

quoted sayings, like "Don't do as I do, do as I tell you," as I loved Nana's cheerfully phlegmatic "You'll swallow a peck of dirt before you die."

The moment of true horror came when my aunt had me into her bedroom one day and opened a drawer in her bedside table, to disclose emptiness, except for a small stony marble rolling around the bottom. I was rather into marbles at the time and this one looked grey-brown, grainy and unusual. I picked it up and fondled its smoothness lovingly, wondering, in the manner of the young with aunts, whether I could cadge it out of her, to use in the school playground Monday morning.

"That," she announced, "is the gallstone that killed your grandfather. They had to cut him open to get it out, and he died."

I dropped the marble as if it were red-hot; my aunt picked it up anxiously to make sure I hadn't chipped the relic, and returned it to its bed in a little box of cotton wool, rather as if it were a specially precious bird's egg.

That was the end of any relationship I ever had

Grandmother Leggett, "as she always was"

with Grandfather Leggett. But I could always feel his sad blue eyes yearning for me, on the back of my neck, whenever I went to my aunt's house. His immobile arms seemed to be on the point of reaching out to draw me into his own peculiar mix of honour, failure, persecution, and death. For all his brains (mother had a terrible way of saying, "You've got your grandfather's brains.") I knew my place lay with the gutsy and life-loving Westalls.

Gran, his widow, was a great lady in mourning for the rest of her life. She wore her widow's weeds till the day she died; they were also somehow the grand clothes of her heyday. Perhaps she'd had them dyed black for the funeral. In the photographs of the 1920s and 30s, my mother's skirts went up and down, her hats went from the cloches of the 1920s (like German soldiers' helmets of the First World War) to the wide-brimmed stetsons of the 30s. Grandmother Leggett never changed: buttoned black shoes, fur-collared black coat down to her ankles, and a huge black floppy hat covered with black cloth roses. She looks like an apparition in a photograph in one of those popular magazines that have titles like *The Unexplained*, and deal with ghostly grue.

She was gentle and unassuming, soft-voiced and never argued with her children, and I *loathed* her. She never took the slightest interest in me, whether I was brilliant or shocking. I think there was only one time she ever really noticed my existence. It was in the summer holidays, and I had spent all day building the most ambitious and amazing machine with my Meccano set. I had it in the middle of the hearth rug (and it was nearly three feet high) when she came ghosting in and put her foot straight on it, bending it very badly; so badly even my father was hard put to repair it. Not only did she fail to apologize, she actually blamed me for placing it there on purpose and with malice aforethought, to trip her up . . . I don't think I ever really spoke to her again, though she lived on five more years. Her only purpose in life seemed to be to live as long as possible. Her recipe for doing this was to take plenty of exercise and "eat hearty to keep your strength up." So she spent her days walking from daughter to daughter at a steady pace, and consuming large meals with gusto (and I seem to remember still wearing her hat and coat or at least her hat, while doing so).

She achieved longevity—she lived to be ninety. I was ever so glad that Nana, who was too busy enjoying life to care whether she lived or died, out-survived her by six years.

So there you have the two parts of me—the rumbustious Westalls, who lived not wisely but too well, and lived longest. And on the other side, Grandfather

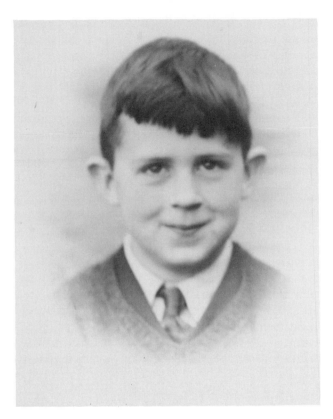

Robert Westall, Jr., age eight, "the 'wonder boy' as yet uncrushed by Mr. Barnett"

Leggett who seemed alive even though he was dead, and Grandmother Leggett who seemed to me to be dead while she had still many years to live. They are quite enough to account for my spooks, and I suppose I should be grateful.

I'm not.

The only Latin I remember from my schooldays is *facilis descensus Avernus*—easy is the descent into Hell.

I fell into Hell educationally when I was eight years old.

When my parents, in 1934, moved to the new Balkwell estate, they were not just looking forward to wide views over the countryside and going to fetch milk straight from the farm. They were also hopeful that they were getting me away from the old junior school in the town centre. And indeed, I spent three happy years at Collingwood Infants, which was modern, airy, and strong on open verandahs, green playing-fields, and pretty young teachers in flowered smocks.

What my parents hadn't realised is that I would move straight from Collingwood Infants to the dreaded Chirton Junior. Chirton stood among the urban slums my parents had escaped from. It looked like a prison, with a tall black perimeter wall, and Gothic windows placed so high up you couldn't look out on anything but Oscar Wilde's little patch of blue sky. Collingwood was built by a state that loved children; Chirton by a state that hated children. Collingwood's floors were shining parquet blocks; Chirton's put splinters of wood into your backside every time you had to sit down on them.

But Hell is not Hell without Satan; and Chirton's Satan was a man called Barnett.

"Bar-*nett*," he told us the first morning. "Remember—a *net* to catch you in." After that, he caned anybody who called him by the much more common name of Barnard.

But then, at Chirton, they caned for practically anything; as the top boy in the top stream, I was caned one stroke for each spelling mistake. Mind you, there were people working in this Hell who tried to help; after all, there were some people trying to help even in Buchenwald and Dachau. The mistresses who took the junior classes were tremblingly kind, when Mr. Barnett wasn't about. And even he couldn't be caning everybody in every class at once, but teacher and class listened together, shaking, for his footsteps in the corridor.

He would burst in; not much to look at. A tubby little man in a brown striped suit, always dapper and immaculate, with black hair smarmed down to a patent-leather skullcap with hair oil. It was the face that gave him away; red as a furnace for ordinary rage; the world threatened to come to an end when it turned white. Behind horn-rimmed spectacles, his eyes roved like homicidal black beetles. It was worst when his spectacles caught the light, and you couldn't tell whether he was looking at you or not.

We did not all suffer equally; we were divided into two camps. The kids from the new estate could be picked out by their highly polished shoes, longish well-brushed hair, and collars and ties. We suffered least; we might have parents who just might complain to the town council if Mr. Barnett went too far. On the average we were caned about once a week; some weeks we mightn't be caned at all. But to the slum kids, with their big heavy, unpolished boots, lavatory-brush hair cut short to avoid the growth of nits, and maroon jerseys done up at the neck with a single button—every day might bring a caning. Their parents would no more dream of complaining than of sailing on the *Queen Mary*. And even among the slum kids, Mr. Barnett had his particular daily chopping-blocks. Like Oswald Hagar. I remember the morning Oswald was dragged onto the school stage, just after the Lord's Prayer had been led by Mr. Barnett. Mr. Barnett told us that Oswald had killed a cat by tying stones round

its neck and throwing it into the river.

"Oswald Hagar killed an innocent defenceless, harmless cat," screamed Mr. Barnett, spitting so hard that a speck of his spittle settled on my cheek four rows back, and it burnt into my cheek as if it were acid and under those mad bulging black-beetle eyes I didn't dare wipe it away.

Then the mayhem started. It seemed to go on forever; but actually only until Oscar had been beaten into a screaming, foaming-at-the-mouth wreck who refused to stand up and be a man and take any more punishment.

I learned to be a coward; to hover in the middle of every group and keep my head down. All my creativity was channelled into not being caned by Mr. Barnett.

But I was not to be left in the middle of my group. Mr. Barnett had heard about me and my genius. Mr. Barnett did not get many pupils into the local grammar school on a scholarship. So he regarded me as the prize pig, the goose which was going to lay the golden egg. He would stop me in the corridor, his face creased into an expression that I think was meant to be joviality, and ask me how my work was going. . . . I began to work extremely hard, wishing desperately that I could have had the courage to do badly.

And as I climbed up the school, things got worse. He gave me a nickname, "Bold Bob." He tried to tell me jokes, which I had to laugh at. In the final year, I was appointed to the great post of Head Milk Monitor, which not only involved going round the classrooms with my daily orderbook, and seeing my sweating minions delivered the correct amount of milk, but actually getting the cashbook to balance and carrying the huge sack of large copper pennies to the local education office on Fridays. In the last few months, after I had honoured his school by duly getting the scholarship to grammar school, I was out of school half the time, delivering his "important letters."

I was much envied; nobody else was ever allowed through the concentration camp gates and there was I, a free man, free to buy a sarsparilla if I had the money, or spend ten minutes peering in toyshop windows in the middle of the morning. But all I could think of was, why was he singling me out? For God's sake, he was almost *fatherly* (he was married but had no children as far as we knew; God help them if he had). Once, when I got overheated after running too hard on an urgent errand, he held my wrists under a cold tap to cool me, and made me lie down on the horsehair-prickly couch in his office. It was creepy; and the more I had to pretend to reciprocate, the more he was making me into a creep. And yet I knew if I once rejected his care, I would face a holocaust worse than Oswald Hagar when he killed the cat. And all the time I was convinced Mr. Barnett was mad, as he twitched with evil rage and black hate, inside that most respectable pin-striped suit. And of course, I was quite unable to tell my parents, because I didn't know what was going on myself. But I got to hate myself more and more. I had to amaze him with my brilliance, constantly, and he was the one person in the world I did not wish to amaze.

And then I twigged what was going on, after the Second World War started, and I saw a newsreel of Hitler playing with his Alsatian dog, and laughing with it, and the dog loving him. Everybody, however mad, however evil, has got to believe that something loves him.

Mr. Barnett was Adolf Hitler in miniature, and I was the Alsatian dog.

It came to a head one morning in his office, while I was giving my correct account of the milk monies. Oswald Hagar and his elder sister Minnie came in late. They were late every morning; they were caned every morning. They were simply especially late that morning, so I was there to see it.

Oswald was already a weeping wreck, shaking from head to foot in anticipation. Minnie pleaded and pleaded to save him the beating. Blame her, she said, cane her. It was she who had wakened late, she who had failed Oswald. Their Mam never wakened up till noon (she was said by some to be the local lady of ill-repute).

Finally, Minnie turned and appealed to me. Wasn't it fair that Mr. Barnett cane her and spare Oscar? I wanted to join in. I wanted to tell dear Mr. Barnett exactly what I thought of him. I think he saw it coming . . . he was no fool. "That'll be all, Bold Bob," he said decisively.

And I turned and went. I have never forgiven myself. In all the years after I left, even when I was an undergraduate I would get these moods of mad rage when I would decide to go back and tell him exactly what I thought of him. But I was still deciding to go when I heard he'd died. He is with me to this day. Always, I am in a plot against those with power; always I am searching for their feet of clay; each one is Mr. Barnett. It doesn't matter what a man is the head of, a communist country or an English district council, the Anglican church or the CIA, Imperial Chemical Industries or the British Army. For a man to wish for, let alone to wield power, makes him evil at the root, to be dragged down from his seat if at all possible. Any man in authority is Mr. Barnett.

It has made a nonsense of my political life; I have voted for every possible party except the Communists; since I reached voting age I have never voted for the same party in two successive elections; always I am seeking the lesser of two evils.

It has left a mark on my writing too. My heroes are all fairly brilliant rebels and subversives. Only my heroines, oddly enough, make desperate efforts to hold my bookish worlds together; but then, when I was a child, all my female authority figures were rather nice, and usually pretty into the bargain. I finally killed off Mr. Barnett nastily, when I was fifty-five years old, in a ghost-story called *The Boys' Toilets*.

Tynemouth High School, which I reached at the age of eleven, was the Kingdom of Heaven. Oak-panelled walls, masters in swirling black gowns, a huge library and best of all, the great honour boards on the walls, stretching back into the remote past of the nineteenth century and stretching forward so that my own name might one day appear on them. Above all, learning for learning's sake. I began to learn about some incredibly ancient people who lived in Ur of the Chaldees, six thousand years ago. What they ate, how they built their houses, how they transported their timber on the Rivers Tigris and Euphrates. My wish to amaze grew no less, but a healthier wish to *know* joined it. I sensed dimly that a great gate was opening in my world that would lead me out from the little place where I was born and had lived till now, into a whole marvellous world of learning. There was even a master called Algie Harrow, and Harrow I knew was also the name of the second-best English public school. I almost felt myself on the portals of the greatest, Eton. . . . I had my troubles at Tynemouth High; I progressed with painful slowness from the fat boy who was hopeless at games to the ferociously muscled monster of the First Rugby XV, but I always felt at home, a fish deeply in water.

There was never any teacher again a hundredth part as mad or bad as Mr. Barnett. Some were a little grumpy; some were real sweeties, but only three men stand out. Only three men shaped and hewed me, and I still carry the mark of their chisels.

Major Joseph Smedley, war-time headmaster, a suitably Churchillian figure with his gown and coat open and his thumbs tucked, Churchill-wise, into his waistcoat pockets. We assumed he smoked huge cigars, but of course, only in private. He caned occasionally, but only for unmentionable thuggery in the toilets, which we all thoroughly approved of. His aim was to make us gentlemen, English gentlemen. He frequently addressed us as "Gentlemen!" When, in the upper sixth, I grew a massive moustache that for some reason drove the unlikeable Head of Biology into public tantrums, Joe had me in for a quiet chat in his study, and asked me to shave it off as a personal favour and for the honour of the school. The appeal worked; and I got my reward in my leaving testimonial, in which he called me "of gentlemanly bearing and manners." I found it the other day, and it almost brought tears to these very cynical hard-bitten eyes.

The best thing about Joe was that sometimes in assembly he would unbutton and talk to us like equals, about some aspect of the war, such as a tragic bombing or a small British victory. He warned us not to expect too much of life; not to count our chickens before they hatched.

"On the 17th of September 1917, my commanding officer on the western front said to me, 'Smedley, I'm putting you up for the Military Cross.' The next day came the great German offensive, and by noon the commanding officer was dead and I was a prisoner of war."

After I left, we corresponded occasionally until he died at the early age of sixty-three. In his last letter he wrote, "Pray for me that I might recover sufficiently to die at my desk in harness." Sadly, he never did. But if there is anything left of an honorable English gent in me, Joe Smedley put it there. If there is a sense of decency in my books, I owe it to him.

Stan Liddell, head of English, captain of the Tynemouth Home Guard, hero of my novel *The Machine-Gunners.* If Joe showed me decency, Stan showed me brilliance. Classical English good looks, the dead-straight nose, the strong jaw that would clamp decisively round a dirty old short pipe, and a moustache like Lord Kitchener's. He also had that raffish dowdiness that was the mark of his class. His was the first sportscoat I saw with leather elbow-patches and leather binding round the cuffs. (When *we* were allowed sportscoats instead of school uniform in the sixth, my mother had to sew cuffs and patches on a brand-new coat . . .) While teaching he would hitch up his faded pullover and stick his thumbs through his braces. He rode to school on the most oily and decrepit old black bike you could imagine, that had a basket on the handlebars and was clearly a relic from his Cambridge days. For he was a Cambridge man, and rumour had it that he had ruined a brilliant career "over some woman" which made him an even more romantic figure in our eyes. He has left his mark on my dress, to the despair of my wife; I have followed his dowdiness while never coming within a mile of matching his elegance. I simply look a shambles. And I judge people by their dress, the opposite way from which most people do. The more sartorially a shambles a man is, the more I take to him. If a man has to wrap himself in a three-hundred-pound suit, an expensive overcoat and a Jaguar car before he can show his face to the world, then he has some weakness he is hiding. Or so says the voice of my prejudice.

Stan had an intellectual arrogance that made him tremendously exciting; he would make some controversial statement, then challenge the brightest in the class to prove him wrong (having told us there was some flaw in his argument, if only we had the wit to find it). We would spend whole periods hurling ourselves at him, like a pack of hounds on some magnificent stag. He had no mercy; if we said something silly, he would send us flying, to the laughter of the rest of the class. We never really caught him out, but he taught me that getting on your feet and debating was the most exciting game in the world; the hours flew. He made me into a public speaker without fear, and has given me a taste for arguing about anything, that has lasted to the present day. One day he said to us that he knew the *inner* meaning of Coleridge's poem, the *Rime of the Ancient Mariner,* and asked us to guess it. We failed; the bell rang and he gathered up his books and swept out before he could tell us. We forgot to ask him next lesson, and we never did find out that inner meaning. But sometimes, when I lie awake before sleep, forty years later, I still try to work out what he must have meant. That's some mark he left on me.

He was the first person who told me I could become a real writer, if only I could stay "honest" long enough. I was thirty years working out what he meant by honesty.

Puggie Anderson was as humble a teacher as Stan Liddell was arrogant. He had crept, in late middle age, from the torment of a slum caning secondary school into the academic peace of the high school, and he had the half-crushed and grateful look of one who knows he has survived with his sanity intact by the skin of his teeth. He was given all the odds and bobs of lessons that other better-qualified teachers didn't want; he was a filler-up of the chinks in the timetable, of which any competent high school needs a couple. He was such a filler-in that we never worked out what he had taken his degree in. But he took sports lessons and library invigilation, and the first-years in almost any subject from physics to religious knowledge. And he took our sixth form for their discussion group in the last lesson on a Friday afternoon.

Puggie's strength in this discussion period was that he never said *anything.* He just sat with his head on his hand and *listened* to us in silence, smiling gently, as we ranted on in our noisy undisciplined way.

And then we noticed something. Sometimes he would give a little tiny nod. What could this little tiny nod mean? Did it mean he agreed with us? But he gave little tiny nods for Socialist points and little tiny nods for Tory points, and even the occasional tiny nod for a Communist point. (A good third of us were Communists at seventeen; when you are seventeen, being a Communist makes you feel strong and brave and forward-looking and uncompromising; it also has the delicious effect of sending your parents into gratifying hysterics. We are all Tory and SDP now.)

Anyway, it slowly dawned on us that the nod meant that we had made a *valid* and logical point. Puggie wasn't after politics; he was after logic and reason. In the same way, if we made a bad illogical point, a look of pursed disgust would drift across his face, as if he had suddenly swallowed a lemon. He would close his eyes and shake his head with an infinitely weary sadness that bore some resemblance to the look on the face of the crucifix in our church. We gathered that unreason and illogic caused Puggie actual physical pain.

And so, with him, we learned not just to shout our mutually contradictory prejudices at each other, but to actually confer together (if explosively) and come to voted conclusions. The most controversial motion we ever passed, in the victorious year of 1945, was that because of the bombing of Dresden and Hiroshima, Churchill and Truman should be put on trial as war criminals, alongside the Nazis at Nuremburg. I think at this point Puggie became a little alarmed at the logical Frankenstein's monster he had let loose on the world, but by then it was too late. One of our lot, Dennis Coe, actually became a Socialist member of Parliament; the rest of us have carried on our anarchistic subversion elsewhere, mainly in pubs, I would guess.

I think I was a bad writer, the worst kind of writer, from the time I could first hold a pencil. I wrote my first novel in the summer holidays when I was twelve. I wrote it because I had lost all my friends from Chirton School; when I went to the high school, they went off to the slum secondary modern, God help them. And the trouble with all my lovely new high school friends was that they lived about five miles away, in much posher houses than ours, and I was desperately shy. So in the boredom of the long holiday I wrote *The Mystery of Dead Man's Bay*. It was execrable. The police inspector got his first clue when the crooks dropped a *crate* of heroin on his foot . . . but it was 12,000 words long, and that showed early stamina if nothing else. In the loneliness of the four summer holidays that followed, I wrote four novels of increasing length and increasingly comprised of hopeless cliches borrowed from bad war movies and my parents' cowboy-novels. I wrote a novel about the Pacific War, but I couldn't bear to let the Japanese have the slightest victory, and in my novel, the Japanese war ended with the destruction of the entire Japanese army, navy, and

air force on Wake Island in 1942. Then the hero (the son of the victorious American commander) walked off happy-ever-after into the sunset, arm-in-arm with his teenage British girlfriend, presumably over a Mount Everest of Japanese corpses. In other words, I had been entrapped by the two classical snares of the teenage novelist, total self-indulgent wish-fulfillment and the re-use of a mass of cliches already third-hand and third-rate. I never dreamt of writing about my own life and times, as I regarded these as being so insufferably dull and boring that no one would want to read of them. Nevertheless, my last teenage novel was 45,000 words of well-spelt and well-punctuated prose, logically arranged in chapters and paragraphs. The matter was rubbish, but the manner was already there.

Then I discovered Tynemouth tennis courts; I invested in a second-hand racket and a second-hand bicycle, and suddenly I had a whole new social life. I didn't go to the homes of my posh friends, and therefore had no reason to invite them back to mine. At our tennis-courts social club we met, played, ate ice creams and drank soft drinks and did some early courting, winter and summer. As my social life increased, my life as a writer vanished to the point where even handing in my school essays became a painful chore. With a couple of exceptions, I stayed dead as a writer for another fourteen years.

The first exception sprang from my need, as ever, to amaze. In the summer holiday of 1948, our entire sixth form were invited to help turn a derelict, stately home fifty miles away into a new conference centre. We were all supposed to travel in a party by bus; but I had a new girlfriend in the party whom I wanted to massively impress, and I knew I couldn't do that by travelling with her in a bus full of yakking kids.

So I decided to ride there solo on my decrepit bicycle. Of course, the damned place happened to be at Otterburn, a hard uphill ride across wild and desolate moors where female taxidrivers had been known to be murdered by their last fare, and left to roast in their burning vehicles . . .

I spent one of the few sleepless nights of my life, pondering on the terror of disgrace. I hadn't ridden a distance anything like fifty miles for several years; it was steeply uphill all the way to the Scottish border at Carter Bar. Suppose my bike gave out; suppose my legs gave out? I had visions of being passed by the bus full of jeering kids, stuck at a crossroads with a collapsed wheel. Or plodding on foot across a moor— under the very eyes of my new and beautiful *inamorata*.

It was not to be borne; I got up at half past five and joined my father at breakfast as he got ready for the morning shift. We left the house together at ten to six. And for the first twenty miles I rode like a dancing dervish, head down, sweating, hair flogging in my eyes, seeing nothing. Then I looked at my watch. It was only seven, my bike had held together so far, my legs were hardly even aching, and I knew I was going to make it.

The whole world changed, as if a wizard had waved his wand; I realised it was the most beautiful morning, cool and sunlit. And I had it almost all to myself on an empty road; everybody else was still asleep. And I rode on more slowly taking in every detail: the wide fields of cut corn, with the stooks sending long shadows across the stubble; the pair of carthorses, looking over a gate, neighed at me and blew long dragonlike streams of steam from their nostrils into the cool air. The hiss of my tyres on the dew-jewelled road, the cobwebs hung with droplets in the sunlit hedges; the blackened colliers returning home on their equally black bicycles, who nodded how-do as if I was an equal. The whole world was mine, because there was no one else who wanted it at that particular moment. A layer of dull grey skin seemed to have been peeled off my eyes for the first time, and I marvelled at everything as if under a microscope. Everything seemed to pass slowly enough for me to enjoy it at leisure. Long before I read the *Centuries* of the mystic Thomas Trehearne, I shared that moment with him.

I had visualised arriving in Otterburn amidst cheers, in time for lunch; I actually arrived before nine, and was offered breakfast . . . everybody, staff as well as students, was deeply impressed. The week, and my relationship with Doreen, got off to a flying start.

Within a month, I was in educational hell again; I had started at the local university at Newcastle to read Fine Art. From being a pretty big fish in a very small pond of 500 kids, I was a minnow in a university of 3,500, all of whom knew exactly where they were going and what they were doing, except me. It felt like a huge education factory, in which for three days I was kept queueing, being interviewed, being addressed in endless streams of jargon by total strangers I never saw again, and pressure-sold things I didn't want, like joining the Officer Cadet Force. In the art school, they had no time for my fancy artistic ideas; day after day I drew the outlines of bottles and, worse, the shapes between the bottles. Three professors prowled round behind our bent backs, sighing and tutting at our incompetence and making very rude remarks to each other . . . from wanting to impress, I was battling to survive. They threw people out without warning, if one line was put wrong . . . they didn't bother to explain the purpose of what we were doing; we were supposed to work it out for ourselves. One girl fainted from the intensity of this emotional pressure cooker; one ran out screaming and never returned. I just kept my head down dully, and went home every night in black rage, and terror of letting down my parents who could no longer help me in this new hell, but who implicitly trusted me to be my usual genius.

This particular night, I got to the bus station in the darkness and pouring rain, and looked up and saw a bus pass with the glowing sign "OTTERBURN."

A wave of bitterness flooded over me like I had never known. How could the world be so treacherous, so wonderful one minute and dreadful the next? And then I decided I would show up this treacherous world for what it was, as a warning to other poor souls like myself. I went home and wrote non-stop for three hours, and I called it *Two Roads to Otterburn*. And in my rage and pain, I captured both the wonder of that particular morning and the horror of that particular evening. It was only published in the "Old Students Section" of our school magazine, but when I next saw Stan Liddell he said "You'll make a writer—if you go on writing honestly about what you *know*."

But I was much too busy carving funny shapes in stone and plaster; stone and plaster were my whole delight, until an evening in 1956, seven years later.

That night again, my emotions peaked. I was a postgrad at the University of London now, still carving funny shapes. But Russia had invaded Hungary, Israel was invading Egypt, the British had landed in the Suez Canal Zone, and Russia was threatening to go to war with us over it. All that day I'd been patting at my clay model in a feeble and pointless way, while we all discussed the coming war. One lad had signed up with some recruiting agency to go and fight in Hungary against the Russians; our gentle Jew had signed up to go and fight for Israel. I, fresh out of doing my National Service with the British Army, was expecting any moment to be called back. I kept on trying to remember bits of my training as an officer cadet. "Actions to take if a Bren machine gun jams," and "The Infantry platoon in attack." I could remember nothing coherently; I knew if the war came I wouldn't last five minutes.

Again, I rode home by bus in the dark and rain. I got off at Westminster Abbey. A street light was shining through the high iron railings onto the lawns within.

The lawns were covered with little tiny white crosses that shimmered in a ghostly way in the lamplight, all the way up to the abbey itself. It was two days before Remembrance Sunday, and the dead of two World Wars had come back to join, or warn, us. I leaned against the railings and thought dully,

"Oh, God, does it *have* to happen again?"

Then a voice spoke up behind me, and I turned to see a bearded Portuguese sculptor I worked with. He said, "We're doing a peaceful torchlight procession past the Russian Embassy, to protest about Hungary. Come and join us."

There were ten thousand students in that procession, and we passed through the West End in an endless silent column. I remember looking up and seeing a wealthy woman standing out on her first floor balcony, holding up her three-year-old son so he could watch. I suddenly had a vision of us, as seen through the three-year-old's eyes, the wet shining street, the long dark silent column, the flickering torches, and I thought, "For him we will be part of history; he will tell his grandchildren about seeing us when he is a very old man."

The procession processed peacefully, and we heard a moving and liberal speech. Then the well-meaning liberal organiser asked us through a loud-speaker mounted on a van to complete our dignified protest by dispersing peaceably. I thought at the time he seemed rather nervous; I remember wondering why.

Then somebody shouted, "To the Russian Embassy!" and in a minute ten thousand people were running blindly, a mob. I suppose we got there because the first person to run knew the way back; nobody else did. Our mood was utterly changed, by a solitary shout. But what was our new mood? Partly, like children, we didn't want the party to end; we wanted more fun. Secondly, we enjoyed being 10,000 strong and didn't want to break up. But mainly, we wanted to make some Russians *very* afraid, as they had made the Hungarians very afraid. I don't think we meant any real harm or damage; but we had this picture of the Russian ambassador cowering behind closed shutters with his staff, white-faced and mumbling prayers, as the sound of our roar echoed.

In any case, the police were there before us, a solid band four-deep across the end of the road. This baffled us immensely. How did they know we were going to attack the Russian Embassy; we hadn't known ourselves ten minutes ago!

I stared at the silent disciplined ranks of coppers with mixed feelings; they had three burly superintendents in front of them, grand in a mass of silver rank-badges and carrying long swagger sticks. Until now, policemen had been my friends; they told you the time, or how to get to places, or showed you across the road when you were small. And though they looked disciplined and silent and impressive, there weren't very many of them. Two hundred to our ten thousand. I felt sorry for them; they were only doing their job. . . .

Then somebody raised a Hungarian flag, and that did it. We hurled ourselves upon the policemen with about as much fury as a crowd elbowing to get aboard a tube train in the rush hour. I swear some of us said, "Excuse me, officer," and apologized for standing on their feet. In the end, it was a kind of rugby scrum of civilised pushing. In between, we rested and talked to the police in a mutually shy way. We asked them if they were getting paid overtime; they replied that they'd much rather be home watching telly. We offered them cigarettes and sweets. It was a very British occasion.

But we did break their ranks twice; twice we got six blokes into the embassy garden, over the high wall. There, being decent English chaps, they hadn't a clue what they wanted to do. They stood and waved to us, and we cheered them wildly. Then the police came and arrested them, and they went away quietly, to more cheers. It might have ended in this good-humoured way, if the superintendents hadn't put the mounted police in to break us up; perhaps they were tired of paying their constables overtime; perhaps there was something *they* wanted to watch on telly.

Mounted police always change the mood. Mounted police are thoroughgoing hateworthy bastards. They push the sides of their horses into your face. They rear their horses' hoofs above your head. From humour, we charged in a second to blind fury. A police horse stood on my foot; all ten hundred weights of him. I punched his belly in agony and fury. He was replaced by a huge superintendent, with a face puce with rage who said, "Touch that horse again, lad, and I'll put you inside."

I screamed back, "When the revolution comes, I'll see you're the first to go." And I meant it; I'd have hanged him from the nearest lamppost at that point; if I'd had a gun I would have shot him. That's what police horses do to you.

It seems ironic, in restrospect, that while I was threatening the Red Revolution, I was actually attacking the Russian Embassy. . . .

Anyway, in the end they broke us up, but not until a police horse had shoved its backside through the window of an expensive dress shop and its rider emerged draped in the latest Paris fashion . . . the horses harried us all the way to the tube station, and we had to fight to the end to protect the girls from harm.

I got home after midnight; my flat was silent, but I was much too worked up to sleep. I imagined all the newspapers printing the story, the police and government version of the story, blackening the names of the naughty students and making us seem like silly children who had misbehaved at a party. Why should *they* have a monopoly of the news?

I sat down and wrote till four in the morning;

exactly how it had been for us. Four thousand words longhand. Then I walked out into the dawn and posted it to my home newspaper, the *Newcastle Journal.*

A week later, my mother wrote to ask when I was being sent to prison; but you could tell the old bird was pleased really; I'd amazed her again. The *Newcastle Journal* had printed the whole thing. Three weeks later, they sent me a cheque for three guineas without a word. That was the first bit of professional writing I ever had published. But I wasn't to publish again for five years; it was just that once again, a moment, a happening, a mood had grabbed the writer in me by the scruff of the neck. If such things had happened to me daily, I might have become a Tolstoy.

My life moved on; I finished my postgrad degree, took up teaching art in a tough inner-city school in Birmingham, got married, got a better job in Yorkshire. In 1960 my son was born, and I moved to Cheshire as Head of Art in a 400-year-old grammar school. Writing couldn't have been further from my mind. I spent the summer holiday of 1961 laying crazy-paving paths all over the garden of my new house. Six weeks doing nothing but handling stones and mixing concrete! Such a waste of creative time seems appalling to me now; I suppose it *was* creative in a way; I was proud of it when I'd finished. But the writing had simply ceased to exist.

It came back to life one day in 1963. I went into the public library, and there was an exhibition of abstract paintings by a young engineer who had tired of building concrete structures and given up all for art. This touched me; besides, the pictures were rather good and very cheap. On an impulse, I walked into the local newspaper office and asked the editor to give the young man a break with publicity. He said, "OK, but nobody knows damn-all about art in this office. You're an art teacher, you write about it."

He paid me two guineas for it, it was well-received, and the young engineer sold half his pictures. Afterwards the editor, Geoff Moore, asked me to write a regular art review. I owe a lot to Geoff; he was a real old-time local editor who lived at his battered typewriter. He used to lean his elbows on it while he talked to you. He had round grooves in his elbow bones that fitted exactly into the frame of his typewriter. Talking on the phone he yelled so hard you learnt to hold the earpiece well away from your ear, to avoid damaging your eardrums.

Geoff taught me brevity, to explain abstract art to the ordinary man-in-the-street in 500 words and not one more (otherwise Geoff would cut my stuff in the most unfortunate places) honed my writing to a razor-edge. I learnt never to use a long word when a short

one would do. I had never been at all a difficult or obscure writer; now all my drive was to connect with the ordinary Joe as efficiently as possible. As the years went by, I spread my wings gently; articles on new public buildings; articles on good old buildings threatened by redevelopment (I managed to save one splendid Regency workhouse from demolition). Then work for magazines—architectural profiles of small towns mainly, with the odd human interest in-depth profile. I spent a while as the northern art-critic of the national *Guardian,* and wrote antiques articles for the national magazine *Homes and Gardens.* As a journalist I learnt to write crisply, interestingly, and even amusingly,—I think as a journalist I became a real pro.

As a novelist, when I began writing novels again, I remained a complete idiot, totally self-indulgent and writing in third-hand cliches about things I neither knew nor understood. I still have, in school exercise books, the tale of an Anglo-Saxon princess travelling through seventh-century England to get married. After 90,000 words of rubbish, she still hadn't reached her husband-to-be. I was later to while away long railway journeys with my son by reading him extracts; it was so comically dreadful that tears of laughter used to stream down his face.

Christopher Westall, about twelve years old

I might have gone on writing trash forever, but for something that happened as his twelfth birthday approached. We had been very close until, one morning in the holidays, a strange group of three boys appeared at our back door. I opened it. The boy at the front was amiable enough; but he had that air of authority and dignity that one sometimes sees in African tribal chiefs. The two other boys stood back at a respectful distance, not from me, but from him. They were obviously followers; even more obviously an escort or bodyguard. The chieftain enquired politely whether my son was in. I called Chris, and the moment he saw this boy, he went berserk. He just grabbed his anorak and left with him, deaf to enquiries as to where he was going, or reminders that lunch was at one and our whole family were going to town that afternoon . . . My wife and I were left with the uncomfortable feeling that we had ceased to exist . . . Christopher was about to be initiated into a gang.

Now do not get me wrong; this was not some dangerous and hooligan gang. I suppose "tribe" would be a better word. Someone has said that childhood is the last primitive tribe that has not yet been conquered by civilisation, and that fits the bill uncannily. In England such tribes find a vacant lot on the fringe of civilisation; it must have no current occupant. An old overgrown garden or derelict allotment is best, with as much tree cover as possible. Here, they build a camp, or rather a house, of hardboard or corrugated iron, filched from rubbish-tips or abandoned buildings; they are not so much thieves as snappers-up of unconsidered trifles such as bricks and sand from building sites.

Here, in the summer, the tribe lives, usually eight to ten strong; it marks out the boundaries of its territory, and is acutely aware of, and usually at war with, the neighbouring tribes. Weapons are bizarre, but not particularly lethal; sticks with nails in, bags of very wet mud or flour, water-bombs. The purpose is to pillage and destroy the enemy camp, and drag away the booty. Frankly, I don't know what they'd find to do, if it wasn't for this warfare, since much of their time is spent rebuilding ravaged camps.

I would never have got to know all this, except that my son's camp had trouble with a persistently leaking roof. The gang leader had read my architectural articles in the local paper, and after a great discussion, my son was sent to invite me to report to the gang headquarters.

I'll never forget approaching the territory at the prescribed hour. I was spotted far-off by a scout up a tree, who went racing off into the dense undergrowth. The chief appeared with two spear carriers, and I was escorted up to the well-hidden camp, feeling like a mixture between a hostage and a visiting ambassador.

Fortunately I managed to spot the cause of the leak swiftly—they had over-lapped their sheets of corrugated-iron wrongly. (Had I failed, I am certain my son would never have spoken to me again.) Afterwards, I was invited into the camp for a cup of rather weak tea, boiled over an open fire. The interior was scrupulously tidy, and hilariously bourgeois—pink armchairs thieved from a tip, a battered washing-up rack and even a battered black-and-white television in pride of place. There was actually a roster of housework, willingly done, though the idea of any of them lifting a paw to help at home would have been risible.

The mixture of bourgeois surroundings mixed with utterly alien tribal coldness (even on the part of my son), can only be likened to that well-known photograph of the tamed Apache chief Geronimo sitting in a Model-T Ford, in his full tribal regalia. It would have been fatally easy to laugh; but had I not kept a perfectly straight face, I would have been banished into outer darkness forever.

As it was, I was awarded honorary tribal membership, and my son was allowed to tell me all the secrets of the gang; otherwise he would have been sworn to a secrecy nothing would have broken. One of the gang had been frequently beaten by his father, in an attempt to find the camp's whereabouts, and had taken all his punishment tight-lipped as an Apache under torture.

I learnt about their tribal laws—they spent nearly as much time law-making as camp-building, and even imported a sixteen-year old, paying him to act as an impartial judge. Punishments were graded from mild to severe, the worst being permanent expulsion from the gang; rather a dreadful punishment as the pariah was left exposed to the brutalities of all the surrounding gangs.

It was after all this that I began my own journey in memory back to the time when I was twelve, in World War II. I wanted to share childhoods with my son. Memories began to surface. A friend said, "Why does the smell of burning kerosene make me feel safe?" and that carried me straight back to the air-raid shelters of my youth. Another time, after a particularly violent TV war-movie, I went to sleep and dreamt, and wakening, said to my wife, "My war wasn't fought with tanks and planes and guns—my war was fought by old men and women and kids." But I couldn't remember the content of the dream.

And then suddenly, the whole time that I was twelve came back to me in one great surge of memory. The smells, the fears, what we ate . . . total recall. And I began to write my first published novel *The Machine-Gunners*. Only it wasn't a literary activity, it was a social activity. I wrote it in longhand, in school exercise-books, and only intended to read it to my son. It was

Robert Westall, about 1974

my gift to him, at the age he had reached; the age when boys in primitive tribes are initiated; the time when Jewish boys have their bar mitzvah. I read him the chapters as soon as I had written them, at Sunday teatime. He was the most savage of critics—if a part bored him he'd pick up a magazine and start reading that instead. The parts that bored him, I crossed out, which is perhaps what gives the book its pace. But I had no thought of trying for publication. After we had finished reading the book out loud, I threw it into a drawer, where it gathered dust for nearly two years. It is, I suppose, ironical that a book written solely for one boy has sold over a million copies.

There is really very little more to tell; since then, it has simply been doing more of the same—it is the story of everyday, and writers' everydays are not thrilling at all—much less than those of pilots or deep-sea divers.

BIBLIOGRAPHY

FOR YOUNG ADULTS

Fiction:

The Machine-Gunners. London: Macmillan, 1975; New York: Greenwillow, 1976.

The Wind Eye. London: Macmillan, 1976; New York: Greenwillow, 1977.

The Watch House. London: Macmillan, 1977; New York: Greenwillow, 1977.

The Devil on the Road. London: Macmillan, 1978; New York: Greenwillow, 1979.

Fathom Five. London: Macmillan, 1979; New York: Greenwillow, 1980.

The Scarecrows. London: Chatto & Windus, 1981; New York: Greenwillow, 1981.

Break of Dark. London: Chatto & Windus, 1982; New York: Greenwillow, 1982.

The Creatures in the House. London: Macmillan, 1983.

Futuretrack Five. Harmondsworth: Kestrel, 1983; New York: Greenwillow, 1983.

The Haunting of Chas McGill, and Other Stories. London: Macmillan, 1983; New York: Greenwillow, 1983.

The Cats of Seroster. London: Macmillan, 1984; New York: Greenwillow, 1984.

The Children of the Blitz: Memories of Wartime Childhood. London: Viking, 1985.

Herbert S. Zim

1909-

ZIM ON ZIM

Monday morning, and the Long Island local to New York was late again! Even before I reached the High School of Commerce, I saw the assistant principal at the door, checking in latecomers. I was a chronic offender. But his "Late again, Zim" came with a smile. He went right on: "Your article yesterday was good, yes, very good." My murmured reply was lost as I started up the stairs to my fourth-floor French class. By floor two I began to understand his greeting, and by floor three, the pieces were falling into place.

About a year earlier, I spotted a notice in the *New York World* (a morning paper long since defunct) inviting readers to a walk Saturday afternoon in Prospect Park, guided by J. Otis Swift. I found twenty or so others at the park's Botanic Gardens, where we learned Swift's story. As an aging city reporter, he felt more and more that New York was the end of the line for people who had once known and loved the farm or the country. He was sure they might be refreshed and renewed by a touch of nature. His editor blessed the idea, and thus I found myself on the second of such walks through the green spots in and near New York. These continued for several years.

Before I was twelve, I was wandering afield, searching and collecting. Scouting awards for birding and the like were my goal. At summer scout camp they liked me enough to invite me back the next summer as a junior member of the staff. At sixteen I was already deep into natural history. A year later, invited to work at a settlement house with the summer program of the Child Study Association, I took East Side boys to a city-run garden patch in an East River park and on trips to explore the wilder parts of the Bronx or Queens. This play-school summer gave me experience and fun.

By the time I met J. Otis Swift, I knew a fair amount about birds, trees, flowers, rocks, and the like. Swift recognized this and kept me right at his side during the weekend walks. His forte was country life and customs, steeped in a humanistic philosophy with religious overtones. He needed my quick response on the names of flowers, uses of trees or the feeding habits of the chickadee or warbler we spotted. By winter, I was with him every Saturday and Sunday, helping and learning at the same time. That year I was a high-

Zim, about 1917

school senior.

Then, in late November, an urgent message reached me from the *New York World*. Swift had pneumonia and was in the hospital. Would I lead the weekend trips for him? I would. And would I send them some notes for the regular report of the trips that appeared every Sunday? I could and did. Sunday night, after the trip, my typewriter was busy, and unconsciously following Swift's style, I wrote of the walk, the weather, the highlights, and plans for the walks in the week ahead. The report was mailed. I thought no more about it.

School work was waiting. Since Swift was still out, I planned more trips for the Yosians, as they were called, trying to find easy-to-reach places where they

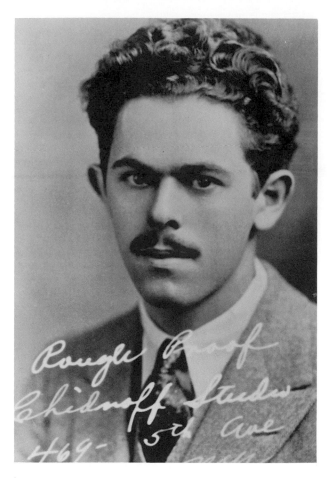

*Herbert S. Zim, age sixteen, high-school senior
and published writer*

and I would feel at home. Back late from the next Sunday hike, I missed the paper, but guessed I might be mentioned in the published report. The *World* did even better. My report was published just as I had put it down, and with a byline. So were the next three that I sent before Swift recovered, and each week, from the *World,* came a check for five dollars.

The first report was the one that the assistant principal had read. At school I became a phenomenon. Even the front office accepted my lateness. It came about as my father, mother, and younger brother left to return to California early that fall. I urged my parents to let me stay until I finished the term. As a senior, due to graduate in January, I was happy with school, with the Yosians, and with Sonia, a girl my age who regularly joined the trips. An uncle in Long Beach offered me a home with his two younger boys. Then my daily train trip to the school started, and so did my record-breaking lateness.

Another incident marked these last school days. Sunnie, as Sonia preferred to be called, was already

working at Pocket Books, a publisher of a series of low-cost popular books. She was finishing high school at night. Her work gave her a choice of defective copies that were returned. With these, I rapidly built up a fine library of damaged Pocket Books. They fitted, row after row, in the small wooden prune boxes that came my way as local grocers threw them out. My reading, with Sunnie's prodding, led me into enticing areas outside the world of nature. Those were happy days.

I was attracted to biography, history, travel, sociology, and education. Pocket Books furnished the content. As my senior term continued, I picked up and read with interest *Education and the Good Life,* by Bertrand Russell. Without a single question I absorbed everything this philosopher had to say about the weaknesses of modern schooling. So when my turn came to make a five-minute speech in the required senior course in elocution, I was ready. This short course aimed to make each graduating senior vocal enough to survive a five-minute job interview.

With my Yosian and play-school experience, speaking was old-hat to me. So when my turn came, I rose and explained, in an overtime five minutes, just what was wrong with American education. This startling topic set well with my astonished teacher, and the faculty knew all about it before the day was over. My place in the school was secure.

I already had a ticket to Los Angeles, a long way by boat, via the Panama Canal. The boat left five days before graduation. I was aboard with my diploma and a small cage of my pet snakes. En route, I indiscreetly took my pets up for an airing. The purser, accepting my story of how harmless they were, insisted that animals, any animals, were taboo in the cabin. My snakes, all three, would be safe with him. They were, for I visited them daily. But this story was passed on to local papers, and even before I landed my parents had seen a brief back-page story of the young naturalist who was bringing a collection of rare snakes to Los Angeles. All these exciting five or six years set my life pattern.

Los Angeles was a disappointment. School had already started. My Commerce diploma did not cover all the courses needed for college entrance. My body soaked in the warmth of the California sun, but each day I missed New York more. The final weeks at school were fresh in my mind, so was the glorious Yosian send-off party. And there was Sunnie, too. She wrote and I wrote. New York seemed further and further away.

As spring came, I saw in my mind's eye marsh marigolds, tender red maple leaves, the returning warblers, and Sunnie. A classified ad in the *Los Angeles Times* listed a car going east that would take paying passengers. I settled for thirty dollars and a quarter of the gas costs. Five of us filled the car, and off we went.

The car, an open touring model, headed east on the new and famous Lincoln Highway that went all the way across the United States. Most of it, west of the Mississippi, was unpaved. Yellow adobe dust flooded the car, making stops to clean the windshield an hourly chore. Ten days later, we crossed the Twenty-third Street ferry into New York. A night at the "Y," a call to Sunnie, and a search for a room all started together. On upper Madison Avenue, a room was vacant, and I moved in. Scanning the papers for a job took precedence. Within a week, I had a place in a West Side hospital, as laboratory boy for a physiologist studying thyroid and parathyroid glands. I washed beakers and test tubes, prepared media, preserved specimens, and ran the autoclave. There was still some time for the Yosians. I went on Torrey Botanical field trips, and those of other scientific societies. Sunnie joined me. Evenings were tied up with make-up high-school courses.

My walks with nature groups led to interesting opportunities. I was asked if I would lead hikes for a youth group that met for weekends on a farm not far from the city. I found the adolescent youngsters bright and interested. Besides our nature hikes, they had a craft program which Sunnie and I joined and enjoyed. The instructor passed on word of an opening in a private school. That interested me, and off I went to be interviewed by Julia Newman, the principal, who asked me to teach a class. In her office, when I finished, she asked, "What do you think of your presentation?" I replied, "It was awful," which it was. Used to working in the field, I gave attention to whatever presented itself, and for that, no organization or planning was possible. A classroom, I discovered, was very different.

My frankness and her need for a part-time science teacher led to a trial, and for two years I worked at the Brooklyn Ethical Culture School, with elementary students. There I got a feeling for what was soon to be called "Progressive Education." Meanwhile, I was catching up with my education. A year at an evening high school gave me an academic diploma that opened the doors of New York City College. Working out a tight program, I continued my schooling as I did my teaching. The New York City examination for laboratory assistant came next, and my passing it gave me status as well as a job opportunity.

My first college program was loaded with French and German. Since I was poor in both, it was a disaster. That semester, the college gave students the Army Alpha test, an early attempt at measurement of intelligence. My exceedingly high score was announced as I

Zim (with hat) leading a geology field trip, early 1930s

flunked out. The president of the college called me in for an explanation, but could only urge me to try harder.

My laboratory license gave me another card to play. As a certified teacher, I could take courses at Hunter College, so I enrolled both in City College (limited only to repeat French and German) and in Hunter College to take courses I wanted to enjoy. In addition, I was hard at work in an experimental branch of the New York Ethical Culture School. John Dewey had a special interest in this little school, and I took over the embryo science program from his son, Sabino Dewey, which meant leaving Brooklyn.

This complex program had another ingredient. I was starting to write papers for educational journals and articles on popular aspects of science for magazines. In the forties and fifties, these totalled about thirty, plus several pamphlets on science and science teaching.

The papers written about my experimental programs and on phases of my beginning research were in journals that only those working in education would read. Or they were presented as reports at meetings that only educators attended. Not many people heard or read what I had to say.

Articles for magazines reached a much larger group. Besides, I was free to let some particular thing or action catch my eye and entice me to round out a story or add an explanation. When Ernie Pyle, the famed war correspondent, was killed on the battlefield, papers reported that he felt that sooner or later there was a bullet intended for him, and that his chances were running out. This suggested that I write an article on the laws of chance and how they might apply on the battlefield. Other events of the war period opened the way for other articles on health, medicine, flight, and rockets.

Earlier in this period, the experimental Ethical Culture Branch School was scheduled to move into a new building in Riverdale, and to become the Fieldston Lower School. I suggested, and then helped plan, a science laboratory for young pupils, based on the program we already had underway. The laboratory was built, and some time later, it was recognized as the first elementary-science laboratory. By now, over two years of teaching experience made me eligible to enter Teachers College at Columbia University.

This put me into a five ring circus: (1) teaching lower-school elementary science; (2) teaching high-school biology and general science under the patient and inspiring Dr. Henry Kelly; (3) evening courses at Hunter College, having worked out a program that fitted Teachers College into late afternoon; (4) finding time to spend with Sunnie by scheduling our Hunter College courses and supper on the same evenings; (5) finally, my master's thesis on *New Techniques in Laboratory Biology* paved the way for an invitation to join the Committee on Adolescents and the Science Committee, both functioning as part of the Eight Year Study in which Fieldston High School played an important role.

Other scheduled commitments were often pushed aside for my enriched research program which addressed questions on the science interests of adolescents and on the activities of science-talented students. To balance this, a number of recognized scientists were asked to recall at what age and with what activities they started toward a career in science. All this, when pulled together, yielded a Ph.D. in science education. *Science Interests and Activities of Adolescents* was published in 1940. The data pointed out areas of interest and concern of young people, which led to the writing of scores of books, and to more pioneer work in science education.

That opportunity soon appeared. Dr. V. T. Thayer, who headed the Ethical Culture Schools, asked me to move down to the main building at Sixty-fourth Street and Central Park West, which had started as The Workingman's School in the late 1800s. The pioneer idea of educating the hand and the mind together stimulated a trend towards a "hands-on" education. However, through several decades, that program of studies, based on ideas of Felix Adler, had moved into set patterns. A new and stimulating direction was needed. Science was a good place to begin.

Early efforts toward sex education had begun at Fieldston Lower, but the senior teachers at the elementary school felt there was no real need for this. They were confident that their students were too young. The opinion of those in science and medicine, plus my own research, showed a strong interest and need for such a program.

We did agree that a cooperating class teacher and I could go ahead with care, caution, and the cooperation of the school's Dr. Beck. Based on fifth-grade experience with animals in school and on a farm, that class moved into a study of all mammals, diverse in form, but all with a common core of anatomy and physiology that sets off mammals as an advanced group. We explored the mammal skeletons, hearts, brains, skin, and finally, without any change of pace, worked into reproduction, with considerable attention to ourselves.

This was an experimental program on which I was keeping detailed notes. Looking at them one evening, Sunnie (already Mrs. Zim for some years) suggested that the study might make a book for all younger readers. With her persistence and editorial help, the manuscript moved along. I came up with the title *We the Mammals* and had the manuscript typed. Sunnie passed a copy around to children's editors she knew. A number sent back appreciative comments, but none sent a contract.

Sunnie was now with Simon and Schuster, and there sought out Clifton Fadiman for an opinion. This well-established editor and author read the manuscript on the train going home that evening. He tried some of it on his own young boys, and reflected their enthusiasm in a written report. Next to see the manuscript was Elizabeth Hamilton at Harcourt, Brace. She took the book on and made only one change—the title. Acknowledging a more famous book of that period, it became *Mice, Men, and Elephants,* and it remained in print for some forty years. After several years of writing articles and reports, this was my start in writing books.

Two other Harcourt books, *Rocks and Minerals* and *Plants* also evolved from school projects, reflecting some student participation.

In between were other titles, stimulated by World

War II, as our American role steadily increased. *Submarines* was almost finished when Pearl Harbor was attacked, and the previously cooperative Navy shut the door on further help.

Later I wrote *Air Navigation, Man in the Air,* and finally *Rockets and Jets* at a time when the bazooka was starting as a common weapon. The "rocket's red glare" of September 1814 came from a simple program of rocket use. Yet within a year or so of my book, rockets adapted to warfare became so common that a large Armed Forces edition of my book was distributed to soldiers and sailors.

Meanwhile, I had begun, with William Morrow and Company some very simple books for younger readers—*Elephants, Goldfish,* and *Rabbits.* All had started from classroom interest. Then from an unusual classroom problem came a new and exciting book, *Codes and Secret Writing.* A teacher had intercepted notes passed by boys, written in a "secret" code. She was a bit worried about the contents, but soon agreed on a possible educational use which could emerge. The boys took over this study, insisting it be kept secret from the girls, who didn't seem to care. I agreed, and even suggested that, by working hard, they might invent a code that even their teacher couldn't decipher. That did the trick. First the boys invented and tried their own codes. Some began to look for ways to make codes more secure. They probed the structure of the English alphabet and the letter frequency in English words and texts.

About a dozen boys worked up codes easy to construct, but difficult to break. They reinforced their codes by using invisible inks made in the laboratory. *Codes and Secret Writing* was a shared project, which duly acknowledged the help of the boys.

But by the time *Rockets and Jets* was finished I had enough of the Pentagon. Our group of top educators was trying to develop educational materials that would help high-school boys who were moving rapidly from school into uniform. We outlined high-school programs in radio, map reading, and other subjects that could contribute to nonmilitary skills which the Armed Forces needed.

Events of the war were moving too fast, and our well-meaning program was soon ignored in army classification and training. As this continued, I resigned from the Pre-Induction Training Division and returned to New York. Soon I was called by my draft board. I registered as a conscientious objector—one opposed to all war. The man in charge listened to my statement, raised pertinent questions, and asked me to return. We talked further. When their decision came, it granted my request. I was assigned to a Civilian Public

Service camp in the Blue Ridge Mountains that form the backbone of Shenandoah National Park. My father and mother moved into our Port Washington, Long Island home, to help Sunnie with our two young sons.

By now, I was thirty-five years old. Early on, I developed three major interests that gave me the most enjoyment. First was the natural sciences, which spread my attention through all the groups of plants, animals, rocks, and minerals, out to the stars and planets. Next came my interest in teaching. With an early start, I found youngsters both a challenge and a delight. Lastly, writing began to occupy more time, and with eight books in print by 1946, I found my two other interests supporting and fused into this one. My teaching experience alerted an awareness of the importance of the student's or reader's interest as a place to begin, and an indication of how far to go. Further, there was a relationship (now well recognized through ecology) so deep that an interest in any single phase of nature soon pulled in others, and new points of view.

My work in Civilian Public Service placed me at the Headquarters of Shenandoah National Park, where I assisted the park forester. There were also other tasks which made my service meaningful. Later, I transferred to the Patuxent Refuge of the U.S. Fish and Wildlife Service near Washington, D.C. There, joining a well-trained team.

I learned that the Fish and Wildlife Service, as part of its research program, had helped to develop a new and potent poison known by its code number—1080. This seemed an ideal way for controlling rats which, in war-ravaged Europe and many other places, were destroying food and supplies, and often carried disease.

The research report was technical and might easily disappear in office files. I urged something more—a simpler report which might alert people to ways this chemical could be used against rats. With permission, I wrote an article for the *Saturday Evening Post.* Soon after it was published, hundreds of worldwide inquiries came in. Later this poison was used to control coyotes and other "pests." Used that way, it began to kill other kinds of wildlife too, and its wide use was discontinued.

We also undertook to summarize about fifty years of research into the feeding habits of American wildlife. Gradually, my experience gave me more responsibility for editing, to help reduce the masses of detailed information into a single book, suited for popular use.

When the manuscript and illustrations were finished, we learned that because of war limitations on paper, only five hundred copies of *American Wildlife and Plants* could be printed by the government. The book had such long-range values for ecology and wildlife

Zim as University of Illinois professor in the "pre-television days," early 1940s

conservation that I suggested commercial publishers might do better than the Government Printing Office. This led to a string of visits to New York to visit publishers and to spend a night at home now and then. McGraw-Hill brought out the book, which later appeared in paperbound editions.

One New York visit brought me to Doubleday, publisher of what were commonly called "The Reed Guides," though other authors were in the series. These books, going back to 1906, had kept two generations supplied with cheap, pocket-sized guides to birds, flowers, and trees. I too had used them, and expressed my appreciation to the Doubleday editor. In return I learned that the color plates for these books were old and worn, that the publication, stopped during the war, would not be resumed. The possibility of a new, fresh series was obvious and in the evening I talked with Sunnie about it. At Patuxent I presented the idea to experts who were working with me. All remembered the "Reed Guides" and saw a place for something new and better. I thought seriously of what those new books might be like.

Starting work on my own, with the goal of writing about the one hundred or so most common birds, trees, and flowers, I gathered data and reviewed all popular writings. The staff at Patuxent were interested because of their wildlife responsibilities. Soon a full outline and sample pages on birds were ready. Sunnie took them to Simon and Schuster. "Let's take this up at the next sales meeting," was the response of Albert Leventhal, the president. Salesmen agreed that the series would sell, and recommended starting with four books. *Birds* came first, since some of it was worked up as a sample. *Flowers, Trees,* and *Insects* were listed next. I was to edit the series and write these four books with backup by Fish and Wildlife experts.

Simon and Schuster negotiated with Western Publishing Company to start the series as a joint venture. Western Publishing would print and both publishers would monitor the writing and illustrations. Simon and Schuster would also distribute and sell. Contracts were signed and work on the books was officially under way. Pocket size was essential, so I went around measuring pockets of friends. Their coats, jackets, trousers, and sweaters gave us data. We came up recommending three satisfactory sizes. One of them turned out to be in exact agreement with what the production people at Western worked out as most suited to their presses. The books were to be one hundred and sixty pages, four inches by six inches, hard bound, and to sell for one dollar.

Birds had started with a goal of about one hundred birds, but this was too arbitrary. Instead we stressed common, but who would say which were *the* common birds? Here we needed expert help, but got very little from the experts. Their advice was to do two books, one on eastern and one on western birds, or one on land and one on water birds. We ignored that advice and started to make our own list. We found eastern birds that were also treated in western books, and vice versa. More data came from the extensive bird files at Patuxent. With help from Chandler Robbins and others there, we compiled a tentative list of one hundred and twelve common birds. When the next expert shook his head on our idea of one small book on the most common North American birds, we showed him our list. Soon we had a group of ornithologists who thought we had done reasonably well, but who still argued strongly about a few more species that might be included.

On Plantation Key, Florida, about 1950. "Lack of shave arouses ire of Coco, our meticulous macaw."

Ira Gabrielson took time from his work as director of the U.S. Fish and Wildlife Service to encourage, review, and advise on birds he knew best. Chandler Robbins and others at Patuxent joined in and argued until we were in basic agreement. My best ally in trying to retain the simple purposes of the Guides was the size of the book itself. Experts always had something to add, but the size of the Guides and their simple treatment demanded that something else be removed before anything new could be added. With this price to pay, we got a thorough study, page by page. In nearly every case the suggestion to add another bird was dropped.

The books moved along, with four overlapping schedules. I did the writing, with suggestions from the experts. As text and art work were completed, *Birds* went to press and was published early in 1949. An immediate success, it produced pressure to use some art already available in *Flowers* but not prepared for the same purpose. This was less satisfying for our needs, but we had a firm promise to replace this art in the next printing. Fifty-eight printings later, we are still waiting!

Each new book added to the success of the series and before the first four books were out, we had started on another group, including *Stars; Rocks and Minerals; Fishes;* and *Weather.* By this time, I was on the faculty of the University of Illinois at Urbana. Expert help from the faculty there, as well as continued help from U.S. Fish and Wildlife, aided the steady flow of titles. Rachel Carson, then with the Service, was slated for a Guide in Marine Biology. But her first book was just out and she was already thinking about the one that would make her famous in 1961, *Silent Spring.* She could not make the time to join the author's group for the Golden Guides.

By the early fifties, over a dozen titles were on the projection board. Already the scope of the series was extending from identification guides to those more directed to an understanding of a natural group or area. In addition to "Nature Guides," some titles were put under the heading of "Science Guides." Others started a group of "Regional Guides," beginning with *The Southwest, The Southeast,* and *The Northwest.* It then moved into areas around specific national parks, such as *Acadia, Everglades,* and *Yosemite.*

With Guides translated and adapted for readers in Europe, it was inevitable that there was special interest in titles that had international use. In addition to translation and distribution of books produced in the United States, Western subsidiaries and licensees developed titles on their own which might be reviewed, adapted, and distributed in the U.S.A. Only a few were.

At about this time, Ridge Press, having already

shown an interest in the Guides, was authorized to develop titles for the series, under my supervision. The overall picture, moving from the fifties into the sixties, reflected the strong and continuing interest in the original Nature Guides and a predictable but varied response to other titles. Early in the fifties the sales curve led to the projection that a sound title could reach the million mark in ten years or so. In fact, these are some Golden Guides and others that have passed the million mark as of 1986:

Golden and Field Guides	Printings	Production in millions
Birds	104	7.3
Butterflies and Moths	31	1.3
Fishes	67	2.7
Fishing	28	1.2
Flowers	70	4.2
Fossils*	67	1.9
Insects	77	4.1
Mammals	64	2.6
Photography*	21	1.1
Pondlife	32	1.0
Reptiles and Amphibians	65	3.1
Rocks and Minerals*	76	5.8
Seashells of the World*	68	2.2
Seashores	58	2.2
Stars*	74	3.8
Trees	78	4.2
Weather	56	2.4
Zoology*	28	1.4
Birds of North America	103	4.5
Trees of North America	62	1.1

Other Books

Encyclopedia of Natural Science*		10.5
Junior Golden Guides*		5.1

*[Books with large foreign printings not included in the total.]

This unusual success may be attributed to a team approach, rather than to a unique talent of the author, expert, or publisher. Open communication and mutual respect of all involved was the key. Printers and pressmen at the Poughkeepsie plant asked to carry through on all phases of printing and binding. "We enjoy doing these books," said their spokesman at a plant meeting. Experts, many of them authorities in their fields, urged their undergraduate and graduate students to use the Guides in addition to the course textbook. "I wish I had these to use when I was younger," was a comment heard from many. The use of the Guides extended widely in the high schools as adjuncts to biology and other subjects, and into lower grades also. With the years, there were increasing reports from young scientists that the Guides were the impetus that sent them into their present life work.

Directed as much as possible on what *readers* wanted to know, the books were also geared for self-teaching. For nearly every topic, both text and art were treated together on a page or spread. Readers were tempted to browse and thumb through their copies. Frequently, when finding a new bird or fish or tree, they already had an orientation that made identification sure and successful. It was this achievement of the reader, learning through his own efforts, that motivated a kind of continuing interest that is rarely found in the classroom.

During these years, Western asked me to take on additional responsibilities in their total program. At various times I had such duties as Editor of Golden Guides, Consultant and Special Editor, Edition Director, Educational Consultant, and Editor-in-Chief. But all this time I was still an independent author, writing books for Harcourt, Brace; William Morrow; and Western Publishing.

One other major project has also occupied my mind since the mid-fifties. At the University of Illinois I was asked to serve as editor-in-chief of *Our Wonderful World,* a new eighteen volume encyclopedia, designed along ideas that developed from my long educational experience. The project was brought to the University of Illinois so as not to interfere with my duties there. Spencer Press of Chicago was producing the set for Sears, Roebuck, and contact with both was essential. As Editor-in-Chief I had a staff recruited mainly from professors' wives who, well educated, often on a professional level, could not be employed by the university. With this team, we searched the history and role of encyclopedias, paying special attention to the *Book of Knowledge,* a favorite of children for several decades. We learned that the first encyclopedias were not alphabetical. Neither was this children's favorite. Its unusual organization came about because it began as a British children's magazine. The encyclopedia was published in the same sequence. Thus a story might continue into several encyclopedia volumes and in following it up, the young readers were exposed to more topics, activities, and stories to enjoy.

We, too, were impressed by the futility of the alphabetical volumes for young browsers and readers. Our approach was something of a free association of ideas into a pattern we called a "tapestry of knowledge." Ideas flowed into one another and were woven into a learning pattern through our specific themes. The story of the many "discoveries" of America might be followed by something on maps and map reading.

This in turn would lead the reader to learn what the New World got from the Old—and what it gave in return.

To enrich our materials still more, we did not use facts gathered and written up by staff. Instead, we searched widely through all kinds of published materials for selections we could use directly. With permission, we cut, edited, and obtained illustrations as needed. So in total, each topic involved three or four or five related selections, with a short introduction and cross reference to other related topics. Every article was a resource from which the interested reader might go further, in one of several directions of his choice.

Albert Leventhal, proud of his achievement with the *Golden Encyclopedia,* an outstanding set for young readers, suggested that I consider a *Natural Science Encyclopedia.* On several visits to New York I discussed this with Albert and his staff. He listened with interest to my report on *Our Wonderful World* and to my plea for a non-alphabetical plan for the proposed *Natural Science* set. His answer was as clear as his approach to publishing—"If it isn't alphabetical, how can we get them to buy the whole set in a supermarket? It's essential for our printing and our distribution." So the Natural Science project went alphabetical.

As the years ticked off at Illinois, I remembered more and more an early plan made soon after I came to the university. My hope was to retire at age fifty-five and devote full time to writing. We had spent time in the Southwest and had been attracted to the mountains

Herbert and Sonia Bleeker Zim, early 1960s

of Southern Arizona. We checked on land near the small settlement of Patagonia. But my needs to be in New York quite often because of my books made these bright Western mountains impossible. The Florida Keys, then only a day's travel from New York, became a greater temptation. By the late fifties, we and our projects were well established there. Winn and Roger, our two sons, attended George School in Pennsylvania, close enough for reasonable contacts. As the Conchs (local Keys people) said, "We had sand in our shoes," and the Florida Keys had become our home.

The sixteen-volume *Natural Science Encyclopedia* came down to the Keys with us. Using our guest house and a separate office, five to eight people worked steadily. Staff from Racine, Wisconsin, and New York came regularly to help, especially Robert Bezucha, who had long experience with large projects. From several universities and governmental agencies we gathered a group of experts, each outstanding in at least one scientific area. With editorial and library help, the project moved steadily along. Problems came up daily and we worked them through. The encyclopedia became a giant jig-saw puzzle with cutting, fitting, and all kinds of adjustments to get the whole natural world snugly, page by page, between the covers.

One real problem arose in the fall of 1960. Hurricane Donna came fast and directly at us. The shore house, bruised and battered as six feet of ocean came through, held its own. The office and library, far back, were not touched by the sea, but a tornado spawned inside the hurricane, tilted the heavy flat roof of the office so neatly that, while everything inside was soaked, not too much was damaged. Manuscripts, records, sketches, art, and layouts had all been packed in plastic "just in case." As part of the cleanup our original house was enlarged and quickly converted into a library and office. Within a month, the hectic pace was normal again. But as editor-in-chief I could not resist the temptation to write a few short entries on my own. Progress continued anyhow.

The first copies of *Natural Science* were ready in June 1963 and in the first two years, some five million books were produced. The ten million mark was passed in 1979. England, France, Spain, Denmark, Switzerland, and Germany each had its own version. A trickle of sales still comes in from Europe.

And through all this, the Golden Guides continued. At any time, about ten were in the works at once, some getting final checks before the presses rolled, others in the first stages of planning. In eleven of these, I had some kind of role as author. And among that group were the first Field Guides of which *Birds of North America* is best known. And Morrow books continued quietly.

Zim family at work, about 1962. From left, Sonia, author of over thirty books;
Roger, age twelve; Herbert; Aldwin; and Ellen Edelen, "then my secretary,
now a publisher at Banyan Books"

Meanwhile another exciting project had developed when Lucille Ogle, an alert and sharp expert on children's books, asked me to look at some art. A large bundle had just come in to Golden Press as illustrations for a children's bird book. The plates were rich, colorful, and full of life. Soon I met the artist, Arthur Singer, and have enjoyed working with him for some twenty-five years. I convinced Western Publishing and Arthur that this art could create a monumental volume on *Birds of the World* for adults, without giving up its value as a book for younger readers.

We found an author in Professor Oliver Austin, a research ornithologist, familiar, through his work and travels, with birds in most areas the book covered. Laying out the art to meet two separate goals was not easy. Arthur Singer made layouts and sketches till all the bird families were represented. *Birds of the World* appeared in 1961 amid much acclaim. It has been printed in five languages and for over twenty years it has been selling well in England, a bird-loving nation. Once again it is also available in America. My edito-

rial task was one I enjoyed to the fullest.

As the fifties gave way to the sixties, the operation of this happy madhouse of writing, editing, planning, and production had a price to be paid. Imperceptibly at first, then more obviously, the goals of all the series were put aside because of pressure of schedules, distribution, and increased production costs. Guides that had started for $1.00, hardbound, were now $2.98, limp. I had taken responsibility for the *Library of Knowledge*, an international set of much promise. But the pace became so fast, and the concerns so limited, that there was neither time nor interest in doing the job as it had been planned. For the first time I withdrew from a Western project, and soon the project itself disappeared.

To help with some of these problems, we shifted the writing to people who would normally have been experts. I still contributed, and some fine books came through with less effort from me. With some others I took on only an editorial role, but that too had its

Updating Birds of North America, *about 1964: illustrator Arthur Singer, co-authors Bertel Brun and Herbert S. Zim*

demands. As editor of the "Junior Golden Guides," I was happy to see short informational books developed on a large scale at low costs. Records are incomplete but by the early seventies over five million copies had gone out. The new Ridge Press books became impossible to supervise from Florida. After the first few titles, they were developed independently. At Western, my role became more that of an editor and publishing consultant than of an author.

We tried doing more and more without the organizational backup we needed, for we were now the equivalent of a small but very active publishing house. During this period it was agreed that I would plan, work, and coordinate with the newly formed educational department headed by Dr. Fred Pinkham, president of Ripon College. Aided by several teachers with writing experience, we began another series of books with a stress on science and the environment. *Second-Hand Water* was our first title. Hardly had our projects taken shape when the new educational department was dropped.

With all this going on, I still felt myself an author

more than anything else. My steady program of writing for William Morrow averaged close to two books a year. Sales passed the million, then the two and three million mark. Some professional writing continued as well, and the textbook *New Worlds of Science* which I did with R. Will Burnett and Bernard Jaffee (for Silver Burdett) was revised. This total program, spreading like an octopus, extended into a variety of books for younger people. They were used in urban and rural schools, in experimental schools, and were especially helpful in depressed areas. They were used in parks, camps and museums, on tours, trips, and in many homes. Constant reports on the values of the Guides were a tonic.

My proposed retirement had more complications, stemming largely from an expanding program at Western Publishing and the personnel changes developing from new management policies and goals. A contract in 1968 limited my responsibilities so I could concentrate my efforts on an acceptable writing program. This seemed to help, but only for a short while. Some of the problems that persisted seemed due to dif-

Sonia and Herbert Zim receiving honorary doctorates at Beloit College, late 1960s

ferences between the home office in Racine, Wisconsin and the Golden Press offices in New York. This seemed to become much more critical after the death of Horace Benstead, Chairman of the Board, a man with a strong and abiding concern with education.

By late 1969 another effort was made to further decrease my responsibilities. This led to an agreement that was considered, reconsidered, and reworked for nearly a year before it was signed in August 1970. It spelled out my retirement as editor of the Golden Guides. I released control of all books in which I was then involved and which were under way. I also released all Golden Guides to be published after 1970. But the agreement clearly and precisely stated that Western could make no changes in any books already published without getting my approval of the changes in advance.

The pros and cons of this agreement have been argued ever since. The publishers insisted that they can pick anyone to revise my books and all I can do is approve or not. After such changes have been made and set in type, they are sent to me. If I then rework or change the changes it is often too late or too costly to get them into the revised book. The decisions of the

Federal District Court went to the Federal Court of Appeals, where, in his introduction to his decisions, Judge Goldberg wrote:

> In the beginning, Zim created the concept of the Golden Guides. For the earth was dark and ignorance filled the void. And Zim said let there be enlightenment and there was enlightenment.

In the ten pages that followed, the generally favorable decisions confirmed that the 1970 agreement was valid. But since 1978, things have not changed, in my opinion. There seems to be an implied suggestion from Western that I can sue them again if I do not like what they are doing. Perhaps I will.

But why all this in an autobiography? Well, it *is* my life story and this is an important part of it because of the principles involved. Writers of text books and any type of "how-to" books (which is what science is all about) watch this with care. Such books must be clear and up-to-date. Readers accept, in good faith, what is between the covers. Publishers know this and demand that authors of such books revise them as needed. Since readers or students cannot judge what is in these books, they depend on the authors.

People often think that an author has a rosy, easy life. Some do. Easy, it is usually not! The work is long and demanding. It takes an author a long time to be satisfied with what he is writing. Problems arise with publishers and publishers have problems with authors. Mine were not unique.

In trying to keep my books as useful as when they were first written, I keep busy. Staying abreast of what is happening in science, or where science is involved, is the biggest task. Television is a real help. Some of the major science programs have much to tell, and no book can substitute for them. By mail I get about twenty-five magazines. I regularly scan them and mark up those articles I want to read. But it may be a month or more before I make any dent in the big pile of magazines close to my desk. Most of what I read in them I read for reference. I miss the joy of picking up some book I like and taking the time to read it from cover to cover. Fiction is also a treat. Most of what I read is nonfiction—informational books.

Of equal importance to what I get from books, magazines, and television are the things I learn from direct contact. I go to museums, zoos, exhibits, and parks. But most of my direct contacts are my mail. A few are by phone and some are face-to-face talks with people, young and old, in this country and abroad. But it is the mail that keeps me busy. Day by day it gets first attention.

Over the years I have received hundreds and perhaps thousands of letters, mainly from young readers—but some from parents, teachers, and other adults. Letters from children seem to come in waves, with a strong drop when schools close for the summer. More seem to show up at the "book week" time of the year, and also about the time when one of my new books gets into schools and libraries.

Schools are very much involved. Teachers or librarians may make it mandatory to "write a letter to your favorite author." When an author is known to send a quick reply, word spreads fast. These kinds of letters are easy to spot, but each one gets a reply—usually a postal card. Every now and then a letter comes through that smacks of something unusual—about the writer, the family, their pets or travel or something just deep and personal. These I try to answer at length. Follow-up letters often come back and we may have a contact that continues for a year or more.

One question asked by nearly all young letter-writers is, "How did you become an author?" Well, that is what this autobiography is all about. If you have read this far, you already know. Many ask, "What other books have you written?" My list is too long to send out, so I let writers know of any book that is similar to the one they have read. I also let them know that librarians have reference books like the one you're now reading, with just that kind of information. At the end of this essay, you'll find a list of my books.

Many young people write to ask for aid in class projects, exhibits, term papers, or science fairs. I often cannot reply fast enough to help them. But again, I tell the writers to go to local sources of help. That might be a high-school or college teacher, a local official or even someone at a factory or business. Local inquiries by young people often get unusually good attention, and make contacts that are far better than those by mail.

Another question turning up often in letters from younger readers is, "Where do you get ideas for your books?" A quick and reasonable answer might be, "From you and your friends, of course." That answer

Visiting with children at the Miami Public Library

Miami-Metro News Bureau

would need some correction, though a number of books have come directly from pupils or other young readers. Some of my books—like *Your Food and You, Codes and Secret Writing,* and *Goldfish*—came from classroom projects with help from students in grades three through six.

Another source of books was the research on *Science Interests and Activities of Adolescents,* which I did within the overall project of *Science in General Education, 1934-1940.* In my part of this major study, I gathered information from about five thousand junior-high-school students in the New York area. Our aim was to present those parts of science which students showed, through reports and through activities we observed, were of the greatest interest to them. A number of students reported on areas of science in dual terms. The strongest pair of these was "very interesting" combined with "disgusting." From these unusual reports evolved a series of books on aspects of biology, physiology, and zoology. The subjects ranged from snakes to your insides, to armored animal, blood, and death—areas which had strong twin responses. Other clues on the interests and concerns of young people came from other parts of this study.

Equally important ideas turned up during the planning for *Our Wonderful World.* At the University of Illinois, Professor Harlan Shores and others conducted studies of reading habits and reading interests in upper elementary-school grades. These studies confirmed and extended our views of what students wanted to know. It also suggested ways in which they said they preferred to get this kind of information. In short, we tried hard to find out from young readers, themselves, just what they wanted to know within the scope of science.

Letters from readers often asked, "What was the first book you ever wrote?" As you already know from the early part of this autobiography, that was *Mice, Men and Elephants.* It was a book that prompted a lot of letters for well over thirty years.

That question is almost always followed by, "Which of your books do you like the best?"—a question that is impossible for me to answer. But I do know the one I like the least. It is always the one I have just finished. That book has been written and rewritten and changed so many times that I am sick and tired of it, even though these changes have made the book better. When it is published and comes to me in a bright, smart jacket, I take a quick look and put it aside. A month or two later, I will read it with care. Then I usually feel much better about it.

One book does bring up strong feelings. It is *Life and Death* (1970), written with Sunnie at the time she was dying of cancer. We tried, as her last message, to tell younger readers what death—and life, were all about.

One last and often-repeated question—"How long does it take to make a book?" Again no simple or easy answer, unless I should say, "too long." The idea for a book may stay in my mind for months or even a year. One special book, still unwritten, has been in my mind, and notes, for ten years. Because it is difficult and important, I keep hoping that someone else will write it and leave me in peace.

Once I decide to write, there may be months of reading, note-taking, outlining, and checking with experts. I try to get more first hand experience, if that is possible, at museums, zoos, National Parks, or in travel. Once I get at the typewriter, an early draft of the book may be ready in a month or two. Then, bit by bit, it becomes a second draft. By that time I have suggestions from the editor, and some of these may need to be discussed. By the third draft, the notes for illustrations may be moved into a rough layout or dummy which shows what is needed and where it may best fit. The editor and artist also get this—with more meetings. Resource material may be needed, though most artists who do illustrations know their sources. Space in the book has to be adjusted for special illustrations that tell more than the text can. All these are fitted into place. Labels and captions are written. The production people have been involved and now take over. Soon we have galleys, sheets of text set in type. These too need correction or fitting. The book is taking shape. Finally we see page proofs or their equal. These say "take a last good look." Then the book goes to press.

Other letters come to tell me about the writer, his school, her family, their pets. These things are good to know. Adults write too. Notes come from parents and suggestions from teachers and librarians. Scientists also write because some feel strongly that young people should know more about *their* science. And, with no modesty at all, let me give credit for much of this writing to thirty years of teaching from pre-kindergarten through the graduate level at the university.

Even more satisfying than suggestions from scientists, teachers, and librarians were those occasions when I could meet and talk directly with park rangers, naturalists, museum workers, field scientists, and other adults with serious natural-science hobby interests. Most had used the Guides in one way or another, or had seen them used in their daily contacts with the public. They were enthusiastic in their comments, and some were vocal about things they wanted improved. From these contacts I learned much about how the Guides worked.

I wish we could estimate the number of young

people who have gone into rewarding occupations or professions because of the interests they developed, helped by "Zim" books, as one of the tools they used. Add to this a much larger number who have enriched some part of their lives with this help. Numbers are not in themselves essential. But every reader needs and can use the best learning tool that the author and publisher can jointly produce.

As I look back I find myself surprised and pleased at the cooperation I have had from scientists—experts in many fields. It seems to stem from their acceptance of the Guides as "a job well done." Even so, it takes a bit of time and, perhaps, a lot of talking to find a way to merge the viewpoint of an expert with that of a person who lacks background or training. Yet the Guides make a real effort to open the door to such readers, and show them the way in. It is a top compliment when a scientist, eminent in his chosen field, thumbs through a related Guide and says, "I really wish I had done this."

Bearing this responsibility to the facts, the Guides try to begin with the reader as he stands. To that end, for example, I never use a glossary. It is a confession that the text is not completely clear. When a term is first used, it is used in a way that is generally understood, or that at least gives one clue to its meaning and use. This changes a bit from one usage to another, so that the reader builds for himself an understanding of the word—one that should change and become more meaningful with time. If a word is not important enough to be used several times, it may not be needed at all. Some other way can be found.

For most books, I had the sincere and constant cooperation of experts. Sometimes we would argue about our special ideas of "accuracy" or "completeness" as applied to books for younger readers. As experts grasped the scope and purpose of the Guides and the Morrow books, they accepted the limits that book size and reading level imposed. Expert help was critical for another reason. The reference books used by teachers and writers are often dated and may be slanted to a special point of view of the expert author. Only another expert can give an opinion on such matters. Because they knew their fields so well, experts often called attention to new data; some not yet in print. In several Morrow books, and with necessary caution, the reader got information that was not only up-to-the-minute, but was a few seconds ahead.

Perhaps more should be said about the Morrow books. In 1946, I began these with Elizabeth Hamilton and later with Connie Epstein. Both editors had remarkable insight. They knew their young readers. After several books for the very young, the series spread into subjects for different and older groups. Sixty "Zim

books" were printed. Including special and foreign editions, these totaled about six million copies. At the top of the list was *Codes and Secret Writing* with 1.5 million, but about 60 percent of all other titles ran to 50,000 copies or more. We experimented a lot. Though praised highly, a group of books about science and everyday occupations did not go over well.

Yet the Morrow series is the one that teachers and librarians like best; and so do I. For forty years the Morrow team has worked as smoothly as basketball champions. We understand and support one another with expert ease, and enjoy our work, year after year. And, for nearly twenty years after 1946, work with Western was about on the same level.

Both publishers had continuous help from experts and from institutions, for the artists as well as for the authors.

Specimens were loaned or sources recommended. Gordon Irving borrowed a number of snakes from the New York Zoological Society to use as he illustrated *Reptiles and Amphibians.* The expert suggested ways to make his work easier. Every snake was kept in a pillow case, tied shut. But when Gordon put it out on the table, the snake would not stay still as he sketched. The expert's advice was to put the bagged snake in the refrigerator for half an hour or so. After the snake had slowed down with the cold, it stayed quiet while Gordon sketched away. We never learned how Gordon's wife felt about finding a snake in with the milk and butter.

In appropriate books and with expert help we decided what things to include as the most common, most widespread, and most important. There still remained the problem of just what to illustrate. A single insect, for example, might be found in four to eight or more forms or stages. Males of some animals differ from females; younger ones from adults; and those living in warm areas from those of colder regions. A single species may exist as two to ten varieties or forms. Plants differ with the seasons and where they grow—and so on and on and on. With expert help we were able to get the best illustration and to make the best use of the space we had. We kept constantly in mind how much readers could learn from pictures and also the art department's demand for clarity, simplicity, and plenty of space for labels and captions.

As I work towards the end of my autobiography, rereading it several times, I can see problems. Some items in my notes have disappeared. Others, not noted, have slipped in at a dozen places. This is to make amends and set things right! I *was* born, in New York on July 12, 1909. Marco Zim, my father, came from Russia as a child. He had no schooling when young. But he had medals and awards for his painting, sculpture, and etchings and he did many other wonderful things. As an artist he found the family name— Zimmerman—too much to put on a painting, so he chopped it down to Zim. Orlo, my mother, was the practical one in the family. She was born and educated in New York but never told us much about her family, which came from Austria. My brother Milton, three years younger, likes to fish and, now retired, fishes near his home, on Indian land in Arizona, along the Colorado River.

Sunnie also came from Russia. Her family escaped when she was very young. She did get schooling here, with a degree from Hunter College and graduate work in anthropology at Columbia University. She translated several books and then wrote about thirty of her own on Indians and other native people of the Americas and Africa. She died in 1971.

As for Grace Kent, my present wife, we met over fifty years ago when I worked with her father who was then director of the Ethical Culture School Camp. She remembered all the new and strange experiences the

Mother, Orlo Zim, about 1918

Father, Marco Zim, about 1918

campers had that summer. Sunnie and I kept in touch with her. Years later, after her husband and Sunnie had both died, Grace came visiting on the Keys. She, too, "got sand in her shoes"—and got me too. So much for a typical, and also a very unusual, family.

Travel, about which I have only given a hint, was really important. Before I was one, my parents moved from New York to a small seaside farm near Mystic, Connecticut. There, early one morning in May 1910, my father took me out in his arms to see Halley's Comet, which just now is back again. I was too young to remember it the first time, and my second look, in 1986, was not impressive. The rest of my childhood was from New York to California and from California back to New York—and repeated. The last return I made alone.

With teaching and writing producing a slight surplus of funds, I invested in an overage Stutz car which soon gave way to a more reliable Chevrolet. Now we got further afield on trips; one time as far as Kansas City for an early summer seminar. At Fieldston, Sunnie and I took high-school students on weekend trips.

At Karnak, Egypt, 1983

Later, with another teacher, we evolved a ten-week summer travel program, taking ten boys around the country on a trip they planned themselves. Later, the early summer session at the University of Illinois gave us a month or more of summer travel with our boys. We went all through the West, with a dip into Mexico which later became a habit that lasted some twenty years.

Once free from Illinois, with our sons in camp or under friendly care, Sunnie and I drove through country roads in Europe, from Italy and Greece up into Scandinavia. Another year, after a Swiss scientific meeting, we went the length of Africa and returned by plane and train. Nearly every year found us in Mexico or nearby Central America for short visits. Sunnie's illness cut these trips off later, but I resumed traveling after her death.

Tours out of London caught my attention. First alone and later with Gracie, I went on camping and other overland trips. I moved from Miami to London, on to Nepal, south through India and Thailand to Malaysia and Singapore. Then our group headed to Australia and through the Outback. I went on to New Zealand, Fiji, and Micronesia before heading home. With Gracie along we next explored Roman ruins in Algeria and Tunisia; big game and early man in Central and East Africa. We went up the Nile in a small boat; later through Canada to Alaska and to the West Indies and other islands.

Zim in Venice, 1984

Time out for photos, on a field trip in Bangkok, Thailand, 1984

Our recent 1985 trip which lasted over three months, was a chance for me to see areas I had visited twelve years before, and which Gracie had never seen. This time it was Miami, New York, London, Bangkok, Kathmandu and then to India and Pakistan. We flew to Greece and started east to Turkey, Syria, Lebanon, Jordan, and Israel. Again up the Nile and to Greece; up through Yugoslavia, Austria, Germany, Belgium, through London once more and home. All this itinerary is mentioned in detail because it was on this trip

The Zims, 1984, "by an undisturbed mountain stream in Agua Blanca, Mexico"

that my autobiography was written. An aging, portable typewriter was at work evenings at our catch-as-catch-can lodgings and in the bus when, on rare occasions, the roads were smooth. What other autobiography has been dragged through sixteen countries and hauled around over thousands of miles?

All this travel has added up to the pages that you have read. At home again, Gracie and I have located missing facts, pulled together stray paragraphs, looked up dates and checked names. My deep thanks to her for all the time she spent; and my thanks to you too for having read this all the way till the end.

BIBLIOGRAPHY

FOR ALL AGES

Nonfiction:

Science Interests and Activities of Adolescents. New York: Ethical Culture Schools, 1940.

Mice, Men, and Elephants (illustrated by James MacDonald). New York: Harcourt, 1942.

Parachutes (illustrated by J. MacDonald). New York: Harcourt, 1942.

Submarines (illustrated by J. MacDonald). New York: Harcourt, 1942.

Air Navigation (illustrated by J. MacDonald). New York: Harcourt, 1943.

Man in the Air (illustrated by J. MacDonald). New York: Harcourt, 1943.

Minerals, with Elizabeth K. Cooper. New York: Harcourt, 1943.

Rockets and Jets (illustrated by J. MacDonald). New York: Harcourt, 1945.

This is Science. Washington, D.C. Association for Childhood Education, 1945.

Elephants (illustrated by Joy Buba). New York: Morrow, 1946; London: Hamilton, 1946.

Goldfish (illustrated by Joy Buba). New York: Morrow, 1947.

Plants (illustrated by John W. Brainerd). New York: Harcourt, 1947.

Codes and Secret Writing. New York: Morrow, 1948; Kingswood, England: World's Work, 1965.

New World of Science, with R. Will Burnett and Bernard Jaffe (illustrated by Robert Doremus, Matthew Kalmenoff, and F. R. Gruger). New York: Silver Burdett, 1948.

Rabbits (illustrated by Joy Buba). New York: Morrow, 1948.

American Birds and Wildflowers, with Alexander C. Martin and I. N. Gabrielson. New York: Golden Press, 1949.

Birds, with I. N. Gabrielson (illustrated by James Gordon Irving). New York: Golden Press, 1949.

Homing Pigeons (illustrated by J. G. Irving). New York: Morrow, 1949.

Snakes (illustrated by J. G. Irving). New York: Morrow, 1949.

Flowers, with A.C. Martin (illustrated by Rudolf Freund). New York: Simon & Schuster, 1950.

Frogs and Toads (illustrated by Joy Buba). New York: Morrow, 1950.

Owls (illustrated by J.G. Irving). New York: Morrow, 1950.

American Wildlife and Plants. New York: McGraw, 1951.

Golden Hamsters (illustrated by Herschel Wartik). New York: Morrow, 1951.

The Great Whales (illustrated by J. G. Irving). New York: Morrow, 1951; Kingswood, England: World's Work, 1964.

Insects, with Clarence Cottam. New York: Golden Press, 1951; London: Hamlyn, 1966.

Stars, with Robert H. Baker (illustrated by J. G. Irving). New York: Golden Press, 1951; London: Hamlyn, 1965.

Alligators and Crocodiles (illustrated by J. G. Irving). New York: Morrow, 1952.

Lightning and Thunder (illustrated by J. G. Irving). New York: Morrow, 1952.

Trees, with A.C. Martin (illustrated by Dorothea and Sy Barlowe). New York: Golden Press, 1952.

What's Inside of Me? (illustrated by H. Wartik). New York: Morrow, 1952.

What's Inside of Plants? (illustrated by H. Wartik). New York: Morrow, 1952.

Parakeets (illustrated by Larry Kettelkamp). New York: Morrow, 1953.

Reptiles and Amphibians, with Hobart M. Smith (illustrated by J. G. Irving). New York: Golden Press, 1953.

Science for Children and Teachers. Washington, D.C. Association for Childhood Education, 1953.

The Sun (illustrated by L. Kettelkamp). New York: Morrow, 1953; Kingswood, England: World's Work, 1964.

What's Inside of Animals? (illustrated by H. Wartik). New York: Morrow, 1953.

What's Inside the Earth? (illustrated by Raymond Perlman). New York: Morrow, 1953.

What's Inside of Engines? (illustrated by R. Perlman). New York: Morrow, 1953.

Dinosaurs (illustrated by J. G. Irving). New York: Morrow, 1954; Tadworth: World's Work, 1984.

Things around the House (illustrated by R. Perlman). New York: Morrow, 1954.

The Big Cats (illustrated by Gardell D. Christensen). New York: Morrow, 1955.

Mammals, with Donald F. Hoffmeister (illustrated by J. G. Irving). New York: Golden Press, 1955.

Monkeys (illustrated by G. D. Christensen). New York: Morrow, 1955.

Seashores, with Lester Ingle (illustrated by D. and Sy Barlowe). New York: Golden Press, 1955.

The Southwest, with Natt N. Dodge (illustrated by Arch and Miriam Hurford). New York: Golden Press, 1955.

Fishes, with Hurst H. Shoemaker (illustrated by J.G. Irving). New York: Golden Press, 1956.

Our Senses (illustrated by H. Wartik). New York: Morrow, 1956.

Photography, with R. W. Burnett (illustrated by H. Wartik and Harry McNaught). New York: Golden Press, 1956.

Comets (illustrated by Gustav Schrotter). New York: Morrow, 1957.

Rocks and Minerals, with Paul R. Shaffer (illustrated by R. Perlman). New York: Golden Press, 1957; London: Hamlyn, 1965.

Weather, with R. W. Burnett and Paul E. Lehr. New York: Golden Press, 1957.

Your Food and You (illustrated by G. Schrotter). New York: Morrow, 1957.

Ostriches (illustrated by Russell Francis Peterson). New York: Morrow, 1958; Kingswood, England: World's Work, 1964.

Shooting Stars (illustrated by G. Schrotter). New York: Morrow, 1958.

Zoology, with R.W. Burnett and H.I. Fisher. New York: Golden Press, 1958; London: Hamlyn, 1965.

Diamonds (illustrated by G. Schrotter). New York: Morrow, 1959.

Giant Little Golden Book of Fish (illustrated by Jean Zallinger). New York: Golden Press, 1959.

The Pacific Northwest, with N. N. Dodge (illustrated by D. and Sy Barlowe). New York: Golden Press, 1959.

The Southeast (illustrated by D. and Sy Barlowe). New York: Golden Press, 1959.

Your Heart and How It Works (illustrated by G. Schrotter). New York: Morrow, 1959.

Guide to Everglades National Park and Nearby Florida Keys (illustrated by Russ Smiley). New York: Golden Press, 1960.

How Things Grow (illustrated by G. Schrotter). New York: Morrow, 1960; Kingswood, England: World's Work, 1964.

Gamebirds, with Alexander Sprunt IV (illustrated by J.G. Irving). New York: Golden Press, 1961.

The Universe (illustrated by G. Schrotter). New York: Morrow, 1961; Kingswood, England: World's Work, 1964.

Rocks and How They Were Formed (illustrated by H. McNaught). New York: Golden Press, 1961.

Fossils, with Frank H.T. Rhodes and Paul R. Schaffer (illustrated by Raymond Perlman). New York: Golden Press, 1962.

Butterflies and Moths, with Robert T. Mitchell (illustrated by

Andre Durenceau). New York: Golden Press, 1964.

The Rocky Mountains (illustrated by Su Zan Noguchi Swain). New York: Golden Press, 1964.

Birds of North America, with Chandler S. Robbins and Bertel Bruun (illustrated by Arthur Singer). New York: Golden Press, 1966.

Corals (illustrated by René Martin). New York: Morrow, 1966; Tadworth: World's Work, 1984.

Sharks (illustrated by Stephen Howe). New York: Morrow, 1966.

Non-Flowering Plants, with Floyd S. Shuttleworth (illustrated by D. Barlowe). New York: Golden Press, 1967.

Waves (illustrated by R. Martin). New York: Morrow, 1967.

Blood (illustrated by R. Martin). New York: Morrow, 1968; Tadworth: World's Work, 1984.

Bones (illustrated by R. Martin). New York: Morrow, 1969.

Hoists, Cranes, and Derricks, with James R. Skelly (illustrated by Gary Ruse). New York: Morrow, 1969; Tadworth: World's Work, 1971.

Machine Tools, with J. R. Skelly (illustrated by G. Ruse). New York: Morrow, 1969.

Mexico, with wife, Sonia Bleeker Zim (illustrated by Virginia Bimel). New York: Golden Press, 1969.

Botany, with Taylor R. Alexander and R. W. Bennett (illustrated by J. Zallinger). New York: Golden Press, 1970.

Cargo Ships, with J. R. Skelly (illustrated by Richard Cuffari). New York: Morrow, 1970; Tadworth: World's Work, 1972.

Life and Death, with S.B. Zim (illustrated by R. Martin). New York: Morrow, 1970; Tadworth: World's Work, 1971.

Orchids, with F. Shuttleworth and Gordon Dillon. New York: Golden Press, 1970.

Trucks, with J.R. Skelly (illustrated by Stan Biernacki). New York: Morrow, 1970.

Armored Animals (illustrated by R. Martin). New York: Morrow, 1971; Tadworth: World's Work, 1972.

Telephone Systems, with J. R. Skelly (illustrated by Lee J. Ames). New York: Morrow, 1971.

Tractors, with J. R. Skelly (illustrated by Lee J. Ames). New York: Morrow, 1972; Tadworth: World's Work, 1974.

Your Brain and How It Works (illustrated by R. Martin). New York: Morrow, 1972; Tadworth: World's Work, 1973.

Commercial Fishing, with Lucretia Krantz (illustrated by Lee J. Ames). New York: Morrow, 1973.

Your Stomach and Digestive Tract (illustrated by R. Martin). New York: Morrow, 1973; Tadworth: World's Work, 1978.

Crabs, with L. Krantz (illustrated by R. Martin). New York: Morrow, 1974; Tadworth: World's Work, 1976.

Medicine (illustrated by Judith Hoffman Corwin). New York: Morrow, 1974.

Metric Measure, with J. R. Skelly (illustrated by Timothy

Evans). New York: Morrow, 1974.

Pipes and Plumbing Systems, with J.R. Skelly (illustrated by Lee J. Ames and Mel Erikson). New York: Morrow, 1974.

Eating Places, with J. R. Skelly (illustrated by Frank Schwartz). New York: Morrow, 1975.

Snails, with L. Krantz (illustrated by R. Martin). New York: Morrow, 1975; Tadworth: World's Work, 1977.

Sea Stars and Their Kin, with L. Krantz (illustrated by R. Martin). New York: Morrow, 1976; Tadworth: World's Work, 1977.

Caves and Life (illustrated by R. Cuffari). New York: Morrow, 1978.

Little Cats (illustrated by J. Zallinger). New York: Morrow, 1978.

Your Skin (illustrated by J. Zallinger). New York: Morrow, 1979.

The New Moon. New York: Morrow, 1980.

Quartz. New York: Morrow, 1981.

Editor of:

Birds of the World, with Oliver L. Austin and A. Singer. New York: Golden Press, 1961; London: Hamlyn, 1962.

Seashells of the World, by R. Tucker Abbott. New York: Golden Press, 1962.

Butterflies, by J. F. G. Clarke. New York: Golden Press, 1963.

"Quiz Me" series, 21 volumes. New York: Golden Press, 1963-71.

Painting, by H. Gasser. New York: Golden Press, 1964.

Washington, by R. E. Smallman. New York: Golden Press, 1964.

A Guide to Fresh and Salt-Water Fishing, with George S. Fichter and Philip A. Francis. New York: Golden Press, 1965.

Insect Pests, by G. S. Fichter. New York: Golden Press, 1966.

The Golden Guide to American Antiques, by Ann Kilborn Kole. New York: Golden Press, 1967.

Pond Life, by George K. Reid. New York: Golden Press, 1967.

Song Birds of the World, by O. L. Austin, Jr. New York: Golden Press, 1967.

Water and Marsh Birds, by O. L. Austin, Jr. New York: Golden Press, 1967.

Zoo Animals, by D. F. Hoffmeister. New York: Golden Press, 1967.

A Guide to Acadia National Park and the Nearby Coast of Maine, by Grant W. Sharpe. New York: Golden Press, 1968.

Seashells of North America, by R. T. Abbott. New York: Golden Press, 1968.

Spiders, by Herbert and Lorna Levi. New York: Golden Press, 1968.

Trees of North America, by Christian F. Brockman. New York: Golden Press, 1968.

Water Birds, with O. L. Austin, Jr. New York: Golden Press, 1968.

Yosemite National Park, by Douglass H. Hubbard. New York: Golden Press, 1970.

Families of Birds, by O. L. Austin. New York: Golden Press, 1971.

National Parks of the World, by K. Curry-Lindall and Jean-Paul Harvey. New York: Golden Press, 1972.

Minerals of the World, by Charles Sorell. New York: Golden Press, 1973.

Editor-in-Chief:

"Our Wonderful World" series, 18 volumes. Chicago: Spencer Press, 1953-60. *Our Wonderful World,* 1953; *Our Wonderful World: Young People's Encyclopedic Anthology,* 1955-57; published as *Our Wonderful World: An Encyclopedic Anthology for the Entire Family,* 1960; *What Is Happening in Our Wonderful World,* four books, 1958-61.

"Fact and Fiction" series, four books. Chicago: Spencer Press, 1958-61.

The Golden Book Encyclopedia of Natural Science, 16 volumes. New York: Golden Press, 1962.

"Golden Bookshelf of Natural History," 3 volumes. New York: Golden Press, 1963-64.

Cumulative Index

CUMULATIVE INDEX

For every reference that appears *in more than one essay,*
the name of the essayist is given before the volume and page number(s).

INDEX

INDEX